5. Solve the following problem in a group: As the chairperson of a high school physical education department, you were instructed in March by the principal to revise the fitness testing procedures to use the following year. Using the eclectic mix of administrative procedures, solve the problem.
6. Review the duties of the athletic director and the department chairperson. Discuss the similarities. What are the differences?

References

DeSensi, J. T., and Rosenberg, D. (1996). *Ethics in sport management*. Morgantown, WV: Fitness Information Technology.

Inside fitness. (1993, February). *Club Industry* 13.

Kidder, R. W., and Born, P. L. (2002, February). Moral courage in a world of dilemmas. *The School Administrator* 59, pp. 14–20.

Mobley, T. A. (1997, April). Leadership in higher education for health, physical education, recreation, and dance. *Journal of Physical Education, Recreation and Dance* 68, pp. 36–38.

Parkhouse, B. L. (ed.). (2001). *The management of sport*, 3rd ed. Dubuque, Iowa: McGraw-Hill.

Railey, J. H., and Tschauner, P. R. (1993). *Managing physical education, fitness, and sport programs* (2nd ed.). Mountain View, CA: Mayfield.

Sattler, T. P., and King, M. J. M. (1997, November). Management: Ready or not? *Fitness Management* 13, p. 22.

Trade talk. (1993, February). *Club Industry* 10.

2

Management Functions in Physical Education and Sport

Many people don't plan to fail, they fail to plan.

Case Study: Chancellor's Decision Not Approved

At a medium-size university, it was decided that a new basketball arena needed to be built. Without input from students, faculty, or the community, the chancellor announced that a new facility, to be called the Student Activity Center (SAC), was going to be built at a cost of approximately $18 million, all of which was to be paid out of an increase in student fees.

Various community citizens, students, and faculty started to criticize the project. People had two main concerns: (1) The facility would not be a real student activity center, because it was suitable only for basketball games, concerts, and graduation ceremonies. (2) There had been no referendum approving the increase in student fees to pay for the facility.

Student and faculty groups protested the project. Both the faculty senate and the student body voted against the proposed arena by wide margins. The protests began campuswide and reached all the way to the state legislature. Due to the lack of support for the facility, the project plans were dropped.

Later when a new chancellor took over, the university appointed a large committee of faculty, administrators, and students to study the facility problem. The committee recommended the building of a facility, to be called the Convocation Center, that would accommodate new laboratories, classrooms, and offices for one of the largest departments on campus (Health, Leisure, and Exercise Science), as well as concerts, graduation, trade shows, and other community events. The structure was estimated to cost about twice that of the previous plan, but the state legislature viewed the facility as an academic building and a community resource and provided $35 million for the project.

The reader should be able to

1. Demonstrate through illustrations or descriptions traditional and futuristic organizational structures for physical education and athletic departments and sport organizations.
2. Describe the relationship of various methods of organizing personnel to function more effectively.
3. Compare and contrast McGregor's theory X and theory Y, quality circles, and theory Z as they apply to sport management.
4. Describe total quality management (TQM) and give examples of how it could be adapted in sport management situations.
5. Compare and contrast the various types of "power" in personal relationships.
6. Describe leadership behavior of administrators in physical education and sport in theory, modeling, problem solving, delegating, supervising, and decision making.
7. Understand the dynamics of supervision in sport management.

■ Organization

The term *organizational structure* is used here to define the manner in which the tasks of a sport organization are broken down and allocated to employees and volunteers, the reporting relationships among these role holders, and the coordinating and controlling mechanisms used within the sport organization (Slack, 1997, p. 6).

The structure of each particular organization should be examined in terms of the following dimensions:

- *Complexity*—how the organization is divided into groups, sports, departments, or divisions that may occur vertically, horizontally, or spatially.

- *Centralization*—the level at which decisions are made. The higher the degree of centralization, the more likely that decisions are made at the top; the more decentralized, the more decisions are made at lower levels.

- *Formalization*—relates to the extent to which policies, procedures, and rules govern the organization. In a highly formalized organization such as a school, the teachers will have little input as to when and how they will perform duties (Amis and O'Brien in Parkhouse, 2001, pp. 75–76).

An organization chart is drawn as a pictorial representation of the entity's formal structure. Some authorities believe that such charts are out of date and promote inflexibility. Experience shows that what is on the chart differs from day-to-day adjustments as alternative and practical lines of communication occur (Miller, 1997).

Because the great variety of programs in physical education and sport create different products, they require different organizational structures. For example, academic programs must ask how well prepared the graduates are and how well they produce on the job. The "physical education" program, athletic department, campus recreation, or a health–fitness business all have different products and thus face unique challenges in determining the optimal organizational structure.

It appears that in the future, physical education and sport programs and businesses will flourish if the organizational structure provides routine communication between staff and management, allows change and innovation, and provides ongoing staff training and development. A balance must be achieved between the amount of control the organizational structure provides the administration and the amount of freedom, shared information, and ability to give input the structure provides for the employees and staff. That is, if a

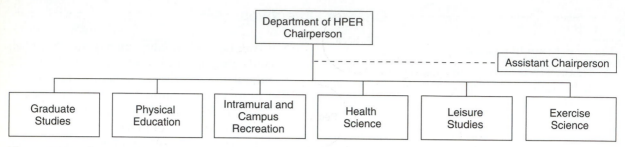

Figure 2.1 Line and staff organizational structure

staff member has a great idea, but the organizational structure doesn't provide an easy path to implement it, the organization and employee suffer. If, on the other hand, the management control is so vague that the staff can follow their own direction without supervision or checks and balances, the organization will again suffer and not be on target to achieve its mission.

Inevitably, this balance will become skewed. When it does, the leadership must recognize the problem and change the organizational structure. Frequently, this occurs only after several years of declining production or profit, losing teams, or decline in the number of graduates, or when a new administrator takes over (Arburgey, Kelly, and Barnett, 1993).

Dimensions of Structure

The size and complexity of the sport organization dictates the amount of differentiation in the structure. The most typical organizational structure found in schools and colleges is a *direct line and staff.* (See Figure 2.1 for an example.) In such an organizational structure, each subunit, such as graduate studies, would have a coordinator or director. Faculty would report through this person to the head.

Some have suggested that a circular model would more effectively serve an educational organization. Such a scheme is illustrated in Figure 2.2. In this structure, all head coaches are on the same level and freely interrelate with each other. The support staff, such as a business manager, are all equally accessible to all coaches.

The organizational structure must reflect whatever enables the staff to perform their tasks best. The structure should *not* be based on an abstract chart from a manual or copied from a successful business. A unique factor in this regard is that frequently there are coaches, teachers, or professors in the department who know more about special areas (such as curriculum, facilities, equipment, or scheduling) than the leader. The organizational structure must reflect this knowledge.

A matrix-type structure (as illustrated in Figure 2.3) encourages taking advantage of others' expertise. This system allows faculty who teach courses to intersect and interact at the circles. Goal setting, curriculum revisions, evaluation agreements, and textbook selection all grow out of the circle clusters.

ORGANIZATIONAL THEORY

Views differ not only on basic organizational structure but also on how the entity should be organized with respect to function and operation. Some organizations simply follow the personal style of the CEO. Others follow the lead dictated by a higher authority, such as the governor of a state, or, in large organizations, the findings of a research and development division that has determined what is best for the organization. Some major companies have combined information systems, human resources, and process management into a super division called the Strategic Resources Group (Davenport, 1993).

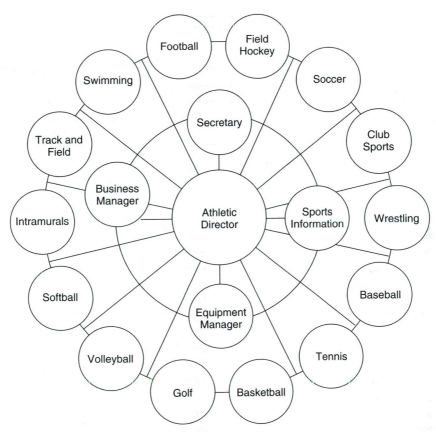

Figure 2.2 Circular organizational structure

ORGANIZATIONAL SYSTEMS

In classical organizational theory, organizations were thought of as similar to machines. From this *scientific* point of view, organizations were seen as "a series of interrelated parts, each performing a narrowly defined set of activities to achieve a particular end product. Like a machine, the organization is expected to operate in a rigid, repetitive, and impersonal manner" (Slack, 1997, p. 9).

A *technical* viewpoint emphasized the *environment.* The organization was compared to an *organism.* Just as organisms change their behaviors to adapt to the changing environment, organizations change their systems. The different systems interact with each other and the environment. These systems were called *input, throughput,* and *output.*

A variation was the *contingency systems* approach. In this approach, the structure of an organization would be contingent on *contextual* factors such as size and the objectives of the entity. A good fit between the structure and the context would be required for efficient operation.

Lastly, with rapidly changing environments, scholars suggested that an organizational structure should emulate the *human brain.* This would allow for ongoing monitoring of conditions with immediate appropriate modification of reactions. The organization would thus *self-regulate.* This theory relies on *cybernetics* for *feedback,* and the organization is viewed as a *holographic system* wherein each unit of the organization has a picture of the *whole,* and thus allows for *self-renewal* (Slack, 1997).

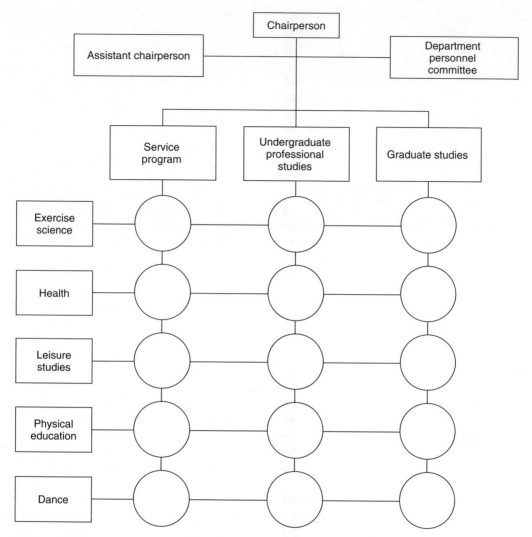

Figure 2.3 Faculty cluster matrix organizational structure

Transparency, Stakeholders, and Sunshine

Transparency in management is truth in management. Stakeholders are all personnel, governmental bodies, clients, spectators, customers, suppliers, agencies, media, alumni, the general public, and owners/shareholders that have an interest in or association with your activity. Sunshine is an old concept in democratic governance of *openness* that has recently been applied to all business as well as nonprofit agencies, including those in sport. *Transparent organizations are struc-tured so that the sunshine beams on all stakeholders.* There are no hidden doors or agendas. Transparency includes fairness, enforcing agreements, and keeping promises (Brown, 2002; CABMA Corner, 2002). While transparency in management has been a growing concept for years, the collapse of several major businesses due primarily to opaque management has certainly sped its adoption.

Transparent management is good for personnel. If a school system says that its policy is to promote from within when possible, and the record shows that in general this has occurred, it will be easier to recruit and hold highly skilled assistants. Transparency will shine light on wasteful practices and bottlenecks so corrective action can be taken. A custodian who happens to have had experience working at a golf course will be more likely to step up and offer cost-cutting means of maintaining fields. Transparent facilities are safer and more easily lend themselves to proactive risk management strategies. Transparent management also leads to enhanced service quality. If a spectator has to miss the entire third quarter because of slow service at the concession stand, and it is known that a timely suggestion to the appropriate athletic official will remedy the problem, the patron will more likely take the time to become involved if there is a record of transparency (Brown, 2002).

■ TOTAL QUALITY MANAGEMENT (TQM)

"TQM is a process of continuous improvement that is focused on responding to customer needs, basing decisions on data, and allowing everyone to participate in the process" (Law, 1993, p. 24). While many organizations have recently established the system, it is not really very new. TQM has grown out of time- and quality- control efforts from the 1920s in entities like Bell Laboratories.

A large number of major U.S. firms committed to the total quality concept in the early 1990s; they reportedly cut costs and improved products and profits. Also in the 1990s, many state governments, agencies, and institutions adopted TQM. Whether it is required from above or not, perhaps TQM is ripe for use in sport management.

TQM is based on 14 principles, which, in order to work, require a critical mass of employees who understand and support the principles (Mawson, 1993). Some of the key elements that drive the TQM process are emphasis on teamwork and investing in ongoing training for all employees.

In implementing TQM in schools and colleges, the emphasis must be on sharing power with teachers, training teachers, and emphasiz-

ing high-quality work for all. Sometimes referred to as "knowledge work," this meaningful work grows out of real-world experiences that help students understand how to apply what they learn (Rist, 1993). Others in education refer to the need to "empower" the entire workforce, who will then strive toward improvement of quality with continuous feedback and evaluation (Herman, 1993). It appears that most successful implementations of TQM in education have occurred in the service and maintenance areas. Some efforts have been made to adopt it in the academic sector, but a major philosophical problem centers on the need for emphasis on meeting the needs of the consumer. Most academicians believe that they, not students, must determine what students need to learn and experience in college (Mangan, 1992).

There are those who believe that TQM is just another fad. Some companies that adopted TQM several years ago now have problems or have dropped the system. One study showed that two-thirds of TQM programs examined had stalled or fallen short of meaningful improvements (De Meuse & Tornow, 1993). One wonders how many of these companies rushed into TQM because they were in serious trouble and were looking for a quick fix. Analysis seems to show that many companies that have experienced disappointing results from TQM never fully bought into the process—it won't work with just lip service or slogans (Holmes, 1992). While some believe that TQM replaces or encompasses McGregor's theory X and theory Y, quality circles, MBO (management by objectives, which will be addressed under evaluation later in the text), and theory Z management, others believe each of these theories is unique and requires study, research, and consideration.

McGregor's Theory X and Theory Y

Douglas McGregor concluded that how managers view workers determines the organizational system followed, which he called theory X and theory Y. McGregor asserted that most administrators unfortunately subscribe to type X. They assume that most workers are lazy and prefer to be told what to

Table 2.1 McGregor's View Related to Human Nature and Behavior as Applied to Educators	
Theory X: The Traditional View of Direction and Control Assumptions	Theory Y: The Modern View of Direction and Control Assumptions
1. Faculty, coaches, and employees in sport businesses have an inherent dislike for work and will avoid it if they can. 2. Because they dislike work, most must be coerced, controlled, directed, or threatened with punishment to perform adequately. 3. Faculty, coaches, and employees in sport businesses prefer to be directed, have little ambition, avoid responsibility, and above all want security.	1. The physical and mental expenditure of energy in work is as natural as play. 2. Faculty, coaches, and employees in sport businesses will exercise self-direction and self-control to accomplish objectives to which they are committed. 3. Achieving objectives is rewarding in itself. 4. In the appropriate setting, teachers and coaches will accept and seek responsibilities. 5. The capacity to exercise a high degree of imagination, ingenuity, and creativity in the solution of organizational problems is widely distributed in the population. 6. In the modern educational setting, only a portion of intellectual potential of teachers, coaches, and sport business employees is utilized.

do. Further, theory X administrators believe that staff tend not to assume any more responsibility than necessary and prefer safety and security above all else. Obviously, this type of executive requires a tight autocratic structure to supervise employees directly (called the "scalar principle"), and the staff need to be consistently pressured to maintain adequate performance (see Table 2.1).

On the other hand, McGregor's theory Y manager would be more positive, and this attitude would encourage greater staff performance. Theory Y management emphasizes the independence, responsibility, and growth of individuals in organizations.

This view holds that the teachers, coaches, and sport business employees are basically self-directed and can be highly self-motivated. Accordingly, if staff members are committed to the goals and objectives of the school, they will perform at higher levels. Naturally, the theory Y administrator holds to a less rigid organizational structure with less direct supervision and emphasizes more professional self-evaluation. One possible problem with theory Y, which McGregor

recognized several years after first promulgating his theory, was that the Y approach usually required the administrator to go along with the consensus of the next lower level of managers or staff. Frequently this represents the popular decision rather than the bold innovative approach required of a dynamic leader. (See Table 2.2.) For theory Y to work effectively in a sport setting, the staff must buy into the concept that they will more likely be able to achieve their own goals by directing their efforts toward accomplishing the goals of the organization.

Quality Circles in Sport

The quality circle philosophy seeks to enhance mutual respect, open communication, and trust within the group and throughout the organization. Quality circles are small groups of individuals who have similar functions and meet regularly, usually one hour a week, to identify and solve common problems. The circles are usually led by a trained facilitator. The chairperson of a department or AD would be a logical leader. In industry, quality circles have led to increased productivity and reduced defects, absenteeism, and turnover.

Table 2.2	Organizational Systems			
System	Scope	Primary Purpose	Adaptability for Sport	Difficulties
TQM (total quality management)	Very wide and complex	Cut costs, improve products and profits	Could be effective for teachers and coaches, but not for students	Requires long-term commitment and considerable cost
MBO (management by objectives)	One-to-one	Performance-based evaluation	Excellent for evaluating teachers and coaches	Identifying how to measure attainments
McGregor's theory X and theory Y	Affects all employees	Increase performance	Easily adapted	None
Quality circles	From a few employees to all	Enhance communication and feedback	Easily adapted	Requires open and honest employees and administration
Theory Z	Culture of whole organization	Improve quality of employees, and thus increase productivity	Excellent	Requires more resources to be devoted to employee improvement

The central concept of the quality circle is that the best ideas for operating or changing an educational program or department come from the teachers or coaches—not from the administrators. With this system, the administrator should have more time and energy to manage and lead, rather than to discipline, evaluate, and solve problems. It requires a self-confident and progressive administrator to loosen the reins of authority enough to make the system work.

An example of applying this concept could be found in a high school athletic department. Each week, the captains of the athletic teams could meet. A member of the administration would be present to act as a facilitator as the group talks about problems and works out solutions.

Theory Z in Sport

William Ouchi, who studied a large U.S. company and coined the term *theory Z*, wrote the book *Theory Z: How American Business Can Meet the Japanese Challenge* and believed that the system could apply to schools very well. McGregor's theory X and theory Y distinguished between lead-ership styles, Ouchi maintained, whereas *theory Z relates to the culture of the whole organization*. Ouchi also believed that quality circles could be compatible with theory Z, but that the latter theory is a larger and more pervasive system.

The theory Z organization would more resemble a clan than a typical bureaucracy because the whole staff would share in establishing goals and objectives. To successfully implement a theory Z organization, administration and employees must trust one another, and the staff must have the best interest of the program at heart. All employees would also need to become knowledgeable about the resources and problems of the whole organization.

Some theorists of leadership are arriving at the same point as the original theory Z, but refer to it as all employees in the *workgroup* or *community* working together. Drath (1996, p. 2) states,

Leadership is a property of a social system, an outcome of collective meaning-making, not the result of influence or vision from an individual. We might call this the idea that leadership is a property of a social system relational leadership, pointing to the way it arises in the systematic relationships of people doing work together.

From a leisure studies approach, this clan or community view of leadership might be referred to as a *holistic ecology-based approach* that promotes new ideas and responds quickly to change. The leader's primary responsibility would be to establish dialogue with others. This would result in a process of influence wherein the administrator, public, and employees would share in the advancement of the organization (Edginton, 1997).

Much of the theory Z concept comes from successful Japanese industry, which has a pervasive tendency toward lifelong employment. This is one reason why this theory may be more compatible with U.S. schools than with U.S. businesses—because of the tenure concept in education. Building on this long-term commitment of teachers through a theory Z organization would result in (1) more thorough screening of initial appointees and more rigorous evaluation before granting tenure; (2) more commitment from the institutions on sabbaticals, job exchanges, funding of workshops, staff development, and job enrichment; (3) more commitment by teachers to solid long-term program development; and (4) more face-to-face contacts (Ouchi and Price, 1993).

From the leader's perspective, in the theory Z operation the administrator would become more of an inspirational leader, with more time to be visible, to visit schools and classrooms. Teachers and coaches would be more likely to question administrators' decisions. Coaches would be given longer contracts (in the absence of tenure) and would be evaluated less on the basis of winning and losing. Because their jobs would be secure, teachers and coaches would feel more commitment to their school and its reputation, program, and future. But because the teachers and coaches would have had a say in the development of the goals of the programs, the problems would be more likely to be minor. There should be less friction between teachers and the administration.

I'm not allowed to run the train
    nor make the whistle blow
I'm not allowed to let off steam
    nor see how fast she'll go
I'm not allowed to set the brake
    nor even ring the bell
But let the damned thing jump the track
    and see who catches hell.

Author unknown

■ POWER

Power is commonly defined as to what extent and in what manner we can get what we want, or what capacity we have to get others to do what we want them to do. Brunner (1997, p. 6) stated, "Most educators defined *power* as power over people," while he suggests more should view power as power with others. It has been suggested that power falls into three categories. The first, *threat power,* is primarily destructive. That is, "If you don't do what I want, something you don't want will occur." (Perhaps your budget will be cut, or you won't receive a raise.) The second type is *exchange power,* which is primarily productive. "If you do something for me, I'll do something for you." This might result in bargaining, conversation, contract, or just an understanding. Destructive potential exists if one party fails to live up to the agreement; but, on the other hand, trust could develop, which would lead to the third level, called *power through integration.* This has the greatest potential and is based on love and trust. Here the power pie gets bigger every time you cut it (Rist, 1993).

These examples might be viewed as *macro* uses of power, while the following could be seen as *micro* examples of power. *Reward power* offers to provide others with something they value. *Coercive power* operates with threats, injury, or abuse to another. It is destructive, negative, and unconditional, and therefore different than discipline. For example, "If you don't win, you're fired." *Legitimate or authority power* is gained through the position one holds. It has limited benefits, restricts group problem solving or synergy, and obviously should be used sparingly and usually limited to emergencies in sport management. *Referent power,* based on mutual respect, develops slowly as values, interests, and personal situations are learned about one another. Investing in listening and sharing will be required. *Expert power* comes from superior knowledge, and while valuable to an organization, it has an advantage to the individual only when the expertise is actually needed (Slack, 1997).

Information power is derived from intelligence, amounts of data, and the accuracy of the information known about the matter at hand or the organization. Sometimes this is referred to as *corporate memory,* which again can be very valuable at specific times to an organization, but powerful to the person only at those times. "Administrators sometimes hoard power because they feel there's not enough to go around and they don't have as much as they need. The paradox is that hoarding power produces divided and powerless organizations. People stripped of power look for ways to fight back through sabotage, passive resistance, withdrawal or angry militancy" (Bolman and Deal, 2002, p. 25).

Group power relates to the power emanating from group dynamics and group synergy, which can be very powerful indeed, and therefore must also be appropriately used so it doesn't emerge into groupthink. *Groupthink* refers to the concurrence-seeking tendency that leads groups to poor decisions. The more *cohesive* the group—that is, the greater the amiability and esprit de corps among the members—the greater the possibility independent critical thinking will be absent. Thus when the cohesion of the group becomes based upon social–emotional factors as opposed to task-oriented objectives, groupthink will more likely occur along with irrational decisions. When this occurs, the driving force of the group becomes keeping harmony, sociability, and the group in-tact, rather than focusing on the power, intelligence, and critical level of the decision or accomplishment of the objectives (Bernthal & Insko, 1993). This might support

zero-based committee strategies wherein committees must justify their existence each year or be eliminated.

■ LEADERSHIP

Warren Bennis, professor of business administration and author of *Why Leaders Can't Lead,* interviewed leaders of all types of companies and not-for-profit organizations. He reported that orchestra conductors and coaches might best represent the metaphor for future leaders. He observed that leadership—the key determinant in the success or failure of any human institution—must be related to the times in which it functions and that almost all organizations are presently caught between two paradigms in how they organize themselves and how they are led. The future mindset will be alignment, creativity, and empowerment—from "macho" to "maestro" (Norris, 1992).

James Houghton, CEO of Corning, also emphasizes that future leaders will differ from those of the past. He believes we must recognize and accept the fact that the Industrial Revolution is over and that we are in the age of information. Alliances will become more and more important. The labor pool will become more diverse and will be more empowered. These factors will shape the structure and behavior of future organizations and leaders (Houghton, 1992).

Former Superintendent George Goens reports,

> Leadership, however, is more than talking tough and "doing" things. The crux of leading and leadership is relationships. Relationships can have positive or negative energy and they can be stimulating or sapping. How productive are relationships based on fear and retribution? How productive are relationships based on forgiveness, compassion, and reconciliation? (2002, p. 32).

The National Center for Educational Leadership has been searching to unravel the mysteries of leadership for several decades. The more they explored, they became convinced that the answers hinge on matters of faith, soul, and spirit.

In the book *Leading with Soul,* the four gifts leaders can bestow are as follows:

- *Authorship*—a sense of pride and satisfaction felt when something unique is created.
- *Love*—the caring or a person's compassion and concern for others—to serve the best interests of the institution and its stakeholders.
- *Power*—the capacity to make a difference and to have an impact.
- Significance—the dual aspects of importance and meaningfulness (Goens, 2002).

Developing a Leader

Leadership at its most basic level is getting others to buy into an intangible idea: the leader's vision of what a company could be. As a manager, if you're asking your members and staff to share your vision, you've got to behave as if you can see, smell, and taste it. In other words, your goals, your stated values, and your action must match. (O'Brien and Sattler, 2000, p. 58).

The leader doesn't order people to "get going," but instead says, "Let's go." The leader is a step ahead leading the way. Competent leaders have necessary technical skills, but also know how to relate well to others. They are "self-starters" with "drive." Effective leaders are willing to take risks and they are flexible; they have the ability to examine and re-examine the performance of areas in the light of changing conditions. The leader must possess poise, wisdom, a quick mind, energy, determination, and the ability to keep on task when frustrated and disappointed.

Tan (1997, p. 30) states, "To date, there is little evidence to suggest that expertise comes primarily through heredity or as a birthright. Rather, expertise appears to germinate from a stable set of characteristics and grows with practice and experience." One position is that young professionals who have "it"—those who demonstrate early in their professional careers that they are self-starters and have special leadership qualities—are quickly identified and given management tasks. As they practice these tasks, they learn more about leadership and are given even more responsibility. The gap widens as these persons continue to soar in executive positions, where success breeds success.

Beyond technical management skills, it has been suggested that the successful leader learn to do the following things well: (1) delegating, (2) learning how and where to get advice, (3) setting life goals rather than just letting things happen, (4) discovering strengths and capitalizing on them, (5) dealing with adversity and moving on, and (6) adapting to rapid change. In the final analysis, successful leaders are the result of both *nature* (natural talents) and *nurture* (environment and skills acquisition). While administrative and interpersonal skills and techniques can certainly be taught and learned, conceptual skills and mental quickness in assessing and solving problems are much more elusive.

Leadership Theories

Through the 1950s, classical leadership theories were based on the *traits* of those studied and therefore held that leaders were essentially born. In the 1960s, Fielder developed the *LPC (least preferred coworker)* approach, the oldest of the *contingency* models. The LPC score was viewed as an indicator of the leader's motivational traits. The instrument required the leader to think of a person who could work least well, and then rate that person on a series of 16 pairs of descriptors, such as "pleasant–unpleasant." (Chelladurai, 1999, p. 168).

Studies out of Ohio State University resulted in the development of the widely used *LBDQ (leadership behavior description questionnaire)*, which has been modified several times. Because this method seldom takes into account situational factors, the results have been inconsistent.

A great amount of research in this area has been conducted at the University of Michigan. These studies have shown that successful leaders (1) are more likely to spend less time doing things subordinates do and more time planning and supervising; (2) are employee-centered rather than product-centered in orientation; (3) allow more latitude in what employees do; (4) develop a sense of cohesiveness among employees; and (5) receive general rather than close supervision from their superiors (Slack, 1997).

In 1971 House promulgated a path–goal theory of leadership, which is based on the leader removing roadblocks and pitfalls from the employee's path so that goals can be obtained and the journey can be more pleasant. In this regard, the leader's role is supplemental. The leader will provide rewards or satisfaction or as an instrument for future rewards.

> The theory focuses on members' personal goals, their perceptions of the organizational goals, and the effective path to these goals. . . . The second proposition of the path–goal theory is that the motivational effect of leadership is a function of the situation that, in turn, comprises the members and the environmental pressures and demands. Members' personality and their perceptions of their ability affect their preferences or reactions to specific forms of leader behavior. Similarly, leader behavior should be varied according to the nature of the tasks; that is, the extent to which they are routine or variable . . . the path–goal theory places greater emphasis on members, their ability, and their personal dispositions (Chelladurai, 1999, p. 166).

In an attempt to synthesize and reconcile existing theories of leadership, Chelladurai constructed a multidimensional model. "Essentially, the model focuses on three states of leader behavior—required, preferred, and actual. It classifies the antecedent variables that determine these leader behaviors into situational characteristics, member characteristics, and leader characteristics. The consequences (i.e., outcome variables) in the model are group performance and satisfaction" (Chelladurai, 1999, pp. 161, 164).

In the 1980s Hersey and Blanchard developed the *situational leadership* theory. It is based on two types of leader behavior: (1) task behavior—the leader structuring how work is to be done; and (2) relationship behavior—providing support to employees and openly communicating with them.

■ DIVERSITY, EMPOWERMENT, AND VISION IN LEADERSHIP

In reviewing the literature and research in leadership, one is struck by the increase in attention and volume of material relating to "diversity, empowerment, and vision." Many businesses, institutions, and agencies recognize that embracing diversity is necessary by law, but it also makes good business sense. By mirroring the diverse customer base, market share can be maintained and cost savings realized, productivity can be increased with better quality, and fairness and pride result (Morrison, 1992a). "Perhaps 85 percent of the net new workers entering the work force before the turn of the century will be from groups other than native-born white men" (Morrison, 1992b).

Diversity. A variety in our patrons, staff, players, or students results in the potential for strength. In sport, we have an excellent record of embracing (sometimes albeit on court orders to begin with) diversity. In the 1950s many colleges and schools included blacks on their squads. In the 1960s there began a wider acceptance of foreign students on teams. Through the impetus of Title IX, women have been included in sport in greater numbers. Through enforcement of the Americans with Disabilities Act (ADA), there has been more (and there should be greater numbers) athletes with disabilities participating in recreation and sport.

The latest frontier appears to be the recognition and acceptance of gays and lesbians as participants, coaches, and leaders. Pat Griffin, the author of *Strong Women, Deep Closets: Lesbians and Homophobia in Sport,* reports that athletic directors and sport managers who do not recognize and plan for this issue will be overwhelmed when it occurs (Rochman, 2002). Administrators in sport, recreation, and physical education need to first become up-to-date on research and information. If possible, talk to others who have been involved with the situation. Become knowledgeable about the legal issues. Meet with superiors both to educate them and to have strategies for dealing with the issues approved in advance. Meet with staff

Table 2.3 New Leadership, Compared to Old Leadership	
Less Emphasis	More Emphasis
Planning	Vision/mission
Granting responsibility	Infusing vision
Controlling and problem solving	Motivating and inspiring
Establishing routine and balance	Stimulating creativity and innovation
Retaining power	Empowering others
Creating compliance	Creating commitment
Contractual obligations	Trust and voluntary effort
Detachment and rationality	Interest in employees and intuition on part of leader
Reactive approach to environment	Proactive approach to environment

Adapted from Bryman, A. (1992). *Charisma and leadership in organizations.* London, Sage.

to openly discuss issues that might arise from athletes, coaches, or administrators becoming public with gay or lesbian lifestyles—such as transportation, overnights, recruiting, and rights of athletes and employees. Encourage the staff to think "out of the box" on other issues and how to fairly treat all situations that could arise. If a leader must make a public announcement in reaction to one of these issues, it would be wise to have the announcement cleared by legal counsel and superiors (Rochman, 2002).

Empowerment.   Empowerment might be considered as preparing a staff for self-supervision—a win–win situation in which managers are helpers, not bosses (Sattler and Doniek, 1993). However, employees cannot be empowered to take initiative and make decisions without a manager who is *involved and knowledgeable* (Sayles, 1993).

Vision.   "There is no more powerful engine driving an organization toward excellence and long-range success than an attractive, worthwhile, and achievable *vision* of the future, widely shared" (Nanus, 1992, p. 3). Shared vision apparently represents a psychological contract between employees and the administration for mutual

benefit (De Meuse and Tornow, 1993). An old proverb states that unless you change direction, you are likely to arrive at where you are headed. Visionary leaders have that long-range vision of where to be headed—they are results-oriented, have an agenda that is attainable, and persuade others to join in the effort to achieve it. They inspire trust and focus on people (Nanus, 1992). The new leadership emphasizing diversity, vision, and empowerment is reflected in Table 2.3.

Leadership is about dreams and possibilities, and at its core, it is about people. Leaders are creators who must make connections with people. Leadership is about dreams (Houston, 2002). Some have called leaders with vision *charismatic;* their behaviors are inspirational, intuitive, and symbolic. "Charismatic leaders transform the needs, values, preferences, and aspirations of their followers, and motivate them to make sacrifices and perform above and beyond the call of duty. Followers of charismatic leaders are generally less motivated by self-interest and more motivated to work toward collective initiatives" (Hadden and Sattler, 2000, p. 60).

Organizational leaders who really make a difference have the vision to *facilitate transitions*—in themselves, in the organization, and in the employees. Such transitions involve letting go of old assumptions and norms, and gaining interpersonal insight by utilizing feedback from others. "Leadership at this level is captured by three powerful words: *courage, discipline,* and *faith*" (Noer, 1996, p. 4).

Bob Lee, president of the Center for Creative Leadership, summarized the core of leadership development by saying that *feedback* is the primary element in personal change. He reports that the vision and focus of the developing leader then "shifts to planned goals, identifiable behaviors, and expected outcomes. And each identifies a continuing process as *the right way to go,* as opposed to just a one-time event" (Lee, 1996, p. 7). Can you think of the many direct applications this process has to sport administration?

Some authorities describe visionary leadership as *shared vision* or *systems thinking*—implying feedback and working *with* employees, not *over* them. This might be called *team learning.* Some refer to this concept as the *fifth discipline* or *systems thinking* (McAdams, 1997). All stakeholders must be motivated to bring the vision to reality (Lease, 2002).

Modeling and Leadership

It can be taken at face value that any sport administrator who presents a healthy and fit image is more likely to have a positive image on customers, employees, or students than one who presents the opposite image. Leading journals such as *Athletic Management* believe in "modeling" to the point that they regularly select and honor outstanding models (Bradley, 1996; Rochman, 1997).

Those who have roles in sport administration have immense exposure. Coaches have even more impact on youth. It is not surprising to see youngsters walking, talking, and dressing like their coaches (Rafaeli and Pratt, 1993). Would it be surprising that these same youngsters would also follow the ethics and value systems of their coaches? It goes without saying that a coach, physical education teacher, or sport administra-

tor who smokes in the presence of youngsters, or who is obese, undeniably fails to model healthy fitness attitudes for youth.

Should physical educators, coaches, or health–fitness staff be required to pass fitness tests similar to those for the military, firefighters, or airline pilots? While this writer has always believed strongly that those promulgating health and fitness should exemplify the best personal health and fitness their makeup allows, there is another side to consider. These persons, in general, are not usually employed to perform, but are employed to teach, motivate, and stimulate others. The question is, does one's lack of health or fitness affect one's competence in those areas?

The answer may be situational depending on (1) whether the employee is meeting the public or is leading/teaching a fitness activity or health education, and (2) the age or sex of the participants.

The American Alliance for Health, Physical Education, Recreation and Dance made it clear in 1998 when it issued the following vision statement:

> AAHPERD envisions a society in which all individuals enjoy an optimal quality of life through appreciation of and participation in an active and creative, health-promoting lifestyle. Members of AAHPERD and its national, district, and state associations are recognized as *dynamic role models* in the realization of this desired future. Members and staff are fully committed to accepting responsibility for continued determination of this future (AAHPERD, 1998).

Marita and Bradley Cardinal sampled 1,036 people on a Likert scale of one (strongly disagreed) to five (strongly agreed) through the Attitude Toward Role Modeling Scale (ATRMS) that contained 16 statements about modeling physical activity and fitness behaviors. The results clearly supported the importance of role modeling as a powerful teaching tool (ranked number 1) followed closely by the notion that they should practice what they preach (ranked number 2). See Table 2.4 for these results (Cardinal and Cardinal, 2001).

Rank	Statement	Mean	Standard Deviation
1	Role modeling is a powerful teaching tool for HPERD professionals.	4.56	0.57
2	It is not enough to simply stay current in the field; HPERD professionals must also "practice what they preach."	4.52	0.62
3	Involvement in regular physical activity at a level sufficient to promote health-related physical fitness is a desirable and recommended behavior for *health education teachers.*	4.48	0.59
4	Involvement in regular physical activity at a level sufficient to promote health-related physical fitness is a desirable and recommended behavior for *physical education teachers.*	4.44	0.58
5	It is important for HPERD professionals to model physical activity and fitness-promoting behaviors.	4.42	0.56
6	Involvement in regular physical activity at a level sufficient to promote health-related physical fitness is a desirable and recommended behavior for *recreation professionals.*	4.26	0.61
7	Involvement in regular physical activity at a level sufficient to promote health-related physical fitness is a desirable and recommended behavior for *dance teachers.*	4.15	0.64
8	To be effective, HPERD professionals must model physical activity and fitness-promoting behaviors.	4.14	0.79
9.5	It is important for HPERD professionals to engage in aerobic activities (e.g., bicycling, jogging) at a moderate-to-high-intensity level for at least 20 continuous minutes, three or more days per week.	4.07	0.76
9.5	It is important for HPERD professionals to stretch the major muscle groups of the body two or more days per week.	4.07	0.76
11	It is important for HPERD professionals to maintain a healthy body fat percentage.	4.00	0.73
12	HPERD professionals who regularly participate in physical activity and fitness-promoting behaviors increase their career opportunities.	3.75	0.84
13	It is important for HPERD professionals to perform at least one set of 8 to 12 repetitions of muscular development activities. (e.g., calisthenics, weight lifting) on 8 to 10 different major muscle groups of the body, two or more days per week.	3.71	0.90
14	It is important for HPERD professionals to accumulate 30 minutes or more of moderate-intensity physical activity on most, preferably all, days of the week.	3.64	0.90
15	To graduate with a HPERD degree, students should pass a health-related physical fitness test.	3.63	0.98
16	As part of their job, HPERD professionals should pass an annual health-related physical fitness test.	3.19	1.01

Table 2.4   Rank Order of Statements on the Attitude Toward Role Modeling Scale*

* The scale's directions read, "Listed below are 16 statements designed to assess your attitude toward role modeling among health, physical education, recreation, and dance (HPERD) professionals. A role model is a person whose behavior and attitude conform to that which society or other social groups expect of a person in her or his position and who has become an example for others to emulate. Please read each statement and respond by circling the most applicable descriptor or associated number."

Source: Cardinal, B. J., and Cardinal, M. K. (2001, April). Role modeling in HPERD: Do Attitudes Match-Behavior? *Joperd* 72, p. 36.

What are the modeling influences in administration? There is little research related to the effects of modeling on leadership. While there are examples of apparently successful athletic directors and school administrators who fail to measure up to commonly accepted positive modeling behavior and images, one would expect these to be exceptions. If a leader fails to give adequate notice about upcoming meetings and starts meetings late, would it not be expected that the coaches and teachers would start exhibiting the same behavior? What kind of dress would be expected from a faculty member if the leader consistently dressed inappropriately? The modeling effect of administrators in physical education and athletics has not been given attention appropriate to its importance.

Change and Innovation

Misoneism may be defined as hatred, fear, or intolerance of innovation or change. Misoneism is sometimes a problem among physical education and sport leaders. This will be fatal in tomorrow's environment. Those who thrive and embrace change will be successful. When technology changes quickly, imitators who learn by watching will leapfrog pioneers (Bolton, 1993).

A problem in management can be defined as a discrepancy between an existing and a desired situation. Problems don't always need solving, but they present *opportunities* to improve a procedure that is presently being accomplished in an average or satisfactory manner. Problems in management are not discrete, but a series of steps. The administrator recognizes that something could be done better, or a problem is evident. The leader has the resources, or it is known that they can be obtained. Action is authorized and the situation is improved, or the problem is solved.

Slack (1997) identifies the following strategies for overcoming resistance to implementing change:

- Utilizing education and communication; knowledge is power.
- Identifying those likely to resist the change, and ensuring their involvement and participation.
- Establishing "change" teams such as problem-solving committees, new venture groups, or interdisciplinary task forces.

- Identifying "idea champions" who are intensely interested in the change and utilizing them in key ways.
- Establishing a supportive atmosphere for those who will be affected by the change.
- Negotiating or bargaining with those who will be adversely affected by the change.
- Manipulating, such as distorting data, which is frequently used but is usually unethical.
- "Co-optation" by absorbing the resisters.
- "Coercion" by threatening dismissal, loss of promotion, or demotion.

In John Kotter's book *Leading Change,* he uses the following eight-step change process to describe the task of bringing about fundamental, radical change in an organization:

- Establishing a sense of urgency.
- Forming a powerful guiding coalition.
- Creating a vision.
- Communicating the vision.
- Empowering others to act on the vision.
- Planning for and creating short-term wins.

- Consolidating improvements and producing still more change.
- Institutionalizing new approaches (Bencivenga, 2002).

Decision Making

A popular way of identifying great leaders is on the basis of how they solve problems by making tough decisions. Farson (2002) believes that is not so because administrators actually make very few decisions. Problems are situations that can be solved, and therefore staffers will have done so. "Predicaments" are permanent, inescapable, complicated, paradoxical dilemmas. These are what administrators face. They cannot be solved, only coped with.

Administrators frequently make decisions by themselves, but at times they might be best served by utilizing groups, as in collective bargaining or in a democratic process with stakeholders. East (1997) outlines four constraints that affect the decision-making process in higher education: (1) time, (2) text (information), (3) context (environment), and (4) constituents. Most of the difficult decisions have a large gray area. In these cases, it is suggested that the administrator view the decision in terms of the *least harm* and the *most good* (East, 1997).

Not all decision-making processes are equally effective. It has been recommended that organizations adopt a process characterized by "inquiry" rather than "advocacy." To achieve this process, attention must be paid to the three C's of effective decision making:

- *Conflict*—vigorous debate and cognitive conflict.
- *Consideration*—all must recognize and believe that all views were entertained.
- *Closure*—becoming adept at knowing when to end deliberations (Tucker, 2002).

Scientific problem-solving methods can help solve all kinds of problems, whether they are personal or concerned with research, administration, or personnel. The concept and methods are the same. Although authorities group the steps differently, the following sequence is recommended:

1. Identify the problem. As an example, let us assume that the problem is a physical education teacher consistently arriving late for school.

2. Gather facts. Determine exactly what degree of tardiness has occurred.

3. Interpret the facts. For example, would there be a different interpretation of tardiness if the person was 64 or 24 years of age, if the first period was a class or a planning period, if the tardiness was 5 minutes or 35 minutes?

4. Evaluate alternatives and select the best solution. Sift through possible solutions; it may be necessary to repeat the previous steps as ideas occur, in order to obtain and interpret more facts.

5. Implement the decision. Let us assume that the best tentative decision would be to hold an informal conference, and gather more facts in order to possibly solve the problem.

6. Measure the solution's effectiveness. For our example, let us assume that it was determined in the informal conference that the person (a first-year teacher) had never been informed that it was necessary to be at the school at 7:45 A.M. rather than 8 A.M., and that she has promised to be prompt in the future. Subsequent reports show that this problem no longer exists.

Decisions do not improve with age. Some administrators struggle with the same problems and decisions for years without turning to alternative solutions. Others avoid making decisions hoping the problem will self-destruct. Effective administrators recognize symptoms leading to problems so that frequently they can take action to prevent the actual problem from materializing. When problems do occur, the leader must take them on and meet them, and not wait for others to bring them up. This is called *proactive* rather than *reactive* problem solving.

On the other hand, one must be able to sense when to "let a sleeping dog lie." In many cases, the effective leader will sense when it is inappropriate to raise a problem by reading the body language and attitude of others—particularly superiors. For example, a coach called an AD on one of the first days of classes in the fall (some of the busiest days of the year) and asked if the AD could be seen about a problem that day. Because the appointment schedule was full, the coach was told that unless it was serious, he could be seen the next day. The coach replied that he thought it was important and wanted to see the AD after hours. The problem turned out to be insignificant. How do you think the AD reacted to being held up after hours? What was the AD's opinion of that coach after learning that the problem was insignificant?

Delegating

Five prominent athletic directors collaborated on the strategies needed today to improve administration in athletics. They recommended delegation as the most important component for management (Hamill, 1997, p. 55). "A common mistake many planners make is giving themselves too much responsibility and the staff too little" (Capell, 1993). What does this mean? It sounds so simple. Why is it so difficult?

Some effective leaders will say delegating means arranging for others to do the work so that you have the time and energy to synthesize and analyze information from within and without, and continue to make sound decisions. There are several reasons why it is so difficult to delegate authority. First, sport management leaders who are promoted to administrative positions are usually conscientious workers, and they feel guilty if they start asking others to do work while they are not physically busy. Second, these administrators are promoted because they are highly effective, and they sometimes feel that no one else can accomplish things quite as well. In addition, they perceive that their effectiveness will be judged on how good the programs or events appear, and to make themselves look good, they want everything done perfectly. Lastly, if the subordinate is to be given the appropriate authority to accomplish a duty, the administrator is giving up a degree of control. This takes a great deal of self-confidence on the administrator's part.

The most difficult of all aspects of delegating authority is recognizing that the person might take a position with which you would not agree. But if subordinates are to grow in experience and confidence, this gamble is necessary. Look at it

this way: Only one bad thing can result for the leader if the subordinate chooses a different course—if the approach fails, the leader is slightly embarrassed. Look at the possible benefits, however: (1) The subordinate's approach may be successful, making the leader look very bright; (2) the subordinate learns from either experience; (3) if the approach fails, the subordinate is embarrassed and will work very hard to show his or her worth; (4) if the approach fails, the subordinate will recognize that the administrator let him or her try and will hold the superior in a very high regard, and greater loyalty will develop; and (5) people worth being concerned about will recognize that the leader has given a subordinate a chance to "try his or her wings" and will not judge the leader as ineffective because of such a failure.

Here are some guidelines for effective delegation:

1. The staff members who have been delegated the responsibility must have the resources and authority necessary to accomplish the task.

2. The work must be appropriate for the personnel. The key is to delegate duties and responsibilities commensurate to the experience and capabilities of employees.

3. Provide clear instructions, and allow for two-way communication. If the responsibility is simple, the communication may be verbal. If it is a long-term goal and quite complex, present the duty verbally, and ask the employee to draft the task in writing, stating the job, authority, resources, and timetable.

4. Address accountability when handing out assignments. To begin, provide the staff members with a clear statement of how the job will be evaluated.

5. Include an end report and evaluation statement. When the project is complete, a clear and concise strategic management report must be written and discussed with the employee (Horine, 1996). The administrator must give full credit publicly for a successful performance, but privately counsel staff members for poor performance.

Supervising

It is difficult to cover supervision in a separate section because it permeates most areas of administration: facilities, communication, equipment, budgeting, public relations, law, and the like. In administration, we are concerned with two forms of supervision. The first deals directly with the supervision of staff and employees. For example, are teachers following prescribed curriculum, are coaches following district rules, are fitness employees prescribing correct protocols? The second relates to the supervision that those employees are rendering to students, athletes, or participants. Are teachers spotting correctly, are coaches teaching required skills, are the fitness employees supervising the workouts of the participants?

In supervision, managers need to develop "emotional wisdom" to deal effectively with other adults. This emotional wisdom requires reaching out to others' perceptions and assumptions. Specifically, psychologists have identified five skills that the emotionally wise person uses in relationships: (1) the ability to accept people as they are, not as you would like them to be; (2) the capacity to approach relationships and problems in terms of the present rather than the past; (3) the ability to treat those who are close to you with the same courteous attention you extend to strangers and casual acquaintances; (4) the ability to trust others, even if the risk seems great; and (5) the ability not to look for constant approval and recognition from others. It has been suggested that internship or site supervisors apply this five C's framework to their visits:

- Credibility.
- Compelling vision.
- Charismatic communication.
- Contagious enthusiasm.
- Culture builder (Dollar and Sagas, 2002).

Keeping in mind the human relations orientation previously discussed, how does the supervisor jump in and get the physical education teachers or coaches "on the ball"? The first step,

oddly, has nothing directly to do with people; it has to do with carefully reading district personnel manuals, athletic activity association rules and regulations, district or school policy manuals, and most of all, employee files. Study personnel records as if you were to be rigorously examined on them. There is no shortcut to becoming prepared: it takes time and tenacity. Next, if direct supervision over others is involved, meet with each staff member to learn his or her goals and anticipated problems before real conflicts crop up. Waiting for personnel problems to develop, and then solving them—reactive problem solving—is counterproductive.

In physical education and athletics, the *group dynamics* of the departments are very important to the supervisor. The teaching or coaching staffs spend a great deal of time together, and the dynamics of the interpersonal relationships will have a direct impact on their performance. The study of group dynamics is a complete discipline in itself and beyond the scope of this section. The following, however, are some considerations for creating a closely knit staff:

1. When hiring a new person, involve several staff members in the selection.

2. Avoid transferring persons causing a problem in a group; do so only when every effort at open communication has been exhausted and the receiving staff is fully apprised of the previous situation.

3. Fully brief the new staff member and assign an established person to act as a resource.

4. If supervising several such groups (such as all coaching staffs), sit in once in a while on their staff meetings (such as a football staff planning meeting) to become more acquainted with the dynamics of each group.

5. If subgroups have an appointed or elected leader, always communicate to others on that staff through that person.

6. Enhance the group's identification and reward the members verbally ("This staff has the highest student fitness scores in the district") or materially with teaching shirts in the

- Observe the participants and their activities and reactions as well as the activity being presented.
- Observe the type of activities engaged in by those vitally interested, and by those who don't seem to be motivated.
- Observe how the leader relates content to real situations.
- Observe to determine if the objectives of the activity are clear.
- Observe the varied techniques and methods used by the leader.
- Observe things that add to the attractiveness of the learning/practice environment.
- Observe the materials/equipment used by the leader to increase effectiveness and motivation.
- Observe how the needs of participants with differing abilities and learning styles are addressed.
- Observe how routine matters are handled.
- Observe what and how assignments are made and evaluated.
- Observe the methods of evaluation.
- Observe how efficiently time is utilized, and how smoothly transitions are made from activity to activity.
- Observe leader techniques in focusing participants quickly.

Figure 2.4 Focus guide for observation of a class or practice
Adapted from *Appalachian State University Reich College of Education Student Teaching Handbook,* 1995.

school colors, or a comfortable coaches' and teachers' dressing room.

A common practice for supervisors is to work out of a central office and to visit various sites. In a young administrator's first supervisory position, a superintendent wisely said, "Your effectiveness will be measured by the amount of time you spend out 'in the field.'" Vary your supervisory visits between "announced" and "unannounced," and ask all staff members to notify you when they are covering something innovative or special, or for any other reason they want you to come. When you go to a work location, always stop to see the person in charge to report that you are there, and to see if there have been any problems or other matters requiring communication. When visiting a class, practice, or game, remain in unobtrusive locations to avoid disconcerting performers, but do not hide, because that might give the impression that you are spying. Never take over a class unless you are required to do so for safety reasons.

If it is possible to do so unobtrusively, take brief notes during the visit. Try to jot down specific examples to illustrate your observations, both positive and negative. Teachers and coaches

will relate to examples better than concepts and generalities. Always communicate, even if briefly between classes, the major items and mention something positive along with the problems. Carry a tape recorder or laptop computer to compose a summary after the visit. If it is possible, arrange for pre- and/or post- visit conferences with the employee. Lightweight and small video cameras allow the modern supervisor to "tape" classes. (See Figure 2.4.)

As soon as possible after the visit, send the summary to the employee with a copy to his or her immediate superior (AD, department chairperson, principal) and file one copy for yourself. These must be honest reports; if the person is having severe problems and the reports show "all is well," the supervisor will be in an untenable position when it comes to adverse action.

Refer to the sample supervisory report shown in Table 2.5. This is a typical report based on an actual incident.

What about criticism? You've probably heard of the saying "a little sugar will get you further than vinegar." Criticism, however, has its place when it is planned and thoughtfully delivered. The primary question is whether the criticism will help the receiver. Criticism should *not*

Table 2.5   Sample Supervisory Report of an Athletic Problem

1. As you requested, the following information is a report of statement concerning the incident at the X–Y football game.
2. I talked to the referee at halftime and all the officials after the game; what follows is their description of the events. Just before the first half ended, the umpire called a penalty against an X player. The referee related the call to the captain and after the completion of the call the X captain asked if the referee would go and talk to his coach. The referee did so, and when asked which player was involved, he called the umpire over to ask him. He reported it was X player number 15. The coach then asked which Y player was illegally blocked. The referee said he didn't know, nor was it necessary or normal to report this information. The coach then called his team over to the sideline and told the referee that the team would stay there until he got the information. The referee turned to the official scorer and gave the forfeiture sign. The other officials reminded him, however, that the rules call for two minutes to get a team ready for play before a forfeiture, so he signaled that they would wait two minutes. The referee said that this was not a team time-out. Just prior to the lapse of the two minutes, the coach sent the team back to playing position. The officials indicated that undesirable language was used by the coach. There was also mention of an unverified statement by the coach before the game that if his team received unreasonable penalties, he would pull the team off the field.
3. The events, as related by the coach at halftime, to the best of my knowledge, were as follows: The coach asked the referee to name the player who committed the infraction. The referee could not tell the coach without asking the umpire. The coach then asked which Y player was involved, and the officials wouldn't or couldn't tell him. The coach said that he was calling the team off the field until they gave him this information. The coach told me that he had a time-out and this was not intended to be a move toward inviting a forfeit, and this is why the referee changed his mind and gave them two more minutes.
4. I informed the coach that whether he was right or wrong in wanting the information, he was not to pull an athletic team off a field for any reason except an emergency. I informed him that the superintendent and I were in agreement that this was embarrassing to the district, made pawns of the players, and had no part in well-run athletics. I told him that his "position" (without defining whether I meant teacher or coach) would be in jeopardy if he pulled another athletic team off the field to protest an official's call.

be used to vent anger, to make one feel superior, or to hurt a person. Ensure that the person being criticized can see that it is in his or her best interest and that the supervisor isn't in the same guilty position. If the supervisor is frequently late, it is a bit ludicrous to criticize an employee for being late. Be sure to know and understand the personality of the employee to know that the criticism will elicit a positive change. If not, try another approach.

For the supervision of participants, the teacher, coach, or activity leader must follow basic guidelines, including being in the immediate vicinity within sight and sound of the participants. The supervisor should not leave without a replacement of equal or higher qualifications. Procedures as to what to look for, where to be positioned, what to lis-

ten for, and emergency plans should be planned and written into lesson plans and guides. The level of supervision must be in concert with the age, maturity, and skill level of the participants and the inherent risk of the activity (Merriman, 1993). Note that any special population will require increased levels of supervision.

Exercises

1. Divide into groups of 7 to 10 and establish the ground rules for functioning as a quality circle. Select one real problem that affects the group and attempt to solve it.
2. Review the material presented under organizational structure. Think of a way to illustrate the organizational structure of either a physical educa-

Critical Thinking

The chairperson of a college physical education department believed strongly in the power of modeling. Majors in physical education were required to pass a fitness and skill performance test before they could enter their student teaching internships. They were required to jog 1.5 miles, tread water, swim one length of the pool, perform some basic gymnastics maneuvers, perform slant position pull-ups (women) or chin-ups (men) and sit-ups, and complete a basic rhythms test. After several years, norms were established for men and women. Students who failed any of the tests were allowed to take and pass an activity course in the failed area, or they could practice on their own and repeat the failed tests the next semester. The assumption was that anyone who was motivated to be a physical education teacher could easily practice and pass. The coordinator for this program had the authority to grant exemptions for anyone with a disability that restricted performance in a particular area.

Based on this requirement in the physical education department, answer the following questions:

1. Was such a program a good idea?
2. Would such a program cause the students to be better teachers?
3. Most highly rated art and music schools require students to audition their talents before they are accepted as majors in that area. Should this be done for physical education?
4. All things being equal, would a fit physical education teacher be a better teacher than one who is not fit?
5. If you were to organize such a program, which of the tests would you not have included? Which others would you have included?

---

tion or athletic department in a completely untraditional way, *not* using any of the standard line and staff charts. Draw the illustration or cut items out of magazines to paste them together to form the illustration. Be creative. (Hint—a spider and web or a baseball field might be utilized.)

3. Review McGregor's theory X and theory Y administrators. Divide the class into two groups, X and Y, and hold a debate with each side defending why its system is best.

4. Divide into small groups and discuss what the physical education department head or athletic director positions will be like in 10 years. What will be the special talents and attributes necessary for successful leadership? Prepare a group written profile. (If you are interested in future leadership positions and you believe your group profile is accurate, you should set your goals now to achieve those characteristics.)

5. Divide into small groups. Prepare a list of the primary leadership characteristics of a school physical education department head or athletic director, and another list for an adult fitness program director. Compare and contrast the two. If they are significantly different, justify why this should be the case.

6. In the section on problem solving and decision making, a case example was presented that was easily solved because the cause of the problem was easily removed. Use the same example, but instead write a difficult problem. Present the new problem to the class and lead the discussion to solve it.

7. This chapter mentions several times that the effective leader delegates authority commensurate with responsibility. Write one example for athletics and one for physical education illustrating how an administrator might issue an order to a teacher or coach to accomplish a task without giving the person the authority commensurate with the duty.

8. Assume that you are the supervisor of physical education for a school district. Visit a school and watch two different teachers instruct a physical education class. Prepare a supervisor's critique of the classes.

References

Arburgey, T. L., Kelly, D., and Barnett, W. P. (1993, March). Resetting the clock: The dynamics of organizational change and failure. *Administrative Science Quarterly*, pp. 51–73.

Bernthal, P. R., and Insko, C. A. (1993, March). Cohesiveness without groupthink. *Group and Organization Management*, pp. 66–87.

Bencivenga, J. (2002, February). John Kotter on leadership, management and change. *The School Administrator* 59, pp. 36–40.

Bolman L. G., and Deal, T. E. (2002, February). Leading with soul and spirit. *The School Administrator* 59, pp. 21–26.

Bolton, M. K. (1993, Winter). Imitation versus innovation: Lessons to be learned from the Japanese. *Organizational Dynamics*, pp. 30–43.

Bradley, M. (1996, October/November). Role models. *Athletic Management* 8, pp. 27–28.

Brown, G. (2002, March). Transparency, truth in management. *Fitness Management* 18, pp. 47–51.

Brunner, C. C. (1997, December). Exercising power. *School Administrator* 54, pp. 6–9.

Bryman, A. (1992). *Charisma and leadership in organizations*. London: Sage.

CABMA Corner (2002, April). *Athletic Administration* 37, p. 45.

Capell, K. (1993, February). Time management: A professional's most underrated skill. *Financial Planning*, pp. 64–65.

Cardinal, B. J., and Cardinal, M. K. (2001, April). Role modeling in HPERD: Do attitudes match behavior? *Journal of Physical Education, Recreation and Dance* 72, pp. 34–39.

Case, R. (2002, March Supplement). A test of the situational leadership II theory in a college football setting. *The Research Quarterly for Exercise and Sport* 73, p. A 109.

Chelladurai, P. (1999). *Human resource management in sport and recreation.* Champaign, IL: Human Kinetics.

Davenport, T. H. (1993, February). Need radical innovation and continuous improvement? Integrate process reengineering and TQM. *Planning Review,* pp. 6–12.

De Meuse, K. P., and Tornow, W. W. (1993). Leadership and the changing psychological contact between employer and employee. *Issues and Observations, Center for Creative Leadership,* pp. 4–6.

Dollar, J., and Sagas, M. (2002, March Supplement). Sport management internships: the impact of site supervisor leadership behavior. *Research Quarterly for Exercise and Sport* 73, p. A 111.

Drath, W. H. (1996). Changing our minds about leadership. *Issues and Observations, Center for Creative Leadership* 16, pp. 1–4.

East, W. B. (1997, April). Decision-making strategies in educational organizations. *Journal of Physical Education, Recreation and Dance* 69, pp. 9–11.

Edginton, C. R. (1997, October). Managing leisure services: A new ecology of leadership toward the year 2000. *Journal of Physical Education, Recreation and Dance* 69, pp. 9–11.

Farson, R. (2002, February). Decisions, dilemmas and dangers. *The School Administrator* 59, pp. 6–13.

Goens, G. A. (2002, February). The courage to risk forgiveness. *The School Administrator* 59, pp. 32–34.

Hadden, C., and Sattler, T. P. (2000, April). The impact of charismatic leadership. *Fitness Management* 16, p. 60.

Hamill, G. (1997, October/November). Speaking on style. *Athletic Management* 9, pp. 55–57.

Herman, J. (1993, April). Is TQM for me? *School Business Affairs*, pp. 28–30.

Holmes, E. (1992). Leadership in the quest for quality. *Issues and Observations, Center for Creative Leadership* 12(3), pp. 5–7.

Horine, L. (1996, June/July). Deciding to delegate. *Athletic Management* 8, p. 13.

Houghton, J. R. (1992, September/October). Leadership's challenge: The new agenda for the '90s. *Planning Review*, pp. 8–12.

Houston, P. D. (2002, May). Elevating dreams to reality. *The School Administrator* 5, p. 46.

Law, J. E. (1993, April). TQM and me: Why is it important? *School Business Affairs*, pp. 24–27.

Lease, A. J. (2002, June). New administrators need more than good grades. *The School Administrator* 59, pp. 40–41.

Lee, R. (1996). Solving a puzzle. *Issues and Observations, Center for Creative Leadership* 16(1), pp. 7–8.

Mangan, K. S. (1992, August 12). TQM: Colleges embrace the concept of "total quality management." *Chronicle of Higher Education*, pp. A 25–26.

Mawson, L. M. (1993, May). Total quality management perspectives for sport managers. *Journal of Sport Management*, pp. 101–106.

McAdams, R. P. (1997, October). A systems approach to school reform. *Phi Delta Kappan* 79, pp. 138–142.

Merriman, J. (1993, February). Supervision in sport and physical activity. *Journal of Physical Education, Recreation and Dance* 64, pp. 20–21.

Miller, L. K. (1997). *Sport business management.* Gaithersberg, MD: Aspen.

Morrison, A. M. (1992a). *Diversity management and affirmative action.* San Francisco: Jossey-Bass.

Morrison, A. M. (1992b). Leadership diversity and leadership challenge. *Issues and Observations, Center for Creative Leadership* 12(3), pp. 1–4.

Nanus, B. (1992). *Visionary leadership.* San Francisco: Jossey-Bass.

Noer, D. M. (1996). Leading the liberated. *Issues and Observations, Center for Creative Leadership* 16(2/3), pp. 1–6.

Norris, M. (1992, September/October). Warren Bennis on rebuilding leadership. *Planning Review* pp. 13–15.

O'Brien, T., and Sattler, T. P. (2000, January). Integrity: The foundation of success. *Fitness Management* 16, p. 58.

Ouchi, W. G., and Price, R. L. (1993, Spring). Hierarchies, clans, and theory Z. *Organizational Dynamics*, pp. 62–91. (Originally published 1978.)

Parkhouse, B. L. (editor) (2001). *The management of sport.* Dubuque, Iowa: McGraw-Hill.

Rafaeli, A., and Pratt, M. G. (1993, January). Impact of organizational dress. *Academy of Management Review*, pp. 32–55.

Rist, M. C. (1993, June). TQM in Tupelo. *Executive Educator*, pp. 27–29.

Rochman, S. (1997, October/November). Role models. *Athletic Management* 9, pp. 29–30.

Rochman, S. (2002, April/May). A different diversity. *Athletic Management* XIV, pp. 43–49.

Sattler, T. P., and Doniek, C. A. (1993, March). How to create an empowered workplace. *Fitness Management*, insert.

Sayles, L. R. (1993). A different perspective on leadership: The working leader. *Issues and Observations, Center for Creative Leadership* 13(1), pp. 1–5.

Slack, T. (1997). *Understanding sport organizations.* Champaign, IL: Human Kinetics.

Tan, S. K. (1997, February). The elements of expertise. *Journal of Physical Education, Recreation and Dance,* 68, pp. 30–33.

Tucker, R. (2002, March). Making decisions. *Fitness Management* 18, p. 6.

3

Communication and Motivation in Sport Management and Physical Education

Management Thought

Achievement is largely the product of steadily raising one's level of aspiration and expectation.

Jack Nicklaus

Case Study: A Teacher's Push

A young physical education teacher took a special interest in her students' skills acquisition, especially that of her troubled students. She provided extra help sessions for the students lagging behind and noticed a difference for the better in their performance. At first other instructors and the supervisor were very pleased, and encouraged her work. Sometimes other instructors sent their troubled students to her.

Because she had so much energy and ambition, she was assigned to six classes and had 45 students per class instead of 30 like the other instructors. The students asked her to sponsor the outdoor club and the cheerleaders, and the supervisor assigned her the unpaid position as director of intramurals. She moved her help sessions to nights and weekends.

During this period she communicated and associated less and less with her colleagues because she was so busy and felt that they were not pulling their weight. Naturally, the rest of the staff thought this lack of communication was because she didn't like them or felt she was better than they. After serving her probationary period, she was considered for, but denied, tenure. She was totally shocked. She learned that about 20 percent of the teachers left their jobs each year.

She quickly landed a job in the management training department of a retail chain with excellent benefits, pay, and opportunity for advancement based on merit competition. She excelled, was promoted, made a good salary, and was moved from one location to another. After a decade she took stock of her life and discovered that the money she made was fine, but she felt that she lacked roots and was adrift. She believed she was not contributing to society; in fact, at times she felt that her marketing and sales skills were taking advantage of shoppers by convincing them that they needed things that were actually frills and of poor quality.

She decided to reconstitute her life and returned for a master's degree to resume teaching. Not surprising, her thesis was on the study of merit pay in education. For her return to teaching, she carefully selected a school system that allowed her to live in a community where she felt she could plant roots, a system with enough schools that one could move from one to another without having to move a home, and one with a merit system for rewarding teaching excellence.

The reader should be able to

1. Identify the barriers to effective organizational communication.
2. Describe the components of effective communication.
3. Explain the importance of nonverbal communication.
4. Become acquainted with written communication needs in sport administration.
5. Learn the essentials of leading meetings.
6. Become acquainted with some of the traditional theories of motivation.
7. Report various strategies that could be followed in motivating staff members to achieve higher performance.

▮ COMMUNICATION

Communicate: (1) to make known; (2) to transfer; (3) to pass news and information to and fro; (4) to succeed in conveying information; and (5) to be connected (Pophal, 2001–2002).

For athletic directors, communicating with employees about delegated responsibilities is key to a successful organization. Hamill (1997, p. 56) states, "Most athletic directors feel that communication is the hinge upon which the success of the departmental delegation swings. If staff are to work with one another toward fulfilling the department's mission statement, they must communicate effectively in order to act in unison. Communication, however, doesn't just happen, it requires organization and structure." Viewed from this perspective, communication is two-way. One communicates *with* others, not *at* others. In addition, one is communicating constantly by what is said or not said, what is done or not done.

Another view is to define *communication* by what you want to happen. Cole (1997, p. 49) said, "Our research with effective communication in organizations has produced the following definitions: (1) Keep people informed; (2) Encourage people to express their ideas; (3) Listen for understanding; (4) Be honest." Fatt (1997a, p. 15) agrees: "The power of words lies in their influence. Managers know how words can be used to build up or tear down a person's image."

Communication is a process, not an event. Here are 10 ways to achieve better communication:

- Understand the purpose of communication—it is designed to achieve a goal.
- Encourage internal customers to get together to discuss the issues.
- Gather additional input.
- Identify your audience.
- Create "key messages."
- Develop a timeline—in what order do your audiences need to know information?
- Develop a plan.
- Start on the inside of the organization first.
- Use multiple tools, multiple times.
- Think circular—start with the end in mind (Pophal, 2001–2002).

According to Stephen Covey, Certain attitudes and behaviors are essential to clearing communication lines:

Attitudes
- I assume good faith; I do not question your sincerity or your sanity.
- I care about our relationship and want to resolve this difference in perception. Please help me to see it from your point of view.
- I am open to influence and am prepared to change.

Behaviors
- Listen to understand.
- Speak to be understood.

- Start dialogue from a common point of reference or point of agreement, and move slowly into areas of disagreement.

When these three attitudes and behaviors are acquired, almost any perception or credibility problem can be solved. Often, once a person understands this, he will change his manner of speech. Instead of saying, 'This is the way it is,' he will say, 'This is how I see it.' Instead of saying, 'Here it is,' he will say, 'In my view'. . ." (Covey, 1992, p. 110.)

Barriers or distortions of a communication exchange that will likely cause misunderstandings are often called "noise." This noise may be either physical or psychological (Olson and Forrest, 1999). Some examples are (1) *physical noise,* such as in a gymnasium full of screaming fans; (2) *distance and time,* as in the ski area manager sending a message via radio to groomers up on the ski mountain, or leaving a message for the snowmakers coming to work later that night; (3) *spatial arrangements,* such as partitions between the coaching staff's desks; (4) *organizational distance,* such as the director of recreation communicating with the groundskeeper; (5) *source of message,* as when the person communicating does not respect or understand the other person; (6) *distraction,* such as very bright colors in an office or an attractive person walking by; (7) *lack of common knowledge,* especially when technical jargon is used ("No wonder we didn't score, he ran a post rather than a sideline"); (8) *lack of concentration* on the part of the listener; (9) *gobbledygook,* which is the smoke-screen type of verbiage designed to overwhelm by use of jargon; (10) *perceptual readiness* that each person has built up through experiences and social contacts that influence the way events, words, and actions are perceived; and (11) *semantics.* The barrier of semantics is demonstrated by the coach who says to his first football team, "You played like a bunch of farmers," which brings incredulous stares because they are all sons of farmers.

The basic components of communication incorporate the following elements:

- *Originator*—the translation of an idea, thought, or description into symbols to convey intended meaning.

- *Encoding*—finding the right symbols, which are most frequently words.
- *Channel*—sending a message by speaking, writing, or gesturing.
- *Receiving and decoding*—for communication the message must be received and then decoded by giving meaning to the message.
- *Feedback*—an acknowledgment that the message was received, such as a nod, frown, statement, or question (Olson and Forrest, 1999).

Evolution of Organizational Communication

Organizational communication has evolved through the following three stages:

1. One-way communication down. Most of our efforts in school administration are directed in this manner. But the preceding material explains that this is not communicating because there is no interacting and little understanding.

2. Administration seeking to determine what staff is thinking. Reports, quick checkups, visits, questionnaires, or suggestion boxes are utilized by management to get a pulse check on staff. Even though this method is shallow and incomplete, it is a start, and many school administrators attempt to use it.

3. Participative management. This form of management involves staff in the process of decision making and will more likely accomplish true communication. However, there can be many obstacles to building the rapport and confidence necessary for the staff to "speak up." Questioning the decisions or proposals of the "administration" may be seen as dangerous to one's promotion and retention. Sometimes management does not oppose input but has not prepared a way to receive it. In other cases, management does encourage and receive input but fails to act on it.

Communication refers to a variety of intentional behaviors consisting of speaking and acting. We use symbols to represent how we think, feel, and believe. The other half of communication is nonverbal. Our identities evolve from how we utilize these two methods of communicating.

In addition, communication is not static and arbitrary, but is always evolving as affected by culture.

Methods of Personal Communication

Staff members can communicate through one- or two-way systems. In "The Anatomy of Persuasion," Fatt (1997–1998b, p. 23) states, "Communication is a two-way, not one-way process. The two (or more) people involved in the communication are exchanging needs, whether they know it or not."

In schools, one-way communication frequently takes the form of signs, faculty notices, and loudspeaker announcements. Two-way communication occurs when the AD sends a notice asking whether Friday at 3:30 P.M. is a good time for a meeting, or when the chairperson asks the staff for suggestions on revising the activity schedule for the coming semester.

Listening. Listening is a vital element in communication, but a skill that sport managers frequently don't find natural and therefore must practice and develop. Think of the total time you spend in communication—likely almost half of it will be in listening. Some studies show that generally we retain only about one-quarter of what we hear. This certainly leaves a great deal to be desired. To improve listening skills, start by talking less, work on putting the speaker at ease, and show that you want to listen. Remove distractions such as a radio playing or a door open to noise. Show empathy, perhaps by nodding, smiling, or leaning toward the speaker. Show complete attention. Don't interrupt to finish slowly developing themes—be patient. Frequently ask questions or ask for a clarification. Be careful to draw a line between a good, active, discussion and an argument. Avoid attempting to communicate when you're angry, as almost no good can possibly occur, and you could do permanent damage to a relationship (Lesikar, Pettit, and Flately, 1996). At times, listening will reveal that both parties of a dispute have, in fact, communicated, and they just have different positions. At this point talking less and compromising more becomes necessary (Stiebel, 1993).

Formal and Informal. Communication can be formal or informal. While formal communication can be either written or spoken, it is usually deliberately planned and documented in writing or by recording, and frequently relates to a legal or policy matter. Informal communication is more spontaneous; frequently the sender doesn't even know communication is occurring. Informal communication vehicles include use of body language, tone of voice, status symbols, and space and height. For example, a supervisor could put himself or herself in a higher or larger chair across an imposing, large desk, as opposed to getting up from such a situation and sitting next to a person in the same type of chair. This writer witnessed an administrator utilize a similar nonverbal maneuver to achieve an advantage in a long and difficult negotiating session with union leaders. After introductions, he feinted as if to remove his coat, but stopped to take the coats of the union people instead and then left his on. One might question the ethics of the maneuver, but not the possible advantage achieved.

Nonverbal and Electronic Communication. There are three types of nonverbal communication: body language, space language, and time language. *Body language* is the physical movement of our bodies, such as waving or folding our arms. Folding the arms will signal that you disagree or feel negatively. On the other hand, leaning forward to listen intently will signal great interest and openness. Along with conveying individual body language, people use *space* language, which grows out of culture. Space language exists on many levels. For instance intimate space extends from touching to about 18 inches away; personal space is from there to about 4 feet; social space is from there to about 12 feet; and public space is from there to a distance of seeing and hearing. Lastly, there is *time* language. This relates to how you give various meanings to time, such as arriving early or late for appointments, prioritizing telephone calls, managing your daily schedule, or preparing an agenda for a meeting (Lesikar, Pettit, and Flately 1996). "Research indicates that as much as 85% of all communication is received through nonverbal channels. In fact, during the first four minutes of an interview, almost 100% of your impressions are based on a candidate's nonverbal presentation" (Henderson, 1989, p. 22).

When we look at a person, we must *see* the person with whom we are attempting to communicate. One must keep one's eyes and ears glued to the other person. Tension, blushing, contraction of facial muscles, fidgeting, undue preoccupation, strained laughter or giggling, and staring in silence are all nonverbal communication (Fatt, 1997a).

Nonverbal communication should be considered from the perspectives of both the senders and the receivers. In the material on listening, several strategies were presented for accomplishing better "receiving" communication—can you recall them? Identify the *spatial* and the *symbol* nonverbal communication from the previous material. In the material on interviewing, were there examples of *temporal* and *body language* nonverbal communication? How are emblems frequently used in athletics in nonverbal communication? Do men and women, athletes and nonathletes, tend to communicate nonverbally in the same ways or differently? Can you think of ways you could improve your evaluation in this class through nonverbal communication?

Athletes seem to have an unusual sensitivity to "listening" to nonverbal cues. Perhaps they have heard so many loud coaches, they look for the nonverbal to read the real message. It is important to remember that our enthusiasm and love for our sport show in our faces and our body language. Unfortunately, so do our indecision, lack of preparedness, or lack of interest in the sport.

Administrators must carefully select the type of communication they utilize. The preferred method is face-to-face verbal communication. Even if one has to walk across a gymnasium to deliver the message, it is probably faster than writing one. Certainly the message gains clarity when questions can be expressed and feedback is generated. Sometimes the manager might believe that she or he is too busy to walk to deliver a message in person; however, one should recognize that to others, this is likely perceived as laziness,

not efficiency. Make excuses to communicate one-to-one, not to avoid it. The second preferred method is via the telephone. Administrators must develop the art of effectively using the telephone so that conversations are neither abrupt nor rambling. A log of important telephone calls is recommended. The third preferred method is to draft handwritten messages, and last, utilize a typed memorandum. If the message relates to a personnel matter or another subject in which a "paper trail" is necessary, however, the typed copy is preferable.

The use of electronic mail (e-mail) accounts for much daily routine interoffice communication in many organizations. It's as easy and quick as writing a note but, at the stroke of a key, is received immediately by one or several people or everyone in the organization. Copies can be made at either end if a file is necessary. When some of the recipients have e-mail and some do not, hard copies can be sent to those not on the system. Once a modem is installed, there is no cost to send these messages, beyond the normal cost of basic telephone service. Studies have shown that the use of e-mail grew by more than 600 percent between 1995 and 2001. Executives were found to spend about two hours a day sending and receiving e-mail, and a little more time in face-to-face communication. Disturbingly, about one-third of the e-mail content was not directly related to the bottom line of the organization—an enormous loss of productivity. The study further showed that about two-thirds of the executives believed face-to-face communication skills had declined due to use of e-mail. Eighty-one percent of the employees preferred both good and bad news to be delivered to them face-to-face (Crowther, 2001).

A great deal of communication coming to chairpersons and ADs is in written form but is not of a legal nature. It is strongly recommended that educators join the progressive practice used in industry and in many government circles of endorsing in handwriting answers or messages at the bottom or margins of the original memorandum or letter. It can be easily duplicated if a record of the response is required.

Innovative Communication Enhancers

An effective strategy to increase communication with the top administration was initiated at a university in two ways. The vice chancellor for academic affairs sent out notices to all faculty that they could sign up to meet with him in small groups for a complimentary breakfast to talk about whatever they wished. Groups of 6 to 10 were arranged until all who signed up were accommodated. This has been done for several years with excellent results. Since there are normally two layers of administration between the faculty and the vice chancellor—chairs and deans—most faculty view this in a positive light. In addition, the chancellor meets once or twice a year with the faculty of each college. For half of the meeting he discusses items of particular interest to the particular college. The remaining time is open for questions from the faculty.

Communication between and among staff members of any organization is vital—if for nothing else than to reduce the number of rumors that haunt organizations with little communication (Feldman, 1993). All information barriers should be eliminated, and employees should be encouraged to keep talking and sharing ideas. Teleconferencing, e-mail at all desks, and newsletters listing the accomplishments of the organization could all be achieved. Open-door policies should be encouraged for all middle- and upper-management personnel.

The Johari Window.   Sport managers may find that communication improves when interpersonal relationships between themselves and their staff are enhanced. A method of achieving this is through the *Johari window* concept. While it is beyond the scope of this text to fully cover the subject, its principle may be summarized as follows: Leaders can enhance interpersonal relations with their subordinates by taking risks through sharing more information, beliefs, and feelings. In turn, they need to encourage and reward subordinates to do the same. As both the leader and the subordinates increase this sharing, interpersonal relationships improve and communication will grow (Horine, 1990).

Conflict Resolution.   Successful administrators know that perception is powerful. If the manager sees a conflict as a problem, a negative mindset is created. If, on the other hand, the manager perceives the conflict as a normal business situation, or as a challenge, it will be easier to solve. The conflict might even be seen as opportunity. Conflict may identify an issue, create motivation to explore it, and provide a medium to move toward resolution. Thus conflict can be changed from a negative to a positive and result in unity and further justice. The following may be considered benefits of conflict management:

- Stimulates creativity.
- Catches mistakes.
- Promotes productivity.
- Increases awareness.
- Strengthens self-acceptance.
- Facilitates personal development.
- Enhances enjoyment in the workplace (O'Brien and Sattler, 2000).

One of the least desirable tasks of the sport manager is the handling of complaints—from "I want my money back [always in the second half of an unequal game] because someone spilled a drink on me" to "I want my lift ticket replaced because someone stole it off me."

Randy Bauer, a human relations expert, conducted a workshop on how to handle angry patrons. The first step is to be a good listener (Suchetka, 1998). Remember the mnemonic device *ART:* Ask questions, Repeat what you heard the person say, and Take notes.

In a situation when an angry person approaches you, use the umbrella visualization—having an open umbrella shields you from taking things personally. Use reassuring phrases like "I really want to try to help you." Thank the person for calling the problem to your attention. If you cannot solve the person's complaint, try consulting with a coworker regarding the situation. If possible, solve the problem on the spot, but if that is not possible, give your reasons and simply state that you are sorry that you cannot meet the person's needs. Don't allow the conversation to drag on or to turn into argument ("Management Notebook," 1993).

Sample Policy: Excuses from High School Physical Education Classes

A student who has an excused absence for the whole day should not be required to make up time missed. Such students may be required to make up written work or skill tests missed and skills that were covered during the absence, however. Parental excuses for only physical education must be honored. These absences should be required to be made up hour for hour by written assignments or afterschool makeup periods.

If a student reports with a verbal excuse of sickness, it may be honored as a parental excuse with the same makeup requirements. Some students become ill after reporting to school. The policy is never to goad, cajole, drive, or demand that a student perform physical activities when he or she claims he or she is not feeling well or that the stunt is beyond his or her capability.

If a student is excused from regular physical activity by a physician for six weeks or longer, an individualized adaptive contract should be arranged in consultation with the physician.

Students well enough to be in school but possessing a parental or medical excuse from active participation in physical education normally will be required to dress in physical education uniform and report for roll call before being excused from activity. If the weather is not severe, it is recommended that these students be utilized as aides for timing and scoring.

Varsity athletes will not be excused from physical education classes. Varsity athletes may be excused from active participation in physical education on the day of a varsity contest, but shall be required to dress in regular physical education attire and attend the entire class period.

Communicating to Participants. This chapter focuses primarily on effective communication between staff and management, but it is just as important to ensure clear communication with participants. For example, in the matter of equipment, exact instructions must be provided to participants about the fit, maintenance, and care of equipment. Clearly stated emergency procedures must be written and communicated to participants. Rules and regulations from physical education instructors to students, coaching skills and techniques to varsity athletes, or instructions on use of complicated exercise equipment in a health–fitness center must be clearly communicated to the participants, and it must be ensured that the participants understand the instructions. An example of the failure to communicate is the case of *Corrigan v. Musclemakers, Inc., D.B.A. Gold's Gym,* Supreme Court of New York, Appellate Division, 258 A.D. 2d 861, February 25, 1999. A sedentary older woman, who had never been to a center or on a treadmill, joined a fitness club. As a part of the membership fee, she received guidance through her first visit with a personal trainer. Late in the visit he put her on a treadmill and set the speed at 3.5 miles per hour for 20 minutes without any instructions on how to adjust the speed or how to stop it. The woman could not keep up with the belt and was thrown from the machine and suffered injuries. Both the trial court and the appellate court held in favor of the woman based on the lack of communicating instructions and dangers (Sawyer, 2002). Refer to Chapter 8, which discusses sport law, and Chapter 9, which addresses risk management, or further information on this matter.

Policies and Procedures
One of the first things an experienced administrator requests when reviewing an organization is, "Let me see your policy handbook or personnel manual." When experienced executives move to a new organization, one of their first major priorities will be to establish or revise these documents.

Sample Policy: Football Health and Safety Policy

1. Preseason conditioning (especially for those who have been working or living in air-conditioned areas) must be emphasized.
2. No player will be allowed to practice until the physical examination is completed.
3. No contact will be allowed until after five days of organized team practices.
4. The uniform for the first five days of practices will be shorts and T-shirts; the helmet is optional.
5. The first five practices must end by 10 A.M. if held in the morning, or start after 5 P.M. in the evening. During the first two weeks, night practices are encouraged.
6. Coaches must know the symptoms of heat illness along with first aid procedures.
7. No practice may last beyond one hour without a water break.

8. No practice may last beyond two hours.
9. Practice games may not be held until after the end of the second week of practice.
10. No player missing school for health impairment on the day of a contest shall be allowed to suit up for the game.
11. No player removed from the contest because of injuries may return to the game without a physician's approval.
12. At game time, the home coach will ascertain that a physician is present, a stretcher is near each bench, and an ambulance is in place. The principal of the home school will decide whether to delay the game if the ambulance or physician is not present.
13. The physician will check with both coaches in the dressing rooms before and after the games.

For an athletic department manual, the following sections have been suggested: (1) general preface and introduction, (2) purpose of program, (3) personnel, (4) finance, (5) travel, (6) purchasing, (7) facility operations, (8) scheduling and contracts, (9) student athletes, (10) public relations, (11) camps and clinics, (12) miscellaneous.

A study of the effectiveness of such manuals concluded that policy books pay for themselves by making the organization work. They provide useful information and help to solve major common problems by standardizing work and cutting down on telephone calls. Some of the problems with the manuals are that users may have trouble finding information because of poor indexing and cross-referencing; they also may have trouble understanding what is intended because of ambiguous writing, or trusting information because it might be out of date.

How does one go about writing a manual? Collect all current policy statements according to the sections just listed and prepare a draft of any others you can think of that are needed. If possible, schedule a retreat for the whole staff so all of these materials can be reviewed and edited at one time without interruption. If this is not possible, distribute all the materials to the staff with a clear, but reasonable, deadline. Because this might appear to be an onerous task for the recipients, select the time prudently and send a covering letter from a higher authority (which you should draft) outlining the importance of the process and mentioning the deadline. Allow the staff to also draft or suggest additional policies. Each new policy must carry the endorsement of the staff or a clear majority of votes. At this point, all new policies must be approved by your supervisor.

Avoid including trivial matters or those that change frequently. After approvals, but before mass production, refer any appropriate policies to specialists such as the legal counsel, safety director, comptroller or budget officer, maintenance director, affirmative action specialist, or a resource person for matters related to the disabled. Organize the manual, including the page numbering system, so that it can be easily revised, expanded, or reduced by reprinting only the affected pages. This requires an easy insertion and removal system. It is mandatory that the manual be reviewed and revised annually so that the staff will have faith in its accuracy and currency. Refer to it often when questions of operation arise, so staff will be trained to seek direction first from the manual.

Communicating with the Staff in Written Forms

Probably the most effective and cost-efficient means of communicating with patrons or a staff that is too large or diverse to meet each week is to send out a periodic bulletin or newsletter. All staff members should be encouraged to contribute notices and reminders to this bulletin to ensure that it doesn't become administrator dominated (McDonnell, 2002).

Another more efficient, but perhaps not as effective, method of written communication is the staff bulletin board. The key to this method is to have one location that is automatically seen by the staff (and yet somewhat removed from most students or patrons) identified for staff or coach information. Only relevant material should be included, and the notices should be removed every few days so that the staff will be more inclined to scan it daily. Memoranda or letters sent to all staff members should be reserved for special topics. For a small staff typically found in recreation agencies or in a fitness center, an effective technique is to establish a policy requiring staff members to initial information after they have read it. Of course, basic policy is best communicated to all staff members through the "policies and procedures" manual.

Personal Conferences

Many school districts and some colleges require the teachers and coaches to have personal conferences once or twice a year with department chairpersons or principals. Although it might seem to the administrators to be a time-consuming task,

experience has shown this to be a wise and valuable personnel action.

It is suggested that these conferences be held during the first six weeks of each school year and again during the last quarter. In the first conference, the major thrust should be to agree on goals and objectives for the year. Frequently, it will help if these goals can be divided into general and specific categories. The means of evaluation should be included in the discussion. It serves no purpose to agree with a faculty member that teaching should be improved without specifying how this goal will be measured. If the staff member is not new, the previous several years' efforts would be reviewed.

In the second conference, the results of the year to date should be evaluated. Keep the discussion open-ended, relaxed, friendly, and very private. This is the time to hang out the shingle that states "Private Conference in Progress— Please Do Not Disturb" and hold all telephone calls. Show the person that she or he is important by giving undivided attention. It is suggested that Mondays and Fridays be avoided—and don't hold these conferences at the end of the day.

Emphasize the positive things accomplished and acknowledge the negatives not as failures, but as areas to work toward improving. Try to analyze shortcomings and discuss why they have occurred. Perhaps part of the reason is administrative—too great a load, poor facilities, lack of equipment, poor schedule, and so on. Provide a written summary of the conference, including the agreements made. One technique is to have staff members submit a preconference summary to the administrator to review before the meeting. When possible, the administrator should move out from behind a desk and sit in a neutral manner adjacent to or across from the person in a similar chair. The administrator should try to let the staff member conclude the conference. Frequently, the most important thing to be said may be held until the last moment.

Contraction and Communication

With difficult economic times often come budget restrictions. In a nonprofit organization budget crunch, the very first item to be eliminated was the newsletter. In a university in similar straits, the first item cut was the faculty/staff popular weekly newsletter. Is this wise? Communication experts think not. Reducing avenues of communication during contraction may cause the following long-lasting negative results:

- Confusion—a vacuum develops.
- Distrust and suspicion.
- Declining productivity.
- Loss of sight—employees can't see the connection between what they are doing and the success of the organization (Warner, 2001).

Committees

Committees of twenty deliberate plenty,
Committees of ten act now and then,
But most jobs are done by committees of one.

The democratic form of administration relies extensively on committees. Administrators must become skilled at establishing committees and ensuring that they are given adequate guidelines. The first requirement is to appoint a balanced group. If it is too diverse, a group spirit will likely never develop. On the other hand, unless the administrator wants the committee to arrive at a predetermined course, the group should not be completely homogeneous. Committees of three to five staff members function effectively.

The administrator should either appoint a committee chairperson, or identify a person responsible for convening the group and arranging for the election of one. In addition, it is imperative that the duties of the committee be made clear and that a date be set for the completion of its work. Experience proves that reasonably short completion times are best, taking into account time needed to gather data and the complexity of duties. The chairperson should appoint someone to record the work of the committee, and this record should be distributed before the committee meets each time along with the reminder of the next meeting.

Leading Meetings

1. Define the purpose. A meeting without a purpose should never be held! A chairperson of a faculty group said at the beginning of a meeting, "I don't know what we are supposed to do today, but as long as we're here, does anyone have any problems they want to discuss?" This is questionable administrative procedure for professionals. The first thing needed was to establish an agenda to distribute before the meeting. If this had been accomplished, it would have been evident that there was no need for the meeting.

Schedule meetings with a reasonable lead time. Usually in a school *no meeting should be called without one week's notice.* People will forget a meeting scheduled too far in advance unless there is a reminder. At the same time, establish an ending time for each meeting. Be aware that individuals will probably not contribute much of value near the closing time of a meeting, so end meetings on time or a little early.

2. Capitalize on what groups do best. Groups can't make decisions, but they are very good at troubleshooting problems, clarifying issues, and critiquing solutions to problems. Of course, frequently committees are "charged" to render a "decision," which is reflected by a vote. Remember, this reflects only what the majority believed, and if a sizable minority had strong opposing views, these should be present in the report. Keep the group's attention on the problem. The leader must summarize and solicit opinions from all members. Avoid meetings lasting longer than one and one-half hours.

3. Rewrite the meeting agenda. The preliminary agenda is only an early guide; frequently the committee chairperson must reorder the agenda or consolidate several items into one discussion. At times the agenda may be stated in terms of an overall goal—for example, the development of a recommendation to the school board for coaching stipends.

4. Avoid common tasks. As the leader, don't call meetings to stall, to shift blame to a group, or to try to create the appearance of team effort for

Table 3.1 Conference Leading	
The Effective Leader	**The Ineffective Leader**
1. Keeps emotions under control.	1. Has temper tantrums.
2. Uses many kind words.	2. Resorts to screams.
3. Gives reasonable explanations.	3. Barks commands.
4. Encourages freedom of expression.	4. Forces arbitrary decisions.
5. Says daily, "How can I improve my tact?"	5. Does not appear to think of others' feelings.
6. Suggests constructive steps.	6. Resists suggestions.
7. Protects the weak and absent.	7. Likes to see others squirm.
8. Prevents ridicule.	8. Holds others up to scorn.
9. Is interested in what conferees say.	9. Acts bored or condescending.
10. Thinks of conferees' comfort.	10. Is oblivious of others' comfort.
11. Uses a persuasive voice.	11. Speaks gruffly.
12. Relaxes facial muscles when not smiling or frowning.	12. Tenses facial muscles; appears nervous.
13. Pays compliments freely and sincerely without flattering.	13. Is stingy with acknowledgments.
14. Overlooks insignificant mistakes.	14. Seizes on errors and makes much of them.
15. Has ideals that she or he practices.	15. Is a doubter and pessimist.

something already established. Be wary of regularly scheduled meetings—they have a way of being held when not really needed, but only because they are already scheduled. In addition, if meetings are scheduled regularly for a set time and then frequently canceled, the staff becomes conditioned to expect meetings not to be held.

5. Eliminate unproductive groups. Periodically, it is necessary to carefully study the reason for a committee's existence. When a new administrator moves into a position, one interesting approach would be to establish a "zero-base" for committees. That is, all groups would be required to petition for their continuance by outlining and justifying their existence. A committee with a record of rendering poor recommendations needs to be disbanded.

6. Define appropriate topics for the size of the group. For a large gathering of more than a dozen or so persons, the topics must be general enough to be of interest to all persons. In a big meeting, people will be bored with general topics not of specific interest to them, and will start finding excuses not to attend future meetings. If a decision must be made by a large group, appoint a subcommittee ahead of time to bring a suggested course of action. Remember that if a committee presents a recommended course of action, this may be considered a "motion" and requires no "second." With small groups of about seven to nine with similar interests, genuine give-and-take discussion can be effective on narrow topics.

Some administrators have had to deal with meetings of large groups that were completely unproductive. Richard Nemec (1997, p. 10) says, "The typical business meeting involving three or more people is a total waste of time."

Becoming an effective meeting leader takes training, a quick mind, and a great deal of common sense (see Table 3.1). If the meeting involves more than a few persons, participants should agree on what procedures will be followed. In large staff meetings, a system of parliamentary law should be followed; however, common sense should prevail. These systems were devised to ensure orderly and fair debate and deliberation of issues. When the system is corrupted so as to prevent this, the leader should step in and make commonsense adjustments. For example, an important curriculum recommendation in one department was made on the basis of a vote of 3 to 2 with 15 abstentions. Does this represent a majority in favor of the change? How much enthusiastic support and commitment to this program do you think the leader can expect in the future?

The calm and positive behavior of the leader while chairing meetings is essential. Losing one's composure, lecturing the staff, or making a snide remark to one of the members who is questioning procedures is out of order. The chairperson of a meeting should not take questions or statements personally, but should skillfully use verbal arguments and reasoning to redirect the discussion back to the issue or problem.

It is imperative that the leader of a meeting present problems and issues in an impartial manner. When a meeting chairperson opens a discussion about an issue with a 15-minute position statement supporting one side of the issue, something is fundamentally wrong in the system. This leader is using the group to generate false support of a predetermined position. Some meeting leaders make a habit of appointing someone else to temporarily chair the meeting so they can freely enter the debate. This is usually counterproductive. As everyone knows, tremendous pressure is exerted on all but the most secure members of a group to go along with whatever position the leader takes.

Opening and Closing Meetings

Set the tone by getting people interested with a short, spirited introduction. Start on time. Explain the agenda and ensure that everyone understands and agrees on the purpose. Either set the ground rules yourself at the start, or have the group do so. Try to get attendees involved in some way early in the meeting. Close the meeting within the announced time span by clearly stating what follow-up assignments and decisions need to be completed (Munter, 1997).

■ MOTIVATION

Related to organizational motivation, Robbins (1997) defined *motivation* as "the willingness to exert a persistent and high level of effort toward organizational goals, conditioned by the effort's ability to satisfy some individual need" (p. 388). In the late 1800s, William James found that hourly employees could maintain their jobs by working at about 25 percent of their ability. Motivation comes about through the process of satisfying physical or psychosocial needs.

Motivation Theories

1. Traditional. According to the traditional theory of motivation, money is the primary motivator. Thus these systems of motivation are based on merit pay or "rate" pay.

2. Maslow's need hierarchy theory. Maslow promulgated this theory in the early 1940s based on the idea that people are motivated on the basis of five classes of needs ordered in a hierarchy of power or force. The first level, *physiological,* centers on basic biological needs such as food, shelter, and the avoidance of pain. The second level is for *security and safety,* which require an orderly, predictable, organized environment in which unmanageable or dangerous things do not occur. The third level is for *love and social needs* to be met. This is achieved through warm interpersonal relationships and friendships and being accepted by others. The next higher level is for meeting *esteem* needs. This relates to a person's desire for recognition and self-esteem—a desire for status, strength, achievement, respect, and confidence. The highest level is to achieve *self-actualization.* The U.S. Army has adopted this level for its motto for every soldier to be everything he or she can be by achieving to the full extent of his or her potential (Chelladurai, 1999). (See Table 3.2.) Continuing interest in these propositions shows with research findings mixed as to the level of support (Chelladurai, 1999).

3. Herzberg's motivation maintenance theory. Herzberg's ideas originated from interviews with engineers and accountants in industry and are also referred to as the *dual-factor or*

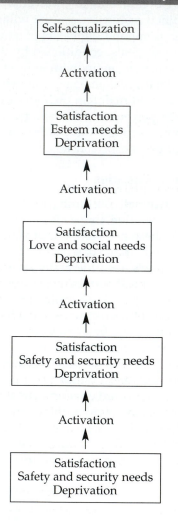

Table 3.2   Maslow's Needs Hierarchy Motivation Theory

Self-actualization

↑ Activation

Satisfaction
Esteem needs
Deprivation

↑ Activation

Satisfaction
Love and social needs
Deprivation

↑ Activation

Satisfaction
Safety and security needs
Deprivation

↑ Activation

Satisfaction
Safety and security needs
Deprivation

Source: Chelladurai, 1999.

motivation-hygiene theory. Some contend that these theories grew out of Maslow's work (Williams and Neal, 1991). Herzberg believed that satisfying the basic hygiene needs would not motivate employees but would keep them from being dissatisfied. For motivation, he advised job enrichment, such as more challenging duties. Research has shown that his theories appear to work for management-level positions, but not for lower-level workers. Interest and research in this theory continue. One such effort is based on utilization of the instrument of the Motivation Assessment and Performance Scale, or MAPS, "which combines importance–performance analysis with the construction of Herzberg's motivation/hygiene theory" (Williams and Neal, 1991, p. 60).

4. Skinner's reinforcement theory. Skinner's theory is based on the premise that if good work is reinforced, it will be repeated. If a teacher or coach produces an outstanding performance and receives a high evaluation or a certificate of merit, the teacher or coach will continue to produce according to reinforcement theory. An example of negative reinforcement would be cutting the coaching pay supplement when the number of wins declines.

5. Vroom's expectancy model. Vroom's model is a hedonistic theory according to which motivation is a drive or force within persons to perform particular actions. According to this model, employees seek to maximize pleasure and minimize pain so that drives are influenced by the outcomes of actions. Outcomes can be immediate and direct, or they can be delayed or indirect. Thus the theory is based on the employees' subjective assessment of the likelihood of certain outcomes. The perceived outcome is termed the "expectancy." If a physical education teacher expects to receive pleasurable experiences from establishing a new curriculum, this expectation will be translated into a drive to accomplish the revision.

6. Likert's linking pins group leadership model. Likert emphasized the importance of groups within the organization. He believed that organizations were interconnected by overlapping groups, with some individuals acting as linking pins by belonging to two groups. He believed that by emphasizing open communication within and between these groups, information sharing and participatory decisions would emerge to motivate individuals within the organization (Euske and Roberts, 1987).

7. Goal-setting theory. "Edwin Locke suggested that conscious goals, incentives, and intentions are related to job performance. The basic premise of Locke's model is that *people set goals concerning their future behaviors.* In this model, the process is influenced by six task/goal dimensions: goal specificity, goal difficulty, participation in goal setting, feedback on goal-directed behavior, peer competition, and goal acceptance" (Wilson, Goodall, and Woagen, 1986, p. 60).

8. Competition. Though there appears to be no major motivation theory named "competition," in practical terms it is widely utilized in industry, education, sport, and recreation. We use ladder tournaments in class, name "coach of the year," "player of the year," or "outstanding ski patroller of the season." It seems obvious that competition must work wonders as a motivator because it is so universally accepted. Is competition such a great motivator? Many authorities think not. There are usually many losers for every winner in sport. When an outstanding staff member is selected in an organization, to various degrees every other person in the organization who has worked diligently may well feel like a loser. A common problem is that it is easier to measure quantitative output than qualitative production. Competition may be more effective when the work is interdependent among workers than it is in most sport-related jobs. Competition as a motivator is likely as effective as the "worth" of the reward. In sport management, the professional recognition is probably more important than the monetary reward.

9. Hackman and Oldham model. Some theorize that when workers experience the three psychological states of meaningfulness, responsibility, and knowledge of results, positive behavioral and affective results will occur. These will include internal work motivation, general satisfaction, and growth satisfaction. Further, it is suggested that increases in skill variety, task identity, task significance, autonomy, and feedback from the work can enhance psychological states. Utilizing a revised version of the Job Diagnostic Sur-

vey, the levels of job satisfaction were evaluated from administrators of physical education, intercollegiate athletics, and recreation/intramural programs. The results showed that these administrators "generally perceived their jobs as more complex, experienced higher levels of critical psychological states, exhibited more positive affective responses, had stronger growth needs, and were more satisfied with the context of their positions than the general working population" (Cleave, 1993, p. 149).

Application of Motivational Theories

Since the majority of the employees that the administrator of physical education, athletics, or recreation will supervise have advanced formal education and training, it is wise to emphasize the meaningfulness of intrinsic motivation. Approach the staff as professionals and provide as much independence as possible to enhance intrinsic motivation. Provide visionary, realistic objectives and recognize staff members as they achieve these goals.

Because the salary and other material rewards for physical education and coaching personnel are usually set by extraneous forces, authorities frequently approach the task of motivating these employees through Herzberg's dual-factor techniques as previously discussed. It has been suggested that symbols used by administrators can influence job enrichment. For example, the AD might often state that the lifelong character of athletic team members is directly affected by the behavior of the coaches. This symbol would impress a coach with a sense of the great importance of his or her job. Job security and intrinsic job factors ranked one and two in Herzberg's studies of job satisfaction. This finding lends additional support to the notion of enriching positions as much as possible so that motivation becomes more intrinsic or self-directed.

What, in fact, satisfies and involves people in their work? Behavioral scientists say people must experience three psychological states: (1) *meaningfulness*—the teacher or coach must perceive the work as worthwhile and important;

(2) *responsibility*—the teacher or coach must believe he or she is personally accountable for the outcomes; and (3) *knowledge of results*—the teacher or coach must have regular feedback and evaluation of the results.

A study comparing the motivational needs of supervisory and nonsupervisory employees found that both groups preferred *less* autonomy, a variety of work assignment, team participation, and altruistic rhetoric. Both groups desired more financial rewards and job security. The supervisory employees considered contributing to decision making an important factor, but they rarely had an opportunity to actively participate in this process (Jurkiewicz, 1997).

A synthesis of research related to teacher and coach motivation shows that administrators who recognize staff achievements will increase the staff's effort. Research also shows that the lack of adequate salaries and job security may result in dissatisfaction but may not affect the staff's willingness to invest effort in work. Job satisfaction is more closely linked to achieving recognition than to salary or job security.

How important for motivation is it to expect people to perform well? Very! A teacher once mistakenly thought that numbers listed on students' records were IQ scores, when in fact they were locker numbers. The students were taught with those expectations. At the end of the year, their achievements matched the mistakenly high and low IQ scores. This result is referred to as the *Pygmalion effect.*

Many studies have shown that students will perform according to the expectations of the teacher or coach. Administrators must encourage teachers to expect greater achievements, based on realistic goals. There is a fine line between the positive effects of high expectations and the negative effects of too much pressure to excel and win. This fine line also exists in regard to administrators' expectations of faculty and coaches.

One of the strongest methods of motivating teachers and coaches is the least expensive—praise and recognition. Why does it seem to be so hard for many administrators to freely give praise? One reason is that they think praising others detracts from their worth; they may think that if they praise good works, the employee may expect a higher salary; they may play the role of the tough boss who is hard to please; or they may feel that if they praise too freely, their job may be in jeopardy. Leaders must accept the fact that the more they praise and recognize staff excellence, the more the employees will strive to improve, which all reflects positively on the administrator. Experience has shown that verbal reinforcement is more effective than monetary reinforcement as a continuing incentive.

Motivational Strategies

Enhancing the social atmosphere of an organization can set a positive note and increase motivation. In one school system, the supervisor for physical education and athletics initiated and sponsored once-a-month Saturday morning golf tournaments for all school administrators, teachers, and coaches. Golf courses contributed reduced rates and small prizes. A social hour and banquet followed the tournaments.

Creativity and innovation can make a staff highly motivated. Creative organizations do not occur in a vacuum; they must be fostered and nurtured. What are the more prevalent stimulants and obstacles to creativity? Research has shown that the stimulants include managers who are good role models, show enthusiasm, have good communication skills, and set a clear direction without managing too tightly. Staff members have freedom in deciding what to do, or how to accomplish a task. Employees view their job as a challenge deriving from the intriguing nature of the duty and its importance to the organization. Those factors that are obstacles include an attitude of managers unwilling to take risks, guarding "turf," an emphasis on standards other than the merit of the job performance, an excessively critical atmosphere, or a lack of feedback.

Critical Thinking

A man returned to graduate school to earn his doctorate after being a high school health and physical education teacher and administrator. After completing his degree, he found employment at a university's physical education department, and went on to be elected department chairperson.

He required all department staff to have their doctorates. The chairperson froze the salaries of staff members who did not have doctorates and had low student evaluations. Some faculty members were angry the chairperson insisted on scheduling more Friday afternoon classes. For some professors, this cut into their Friday afternoon recreational time, which had become a tradition. Obviously, he did not consult with the majority of the staff when he made these changes.

When he was making these changes, he did not get along with his direct superior, the dean. The chairperson believed the dean was showing favoritism toward her previous academic department to the detriment of the other departments at the college. The chairperson and supporters went over the dean's head for a conference with her superior, the vice chancellor for academic affairs. Meanwhile the chairperson's staff evaluated his effectiveness in the department. Most individuals on the elected review committee were not happy with the department changes.

The committee recommended that the chairperson be removed from his position and produced a list of problems in the department. The chairperson rebutted every complaint in writing and reminded the vice chancellor that he had the highest of evaluations for the previous two periods. The dean reviewed the committee's findings and recommended that he be removed. A petition signed by 80 percent of the faculty in that department recommended that he not be removed as department chair. The vice chancellor acted to remove the chairperson because the review committee and the dean's decisions agreed.

He went back to full-time teaching. A few years later he was selected for an administrative position higher than the dean's.

1. What were the major mistakes made by the chairperson before the evaluation? What could he have done differently?
2. What were the major mistakes made by the other officials?
3. How would you evaluate the system that concluded with the removal of the chairperson?
4. If the evaluation committee was not representative of the faculty, how did they end up being elected?
5. What could the chairperson have done just prior to the election of the review committee to ensure a representative committee?
6. Should the chairperson have resigned, as requested, to save himself the humiliation of being publicly removed?

Exercises

1. Describe barriers to effective communication you have experienced in sport or recreation.
2. Identify a sport or physical education example that illustrates each of the basic components of effective communication.
3. List five examples in sport or recreation of nonverbal communication.
4. Write a sample policy statement for some specific sport or physical education activity.
5. Structure the group to act as if it is a coaching staff or a physical education department faculty. Prepare a list of all the various roles or characters one could find in such a group (know-it-all, talks too much, doesn't talk at all, old-timer who says we've tried it all before and it didn't work, and so on).

Assign each member to play a role. Plan a typical meeting agenda and rotate the chairpersons to experience leading the group.

6. You are the chairperson and AD for a high school. An excellent coach with a winning record has the lowest teacher evaluation in the physical education department. He used to teach well, but lacks motivation. In small groups, discuss this situation and then list motivational strategies the administrator could try.

7. Report a strategy to motivate staff members other than those already listed.

References

Chelladurai, P. (1999). *Human resource management in sport and recreation.* Champaign, IL: Human Kinetics.

Cleave, S. (1993, May). Applicability of job diagnostic survey to administrative positions in university physical education and sport. *Journal of Sport Management,* pp. 141–150.

Cole, L. (1997, August/September). To see communication it has to be measured. *Communication World* 14, pp. 49–51.

Covey, S. R. (1992). *Principle-centered leadership.* New York, NY: Fireside.

Crowther, G. (2001, August/September). Face to face or email? *Communication World* 18, pp. 23–26.

Euske, N. A., and Roberts, K. H. (1987). Evolving perspectives in organizational theory: Communicating implications. In F. M. Jablin, L. L. Putnam, K. H. Roberts, and L. W. Porter (eds.), *Handbook of organizational communication.* Newbury Park, CA: Sage.

Fatt, J. P. T. (1997a, August/September). Affecting the senses. *Communication World* 14, pp. 15–17.

Fatt, J. P. T. (1997–1998b, December/January). The anatomy of persuasion. *Communication World* 15, pp. 21–23.

Feldman, E. (1993, February). Is your department rife with rumors? *Cleaning Management,* p. 62.

Hamill, G. (1997, October/November). Speaking on style. *Athletic Management* 9, pp. 55–57.

Henderson, P. E. (1989, January). Communication without words. *Personal Journal* 68, pp. 22–29.

Horine, L. (1990, August). The Johari window: Solving sport management communication problems. *Journal of Physical Education, Recreation and Dance* 62, pp. 49–51.

Jurkiewicz, C. L. (1997, Fall). What motivates municipal employees: A comparison study of supervisory vs. non-supervisory personnel. *Public Personnel Management* 26, pp. 367–389.

Lesikar, R. V., Pettit, J. D., and Flately, M. E. (1996). *Lesikar's basic business communication* (7th ed.). Chicago: Times Mirror Higher Education Group.

Management notebook. (1993, March). *Club Industry,* p. 43.

McDonnell, A. B. (2002, March). Using a newsletter to better reach your members. *Fitness Management* 18, pp. 32–34.

Munter, M. (1997). *Guide to managerial communication.* Upper Saddle River, NJ: Simon & Schuster.

Nemec, R. (1997–1998, December/January). Get rid of business meetings. *Communication World* 15, pp. 10–11.

O'Brien, T. and Sattler, T. P. (2000, May). The benefits of conflict. *Fitness Management* 16, pp. 54–56.

Olson, M., and Forrest, M. (1999, 5th ed.). *Shared meaning: An introduction to speech communication.* Dubuque, IA: Kendall/Hunt Publishing Company.

Pophal, L. (2001–2002, December/January). Ten steps to better communication. *Communication World* 19, pp. 16–19.

Robbins, S. P. (1997). *Essentials of organizational behavior* (5th ed.). Upper Saddle River, NJ: Prentice Hall.

Sawyer, T. H., ed. (2002, October). Considerations for training beginners on the use of treadmills. *JOPERD* 73, pp. 10–11.

Stiebel, D. (1993). The talking trap. *Executive Educator,* pp. 33–34.

Suchetka, D. (1998, January 15). Taming a tantrum. *Charlotte Observer,* pp. 5E, 8E.

Warner, S. B. (2001, October/November). When times get tough. *Communication World* 18, pp. 20–22.

Williams, A. E., and Neal, L. L. (1991, Summer). Motivational assessment in organizations: An application of importance-performance analysis. *Journal of Park and Recreation Administration,* pp. 60–71.

Wilson, G. L., Goodall, H. Jr., and Woagen, C. L. (1986). *Organizational communication.* New York: Harper & Row.

4

Human Resources in Sport Management and Physical Education

———— Case Study: Hasty Decisions Lead to Litigation ————

One autumn, as the school year opened, the women's volleyball coach resigned for personal reasons. The volleyball team had already been practicing for over a week. The athletic director quickly announced the vacancy and advertised the position. It was a large school competing in the highest division of competition, and several other fall sports, including football, were in season and demanding a great deal of the AD's attention.

A middle school teacher called the AD, asking for an appointment to discuss the position. The AD called the principal of the middle school to inquire about the candidate's background. She was told that the teacher was new, came from out of state, and had been hired because of his excellent academic preparation and recommendations.

During the interview the AD was impressed with the applicant's enthusiasm for the position and noted he had volleyball experience. Because the volleyball team had been without a coach for several days, the AD hired the man.

The next week, in practice, during an unorthodox and dangerous drill, a student was seriously injured. She sued the AD and the new volleyball coach. Investigation revealed that the coach had no coaching experience and that his volleyball experience was limited to beach volleyball. Practice plans had not been required or approved by the AD, nor had she visited any of the practices.

The reader should be able to:

1. Apply equal opportunity employment and affirmative action concepts to physical education or athletic personnel actions.
2. Demonstrate effective interviewing skills.
3. Relate humanistic personnel relations to administration in physical education and sport.

4. Outline modern applications of supervision, staff development, and time arrangement to physical education and sport.
5. Explain the relationship between stress and teacher, coach, and administrator burnout and how each can cope with stress to prevent it.

■ AFFIRMATIVE ACTION AND EQUAL EMPLOYMENT OPPORTUNITY

We often hear about the concepts of affirmative action and equal employment opportunity, but have you ever thought what they mean? *Equal employment opportunity* (EEO) means that everyone has an equal chance for employment based on qualifications. Discrimination based on race, color, religion, sex, national origin, or handicap is prohibited. This concept also applies to training, promotion, position assignment, benefits, discipline, and discharge as well as initial recruitment and employment. *Affirmative action*, as the term suggests, goes beyond EEO because it requires that employers make an extra effort to attract, employ, and promote members of minority groups. Affirmative action means to act, rather than to merely react, to minority employment. Affirmative action may be defined as a proactive process of evaluation and corrective action to eliminate past and future discrimination.

Origins of EEO and Affirmative Action

The basis for these programs might be traced to the Constitution itself, along with subsequent laws and executive orders, but EEO was specifically created through the 1964 Civil Rights Act. For the first few years, results were meager. In 1972, however, the act was expanded to cover 15 million state and federal employees. In addition, procedures were changed so that discrimination was viewed not as a single, isolated act, but as *systematic discrimination* over time.

In addition, the Age Discrimination in Employment Act (ADEA) was passed in 1967, and amended in 1978 and 1986. This act prohibits discrimination against employees over 40 and prohibits mandatory retirement ages.

Employees have a prima facie case of age discrimination if:

- The individual is a member of the protected class.
- The individual was terminated or demoted.
- The individual was doing the job well to meet his/her employer's legitimate expectations.
- Others were treated more favorably. (Miller, 1997, pp. 102–103)

Although race, gender, and age have been terms under which people file discrimination suits, religious discrimination in employment is on the rise. For a successful claim, the plaintiff must prove the following:

- A bona fide religious belief that conflicts with an employment regulation.
- The employer is informed of this belief and the resultant employment conflict.
- The employee was disciplined for failure to comply with the conflicting employment regulation. (Miller, 1997)

Rather than debate whether EEO is right or wrong, it is better to consider affirmative action as a positive opportunity to solve an old problem. Three general types of actions are considered discriminatory and are prohibited:

- *Disparate treatment*—treating a group or a member of a group differently, as in race discrimination.

- *Disparate effect*—applying policies equally to all groups, which actually penalizes some groups. For example, not hiring anyone who has been arrested (as opposed to convicted) penalizes nonwhites because statistics show that nonwhites have higher arrest levels.
- *Present effects of past discrimination*—for example, using seniority in releasing high school teachers when enrollments drop while statistics show that discriminatory practices long ago resulted in a low ratio of women hired, so that women hired recently would be released in greater numbers under a seniority basis of retention.

Diversity

Diversity in the workforce is being mandated from a variety of directions. Many social scientists agree that we stimulate higher achievement and enrich lives where diverse groups work together. As the world shrinks, this is most important in relation to being exposed to other cultures. Most institutions in higher education are striving to maintain a diverse faculty and student body.

Problems have emerged, however, when either staff or students are employed or admitted who don't have adequate preparation or skills to succeed. It would appear that the solution is to provide special training for these employees or students so that diversity can be maintained, but also high standards may be achieved. Some gifted athletes are able to follow this avenue by enrolling in private secondary schools on scholarships. Another example is the West Point Military Academy Prep School. Overall, graduates of this school raise their SAT scores some 110 points (Dickerson, 1998).

To ensure success of minority graduates and others who don't feel ready for a regular position, noncredit graduate internships should be available. They could be modest-paying, teaching/coaching positions of guided practical and applied on-the-job training. These internships could also be developed in wellness, fitness centers, golf and tennis clubs, and recreation departments (Handley, 1997b).

Justice for All or Preferences for Some

Some may argue that if discrimination is wrong, then reverse discrimination must also be wrong. They also postulate that for one to suffer now for injustices in the past is not fair. Many other similar contentions, mostly spurious, have been advanced to contest affirmative action programs.

Those presenting the case for affirmative action point out that the concept simply tries to break white male dominance, especially in the professional ranks and the boardrooms. Voluntary methods have not worked, so this *proactive* system is necessary. Those supporting the concept emphasize that affirmative action is intended to *ensure that the best, most qualified person is employed*, regardless of gender or race.

Affirmative Action Guidelines

Guidelines require an employer (for an example, a school district) to perform a work analysis to determine if any minorities or women are being underutilized in a group of jobs with similar duties. The key is to determine *underutilization*—having fewer persons in a specific type of position than would be expected by their statistical availability.

To comply with an affirmative action plan in one university, the employment and recruitment procedures must meet these three conditions: The vacancy must be advertised locally and nationally; all screening procedures must be as objective as possible; and job offers must reflect equitable compensation considerations (Howe, 1997). In addition to these conditions, the department must be able to demonstrate that a qualified person was employed.

If the agency or institution is large enough to have an EEO officer, it should be standard operating procedure for this person to attend search committee meetings. At the start, it should be emphasized that all matters and materials are confidential, and that the chair of the search committee is the official spokesperson (Howe, 1997).

Many questions become illegal only when they are used to discriminate. In some situations, to carry out affirmative action, information covered in some questions might be necessary and proper. (See the list of questions in Table 4.1.)

Table 4.1 Employment Application Form or Verbal Questions That May Be Considered Unlawful Discrimination

1. *How old are you?* Discrimination based on age is prohibited by the Age and Discrimination in Employment Act specifically for persons between the ages of 40 and 70.
2. *Have you been arrested?* As previously stated, minorities have a greater proportional rate of arrests, but this fact cannot be directly associated with criminal guilt.
3. *Will you work on weekends?* This could be discriminatory toward persons of some religions. Of course this must be asked if the position requires weekend duty.
4. *How many children do you have, and what are their ages?* This obviously will lead to discrimination against women with young children because most employers think these women are more likely to miss work, or against women of some religions who tend to have more children.
5. *Have you been convicted of a crime?* While it is possible to exclude persons from some areas of work for some crimes, a general question of this sort will discriminate against minorities.
6. *What is your financial status?* Frequently this question is implied by asking what charge cards the applicant carries, whether a home is rented or owned, what is owed on automobiles and furniture, whether pay has ever been garnished to cover debts, or whether a fidelity bond has been refused. These inquiries may discriminate against minorities and women and have no relationship to teaching physical education or sport positions.
7. *Do you have close friends or relatives employed by the district?* This question might lead to discrimination either way—by favoring those who say yes, or, in some districts, refusing employment because a close relative is already in the organization.
8. *What are your physical characteristics?* The color of eyes or hair might lead to discrimination by race, and size has been used in the past to restrict employment without merit. *What is your height or weight?* Either may be discriminatory against some nationalities and women.
9. *What is the lowest salary you will accept?*
10. *What is your marital status, prior married name, spouse's name, or work? Are you widowed, divorced, or separated? Maiden name? Mr., Mrs., or Miss? What is the name of your spouse? What does your spouse do?* These questions have nothing to do with the position for which the person is being interviewed.
11. *Do you have a disability?* The disabled person may be excluded only if not qualified to safely and effectively perform duty required with *reasonable* accommodation by the employer.

Source: Adapted from Howe, 1997.

Job Descriptions and Advertising Positions

The first step in the process is to conduct a needs analysis to determine what tasks within the organization need to be accomplished. You can then write the job description to be advertised. For positions below higher education, this is a straightforward task that will include the subject(s) to be taught and whether any coaching assignment is included. In higher education this description must be carefully worded to include courses that must be taught, those that may be taught, the degree required or preferred, special competencies required (such as leading research or curriculum studies), or the ability to perform service functions such as directing a laboratory or advising students.

The *exact wording is important* so as to attract the candidates desired, but also because the *interview questions and judgment of the candidate must be based on the job description.*

The notices for vacancy must be placed according to the location of the pool of applicants. The application deadline must be indicated and must be of a reasonable length of time from the initial announcement, usually 30 days. For positions in elementary and secondary schools, it is recommended that notices be posted in all schools in the district, placed in the local paper(s), and sent to placement offices for institutions in the region that graduate majors on the level of the position. For positions in higher education, it is recommended that the notice be placed in local paper(s), the institution's faculty newsletter, a general educational newspaper such as the *Chronicle of Higher Education,* or a journal of the specific field such as *AAHPERD Update,* and that it be sent to the individual institutions, particularly those that graduate large numbers of minorities.

Since the inception of the World Wide Web, most organizations also post vacancies electronically. Most organizations have constructed and manage websites associated with their organization or school. These sites typically contain pages that advertise vacancies within the organization and often allow applicants to submit materials electronically. Independent websites also exist offering a vast array of positions in the sport, fitness, and physical education fields. The majority of these sites will accept position vacancy announcements and post them at no charge to your organization.

Applicant Screening and Interviewing

An effective screening process can help avoid negligent hiring suits. A recent study of the practices used by school districts to screen applicants resulted in the following guidelines:

- Draft a legally sound application balancing the rights of the applicants and the district's duty to conduct investigations to protect the safety of students.
- Write a tight job description with explicit job requirements, qualifications, and standards of expected performance.
- Verify all information such as past employment history, credentials, certification, possible criminal record, and personal characteristics. This is critical given the recent incidence of high-profile situations where candidate résumés have been found to have fraudulent or misleading information. It is therefore imperative that administrators carefully review the materials submitted by applicants for accuracy.
- Keep all employees involved in the screening process fully informed as to annual changes in proper procedures ("An Effective Screening Process," 1997).

Selecting the Candidate

In addition to members of the search committee, anyone who visited with the candidates should have an opportunity to present opinions to the search committee. After committee members have studied their notes from all the interviews, members should all have an opportunity to present their views. It is suggested that each present their findings by listing the strengths and weaknesses for each candidate. Some processes will require that each member rank the candidates. At this point, if possible, the chair of the search committee should attempt to bring the group to consensus to avoid a divisive vote (Thomas, 1997). Griffin (1997, p. 30) states, "The key factor in hiring staff is making sure that the 'fit' is right. Is this person going to respond to the challenges of our program? Is this person going to contribute to the chemistry of our team?"

Selecting staff for the nonschool sport businesses has evolved from selecting those who will work for the least money to selecting those with enough maturity, training, and personality to provide appropriate services to a maturing clientele. Plummer (1997, p. 33) states, "Winners in the gym wars will be clubs that understand long-term service is replacing high-pressure sales as the central operating strategy." He suggests that tomorrow's success will depend on offering salaries high enough to attract employees who meet higher standards, provide better working conditions, and put more into ongoing training and performance evaluation. Changes toward more flexible benefits and work schedules also need to be considered.

Who Should Be Interviewed?

A difficult task for the administrator and search committee is screening the applicants to determine who should be interviewed. A quick and easy first step is to eliminate any who have not met the deadline, have incomplete applications, or do not meet minimum requirements such as a specific degree. The search committee could then cull the applicants to a group of 8 to 10. The committee should meet to identify the "short list," and each of these applicants should be called.

They should be informed that they are on the short list, confirm that they are still interested in the position, and be notified that their references and other professionals will be called (Howe, 1997).

Those not on the short list should be informed that they are no longer being considered. During this time, all committee members should be involved in the calling process, but all should use the same format, ask the same questions, and take copious notes. The supervisor of every candidate can be called, if listed as a reference or to verify employment. From the reference calls and previous information, the short list should be narrowed to two or three by the committee and invited for interviews. Experience has shown not to expect to learn a great deal more about a candidate from the interview if the previous exercises have been thorough. If the candidate is not doing 75 percent of the talking in interviews, the leader must step in and rectify the situation (Howe, 1997).

The Interview Process

Remember that the interview is not only a period of assessing the candidate, but also of "selling" the organization. Frequently your number one candidate is also the primary candidate for several other positions. Usually the salaries do not differ significantly, so how the candidate feels about your organization will determine her or his acceptance of your offer. It is certainly frustrating to go through this six-month process only to have your primary candidates turn you down, and have to start the whole process over. The interview visit is the time to show "your best face."

The actual interview can range from an informal one-to-one for a local entry position to a full committee interview for a professional position. For the latter, the committee should form the questions ahead of time, and each candidate should be asked the same questions. One strategy is to have each committee member responsible to ask a specific question. Follow-up questions directly related to the questions or the answers given can be asked by anyone. Try to balance the number of follow-up questions among the candidates.

The interview should begin with questions that allow the candidates to relax and accentuate their qualifications. The interviewer should ask the candidates to recap their most significant career accomplishments. This increases their confidence and sets a positive atmosphere for the interview. Many administrators also like to follow with a question such as "Why do you think you were successful in accomplishing those tasks?" This gives the interviewer a sense of how the candidates think about the processes and people involved in their success.

One of the worst interview questions is "Tell me about your weaknesses." This puts a candidate on the defensive and typically reveals little of value to the interviewer. Savvy candidates will handle such a question with "I'm too much of a perfectioinst" or "I put in too many hours on the job and don't have much of a social life." A better question would be "All of us have encountered situations where the results did not measure up to our expectations. Could you provide any examples where this may have happened to you?" Again, a follow-up question should be directed to the attribution for this problem. "Why do you feel that more positive results were not obtained?" In listening to candidates respond to these sets of questions, be particularly cautious if a candidate takes all of the credit for successes and blames failures on everyone else.

Subsequent questions should focus on the specific tasks noted in the job description or listed in the vacancy announcement—questions like "How do you do your planning?" or "What teaching (or coaching or management) styles have you found to be most effective?" Many administrators also like to ask situation-based questions, which pose a scenario to the candidate and ask how he or she would respond. Again, this type of questioning will allow you to better understand if the candidate has the skills and personality to fit with your organization.

At the conclusion of the questions, always ensure time for questions by the candidate. (Note that *before the committee interview,* it is necessary for the applicant to have *completed a session with the administrator* of the unit to cover many of the things a candidate wants to know such as office space, computer availability, promotion policy, housing, transportation, and salary.)

The committee will usually be required to recommend two candidates for a position, perhaps in order of preference. Immediately upon receiving a written confirmation of acceptance by a candidate, call the others who were interviewed, and write the others on the short list. If the top two candidates did not accept the position, the committee must decide whether to reevaluate the remainder of the short list, or to readvertise and reopen the search.

The Successful Interview from the Candidate's Perspective

The following guidelines for job interviews have been suggested for candidates who have limited professional work experience: Learn all you can about the organization. If possible, talk with someone already working in the program. When meeting the interviewer, make good eye contact and offer a warm, firm handshake. Listen to the questions carefully and, if necessary, ask for clarification, or rephrase the question back to the interviewer to ensure understanding.

Dress and be groomed appropriately for the position for which you are interviewing. Be early—Murphy's law will likely take effect with an elevator that is inoperative, or a bus that gets locked in traffic. Use the extra time to do some mental practice and relaxation drills. Show positive body language by being open (no crossed arms), and be relaxed. Being mentally prepared will help make you feel confident. Doing practice interviews is a good idea. Remember, experience shows that the interviewer is listening to your "personality" more than the details of your answers. End the interview in an upbeat manner, and, if appropriate, follow up the interview with a letter or a telephone call.

▨ PERSONNEL SERVICES

Human Relations

Sport administrators in education, recreation, and commercial sport must sharpen their abilities in human relations. In our increasingly service-oriented economy, "people skills" will be of para-mount importance. To be a leader in human relations, one must balance being responsive to a business's or department's goals and objectives and remaining an advocate for the needs, feelings, and desires of the staff (Fraze, 1989).

To enhance positive human relations, the sport manager must affirmatively plan and embrace humanization. "The process of humanizing any area . . . involves special attention to basic needs such as recognition, caring, acceptance, self-esteem, identity, security, freedom and power to achieve goals, and clear values. Humanizing means being sensitive to the needs of people as they develop competencies" (Knapp, 1989, p. 40). Humanistic education (1) accepts the learner's needs and purposes; (2) facilitates self-actualization; (3) fosters the acquisition of necessary basic skills; and (4) personalizes educational decisions. This humanistic manager resembles McGregor's type Y administrator, previously discussed.

It has been suggested that humanistic management in industry will outproduce the traditional models by 20 to 40 percent and yield healthier and more satisfied employees. It appears that these assertions also hold true for physical education and athletics. In many ways, sport resembles a highly competitive business, and the players are like workers.

The most significant force operating today is *social trends*. One major trend is the reduction in the proportion of white males in the labor force, who now are in the minority. Society appears to be lessening its individualistic, "what's-in-it-for-me?" focus and placing more emphasis on humanism and the general welfare of society. It is generally agreed there is an evolution of authority based on consent. If, or when, this permeates sport, what effect on administration in physical education and athletics will it bring?

Some assert that because of rapid changes in society, today's students, players, teachers, and coaches might be sensitive to being "put down" by negative remarks and actions and might develop internal anger. If that anger is not expressed through the proper channels, it will somehow adversely affect performance. It has been suggested that the teacher, coach, and administrator should develop skills in the following dimensions:

1. **Encoding skills**—human relations, being personal.

2. **Decoding skills**—listening skills, getting into the other person's world.

3. **Cybernetic skills**—feedback, communicating through body language, eyes, words, summarizing what you think the other has said.

4. **Channel skills**—setting appropriate mood, tones, and atmosphere.

5. **Confrontation skills**— airing both sides of issues, not necessarily solving all problems or even deciding exactly what to do, but placing the issue out in the open.

Management by Participation

Participative management techniques have produced dramatic results. Does this concept have a place in sport management? The author believes it does. In essence, this means emphasizing democratic administration techniques as outlined in Chapter 1. The key is to ensure that all employees are fully informed on the matter at hand. Then, the more they are involved in the decision-making process, the more the organization should expect loyal and dedicated support from the group (Zeigler, 1987).

Staff Development

Assuming that everything has been done to employ the best staff, the major avenue open for improving performance is through staff development. What is it? *Staff development* includes individual and group efforts; it encompasses any planned or unplanned activity that results in improved performance. This might mean eliminating personal problems or learning a technical skill such as a new teaching method.

For employees, demand the best, and then train them well. Start with a manual that is clearly written, concise, and easy to understand. Once employees learn the routine works, ongoing training must have a high priority. All clubs must have a continuing education budget. Make it a

priority for employees to be certified, and then recognize those that are ("Employees," 1997).

Administratively, many vehicles are open for staff development. The author stumbled into one of the most successful when a new position for an elementary physical education teacher was authorized too late to have the teacher processed before the school year had started. Because no school had been promised the position and the employee had no previous experience, he was rotated for six weeks between two schools thought to have strong in-service training programs. In his evaluation of the experience, the teacher suggested that he could learn a great deal more if he could spend some time at each elementary school in the system. This rotation was scheduled, and the physical education teacher(s) from the schools he rotated to visited other schools while he was there. This continued until all elementary physical education teachers in the system had visited at least one other school. The increase in enthusiasm, communication, cross-fertilization of ideas, and esprit de corps was phenomenal. In addition, the new teacher packed years of experience into one semester.

Formal staff development plans could include the following:

- Have a teacher and coach from one school visit another to tell and show how "we" do it.
- Have a particularly strong teacher put on a clinic for the teachers and coaches in the same school.
- Bring specialists in from the central office of a large system, state office, or a college.
- Schedule group projects so that every teacher and coach is responsible for researching a specific part of the program.
- Arrange to visit other schools or special centers; employ substitute teachers to cover classes.
- Arrange after-school or night courses at the school itself.
- Rotate equipment or materials among appropriate personnel.
- Attend workshops and conferences.

The utilization of formal and informal written and verbal critiques is another excellent means of staff development. For example, after the conclusion of each grading period, call a meeting of all physical education teachers to evaluate that period. Have them list positive things to encourage and continue, and make recommendations for solving or reducing each problem. The same method can be applied to hosting any athletic event (or a whole season) or a special physical education program.

In-service training that improves service and also creates opportunities for upward mobility is vital in the club industry. For one thing, it's too time-consuming and expensive to keep hiring for the same position. Some clubs have incorporated in-service training even in the interview and initial employment process. For example, each new employee could visit a competitor's establishment and prepare an evaluation report. One chain of fitness centers requires a 40-hour program that includes certification, audiovisual presentations, and role-playing ("High-Stakes Headhunting," 1993).

While budget restrictions might prohibit purchasing large numbers of journals and books, it is recommended that the materials obtained be circulated among the schools. For example, if there were seven elementary schools in a district, every book published relating to elementary physical education could be purchased and rotated among the seven schools. The cost would be only about one book per school per year. The materials could be available to all in a central location after the initial circulation.

Employee Benefits

In most public institutions, all full-time employees will fall under the greater organization's umbrella coverage for benefits. In sport, however, many part-time employees miss coverage. Sometimes if employees' duties can be increased to three-quarter time, they will be included. In the commercial arena, providing wholesome benefits at a reasonable cost will provide many long-term gains in more productive personnel and less lost time.

There are four types of health care plans from which to choose:

- Health maintenance organization (HMO).
- Preferred provider organization (PPO).
- Indemnity plan, which allows patients to visit the doctor of their choice, but tends to be more costly than managed plans.
- Medical savings account (MSAs), which is a private account funded by the employee's pretax contributions.

When investigating plans, ask the following questions (Handley, 1997a): What are the costs? Can I choose my doctor? Does it offer access to specialists? Are there coverage limits? How much of the premium dollar is spent on health care? Does the plan have a good reputation? Can it provide excellent educational materials? Does it deliver what it promises?

Time Management

How do some CEOs of the world's largest corporations get everything done, even when working only half a day? One expert says that they reserve their serious work for "prime times" when their energy level is at its highest. They multiply their time by using a strategy called "leveraging by rapidly processing and filtering large amounts of information." As some conferences or meetings drag on with no new information being presented, you might have thought, "Would the leader just bring this thing to closure?" Effective and efficient CEOs possess a "compulsion to closure." They can't stand a nebulous ending. They'll say, "What's the bottom line? Let's get on with it" (Palmer, 1997).

Like most managers, sport management leaders have more responsibilities than time available in a week to get everything done well. This is when delegating work to a well-organized group of students can relieve the manager from tedious duties. And there are now more people over 65 years of age than there are teenagers; sport leaders should take advantage of this pool of talent for volunteer assistance.

To learn how to manage your time, consider the following points:

1. Face the fact that managing time is a skill you must develop. It will take effort to read, think, and assess what you have to do, what you are doing, and what you want to do.

2. Develop a more realistic sense of time to determine what you are doing with it. Keep a record of your expenditure of time by maintaining a log of your activities for the day and night.

3. Plot the log by grouping activities into sections such as "talking to students" and "talking on telephone," and list the percentage of time for each. Evaluate your goals and objectives and compare them to the time expenditures.

4. Learn to say no. Unless the request is for an obvious obligation, learn to say "Thank you for asking; I'll check my schedule and think about it. Contact me in a few days and I'll let you know." One can then assess how the request fits goals and time available.

5. Get organized! Discard materials that are already filed somewhere else, or those no longer essential.

6. Handle paperwork as little as possible. Have routine requests for information screened out by a secretary before they get to you. Refer appropriate telephone calls to subordinates. Utilize form letters and memos that can be easily noted and returned to the secretary.

7. Master the telephone. Be polite and social, but control the time.

8. Study and control your calendar. List the priority items on the schedule. When you know from experience that the day before home games or the last day of the grading period is hectic, mark off that whole day for that purpose and hold to it except for emergencies. Salespersons, students, or parents who don't have previous appointments will adjust to the fact that your calendar is filled.

9. Delegate all appropriate matters.

10. Relax. To be fully efficient, you must have time for yourself. A psychiatrist who was director of student health services for a college made a practice of taking the telephone off the hook, locking the door, turning off the lights, and putting his feet up on the desk for 10 minutes twice each day.

Adopting modern office communication and organization will greatly impact the time of the administrator. Effectively utilizing personal computers and simple filing systems will save large amounts of time. Wisely organizing on the computer data such as mailing lists, names and addresses of firms who take out advertisements in programs, equipment or book suppliers, and eligibility rosters will also save time (Olson and others, 1987).

The administrator's bane is the constant minor interruptions to answer insignificant questions or to solve small problems. To avoid this, experienced managers suggest publishing an operations manual. (For details, refer to "Policies and Procedures" in Chapter 3.) Such a manual not only saves the administrator's time, but saves the staff member time and can be used very effectively to save training time for new personnel (Renner, 1998). (For further information on fitness management, visit http://www.fitnessworld.com.)

Unorganized managers frequently run out of time because they are reacting to problems and overlooked deadlines. A method to reduce these "put-out-the-fire" drills is to maintain a "tickler" calendar on a computer. This is done by listing what deadlines occur, or what projects or notices need to be accomplished during every week of the year. The list in the first week in May might include notes to ensure that all budgets for the following year have been received; to send a memo to maintenance to remove all tennis and outdoor basketball nets on the last day of classes; and to send letters of thanks to all sponsors advertising in game programs during that year. It will take over a year to refine this system, but it is well worth the effort.

Conflict Resolution

Personnel conflict is inevitable in the fast-paced work of sport administration. Management must regard conflict like any other problem—as providing an opportunity to make the organization better by resolving it.

A conflict might stem from an individual or between individuals. Pinpointing the origin of the conflict is a step toward resolution.

Most of the time, conflict grows out of lack of communication or differing performance standards between areas. For example, the sales force might be happy with an increased membership, but the exercise leaders and locker room attendants might be unhappy without any more help.

Another constant source of conflict is the incongruity between "supervisory" or "management" level and working staff. Here is an excellent place for quality circles (see Chapter 2) to work. The final resolution of any conflict should result in everyone winning, not in one party giving in (Sattler and King, 1998).

The following guidelines are suggested, to travel from discord to harmony (Cocchi, 1998):

- Always keep your door and mind open.
- Hold regular meetings.
- Become a good listener.
- Empower your personnel.
- Provide adequate training.
- Create a policy guide.

Ombudsperson

An ombudsperson is one to whom any staff member may turn for answers, directions, or clarification, and sometimes to initiate relief for situations arising out of bureaucracy or maladministration. The scope of the duties of an ombudsperson include being independent; dealing with complaints or injustices; having power to investigate, criticize and publicize, but not to reverse administrative action; and serving students, athletes, staff, and faculty.

Some specific types of situations in which an ombudsperson might become involved include (1) faculty, staff, or administrative mistakes, errors, or oversights; (2) failure of persons of authority to impart sufficient information or adequate explanations; (3) the complainant being given inaccurate information or misleading advice; (4) misapplication of the rules and instruction; (5) peremptory or inconsiderate behavior on the part of officials; and (6) unjustifiable delays.

In schools and colleges, establishing ombudspersons became popular in the 1960s, with the first appointed at Eastern Montana College in 1966. By 1974 there were more than a hundred in action. It appears that the first such appointment in a department of health, physical education, and recreation was at Appalachian State University in 1973 (Horine, 1987).

As schools, recreational agencies, and colleges become larger and more complex, there develops an inherent distrust by staff and the persons being served. When an organization actively advertises that there is an ombudsperson to address unfairness or bureaucratic complexities, the staff and public will perceive that agency in a more positive and less adversarial light. Inevitably in complex organizations, wrongs occur for which existing appeal boards and grievance committees simply don't provide relief. Utilization of an ombudsperson is cost effective. Litigation and hearings involve groups of people and take many more "person hours" than an ombudsperson. It should be emphasized that the ombudsperson does not take the place of existing hearing or review boards. Remember that the complainant's name should not be used without permission. Frequently the complainant has received contradictory information and simply wants an authoritative answer. While the ombudsperson is not a counselor, frequently there will be a cathartic effect from voicing the problem to a neutral person even if no further action occurs.

■ STRESS AND BURNOUT

University of Colorado scientists have initiated experiments that subjected rats to loud noise. In each pair, one rat could stop the noise by pushing a wheel, while the other could not control it. The rats in charge of the noise were fine, but not those without control—they had "learned helplessness." These types of experiments have shown that some mind-body connections are "hard-wired" and form a new area of investigation called *psychoneuroimmunology.* "The body's immune response is a subtle, complex dance between the thymus gland

and the spleen, bone marrow, lymph nodes and special white blood cells carried by the bloodstream that reach every cell in the body" (Somerville, 1993, p. 6).

What Are Stress and Burnout?

Stress may be defined as the *strain* or *discomfort* resulting from *force* acting on you. This is a *stimulus* definition, derived from physical sciences. Stress is like a force of water straining the dam holding it back. The dam could give way from a sudden storm, or it could collapse from a gradual overload that causes constant and prolonged strain without any additional force. On the other hand, stress could be defined as the physiological or psychological response to an external event. The external event or condition is termed the *stressor*. This is a *response* definition. In this definition, the important thing is not the stressor, but how the individual responds to it.

> Stress can be best understood as a discrepancy between the perceived demands of a situation and the perceived abilities to cope with and adapt to those demands. When the demands of a situation outweigh the resources one has to handle the situation, the result is a perception of negative stress. The greater the perceived mismatch between the demands and resources, the greater the resulting physiological, psychological, or emotional response (Kelly and Gill, 1993, p. 94).

One negative response is "burnout." Some view burnout as the response one has to the consistent emotional strain of working with persons with problems. Another view is that burnout is "a multidimensional syndrome characterized by feelings of emotional exhaustion and depersonalization and a reduced sense of personal accomplishment about one's work" (Kelly and Gill, 1993, p. 94).

Type A Behavior

Type A behavior has been associated with increased health problems. Type A personalities are characterized by anxious, aggressive, and impatient behaviors; specific or overt behaviors such as muscle tensions, alertness, rapid and emphatic speech, and

fast pace of most activities; and emotional responses of anger, hostility, and irritation. Studies show that the achievement-striving dimension is positively related to performance, whereas anger and hostility are positively related to anxiety. Obviously, increased anxiety is believed to be related to health problems. Thus it is suggested that administrators should focus on intervention strategies and programs that modify the anger and hostility factors of employees with Type A personalities (Lee, Ashford, and Jamieson, 1993).

Fight or Flight?

For survival, the human body is designed to react to danger by a series of accelerated bodily changes. Long ago, these responses prepared one to either stand and fight or to flee for survival. These biochemical changes occur mostly under the direction of the hypothalamus gland, and, in part, lead to muscle tension, a surge of adrenalin and other hormones, slowed digestive processes, dilated eyes, reserve sugar supplies being pumped into the blood, increased red blood cell production, increased heart rate, and activation of blood-clotting mechanisms. This system is still operating for us, but in today's world it is seriously flawed. Teachers and coaches, for example, are constantly challenged by stressful situations that call for fight or flight, but they are restricted to reacting calmly and talking about the situation. Of course, while they appear to be calm, their autonomic systems are raging, a programmed response that is inappropriate.

Physical Education Teachers and Burnout

As previously defined, first the teacher feels "hurt" personally by the overload of stressors. Burnout is circular and feeds on itself. Once the teacher becomes lethargic and depressed, his or her schoolwork and interpersonal relations deteriorate. The teacher starts to ask, "What's the use? Parents, students, administrators don't care—I'll just roll out the ball." In addition to the difficulties just listed, the physical educator might experience insomnia; over- or undereating; sexual dysfunction; inappropriate use of drugs or alcohol; diarrhea, cramps, or constipation; overuse of sick leave; irritability, depression, ulcers, chronic back pain, or frequent headaches.

Causes. Danylchuk (1993a, 1993b) has utilized two different instruments (the Stress Diagnostic Survey and the Maslach Burnout Inventory) in studies to measure the occupational stressors and burnout among physical education faculties. Results show that the greatest stressors are qualitative overload, role ambiguity, and role conflict. Females perceived gender discrimination, quantitative overload, and time pressure as greater sources of stress than did males. Burnout was reported greater in females, faculty under 39, single subjects, coaches, and nontenured faculty than in their counterparts. Emotional exhaustion was most related to quantitative overload, job scope, and time pressure. The organizational structure contributed the most to depersonalization (Danylchuck, 1993a, 1993b).

Responses to stress can be *cognitive, behavioral,* and *physiological.* Physiological reactions to stress can be managed through relaxation training, autogenic training, systematic desensitization, and biofeedback. To manage cognitive reactions, techniques include cognitive restructuring therapies and thought stopping. Behavioral reactions can be reduced through the use of reinforcement of approach behavior or modeling techniques. All such methods require special training. Some researchers believe that stressed employees might be more likely to abandon problem-solving, proactive coping strategies in favor of emotion-focused and avoidance tactics. Thus programs that teach understanding of the process of stress and burnout will be more successful with interventions that enable employees to choose coping behavior over unproductive avoidance actions (Lee and Ashford, 1993).

A prescription for reducing burnout in physical educators is to arrange "time-outs" away from students. These might involve exercising or play periods; spending time with adults; originating new creative projects by preparing materials, researching projects, or creating something in the arts; making a change in teaching strategies or methods; meditating;

engaging in family projects or short vacations; and reducing drug and alcohol consumption.

For teachers to cope with stress, they must eliminate the myth of the "superteacher." They must understand that they cannot continue to give without replenishing. Teachers must take time for themselves and learn to say no to extra duties when they are overcommitted. Teachers need to take time off, and students deserve teachers who have. We need educational environments that allow teachers to admit failures.

Burnout and Athletic Coaches

Coaching is fraught with emotional ups and downs. The pressure to win, whether external or self-imposed, can be enormous. As a result, many coaches find themselves in a constant struggle to balance the highs and the lows in their lives. Research shows mixed levels of burnout in coaches. Kelly (1994) has reported that college baseball and softball coaches were more burned out than practitioners in other helping professions.

The causes of stress and burnout for coaches are similar to those of teachers, but with some differences:

1. Except for the higher levels, athletic coaches can quit and still maintain their full-time teaching positions with little adverse effect, either economically or professionally.

2. The athletes themselves have volunteered to participate, and therefore bring a different attitude to the activity than the in-class student.

3. A coach has almost dictatorial authority for discipline and can easily cut an athlete out of the activity, whereas a teacher has little power to eliminate problem students.

4. A coach receives constant reinforcement from the public and students about the worth of the activity and the need for it.

5. A coach has many opportunities to communicate with other adults, especially if there are other coaches on the staff.

6. It is acceptable for a coach to yell at players, officials, and fans, and even to the heavens, if there is no one appropriate to blame when adverse results occur.

7. It is acceptable to show other forms of emotion not possible for teachers, such as hugging, patting, and even crying in public.

With all the preceding coping or prevention techniques built into the job, why do we hear so much about the pressure and stress illness experienced by coaches? In part, the following might be the reasons:

1. Coaches put an impossible burden on themselves to win. Few coaches will accept and internalize the reality that for every winner there is a loser.

2. Coaches assume awesome workloads, particularly the vast majority who teach a full class load and then coach one or more sports.

3. It's difficult to live up to the "all-American" model expected by students and the public.

4. Coaches frequently experience role conflict because they are confronted with simultaneous situations for which opposite behaviors are expected.

5. Role ambiguity— frequently, clear and consistent information is not available regarding rights, duties, and responsibilities.

Along with the conflicts of the last two items, coaches must try to reconcile the two inconsistent approaches to athletics: one is based on educational and scientific principles; the other advocates winning at all costs. Other stressors are low pay, lack of job security, unrealistic performance expectations by parents and media, evaluation based on the performance of others, poor player–coach relationships, and recruiting.

Sometimes, the unique occupation of teacher and coach can produce unavoidable conflicts. The greater rewards resulting from coaching success naturally draw coaches to emphasize that role over the teacher role. From their professional training in education, coaches may realize this approach is not in concert with their true beliefs, causing long-term stress that frequently is not consciously recognized by the coach.

Coping Techniques for Coaches

Studies of burnout in coaching have generally found that the perception of burnout in coaches might be greater than is actually the case. Most studies seem to show that their burnout, while still a problem, is less than in other helping professions. Research results are mixed as to whether female coaches have greater rates of burnout than males, but research seems to support the view that they, in fact, do. This might be more the result of outside forces—such as working in what is essentially a man's environment, having "extra" or dual roles in the family, and having less experience in coaching, participation, and training—than the stress of the coaching itself. More research is needed (Kelly and Gill, 1993; Pastore and Judd, 1992; Danylchuck, 1993a, 1993b).

To head off burnout, coaches should familiarize themselves with intervention strategies. Research shows that professionals can constructively analyze and communicate their feelings to others and reduce burnout. The first step is awareness. Coaches can learn stress management techniques and utilize meditation, progressive relaxation response, autogenic training, self-hypnosis, yoga, and biofeedback. Frequently, altering a lifestyle to include appropriate exercise, nutrition, and adequate rest will help. Some authorities have recommended the elimination of all caffeine, while others have emphasized group activities and attending professional clinics and conferences.

Burnout must be of concern to the AD. Some research suggests that the administration itself is one source of stress, so everything that can be done to eliminate administration-related stress should be accomplished. A policy should be initiated of supporting (to the greatest possible extent) coaches attending meetings; providing support groups for coaches; providing superior facilities, equipment, offices, and travel arrangements; providing automatic systems for input by coaches in decisions that affect their worlds; and providing liberal praise for jobs well done (Pastore and Judd, 1992).

However, if the imbalance between the demands of the situation and the available resources is minimal, coaches will likely perceive this as a challenge, not stress. If the demands are easily exceeded by the resources, the coaches will likely be bored (Kelly and Gill, 1993).

Burnout and Administrators

Burnout of administrators may be approached from four perspectives:

1. Awareness. Accept the fact that stress drives administrators toward success and over-drives some into incapacity. Study stress to understand it and use it intelligently.

2. Tolerance. Part of the administrator's tolerance to stress is determined by the stressor, but a great deal is also determined by his or her style of reacting.

3. Reduction. Become aware of the stressors; this alone may reduce their effects.

4. Management. While the symptoms of burnout are similar for coaches, teachers, or administrators, the causes differ somewhat. School administrator burnout can be caused by the stress associated with making group decisions when one is accustomed to making independent decisions. Special legislation, layoffs, schools assuming larger social roles, administrators confronting the realities of their own individual life stages, and rapid societal change also add to burnout.

Midmanagement administrative positions might be the most stressful because middle managers frequently must resolve conflicts that affect a variety of groups with competing needs and interests. For example, reports indicate that teachers and department heads felt more stress than principals (Lee and Ashford, 1993). Some who have been in the positions believe the same applies to public school supervisors and to chairpersons in higher education.

Coping Techniques for Administrators

Most of the techniques used by teachers and coaches can and should be used by managers and administrators. Certainly, wholesome lifestyle habits regarding exercise, diet, rest, and relaxation all apply. On the other hand, restricting inappropriate ingestion of alcohol, drugs, tobacco, or caffeine might apply even more.

It has been recommended that leaders in sport and physical education cope with stress for themselves and their staff by building self-esteem with praise and recognition; emphasizing the positive, and developing opportunities for promotion and growth; integrating individual, program, and school-system goals; developing effective interpersonal relations for the staff; practicing effective leadership skills in such areas as the amount of meetings and paperwork required; and communicating.

Some strategies apply more directly to administrators. One is exercise. Teachers, coaches, and fitness leaders all are bound to get some activity, while administrators frequently have reserved parking and barely move all day long. Two opposite strategies might help—one is to force oneself out of the office to walk around the building each midmorning (especially if stairs can be incorporated), and the other is to lock the door and meditate for a few minutes twice a day.

Two additional means of reducing stress in administration include facing and solving problems in a timely manner. Problems are not like wine; they won't get finer with age. If one has all the information that will be forthcoming, and all whom should be consulted have been, give yourself an ultimatum to make the decision before leaving the office. A compromise to this, if it is a very serious matter, is to write the decision out, but leave it in your desk overnight. The overnight stress is gone, but you still have time to look it over the next day to make adjustments. Delegating is the second unique opportunity the administrator has to reduce stress.

Exercises

1. Contact your placement office to get suggestions for preparing a résumé; write it.
2. Draft a job description announcement for the position for which you would be best qualified. Prepare a letter of application for this position.
3. Write a simple job description for a physical education or coaching position. Next, write the four most difficult questions you can imagine being asked if you were interviewing for it. Pair off and, after reading the job description to your partner, ask the questions as if you were the interviewer.
4. Write a job description for a physical education teacher's or coach's position that could be filled by either sex. Prepare 10 questions, half of which are inappropriate or illegal. Pair off and allow your

Critical Thinking

The following is a typical in-box, out-box situation. Assume that you are the head of the high school physical education department and the athletic director. You have access to a secretary who also handles work for a vice principal and two full-time counselors. The time is midfall. You teach three 50-minute physical education classes per day, with three periods free for administrative duties and planning. The school has about 1,500 students, ninth through twelfth grades, with physical education elective at upper grades. You have five years of teaching experience.

The staff:

Teacher A: Female, teaches part health and part physical education six periods a day. No coaching. Eighteen years in that school.

Teacher B: Female, teaches six periods of physical education per day, coaches volleyball and softball. Total teaching experience: two years.

Teacher C: Male, teaches same as "A," 22 years teaching experience (15 years at that school). Coaches wrestling.

Teacher D: Male, teaches same as "B," first year of teaching. Is assistant football coach and coaches baseball.

Meetings: You have a standard meeting of all chairpersons and vice principals at 3 P.M. every other Thursday, and a physical education staff meeting the alternating Thursdays at 3 P.M.

Directions: It is a Wednesday and you have taught three straight physical education classes. The last football game and women's volleyball game are the coming Friday, football at home and volleyball away. Men's cross-country and women's tennis seasons have ended. Your last class of the day was over at noon; before going to lunch, you find the following in your mailbox. Read all messages first. On a separate sheet, list the order in which you would handle the messages (by item number) and write a few lines after each item, describing how you would handle it.

1. Telephone message from chairperson of nearby college physical education depart-

partner to read the job description. Ask the questions you have prepared. Your partner should indicate which questions are unfair, but assume that because the job is desperately desired, go ahead and practice answering them in such a way as to be honest and yet obtain the job.

5. Write a paragraph that describes how a coach or physical education teacher has been wronged by an administrator, resulting in hurt and anger. For example, the administrator has assigned one teacher six classes while the other three have only four. Read the description to a partner who is the responsible administrator and act out how to handle the situation.

6. Assume that you are the coordinator of physical education for five elementary schools. Classroom teachers teach all physical education classes, and you spend one day a week at each school. The principals of the schools have agreed to allot you two hours at each school the week prior to school open-

ing in the fall to present staff development programs. Outline the two-hour program you would present at each school.

7. Describe the most stressful time in your life and how you handled the stress. From information presented in this chapter, report other techniques you might have employed.

References

An effective screening process can help you avoid negligent hiring suits. (1997, February 14). *Your School and the Law* 1, p. 4.

Cocchi, R. C. (1998, January). Conflict resolution. *Club Industry* 14, pp. 34–36.

Danylchuk, K. E. (1993a, January). Occupational stressors in physical education faculties. *Journal of Sport Management*, pp. 7–24.

Danylchuk, K. E. (1993b, May). The presence of occupational burnout and its correlates in university ment requesting permission to use the high school gym for cardiac rehabilitation program for heart patients on Monday, Wednesday, and Friday from 5 P.M. to 6 P.M. all year, starting next month.

2. Telephone message from Jerry Smith of a local realty firm asking if you and the principal can play doubles tennis tomorrow at 4 P.M.

3. Telephone message from Mrs. Washington; her son's lunch was stolen from his physical education locker. She wants to know what you are going to do about it. Please call her.

4. Letter from a mother of a girl on the volleyball team complaining that the football team had two free dinners given for them, but the volleyball team had none.

5. Note from the vice principal stating that several teachers recently had discipline problems with three football players.

6. Letter requesting that a women's basketball game be scheduled.

7. Request from the cheerleaders asking you to speak at the pep rally on Friday.

8. Note from the football coach requesting that the stadium grass be cut tomorrow rather than on Friday because rain is predicted.

9. Telephone message from Jim Burns representing Big-Time Sporting Goods World; he wants to see you on Friday afternoon about winter equipment orders.

10. Memo from chairperson of Accrediting Association Self-Study Committee for the school reminding all department chairpersons that a preliminary draft of each department's report is due by the end of next week.

11. Catalog arrived from Rawlings Sporting Goods Company.

12. Forms arrived from the state athletic association for winter sports. They must be returned by December 15.

13. Note from the father of one of your students asking why his child failed physical education class. The note ends with, "How can somebody flunk gym?"

physical education personnel. *Journal of Sport Management*, pp. 107–121.

Dickerson, D. (1998, January 5). How to keep elite colleges diverse: An army-style prep school for minorities. *U.S. News and World Report*, pp. 73–77.

Employees: Demand the best, then train them well. (1997, August). *Club Industry*, pp. 13, 20.

Fraze, J. (1989, January). The "H" stands for human. *Personnel Administrator* 34, pp. 50–55.

Griffin, P. (1997, August/September). Winning the management game. *Athletic Management* 9, pp. 30–33.

Handley, A. (1997a, August). Employee benefits. *Club Industry*, pp. 27–28.

Handley, A. (1997b, September). Small club management: How to start an internship program. *Club Industry*, pp. 36–37.

High-stakes headhunting. (1993, March). *Club Industry*, pp. 24–31.

Horine, L. (1987, March). Ombudsman: Champion of compromise. *Athletic Business* 11, pp. 44–45.

Howe, R. D. (1997, October 7). *Revised equal opportunity charge.* Unpublished institutional memorandum, Appalachian State University, Boone, NC.

Kelly, B. C. (1994, March). A model of stress and burnout in collegiate coaches: Effects of gender and time of season. *Research Quarterly for Exercise and Sport*, pp. 48–58.

Kelly, B. C., and Gill, D. L. (1993, March). An examination of personal/situational variables, stress appraisal, and burnout in collegiate teacher-coaches. *Research Quarterly for Exercise and Sport*, pp. 94–101.

Knapp, C. E. (1989, February). Humanizing outdoor education: Exploring the affective domain. *Journal of Physical Education, Recreation and Dance* 60, pp. 40–43.

Lee, C.; Ashford, S. J.; and Jamieson, L. F. (1993). The effects of Type A behavior dimensions and optimism on coping strategy, health, and performance. *Journal of Organizational Behavior* 14, pp. 143–157.

Lee, R. T., and Ashford, B. E. (1993). A further examination of managerial burnout: Toward an integrated model. *Journal of Organizational Behavior* 14, pp. 3–20.

Miller, L. K. (1997). *Sport business management.* Gaithersberg, MD: Aspen.

Olson, J.; Hirsch, E.; Breitenbach, O.; and Saunders, K. (1987). *Administration of high school and collegiate athletic programs.* Philadelphia: Saunders.

Palmer, D. (1997, September). How America's most successful executives accomplish so much in so little time. *Executive Focus,* p. 23.

Pastore, D. L., and Judd, M. R. (1992, May/June). Burnout in coaches of women's team sports. *Journal of Physical Education, Recreation and Dance* 63, pp. 74–79.

Plummer, T. (1997, September). Staffing for success. *Fitness Management* 13, pp. 31–40.

Renner, M. (1998, January). Innovation: "Operations manual" organized policies, procedures, program samples, suppliers and equipment contacts into one book. *Fitness Management* 14, pp. 38–39.

Sattler, T. P., and King, J. M. (1998, January). Understanding organizational and personal conflicts. *Fitness Management* 14, pp. 20–22.

Somerville, D. (1993, May). Mind, body, and health. *Colorado Alumnus,* pp. 6–7.

Thomas, J. R. (1997, May/June). Vision and leadership for selecting and mentoring new faculty in higher education. *Journal of Physical Education, Recreation and Dance* 68, pp. 38–40, 46.

Zeigler, E. (1987, January). Sport management: Past, present, future. *Journal of Sport Management* 1, pp. 4–24.

5

Public Relations, Partnerships, Marketing, and Promotion in Sport Management and Physical Education

---

Management Thought

Of all the things you wear, your expression is the most important.

Case Study: Enrollment Increases after a PR Audit

A medium-size university located in the mountains hired a consulting firm to initiate a yearlong public relations audit. The firm sent questionnaires to alumni, administrators, students, and members of the community, asking questions regarding their demographics and geography. For example, where did graduates live and where did they work?

Many of the findings were used to develop new marketing and PR strategies and a new logo. The new university publications would emphasize the beauty, nature, and leisure opportunities in the area such as skiing, camping, and hiking.

The athletic program was found to be mostly on target. The study showed that the new marketing focus on the niche of outdoor recreation attracted a student body more interested in personal recreation and fitness, but the campus itself lacked the programs and facilities to accommodate the students' needs. This provided the impetus to create a new recreational facility and increase the staff and resources for campus and outdoor recreation offices.

An interesting finding related to the physical education department's activity courses. A couple of beginning skiing sections were offered at a ski area 15 minutes from campus. The PR audit found that about 60 percent of the incoming students had ranked snow skiing as one of their highest priorities for enrolling in the university. However, graduates reported that only about 10 percent had actually skied during their years at the university. Accordingly, many of the graduates left with a negative feeling about their stay, even if they didn't know why. From this response, the university decided to increase the opportunities for students to ski.

The majority of students could not afford skiing lessons and did not have the required equipment. The physical education department decided to offer skiing as an activity class. Because there were no staff available to accommodate greatly expanded classes, the solution was to arrange a financially attractive package with the ski area based on producing large numbers of students Monday through Thursday nights when the slopes were not busy. The package included ski rental, lessons, and a lift pass. A bus provided transportation for all the students. Additional classes were added for intermediate skiing, ski patrolling, and ski instructing. The annual enrollment grew from about 30 to about 500.

The reader should be able to

1. Define *public relations (PR)* and common terms associated with it.
2. Describe the scope and importance of PR in physical education and sport and how a PR assessment could be completed.
3. Relate the principles and guidelines of PR to physical education and sport management.
4. Differentiate product, price, place, and promotion within the marketing mix.
5. List the guidelines of fund-raising and give examples of how they apply to physical education and sport.
6. Describe examples of partnerships in sport and physical education.
7. Identify effective means of improving concession operations and profits at the institution you are attending.
8. Identify examples of PR programs in physical education.
9. Identify examples of PR programs in sport.
10. Identify examples of PR programs in fitness and wellness centers and in recreation.

■ ELEMENTS OF PUBLIC RELATIONS

Public relations (PR) is the function of top management. The head of the organization must be the "point person" to set direction, goals, and policy to establish an effective program. A good PR program depends on systematic and purposeful evaluation of public attitudes. The relevant in-depth data are developed by skillful experts using appropriate instruments and methods. A public relations program should be active, centered on the public interest, and, if the organization is large enough, carried out by quality practitioners.

School athletics and physical education are not commercial enterprises. The bottom line is not to sell a product, but rather to build an efficient program based on policies, regulations, and laws. The public must be kept informed of how the programs are meeting these objectives. All teachers and coaches must be aware that their programs are really owned by the public.

Even in commercial sport organizations, today's consumers want to make educated decisions about their fitness and health objectives. Therefore price discounting, hard-sell techniques, and hard-body-type marketing and advertising will no longer be effective. Instead, utilize the fitness-for-health educational theme that a lack of physical activity is detrimental to health. "If you want to broaden your membership base, you have to market to a more diverse group" (Cioletti, 1997).

The PR Audit

"You can't get where you're going unless you know where you have been." A *PR audit* is an examination of the program, its objectives, and results to determine how various constituencies feel about the program and what they know about its accomplishments. Sound marketing is based on timely information (Tadlock, 1993).

Audits have the following four general categories: (1) identifying the relevant publics, (2) determining what these publics think of the organization, (3) measuring what the publics believe are important issues or concerns, and (4) evaluating the publics as to their importance and power. This process has been summarized as finding out what "we" (the organization) think; what "they" (the publics) think; measuring the distance between the two; and adopting policy to diminish the difference (Baskin and Argonoff, 1988).

Communication audits include the following five steps: *Communication climate surveys* determine how open the publics perceive communication channels to be. *Network analysis* measures the frequency and importance of interaction within the organization. *Readership surveys* determine reading patterns of publics and the employees within the organization. *Content analysis* measures the amount of favorable and unfavorable media coverage the organization receives. *Readability studies* determine the clarity of the written words utilized within the organization and to the publics (Baskin and Argonoff, 1988).

Once the audit has been completed, you must integrate the audit with strategy. Irwin, Sutton, and McCarthy (2002) have suggested a five-step process for integrating PR, communication, and promotion (Figure 5.1). The first step in the process is to conduct a thorough *assessment* of the situation. Each sport organization will function in a different set of circumstances that will vary across time. Thus the current status of PR, communication, and promotional activities will serve as the baseline measure.

The second step of the Irwin et al. model is *alignment:* the process whereby all constituencies are brought together "on the same page." This is critical to ensure that all PR, communication, and promotional activities are consistent across the organization. In addition, the process of alignment will enable the assignment of specific tasks to various units and people within the organization.

Based on the previous two steps, *design* a campaign that brings all of the elements together. Specifically, components focused individually on PR, communication, and promotion need to be developed side-by-side to ensure that content, timing, and execution are coordinated.

Activation involves putting the design into motion. Again, according to Irwin et al., the key to activation is setting a timeline and checking to ensure that all activities are on track and operating according to the designed plan. As with any plan always consider the possibility that everything might not go as planned; a good administrative practice is to develop contingency plans that can be activated if the original plan encounters problems.

Finally, measure the effectiveness of the entire program. *Measurement* is often difficult and

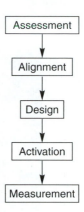

Figure 5.1   Adapted from Irwin, R. L., Sutton, W. A. and McCarthy, L. M. (2002). Sport Promotion and Sales Management, Champaign, IL: Human Kinetics Publishers, p. 18.

time consuming. However, it is the key to success. Measurement not only aids in identifying issues with the existing campaign, but also provides feedback for future adjustments to PR, communication, and promotional activities.

■ PUBLIC RELATIONS: SCOPE AND IMPORTANCE

Much expertise in PR is derived from industry. Some of these methods are excellent and easily adaptable to school programs. Industrial PR is a new field and thus is still evolving and maturing. To many, PR means publicity and is a brassy means of calling attention to a product, team, or person. But these methods are just a small part of PR.

A major problem common in industrial PR, as well as in physical education and sport PR, is the tendency to overstate the benefits of products. Whereas industry must strike a balance between the profit motive and social responsibility, administrators in physical education and sport must ensure that only scientific and professionally sound claims are made on behalf of programs. For example, if a football program is promoted as building character, citizenship, and sportsmanship, the administrator must see to it that the program does just that!

The foundation of a successful PR program is a well-rounded physical education and/or athletic program, which promote lifetime activities.
Credit: Appalachian State University Sports Information Office, Boone, NC.

PR is needed for a variety of reasons. Physical education and sport are constantly evolving, and the public needs to be informed about the changes and new programs. PR programs help raise financial support, an important factor because funding for physical education and sport is being restricted. In a democracy, the public has a right to know how their contributions are being spent, and through good PR they can find out. Lastly, the two-way communication PR provides enhances the staff's morale because their performances are recognized. At the same time, they are motivated toward greater achievements because they know that the results will be noticed.

The number of administrative positions in PR in sport is increasing. In addition, all colleges have sport information directors.

■ PRINCIPLES AND GUIDELINES FOR PUBLIC RELATIONS

Principle 1. *The foundation of a successful PR program is an excellent product.* A poorly operated program patched to look smooth will sooner or later become unglued and disintegrate. A sound program is for PR what a solid foundation is for a house. As storms come and go with lean budget years, losing seasons, or personnel problems, it is the foundation that counts.

An important aspect of an outstanding program or business is great service. Whether a business or nonprofit entity, the staff needs to be constantly reminded that job number one is to serve the public.

Principle 2. *PR must be based on the truth and the premise that the public has a right to be informed about the programs.* Any misrepresentations of facts or material will ultimately come out and result in a negative reaction greater than would have resulted from an honest report. Downgrading the players' abilities to make the coach look better is dishonest and counterproductive. The public can see through these smoke screens. Listing incorrect heights or weights is also deceptive. This sham serves no long-range purpose other than to destroy the credibility of the coach and school. A PR program must win the public's confidence through honesty, and good reputations must be jealously guarded.

Sometimes problems occur that PR specialists might like to ignore. Avoiding problems is neither honest nor professional; it is not even good PR. If the physical fitness scores have gone down, "tell it like it is." If funds have been lost, or a student has gone astray, protect the privacy of the individuals involved but report the story.

Principle 3. *PR programs must be continuous.* Although it is extremely difficult to accomplish this, the head administrator must adopt long-term plans for PR. It is easy to procrastinate because of the immediate workload, and small problems can seem more important. Then a major problem develops, such as budget trouble, and a PR campaign is launched to try to save the ship from sinking. An effective PR program is planned year-round and frequently several years in advance. Campaigns, special drives, or special events are not thrown together to put out a fire, but are planned with forethought and reason. They occur at the right time for the right reason and are mounted on a solid base of previous work and accomplishments. Administrators should develop a PR "tickler" schedule. This is a calendar for the whole year on which the dates are marked showing when notices, press releases, thank-you letters, and the like should be sent.

Principle 4. *A major responsibility is to represent the physical education and/or athletic programs to the public—to be an advocate and spokesperson.* This means that the PR program has an educational facet as well. To many, athletics reflects aggression or force, the win-at-any-cost ethic. The public should be informed of the enormously positive side of sport that should be cultivated and nurtured—its beauty and its potential to engender cooperation, sportsmanship, and the quest for excellence. How many people on the street understand what a balanced physical education program is or its potential for enriching the quality of life? PR programs should inform the public about how their support can make that enrichment possible.

Principle 5. *The PR program must be based on two-way communication.* When the information is just going out, it's publicity at best and propa-

ganda too often. An important requirement is to know what the public does and does not know about the program and, even more important, what they think about it. An administrator who listens to ideas, suggestions, and criticisms will be way ahead. After all, everyone has been a student, and many have been athletes. It is likely that they would have good ideas for improvement. Remember, many have spent a lifetime developing expertise in specialties such as insurance, food service, or equipment and should be in a position to offer meaningful suggestions. The PR-oriented administrator doesn't resist or discredit someone who complains, but instead accepts the criticism, perhaps saying, "That's an interesting way to look at the situation" or "I don't agree with your criticism, but I'll think about the situation and talk to some others about it." All personnel in physical education and sport, but especially administrators, must strive to improve listening skills. Because of their aggressive coaching backgrounds, far too many administrators are talking when they should be listening.

Principle 6. *The PR program must explore the use of all forms of media and communication avenues.* Naturally, television, radio, and newspapers need to be fully utilized. But effective PR means being creative. It is possible to communicate through alternative forms, such as dance presentations, group meetings, professional publications, open houses, bulletin boards, newsletters, letters to parents, or even motion pictures, videotapes, or slide-and-sound programs. Frequently other faculty will be willing to assist when they are encouraged to use their creativity. Students are especially useful.

Principle 7. *Positive human relations must be developed for a PR program to be successful over the long term.* Set high professional standards; avoid reporting the negative actions of subordinates, even if it means you must take the "heat." Cooperative planning involving a variety of school people also enhances positive relationships. Such planning encourages one-to-one relationships and results in face-to-face encounters. The image

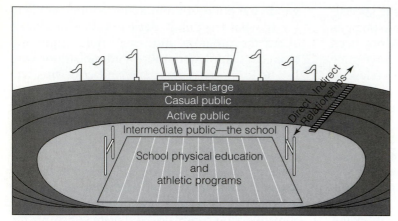

Intermediate public — Students, teachers, and staff

Active public — Parents of athletes, students, sports people, and spectators who regularly attend contests

Casual public — Ex-sports people and fans who follow records of teams and attend occasional contests

Public-at-large — Public who have never been interested in physical activity and have no present interest in progress of school teams

Figure 5.2 The "publics" of physical education and athletics.
(Adapted from Unruh, A., & Willier, R. A. (1974). Public Relations for Schools. Belmont, CA: Lear Siegler/Fearon Publishers, p. 65.)

of the coaches, physical education teachers, and administrators becomes extremely important when the public sees these people "up close and personal." This personal visibility is extremely valuable PR. Recently, a college coach who was receiving extremely critical newspaper reports visited an administration class to "tell his side" and won a classroom of supporters for his candor with them.

Principle 8. *Define the particular public groups whose opinions affect the program and structure the PR program to reach them.* A particular public is made up of those who are concerned with the program directly or indirectly. (See Figure 5.2.)

Note in Figure 5.2 that there is a hierarchy of influence within the general public. The immediate public directly affects the program, whereas the public-at-large only remotely affects the program. It is necessary to recognize the importance of the students and school staff. The majority of the PR endeavors should be aimed at the public most directly associated with the programs. Frequently,

PR efforts are directed at the public-at-large despite the fact that students, staff, and parents are much more important than the general public.

It must be recognized that every power structure is different; the public at a particular school might differ from another school's public. The school board, town council, or booster club might be included in the immediate public for high schools. In colleges, sometimes an alumni organization, booster club, or trustees have this role. The PR program should be aimed at the people directly related to the sport program. Some have described this as the "frequency escalator." This concept breaks down the audience into four categories:

- Indirect and nonconsumers who do not attend yet.
- Light users who occasionally attend.
- Medium users who buy numerous single-game tickets.
- Heavy users are season ticket holders or businesses that buy blocks of tickets (Sutton, McDonald, and Milne, 1997).

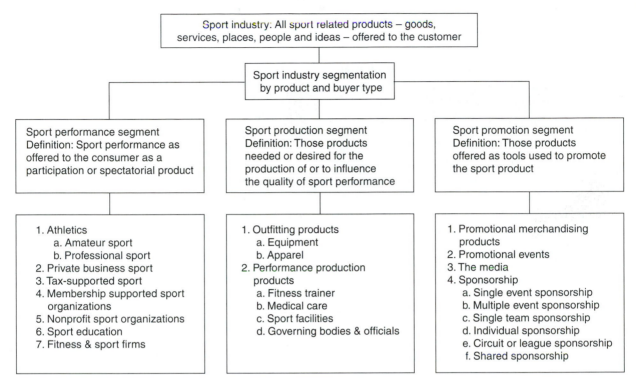

Figure 5.3 Pitts, B. G., Fielding, L. W. & Miller, L. K. (1994). Industry segmentation theory and the sport industry: Developing a sport industry segment model. Sport Marketing Quarterly, 3(1), 15-24.

To make all the "publics" aware, the PR department may have to ask fund-raisers for support. Before the PR efforts begin to ask for funds, guidelines need to be set. The fund-raisers should understand two factors: the motivation behind the contribution, and the quid pro quo (what do they get for what they give?). The "give" and "get" may derive from desiring change, commitment, curiosity, involvement, material benefits, power, results, recognition, or social benefits (Robinson, 1997).

■ MARKETING SPORT AND PHYSICAL EDUCATION

Marketing
Strategic sport marketing is the process of designing and implementing activities for the promotion and distribution of a sport product or service to the consumer, the result of which satisfies the consumers' desires and the organization's objectives. This re-

sults in an ongoing strategic fit between the goals and resources of the organization and constantly changing market opportunities (Stotlar, 2001A).

The key to applying marketing concepts to sport and physical education programs is to first understand the scope of the industry and where your organization fits within that industry. Pitts, Fielding, and Miller (1994) developed the first comprehensive model (Figure 5.3) of the sport industry. It encompasses the vast array of sport businesses, programs, and activities including athletics, physical education, recreation, and fitness. Thus sport marketing efforts across this industry are just as varied as the components of the model.

Developing a marketing plan for your sport organization is critical to success. Unfortunately, many sport managers never take the time to develop a plan, and their marketing efforts are disconnected and ineffective. The principal steps in developing a marketing plan are outlined next.

Marketing Plan Outline

Executive Summary. The executive summary introduces the product or service being marketed and presents an overview of the entire marketing plan.

Introduction. The introduction section tells the reader about the organization's *mission statement*. A mission statement clarifies the organization's reason for being. Other key issues addressed in the introduction typically include answers to the following questions: What does your sport organization produce and market? What is the existing demand for these sport-related products and services? Who are the sport organization's customers? How do you plan to use the sport organization's resources to market your products/services to meet this customer's demands?

Situational Analysis. Sport organizations do not operate in a vacuum; therefore, marketing plans must be based on an analysis of the environment in which you will conduct your activities. Identify the strengths and weaknesses of your organization (program/team/department). Just like a good game plan, the marketing plan will address specific strengths and weakness for each of the following building blocks of your organization: products/services, employees, budget and finances, and customers. Other environmental factors should also be included in your analysis. These include economic climate, technological trends, government and public policy, and competitor analysis.

Customer Analysis and Target Market Identification. Because the purpose of marketing is meeting consumer needs, it is imperative that you gain as much insight as possible about your customers. Information about the customers is often classified by demographics. These factors traditionally include age, gender, ethnicity, income, and geographic location. Additional factors to be considered are lifestyle, type of product/service desired, personal activities, in-terests, opinions, purchase frequency, and level of team/product loyalty.

Once these consumers have been identified and information about them has been collected, sport marketers engage in *market segmentation:* dividing the customers into groups based on their characteristics and behaviors. The resulting groups of customers are referred to as the *target market(s)*. These are the people that are most likely to purchase your products/services and attend your sports events.

Goals and Objectives. Marketing objectives must be developed to help your sport organization achieve its goals. Objectives can be written regarding market share, sales volume, and position in relation to price and quality of other products and services. State them precisely.

Strategy and Tactics. *Marketing strategy* details what you will do to achieve your marketing goals and objectives. Your strategy may be trying to differentiate your product from the competition, segmenting the marketing differently, positioning (or repositioning) the product relative to competitors, or the like. This section explains what you are planning to do strategically, given the current position of your product in the product life cycle. Be sure to consider how your main competitor(s) will likely respond to your marketing strategy (if applicable) and what you will do to counter this (avoid threats and exploit opportunities). Marketing tactics differ from strategy in that *tactics* are how you will implement the strategy. Tactics include every action required to implement the strategies. Tactics have traditionally been built around elements called the marketing mix: product (or service), position, price, and place (distribution).

Implementation and Control. Marketers and managers need to have an action plan for controlling marketing plan activities. This necessitates the development of a calendar or chart showing what activities are due to be completed at specific intervals. In addition, information about marketing costs and the ultimate evaluation must be presented.

Summary. The summary section of the marketing plan offers the reader a concise overview of the plan features and benefits that can be attained for the customer. It also presents a summary of the expected profits, market share, and sales volume.

Marketing Mix

Product. Even though much of product in athletics may be in the general service realm, the axiom that the ultimate goal is "to meet the needs of the consumer" still holds true. This includes services, such as halftime entertainment, parking, and ushers, to products such as concessions, seat cushions, and programs. One might view the ticket, not the contest, as the product (Stotlar, 2001A). In the fitness center, the "experience" might be the product.

Marketing and promoting nonrevenue sports is always a challenge. A strategy that became common during the period of the Atlanta Olympics was to call these *Olympic Sports*. While there are exceptions, like basketball, most nonrevenue sports do fit the title. The University of Washington used the theme of Excellence in Education to market its Olympic Sports by targeting elementary school students. Schools were given bulk tickets to be used by teachers as incentive awards for attendance and the like. Another similar approach used at Duke was to allow parents to apply for tickets to Olympic Sport contests for birthday parties (McDonald and Sutton, 1998). Remember, hook a youngster as a fan and you likely will get one or more parents in the short run and the youngster for life.

In the sporting goods and facility construction businesses, the products are more traditional. In ski areas, golf courses, aquatic centers, and the like, the "activity" experience may be the drawing factor, but sales of such things as golf cart rentals, lessons, equipment, and concessions are direct products that generate substantial income.

Price. Price is important, but not most important, in the marketing mix; otherwise nonrevenue sports with no admission would outdraw all revenue sports. Price is elastic, but only to a point. For example, if one could attend a movie for less than it costs to attend your high school ball game, you would likely be overstretched. The price for providing the services of an athletic event must be balanced with many factors, not the least of which is how important it is to draw a large crowd. A 30 percent increase in admission that resulted in a drop in attendance of 15 percent might seem to be wonderful economics—but not if the smaller crowd caused a loss of the game due to less crowd support.

In sport product pricing, the price will often be based on the final cost of production plus a required profit. This is called *markup pricing*. The *keystone* method of pricing is wholesale cost, doubled (Stotlar, 2001A).

Many high schools and colleges determine costs for admission and concessions based on what others in their conference, or area, charge. If the school is the primary sport draw in the area, or if the team has been a consistent winner, perhaps the fee is increased. Guessing like this is not very astute.

Place. This component is fairly static because there is little choice in the venue or facility to deliver sport programs. If the sport business is new, such as a sport retail store, note that the three most important factors will be location, location, and location (Stotlar, 2001A).

Even though the facility remains static, many related facets are controllable. Such items as parking, gate entrances, crowd flow, toilets, concessions, public address systems, seat configuration, and scoreboards are but a few of the location's subconsiderations that can be adjusted, reorganized, or improved.

In order to decide the right mix between product, price, and place, three common methods are used in market research: surveys, experiments, and open-ended explorations. Surveys ask questions, which gather data and make judgments based on these findings. In experimental market research, the researcher divides subjects into two groups: the treatment group and the control group. After testing the variables on both groups, the differences are studied. Open-ended explorations use in-depth interviews, focus groups, participant observations, projective techniques, and similar strategies (Brooks, 1994).

Promotion and Advertising

"Promote or Perish" might be an appropriate slogan in today's athletic world. How do promotional ideas develop? The promotional idea should grow out of a need to meet an objective or solve a problem. We are limited only by our imagination and the philosophy and policies of the organization.

Promotion is the overall activity of furthering or advancing business, particularly through increasing the sales of its services or products. Advertising is mass communication paid for by the organization. Sales promotion is a catchall term for any types of promotion not covered by the other forms, such as newspaper coupons for half-price tickets. The school or institution has direct control over these promotions. The organization has little direct control over the fourth promotional activity, publicity. Sport managers, while pleased to see positive and complimentary publicity, naturally blanch when the same degree of media attention focuses on problems.

Some experts believe that any publicity is good, whether it is negative or positive. Many sport administrators believe, however, that in nonprofit and service organizations, it is not professional to capitalize on and promote negative publicity. The blend of the promotion, advertising, personal selling, and publicity is called the *promotional mix*.

The administrator for a physical education or sport program is frequently unable to *market* it effectively because of the constraints of league schedules, prescribed times, dictated ticket prices, and the like. Therefore, *promotion* should receive the most attention. Many fine examples will be presented in the next section of this chapter, but new and innovative ideas need to be found.

In the fitness industry, several examples of successful promotions can be seen. Many fitness centers offer "bring a friend" days when current members are encouraged to bring a friend to work out with them in hopes that the friend will enjoy the activity and join the center. Wellness centers and fitness clubs also conduct "health fairs" to promote their operations. In this promotion, the wellness center invites health-related businesses to exhibit their products and services within the center. For members, this is often seen as a benefit, yet it also attracts new members to the enterprise.

Physical education programs for many years have conducted "field days." Typically these evenings allow the children to exhibit the sports skills that they have learned in classes (such as golf). In other examples, the parents are asked to join in or are given free instruction from the PE teachers in the sports so that they may enjoy them with their children.

Promotional activities in competitive sports are many and diverse. Most sport programs designate certain games as promotional games where items are given away to fans. These "hat day" type promotions have a reasonably good success rate for increasing attendance. Another type of promotion used in competitive sport is the declaration of a special day (such as Scout Day) where identified groups are recognized for their civic contribution. This has also increased attendance for most activities.

Another promotional activity that crosses the boundaries of many sport activities is the speaker's bureau. A speaker's bureau can be established to detail the expertise of the sport organizations employees. The material is then distributed within the community so that civic and other groups can contact individuals as potential speakers. This gives the civic group an informational speaker and provides positive PR for the sport organization.

Creative advertising can be a key element in promoting athletic programs. For example, schools are finding that even on the high school level, money can be made on signs. In track, the hurdles always present popular shots for photographers, so advertising on hurdles can be sold. Appropriate signs in baseball and football fields and basketball gymnasiums are possible. Score-

Hurdles are potential vehicles for promotional signs.
Photo courtesy Watauga Democrat.

boards are particularly valuable assets. Schools have found sponsors to pay for the scoreboards with an agreement for free advertising for a few years, after which the school owns the scoreboard and will be able to sell the space. Thus, not only does the organization get a free scoreboard, but it will make money after a few years. The amount of money that can be realized from scoreboard signage varies from a few hundred dollars in a local recreation facility or school gymnasium to several thousand dollars at the collegiate level. Professional teams often use signage contracts with sponsors in the millions of dollars.

Five common marketing mistakes occur in sport: (1) failure to determine a unique marketing message; (2) not finding out exactly what customers or patrons need, want, and expect by asking them directly; (3) lack of testing all marketing and advertising messages for sales or attendance results; (4) failure to make all mar-

keting and advertisements direct response; and (5) failure to provide superior customer or patron service (Gerson, 1993).

Naturally, in commercial sport enterprises, advertising is prominent. From an ethical perspective, it is necessary to keep a balance between making a profit and acting in a socially responsible, legal, and ethical manner (DeSensi and Rosenberg, 1996). Several examples of school sport programs selling advertising have been subject to criticism. In Colorado, one of the first school districts to sell stadium and school product rights to a soft drink company received national attention. In Illinois, sports announcers will make public address announcements about the equipment maker just in case the fans miss the banners hanging in the gymnasium. One elementary school even sold naming rights to its gym for $100,000 (Gordillio, 2002).

With an enormous increase of sports on television, sport figures frequently endorse products. Turner and others (1995) reported a study that involved 35 hours of television sport broadcasts and 35 hours of nonsport programs. The types of commercials advertising products and the names of famous individuals in the commercials were recorded on a tally sheet. The data indicated that sport figures were used as endorsers of products in only 11 percent of the total 872 commercials. Of the athletic figures employed in the commercials, 97 percent were male. During professional basketball games, 36 percent of the advertisements had sport figures endorsing a product. Professional football was a distant second with a 21 percent use of sport figures in commercials. Nonsport broadcasts were third, employing sport figures in 19 percent of their advertisements. The major conclusion of this investigation was that in advertisements, female sport figures are relegated to a position secondary to that of male sport figures (Turner and others, 1995, p. 27).

Managers of both professional and amateur sport programs should be very careful when athletes are used for commercial advertising. All of the professional sport leagues have language in their collective bargaining agreements that restricts the use of player images to advertise products or services. In general, team photos and groups of players can be used to advertise or promote upcoming games, but the team cannot use a single player image to promote a product. That right belongs to the player. Similarly, players cannot sell rights to advertising on their uniforms. Those rights belong to the team or the league. Just in case you are wondering, the athletes' shoes are not typically included as part of the uniform.

Amateur sports have rigid rules about commercialism. At the high school level these are normally controlled by the state athletic association and at the collegiate level by the National Collegiate Athletic Association (NCAA). In a recent case involving a college football player, the NCAA refused to allow the athlete to appear in advertising for a leading clothing manufacturer under its commercialization rules. The athlete ultimately decided not to pursue the advertising opportunities and continued to play football (Kiszla, 2002).

■ PARTNERSHIPS AND FUND-RAISING

General Guidelines

To understand and plan for funding, it is necessary to evaluate how the public relates to the products—sport and/or physical education. What are they worth to the public? Since the beginning of the century, every time there has been a financial squeeze, the arts, physical education, and athletics have been considered frills, and funding has been cut.

Fund-raising for nonrevenue sports is especially challenging. In this area, quality programs are vital. There must be a product analysis for each program to determine what may be of interest or value to consumers or donors. Cost-effective solicitation is measured and evaluated on the basis of maximum return of funds for effort and money expended. Be patient.

It may be easier to raise money than it is to sell tickets. It sometimes takes a winning team to sell tickets, but you can raise money whether you're winning or not. Frequently gate receipts

are shared, whereas funds raised remain entirely at "home." Here are some recommended strategies:

1. Obtain legal and accounting counsel, particularly related to requirements to meet Internal Revenue Service standards.

2. Don't give away too much, such as too many tickets, to entice donors.

3. Maintain an ongoing communication system with donors, such as weekly newsletters.

4. Involve as many people in the drive as possible—people give to people.

Once it has been determined that the need justifies a fund drive, the resources are available, and the program has been administratively approved, set a target that is expected to be exceeded by about 10 percent. Oversubscribing a drive lifts the spirits of the workers and donors and sets the momentum for future drives. If the expected amount is not raised, it will more likely meet, or be close to, the announced goal.

If the goal is a major gift program, the first step must be to develop a list of major donor prospects, as well as the volunteers and staff to cultivate and solicit them. The essential elements of a major gift program include these:

1. The gift committee should reflect the segments of society from which the donations are expected.

2. All members must understand the goals and the protocol of solicitation.

3. A pool of target donors should be provided for each committee.

4. A strategic plan must be developed to cultivate major donors, including invitations to special events, birthday cards, newsletters, and the like.

5. Comprehensive records must be maintained, recording contacts and initiatives.

6. Involve the CEO (AD, chair, dean, director) as well as potential donors in the "inner circle" of advisers and friends of the program (Clontz, 1992).

Because it costs money to raise money, and one needs to raise money because of its scarcity, the experts advise avoiding TV, radio, and expensive brochures. Instead, try personal contacts and direct mail. Avoid utilizing items with built-in obsolescence and instead be innovative.

The best way to approach a businessperson for a donation or to sponsor an advertisement is to put yourself in his or her position. Think of ways your school or athletic program could be of use to the business. The timing of a request is important. Learn the fiscal spending year of your target and then make your request early in that year. In addition, make your request several months before you need the funds. Whom should you see? If the firm has a promotions department, that's your target; if it's smaller, see the person in charge of marketing or advertising. Frequently, national chain stores are unlikely to support funding requests. Banks and insurance firms are usually good sources for funding.

There are three general strategies for fund-raising: 1 stage a "quick fix" event such as a jog-a-thon or flea market; 2 employ a professional; or 3 develop an annual fund-raising campaign with professional consultation and community assistance. Because the staff will quickly tire of repeating the first strategy, and the second will cost up to half of the gross, the last plan is recommended.

To initiate an annual fund-raising campaign, identify a popular cause that will capture interest and commitment. Before announcing the campaign, the target amount, or the timetable, initiate a fact-finding study to determine where the money will come from, how much to expect, and how soon to expect it. Experience shows that one-third of the total contributions will come from a handful of donors, another third will come from about a hundred people, and the remainder will come from all other sources. Almost all of the initial big givers should already be pledged; a substantial number of the next hundred should also be committed. In this way, most of the goal amount is already pledged and a successful campaign is ensured. Establish consultants who have the necessary experience and connections to achieve the results, and have community campaign workers committed, coordinated, and scheduled. The campaign workers will respond to a well-organized schedule. Recognize that a few workers will do outstanding work independently and a few will not get the job done no matter what motivation is offered.

The primary reasons given for not employing professional fund-raisers is the cost and loss of control. But it is in the best interests of the institution to employ professionals to raise $200,000 or more. Members of the American Association of Fund Raising Council are reimbursed at a set fee determined in advance, not on a percentage of the funds raised. The following reasons are advanced for employing a professional to raise large sums:

1. The campaign will be faster and cheaper.
2. The professional's experience will dictate the most effective and cost-efficient procedures for a campaign.
3. The professional draws on his or her knowledge of numerous similar campaigns to develop the best plan of action.
4. If the campaign director becomes incapacitated, the professional consultant will see that the replacement is competent to maintain continuity.
5. Competent and experienced personnel will frequently volunteer their services contingent upon the employment of a professional fund-raiser.
6. The employment of a professional with known successes tends to create a spirit of confidence, which can become a self-fulfilling prophecy.

Fund-Raisers

Allowing the public to utilize the school's facilities after hours can raise funds whether or not there is a charge. For instance, free use can improve community relations and generate support and the votes to ensure consistent funding. On the other hand, colleges frequently raise substantial funds from establishing user fees for facilities.

Many sport businesses fail to realize the profit they could and should generate from concessions. The first step should be a feasibility study. Then, assuming that a potential for profit is discovered, a sufficient budget must be allocated to do the job right. (The old adage "You have to spend money to make money" applies here also.) It pays to hire a consultant for advice about a menu selection that is simple, fast, and priced to sell and about the design of the space to achieve maximum efficiency. Market and promote the concessions and let people know that you are committed to the business. Ensure that the concessions operation is staffed by customer-oriented, trained, and honest employees (Hilkemeyer, 1993).

A concession professional offers the following advice to maximize revenue (Bigelow, 1989):

1. Sell highly recognized brands, avoid undersizing, and offer a better price value for the largest sizes to increase per capita spending with the same labor cost.

2. Use quality equipment and locate it to avoid extra steps or constantly turning around.

3. Train employees and assign each new one a mentor.

4. Select purveyors carefully and fully utilize them for developing standard recipes, portion controls, and equipment maintenance.

5. Provide a high-quality "designer" item or two at a higher price.

6. Employ a subcontractor with a detailed contract as to insurance, quality control, pricing, and health requirements.

7. Piggyback items to a holiday or special event, such as homecoming.

8. Use cash registers.

9. Have supervisors look at the operation through the customer's eyes to find ways of improving the operation.

Booster Clubs for Fund-Raising

As funds dry up because of declining enrollments and escalating costs, raising funds through booster clubs has become more common. The disadvantages of establishing a booster club are loss of control and its interference with general education fund-raising. To avoid these problems, turn to solid, well-established local businesspeople to serve on the steering and organizing committee. Have well-publicized, open meetings in which a constitution and bylaws are formally adopted. Ensure that the regulations stress that all booster club activities must be approved by the school administration and that all funds raised must be donated to the school athletic department for needed use as determined by school

officials. Make sure that legal and accounting consultants approve procedures.

The number one potential problem for the administrator is the possible loss of control of the booster club or interference in athletic activities from booster club members. Club members must not influence coaching and administrative matters more than any other citizens. On the other hand, a tax-paying citizen shouldn't lose rights just because she or he is a member of the booster club. Monday morning quarterbacking is a great temptation for booster club members. The solution: do not allow coaching to be a topic of conversation at booster club meetings. Recognizing the efforts of booster club workers at halftime could head off some criticism, and a coach or school administrator could serve as the president of the booster club. In addition to the sound administrative structure of the club itself, mentioned in the previous paragraph, a key element of control is communication. Keep the booster club members informed. Have coaches and administrators meet regularly with the club to help plan and inform members before a problem or crisis arises.

The most important function of the booster club is to make the public aware that athletic programs should be fully funded from general tax revenues. Until that day arrives, booster clubs should supplement the athletic budget, not sustain it.

In some communities, the booster club's primary fund-raiser is its membership fees. To raise funds, members sell advertisements for the football program; offer reserved seats and parking; sell hats, T-shirts, and bumper stickers; operate concession stands; and solicit donations year-round. Stier (1997) describes 70 step-by-step opportunities for raising funds for sport and recreation. The fundraisers are divided into four groups based on how much they are expected to raise: up to $3,000, $3,000 to $5,000, $5,000 to $10,000, and over $10,000. For each of the 70 fund-raisers, Stier discusses level of complexity, description, scheduling, resources needed, time, expenditures, personnel needed, risk management factors, permits/licenses, and hints.

Sponsorships

The phenomenon of corporate sponsorships in nonprofit sport generates some controversy and criticism, but it has become a growing fact of life. Reports indicate that annual increases up to 15 percent per year have recently occurred, yet smaller annual increases per year can be expected. For example, spending on sponsorships in North America for 2001 was $9.57 billion, up 2.9 percent from 2000 (IEG Projection, 2001). Spending in 2002 also slowed because of the economic downturn in the United States.

Most nonprofit sport organizations, such as schools and colleges, cannot allow tobacco companies as sponsors, and some voluntarily extend this prohibition to companies involved with alcohol. Sponsorships of the football bowl games and shoe contracts for basketball coaches have caused considerable concern. An innovative approach, developed by the University of Southern California, has originated endowments to fund scholarships for various positions or to pay coaches' salaries from the interest earned on the endowment (Stotlar, 2001b).

In the past, many sport managers would develop "gold, silver and bronze" packages to offer benefits to sponsors. At the grassroots level (high school or local events) this may still be effective. However, more sophisticated sponsorship proposals are needed as the size of the investment and the scope of the event increase. "Boilerplate" proposals won't work; companies are looking for sponsorship proposals that are tailored to their specific needs. Therefore, sport managers must carefully examine potential sponsors and craft sponsorship opportunities that meet the companies' needs.

Case in Point. As the coordinator of a four-county senior games program, the author needed a sponsor. The primary sponsor for the state senior games, one of the largest banks in the country, also had one or more banks in each of the counties served by the local games. The state senior games officials were confident that the bank would happily sponsor the local games. Because the amount of sponsorship was quite modest, a succinct proposal was presented to the president of the local bank. After a considerable time the bank president indicated that the request should be made to the regional office—which promptly sent a negative reply. At this point, a friend determined that a smaller, state-level bank with local offices was eager to be a sponsor. As a courtesy and to avoid interfering with the state-level sponsorship, the first bank's regional office was informed of the tentative move to accept sponsorship from their competitor unless they could work something out. Apparently, upon consultation with the state headquarters (which is also the national office), the decision was reversed and the sponsorship was granted. Was the entry point incorrect? How would you have approached the problem?

Don't pay for anything that someone will sponsor. Allow firms to advertise on your tickets by paying for the cost of printing the tickets. Have products donated for raffles or giveaways. Educators used to fear that sponsors would interfere with operations. Corporate sponsorship no longer presents a problem for high school administrators. Businesses are pouring millions of dollars into high school activity programs in almost every state.

The promotional opportunities offered by NCAA Division I and II athletic programs through sponsorships include utilizing public address announcements and complimentary tickets. More than three-quarters offer facility signage, souvenir program advertising, and back-of-ticket advertising. A little over half include coupon distribution at events, on-air broadcast mentions, and booster club memberships. Only 20 percent utilize hospitality privileges (Irwin, D., 1993).

What do companies look for in sponsorships? Representatives of the 12 official NCAA corporate sponsors were interviewed to try to answer this question. The companies indicated that their motivations were affiliation with sports (67 percent), access to college athletes (50 percent), media exposure (58 percent), ticket access to championship events (42 percent), and product/service exclusivity (42 percent). Ten of the 12 sponsors reported that they were satisfied with the program and cited a specific demographic group as an important factor in their sponsorship (Stotlar and Kadlecek, 1993).

Another form of sponsorship is to convince firms to put up a valuable prize, such as a car, for a hole-in-one or making a shot from half-court at

	Cost	City Agency Cost	School District Cost	Joint Cost
	Table 5.1 Cost Analysis Budget for Construction and Operation of Independent versus Joint Programs for a Sports Center			

	Cost	City Agency Cost	School District Cost	Joint Cost
1.	Land	$ 200,000	$ 200,000	$ 200,000
2.	Senior citizen kitchen and meeting area	50,000		50,000
3.	Toddler playground	15,000		15,000
4.	Four tennis courts	35,000	35,000	35,000
5.	Stadium and track	300,000	300,000	300,000
6.	Annual maintenance and supervision	100,000	100,000	100,000
7.	Baseball field	50,000	50,000	50,000
8.	Two softball fields	50,000	50,000	50,000
9.	Swimming pool and dressing rooms	200,000	200,000	200,000
10.	Parking	100,000	100,000	100,000
		1,100,000	1,035,000	1,100,000

Summary
A. Each agency develops own; total outlay to community at large equals $2,135,000.
B. If agencies split cost on items both needed, school district would spend $512,500 instead of $1,035,000; city agency would spend $592,500 instead of $1,100,000.
C. Savings to community would equal $1,035,000 for land purchase, construction, and operation in the first year.

halftime. Small businesses can do this without much expense by purchasing insurance to cover the cost of the prize in case it is won (the insurance covers the sponsor's "loss"). By paying a relatively modest amount for the insurance, the firm can gain all the publicity as if they actually donated the large prize. Call SCA Promotions at 888-860-3700 for more information.

Partnerships

As cries for accountability become more common, community cooperation also will become a requirement, not an option. Frequently school physical education and athletic personnel cooperate informally with such agencies as recreation departments and with private industry. But to ensure that these joint programs are retained even when personnel change and to ensure legal protection for all parties concerned, formal agreements should be written.

The following steps have been suggested to open communication between two agencies:

1. Issue joint policy statements.
2. Attend each other's board meetings.
3. Establish a coordinating committee.
4. Conduct joint board meetings to evaluate programs.
5. Establish a coordinator for each agency.
6. Review new programs jointly.
7. Publish appropriate brochures jointly.
8. Sponsor in-service training jointly.

There are many benefits for a partnership. Hastad and Tymeson (1997, p. 47) state that forming a partnership can result in

• Coping with reduced funds and personnel.
• Refocusing initiatives.
• Maximizing external relations through volunteerism.
• Linking with other organizations to achieve mutual goals.

When two agencies are ready to form a partnership and sponsor a program (as illustrated in Table 5.1), they should cite the legal codes authorizing the joint venture; list the purpose of the agreement; state the roles and responsibilities of each agency; cite the supervision requirements; list the responsibility for liability insurance; cite the use of priorities for the facility; state all terms and conditions; and establish and list the procedures for evaluation. The proper evaluation of cooperative programs is extremely important. This process should include cost (efficiency and effectiveness), community needs, involvement of other resources, personnel (their effectiveness, as well as the effect of the program *on them*), and community service delivery.

Partnerships between a coalition of businesses and one or more school systems are a growing reality in which athletics are included. For example, in Fairfax, Virginia, more than 160 local businesses and public schools have forged partnerships ("Partners in Education," 1997). In addition, there are increasing partnerships forming between towns to share facilities such as a swimming complex (Sherman, 1997a and 1997b).

■ PUBLIC RELATIONS EXAMPLES IN PHYSICAL EDUCATION

From time to time, the National Association of Sport and Physical Education (NASPE) prepares public service announcements (PSAs) for the media. In August 1997, NASPE sent 500 letters to radio stations with a 30-second announcement reporting on statements by the U.S. surgeon general that physical activity reduces the risk of developing some of the leading causes of illness and death. In addition, NASPE sent notices to 210 television stations announcing similar 30- and 60-second tapes for television.

In March 1997 the Centers for Disease Control and Prevention (CDC) produced a six-page pamphlet, *Promoting Lifelong Physical Activity,* that has very useful and accurate facts about the benefits of exercise. This pamphlet can be reproduced and adapted without permission. (The CDC pamphlet is available online at http:www.cdc.gov.)

National Sport and Physical Education Week

National Sport and Physical Education Week was originated in 1976 and is now the first week in May each year. Proclamations announcing the event have been made by the governors and the state superintendents of public instruction.

Shopping malls have enormous potential for holding demonstrations or promoting programs. Experience has shown that afternoon demonstrations reach more people and that music attracts crowds. Schedule the demonstrations with mall promotion directors early in the year because their calendars fill up rapidly. Publicize the programs heavily so that the students perform for large crowds, but also so that the mall directors will view the demonstrations as good business.

When it comes to National Sport and Physical Education Week, don't overlook persons with disabilities. By adapting the activities, students with any disability can be included. The emphasis could be on a variety of activities that offer instruction to as many persons as possible. Workshops, clinics, films, and speakers should be utilized.

An overlooked area for marketing in physical education is the recruitment of both students and faculty. Because personal recruitment is usually the strongest type, each teacher training department should use their majors and young faculty as recruiters. One of the most effective strategies is to send junior physical education majors back to their high schools to recruit. Usually they have been well-known athletes and would be highly respected by juniors and seniors who are in the active stage of planning their careers.

In support of the National Sport and Physical Education Week each May, NASPE produces a promotion kit that includes a colorful poster with the program's theme for that year. Call 800-321-0789 to order (NASPE, 1998b).

Special Public Relations Programs

Various forms of dance have a great deal of PR potential. In many areas of the country, tap dancing has regained popularity and performances gener-

Get your product's name in front of the public as much as possible.
Credit: Appalachian State University Sports Information Office, Boone, NC.

ate immediate attention. Aerobic dance classes have attracted huge numbers and present an exciting opportunity for performances. Many colleges and secondary schools have performing dance troupes of various types (cloggers, ballet, modern, jazz) that help interpret movement to the public. Note that the National Dance Week in late April each year is an excellent time to show off dance and physical education programs.

In the interest of expanding fitness activities for youngsters, AAHPERD has been promoting two programs that generate a great deal of enthusiasm from children and the public. The two programs are Jump Rope for Heart and Hoops for Heart. To get the latest information on events, ideas that work, and problem-solving solutions, access the newsletter through the AAHPERD Web pages at www.aahperd.org, then click on AAHPERD, then Programs & Events, and then click on the Jump Rope for Heart/Hoops for Heart sections (Jump, 1997).

The aerobics movement has provided the opportunity to present dance-a-thons, jog-a-thons, swim-a-thons, and cycle-a-thons. These events have been used to raise funds for a variety of causes, but they also provide an excellent opportunity to draw attention to the entire physical education and sport program. In addition to fostering good PR with the public, the special events frequently motivate many students during the prolonged training period before the event. As stated by Schneider (1992),

> If physical education really does add to quality of life with benefits for health, physical fitness, and psychosocial growth resulting from participation in active games and sports, then participants and parents must understand how these occur. If the new physical educator really has changed the "throw-out-the-ball" teacher image, the community deserves to know about it (p. 70).

ACES (All Children Exercise Simultaneously) aims to educate children about the importance of leading a healthy lifestyle. Each school organizes its own activity for 15 minutes. Millions of children from all over the United

States participate each year along with children from 50 other countries. The day is celebrated in the first week of May each year.

Parent Involvement and Community Relations

Parent participation nights can add a special dimension to physical education programs. They have evolved into a hands-on experience in which parents are offered the opportunity of a lifetime: to drop years off their ages and become kids again. Rather than inviting parents to come to the school to see what their children have been doing, they come and participate with their youngsters.

Other means of involving the parents are to establish a bulletin board near the gymnasium where parents can see it as they drop off or pick up their children, and to write a newsletter to parents that outlines upcoming activities.

Commercial firms are also seeing the PR potential in parent/child competition. It is often easy to find sponsors to underwrite the costs of such programs. Life insurance companies have sponsored national family competitions in skiing and tennis.

Due to the special character of the physical and psychological experiences of students with disabilities, it is imperative that parents and, if possible, siblings be involved in adaptive physical education programs.

Another way to enhance community relations is for school and college physical education personnel to become involved with programs for the aged. To contact existing programs, consult the area or state office on aging. The community relations potential is enormous, as are the possible benefits of obtaining volunteers to be physical education aides.

Another new promotion to get families involved in fitness activities is Family Health and Fitness Day, USA. Growing out of the U.S. surgeon general's report on physical activity and health, which was issued in 1996, the inaugural celebration was held in the fall of 1997. This event encourages organizations to host noncompetitive family health and fitness activities across the nation. It is scheduled to be an annual event taking place on the last Sunday in September ("Family Health and Fitness Day," 1997).

■ PUBLIC RELATIONS EXAMPLES IN SPORT

A team concept for promoting athletics succeeds particularly well in small towns. Team leaders select a number of assistants and compete for donated prizes for selling season tickets. On the college level, the team approach might involve the coach, ticket manager, and sport information director. Particularly on the college level, the locations and hours of ticket offices need to be widely advertised. If the program is large enough, it might be good business to utilize several local businesses, such as banks or sporting goods stores, for ticket sales. Promotions work most effectively when they combine print media (or direct mail) with radio or television promotion and publicity. Radio shows often use event tickets as prizes—and gladly "talk up" the event on the air in exchange for complimentary tickets to award to their listeners. Every game that isn't expected to be a sell-out should have a special promotion. Take advantage of local interests and talents. As often as possible, arrange special promotions or events that in themselves also increase profit. For example, a well-conceived long-distance run finishing in the stadium before a game would not only draw attention to the contest but could probably operate at a small profit.

Ohio University reports phenomenal grade point averages and graduation rates by athletes. In addition to the usual efforts such as study tables and the like, several special initiatives are involved. One is a mandatory class in responsible decision-making. Another is a 10-hour stint in a career-planning resource room. Athletes are encouraged to interact with other students by using services available to all students. The capstone is an invitation to a private breakfast for the 15 athletes with the highest grades from the previous semester (Bradley, 1993).

A nationwide public relations program that has been very successful is National Girls and Women in Sports Day, promoted by a variety of organizations including the Girls Clubs of America (GCA), National Association for Girls and Women in Sport (NAGWS), Women's Equity Action League (WEAL), Women's Sports Foundation (WSF), and Young Women's Christian Association (YWCA). A community action kit, prepared for national distribution by NAGWS, is used by volunteers from each state to coordinate activities and arrange for gubernatorial proclamations.

To stimulate the opportunities for women to experience sport, NAGWS has initiated a never-ending promotion called Be A Winner. It is a fund-raising program that can be used to help local programs as well as NAGWS. Products such as T-shirts, hats, water bottles, and sweatshirts with the Be A Winner logo are available. ("Promote Your Sports Program," 1997.)

Most colleges have entered into merchandising any product that can carry their colors, a picture of their mascot, or their logo. Typically these include T-shirts, sweatshirts, caps, glasses, cups, and bumper stickers. Fad items might include cowboy hats or leather products. Specialty items include cocktail glasses, Christmas stockings, and limited-edition paintings, prints, rugs, and clocks. They change these items frequently and test new ideas, such as coloring books, puzzles, napkins, or sport dolls.

The cornerstone of financial success at the University of Michigan is its heavy reliance on direct mailing. The fact that educational institutions receive a nonprofit mailing rate allows bulk rate mailing at less than half the cost to businesses. Also, compared to businesses, the targeted public is much easier to identify. Addresses frequently can be obtained at no cost, whereas businesses must purchase lists. In addition, the seat you are selling costs nothing to produce and can be sold over and over. It is suggested that the name and address of anyone buying a ticket, requesting a schedule, or showing any interest in athletics be recorded into a computer for future mailings. Before organizing a mailing, check with the post office, because regulations change from time to time. Following prescribed rules can result in substantial savings. Frequently one can "piggyback" a direct mailing by enclosing written material in the monthly statements sent out by a large business or public utility. Because the piece of material mailed is a major cost of direct mail, take time to develop it, soliciting expert assistance along the way. It is useful to use two strategies to promote ticket sales. The first is to market season tickets as aggressively as possible. This tactic provides insurance against poor weather, losing records, or a poorly drawing visitor. The second strategy is to encourage group ticket sales for contests not expected to sell out. Target youth groups, civic organizations, church groups, corporations, and associations.

Many universities have found that it pays to develop special student athletic support groups. (Frequently the catalyst is woeful attendance or losing teams.) Other successful ideas include

- Holding spirit banner contests.
- Making "table-tents" out of folded four-by-six-inch cards with appropriate notices on cafeteria tables.
- Working within dormitories, clubs, or fraternities/sororities to have group attendance at athletic events.
- Reinforcing an active pep band.
- Finding ways of getting coaches personally involved with student groups.
- Selling face painting services or giveaways (of something donated) for students in school colors.

Notre Dame University initiated an interesting concept that recruits young fans and encourages art at the same time. Grade school students compete in a contest of drawing their interpretation of Notre Dame basketball. The artwork of each winner has been featured on one of the basketball tickets, and each artist has been recognized at the halftime ceremonies (Herzog, 1993).

A well-run community tennis association (CTA) is one of the best ways to bring in new tennis players. Information on how to form a CTA can be obtained through your sectional U.S. Tennis Association office. Request a Community Tennis Association Kit that includes "How to

Form a Community Tennis Association: A Step-By-Step Guide" (Blume, 1997).

■ PUBLIC RELATIONS IN RECREATION, WELLNESS, AND FITNESS CENTERS

One of the best PR functions for health, fitness, and wellness centers is the "fitness fair." This promotional event consists of an exhibition or trade show with local health-related businesses staffing information booths for fair visitors. Fitness center managers typically canvass the community for participants to purchase a booth where their products and services can be displayed. Vendors can range from health food and nutritional supplement suppliers to home exercise equipment retailers.

For a fund-raiser with little risk and a great deal of entertainment, hold an auction. One highly successful effort featured both sport and nonsport donated items. Potential donors are notified that they will receive a receipt for tax purposes. Professional athletes, retail stores, coaches, and television personalities are solicited for game uniforms, autographed items, and new sporting goods. Even services from current coaches and athletes can be solicited (Hoch, 1993).

The following questions can indicate whether a fitness center is reaching and serving the adult health/fitness market:

- Does your adult program have the support of management?
- Does the program have a dedicated budget? Is the program ageless?
- Does the program incorporate self-actualizing values?
- Does the program address the diversity of the market segment?
- Is the program user-friendly?
- Does the program offer choices?
- Does the program speak to possibilities in the aging process, as opposed to limitations?
- Does the program offer a progression of experiences that challenge individuals to reach their full potential?
- Does the program offer opportunities for both individual and group activities?
- Do entry-level programs and classes emphasize fundamentals?
- Does the program emphasize that the higher levels of function participants can attain through exercise can enhance their lives?
- Does the program have motivated leadership?
- Is there an evaluation system in place?
- Are you selling feelings, emotions, and experiences?
- Do you walk your talk? (Rude, 1998)

Promote your department via a special annual event. This might be a field day, founders' day celebration, or any other event that attracts media attention and a good crowd. In Westbury, New York, the recreation department accomplishes this by promoting "June Is Recreation and Parks Month" (Walsh, 1993).

The Baptist Memorial Hospital in Memphis has reported a highly successful PR program called the "Summer Meltdown." About 75 departments involving 600 people have participated with a team approach of earning points in aerobic or walking classes and for pounds lost. (Other health–wellness information is incorporated.) A team award of a riverboat trip serves as a major incentive (Miller, 1993).

For profitability, fitness clubs must constantly attract new members. For this reason, studying their use of the media is instructive. A constant seems to be "change." They constantly employ new strategies—hot-air balloons, new publications, cash register receipts, coupon books, and new technologies such as laser disks and multimedia computers. They eagerly watch for interactive television programming. They value frequency of ads rather than size; yellow page use; and direct marketing, including invitations, newsletters, brochures, and postcards. Most fitness clubs also support websites that promote their products and programs to new and existing members. The new concepts for marketing in this decade are co-promotions and tie-ins. Promoters are combining forces with strategic allies to jointly promote both products (LeCompte, 1993).

The following marketing tips are suggested for capturing more corporate accounts for a fitness club:

- Use statistics to show that frequent exercisers have a substantially lower absenteeism rate (as reported in "The Economic Benefits of Regular Exercise" by the International Health, Racquet and Sportsclub Association, Boston).
- Reference the surgeon general's report on physical activity and health (Healthy People 2010, www.health.gov/healthy people/). The stamp of approval by the U.S. government will carry considerable weight.
- Use testimonials from satisfied CEOs.
- Determine what the specific needs are of a firm and offer a package that meets those needs.
- Go to the worksite to offer education and wellness information first and then offer a program when the benefits are understood.
- Based on size of operation, decide whether to use specifically trained salespeople to sell corporate accounts.
- Be flexible and creative in offering a variety of payment options to the corporation and employees.
- Hold open enrollments for a relatively short period of time (perhaps 30 days) to create a sense of urgency.
- Assess and evaluate participation and publicize back to the firm the positive results.
- Exhibit at corporate health fairs.
- Exhibit at business expositions through local chambers of commerce or trade associations (Lolye, 1997).

For marketing and promotion ideas, review the articles and archives of *Fitness Management* magazine at www.fitnessworld.com/.

■ NEWSLETTERS, SPORT BROCHURES, AND PROGRAMS

A sport newsletter is an excellent PR initiative. With the advent of word processors and desktop publishing, any coach can print a newsletter. For example, a track coach could produce a newsletter after each meet and send it home with each squad member, post it on school bulletin boards, and send one to each lower school in the district with the names of graduates of the school highlighted.

A high school baseball coach promoted his program through the usual newspaper coverage, but also used the photographs on the school bulletin board and produced a bimonthly baseball newsletter. For special incentives, he scheduled a three-to-five-day spring trip and invited a team for a three-day weekend and a three-game series. A vital part of the promotional effort was a handbook for the squad members that included philosophy, offense, defense, and off-season conditioning drills and requirements. This coach also suggested that scheduling one game each season on a college campus both motivated and promoted the team.

Whether or not a colorful and informative program generates any income, it will always be promotional. But to make money, the sport will need to draw appropriate crowds, have rather large squads, and usually charge admission. At high schools, program development and marketing are natural for a booster club. The ratio of advertising pages to nonadvertising pages in a game program should be from 50 to 70 percent. Also recommended is the use of color, at least black with one solid color, and the use of black-and-white photographs with appropriate captions. Schools can do some or most printing; if not, the booster club can try to arrange for printing at cost from a local business. Carefully study advertising rates for ads to generate as much as the market will bear, and offer advertisers several choices. Small schools frequently use the free, four-page program blanks supplied by soft-drink firms to advertise their products. Other schools use the free program only for the roster sheets inserted in the middle of their own programs. While attendance in NCAA football and basketball has dropped, sales of game programs have increased by 18 and 35 percent—accomplished partly by new, less expensive production costs, and such innovative approaches as producing "collectibles" in the programs, and redeemable cents-off coupons, trading cards, and "lucky" programs that win prizes (Irwin, R., 1992).

Here are some guidelines for developing marketing brochures:

1. Define your offer and its major benefit in the headline.

2. Use the front page of the brochure to attract attention with a dramatic photograph.

3. Use editorial-style layouts and simple graphic design for credibility.

4. Use photography to show the consumer the product or service in action.

5. Use a type style that is easy to read.

6. Use photo captions and sidebars to emphasize key benefits.

7. Support your ad copy with testimonials and case histories.

8. Use coupons or return mailers to make it easy for the customer to respond.

9. Develop trust between you and the consumer with guarantees.

10. Use full-color printing and quality paper to convey a first-class image.

▮ MEDIA

It's easy to blame the media when teams or events don't receive the proper coverage, or when an insignificant problem is blown out of proportion for a sensational story. Before placing blame, investigate to see if the proper cooperation and professionalism have been provided to the media (Robinson, 1997). Keep in mind that there is tension between sport organizations and the media. Media personnel often judge those providing information from sport organizations as amateurs (and sometimes they are) who are trying to get free advertising, framing it as "news."

The media have enormous power to influence the PR program. Institutions and agencies at all levels must cultivate a positive working relationship with all representatives of the media. Some universities have arranged for 30-second free public service TV clips of their athletic programs during newscasts. Athletic directors should personally introduce new coaches to media firms—an action that could subsequently result in interviews.

Some universities with a wide listening audience have found it possible to sign multiyear TV contracts that cover all revenue sports. Frequently these contracts include professional services, such as developing press guides, producing highlight shows, advertising spots, billboard advertising, and consulting services.

Cable channels and public television provide other avenues for gaining exposure. These can be extremely important in generating future media financial gains. Nonrevenue men's and women's sports can reach a wider audience on cable TV and public television. Most experts believe that cable television will grow and become an important PR vehicle for schools and colleges. The emergence of "sport only" channels is evidence of this trend. Ask local cable companies to cover your events without payment to the school to increase visibility. Investigate the legal aspects of the television for both home and away games or events. Many universities also offer webcasts of their games and events. This allows supporters across the nation and the globe to access their favorite teams. As the technology for video streaming improves, this avenue of promotion and distribution will certainly enhance the promotional capabilities for many sport organizations.

Athletic administrators must recognize that media coverage is based on predictable criteria. For example, newspapers will give space based on game attendance, the closeness to home, and the uniqueness of the event. Television will base coverage on similar criteria, except that known exposure and past visibility become more important, as well as intangibles such as sex appeal. The media are insatiable for the unique—for a different slant. If it's media coverage and exposure you want, think "unusual." Often the story is right there and doesn't have to be contrived. For example, has interracial cooperation on a team helped build more harmonious school spirit? Why not say it? Are there brothers on the same squad? Brother and sister playing on respective teams at the same time? A beauty queen on a team? Players on the team at the same school where their fathers

Critical Thinking

A high school has 1,200 students. In the spring, a new football/soccer stadium was completed. It seats about 1,000, whereas the old stadium had room only for 700. This construction project resulted in cost overruns, and planned items had to be cut out. The new stadium has no visitor's restrooms or concessions stands and no scoreboard; the new expanded parking is gravel instead of pavement. Internally, there was barely enough money to maintain the old equipment and the old supply budget, let alone buy new things. The municipal authority and the Quarterback Club worked intensely for three years to gather enough money to get the stadium built, so there is no hope of obtaining more funding from them. People involved with the project feel horrible to ask for money once again because the fund-raising has been going on for three years.

The principal, athletic director, superintendent for business affairs, and football and soccer coaches brainstorm on future funding. It is your responsibility, as the new assistant soccer coach, to report back to the AD within a month with a strategic plan to solve the funding problem. The stadium has no specific name, nor are there any advertising signs. No sponsors had even been associated with the athletic program.

Consider the following points when preparing your plan:

1. What could you give and receive for signs and banners in the stadium?
2. What could you receive for using a business or product name for the stadium?
3. What could you give for someone to print, free of charge, commercial programs for the athletic department to sell?
4. What could you give to have some or all of a scoreboard purchased?
5. What could you give to have a construction or plumbing contractor build visitor's restrooms?
6. What could you give to have anyone pay for or construct a concession stand?
7. What could you give and receive to have firms or product suppliers sponsor a team or some aspect of the athletic program (for example, finding an official sponsor for the band, athletic training program, or the soccer team)?

In your report, also include any dangers or possible negative sides to your proposals.

---

or mothers played? Most important, show interest in the media and supply them with timely details—not that South beat North 15–5, 15–10, 15–9 in volleyball—because that and nothing more will be what is reported.

Hessert (1997) reports that the two primary strategies for working with the media are to first understand the media and their job. Determine where the interviewer is coming from and what is needed from the medium's point of view. Second, be prepared to promote your own agenda. Create an "interview prep checklist" that will aid you in presenting facts accurately and hitting all of the important areas you want to promote. Here are some general guidelines:

- When the focus is on the negative, hit it head-on quickly and don't repeat it.
- In television interviews, demeanor and eye contact are as important as words.
- Offer information that fits the needs of the reporter's medium. For example, for television the average interview lasts 20 seconds or less.
- Don't be baited.

Exercises

1. Assume that you are a teacher and coach on a middle school staff (grades 4–8) with three other physical education staff members. The chairperson says that the principal has directed the unit to come up with a PR program, and you are appointed to be in charge of it. Describe how you would accomplish this assignment.

2. The coach of a high school football team has a starting line that will outweigh every team in the conference. To avoid being singled out as the team to beat, he reports the weights as less than they are. Is this good PR? Why?

3. You are the new baseball or softball coach of a 2,000-student high school. In the last several years, the team has lost two-thirds of its games. The budget, existing equipment, and facilities all appear to be in worse-than-average condition for teams in the conference. Prepare a list of things you would attempt to do over a three-year period to establish a first-class PR program for baseball and softball.

4. The faults and problems of school athletics are well publicized. Frequently the positive side of athletics (other than winning) is not promoted. Assume you are the basketball coach of a junior high school with 2,000 students. Develop a list of strategies you would follow to promote the positive side of athletics. Be specific: don't report that you would build good sportsmanship—report how!

5. Although there have been highs and lows over the last three decades, generally it has become more difficult to fund athletic programs from state or school district budgets. Thinking back on the high school you attended, select three specific projects or strategies that might have been followed to raise funds in a professional manner.

6. Develop a media presentation to promote the athletic department. Utilize a slide-and-sound approach, video, or movie film.

7. Develop a series of activities for different populations to promote National Sport and Physical Education Week.

8. For high school basketball, you decide to gain more revenue by increasing admission by 20 percent from $2.00 to $2.40, even though you calculate the "gate" will decrease by 20 percent. Is this a smart move?

References

Baskin, O. W., and Argonoff, C. E. (1988). *Public relations* (2nd ed.). Dubuque, IA: Wm. C. Brown.

Bigelow, C. (1989, January). Spicing up your concession profits. *Athletic Business* 13, pp. 42–45.

Blume, B. (1997, November/December). It takes a community. *Tennis Industry* 25, pp. 42–43.

Bradley, M. (1993, March). Blending in. *Athletic Management* 5, p. 16.

Brooks, C. M. (1994). *Sports marketing.* Englewood Cliffs, NJ: Prentice Hall.

Cioletti, J. (1997, August). Checklist for success. *Club Industry* 13, pp. 17–19.

Clontz, L. (1992, June). Maximize your fund-raising campaign. *Athletics Administration* 27, pp. 14–16.

Cohen, A. (1993, January). Research for tomorrow. *Athletic Business* 17, p. 16.

DeSensi, J. T., and Rosenberg, D. R. (1996). *Ethics in sport.* Morgantown, WV: Information Technology.

Ellis, M. J. (1988). *The business of physical education, future of the profession.* Champaign, IL: Human Kinetics.

Family health and fitness day USA set to debut. (1997, Summer). *USSA Sport Supplement* 5, p. 5.

Gerson, R. F. (1993, March). Five costly marketing mistakes to avoid. *Fitness Management* 10, pp. 53–54.

Gordillio, J. (2002, June 14). Naming rights could be prep gold mine. *Southern Illinoisian*, p. 4D.

Hastad, D. N., and Tymeson, G. (1997, May/June). Demonstrating visionary leadership through community partnerships. *Journal of Physical Education, Recreation and Dance* 68, pp. 47–50.

Herzog, B. (1993, March). Research for tomorrow. *Athletic Business* 17, p. 13.

Hessert, K. (1997, October/November). Surviving the spotlight. *Athletic Management* 9, pp. 16–17.

Hilkemeyer, F. (1993, May). Food for thought. *Athletic Business* 17, pp. 40–43.

Hoch, D. (1993, March). Do I hear $100? *Athletic Business* 17, p. 16.

IEG Projection. (2001). Sponsorship spending will lag predicted economic rebound. *IEG Sponsorship Report.*

Irwin, D. (1993, May). In search of sponsors. *Athletic Management*, pp. 11–16.

Irwin, R. (1992, May). Reading between the lines. *Athletic Management*, pp. 15–18.

Irwin, R. L.; Sutton, W. A.; and McCarthy, L. M. (2002). *Sport Promotion and Sales Management.* Champaign, IL: Human Kinetics Publishers.

Jump and hoop coordinators can express themselves again. (1997, November/December). *Update*, p. 11.

Kiszla, M. (2002, August 21). Bloom's choice not so crazy. www.denverpost.com/stories, 8/21/2002.

LeCompte, D. (1993, March). Media mix? *Fitness Management*, pp. 44–46.

Lolye, D. (1997, September). In good companies. *Club Industry*, pp. 19–22.

McDonald, M. A., and Sutton, W. A. (1998, December/January). A grassroots approach. *Athletic Management* 10, p. 24.

Miller, M. (1993, April). Summer meltdown. *Fitness Management*, pp. 42–43.

National Association for Sport and Physical Education. (1998a, Winter). Join project ACES. *NASPE News,* p. 6.

National Association for Sport and Physical Education. (1998b, Winter). Promote May with NASPE kit. *NASPE News,* p. 7.

Partners in education. (1997, February). *Journal of Physical Education, Recreation and Dance* 68, p. 6.

Pitts, B. G.; Fielding, L. W.; and Miller, L. K. (1994). Industry segmentation theory and the sport industry: Developing a sport industry segment model. *Sport Marketing Quarterly* 3(1) pp. 15–24.

Promote your sports program—Be a winner. (1997, November/December). *Update,* p. 12.

Robinson, M. J. (1997, March). The motivation behind the money. *Athletic Management* 9, pp. 45–48.

Rude, J. (1998, January). Making the mature decision. *Athletic Business* 22, pp. 31–37.

Schaaf, P. (1995). *Sports marketing.* Amherst, NY: Prometheus Books.

Schneider, R. E. (1992, May/June). Don't just promote your profession—market it. *Journal of Physical Education, Recreation and Dance* 63, pp. 70–71.

Sherman, R. M. (1997a, August). Soccer success. *Athletic Business* 21, pp. 28, 30.

Sherman, R. M. (1997b, December). A strategy of sharing. *Athletic Business* 21, pp. 32–33.

Stier, W. F., Jr. (1997). *More fantastic fundraisers for sport and recreation.* Champaign, IL: Human Kinetics.

Stotlar, D. K. (2001a). *Developing successful sport marketing plans.* Morgantown, WV: Fitness Information Technology, Inc.

Stotlar, D. K.(2001b). *Developing successful sport sponsorship plans.* Morgantown, WV: Fitness Information Technology, Inc.

Stotlar, D. K., and Kadlecek, J. C. (1993, April). What's in it for me? *Athletic Business* 17, pp. 32–36.

Sutton, W.; McDonald, M.; and Milne, G. (1997, February/March). Escalating your fan base. *Athletic Management* 9, pp. 4–6.

Tadlock, L. S. (1993, May). Marketing starts with information. *Parks and Recreation,* pp. 46–50, 79.

Turner, E. T.; Bounds, J.; Hauser, D.; Motsinger, S.; Osmore, D.; and Smith, J. (1995). Television consumer advertising and the sports figure. *Sport Marketing Quarterly* 4 (1), pp. 27–33.

Walsh, E. R. (1993, June). Promotable events. *Parks and Recreation,* pp. 74–77.

6

Financial Management in Physical Education and Sport

─ **Case Study: Financial Exigency Hits Three High School Athletic Programs** ─

The county had been providing 30 percent of the funding for three high school interscholastic programs. A conservative coalition was elected to the county commissioners and voted to remove that subsidy for the next school year. The programs had been operated in an austere way for years. Each school has had strong support from booster clubs, fund-raisers, sponsorships, and advertising. There will be no substantial increase in funds from any source. The supervising director for physical education and athletics for the county called the three ADs and the three principals in to discuss the emergency. In the meeting it was quickly decided that with fine-tuning, perhaps 5 percent could be saved, and the group decided to list strategies that could be used to save the other 25 percent. After hours of discussion, the following list was constructed:

- Greatly reduce the number of assistant coaches.
- Switch from professional to volunteer lay assistant coaches.
- Reduce about half of the nonrevenue sports.
- Reduce all nonrevenue sports that have the largest equipment/operating budgets.

- Reduce the sports that have the lowest number of participants but high budgets.
- Drastically reduce the distance teams can travel.
- Drastically reduce the number of contests each team can schedule.
- Require teams to travel together even if different sports and playing at different times of the day.
- Drastically increase prices of admission, programs, and concessions, and adding a parking fee for all contests.
- Add charges for admission of all children, students, and adults to all events, including nonrevenue events.
- Drastically reduce the number of participants allowed to be carried on each team.
- Require all athletes to buy and clean their own equipment.
- Substantially reduce all coaching stipends.
- Drastically reduce the equipment and supply budgets for all teams.
- Drop basketball for both girls and boys.
- Drop football.

After a subcommittee studied the money expected to be saved by all of these possibilities, it was reported that it would require instituting most of the above strategies to achieve a 25 percent savings, except for the last one. *Dropping football alone would achieve this.* The committee voted to drop football, against strong objections from the principals, who said that discipline, attendance, and spirit would be adversely affected. The vote was presented to the next county school board meeting, and the matter was tabled for more thought and public reaction. The public outcry from parents, students, and the business community required an emergency meeting for the county commissioners, who almost without discussion rescinded the vote to abolish the subsidy and increased the subsidy to 35 percent.

Chapter Objectives

The reader should be able to

1. Prepare an athletic or physical education budget.
2. Define and use appropriately the terms common to school financial management.
3. Describe the ways in which educational accounting is more complicated than simply reporting and recording figures.
4. Compare and contrast the accounting systems of *object, function,* and *program* recording.
5. Describe controls in financial management in physical education and sport.
6. Explain the purposes, principles, and steps of budgeting.
7. Discuss the options of the physical education or athletic administrator in the event of an immediate financial need.

■ COMMON FINANCIAL TERMS

Definitions

Account. A financial record containing information about transactions related to expenditure, receipts, assets, fund balances, and liabilities.

Accrual accounting. A system in which revenues are recorded when appropriated rather than when received, and expenditures are recorded when ordered, rather than when received and paid for.

Appropriation. The amount of funds, according to the budget, set aside in an account and authorized to be expended during the year for a specific purpose.

Auditing. An official examination and verification of accounts to determine whether an agency has spent, or is spending, appropriated funds in accordance with the budget.

Budget. A statement of the estimate of receipts and disbursements for a period of time.

Capital outlay. An expenditure for property or equipment that has permanent use and value, such as land, buildings, permanent equipment (not supplies), and fixtures.

Contingency fund. Funds and other resources held in reserve within each budget year to provide for unforeseen problems or emergencies, or for anticipated expenditures of uncertain amounts.

Contractual services. Services performed on order under an agreement with an outside organization for a set fee, such as paying a fee for an equestrian center to provide horseback riding lessons for physical education classes. (Sometimes referred to as *outsourcing.*)

Credit. An increase in funds usually listed on the right side of an account, or a deduction from an expense account.

Debit. A decrease in revenue or net worth usually listed on the left side of the account, or an addition to an expense account.

Debt service. Expenditures to retire debts or to pay the interest costs of loans.

Direct costs. Costs related to a specific program or group of programs.

Discretionary funds. Money for incidental expenses raised from nongovernmental sources, such as donations or fund-raisers, to be used at the discretion of the custodian of the account.

Exigency, financial. An immediate financial need in which action must be taken to reduce expenditures, such as a decree by the board of education to reduce the total budget by 20 percent.

Expendable outlays. Equipment and supplies that have a short life and low cost per item. They include such equipment as balls and uniforms, and supplies such as paper and fertilizer.

Fiscal year. Any one-year period at the end of which the school or athletic program closes its books and determines its fiscal condition. In most schools and colleges, the period runs from July 1 through the end of June.

Fixed charge. A financial obligation of a recurring nature incurred at a fixed rate which appears as overhead such as rent, insurance, utilities, and contributions to employee benefits.

Indirect costs. Costs that are not directly associated with a specific program, such as overhead or general support.

Managerial accounting. The system that "includes cost accounting and the generation of information for decision-making using accounting data" (Engstrom and Hay, 1994, p. 239).

Petty cash. A small fund, frequently a maximum of $100, available for paying modest obligations—usually under $25, for which issuing a formal purchase order would be time-consuming and expensive.

Purchase order. A written request to order the purchase of material or service at a price outlined in the document.

Reserve fund. A fund that remains on hold from one budget year to the next which is invested and thus continuous to grow. This fund is used for major or unforeseen calamities such as a natural disaster that destroys a gymnasium. This is sometimes merged with the capital fund.

Sinking fund. A fund that is used to liquidate an obligation, usually with payments on a scheduled basis to complete the payment at a specific time.

■ STRATEGIC MANAGEMENT

Sport is big business. The sport industry has been estimated at well over $200 billion per year in the United States. Whether part of a commercial sport business or a small school or institution, fiscal long-range or strategic planning is required. Strategic planning is necessary for all areas of sport such as programming and facilities, but none will be realistic unless tied into long-range fiscal planning. Leaders must have a vision of where they are heading, and the strategic plan is a map that outlines how the resources will be managed to get there. Typically fiscal strategic plans are for the future 3 to 10 years. Budgets and accounting for the expenditure of funds will grow out of these plans (Alden, 2000).

Strategic planning is a thorough and lengthy practice. The whole staff needs to be involved, but the leader must believe that the process is vital. Once written, plans must be as widely disseminated as the size and complexity of the organization dictates. One university made 30 public presentations of a five-year plan throughout the state, sharing it widely with the media. This institution decided to focus on three areas: cost containment, revenue enhancement, and facility improvements. For example, university planners expect to increase revenue through a new approach of outsourcing all of their marketing endeavors, creating an annual giving program, and increasing their profits on reserve funds (Alden, 2000).

The following categories have been suggested to be included in a strategic plan:

- The mission goals and objectives of the organization.
- An analysis of the program's current financial status.
- An analysis of revenue versus expenditure projections.

- An analysis of capital projections in priority order.
- Specific information regarding the intended financial state of the end of the study period (Koteen, 1997; Alden, 2000).

There are reports that strategic planning in industry has never lived up to expectations and that it is really nothing more than good management (Mintzberg, 1994). On the other hand, Koteen (1997) reports that strategic management has been used successfully by the Internal Revenue Service and the American Red Cross. The U.S. Congress has mandated that strategic management be used extensively throughout the federal government.

The key concepts of strategic management are *distinctive competence* and *competitive advantage.* The former means to do what you do well. Make good use of unique capabilities and natural advantages. If your university has turned out strong wrestling teams for decades—you're in an area with long, bleak winters and rich high school wrestling talent—it doesn't take much imagination to determine that it would be a wise move to emphasize wrestling. Competitive advantage means that you could choose competitors to schedule or products to sell that would provide positive returns. These positive returns could be a good chance for a victory, excellent exposure, greater gate receipts, more chance for television income, association with an institution or school with an excellent reputation, an increase in clients or patrons, or simply more income.

For long-range strategic planning, experts suggest that a broad-based planning group be appointed with membership reflecting all constituents. This group should frankly and openly discuss changes that might make the program more effective. Discuss the goals and the values that the program should uphold. These thoughts can be crafted into a mission statement. Based on this statement, priorities and objectives should be identified as strategies and measured against the likelihood of advancing the mission. Strategic planning is continuous and flexible. Appointments to the planning group must therefore be staggered (Dlugosh, 1993). When a lack of progress is blamed on the notion that there wasn't enough time, money, or staff, it actually indicates that financial strategic planning was not achieved (Pitts, 1993).

What if strategic management analysis shows the organization is off course? For instance, a fitness center is oriented toward aerobics, but a market analysis has shown that it should be heavily directed toward weight training. Or an academic department has been investing its resources in an exercise science program, but analysis shows it should be directed at leisure studies and tourism. It is always difficult to change directions in an organization.

Like crises, change can present opportunities for an organization. When strategic management planning signals a need for an adjustment, organizations react in a variety of ways. Some look backward and keep doing things the same. Others are reactive in that they look at past data and make small incremental changes. A stronger position is to anticipate changes, predict problems, and try to correct deficiencies through systematic analysis of their causes. Organizations that react by exploring make a primary effort to identify the problem and then create new alternatives. Similar to exploring, some organizations go further: they look for new solutions and move in uncharted directions fostering innovative behavior (Koteen, 1997).

■ FISCAL MANAGEMENT

Fiscal management includes three steps: (1) top management setting goals and objectives and appropriating the funds to execute the program, sometimes called a *fiscal strategic plan;* (2) fulfilling *fiscal responsibility* by certifying that funds have been expended legally and efficiently; (3) carrying out the technical and mechanical arrangements of accounting and security of the *fiscal structure and the budgetary process.*

The benefits of effective financial planning are many. Decision making is proactive and systematic rather than reactive. Employees are linked throughout various levels of organization because they must communicate with one another. Employees are motivated to meet the challenges that arise. Risks are reduced and the organization's competitiveness is increased. And the organization achieves adequate control.

Accountability is the name of the game. The American public has always been prudent when allocating money for education, but now it is frugal. Schools must have sound financial management to survive. Many states have enacted laws in recent years restricting the amount allocated to education in general, and recreation, physical education, and athletics in particular. In many areas, special bonds to fund capital projects have been defeated. It is imperative that the most ethical and professional methods of managing the financial resources be applied. At the slightest hint that funds are being mishandled or that there is an impropriety in a program's financial management, a loss of credibility could produce financial reductions.

■ ACCOUNTING

... accountability in fiscal terms means that people responsible for some activity involving money must provide evidence of appropriate care as conservators, which is now taken to include *wise use* of all resources. . . . it describes the practice of good business principles, when handling money. . . . At broader levels, accountability has come to mean wise use of all resources purchased by the district. This includes accounting function, but it also includes the decision-making process by which funds are spent and the outcomes resulting from such expenditures" (Thompson and Wood, 2001, pp. 106–107).

School accounting has two primary categories: statistical and financial. *Statistical accounting* includes pupil attendance figures, inventories of equipment and supplies, and similar types of records, all of which are important and will be discussed further in relation to purchasing and maintaining equipment. In this chapter we are concerned only with *financial accounting*, which involves all transactions involving money and which, in turn, affects all dimensions of physical education, athletics, and other sport organizations.

Accounting is a broad field. In relation to schools and sport, it includes all aspects of computation and uses of financial data. Accounting is the tool to control finances (income and outlays).

Accounting is more than reporting and recording finances; it is not an end in itself. Accounting serves management in a variety of ways to maximize the efficiency of the organization. For example, let us assume that the athletic budget is based on substantial income from concessions during football. The amount listed in the budget is based on past history and estimates about the crowds expected for this year's home games, as well as other related factors. Accounting procedures might show after three games, however, that the income from concessions is substantially lower than budgeted. Meanwhile, all spending is based on the premise that the additional money will be forthcoming. Naturally, the athletic director takes action first to try to determine why concession sales have fallen off and to increase them. The director also begins to restrict expenditures to balance the account. In this example, accounting is a management tool for the director.

Almost all colleges, large commercial recreation businesses, recreational agencies, and professional sport organizations have put all of their financial operations on computers. Many high schools have yet to make this adjustment and continue to accomplish their accounting by hand, which causes difficulties. In hand accounting, even when following an encumbrance system on expenditures, one generally must wait for a minimum of 45 days to see financial results because income frequently goes through a central collecting office. This time lag occurs because the books usually are not closed until the end of a monthly reporting period, and then it takes about two weeks to computed all the data. In the example cited in the previous paragraph, the results from hand accounting would be too late to solve the problem or even to restrict spending. This time lag is why spring sports frequently must cut budgets and "take up the slack" when football or basketball have had financial problems. The answer lies in computerized data processing, so that a complete accounting can be provided the day after any game.

Governmental and nonprofit accounting systems are not based on profit and loss, but emphasize the social and political objectives and constraints. Accounting is a service function. Meeting demands in governmental and other nonprofit organizations means giving the public data and information to show that there has been adequate *control and accountability* in the handling of financial resources.

The Objectives of the Accounting System

1. The financial information system should provide data so that planning several years into the future is possible. The information should be program oriented.

2. There must be an orderly system of financial records relating to all phases of the program.

3. There must be an orderly and professional method of authorizing expenditures.

4. Authorized forms must be prepared and a system of procedures established so that contracts and purchase orders are standardized and leave "paper trails."

5. A system must be established to ensure that services, goods, and facilities have been received and are acceptable before payment is authorized.

6. The preceding transactions must be recorded in such a way that independent examiners can determine to whom payments were made and for what purpose.

7. It must be ascertained that sufficient revenue is received to meet authorized fiscal obligations. These receipts must be properly recorded, showing the source and in which fund or account each is to be listed.

8. All special funds not maintained through the central business office must be recorded and accounted for in accordance with the school district or college operation so that the records will allow the superintendent's or college president's representative to supervise or administer all subareas.

9. Because all accounts will be audited, the financial accounting system must provide all the information necessary for adequate auditing. The leadership must be able to show from the financial records that all funds have been accounted for and none have been misused, lost, or stolen.

10. The accounting system must be appropriate to the size and complexity of the program and provide necessary information to report to the public.

11. Because financial reports must be made to other agencies and associations, accounting systems and procedures must be in accordance with the guidelines of these units.

12. The accounting system must provide the necessary data for research to evaluate business management policies. Cost analysis, which is described next, is especially useful in evaluating the policies.

In summary, the proper accounting system in schools will

- *Create a complete record* of all financial transactions at school and district levels.
- *Summarize activities* of the schools in financial reports required for proper, effective, and efficient administration.
- *Provide information* used in budget preparation, adoption, and execution.
- *Provide safeguards* on use of money and property, including protection against waste, inefficiency, fraud, and carelessness.
- *Create a longitudinal record* to aid administrators, teachers, boards, and laypersons in program decision processes (Thompson and Wood, 2001, p. 113).

Managerial Accounting

Managers use accounting data to make decisions. Managerial accounting is a system that attempts to evaluate the benefits of services received in terms of measurable units. Sometimes cost accounting is called *cost effectiveness* or *cost–benefit analysis*. Its purpose is to help managers maintain a precise focus on the most efficient use of funds. This method has been described as an analytic tool that permits managers to relate program costs to organizational effectiveness. The main purpose is to help managers minimize costs and maximize effectiveness. (Horngren, Sundem, and Elliot, 1999, p. 193).

For example, in physical education, one could analyze the comparable costs of similar programs by dividing the total budget for physical education by the number of students served to calculate the cost per pupil. Before drawing conclusions, one would need to carefully analyze many variables, including the type of program and activities; the age and size of the school; the socioeconomic background of the school population; the age, experience, and education of the teachers; and the success level of the programs. The bottom line is performance levels and gains in the largely unmeasurable *affective domain* (socioemotional) for a given cost per student.

An example of cost accounting in athletics is to compare the costs of two football programs by total program costs or per participant costs. Again, in its simplest but largely inaccurate form, this could be done by comparing the win–loss records and the budgets between two comparable schools, or better, but still lacking, the cost per participant. At the very least, such comparisons must be computed over several years. The figures must reflect many of the variables listed in the previous paragraph, as well as the quantity and quality of the equipment and facilities. In particular, the socioeconomic structure of the community is important because it affects the community's desire to support the program. One must be cautious when adopting an industrial fiscal model, such as cost accounting, in an educational setting.

Accounting Records and Procedures

Although each institution of higher education has its own accounting system, the current trend encourages state systems of higher education to follow a standard system. A series of handbooks on school financial management, published by the U.S. Office of Education, has influenced most primary and secondary schools to follow the same recording and reporting systems. This system of line-item budgeting is built on the idea of *function*, *program*, and *object* categories.

What do the words *function, program,* and *object* represent? This kind of accounting is as elementary as numbering football plays. The *functions* refer to

the particular area of performance, or the purpose for which a thing exists. For example:

1000 Instruction
1100 Regular programs
1200 Special programs

For *program* accounting, the third and fourth digits of the functions are coded, as the following illustrate:

1106 Foreign and classical languages
1108 Health and physical education
1130 Student activities

and so on, through 21 additional classifications in the "regular programs" function. These program designations refine the previous *function* classifications. Program budgeting is particularly useful for persons removed from the details of the organization.

The third recording area is called the *object* and refers to the services or commodities received through the transaction, as the following illustrate:

100 Salaries
200 Employee benefits
300 Purchased services
400 Supplies and materials

Just as football players know that play number 27 means that back number two is running through hole number seven, the administrator knows that "1108–400" refers to an expenditure of supplies or materials for physical education or health.

The Balance Sheet

A major part of the accounting system is the balance sheet. It is like a snapshot of the financial status of an organization at a specific instant of time. Recently the terms *statement of financial position* or *statement of financial condition* have been substituted for the balance sheet. "The balance sheet has two counterbalancing sections. The left side lists assets, which represent the resources of the firm (everything the firm owns and controls—from cash to buildings, and so on). The right side lists liabilities and owners' equity, which represent the sources of the resources used to acquire the assets. Liabilities and owner's equity might be thought of as claims against the resources" (Horngren, Sundem, and Elliot, 1999, p. 8).

Controls

Controls in financial management are policies and regulations relating to the expenditure of funds to ensure that they are handled in an efficient, safe, and correct manner. Controls are to accounting what the thermostat is to the furnace. Controls should be viewed as a positive force to create a climate of trust, a high esprit de corps, and efficient working conditions. The management practice of "controlling" the purchase of equipment to the point that teaching is ineffective is as bad as allowing employees to purchase anything they want even if it does not further the organization's objectives. "The issue is how to selectively determine where to put control emphasis to get a quality job done and yet do it within reasonable amounts of effort compared with the benefit gained" (Koteen, 1997, p. 306).

Financial control is balance. Applying the least amount of control to maintain high professional and ethical standards is the goal. Controls should allow a coach to obtain equipment and supplies by following simple, prescribed steps. But the coach should not be allowed to purchase a type or amount of material not budgeted or approved, and she or he must safeguard the equipment once in possession.

The elements of controls are these:

1. Meaningful standards and guidelines for financial management that are comprehensible to all and are measurable.

2. An efficient and well-tuned system of controls that strikes a balance between control and smooth function, designed so that unacceptable practices are detected early enough for simple correction.

3. A system designed so that controls are reapplied as soon as possible after corrections have been made.

What qualities should be found in controls? Controls should be economized—the fewer the better.

Transactions or events must be meaningful before they are controlled. The controls should be specific and appropriate to the event, especially in athletics because unusual transactions take place at very unusual times. Controls in themselves have to be cost-efficient and match the event being controlled because the more the controls, the costlier the system. Controls must be applied at the most propitious time during the transaction—too early or too late results in no control at all. The most effective controls are the simplest. A high-quality control must help the administrator make appropriate decisions efficiently.

Athletic fiscal management needs careful controls because the majority of the income does not originate from state or municipal funds, and thus does not necessarily have to be managed in the same manner. Frequently some income comes from donated sources, which carries the danger of outside interference. Coaches are often outspoken, aggressive, and, in rare cases, "spoiled" to the point of demanding too much. Some coaches do not have the experience or training to recognize proper financial management. Because most athletic competition does not take place during normal work periods, transactions occur at odd times (Friday nights, Saturday and Sunday afternoons, and during holidays). Sporting goods and facility markets are high-markup, aggressive business areas in which salespersons might be tempted to suggest shortcuts to achieve quick sales or to offer coaches complimentary equipment if orders are placed with their firm.

Some commonsense controls in athletics are these: Require at least two signatures for every transaction. Have all revenue go to the treasurer or business manager for the district or institution, just as all other school income does. Have all bills paid by the same office and person, but only after signed invoices are presented by the responsible faculty member. (Nonfaculty assistants or nonpaid equipment managers should not sign for incoming equipment and supplies.) Require coaches to itemize large orders and to inventory the complete order before signing the invoice. Require precise inventories at the conclusion of each session; send reports to the AD and the business manager. Insist that all equipment be accurately marked and properly stored. People handling cash should be bonded for the largest amount they will handle all year, and security for handling cash should be thoughtfully planned. The coaches should receive timely accounting reports of the status of the budget they control. Accrual (or modified accrual) accounting systems explained in the following section should be utilized, and internal and external audits must be initiated on regular and irregular schedules.

Accrual Accounting. Accrual accounting is a simple control recommended for physical education and athletics. In this system, revenues are recorded when appropriated and not when they are actually received, whereas expenditures are recorded as soon as money is obligated, such as for a purchase order. A modification of this method records income when it is actually received rather than just appropriated (Engstrom and Hay, 1994).

In school athletics, there is almost no income in the third and fourth quarters of a fiscal year unless appropriations are made quarterly. Thus there are few ways to make major financial adjustments from March through June if accounts become overdrawn. Programs can develop problems when several coaches place large orders in the spring, with the understanding that they won't be billed until after July 1. What happens if the coach is terminated, the sport is discontinued, or the budget is drastically cut? Following accrual accounting would prohibit such poor practices.

Essentially in accrual accounting, there is an attempt to match revenues and expenses in a certain time period. Recently Bally Total Fitness, the largest fitness company in the country, was required to shift from a system of accounting used by retail businesses to a revenue recognition system used in the service industry that is close to accrual accounting (Cioletti, 1997).

Concurrent Auditing. Controls are sometimes referred to as a type of concurrent auditing. Under this method, checkpoints and approvals are established before the expenditure is even au-

thorized. In this way, auditing is concurrent to the transaction to ensure that correct budget codes are listed, funds are available, and the appropriate signatures and approvals have been entered. Obviously, this preauditing control is advantageous because mistakes are rectified before they happen rather than after they happen, as in the postaudit system outlined in the next section.

Audits

"Auditing is the independent examination of accounting systems generally, and specific accounts in particular, to ensure the accuracy and completeness of the accounting records in a district" (Thompson and Wood, 2001, p. 130). Audits are required to verify that all transactions and record keeping in financial management have been in accordance with policy and law affecting the operation of the program (see the definitions at the beginning of this chapter). To accomplish this verification, accountants from within an institution (internal auditors) or from outside (external auditors) examine the books to trace original documents and entries to certify that the system is sound and has been followed.

Audits will never be ranked as a top-ten experience, but they need not be feared. Audits are a natural part of the administrator's job. The following are some suggestions for how to limit the aggravation: Keep in mind that audits occur to verify the financial records, not necessarily to find errors. Require all clerical and staff members to maintain accurate records and to follow the prescribed protocols to the letter. If this is standard operating procedure, audits will be a breeze. Work with the auditors on a schedule that fits into your operation and, if the operation is complex, arrange for an accountant familiar with the system to be available during the period. Maintain your composure, communicate clearly, and don't be concerned if you are asked to repeat the same explanations. As always in administration, try to delegate as much as possible, and don't assume that an auditor's finding is correct—auditors make mistakes also (Sattler and Mullens, 1993b).

Audit reports vary, but if a variance is discovered, it becomes a legal matter and must be reported and corrected immediately. Most reports will provide suggestions for changing procedures or recommend areas for study. The reports might question why such a low interest rate is being received on reserve funds or point out that hand calculations are being made in an area better served by electronic data processing. The third section of a few reports expands on the two preceding areas, combining and comparing accounting records with auditing records to establish *cost–benefit analysis*, previously covered under cost accounting.

Petty Cash, Revolving Funds, and Discretionary Funds

Petty cash, revolving funds, and discretionary funds are similar in nature, use, and amount of money involved. (See the definitions at the beginning of the chapter.) Petty cash and revolving funds are synonymous; the primary difference between them and discretionary funds is that discretionary funds are usually nonappropriated (gifts, revenue from school fund-raisers, staff contributions, and the like) while petty cash is a revolving fund of money from regular appropriations. It is said to "revolve" because the money spent is charged against regular accounts, and when this recording is completed, the cash is returned to the fund. Because it may cost about $10 to process each purchase order, this fund is used to pay for items costing less than $10. But regular receipts must ultimately show which accounts were debited. The total petty cash fund is usually $100 or less (Thompson and Wood, 2001, p. 248).

On the other hand, the discretionary account is used at the discretion of the custodian of the account (AD, chairperson, principal); receipts are required, but frequently they are informal or self-generated. For example, this fund may be used to pay for a disadvantaged student to have a physical examination required for team participation. So that the student is not embarrassed, a counselor or AD might sign a receipt signifying that this money was paid by the principal. Thus the audit will indicate only that all funds were properly accounted for and not attempt to determine the correctness of the expenditure so long as it

was for the good of the school, program, staff, or students. Frequently the discretionary fund is used to send flowers or sympathy cards, pay for small COD charges, and snap up special cash-only inexpensive sale items needed by the school.

Proprietary Funds

Funds in schools that do not come from the government are considered proprietary and require a separate accounting system. These funds are generated from fees for services or from activities for which there is a charge similar to a for-profit business. Proprietary school funds are typically divided into two categories. *Enterprise funds* are generated from athletics along with other similar activities such as selling school newspapers or sales from a bookstore. *Internal service funds* are derived from such things as a central printing or maintenance shop (Thompson and Wood, 2001, p. 115).

■ BUDGETING

Budgeting is an approved plan for how revenue will be expended so that the end result is that *revenue equals expenditures*. Different organizations seldom use the same budget process. The budget system should reflect the organization's unique environmental factors and circumstances. The important thing for students to remember is that the budgetary process is designed to provide data for administrators to make decisions or reflect decisions already made. Miller (1997, p. 206) has summarized the differences between accounting and budgeting by stating, ". . . accounting statements represent what has happened, whereas the budget represents what is expected to happen."

The benefits of good budgeting are many. Waste and runaway costs are reduced. The organization stays focused on strategic planning. Employees are educated about resource limitations, and they are empowered by such knowledge. And product pricing decisions are easier to make (Miller, 1997, p. 206).

Cash Flow

An important part of the budget process is the timing of when you are paying bills and collect-

Table 6.1 Sample Cash Flow Chart for a Sponsored Televised Tournament

	April	May	June	July	August	September	October	November	December
Revenue									
Title sponsor				✓			✓	✓	
Presenting sponsor						✓		✓	
Other sponsors		✓	✓		✓	✓	✓	✓	
Ticket sales				✓	✓	✓	✓		
TV commercial sales								✓	✓
Merchandise							✓		
Expenses									
Personnel	✓	✓	✓	✓	✓	✓	✓	✓	✓
Facility				✓			✓		
Printing		✓	✓			✓			
Travel	✓	✓	✓	✓	✓	✓	✓	✓	
Prize money							✓		
TV production					✓		✓	✓	
Labor (crew)						✓	✓		
Hotel	✓	✓	✓	✓	✓	✓	✓	✓	✓
Advertising				✓	✓	✓	✓	✓	
PR		✓			✓			✓	
Parties							✓		
Promotion					✓		✓		
Merchandise						✓			

When planning your event, realize that expenses come prior to revenue being received, so plan accordingly.

Source: Solomon, J. (2002). *An insider's guide to managing sporting events.* Champaign, IL: Human Kinetics.

ing revenue, which is called *cash flow.* It is important to know when you must pay bills and when the revenues will be received. Thus you will have the capital on hand to pay bills in a timely fashion without having to borrow and incur interest charges or dip into reserve funds. To plan your cash flow, follow these guidelines:

- Develop a chart that graphs the income and expenses by dates.
- Determine the amount of seed money or start-up funds needed.
- Try to schedule payments as late as possible without penalties of ill will.

- Recognize that larger firms are usually the slowest to pay for services rendered (Solomon, 2002, p. 35).

See Table 6.1, which shows a sample cash flow chart for a sponsored televised tournament.

Opportunities and Advantages of Budgeting

The inexperienced administrator might incorrectly view budget making in negative terms. The process is actually both necessary and potentially positive. It presents a systematic manner of objectively reviewing current programs and a vehicle to arouse staff members to constructively channel their concerns and requests for additional support. The budget process provides an orderly way to change programs or eliminate weak or unprofitable areas. It presents an opportunity to develop long-range strategic plans and present the needs to the public or review boards. The budget process also provides an excellent time to evaluate programs since the last budget cycle, to ensure that all areas have the necessary support, or to transfer resources between areas.

Purposes and Principles of Budgets

The budget should grow out of the needs of the program. Don't start by asking, How much money do we have? How should we budget to spend it? But be realistic; refrain from planning programs for which there is no hope of adequate funding no matter how strong and well documented the justifications might be—that would be irresponsible. The past levels of funding, the economics of the time, and the political climate of the region must all be weighed.

The general principles to follow in building a budget for a nonprofit organization are these: Be conservative; you are the custodian of public funds. Base expenditures and income over at least the past three years, and take into account unusual conditions or events (rainy weather, new coach, winning season) that might affect income or expenses. Plan for at least 10 percent for contingencies, and involve all people directly affected in the planning process. Ensure proper approvals by higher authorities; and follow through to ensure that the budget is interpreted to the users in the field. Be aware that most budgetary systems are eclectic; that is, they incorporate parts of several systems as required by their unique situation. One budget could incorporate parts of all of the following systems.

■ TYPES OF BUDGETS

As previously discussed under accounting, schools and colleges primarily use two types of budgets, *line-item* (two subtypes of *functional* and *object budgets*) and *program* (or *performance*) *budg-*eting*. Program budgeting is a newer method. The larger the institution, the more it is necessary. It is an excellent way to describe budget items to review boards that are not familiar with the organization's details.

Multilevel Standards Budget

This is a simple procedure that consists of new budgets based on one of the following:

- Amounts of expenditures based on the same as the previous year.
- Amounts of expenditures based on the same as last year, but increased for inflation.
- Amounts of expenditures based on the same as last year, increased for inflation and for new increases for approved new programs or services.

Index Budgeting

This form of budgeting is mandated in some states or school systems in which ceilings are established for spending. Frequently this system will be established from a set year as a base to limit increases to the rate of inflation and population or client increases.

Formula Budgeting

This system of budgeting is usually set from the top and dictated down the line, rather than being developed from the bottom users upward. The total amount of money available to budget will be based on head counts with a set formula for allocating the total funds.

PPBES

An example of program or performance budgeting is *PPBS* (planning, programming, budgeting system), which became *PPBES* when the function of *evaluation* was added. PPBES was a formal attempt to couple strategic planning with programming and budgeting into a single system.

Step one of PPBES is to make *long-range plans.* This step requires the administrator and the staff to analyze the program and its objectives several years into the future and to put the plan into writing. The second step translates the plans into *spe-*

cific programs reflecting which parts of the long-range program are the most and the least important. Step three is to *budget* for the programs, weighting the financial support for each program in proportion to its importance as stated in the planning and programming stages of planning. Step four is to *evaluate* how effectively the organization used the resources available to meet the plans outlined in the first step.

Many authorities seem to agree that the PPBES system never worked. It has been difficult to agree on what each of the elements meant, and planning, programming, and budgeting were really never put together. It is an interesting theoretical system to study, but probably not suitable for school or sport organizations (Mintzberg, 1994).

Zero-Base Budgeting

Zero-base budgeting was developed in 1969 by Texas Instruments, Inc. This method was publicized in 1973 when the then-governor of Georgia, Jimmy Carter, adopted it for his state. The basic concept of zero-base budgeting is that organizations or programs must justify their entire fiscal request, not just the increases. In standard budgeting, an organization simply takes the previous budget and requests increases for new or expanded aspects, along with an inflation figure. Only in very unusual circumstances will an organization ask to drop a service or program and reduce its budget.

The process of zero-base budgeting entails the following:

1. Identifying decision-making units. These units are any entities within the organization for which the authority and responsibility for planning and controlling are self-standing. For example, in a physical education organization a unit might be the intramural program, or in athletics it could be basketball for women.

2. Analyzing decision making in a decision-making package. This step aims to measure oranges against other oranges. Each unit must study its goals and objectives and then decide how all subunits will evaluate their process to meet the end result. Obviously, a standard measuring device must be identified so that the reviewers can compare each subunit. This device might be cost per player, weighted to account for equipment differences, gate receipts earned, win–loss record, numbers of participants involved, or perhaps several of these. This statement must identify the cost difference between funding input levels and production accomplishment, or output. In addition, this statement must identify alternative means of accomplishing the objectives.

3. Evaluating and ranking all alternatives within decision-making packages. The administrator or reviewing group must rank the alternatives, assigning priorities to them as they benefit the organization. This is the crux of the zero-base concept because it allows (or forces) the manager or reviewing group to systematically analyze, according to standard criteria, each of the forces competing for money.

4. Preparing a detailed operational budget. Once the alternatives have been ranked, a detailed budget can be built on any of the previously reported types. As one can see, zero-base budgeting is a long-range program that requires a well-prepared staff to adjust its thinking and habits over time. Strong leadership is also needed to keep the process on a steady course (Farmer, Mulrooney, and Ammon, 1996).

Fund Budgeting

A fund is an independent account in which costs and revenues balance out. It relates to specific activities with special objectives. Fund budgeting serves an important internal accounting function but is most useful in presenting financial reports to higher authorities, such as school boards or athletic councils. (See Table 6.2.) Fund accounting requires no additional records or forms, but it organizes the reporting of existing data into a form that compares each fund to others. If there are too many funds, or if funds vary greatly in size and scope of services, it tends to limit their usefulness.

An example of fund budgeting is shown in Table 6.3. One can quickly see how this type of budget could serve as an internal control. In addition, people on review boards who are not fa-

| Table 6.2 | Sample Cash Balance Report for Activity Fund Accounts |

Account Number/Title		Beginning Cash Balance	Current Month Transactions	Ending Cash Balance
109 xxxxx xxx xx xxx x	Season tickets	$ 1,362.03	$ —	$ 1,362.03
110 xxxxx xxx xx xxx x	Activity tickets	$ 11,235.09	$ —	$ 11,235.09
111 xxxxx xxx xx xxx x	Concessions	$ —	$ —	$ —
112 xxxxx xxx xx xxx x	Parking permits	$ 8,739.84	$ 565.00	$ 9,304.84
114 xxxxx xxx xx xxx x	Football	$ 4,114.05	$ 1,871.20 −	$ 2,242.85
116 xxxxx xxx xx xxx x	Boys' basketball	$ 10,131.35	$ 3,182.17 −	$ 6.949.18
117 xxxxx xxx xx xxx x	Baseball	$ 161.84	$ 187.10	$ 348.94
118 xxxxx xxx xx xxx x	Boys' track	$ 140.00	$ 490.00	$ 630.00
119 xxxxx xxx xx xxx x	Soccer	$ —	$ —	$ —
120 xxxxx xxx xx xxx x	Wrestling	$ 8.42	$ —	$ 8.42
122 xxxxx xxx xx xxx x	Cross country	$ —	$ —	$ —
124 xxxxx xxx xx xxx x	Boys' tennis	$ 308.86	$ 120.00	$ 428.86
126 xxxxx xxx xx xxx x	Golf	$ 17.50	$ —	$ 17.50
128 xxxxx xxx xx xxx x	Boys' swimming	$ 2,788.38	$ 109.03	$ 2,897.41
130 xxxxx xxx xx xxx x	Girls' tennis	$ 469.02	$ —	$ 469.02
131 xxxxx xxx xx xxx x	Girls' soccer	$ 33.68	$ 426.10	$ 459.78
132 xxxxx xxx xx xxx x	Girls' volleyball	$ —	$ —	$ —
134 xxxxx xxx xx xxx x	Girls' basketball	$ 6,745.51	$ 1,282.03 −	$ 5,463.48
135 xxxxx xxx xx xxx x	Softball	$ 32.97	$ 111.32	$ 144.29
136 xxxxx xxx xx xxx x	Girls' swimming	$ 1,603.06	$ 129.45	$ 1,732.51
138 xxxxx xxx xx xxx x	Girls' gymnastics	$ —	$ —	$ —
140 xxxxx xxx xx xxx x	Girls' golf	$ —	$ —	$ —
141 xxxxx xxx xx xxx x	Weight training	$ 7.035.23	$ 4.076.40 −	$ 2,958.83
142 xxxxx xxx xx xxx x	Tournament account	$ 925.26	$ 1,008.58	$ 1,933.84
143 xxxxx xxx xx xxx x	Writers' club	$ 1.64	$ —	$ 1.64
144 xxxxx xxx xx xxx x	Student support group	$ 16,602.31	$ 11,040.44 −	$ 5,561.87
145 xxxxx xxx xx xxx x	City basketball	$ 3,551.84	$ 110.00 −	$ 3,441.84
146 xxxxx xxx xx xxx x	Dramatics	$ 1,834.92	$ 41.00	$ 1,875.92
147 xxxxx xxx xx xxx x	Drama trip	$ 19,998.54	$ 14,780.01 −	$ 5,218.53
148 xxxxx xxx xx xxx x	Thespians	$ 656.88	$ 16,008.06 −	$ (15,351.18)
150 xxxxx xxx xx xxx x	Debate	$ 920.35	$ —	$ 920.35
151 xxxxx xxx xx xxx x	Scholarship bowl	$ 825.00	$ —	$ 825.00
152 xxxxx xxx xx xxx x	Cap and gown	$ —	$ —	$ —
154 xxxxx xxx xx xxx x	Needy student	$ 355.42	$ 5.00	$ 360.42
156 xxxxx xxx xx xxx x	Newspaper	$ 1,400.00	$ 848.00	$ 552.00
158 xxxxx xxx xx xxx x	Music contest account	$ 216.12	$ 195.19 −	$ 20.93
160 xxxxx xxx xx xxx x	Music support group	$ 1,517.89	$ —	$ 1,517.89
161 xxxxx xxx xx xxx x	Variety shows	$ —	$ 1,347.05	$ 1,347.05
162 xxxxx xxx xx xxx x	Special music	$ 1,916.19	$ 100.00	$ 2,016.19
164 xxxxx xxx xx xxx x	Chorale	$ 4,817.36	$ 4,817.36 −	$ —
166 xxxxx xxx xx xxx x	Schoolwide talent	$ 134.92	$ —	$ 134.92
168 xxxxx xxx xx xxx x	Jazz group	$ —	$ —	$ —
170 xxxxx xxx xx xxx x	Orchestra	$ 263.00	$ 50.00	$ 313.00
172 xxxxx xxx xx xxx x	Choir fundraising	$ 9,679.28	$ 10,530.00 −	$ (850.72)
173 xxxxx xxx xx xxx x	Pep club	$ 1,924.66	$ 192.24	$ 2,116.90
174 xxxxx xxx xx xxx x	Cheerleaders	$ 598.73	$ —	$ 598.73
178 xxxxx xxx xx xxx x	Student council	$ 12,338.69	$ 2,104.76 −	$ 10,233.93
			Fund balance =	$ 69,442.08

Source: Thompson and Wood (2001), p. 250.

Table 6.3 Sample High School Athletic Program Operating Fund Summary Statement (Expressed in Thousands)								
	Football		Basketball		All Others		Summary	
	$	%	$	%	$	%	$	%
Revenues								
Gate receipts	$20	33%	$10	46%	$ 5	17%	$ 35	32%
Concessions								
Programs	15	25	2	09	2	07	19	17
Parking								
Radio	5	08	2	09	1	04	8	07
Donations	10	17	4	18	5	17	19	17
Subsidy from district	10	17	4	18	16	55	30	27
	$60	100%	$22	100%	$29	100%	$111	100%
Expenses								
Administrative/travel	$10	17%	$ 6	27%	$ 7	24%	$ 23	21%
Maintenance	13	22	2	09	2	07	17	15
Supplies/equipment	15	25	5	22	7	24	27	24
Officials	2	03	1	05	2	07	5	05
Concessions/printing	5	08	1	05	1	03	7	06
Advertising	2	03	1	05	1	03	4	04
Salary supplements	10	17	4	18	6	21	20	18
Miscellaneous	3	05	2	09	3	10	8	07
	$60	100%	$22	100%	$29	99%	$111	100%

miliar with details can get a different perspective on the budget from a fund statement. One of its most useful elements is its comparison by percentages. Note in the sample that football earned 25 percent of its revenues from concessions, programs, and parking, whereas basketball earned 9 percent from these areas and the other sports earned 7 percent. A board might look at these figures and reflect, "We can see how the mostly non-revenue sports might be this low in the income from these areas, but why does basketball show a low percentage?" This observation could lead to a study of the sales, charges, and marketing of the concessions, programs, and parking in basketball. The study might find that actually the concessions were healthy, but the parking and programs were free, when charges could be made for both.

Compare the costs for maintenance and supplies across the board, and note that the average for all three areas is 15 percent. While basketball is, as expected, less in both dollars and percentage

than football, note that in the nonrevenue sports, only 7 percent of their budgets is spent in this area. When reflecting on the costs for such sports as baseball/softball and track and field, the AD might decide that these areas need to be studied to determine whether the support in maintenance and supplies needs to be increased. Fund budgeting also helps review committees to decide how the financial resources should be divided. Note that the summary column on the far right is an excellent way to see at a glance where resources originate and how they are utilized.

■ TRADITIONAL BUDGETING PROCESS

Although the type of process and size of the budget will dictate how much effort and time is expended on each phase of budget building, there are universal steps through which the budget must pass.

Step I: Gather Data

In all but the smallest of units, this process starts on the day the previous budget was implemented. For recreational sport programs, it includes gathering statistics on the numbers of participants and equipment checkouts. For various athletic teams, and it means ascertaining the numbers on the squads and the win–loss records; appraising the facility; noting the honors won by individuals, the numbers of spectators, and the gate receipts; inventorying the equipment; and reporting expectations for the following season. For physical education, the process includes pre- and posttesting of various skills or fitness, ascertaining the average class sizes, reviewing the facility and equipment, studying the curriculum, reviewing teacher evaluations, and having students evaluate the program. Frequently it will be wise to draw together the persons affected by the budget to analyze how these data relate to the organization's goals. In larger units, administrators need to meet only with representatives from different segments. For example, in colleges the AD might meet with representatives from women's sports, the business manager, football, men's and women's basketball, and nonrevenue men's sports. In high schools it might be a representative from men's and women's fall, winter, and spring sports. One way or another, everyone affected *must* have a voice in the process, and it must be continuous throughout the year.

Step II: Analyze Past Budgets, Facilities, and Equipment Inventories and Compare to New Requests

Use a three- to five-year period for study. Three-year studies are usually satisfactory for equipment and supplies, but capital items and personnel needs require longer periods for review. The administrator or the review group must study the trends and compare the results to the previous budgets. How extensive were past increases? Do the data from Step I reflect appropriate production gains? Do changes in socioeconomic conditions need to be considered? For example, how many high school programs failed to reflect the past increase in interest and demand

for tennis, golf, or soccer and failed to budget for courts or fields and equipment to meet this interest? Do the past budgets and participation figures show sufficient progress in women's sport to satisfy the legal and professional obligations? What level of inflation is predicted?

Step III: Construct the Budget

Follow the form or type required by the system, make decisions, and list amounts. If the details of the system are not prescribed, budgeting in the three separate but related areas of *personnel, operations*, and *capital accounts* is quite effective. For public administrators it is important to become familiar with governmental accounting. To construct a budget in governmental agencies, the funds are usually classified into four categories:

1. The general fund, which includes most basic services and anything not in the next three categories.
2. Special revenue funds, which are legally restricted for a specific purpose (for example, if a school system opened an account to fund the purchase of an activity bus for athletics).
3. Capital project funds, which take in all major projects other than those funded by proprietary or trust funds.
4. Debt service funds, which account for the payment of the principal and interest on general long-term debt (Engstrom and Hay, 1994).

Athletic and school administrators often think only in terms of operations budgets, and tend to leave the remainder to the higher authorities. Honesty is the only professional policy— *don't pad budgets*! Develop a reputation for absolute credibility; be able to justify every dollar requested. Get actual figures when possible rather than estimates. For example, if you are drafting a budget in February that is due in April, call suppliers and see if they have quotable prices for the next season; see if officials' fees have been set rather than guessing at increases. While it is not usually required to budget for revenues in physical education, income estimation is vital in athletics. Use figures from the past three years and, if in doubt, err on the low side for income.

Step IV: Justify the Figures and Present the Budget

More administrators fall down in this step than in others. There is never enough money to go around. While athletics are often not competing for the same dollar as other school programs, certainly physical education and intramurals will be. Often the review board or superintendent will approve funding based on the justification. In some situations, only the figures are reviewed and the justification is verbal. If so, go to that meeting with facts and figures logically organized, rather than speaking from memory. Use graphs and other visual aids to illustrate the need and to show past successes. If there is a special capital request—for example, for new lighting for a baseball field—have experts in lighting attend the meeting. Use a soft-sell technique and be organized. Not many superintendents or boards will respond to an aggressive, fast-talking administrator. Base all justifications on what's best for the students, not for the coaches, teachers, school, or for winning more games. Ensure that the budget has been shared, and, if possible, endorsed by all affected before it is presented to higher authorities. Make sure it contains no hidden agendas! Frequently, teachers or coaches will have an opportunity to share their opinions about the budget with people who may have influence. The better informed they are, the more intelligently they can speak about it.

Step V: Interpret and Evaluate the Budget

If the budget is not too complicated and the staff number about 25 or fewer, each member should receive a copy of the budget. It is recommended, however, that the staff receive the budget in a meeting, at which time the process should be reviewed and questions and criticisms openly entertained. If people have questions or criticisms and are not encouraged to voice them in a staff meeting, they will do so otherwise in a negative fashion. In an open meeting, explanations can be made to reduce friction. Budget evaluation is a continuous process that begins as soon as it is implemented. Through the controls previously covered, the budget is monitored for sound management throughout the year. In addition, the criteria used to determine the budget are also used to evaluate the extent to which each section or sport meets its stated goals. These evaluation results once again become the database for planning the next budget. (See Figure 6.1.)

■ FINANCIAL EXIGENCIES

Financial exigencies are critical financial situations requiring immediate action. Unfortunately, in these days of taxpayer revolt there will be periods when unexpectedly drastic and immediate spending cuts must be made. The administrator will probably not have planned for this. In the pressure and emotion of the situation, unwise or even illegal decisions are sometimes made.

Case in Point. The college athletic department has gone into the red for the third year in a row, and the reserve fund is exhausted. A plea is made in the spring to increase the student athletic fees, but it is quickly rejected by the board of trustees. Without time or energy for a thorough systematic review, a decision is made to drop both baseball (men) and softball (women). The softball players sue, on the basis of title IX and the court rules in their favor the next spring. The institution receives a great deal of negative publicity; both the men and the women are upset; the institution is left without varsity baseball; and the same budget crisis is present, but worse, because no funds were budgeted for softball, but the court-ordered program must be funded.

Reducing a budget can and should be an orderly, productive process based on strategic planning and a clear statement of the mission and goals of the unit. The rationale for reductions should be made according to guidelines that clarify all the reasons for the review board's final process, and all affected people or groups should have input about the budget. After all public hearings, the review board should be presented with several clear options. When the review board has made its decision, the CEO (AD, chair, director) should privately counsel any sub-unit head (such as the football coach) whose budget

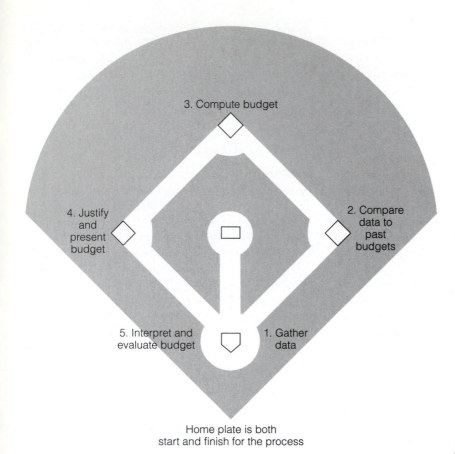

3. Compute budget

4. Justify and present budget

2. Compare data to past budgets

5. Interpret and evaluate budget

1. Gather data

Home plate is both start and finish for the process

Figure 6.1
The continuous budget cycle.

has been adversely affected, and then announce the results. Depending on circumstances, it may be wise also to announce if unit heads have supported or not supported the decisions. Naturally, if a unit head agrees to support such a decision, generous praise would be provided for support from such a person.

For physical education, the following are some of the types of changes that could be considered (even though many are unappealing) to reduce budgets:

- Increasing class sizes.
- Increasing the number of classes each instructor teaches.
- Using paraprofessionals or aides to teach some classes.
- Reducing the course requirements.

- Increasing the standards of elective classes so fewer marginal students will elect to take the classes.
- Changing the activities from those that require small numbers to those that can accommodate large numbers.
- Changing from activities requiring costly facilities and equipment to those that require little.
- Changing the schedule so more classes can meet within a given time.
- Reducing the number of classes that require transportation.
- Adding classes for which a fee is paid for an adjunct instructor to teach, such as scuba class.
- Reducing nonessential maintenance.
- Purchasing less expensive equipment or using discarded equipment.

There are pitfalls in almost every area of budget reduction, but the most dangerous is to make a cut that results in a hazardous situation. If you can't do it safely, don't do it! For this reason, most colleges opt for dropping sports entirely rather than bits and pieces of all the preceding items.

■ BUDGETING IN PRACTICE

University Campus Recreation and Intramural Program: An Example

The funding comes from student fees. An application for support is made to the student affairs budget council. The council allocates funds according to a system that resembles zero-base budgeting. All other organizations, such as the student newspaper, must apply in the same manner. The budget council is very carefully structured with a balance of professionals and students. The vice chancellor for student affairs has final authority, and the council is only a recommending body.

The intramural program director begins gathering data in the fall and builds this database throughout the year. These data are compared to the past several years to plot which programs and activities are growing and need more support as well as those that are perhaps losing appeal. With this information in mind, the *line-item and object budget* is completed. A summary of the budget request is submitted along with the previous year's approved budget. (See Figure 6.2.) Justifications for all major areas are compiled, and a job description for every position is forwarded. The director appears before the council to present the case and answer questions. The final approved budget is received before the conclusion of the school year. Purchases and recruitment for the fall semester are begun immediately.

A Medium-Size High School Athletic Budget: An Example

At the conclusion of a season, each coach inventories equipment and assesses the program for the next year. Lists of the equipment needed for the next season are prepared. Each coach has a conference with the AD and reviews this material. The AD may suggest adjusting the order or changing the quality of equipment. The aim is frugality, but also to ensure that everyone is supported at an adequate and safe level. For example, if the men's or women's track team requests fancy high-priced warm-ups when plain cotton would be warmer, less expensive and longer-lasting, the AD would advise the coach to change the item. The AD makes the final decision in consultation with the principal. See Table 6.4 for a line item budget example.

Because the AD does all the scheduling, he or she can control the transportation budget. The principal signs all checks for purchases after the appropriate PO (purchase order) has been signed by a coach and the AD. The district pays half of the coaching supplements. The remainder of the operating funds are derived through gate receipts and family and business season ticket purchases. The budget is based on *need*, and a reserve fund of $5,000 minimum is maintained for emergencies. In addition, five-year plans are maintained and revised annually for capital expenditures, such as the cost of a new activity bus. Thus fund-raisers are planned for several years in advance of their needs. If the item is major, such as installing a new all-weather track, the school may receive matching funds from the county. A low-key, but professionally operated, booster club exists to provide assistance for ongoing fund-raisers and small maintenance and building projects.

Where does the income come from for funding high school budgets? One survey of 187 schools in 45 states reported that 37 of the schools received less than one-fifth of their funding from school boards. This is an alarming figure, because these school boards are saying that the athletic program either has little value or is not educational. These schools rely on ticket sales (about 70 percent), booster clubs (11.5 percent), and miscellaneous sources such as fund-raisers, soda machines, and activity cards (8 percent) (Cohen, 1993).

Student Activities Budget Council Sample Worksheet

Name of Organization <u>Recreation and Intramurals</u>

Expense Object Code	Name of Account	Last Year's Approved Budget	Next Year's Requested Budget
1412	Temp. emp. Nonstudents		1,600
1452	Temp. emp. students	81,850	96,751
1812	FICA		120
1990	Contracted personal services	2,450	1,250
2130	Clothing		7,430
2400	Repair supplies	300	1,280
2600	Office supplies	2,663	3,200
2510	Gas and oil	500	642
2910	Data processing supplies	500	810
2990	Other supplies	1,953	7,977
3100	Travel	2,297	4,109
3210	Telephone		3,000
3250	Postage		210
3410	Printing	1,800	2,800
3520	Equipment repair	400	1,420
3600	Freight		80
3700 3910	Advertising (revenue) Advertising (no revenue)	1,915	1,600
3950	Conference fees	390	600
3990	Other services		
4400	Maintenance contracts		1,108
4210	Vali-dine		650
4900	Other fixed expenses	180	432
5100	Office equipment		345
5590	Other equipment		16,695
8153	Work/study wages	3,359	1,841
8902	Transfer to reception fund		50
4390	Equipment rental	100	
	Expense total (A)	100,657	156,000
	Revenue total (B)		
	Allocation (A−B)		

Figure 6.2 Example of planning next year's budget.

A Public School District Physical Education Program Budget: An Example

The two factors that appear to affect the budget for physical education are (1) the level or grades involved (elementary, middle school, secondary), and (2) the number of students involved. Frequently these factors result in the budget dictating to a large degree what program evolves, which is not the correct way to plan a program.

| Table 6.4   High School Football Line Item Budget Items | |

Expenditures	Revenues
Supplies	Booster club donations
Office supplies	School board contribution
Training room	Game program sales receipts
Game ticket and program printing	Game concessions sales
Replacement lights for stadium	Game ticket sales
Stadium rest room and locker room supplies	Advertising receipts
Stadium field maintenance, fertilizer,	Student association contribution
grass cutting, and marking	
Bleacher cleaning and maintenance	
Periodicals and books	
Leasing fees for office equipment (copy machine, etc.)	
Videotapes	
Gas	
Equipment	
Game uniforms	
Helmets and pads	
Practice uniforms, towels, etc.	
Game warm-up capes	
Balls	
Practice device replacements (blocking sleds, etc.)	
Weight training replacements	
Utilities	
Water	
Electricity	
Telephone	
Personnel	
Coach's stipends	
Office employee salaries	
Maintenance employee salaries	
Bus driver salaries	
Announcer salary	
Game officials	
Other	
Laundry costs	
Insurance	
Reserve fund set-aside (emergencies)	
Future capital projects set-aside (such as new press	
box or activity bus)	

This typical example shows how to arrive at a budget for physical education. The principal sends the chairperson a note stipulating the budget for the coming year. If the figure is based on numbers in physical education classes, it must be followed. In many situations, the total school budget will be based on the average daily membership (ADM) for that school. In this case, the principal may discuss the needs of each department with chairpersons and establish budgets based on need, considering previous budgets and changing factors. In either case, once the department allotment is fixed, the chairperson usually will discuss the equipment and supply needs for the coming year with the whole staff, individually, or accept written requests for equipment and supplies.

The decision of precisely how the dollars will be spent is usually based on the previous several budgets, inventories of existing quantities, and considerations of what areas need more. Typically the purchases are made from a purchase order originated from the chairperson, signed by the principal, and actually processed by the district business manager.

A University Physical Education Department Budget: An Example

In the past, most college physical education budgets were established by the chairperson sending a budget request with justifications to the next higher level, frequently a dean. After discussions and reviews by higher authorities, the final approved budget was sent down.

The recent trend has been for the budget to be established automatically by formula. In this process, the primary driving force of the formula is *credit hours generated*—thus the struggle for each discipline to attract students. The theory is that the free marketplace (students) dictates which department receives the support. The problem is that vigorous, demanding disciplines might be left at the starting blocks, whereas programs perceived as fun and easy might be rewarded. To try to control this factor, most formulas have an index to account for special equipment and other subjective factors.

Typically each spring the chairperson will consult with key people (frequently coordinators), comparing the previous budgets with the needs and totaling the figures for the new budget. Changing factors that might affect the various line items are solicited. For example, several new academic courses may have been added, so perhaps increases in paper and audiovisual supplies might be in order. Perhaps a new course has been added and the cost of start-up equipment needs to be reflected. In the end, the chairperson juggles the figures while reflecting on the past, considering the future, and listening to advice. Finally, he or she computes the budget for the coming year.

A University Athletic Department Budget: An Example

The university AD frequently utilizes assistants to help build the budget. All coaches prepare budget requests, and then the AD and the assistants begin to estimate revenues.

The revenue expected from student athletic fees can be predicted quite easily. Booster club revenues are difficult to predict. How will this year's athletic teams' (primarily football and basketball) records affect giving? What will be the state of the economy and how will that affect contributions? Keeping these factors in mind and studying the record of the last three years results in a realistic figure. If more is raised than predicted, it goes into the reserve fund, and only the interest earned will be spent. Parking, concessions, and program sales are estimated from past records. Gate receipts are extremely difficult to estimate because the weather and the win–loss record become so important. And estimating the very important television revenue is vital. In a small university, the TV revenue can vary widely. Finally, a total is determined for income.

By midspring, all coaches will have turned in their budget requests and personally consulted with one of the budget review committee members. Usually the AD will confer with the football coach and men's basketball coach; the assistant AD for men with all other coaches of men's teams; and the assistant AD for women's athletics will confer with all coaches of women's teams. The university's scheduling policy will control this aspect of the requests. Each coach will request funds in prescribed line-item areas such as telephone, recruiting, equipment, official fees, travel, and scholarships. In large institutions, women's basketball is now a revenue sport, but it frequently still remains under the budget control of the AD for women's athletics.

The review team will study each sport, comparing the request to the last several years, the spending record by line item over the years, the record of the team, the future of the team, and other special situations. When there is agreement that the requests are not in line with policy or need, adjustments are made both up and down. The budgets are totaled, and if they don't exceed the estimated income, the process is completed. Almost always this is not the case. If so, all sports are reviewed again to make reductions anywhere possible. Coaches frequently will be asked what they would like to be cut. In some instances it is impossible to reduce the budgets further and still remain competitive. When this occurs, the matter must be taken to the athletic council and the chancellor. If reserve funds are not adequate and no further institutional resources are available, policy changes are necessary, such as reducing the number of nonrevenue contests or dropping one or more sports from the program.

A Sport Business Budget Procedure

As required for the preparation of any budget, compiling information and documents is the first step. Unlike nonprofit organizations, items such as unemployment rates, market trends, wage and salary plans, and customer or membership data will be important, along with information such as equipment and supplies expenditures emphasized in nonprofit programs.

Next a revenue budget representing all the money coming into the business is computed. The internal factors controlled by the business, such as risk objectives and management style, are identified; the external factors not within the control of management, such as inflation, the economy, and interest rates, are also recognized.

The next step, budgeting expenses, includes both fixed expenses, such as utilities and rent, and variable or uncontrolled expenses such as the payroll.

Finally, compute the result of revenue minus expenses. Rather than profit, this should be considered the capital budget to accommodate equipment or facility improvements or expansion, or to improve services. As in all types of operations, the day the new budget is put into service, an evaluation program should automatically swing into place (Sattler and Mullens, 1993a).

■ FINANCING

Nonprofit sport organizations such as schools, colleges, and recreation programs will be financed by a combination of sources. Operation fi-

nancing will typically be from municipal, district, or state funds augmented by fees, and to a lesser extent by sales. At times bonds are floated, especially to finance major capital projects, and special assessments against a student body are frequently authorized. Higher education athletics also obtain funding from student fees, donations, media payments, sponsorships, and gate receipts. See Chapter 10 for further material on financing capital projects.

For private facilities, financing is another matter. Some organizations, like Bally Total Fitness, the largest fitness business in the United States, are traded as public commodities. Issuing public or private stock is a cumbersome strategy suitable for only large companies. For the average club, however, financing a new facility, improvements, or operating capital is another story.

One option is to look to banks, but remember that banks view the fitness industry as "faddish" and thus treat their loan applications as high risk. In addition, a fitness facility is not easily converted to other businesses, should it fail. Frequently banks will expect the owner to provide about 40 percent of the amount needed, which is called *equity capital*. Prepare materials that address the following questions:

- Will the club's cash flow cover debt service with a 30 to 60 percent surplus?
- Does the business have assets the creditors can secure?
- Who loses in case of a business failure?
- Is the equity investment sufficient to cover the banker's risk?

Alternative sources of funding are private investors. These groups or people have money to spare, have an entrepreneurial spirit, and are called "angel" investors. Sometimes venture capitalists can be found on the Internet. Another source is through the Small Business Investment Company (SBI). Buying into a franchise is sometimes an attractive option because franchises are several times more likely to succeed than new independent businesses. Another strategy is to lease rather than purchase equipment (Morris, 1997; Loyle, 1997; Miller, 1997).

Critical Thinking

It is interesting to think about the major league franchises from many points of view. Many owners say year after year that they are losing money, but each year the cost of purchasing a major league franchise goes up. Some writers have summarized this phenomenon by focusing on tax write-offs. Anyone buying a franchise must be wealthy. Such a person is always looking for the best way to lessen tax bites. One possible way is to find a business that shows paper losses but will sell later for an amount in excess of the original purchase price. There are intricate tax rules for writing off losses against other income activities and for handling capital gains on a subsequent sale. Major league franchises seem made to order.

Let's say you are wealthy and like to be involved in sport. You pull together some other wealthy friends and buy a major league franchise for $150 million. After a couple of years of minor losses that you claim to have (you're not about to actually open your books for this to be verified), you go to the local or state authorities and tell them you need a new stadium with more luxury boxes, and more parking and concessions, otherwise you'll move the team. The astute politicians say they must protect the citizens and say they'll pay for only half the cost. You reluctantly agree after getting an even bigger cut of the concessions and parking and more luxury boxes. The politicians look good and the voters reelect them, and the public thinks you are wonderful for paying some of the cost and keeping the team "at home."

You keep the team for a few more years, always claiming to be either losing money or breaking even. When you actually have losses, you take full advantage of business tax deductions. During that time you consistently raise ticket prices, along with prices for parking and concessions. Naturally, every few years there is a new, bigger television contract from which you gain handsomely. After all this financial "hardship," you decide to sell, and to your surprise you find that another group is willing to pay $200 million for this losing business.

1. Because of the antitrust agreement, baseball is the only major league sport that allows the owners to decide when a team can relocate. Thus there has been little franchise movement in the last couple of decades. Is this good for baseball? The taxpayers? The players? The owners? Why don't the owners vote to allow more moves so that they maintain more of a threat when they say they will move to another location if they don't get the citizens to give them whatever they want?

2. The franchise moves for the other major league sports occur so often that even hard-core fans have trouble keeping up with where teams are located. Is this good for the taxpayers? The owners? The players?

3. Can you think of other examples in which taxpayers vote to directly subsidize businesses?

Exercises

1. In the intramural budget shown in Figure 6.2, several items common to all budgets of this sort are omitted. Discover what is left out. (The items were not forgotten; they happen to be provided by the physical education department or general university funds.)

2. Discuss the relationship between the riddle "Which comes first, the chicken or the egg?" and programs and budgets.

3. In some cases, Title IX studies have been based on determining the cost per athlete. What problems could result from this procedure?

4. Assume you have a physical fitness competition night for your junior high school. Because a large

crowd is expected, admission will be charged. Describe how you would arrange the charge system to ensure that adequate, but not more than necessary, controls are present.

5. Describe the dangers of petty cash and of discretionary funds.

6. You are the AD at a high school for which the school district pays all the coaching supplements, which amount to 25 percent of the total athletic budget. During the summer a series of major problems hits the school district, and the board decides it cannot pay the coaching supplements. Assume that you have been operating on an austere budget and have been active in fund-raising just to break even. What would you do?

7. Assume you are the softball or baseball coach for a large high school. You are to prepare an expense budget. Your field facility (the diamond and fences) is satisfactory, and you concluded the last season with just enough equipment and supplies to get by (bats, balls, and so forth). Your basic game uniform is three years old and is projected to be used for five seasons. Estimate the cost of all items unless price data are made available to you.

References

Alden, E. (2000, June/July). Forecasting finances. *Athletic Management* XII, pp. 33–38.

Cioletti, Jeff. (1997, September). Bally changes accounting methods. *Club Industry* 13, p. 6.

Cohen, A. (1993, May). School daze. *Athletic Business* 17, pp. 24–32.

Dlugosh, L. L. (1993, February). Planning makes perfect. *Executive Educator*, pp. 63–64.

Engstrom, J. H., and Hay, L. E. (1994). *Essentials of governmental accounting for public administrators.* Burr Ridge, IL: Richard D. Irwin.

Farmer, P. J.; Mulrooney, A. L.; and Ammon, R. (1996). *Sport facility planning and management.* Morgantown, WV: Fitness Information Technologies.

Horngren, C. T.; Sundem, G. L.; and Elliot, J. A. (1999). *Introduction to financial accounting* (7th ed). Upper Saddle River, NJ: Prentice Hall.

Koteen, J. (1997). *Strategic management in public and nonprofit organizations* (2nd ed.). Westport, CT: Praeger.

Loyle, D. (1997, July). Bally's new "numbers guy." *Club Industry* 13, pp. 31–37.

Miller, L. K. (1997). *Sport business management.* Gaithersburg, MD: Aspen.

Mintzberg, H. (1994). *The rise and fall of strategic planning.* New York, NY: Free Press.

Morris, B. A. (1997, December). Dealing dollars. *Club Industry* 13, pp. 27–31.

Pitts, E. H. (1993, April). Stretching to strategic aspirations. *Fitness Management* 9, p. 6.

Sattler, T. P., and Mullens, J. R. (1993a, February). How to budget simply, effectively. *Fitness Management*, p. 9.

Sattler, T. P., and Mullens, J. R. (1993b, April). How to limit the aggravation of audits. *Fitness Management*, p. 9.

Solomon, J. (2002). *An insider's guide to managing sporting events.* Champaign, IL: Human Kinetics.

Thompson, D. C., and Wood, R. C. (2001). *Money and schools* (2nd ed.), Larchmont, NY: Eye on Education.

7

Purchasing, Maintenance, and Security Management in Sport and Physical Education

———————— Case Study: Purchasing Equipment: Be Specific ————————

Purchasing sport and recreation equipment, supplies, and uniforms is a major duty for those in sport administrative positions. In this chapter you will learn about correct purchasing strategies. Mistakes can and will be made; your job is to minimize purchasing mistakes by asking specific and detailed questions.

Here is an example of a purchase gone awry. One city supervisor ordered a gross of footballs to meet the needs of all the high schools in the district. When the footballs arrived before practice, he found they were all small sizes. Another supervisor placed an order for high-quality baseballs. He was pleasantly surprised at the price from one vendor and quickly accepted it. The baseballs appeared to be fine until the team started practice hitting—they were "dead" balls. The supervisor found out that the baseballs had been sitting in a warehouse for several years.

From these problems it became standard operating procedure to add this disclaimer to purchase orders: the equipment must have been manufactured within a specified period.

—————————————— Chapter Objectives ——————————————

The reader should be able to

1. Demonstrate how to properly identify equipment needs in physical education and athletics.
2. Describe the entire purchasing process, including the pros and cons of central versus individual purchasing and of direct and bid-basis purchasing.
3. Write a specification for an item of equipment.
4. Outline a system of receiving, labeling, inventorying, storing, and issuing equipment.
5. Report special concerns related to the purchase and maintenance of major items of equipment, such as uniforms and balls.
6. Design security systems for physical education and athletic facilities.

In purchasing management, the bottom line is value. The value of a piece of equipment is found somewhere between the price of the object and the cost of producing it. In physical education and athletics, the value is frequently more complex to measure than might be the case for other types of equipment. For example, the feel of a ball or bat might be extremely important. And the safety of a helmet is more important than its price or how long it will last. Conversely, for an elementary school, the life of a basketball compared to price is what counts. The administrator must rely on judgment and experience to get the best value. It has been said that a dollar saved in purchasing is 100 percent profit.

Sport equipment and supply purchasing is a highly developed activity frequently controlled by institutional policies and regulations. In the public schools, the procedures are usually established by the central business department. The facets of purchasing—from determining what is needed, to the mechanics of the paperwork and the storage and distribution of the objects—will be discussed in this chapter.

■ PURCHASING

Although both the needs and the complexity of the purchasing system depend on the size of the school and whether it is involved in a central purchasing organization or an independent method, common principles and guidelines apply.

1. **Standardize.** Carefully select conservative items of equipment to standardize so that even with changes in coaches, the products will be well received.

2. **Quality.** With careful security, proper storage, purchasing, and maintenance, high-quality equipment is the most economical in the long run.

3. **Prompt payment.** Order only what can be afforded with timely payments of bills, in order to gain a positive professional reputation and take advantage of "early pay" or "prepay" discounts.

4. **Early-bird ordering.** This policy allows for discounts and equipment to arrive early so inventorying, marking, and fitting players can all be accomplished in an orderly manner.

The sport administrator must be an expert on football equipment and football/soccer field maintenance.
Source: Charleston (SC) Swamp Foxes Media Relations Office.

5. **Professional and personal relationships with vendors.** Develop positive and professional relationships with all vendors with an emphasis on hometown suppliers.

6. **Businesslike approach.** While being friendly, negotiate for the best price, taking full advantage of all discounts, and scrupulously avoiding any personal gains.

Equipment Needs Based on Program

The program itself should determine what equipment and supplies are necessary. The three guiding principles of ordering equipment are quality, cost, and service. Not only the type, but also the level, of activities should dictate these needs. For example, if the high school physical education program includes golf as a short-term elementary minicourse, perhaps only three inexpensive irons and one wood need to be purchased for the average number of students in each section. If the course is advanced, however, probably double that number of better-quality clubs need to be purchased. As previously stated, when it comes to physical activity and equipment safety, the administrator has no decision to make. *The quality of the equipment must be sufficient to be safe or the activity should not be scheduled.* When safety is not the consideration, however, the administrator's judgment comes into play.

It pays in the long run to buy high-quality equipment. It is difficult to justify paying considerably more for an item when other like objects look similar (for example, two basketballs), but if the situation meets the following qualifications, the better equipment should be purchased:

1. Experience or valid testing has proven the difference in quality.

2. The item is standard and is unlikely to be made obsolete by a rule change or the like.

3. The personnel who use the object believe in its quality and are likely to continue to be the users.

4. The object will not be subjected to abuse.

5. Security for the object will be sufficient.

In one case, class use determined that good golf balls lasted more than twice as long as cheaper balls but did not cost twice as much. Particularly because the teachers and the students liked the better balls, it was an easy decision to continue to purchase the high-quality balls. Records began to reveal, however, that although the numbers of students remained constant, the number of balls needed increased substantially. The problem was security; no matter what was tried, one way or another the balls vanished. When the cheaper balls were purchased again, the problem of security disappeared.

Equipment Needs Based on Inventories

Before making decisions about buying equipment, the administrator must study the inventory records. The inventory is vital to identify and locate items on hand, to estimate the value of these items, and to provide information on the serviceability of the equipment. Two kinds of inventories commonly used are the perpetual inventory and the periodic inventory. As the words suggest, the *perpetual inventory* is constant and reflects changes every time an item is added or deleted,

while the *periodic* method results in a status report at specific intervals, usually monthly, quarterly, or annually (Strauf, 1989).

An example of an annual (periodic) football equipment inventory would start by interviewing returning players at the end of a season. They would be remeasured for any size changes. Each piece of equipment would be discussed with the athlete to determine if it still fits properly and performs adequately, if anything needs to be replaced, and what equipment can be used again next season. The inventory is divided into three parts: (1) the in-stock inventory, which covers items not checked out to athletes, such as balls or extra shoes; (2) the in-use inventory, which covers things checked out to the athletes; and (3) the projected needs inventory. Under this system, athletes who will return next season keep their equipment in their lockers until then.

Bar-coding athletic equipment for control and inventory is fast and accurate. In most colleges, students, faculty, and staff already carry bar-coded identification cards, so it is simple to label and scan athletic equipment. Once the system is operating, it is easy to form other linkages. For example, students can be billed for lost equipment through the university's student account system. All kinds of data can be applied to the bar code to help track equipment and make purchasing decisions. Four primary benefits of bar-coding athletic equipment are that it saves time from loading dock to checkout window to purchasing period, reduces the amount of lost equipment, saves money, and holds athletes liable for the equipment they use (Cohen, 1997).

Athletic equipment should be inventoried annually at the end of each season, but physical education equipment, which is used throughout the year, often requires a perpetual inventory. Much depends, however, on the size and complexity of the operating unit, as illustrated in the following examples.

Case I. A middle school consisting of 1,000 students and two physical education teachers is given an equipment and supply budget based on the number of students. At the conclusion of each

Sample Inventory Form

Sport_____   Date_____

Inventory completed by_____

Item	New	On Hand			Missing	Number Needed	Date Needed
		Excellent	Adequate	Discard			

year, the teachers prepare their purchase requests based on their program and inventory, restricting the order to the limits of their budget; thus they are on a periodic inventory.

Case II. A high school of 1,500 students, four physical education teachers, and the usual complement of coaches has separate budgets for physical education and athletics. The physical education program is designed so that each nine weeks instructors rotate among the teaching stations depending on the weather. For instance, basketball is taught for four nine-week units. All nets, balls, and other necessary equipment are inventoried during that period using an adjusted perpetual method. The instructor inventories 20 days before the end of each nine-week unit and places necessary purchase orders to maintain the required level of equipment for the next instructor. On the other hand, in athletics, each coach prepares equipment requests immediately after the season ends and presents the needs to the athletic director.

Case III. This is a city system with three high schools, five junior high schools, and 20 elementary schools. All equipment and supplies are purchased through a central office. A complex system is utilized for both physical education and athletics, involving the school system's warehouse.

Items used mainly in physical education, but including some athletic equipment, are standardized. These standard items include game footballs and synthetic-covered teaching footballs, but not rapidly changing and individualist objects such as helmets or jerseys. For standard items, the coach or the chairperson of the department simply calls the warehouse and requests the item; it is charged against his or her account and sent. Every standard item has a minimum and maximum stock level, with as much spread between the two as possible to allow for purchasing in quantity. In addition, most standard items have a "full inventory date" listed so that just before the season when large amounts of a certain type of equipment are likely to be drawn, there is automatically an adequate supply. Obviously, this system is computerized, and each responsible person receives periodic balance sheets. For the nonstandard equipment, the coaches prepare purchase requests after their seasons end.

After the physical education or athletic administrator in a large school system places an order, it goes to a purchasing manager. The purchasing manager will screen orders to ensure that they are either standard items or that a special item is clearly justified. The basic objective amounts to maximizing buying power while minimizing costs. To accomplish this goal, managers must purchase equipment of the correct quality and quantity, at the best price, from the best source, at the most auspicious time. The objectives of the purchasing officer should be to support the educational needs of the program; to buy on a competitive basis; to minimize losses due to obsolescence, theft, or deterioration; to develop alternative sources of supplies; to maintain positive, open relationships; and to continually evaluate vendors and products.

▮ THE PURCHASING PROCESS

Steps in the Purchasing Process

As previously stated, each school operates under a unique purchasing plan. This section discusses a variety of guidelines and common issues found in most situations. What does a teacher or coach do to start the process of obtaining a desired piece of equipment, and what steps are involved?

1. As outlined in the previous section, the need must be established.

2. The immediate supervisor (AD or department head) is consulted. At this point the option to rent or lease the equipment rather than purchase should be discussed. For example, many sport organizations have found it best to lease equipment, such as scrubbers, that would be obsolete in a couple of years if purchased. Another product frequently leased in schools and universities is the copy machine (Mintz, 1997).

3. A *requisition* is completed and signed by the designated authority, usually the AD or department head, but sometimes the principal. In some small schools, the AD will have a check made out for the principal's signature if the price is small, rather than complete a purchase order or requisition. See Figure 7.1.

4. Appropriate authorities act on the requisition by rejecting, adjusting, or approving it as written.

5. Depending on the policies of the system and the size of the order, the requisition will be processed as a *direct purchase* from a suitable vendor, or the item will be *bid*. (A detailed discussion of these systems will follow.)

6. A *purchase order* with the necessary number of copies will be completed.

7. In many systems, the organization's own form called a *voucher* is sent to the vendor in duplicate with the *purchase order*. When the voucher is returned by the vendor, payment is made. Other systems will pay only when the equipment is received with a document called an *invoice*.

8. When the equipment is received, the merchandise is checked in and inspected. In some cases, all equipment is received and inventoried at a central warehouse, but in others, it comes directly to the requestor.

9. The bill is paid after two steps are completed. The purchasing agent, who in a small school might be the AD or principal, receives written notice that the item has been received and

Purchase Requisition

The office of the business manager is vested with sole authority to order materials and contract for services. The university will assume no obligation except on duly authorized purchase orders. Please use separate requests for different types of material—stationery, repairs, furniture, electrical goods, etc. Original to business office; duplicate for department.

Business Manager: Please order the following   ☐ Supplies   ☐ Equipment   ☐ Services

To be used for _____ Date needed _____

Office Use Only	Date		No.

Suggested source (if any) _____

_____

Deliver to _____

No. | $ _____

Budget information   Person requisitioning _____

Budget name   Person in authority _____

Catalog No.		Quantity	Article (Describe Fully) Attach Quote If Already Obtained	Firm Price

Filled By	Received By	Date	Filled By	Received By	Date

For Business Office Use Only

VUA—Northern Ind. Bank & Trust

☐ Check request amount _____ $ _____

☐ Work order number _____ P.O. no. _____

VUA—Systems

☐ Membership entered _____ Audited by _____

Budget approved

Vice president for business affairs _____

Asst. business manager _____

Figure 7.1 A sample of a purchase requisition form.

is acceptable. Frequently this step is accomplished by the teacher or coach signing and dating the invoice that accompanies the equipment. Second, the vendor will present a bill or a copy of the invoice showing that the material was sent. When both conditions are met, payment is made.

10. Delivery of equipment is made to the ultimate user if it was originally received at a central warehouse. The equipment is inventoried and correctly labeled.

Central or Individual Purchasing

In central purchasing, a purchasing agent rather than the AD, teacher, or coach completes the buying process. This system is most often found in public school districts or universities that buy in volume for all their educational units. The advantages are that volume purchasing results in lower prices; larger orders attract more bidders and thus more competition; the central purchasing office is set up to handle purchases in a more businesslike manner regarding forms, correspondence, warehousing, and payment of bills; and the system allows standardization of equipment.

When each school or even each coach or teacher handles the buying, it is called *individual* or *distributive purchasing.* The advantages of individual purchasing are that one can take advantage of sales or "specials" on short notice; specific models of equipment may be identified; direct purchases can be made with dealers known to the buyer in order to develop quick and reliable service; bid notices can be sent to dealers of the individual's choice; and purchases can be made as needed and not far in advance.

■ DIRECT AND BID PURCHASING

Direct Purchasing

To protect the public's tax dollar, most governmental units, including school systems, greatly restrict direct purchasing. Direct purchasing is simply buying what is wanted from whoever the person thinks is the best supplier. Many schools have a $500 limit on direct purchasing. This is an anomaly because direct buying is what drives capitalism and has created the greatest industrial system in the world. The difference between schools and industry is that the profit motive of private business keeps inept buying in check.

Direct purchasing has several disadvantages. First, it is likely that higher prices will be paid. It is easy to show favoritism and purchase on the basis of personality rather than on the worth of the product. It is possible to give business to friends or relatives. And if the purchaser is not a technical expert on the specific piece of equipment needed, he or she may buy something of inferior quality without realizing it.

Direct buying also has many advantages. It is quick; the purchase can be made in minutes if a supplier is available locally. It is frequently easier to match up equipment by dealing directly with the vendor rather than by writing the specifications. One is more apt to get better-quality items as long as the buyer is a technical expert. Local purchases stimulate the businesses that frequently contribute to the program. Purchases can be made from dealers who are known to stand behind their products and to provide reliable service. And usually vendors are paid more promptly, creating positive business relationships.

To Bid or Not to Bid?

For most administrators, the question of whether to take bids is answered by regulations or laws that prescribe the bidding process for any order over a set amount. The bidding process begins when the intention to purchase equipment is advertised; the exact specifications are prescribed. Vendors calculate the lowest price they can sell the item for and submit this figure as a bid.

The disadvantages of the bid process are many. Quality can suffer. (Astronaut Alan Shepard is said to have quipped that he would have felt better on the launch pad if he didn't know that all the hardware under him was supplied by the lowest bidder.) The bid system sometimes adds to equipment costs if the item is rather inexpensive but the purchase system is complex, requiring a great deal of paperwork. The system is slow, with waiting periods throughout the process necessitated by writing the specifications, advertising, reviewing the bids, and making the decision. The system can discourage purchases from small local dealers who don't have the capacity to process the paperwork or the variety of products necessary to meet specifications. The system can encourage vendors to compete to see who can cut the most corners and still meet the technical requirements. Frequently, when the product delivered doesn't meet the specifications, the goods are not returned because the equipment is needed immediately, and something inferior is better than nothing; or the vendor is allowed to supply some additional items to make up for not meeting specifications. Either of these situations degrades the system.

However, the bid system has advantages. It can stimulate honest competition among reputable vendors, resulting in lower prices. It can result in on-time delivery of products that meet the needs of the consumers. It can stimulate the competitors to include warranties and reliable service. Bidding spreads the purchasing among vendors. It will ensure that purchasing is not based on friendships or relationships. It will lessen the possibility of mistaken judgments on the technical quality of equipment or merchandise.

Types of Bid Systems

Competitive Sealed Bidding. Sealed bidding is the most frequently used system and the most recommended. Most bidding systems require that the important aspects be advertised for a prescribed time, usually from 7 to 21 days of open bidding. The best bidding processes require a public announcement to indicate which firm received the bid, and sometimes require an explanation of why the bid was so awarded.

Competitive Negotiation. This is similar to sealed bidding, but it is not as specific. Instead of detailed specifications of each item, it describes what the equipment is to accomplish.

Competitive Negotiation after Competitive Sealed Bidding. If an item to be purchased is expected to draw bids that exceed the available

funds, this method is used to avoid costly rebidding. The purchasing agent can negotiate with the bidders after it is determined that all bids exceed the funds available.

Noncompetitive Negotiation. This method is used when there is not time to bid—for example, when a specific replacement part is required, or equipment is needed to match other pieces, or if it is known that there will not be several bids entered. Many purchasing codes outline which types of equipment or services are allowed under this category.

■ SPECIFICATIONS

The notice sent to vendors inviting their bids is frequently called a *bid sheet*. The exact details of the required equipment are the specifications. On occasion, specifications are not written in sufficient detail to guarantee receipt of the exact product; however, it is possible to be too narrow. In that case, the item might not be bid and then it must be ordered specially, and the cost is substantially higher. The middle ground is to be only as specific as necessary to restrict the product to what is required. For example, The chairperson of a physical education department decided that, even though the arrows being purchased for archery were of average price, they were breaking so rapidly that cheaper ones would probably last as long. The specifications stated only the required length, and as expected, very low prices were quoted. Before the arrows could be used in the fall, however, they warped so badly that they were too dangerous to use and were discarded.

The challenge is to write specifications as concisely as possible. Every word should have a purpose. List colors precisely, not as blue or red, but as Carolina blue or cardinal red. Specify size, weight, materials, and perhaps design factors. If there is a national standard, such as for football helmets, be sure to require that the equipment meets the standard. Attempt to determine why a coach likes a specific model and list those reasons rather than specifying that model. Experience has shown that one tip for getting better bids is to specify that the item must meet or exceed the quality of model X of brand Y. This gives the vendor and the coach a simple and quick standard.

Examples of Specifications

1. Balls — playground-utility type — 13″ diameter—special antioxidant construction—heavy gauge, rubber with stipple finish—ball shall have a self-sealing valve—each ball to be individually packed in plastic bag—all balls to be tested for ozone—deflated (followed by a list of three approved balls).

2. Net, basketball, goal, chain-type, body of net to consist of hot-dipped galvanized chain not less than 14 ga. .083 equal of inco #3 breaking strength approx. 400 lbs.—with twelve 10 ga. .134 galvanized #40 hooks 1 1/16 inches long.

3. Tennis balls—official, heavy duty for asphalt courts, new fresh stock, packed three balls to a vacuum-sealed container. Shall be first quality, approved by U.S. Tennis Association. Yellow. (Followed by a list of five approved manufacturers.)

■ TESTING, RECEIVING, AND STORING

Need

Testing and evaluating equipment is necessary for the following reasons: (1) In order to determine what factors should be listed in specifications, the satisfactory item should be evaluated. (2) When the products are received, they should be evaluated to ensure that they meet specifications and also to see whether the specified standards were too low or too high for actual needs. (3) An evaluation should be made to determine whether an alternative or substitute item not on a qualified list is adequate.

Approaches

There are several possible approaches to testing or evaluating equipment. One is to communicate with several companies producing acceptable models of the item to determine the manufacturer's specifications. By removing trade names, these descriptions can be useful in writing speci-fications. Another avenue is to study the standards listed by the National Federation of State High School Associations. If the system is large and has a purchasing department, athletic specialists and personnel from that department should actively test products. In medium-size districts, some selective testing is possible when an item is going to be purchased in large quantities or if the product will have a long life.

One testing method is to request that specialists within the school, or people friendly to the school, analyze items and assist in identifying key specifications. For example, home economics teachers can frequently evaluate towels or uniforms. In order to determine which shorts, supporters, towels, T-shirts, and uniforms should be on an approved list, equivalent quality samples from several well-known companies can be requested.

An excellent method of evaluating items for future orders is to purchase small quantities of several equivalent items or to request testing samples from the companies. Put all the items to equal use for a season. Evaluate them at the conclusion of the season. When evaluating the results or performing active testing, invite users such as coaches and teachers, to participate. Another simple method of testing, but much more subjective, is to order equivalent items for two separate schools with similar use demands, and compare the results at the end of the year or season.

Alternatives or Substitutes

When notices for bids are advertised, information on acceptable substitutes and alternatives should be included. The information should clearly state if a designated brand and model is the only acceptable bid for each item or whether equivalent models may be bid. The supplier should be required to furnish catalog information including a picture and specifications for any substitutions for an alternative bid. In many cases, the vendors are requested to send a sample of the alternative. The institution may state that it must be sent to the school at no cost, and that it will not be returned whether or not the bid is accepted. Naturally, if the product is expensive, this demand is unreasonable and would greatly reduce the number of bidders and eliminate free competition.

Product Endorsements

The National Federation of State High School Associations licenses athletic products in two categories: (1) *Approved.* This means that the item meets the specifications of physical dimensions, weight, and design as stipulated in the federation's handbooks. The approved label also denotes that the product has been field-tested for durability, performance, and other factors. (2) *Official.* This term means that the product meets the federation's specifications, and it allows the manufacturer to advertise the product as "official." Only one product in each category (e.g., baseballs) can be selected. The company pays a fee to the federation for being included in either category.

Receiving Goods

Many serious problems result from failing to follow proper procedures when goods are received. The first task is to unpack the goods promptly. If possible, they should be unpacked by the coach or teacher who will be using the equipment. In order to claim concealed damages of goods, the Interstate Commerce Commission requires that the claim be made within 14 days.

After the goods are inspected and found to be satisfactory, the items should be carefully listed on the inventory, as previously discussed. At the same time, however, it is imperative that each item be labeled and permanently identified. It is suggested that balls be inflated for about a week before marking to make them easier to replace in the event of defective valves. Frequently, identical equipment will be used by many schools and youth teams and sold in retail stores. When equipment is lost or stolen, the school must have a permanent identification mark on the goods to claim them. In addition, labeling each piece with the purchase date is the only way to evaluate how long it lasts. So that the identification cannot be obliterated or removed, it should be burned or scratched into most equipment. If this is not possible, it should be boldly lettered with permanent ink in a spot where it won't wear off. The identification should list the initials or name of the school and the year the item was purchased.

Vendor Payment

Vendors range from suppliers of physical education, recreation, or sport equipment to those providing services such as field turf management, laundry, or providing meals to a team. Contracts should be signed for each. Remember that the vendor's attorney will have worded contracts to protect the vendor, so don't hesitate to amend these contracts. The vendors will resist this, but if it is of importance, remain steadfast. If the vendor wants your business, it will likely adjust. In addition to getting things done in a professional manner, as reported earlier, one will likely transfer liability to the vendor if the contracts are properly constructed (Parkhouse, 2001, pp. 206–207).

In general, schools and colleges have earned very low marks in paying equipment bills. Administrators must understand that slow payment of just bills causes undesirable results. First, Vendors will have to borrow money to cover the merchandise delivered, and the cost is ultimately added on to future sales. The dealer will avoid doing business with slow-paying schools, and may go out of business. Merchandise delivered but not paid for until 30 to 60 days later causes cash flow problems. One reason why direct purchasing generates great price reductions is because the merchandise is paid for at the time of the sale, eliminating the cash flow problem. Dealers prefer to rely more on retail sales because of concerns about prompt payment.

Equipment Storage

To a great extent, the life of equipment and uniforms directly relates to the preventive maintenance, cleaning, and storage they receive. How many times have you been to the season's opening game only to see that the scoreboard was inoperative or half the lights were out? Have you heard of the baseball coach who tossed all the gloves into a box and left them that way until the following season? What would be the condition of football helmets if they were thrown in a box for storage? The following general guidelines for equipment storage are recommended:

- Maintain good security.
- Routinely deal with all related equipment after each season.
- Plan storage according to a central concept.
- Maintain a proper storage environment.
- Maintain appropriate access to the storage area.

Physical education teachers must follow the same procedures at the end of units.

Coaching stipends should not be paid until all equipment is inventoried and properly stored. Once a season or unit is over, it is easy to lose interest in the equipment and record keeping.

The maintenance of a proper environment is essential to ensure the longevity of the equipment. Both humidity and temperature must be controlled, but it is more essential to control humidity. In many sections of the country it is wise to operate dehumidifiers to reduce the amount of water in the air. Rubber, leather, and electronic equipment are particularly vulnerable to deterioration in an uncontrolled environment.

Monitoring access to storage rooms is a sensitive problem. Every coach, instructor, manager, and maintenance person thinks he or she should have free access. Administrators frequently must issue stern orders to control the access while ensuring that those who need equipment are served promptly.

The Equipment Manager and Special Equipment Storage Considerations. The most desirable plan is to have a paid full-time equipment manager. If this is not possible, work toward a paid part-time equipment manager. At some small schools, a successful plan has been to combine a physical education and athletic equipment manager, sometimes even including some maintenance duties to justify the position. Sometimes a teacher or coach may have to perform these duties. In this situation, it is recommended that individually secure cabinets or lockers within a general storage room be devoted to each sport, and for physical education equipment. Make ex-

tensive use of student equipment managers, but ensure training and supervision.

The structure, organization, and lighting of the storage room are critical. Fire walls should be installed. Large, bulky items should be stored in the center of the room. Entrance doors should be double; the lighting should be ample and well-located. The shelving system should ensure that equipment stored the longest is used first. If the equipment is ordered without the aid of a computer, it may help to have a card on the shelf in front of each type of equipment showing the minimum quantity to have on hand as a reminder for reordering.

Issuing the equipment requires exact planning. Ensure a balance of controls to avoid an avalanche of paperwork and long lines for an athlete to receive equipment, or the other extreme of just handing equipment out on the "honor" system. At the least, each athlete should sign for all equipment, have it properly fit, be clearly notified on how to care for it, know what to look for in deterioration or malfunctioning, and be instructed to promptly return for replacement any defective equipment.

■ SPECIAL EQUIPMENT PURCHASING

Uniforms

What successful college and professional athletes wear (such as Lycra inserts, color blocking, and baggy basketball shorts) drives the uniform market. In football uniforms, function dictates style to a certain extent, as uniforms have become snugger and sleeker to minimize grasping. Adding a small amount of Lycra allows additional freedom of movement without other restrictions. Sublimated fabric, which has a print pattern dyed into the material, is also becoming more popular, especially with volleyball, basketball, and soccer apparel (Catalano, 1996).

Athletic uniforms hold a unique position in the garment industry because they must look fashionable, be functional, and still possess the durability of rugged work fabrics. As some firms exit the business of selling custom team uniforms, more attention will be required in preparing orders to ensure matching (Mendel, 1994).

In rare instances, physical educators and designers have worked together to design uniforms according to the principles of biomechanics and motor learning. When this opportunity presents itself, important considerations are the degree of restriction of movement, heat dissipation, and feel. Of course, the coach and administrator are also interested in the appearance of the garment. One such design, for a one-piece baseball uniform that looked like the traditional socks, pants, and jersey, was an attempt to keep the socks from falling down and the shirttails from coming out.

Attention to fashion has been on the increase. When the New Orleans Hornets of the NBA needed a new uniform, they turned to a leading New York City fashion designer. Sport equipment manufacturers follow fashion emphasis by moving toward fashion colors and splashy, free-flowing graphics.

Uniform Raw Materials

By knowing the properties of the raw materials, the teacher, coach, or administrator may more intelligently match the need to the material. Many school officials seem to go through the following stages as their primary basis for selecting uniform changes over time. First they ask themselves, "What looks best?" Then, "What lasts longest?" And finally, "What's the best price for what looks acceptable and lasts long enough to serve the purpose of the garment?"

Nylon Filament.   Nylon is a petroleum-based product. About 12 pounds of crude oil are required to make 1 pound of nylon, and the process is energy intensive. Nylon, the strongest fiber known, is used in sport clothing in filament form and textured yarn form. Nylon filament yarns have been used the longest and frequently have been combined with cotton. Nylon's advantages include strength and bright colors, and its disadvantages are little moisture absorption (wickability), lack of stretch, degradation due to light, yellowing, and wrinkling.

Stretch Nylon.   This yarn seems to be the perfect raw material for athletic clothing. The yarn is made by texturizing the nylon filament by heating it close to the melting point, distorting the filaments, and then cooling. The result is a material that is abrasion-resistant, absorbs moisture, holds bright colors, and has stretch properties. However, the price of such materials is high.

Polyester.   Polyester is a derivative of petroleum, but only about seven pounds of crude oil are needed to make one pound of polyester. Polyester uniforms never need ironing. New specially treated polyesters have improved their ability to absorb moisture. Its greatest value is that it is inexpensive. On the negative side, polyester does not have stretch properties. It is sometimes difficult to effectively print numbers on polyester, and, because it has low heat tolerance, it is difficult to wash at high temperatures. It is generally not as strong as nylon.

Acrylic.   This is a synthetic yarn usually produced by spinning. It is similar to wool. Bright colors show and hold fast, and acrylic is stronger than wool. Acrylics are softer but heavier than stretch nylon and react poorly to extreme heat.

Cotton.   Uniforms of cotton remain favorites because of their fine feel and because they absorb moisture very well. Cotton's primary disadvantages are that it is not as strong as the other fabrics, and it is difficult to launder light colors without using bleaches, which weaken the fabric. For this reason, avoid ordering cotton fabrics in white.

Three types of fabrics are generally used in uniforms. Woven fabrics are created on a loom that intertwines the yarn lengthwise and crosswise, resulting in a stable fabric that fits well but has little stretch. Jersey knit is created by "weft" knitting; it results in a fabric that can "run" if damaged but has excellent stretch properties. Double-knit fabrics are made in processes similar to those preceding, but instead of one needle, two are used to tie the yarn in a crisscrossing pattern that reduces the "running" problem.

Buying Uniforms

The best approach to buying uniforms requires a year-round system. The person responsible for the purchasing should contact vendors or companies during the season asking for samples and information about the next season's products.

In addition to selecting the raw material, the fabric type, color, and design, two additional administrative questions must be answered: How many should be bought at one time? When should they be purchased?

A simplistic answer to the first question is to buy the number required each season. The problem with this solution is that budgets often can't accommodate buying 10 uniforms one year and perhaps 30 the next. Also, because of changing styles and fabrics, as well as for psychological reasons, coaches periodically want to change a whole set of uniforms.

One solution is a revolving seven-year purchasing cycle. Assume that a football program requires 36 uniforms for each team—varsity, junior varsity, and freshman, and that a jersey of suitable quality could be purchased in year one, passed on to the JV in year four, and—showing considerable wear—on to the freshmen in year seven. Remember that inflation increases the cost each year.

In the revolving seven-year plan, the same number, 36 jerseys, could be purchased over seven years, allowing for the same amount of inflation. One would purchase 12 jerseys every year. Note that to utilize this plan one would have to continue the same style and color of uniforms worn prior to the seven-year cycle, while in the traditional model, there could be a new type. A considerable savings could be realized over the seven-year period.

Another factor in purchasing uniforms involves timing. Team uniforms are actually a special order and, as such, require much more lead time than most coaches and inexperienced administrators imagine. Because of unhappy results of schools receiving new uniforms after the home opener, as well as the business problem of adequate cash flow on the part of the dealers and manufacturers, the current trend gives substantial discounts for prepaid early orders. For example, the school might receive a 15 percent discount if football uniforms are ordered and prepaid in the spring.

A general guideline for placing orders follows: for fall sports, order by April 1, the previous spring; for winter sports, order by the previous July 1; for spring sports, order by December 1.

The time for the coach to complete the entire order for the next season is within weeks of the completion of a season. Then the AD must decide if it can be afforded. For costly football uniforms, the ordering period is frequently about halfway through the basketball season. This problem shows the importance of having a reserve fund so that the AD can place orders early, take advantage of sales and discounts, and yet remain confident that if an emergency occurs or the basketball team goes on a losing streak, the bills can still be paid. Some manufacturers who have had frequent business dealings with a school will accept and process an order without the final budgetary approval, and hold the order so the school can still rescind it without penalty. Sometimes this is called a "checked-in-place-and-ready-to-go" order.

Details are the downfall of many coaches when it comes to uniform orders. The AD and purchasing agent, if there is one, must train themselves to look for common errors. For example, frequently an order for 12 jerseys may specify only 11 numbers or 11 sizes. Another common error omits specifying the trim or the trim size. One manufacturer reported that if any part of an order is in question, the whole order goes back to the school. Another stated that about 15 percent of all orders must be returned for clarification. Spend time studying that order as if it were your money! Ask an experienced person to review it.

Buying Inflated Balls

One of the most difficult decisions for the administrator is what types of inflated balls to purchase. Understanding the basic construction of balls is vital; then the administrator must assess which ball is best for a particular use. Two primary questions are related to this assessment: How will the ball be used, in varsity games or on the playground? And what surface will the balls be used on—deep grass, polished hardwood, concrete, or gravel?

Basketball Construction. Most basketballs today are constructed around a core of a butyl compound bladder that holds the air. The bladder is wound with nylon. Some companies use a programmed uniform winding system such as the patented icosahedron winding system. Other cheaper models are randomly wound. In addition, experts state that high-quality balls should be wound with nylon thread made especially for this purpose and not with ordinary garment-type nylon thread, which some inexpensive balls contain. Some cheaper balls are wound with polyester or a rayon and cotton blend, neither of which is as durable. In addition to the quality and type of winding, the third factor affecting the ultimate quality of the ball is the amount of winding. The National Sporting Goods Association suggests that medium-quality balls should be wound with at least 2,000 yards of nylon thread, whereas a high-quality ball should be wound with 2,500 yards or more.

After the winding, covers are put on the balls. Covers are made of the following materials:

1. Leather. These balls are made for indoor use on a smooth synthetic or hardwood floor.

2. Synthetic leather. These balls are made of vinyl polyethylene, which looks and feels like leather. It is said that this material outlasts leather but wears differently from rubber or vinyl. Synthetic leather balls can be used on any smooth surface inside or outdoors.

3. Vinyl. These balls can be used indoors or out and can be used on any surface including asphalt, but they lose some resiliency in cold weather.

4. Rubber. Rubber balls also are used on any surface. They are not as slippery and hold their resiliency better than vinyl.

Many believe that the best ball for all-purpose use is a vinyl and rubber ball.

Not only is the cover material important, but so is the way it is applied to the core. There are three common methods: hand-sewn panels, molded rubber, and nylon wound. Most authorities agree that the hand-sewn leather ball is the best, whether it is a football, basketball, or soccer ball. Molded rubber balls have been useful for practice but not as a game ball. The nylon wound cover is the latest style, is cheaper to produce, and is being used more as technology improves.

Football Construction. Because the outside specifications and weight for footballs are so exact, manufacturers are attempting to improve the feel and the inside. Most bladders are made of butyl rubber, while some are now made with polyurethane, which is reported to be stronger and more consistent in cold weather. Additional treatments to the exterior make the leather more water-repellent. One manufacturer utilizes a cotton lining, and another uses only the backs of animals for the leather with the finest feel.

Scoreboards

Because of electronic advances and timing devices, scoreboards are rapidly changing. Administrators should review the latest information in various journals if they are purchasing new timing devices or scoreboards.

There appear to be some persistent trends in the new timing devices. First, one timing device can be adapted for many sports. Radio remote controls are now capable of operating scoreboards in various locations from a central unit. Modular units are available, enabling a school to start with a basic board and then add to it as finances permit. The advertising capabilities of scoreboards have increased to the point that the cost of the board can be met. In one case, the company supplied the advertising panels free and retained the income from them for the first year. Solid-state electronic engineering provides greater flexibility in circuitry and longer warranties. Scoreboards are lighter and use more microprocessors.

Shoes

The key is to buy the right shoe for the sport and surface. The administrator must listen carefully to athletes, coaches, and shoe specialists. Most coaches have found that buying high-quality shoes pays. On the lower levels, when the athletes must provide their own shoes, coaches can frequently arrange with local distributors for the athletes to purchase a good shoe for a reduced price. This encourages the athletes to buy better shoes, producing a positive effect on their performances and safety. Poorly fitting shoes harm performance and could lead to injuries. Inexperienced coaches should consult with shoe representatives and read material from the company producing the particular shoe.

Trends come and go as to what is popular in athletic shoes. Health club members frequently look for a cross-training model. Bright-colored fashion models have shown strong sales. Shoe companies are directing their advertising to the nostalgia of "the good old days," which seems to pay off in increased sales.

Football Equipment

Because of the number of players involved, the cost of the equipment, and the danger involved, every AD must be an expert on football equipment. Most authorities agree that the most important aspect of football equipment is proper fit. Maintaining correct fit starts with the original purchase. Don't try to start a freshman or junior high school football program with hand-me-down large varsity pads. If correctly fitting equipment cannot be purchased, drop the program.

Two key points in proper fit are to (1) purchase pads by position, so that a linebacker has distinctly different pads from a blocker, and (2) measure each athlete individually. The quality, fit, and recertification of used helmets have received considerable attention.

The National Operating Committee on Standards for Athletic Equipment (NOCSAE) has lowered the Severity Index requirement on football helmets from 1,500 to 1,200. According to NOCSAE's most recent records, the proportion of helmets that are recertified annually has been in the 84 to 96 percent range, which is not expected to change much with the introduction of the new Severity Index standard (Plass, 1996). Typically all helmets sent to reconditioners are visually in-

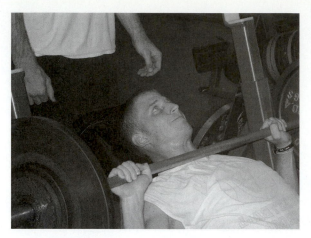

Sports Administrators need to be experts on purchasing strength-training equipment.
Source: Appalachian State University Sports Information Office, Boone, NC.

spected for cracks or wear, and about 15 percent are rejected (Strauf, 1996; Plass, 1996).

Purchasing Other Specific Equipment

How does the administrator, coach, or teacher find the best buy on swimming products or soccer or weight-lifting equipment? The following strategies are recommended: read journals about the subject; communicate with manufacturers of the equipment; talk to coaches; visit teachers and coaches at other schools to evaluate their opinions of the equipment they have purchased; talk to equipment managers; and talk to players.

Strength-Training Equipment.   While it is beyond the scope of this text to provide details of purchasing equipment for all kinds of sport, the following may serve as examples. Related to weight training, the first step is to evaluate equipment and determine what muscle groups cannot be strengthened through the use of existing machines (see Table 7.1). Then contact companies and ask if they will provide a floor plan for optimal use of the facility, whether they provide "use" material for each machine they sell, what warranties are included, why their product is better than others, and what their best price is.

Table 7.1   Comparison of Four Types of Strength Machines

| | Price Range | Velocity | Resistance | | Work/Power Evaluation |
			Type	Magnitude	
Traditional	Low	Controlled by exerciser; usually acceleration is variable	Concentric and eccentric muscular contractions	Hardest at start and progressively easier until momentum prevails	Estimation: weight × distance and timed sets
Velocity-controlled	Moderate	Exerciser selects speed: constant 50 to 75% of range	Either concentric or eccentric mode	Exerciser determines effort against the machine	Estimation: load × distance load × velocity
Resistance-controlled	Moderate	Acceleration is somewhat restricted	Either concentric or eccentric mode	Adjusts to create maximum resistance	Assumption is that maximum work is done
Computerized/programmable	High	Adjustable—constant or variable	Either concentric or eccentric mode	Multi-adjustable	Calculates and displays (screen or printout)

Source: Adrian, 1989a.

With a wider spectrum of users of weight-training equipment, one trend is the addition of enhancements to variable-resistance equipment to make it more user-friendly. New advancements include "the addition of smaller weight increments; range-of-motion limiters . . .; scientifically engineered cams that mirror the way the human body moves; seat adjustments that conform to almost any body height and type; and weight stacks designed to reduce noise" (Connor, 1997).

See Appendix A for names and addresses of some strength-training equipment vendors.

Reducing Purchasing Costs

In addition to getting the best buy for the money (which was previously discussed) and the maintenance and security (to be discussed subsequently), what other methods might be considered? When purchasing equipment in large quantities, have it colorfully engraved with the school system's logo to discourage thefts. Buy manufacturers' overruns or closeouts. For classes, purchase slightly blemished equipment. Rather than purchasing first-aid kits, buy lightweight containers and assemble the kits from common materials. Utilizing homemade or school-made equipment may result in considerable savings. For example, physical education scooters can be made from discarded desktops by attaching small wheels. Another big saver is for schools to make their own awards, using such items as helmets that must be discarded. (See Table 7.2 for a sample equipment checklist.)

■ MAINTENANCE

Ask any administrator, "What is your most difficult task?" The most frequent reply will be, "Main-

Table 7.2	Checklist of Selective Items to Consider in the Purchase and Care of Supplies and Equipment	Yes	No
1.	Selection of supplies and equipment is related to the achievement of the goals and objectives of physical education and sport programs.	_____	_____
2.	Supplies and equipment are selected in accordance with the needs and capacities of the participants, including consideration for age, gender, skill, disability, and interest.	_____	_____
3.	A manual or written policies have been prepared regarding the procedure for purchasing, care, and control of all supplies and equipment.	_____	_____
4.	Mechanics of purchasing such as the following are used: requisitions, specifications, bids and quotations, contracts and purchase orders, delivery data, receipt of merchandise, audit and inspection of goods, vendor invoices, and payment.	_____	_____
5.	The relationship of functions such as the following to purchasing is considered: organizational goals, programming, budgeting and financing, auditing and accounting, maintenance, legal rules and regulations; ethics, and organizational philosophy.	_____	_____
6.	Principles of purchasing such as the following are adhered to: quality, safety, quantity, storage, inventory, control, and trade-in or carryover value.	_____	_____
7.	A close working relationship exists between the department chairperson and school or college business manager or athletic and activities director and the equipment manager.	_____	_____
8.	Participants provide and maintain their own equipment and supplies when appropriate.	_____	_____
9.	Merchandise is purchased only from reputable manufacturers and distributors, and consideration is also given to replacement and the services provided.	_____	_____
10.	The greatest value is achieved for each dollar expended.	_____	_____
11.	Management possesses current knowledge and understanding of equipment and supplies.	_____	_____
12.	Management is receptive to advice and suggestions from colleagues who know, use, and purchase supplies and equipment.	_____	_____
13.	The coach of the sport is contacted when ordering merchandise for his or her activity, and specifications and other matters are checked.	_____	_____
14.	The director of physical education and athletics and activities consults with the business manager when supplies and equipment are needed and ordered.	_____	_____
15.	Regulations for competitive purchasing are followed.	_____	_____
16.	Supply and equipment purchases are standardized whenever possible to make replacement easier.	_____	_____
17.	Management is alert to improvements and advantages and disadvantages of various types of supplies and equipment.	_____	_____
18.	Brand, trademark, and catalog specifications are clearly defined in the purchase requisitions.	_____	_____
19.	Purchase orders are made on standardized school or institutional forms.	_____	_____
20.	Functional quality of merchandise and the safety it affords are major considerations.	_____	_____
21.	The inventory is computerized and is used to plan for replacements and additions.	_____	_____
22.	Complete and accurate records are kept on all products purchased.	_____	_____
23.	New equipment and supply needs are determined well in advance.	_____	_____
24.	New materials and equipment are tested and evaluated before being purchased in quantity.	_____	_____
25.	New equipment complies with minimal safety requirements.	_____	_____
26.	Honesty is expected in all sales representations.	_____	_____
27.	State contracts are used when they are available.	_____	_____
28.	Management is prompt and courteous in receiving legitimate sales and business people.	_____	_____

	Yes	No
29. All competitors and vendors who sell merchandise are given fair and equal consideration.	____	____
30. Gifts or favors offered by salespeople or manufacturers are refused.	____	____
31. Materials received are checked with respect to quality, quantity, and safety and whether they meet specifications that have been indicated on standardized requisition forms.	____	____
32. Prompt payment is ensured on contracts that have been accepted.	____	____
33. All orders are checked carefully for damaged merchandise, shortages, and errors prior to officially signing for the shipment.	____	____
34. Policies have been established for designating procedures to be followed when there is theft, loss, or destruction of equipment.	____	____
35. People who are issued supplies and equipment are held accountable for them.	____	____
36. Inventories and audits are taken periodically to account for all materials.	____	____
37. A uniform plan is established for marking and labeling supplies and equipment.	____	____
38. A written procedure has been established for borrowing and returning or issuing and dropping off supplies and equipment.	____	____
39. A procedure has been established for holding participants or users accountable for equipment that is not returned.	____	____
40. Proper storage facilities have been provided for all purchases.	____	____
41. Equipment is cleaned and repaired when necessary before replacements are ordered.	____	____

Source: Bucher and Krotee (2002), pp. 376–377.

tenance and cleaning." Maintenance personnel are frequently shortchanged; they are understaffed, and they do not get enough pay or respect from superiors. They must cope with insufficient storage space and supplies. New sport facilities should include a central maintenance/custodial complex. If possible, this should be centrally located, be hard-wired for the latest communication equipment and computers, and have appropriate storage capacity and a repair workshop area. Either the custodial/maintenance staff should be welcome in the same break area for others in the facility (which is preferred), or there should be one dedicated for them (Sawyer, 1999, pp. 97–101). Maintenance personnel should be referred to as "custodians" or "maintenance persons," not as "janitors." In larger facilities the title of "maintenance engineer" or "maintenance director" has found favor. Just as preventive medicine is much more economical than waiting for an illness that requires surgery, preventing a mechanical problem is much more efficient than fixing it after the fact.

In most areas of the United States, late summer or fall is the best time to accomplish major preventive maintenance. Winter is no time to have a roof leak or a heating system fail. Ensure that all belts have been inspected or replaced and filters cleaned. Such things as re-lamping and vacuuming girders are best done at this time before all the attention returns inside (Martin, 1997).

Like all other sport facilities and equipment, playground equipment must be regularly serviced and maintained. The National Playground Safety Institute has originated a training course to this end. Information may be found on the NRPA website, www.nrpa.org (Christiansen, 2002). To reduce injuries and preserve expensive outside synthetic or turf fields and inside synthetic or hardwood floors, more facility directors are turning to floor covers. The outside covers have become lighter and thus less expensive, while the trend for inside covers appears to be heavier covers in narrower strips for ease of rolling in and out ("Surfaces and Covers," 2000).

A trend in maintenance and housecleaning is *outsourcing:* contracting with an outside firm to provide the services for a fee. From an administrative point of view there are pros and cons for either plan. In recent years, outsourcing seemed inevitable for schools and colleges.

To efficiently maintain facilities, a maintenance system must be planned. Each facility should be inspected by a team, including several staff members who regularly use the facility and at least one maintenance person, to determine the goals and objectives of the cleaning and preventive maintenance. The team should then write a plan that establishes what needs to be accomplished, how often, special supplies or treatments required, and who will accomplish the tasks. After this plan is approved by the supervisor who can ensure resources to achieve the ends, the system should be entered into a computer program and posted in the facility. The master maintenance-system program should be reviewed weekly by the supervisor prior to inspections, and a team with staggered multiyear appointments should review and revise the plan each year.

Once you have developed a high-performance maintenance team, follow these guidelines to ensure efficient results:

- Maintain communication with your cleaning workers and administrators, and regularly evaluate their work.
- Reiterate program goals—job security and improved efficiency.
- Review program priorities: customer service and satisfaction, and a clean, healthy, safe environment for students, faculty, administrators, and workers.
- Have a consultant develop an evaluation and procedure for assessing building cleanliness every two weeks (Pellerin, 1997).

Sport administrators should be aware that increasingly, cleaning materials that are more environmentally friendly will need to be used. In the maintenance industry, these are referred to as "green" products. Many believe that if the prod-

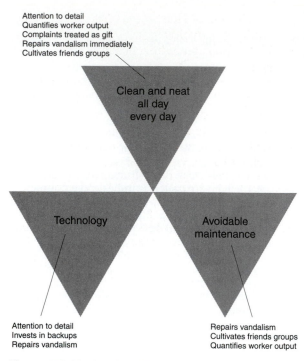

Figure 7.2 Model of world-class maintenance
(Source: Plantera, M.J. (2002, January) p. 55.

uct is not toxic, it can't clean as well; so supervisors must be prepared to overcome resistance (Cummings, 1997).

Maintaining Existing Facilities

In a nationwide study of what maintenance activities separate world-class parks from others, researchers found three overriding practical components (see Figure 7.2). These activities can be applied also to maintenance of any sport facility. The first lesson can be summarized as "clean and neat all day, every day":

- Pay attention to detail.
- Quantify worker output.
- Treat complaints as customer gifts.
- Repair vandalism immediately.
- Cultivate "friends" groups.

The second lesson learned was to eliminate avoidable maintenance:

- Apply weed killers on select areas in late summer to avoid weeding in the spring.
- Pave under team benches and other similar spots.
- Encourage all employees to provide input to every routine task and for each capital project.
- Maintain computerized maintenance schedules and rate worker output.
- Utilize "dry water" to reduce labor costs associated with newly planted trees.

Lesson number three was to utilize state-of-the-art electronic and computer devices:

- Pay attention to detail by using such devices as palm computers.
- Invest in back-up systems for such things as the swimming pool pump.
- Keep accurate records (Pantera, 2002).

Maintenance Schedules

There are many types of maintenance schedules, and they all present difficulties. One concept is to do as much of the work as possible when the students are not in class or practicing. The problem with this approach is that it requires people to work at odd hours, which complicates the problem of attracting and retaining good workers in marginally paying jobs. The other concept is to schedule maintenance crews at regular hours and have them work around the activities. The teachers and coaches generally like this arrangement, and the maintenance personnel obviously prefer this schedule. The problem is that it is inefficient. Coaches and teachers tend not to plan set-ups and other needs in advance. They typically interrupt the staff to pull out bleachers or set up the volleyball standards. It is also handy, for example, to have maintenance persons carry blocking dummies in and out as long as they are on duty. Some small elementary schools have tried to solve the problem by paying a premium wage to one custodian and setting up a split shift with four hours in the morning and four hours after school.

Experience has shown that in larger units a modification of the two systems works out best

in the long run. One person starts with a very early eight-hour shift. That person attacks special problems that might have developed overnight and does routine tasks such as mopping wrestling mats or watering fields that must have time to dry before use. The main crew starts a normal, but early, eight-hour shift to accomplish the usual set-ups and cleaning before classes start. One person starts a late shift just before the main crew goes off duty. This person will be able to clean classrooms after students are finished for the day and after each varsity or intramural activity concludes.

It is difficult to judge the number of people it should take to clean and maintain physical education and sport facilities. Mostly, the administrator must act on a balance of subjective judgment, the advice of staff, and past experience. It might be reasonable to assume that one person could adequately maintain 15,000 square feet of interior space or two acres of school grounds. Supervisors must insist on adequate and efficient work performance, but also must be reasonable and protect employee rights and privileges. Remember that the demands of maintenance personnel in physical education and sport differ a great deal from demands in other educational settings, and this must be communicated.

Laundering

The type of laundering uniforms and towels receive greatly affects their wearable life and appearance. Whether the laundry is done on the premises or elsewhere directly affects the quantity and quality of the material one purchases.

It might be in the best interest of the school to purchase equipment and do the laundering at the gymnasium. Here are some reasons:

- A smaller inventory of towels, physical education uniforms, and practice articles is needed.
- Articles such as athletic supporters or game uniforms can be laundered with special attention given to the degree of hot water used and how long they are dried.
- When the school has one set of uniforms and back-to-back games, laundering can still be

accomplished.

- Laundry can be done on weekends and holidays.
- In many cases, losses will be reduced.
- Time for loading, unloading, and inventorying laundry are eliminated.

Disadvantages or possible problems with a laundry on the premises are these:

- In some situations, the laundry will be done by an institution, such as a college or hospital, and thus there would be competition between two tax-supported units.
- Frequently, planners overlook providing the extra space required for the laundry facilities and the subsequent cost.
- The utilities cost money, especially the hot water and electricity.
- Not only the machines must be purchased, but also detergents and bleaches.
- Maintenance, repair, and replacement costs of machines must be budgeted.
- There are also labor costs for operation.
- There is an increased load on the sewer system.

After weighing the advantages and disadvantages, frequently it will be determined that considerable savings will be generated by installing a laundry on the premises. Administrators are urged to not reach this decision based on coaches and teachers doing the laundry to save labor costs. This would be a misuse of a professional's time and duties. The greatest mistake made in purchasing laundry equipment is to buy machines designed for home use, which will not hold up. Heavy-duty institutional equipment must be purchased. Industrial wash machines can hold from 50 to 250 pounds, and dryers from 30 pounds to 150 pounds. It is advised to get a dryer slightly larger than a washer. A decision must also be made as to electric or gas models. Gas models appear to be cheaper to purchase and to operate. Compare the warranties carefully.

Energy Conservation

Sport facilities are enormous energy users. Every-thing that can be done to reduce the drain of this precious resource must be accomplished, both when the facility is built and through retrofitting and administrative creativity. Schedules to perform regular preventative maintenance on furnaces and cooling/heating systems not only save energy, but are cost effective. Broken windows must be replaced immediately with break-resistant material, and storm windows and doors should be installed. In high-traffic areas, such as gymnasium entrances, add an entrance foyer with an air lock.

Some energy savers might adversely affect programs, but they should still be considered. These include such strategies as scheduling athletic contests centrally and consecutively during the day. Showers constitute a great energy drain. Consider reducing the rate of water flow and the temperature of the water-install water-saver shower heads; consider spring-loaded shower controls; and promptly repair leaks.

Consider curtailing night, holiday, or weekend practice, or require teams to dress and shower at home during these times. For physical education, consider scheduling more activities that don't require showering, or schedule some days each week as "no shower" days. In warmer weather, consider shutting off hot water.

Study the possibilities of new technologies in weatherproofing, installing solar heating systems, using heat pumps and other systems to reclaim energy, and burning oil wastes from activity or school buses in heating/cooling systems.

Maintenance for Special Areas

Turf. An area of great maintenance concern for schools of all levels is that of natural turf. With the constant abuse playfields receive, special maintenance is required. Administrators are urged to consult with golf course maintenance engineers, professional baseball park maintenance supervisors, and turf nurseries in the area. The soil composition and natural environment are so unique to each school that following the instructions of maintenance from a source located hundreds of miles away is folly. General trends in maintaining natural turf are to avoid an overdependence on fertilizers and to expend more effort on reseeding and aerating the roots, and utilizing tine harrows (a drag linked together like a blanket or section of fencing with steel tine teeth). The best time for seeding is late summer, and the second best is early spring. If the field must be used for baseball and softball in the spring and soccer and football in the fall, however, dormant seeding can be done between Thanksgiving and Christmas.

Agronomists have recommended the following turf management program:

- *Fertilize* both early and late in the season.
- Never *mow* more than one-third of the length of the grass blade at one time. The height depends on the type of grass and the type and amount of activity; the length should be longer during hot weather.
- Use as little *water* as possible to maintain healthy turf.
- *Cultivate vertically* and *aerate*.
- *Overseed* or *resod*.
- Apply a *tarp covering* when the grass is dry.
- Test for *compacted soil*—use permeability tests to measure. The recommended soil mix is 75 percent sand, 15 percent silt, and 10 percent clay.
- The *grass type* should usually be a mixture of bluegrass or Bermuda.

Swimming Pools. No area is more difficult to maintain than a swimming pool. Not only are there the usual maintenance demands of properly cleaning the facility—decks, fences, lights, and shower rooms—but there is also the very technical chemical maintenance of the water. Myths about proper water balance abound. For example, eye irritations and chlorine odor usually result from insufficient chlorine, not too much. One competitive swimmer excretes more ammonia through perspiration than a small child does by urination. For indoor swimming pools, the cleanliness of the swimmers and the amount of physical exertion affect the chemistry of the water the most. In outdoor pools, the sun has the greatest ef-

fect. An overlooked factor in operating pools with poor water chemistry, particularly with too much chlorine, is the damage to the mechanical equipment and lines. Because the water chemistry changes from minute to minute, water test kits are only guides. It is recommended that institutional pools have automatic chemical control.

Gas chlorination systems have been used extensively and have always presented dangers. Chlorine gas leaks have injured people; in rare instances, serious injuries have resulted from explosions of these tanks. Some authorities have recommended that the new system of generating sodium hypochlorite on site by electrolysis be used instead of chlorine gas. It seems to be a win–win situation from which swimmers gain a more healthy environment; it is convenient, safe, and less expensive to operate.

From a maintenance perspective, spring cleaning of a pool is the optimal time to accomplish preventive maintenance. This may also be an excellent time to switch to new maintenance equipment.

Wood Gymnasium Floors. Maintenance of wood gymnasium floors is another common administrative necessity. If planned and performed regularly wood floor maintenance is simple and inexpensive. The two most important factors are these: (1) Restrict the amount of dirt and grit entering the gymnasium through educational efforts (signs, announcements, and discipline), require the proper shoes, and control open windows and doors. (2) Sweep daily with a treated dust mop or more often when there is heavy use. Use water only when needed to clean up a water-soluble substance such as a soft-drink spill, and do not wax (Brickman, 1997).

Annual planning and budgeting for wood floor maintenance is a must. This cost is frequently overlooked by administrators in long-range planning, and then put off year after year because no funds are available. The following has been a successful maintenance plan for gymnasium wood floors for a school district with eight such facilities. The plan called for schools to rate their gymnasiums as receiving low, medium, or high use. Those with *low use* were scheduled to be resanded every nine years; they were to have their seal removed and were to be scrubbed during years three and six (second method), and scrubbed or dry-cleaned (third or fourth method) as needed in all other years. Those in the *medium-use* range were scheduled for resanding every six years; removing seal every other year, and scrubbing or dry cleaning every year. Those classified as *heavily used* were sanded every three years, the seal was to be removed the second year, and they were to be scrubbed and sealed the first year. A matrix for budgeting these costs was put into long-range planning. If a gymnasium floor did not need a more costly treatment because of excellent care or less use, the schedule would be delayed a year, and that school could use the funds saved for another project. Some floors that are installed to restrict moisture buildup and have limited use might require sanding only every 20 years (Brickman, 1997).

Synthetic Playing Courts.   Synthetic playing courts made out of polyvinyl chloride or urethane in smooth or pebbled surfaces have become popular. These floors, however, also require regular maintenance, or they will crack or peel and allow abrasive agents to erode their appearance. Previously, the products used to prevent damage were acrylic copolymer coatings and sealants. A newer method is to coat the floors with two applications, which results in a more durable bond. This procedure requires a great deal of preparation. Regular maintenance of a synthetic floor calls for dusting twice a day and scrubbing once a week. The recoating needs to be done annually.

Synthetic Turf.   Keeping an artificial turf field clean will add as much as 30 percent to its life. Debris should be picked up by broom or motorized vacuum cleaner as often as needed. Once or twice a year, sand, grit, and dust need to be flushed out. Snow should be removed, but allow a one-centimeter film to remain. Covering an artificial turf field should be considered. The best

cover is a light-colored coated nylon fabric. Just as in covering natural grass, don't cover artificial turf when it is wet.

Rest Rooms.   In a 1997 study, higher education institutions received complaints about rest room cleanliness (60 percent) and rest room supplies (35 percent). The frequency of complaints for schools was 43.9 percent for rest room cleanliness and 37.9 percent for rest room supplies. If you want to please people who use your rest rooms, ensure that these steps are all followed:

- Sweep the floor, empty wastebaskets, and fill soap dispensers.
- Spray inside and outside toilet bowls with quaternary disinfectant solution.
- Swab the inside of the toilet bowls and flush them while still swabbing.
- Spray the tops and undersides of toilet seats, fixtures, and the wall behind toilets, and wipe dry.
- Spray the outside of the urinals and swab the inside while flushing. Wipe the outside of urinals with a clean cloth.
- Spray disinfectant cleaner on walls, pipes, the underside of basins, soap dispensers, mirrors, and wall-mounted fixtures. Work from the ground up.
- Protect against graffiti and uric acid by spraying a thin film of cleaner or polish on the fixtures each day, and wipe with a soft cloth.
- To control objectionable odors, especially those of urine and mildew, spray an odor counteractant around the toilets and urinals.
- Mop the floor with disinfectant solution (D'Iorio, 1997).

■ SECURITY

Similar to other management concerns, the best place to start planning for security is to analyze the present situation and develop strategic plans to correct problems. If security problems are already serious, a security consultant should be employed to assist in the process.

The type of security required for each facility is highly individualized. A small rural school will be entirely different from a large school in an urban setting. The level of students from early childhood to adult learners will also impact the amount and type of security required. In the wake of terrorist attacks and shootings in schools, administrators must draw up plans of action (which need to be reviewed and practiced each year) for such an emergency as well as standard operating procedures to handle everyday situations. In many communities, the local police will direct traffic at schools in addition to providing full-time police on duty in schools. If not, outsourcing these duties should be considered. Students should refer to "Risk Management" in Chapter 9 for more information.

Facilities designed for security and safety from the start offer the best and most cost-effective course of action. Commonsense building styles and materials should be considered with security in mind, such as steep, sloping roofs; windows designed with expanded metal or woven wire screens; and electromagnetic doors that cannot be opened from the outside, but automatically open when an alarm sounds. Liberally use heavy masonry construction materials such as fully reinforced concrete block, even for toilet partitions, and interior walls coated with a durable substance, such as thermal liquid tile ("Security by Design," 1993; Alvord, 1993).

Security Solutions

Over the years, the military has learned that no matter how many technical and mechanical devices there are, ultimately the degree of security depends on the education and will of the personnel involved. If the student body and staff take pride in school property and respect it, the need for sophisticated security equipment greatly diminishes, other than to restrict nonstudents from entering the premises.

You can't have an open facility that's also a secure facility, but you can have an "open-looking" facility (Cohen, 1993). If one compared the entrance to our campuses to those in other parts of the world, there would be great pride in our freedom. Unfortunately, in some locations, primarily in the inner cities, tight security is required. Some schools, particularly private institutions, are turning to professional security forces. Some have also installed sophisticated security equipment such as sonic motion detectors in areas containing valuable equipment and on first-floor street windows. Television surveillance systems are frequently used to monitor parking lots, hallways, entrances, and exits.

Administrators must study the strategies that are open to them for security enhancement, balanced against cost and intrusion on individual rights. A good place to start is to check with insurance companies to see how better systems will lower insurance costs. Everyone has different security needs.

> When you buy a system, you have to consider a number of environmental factors. These include the configuration of doors and windows, the positioning of ventilation ducts, and neighborhood crime statistics and patterns. Security systems are designed to provide three levels of protection—perimeter, interior, and dedicated. Perimeter security utilizes technology that has been around for decades. The second line of defense consists of a system of interior traps that detect motions made by burglars who move around after business hours. Of the technologies that trap interior motion, the most popular are passive infrared and microwave. The former detects body heat from a person moving amid cooler room temperatures, triggering an alarm. Microwave, by contrast, detects the motion of the burglar. Glass-breaking sensors come in the form of audio sensors that are usually installed in the ceiling. (Perry, 2002).

> Since the September 11 attack, highly sophisticated electronic surveillance systems have been used at large attendance sporting events. "The thorny legal issue confronting sports facility operators who consider implementing any new security measure involves the Fourth Amendment right of individuals to be free from unreasonable searches." (Miller, et. al, 2002)

One of the biggest security problems facing administrators in physical education and athletics is the lockers and locker room. An open shower room that can be seen throughout by the attendants helps tremendously (Horine and Turner, 1979). Mirrors have been installed to see around corners, and television monitors could be used.

The administrator concerned about security needs to be aware of the different types of locks available. Generally, there are three types of locks. The least expensive and the least protective lock is the simple, hollow-shell padlock. The lock affording average protection at a medium price is the laminated warded lock, constructed of layered hard steel that is keyed with an identical squared-tooth pattern on each side. The best lock is a precision pin tumbler padlock that is distinguished by its key, which is flat and smooth on one edge, with irregular serrations along the other edge. Twin, hardened-steel locking levers double lock and hold the padlock shackle tight until precisely the right key is employed.

Sport complexes need security lighting for exterior areas. The Columbus, Ohio, school district determined that its security lights needed attention. The district replaced outside lights with *low-pressure sodium fixtures* with polycarbonate lenses, which resist breakage. These lights, referred to as "LPS," have a lower wattage and so use less energy and last much longer. Users of these lights should recognize that they cause most colors to appear either gray or yellow. In another school, the mercury vapor lights were replaced with *high-pressure sodium fixtures* (HPS). In the process the wattage was reduced from 40,800 to 9,000.

Whether the operation is commercial, recreational, or campus, security is necessary. If an unauthorized person enters and gets hurt, the organization could be liable. Unwelcome guests also increase the likelihood of thefts. Membership cards that are passed through a computer are common, but catching those who pass cards around is difficult and time consuming. A newer system prompts a digital photograph of the cardholder on the computer screen. The bar code card can be so small it can fit on a key ring. The YMCA of Ashland, Ohio, has installed a hand-recognition system that takes less than two seconds (Cioletti, 1997; Patton, 1997).

In designing the control station, great care must be given to the lines of sight that it allows. Raising the control station will be helpful. Touch pads in special areas with card swipe readers of code numbers can be effective. Door alarms and controls along with videocameras will also improve security. "Simple contact switches, coordinated with reporting/control software, allow staff to monitor usage of activity spaces, locker rooms, and so on. In addition, entire buildings can be 'shut down' at the end of the day in an automated time-driven process from a central campus or building location" (Patton, 1997, p. 67).

Playground Security

There is a national building code for play areas, published in Section 15.6 of the Americans with Disabilities Accessibility Guidelines, which provides guidelines for new construction or alterations to existing play areas. Several themes continue to emerge in relation to playground security and safety. One is that height does seriously matter. The farther one falls, the greater the risk of serious injury. The second is the need for consistent but forgiving playing surfaces (Malkusak et al., 2002; Frost et al., 2002; Hendy, 2002; Peterson, 2002). See Chapter 10 for further material.

The School Safety Center of the California Department of Justice has published a handbook that suggests the following measures:

1. Playground equipment should be durable, with a minimum of movable parts, and should have tamper-proof fasteners and bolts.

2. Playground equipment should be clearly visible to neighbors, school personnel, and security forces.

3. Drinking fountains should be recessed into walls.

4. Students, parents, and school staff should be involved in planning playgrounds.

5. Playgrounds should be fenced separately from school buildings.

6. Bicycle racks should be in a secure and monitored area.

7. Play areas should be constructed so that natural barriers or fencing restrict vehicles from sport and play areas.

8. Special efforts need to be made to keep motorcycles and automobiles off the running tracks, large grass fields, and tennis courts.

9. Narrow gaps should be installed in fences to allow entry and discourage fence climbing.

Critical Thinking

At the end of a school year, a high school physical education department voted to purchase two treadmills for the next year. They believed that these machines could be used with partially disabled students, to prescribe individualized exercise plans for other students, and for rehabilitation of some injured varsity athletes. As the chairperson of the department, you study the budget, and it looks like you could accommodate this request. The school system does not have a firm policy on bidding or direct purchases, so it is up to the principal to decide. You meet with the principal and she supports the idea, but it will be a substantial purchase. She asks you to get at least three bids for national suppliers and three price quotations from local businesses, and present them to her along with your recommendations.

Upon investigation you find that the treadmill that would meet the needs of the students will run about $3,000. For equal-quality models, the local suppliers quote $2,800, $2,900, and $3,000 each. The first supplier reports a 90-day warranty and will commit to a $200 donation to the booster club; the second one reports a six-month warranty and suggests that he will sponsor a dinner for the football team; and the third reports a one-year warranty. All other related matters as to service and reputability are equal. The bids from out-of-town national suppliers come in at $2,600 with a 90-day warranty; $2,700 with a six-month warranty; and $2,800 with a one-year warranty.

1. Analyze the local offers.
2. Analyze the national bids.
3. List your first and second choices for the principal, and give your justification for each.

---

10. Designers should avoid creating areas for natural "hangouts" that will result in litter, grafitti, and other problems.

11. Sufficient trash receptacles should be supplied, anchored to posts.

12. Signs should be embossed or enclosed in concrete or other sturdy material and located above reach.

College Complexes Increase Control for Security

Most large institutions have initiated some type of automated-entrance security system that easily controls who has access to facilities. These may include identification cards utilizing bar codes and scanners, magnetic stripes, integrated microchips, radio relays, and laser beams. Leading the technology in this area seems to be the ski industry, which is not only controlling access with these devices, but is building a marketer's dream of data, with the capability of immediately identifying "hot" cards ("Ticketing and Access Control," 1993).

Equipment Cages

Many schools and colleges have found that employing an equipment manager and operating a checkout system through an equipment cage assists the inventory system, improves security, and reduces maintenance costs. Frequently the savings in these areas will more than offset the salary required.

Exercises

1. For equipment orders, many times you will be given a total amount you can spend and you buy what you can afford. What is the matter with this?
2. List, in order, the best things about the bid method of purchasing. List, in order, the problems associated with bid purchasing.

3. Two common reasons were given to explain why coaches may request a special brand and model of an item of equipment and not accept any substitute. Try to think of any other reason you might accept if you were the administrator.

4. Several examples of specification statements were outlined in this chapter. Select a piece of equipment with which you are familiar and write a specification.

5. Assume you are to start a new soccer team for a junior high school (grades 7–9) and, without knowing who will try out for the team the following fall, you must place an order for the uniforms by May 1, the previous spring. Write an order for 25 soccer uniforms, in part listing sizes, numerals, colors, trim, raw product, fabric, style, and design.

6. When it comes to purchasing inflated balls, what three factors in the winding of the bladder affect the ultimate quality of the ball? Rank the three in order of importance and explain why.

7. Assume that you are the administrator who has the responsibility of maintaining a field used heavily in the fall for field hockey, soccer, and classes in physical education, but used only a few hours a day for classes in the late spring and the remainder of the year. Outline a one-year maintenance schedule for that field.

8. Inspect the main gymnasium of the school you are now attending and write the following two reports: a maintenance list of items needing attention in *order of priority;* and a security evaluation with recommendations for improvement.

References

Adrian, M. (1989a, January). Weighty decisions. *College Athletic Management* 1, pp. 21–22.

Alvord, M. (1993, February). Burbank's wilderness-style restroom is vandalism resistant. *Park/Grounds Management* 8, pp. 4–5.

Brickman, H. (1997, November). Helping hardwood perform. *Athletic Business* 21, pp. 67–72.

Bucher, C, and Krotee, M. (2002). *Management of physical education and sport* (12th ed.) New York: The McGraw-Hill Company.

Catalano, J. (1996, February/March). Following the fashions. *Athletic Management* 8, pp. 38–44.

Christiansen, M. (2002, April). Playground maintenance. *Parks and Recreation* 37, pp. 84–91.

Cioletti, J. (1997, July). Your front line. *Club Industry* 13, pp. 39–45.

Cohen, A. (1993, March). Security check. *Athletic Business* 17, pp. 41–44.

Cohen, A. (1997, August). Keeping track of everything. *Athletic Business* 21, pp. 43–48.

Connor, D. (1997, July). Selectorized strength-training equipment. *Club Industry* 13, p. 50.

Cummings, S. (1997, September). Changing times. *Cleaning and Maintenance Management* 34, p. 64.

D'lorio, K. (1997, November). The rest(room) of the story. *Cleaning and Maintenance Management* 34, pp. 46–50.

Frost, J.; Sutterby, J.; Therrell, J.; Brown, P.; and Thornton, C. (2002, April). Does height matter? *Parks and Recreation* 37, pp. 74–83.

Hendy, T. (2002, June). Playgrounds for the mind, body and spirit. *Parks and Recreation* 37, pp. 64–71.

Horine, L., and Turner, E. (1979, December). Appalachian State's locker room renovations provides open atmosphere. *Athletic Purchasing and Facilities* 3, pp. 20–23.

Malkusak, T.; Schappet, J.; and Bruya, L. (2002, April). Turning accessible playgrounds into fully integrated playgrounds. *Park and Recreation* 37, pp. 66–69.

Martin, J. (1997, September/October). Preparing your club for the indoor season. *Tennis Industry* 25, pp. 30–31.

Mendel, B. (1994, February/March). The team uniform industry. *Athletic Management* 6, pp. 36–39.

Miller, L. K.; Stoldt, G. C.; and Ayers, T. D. (2002, January). Search me. *Athletic Business* 26, pp. 18–21.

Mintz, J. (1997, December). To buy or not to buy? *Cleaning and Maintenance Management* 34, pp. 50–52.

Pantera, M. J. (2002, January). 25 keys to world-class maintenance. *Parks and Recreation* 37, pp. 49–59.

Parkhouse, B., ed. (2001). The management of sport (3rd ed.). New York: The McGraw-Hill Company.

Patton, J. D. (1997, August). Mission: Control. *Athletic Business* 21, pp. 63–68.

Pellerin, T. J. (1997, November). Higher education saves a cleaning staff. *Cleaning and Maintenance Management* 34, pp. 40–43.

Perry, P. M. (2002, April). Security first. *Athletic Business* 26, pp. 40–44.

Peterson, J. A. (2002, April). Eliminate playgrounds? You must be nuts. *Parks and Recreation* 37, pp. 92–95.

Plass, T. (1996, June/July). New NOCSAE standards. *Athletic Management* 8, p. 37.

Sawyer, T., ed. (1999). *Facilities planning for physical activity and sport.* Dubuque, Iowa: Kendall/Hunt Publishing Company.

Security by design. (1993, January). *American School Board Journal* 180, pp. 37–39.

Strauf, D. L. (1989, January). Anatomy of an efficient equipment purchasing system. *Athletic Business* 13, pp. 48–54.

Strauf, D. L. (1996, June/July). Helmet check. *Athletic Management* 8, pp. 36–41.

Surfaces and covers. (2000, Aug./Sept.). *Athletic Management* XII, pp. 58–63.

Ticketing and access control. (1993, May). *Ski Area Management* 16, pp. 78–81.

8

Law and Physical Education and Sport

──────── Management Thought ────────

If a man has common sense, he has all the sense there is.

Sam Rayburn

──────── Case Study: Player Negligence ────────

The legal case *Bourque v. Duplechin* (1976) is often cited for findings in sport negligence, player-on-player liability, and even rule changes in high school baseball and softball. The other key cases that common law follows in this country include *Nabozny v. Barnhill* (1975) and *Hackbart v. Cincinnati Bengals, Inc.* (1977).

Bourque, the plaintiff, filed a suit to recover damages for injuries he received while playing second base in an adult softball game. Duplechin was on the opposing team and inflicted the injury onto Bourque. The trial found in favor of Bourque, but Duplechin appealed the verdict.

Bourque was playing second base. Duplechin hit the ball and advanced to first base. The next batter hit a grounder and Duplechin sped to second. The ball was fielded by the shortstop, who flipped it to Bourque, who stepped on second base and continued into the infield away from the base. Duplechin veered away from the baseline and collided with Bourque

five feet away from the bag. As he hit Bourque, he raised his arm and caught him under the chin. Duplechin was removed from the contest by the umpire. At the time of the incident, Bourque was 22 and five feet seven inches tall. An expert witness testified that softball is a noncontact sport and the accepted way to break up a double play is to slide into second base.

Duplechin admitted that he ran into Bourque at full speed while standing up, but stated that the cause of the accident was Bourque's failure to get out of the way (Bourque had assumed the risk of being hit if standing in the basepath, but not of being run into five feet away from the base). The trial court's conclusion was that Bourque did not assume the risk of Duplechin's negligent act.

Bourque had a broken jaw, lost seven teeth, and required plastic surgery. He was awarded $12,000 for pain and suffering and $1,496 for special damages. The Louisiana Court of Appeals upheld the trial court findings (Yasser, McCurdy, and Goplerud, 2000).

The reader should be able to

1. Explain the origins of law in the United States and how it applies to the specific fields of physical education and sport.
2. Demonstrate the ability to apply legal concepts and legal terms frequently associated with sport and physical education.
3. Describe the basis for lawsuits against teachers, coaches, and administrators and the possible defenses.
4. Identify the association between law and physical education and sport as it applies to product liability, facilities, equipment, supervision, and discipline.
5. Explain the relationships between law and specific areas of interest in sport, such as amateur standing, rules and regulations, associations, contracts, violence, personnel, the media, drug testing, sexual harassment, and Title IX.

A graduate student who had taught for two years said, "I still get a cold sweat when I think of the things I did in my first year—that I didn't get sued was just plain luck!"

Many readers are thinking to themselves at this point, "What's the problem? Teachers and coaches can't be sued." Not so! Every teacher, coach, sport leader, and administrator can be sued. The fact is, they are more vulnerable than most other occupations or classroom teachers. There is a dangerous view in today's society that for every injury or poor outcome, someone must be responsible and pay. Because of this, at times it has been difficult for physical education teachers, coaches, and sport leaders to obtain reasonable liability insurance.

In addition, there has been concern that court decisions dictate rules and policies affecting physical education teachers, coaches, recreation leaders, and associations. These decisions sometimes are not in the best interest of the athletes or students and frequently put an undue financial burden on the organization.

■ DEFINITIONS

Attractive nuisance. Maintenance of a condition likely to attract children at play to a dangerous situation.

Governmental immunity. Common-law principle that it is not in the public interest for governmental agencies to be sued except where waived or permitted by law.

In loco parentis. In place of the parent.

Liability. The condition of being responsible either for damages resulting from an injurious act or for discharging an obligation or debt.

Libel. Written defamation (not necessarily published).

Litigation. Lawsuit. Court action.

Malfeasance. Commission of an illegal act.

Misfeasance. Improper or unlawful performance of a lawful act.

Negligence. Lack of ordinary care in one's actions; failure to exercise due care.

Nonfeasance. Failure to perform a duty that was legally required.

Plaintiff. Initiator of a legal action.

Proximate cause. The reason, under law, for the injury.

Respondeat superior. Common-law principle that the employer is responsible for the employee.

Save harmless. Law or guarantee giving "respondeat superior" protection to public employees accused of civil wrong associated with their official duty.

Tort. Civil wrongs (as opposed to criminal), not arising from a breach of contract (Clements, 1988).

■ LEGAL TRENDS IN PHYSICAL EDUCATION AND SPORT

The area of law and sport has changed and expanded more than any other subarea studied in sport management. There are now sport law centers or institutes within law schools, while just a few decades ago only a few physical education teachers or ADs published materials in sport law. Today new sophisticated textbooks on the subject are printed every year.

Because sport reflects society in general, the litigious nature of society has also been reflected in sport. People injured in sport and physical activity often believe that the sport organizers can and should guarantee their complete safety. This is not the case—accidents and injuries can and do occur in sport. However, this fact does not stop injured participants from filing litigation. "Litigation in physical education and sport has increased in recent years and was, until sexual harassment complaints, clearly the number one area for litigation in schools" (Bucher and Krotee, 2002).

Why Are There More Lawsuits in Physical Education and Sport?

The popularity of sport has never been as high as it is today. Organized sport for youth exists from the soccer fields to climbing camps; leagues for men and women of all ages proliferate in recreational, school, and club settings. As a result, some participants get injured and subsequently file suit.

Coupled with the preceding items, more cases are going to court because of sweeping changes in the interpretation of product liability as it relates to sport equipment. Another recent factor is the availability of free legal assistance or prepaid legal service. Also, lawyers taking cases on a contingency-fee basis make it more attractive for persons to gamble and sue. The tremendous amount of money awarded in some cases attracts others. In addition, there has been an increase in the awareness of individual rights, which translates into more cases. And the eagerness of insurance companies to settle cases out of court has made it more attractive to sue.

Negligence

What Constitutes Negligence?

Negligence is either doing or failing to do what a reasonable and prudent person would have done under the same circumstances. It is the failure to exercise reasonable and ordinary care.

In general, you must ensure the safety of students, including providing safe facilities and equipment; teach and enforce appropriate rules; teach appropriate and necessary skills; provide proper supervision in a reasonable and prudent manner; and be aware that even if the participant is careless and contributes to the accident, you may be liable. Note that these factors apply equally to school, recreation, or commercial sport activities.

Determining Negligence.

Three factors will be considered to determine *whether* negligence has occurred: extent and nature of the risk involved; social value and utility of interest advanced; and alternative course of action availability. "The following four elements must be *proved* by the plaintiff in order for an action to be considered negligent: (1) duty of care owed, (2) breach of duty, (3) actual or proximate causation, (4) damages" (Cotton and Wilde, 1997, pp. 26–32). All of these elements must be proved for the sport manager or teacher to be negligent.

The first element (duty) is concerned with whether there was a duty to act, or not to act in an unreasonable manner. For example, in *Edison v. Uniondale Free School District*, 1995, the court held that the school did not violate the duty it owed to a student wrestler by allowing him to wrestle an opponent in a greater weight classification. The key facts in the decision were these: (1) The student voluntarily participated. (2) He knew ahead of time that he would wrestle a larger opponent. (3) The blow to the jaw that caused the injury was not related to the weight difference. (4) Wrestling beyond a medical time-out for evaluation had no effect on the damaging injury ("School Liability," 1996).

The second element (breach of duty) can be proved by direct evidence, violation of a statute, or *res ipsa loquitur* (allowing the plaintiff to recover on the basis of what probably happened on the basis of circumstantial evidence). For example, in the first instance, the coach plays a participant when the trainer has ruled that she should not play. An example of the second type would be a teacher using an activity not included in the approved curriculum. Breach of duty is typically measured by the notion of *standard of care.* Standard of care measures the actions (instruction and supervision), facilities, and equipment provided against the generally accepted practice of other sport professionals. In many situations, professional organizations such as the American College of Sports Medicine (ACSM), National Strength and Conditioning Association (NSCA), and American Council on Exercise (ACE) provide guidelines for professional conduct or protocol for specific activities. ACSM has also published guidelines for sport and fitness facilities. Another source to which your professional conduct could be compared is work published by experts in the field. If specific references cannot be located, lawyers often call in "expert witnesses" to review your conduct and testify how it did or did not meet the standard of care.

Cotton and Wilde defined contributory negligence as "conduct on the part of the plaintiff, contributing as a legal cause to the harm suffered, which falls below the standard to which plaintiff is required to conform for his [her] own protection" (Cotton and Wilde, 1997, p. 45). In the few states that allow contributory negligence, a plaintiff who plays a role in his or her own injury is barred from recovery.

The third element (actual and proximate cause) requires it to be determined that the plaintiff's harm or injury was legally caused by the defendant's negligent act.

> If the same harm would have resulted if the negligent act had never occurred, then the act is not the actual cause of the harm. This is sometimes referred to as the "but for" test; the particular harm in question would not have been suffered "but for" the negligent act of the defendant (Wong, 1994).

For example, a maintenance person uses unslaked lime in marking a recreation field, and a participant is blinded from the substance burning the eyes. The use of the unsafe material was the proximate cause of the damage.

Last, the plaintiff must prove that actual damage has occurred as a direct result of the defendant's negligence. The plaintiff may seek recovery for past, present, and future pain and suffering, medical expenses, loss of earnings, and loss of consortium (spouse's companionship). For example, a woman injured her knee skiing. She had arthroscopic surgery, missed several days of work, and claimed she could no longer enjoy skiing.

Defenses against Negligence.   The best two defenses are to either plan your programs so that injuries do not occur, or show that one or more of the four elements were not present. In addition, there are the following defenses: contributory negligence, comparative negligence, assumption of risk, act of God, and immunity.

Contributory Negligence.   Consider the following situation: You are the playground supervisor and leave the playground unsupervised. The students decide to walk on the top of a fence. After about 10 minutes, one student slips and breaks an arm. A six- or seven-year-old would not be considered contributorily negligent. If the student were 12 years of age, however, you might be held negligent, but you could try to show that at that age the student contributed to the accident and you should not be held solely responsible. You would show that the child should have appreciated the danger. If the student were older, it would be easier to show contributory negligence. In athletics, contributory negligence frequently results from the injured person exposing himself or herself to danger intentionally or unreasonably.

According to Cotton and Wilde, "comparative negligence is not a true defense against liability for negligence. More appropriately it is a method for apportioning blame or the relative degree of responsibility for the injury" (1997, p. 47). As an example, a basketball coach sent two of his players out for a training run on public roads at 6:30 A.M. The team had agreed to do the runs on Friday mornings to free up afternoon practice time. The route was heavily trafficked and without sidewalks. Some team members had asked for the coaches to set an alternative route, but the coaches refused. One morning two of the players, while running on the incorrect side of the road, were struck by a truck. One player died and the other was seriously injured. In its findings, the court ruled that the driver of the truck was 46.6 percent responsible, the college was 24.8 percent responsible, and the players were 28.6 percent responsible (*Howell v. Kansas Newman College*, 1 P. 3d. 310).

Comparative Negligence. The majority of states have passed legislation to allow for the use of comparative negligence. Comparative negligence is a doctrine which assesses the amount of negligence on either side and then apportions the damages based on the amount of negligence by the two parties.

Assumption of Risk. Assumption of risk results from the voluntary assumption, expressed or implied, of a known and appreciated risk. A participant or a spectator who assumes the risk created by the conduct of another cannot recover when harm occurs. Assumption of risk was (and still is in most of the world) a standard defense in the United States until recent years. For example, in skiing, until about two decades ago, it was held that anyone who would put long boards on their feet and fly down an icy mountain certainly assumed that sooner or later a crash would result in injury, with no one to blame but themselves. Not now!

On the other hand, while the facility owner is not an insurer of safety, patrons do not assume the risk of unsafe or hidden hazards. Participants do not assume risks from actions outside the rules of the game, or by third parties. Spectators do not assume the risk of unreasonable actions such as a baseball player intentionally hurling a ball at a person in the stands.

An examination of one case (*The Regents of the University of California v. Roettgen*, 41 Cal. App. 4th 1040) may help to clarify the principle. A student in a rock climbing class was killed after a fall; his widow filed suit, claiming that the course in-

structor and the university were negligent and responsible for his death. The suit alleged that Norman Roettgen's fall was due to the negligent actions of his instructor in placing all four anchors into a single crack system. The court stated that "as a general rule, persons have a duty to use reasonable care to avoid injury to others and may be held liable if their careless conduct injures" (p. 1,045) However, the court noted that the scope of the duty owed also depends on the defendant's role in the injury. The court found that Roettgen was an experienced climber, knowledgeable of the inherent risks of climbing, and was not taken beyond his abilities—and that the inherent risks of rock climbing cannot be eliminated without destroying the very nature of the sport. Therefore, the assumption of risk doctrine protecting the college from liability was applicable.

An Act of God. Quite obviously, this defense rests on the notion that something beyond the control of anyone has occurred. An example would be if a sudden gust of wind forced an activity bus off the road. Some believe that this constitutes the "bolt of lightning" defense. However, you need to be aware that this defense can be used only for unpredictable and uncontrollable acts of nature. Thus if a coach were to keep a team out on the practice field when a thunderstorm was approaching, this defense would certainly not be valid.

Immunity, Statute of Limitations, and Good Samaritan Statutes. Governmental immunity comes to us today through our legal system based on "common law" from England. The roots of immunity evolve from the days when the king was the government. Because the king could do no wrong, suing the government was not permitted. In states still following this doctrine, the school cannot be sued because it is considered to be part of government. The trend, however, is for states to abrogate or modify their immunity because it is believed that one should not have to bear the cost of treatment and suffering of injuries caused by negligence, even though that agency may have been traditionally protected by governmental immunity.

If the plaintiff has not filed a complaint within the state's prescribed time, this will bar recovery. Note, however, that there are different time limitations for various torts, so the plaintiff may bring suit on another tort with a different limitation. In some cases, the claim must be made in writing within six months.

Good Samaritan laws protect those offering first aid to injured people. The laws among the states differ widely. They do not hold if treatment is reckless or wantonly harmful. Some states, such as North Carolina, cover only the highways; and, strangely, New York covers only dentists. In Massachusetts, registered members of the National Ski Patrol are provided specific protection (Wong, 1994).

Two examples from the same activity, shot-put injuries, resulted in opposite immunity rulings. In *Hedges v. Swan Lake and Salmon Prairie School District,* 1992, a student was asked by a teacher to mark where shot puts she was throwing landed. The student was struck by one, was injured, and sued the teacher and the district. The trial court granted the defendant's motion for summary judgment on the basis of immunity. On appeal, however, the Montana Supreme Court ruled that the defendant's negligence did not arise from the lawful discharge of official duties associated with legislative acts as provided in the immunity statute, and therefore reversed the trial court's decision and remanded the case for trial.

In *Rankey v. Arlington Board of Education,* 1992, the plaintiff was attending her son's track meet at the school of the defendant. On the way to the stands she was struck in the face by a shot put thrown by a student who was practicing. She sued the district, superintendent, AD, and track coach, contending that warnings should have been present. On the other hand, the defendants sought immunity, which was granted by the trial court. This finding was affirmed by the court of appeals.

Save Harmless. Review the definition at the beginning of the chapter. In most states, *whether the school district enjoys immunity or not, the teacher or coach is liable for his or her own torts* and should be prepared to pay for judgments. Some states, how-

Safe playground equipment is vital. Note sturdy heavy-duty construction, smooth surfaces, and sand under the equipment. The U.S. Consumer Products Safety Council publishes guidelines for playground safety. *Courtesy of the Hardin Park Elementary School, Boone, North Carolina.*

ever, have given school districts permission to "save teachers" from this expense and pay the teachers' "harmless" judgments.

There will seldom be a clear case as to whether the teacher or coach is "saved harmless," owing to the myriad possible conditions. This may depend on the status of the law of the particular state, including the following factors: Are districts allowed to purchase liability insurance? Was the tort associated with a specific area covered by the insurance? Was the injury associated with a "proprietary" (business-oriented) function? (This sometimes includes athletics.) And, regardless of the particular state law, was "reckless" negligence involved? Employees should determine exactly what their "master–servant" relationship is.

Product Liability

Product liability imposes liability on the manufacturer, wholesaler, retailer, and supplier for defective products placed on the market that cause injury. This liability theory is based on the concept that the manufacturer, or seller, is in a better position than the consumer to become aware of and eliminate the defect and to absorb whatever loss occurs (Clements, 1988, p. 77).

Manufacturers must use *reasonable* care in manufacturing and designing equipment so that if it is used in the intended manner, it will be safe. If equipment will be dangerous even if properly used, it is the duty of the manufacturer to warn of this danger. Manufacturers are typically not required to make completely safe products. In court similar products are often used to help determine what a "reasonably" safe product is.

Cotton and Wilde (1997) noted that the three most important elements to be examined in product liability were improper design, improper construction, and failure to warn. In one particular case, *Arnold v. Riddell,* a court awarded a $12 million verdict to a football player when the court held that the manufacturer had a duty to warn players about the dangers of the PAC-3 helmet. At trial Riddell was found to be 63 percent at fault for Arnold's injuries (*Arnold v. Riddell,* 882 F. Supp. 979).

Facilities and Equipment

As funding athletics has become more difficult, many institutions have turned to renting or leasing their facilities to special groups. The legality of such a practice has been questioned. In Arizona and New Jersey, the use of facilities by religious groups was challenged. In both cases it was held that this was merely a business transaction and was allowed. In Wisconsin, the courts stated that a high school gymnasium could be rented to religious or political groups, but the activities must be nonpartisan and nondenominational. Frequently commercial groups have rented, leased, or shared in the gate receipts for use of athletic facilities. Is it legal for private schools to rent or lease public athletic facilities? In Montgomery, Alabama, this question was tested in court because four all-white private schools were utilizing a municipal stadium. The court found in this case that the municipal stadium could not be used, but this did not apply to private school students individually utilizing city recreational facilities.

One particular situation shows that sport managers should be aware that freedom of speech issues can arise. In 1997 a University of Mississippi fan was instructed to put away a large Confederate flag (the University of Mississippi nickname is the Rebels) and refused. The stadium managers noted their policy prohibiting banners or flags more than 12 feet by 14 feet. While the fan believed that he was being denied his freedom of expression guaranteed under the First Amendment of the Constitution, the stadium managers noted that they had developed the rule for the safety of fans and that the fan could have displayed his team logo in other ways (*Barrett v. University of Mississippi,* 531 U.S. 1052).

Prayer in conjunction with athletic contests has also been reviewed in the courts. The landmark case, *Santa Fe Independent School District v. Jane Doe* (530 U.S. 290), found that such activities, even if voluntary, are unconstitutional.

To avoid legal problems arising through the use of sport facilities, it is recommended that institutions

- Establish written standard operating policies.
- Develop a written emergency care or crisis reaction plan that is included in any contract with outside users and is frequently reviewed with in-house users.
- Ensure that strict supervision is present for all uses.
- Refer all unusual requests to legal counsel for advice.
- Ensure that all supervisors of events are familiar with the general use and emergency care procedures and policies.
- Require appropriate insurance.

Although suits are often filed as a result of injuries related to play and sport facilities, it is surprising there are not more. If you were to inspect the nearest playground or athletic stadium, you could probably spot several potentially dangerous conditions. Think of some of the facilities you have used recently. It is impossible to make facilities "fail safe," but it is the duty of the professional teacher, coach, and administrator to foresee these potential hazards and eliminate them before injury results.

Attractive Nuisance. Another specific legal concept frequently encountered in unattended play or sport facilities is the "attractive nuisance." The courts generally hold that the typical youngster will be attracted to any type of play area and will not be mature enough to see that the area may be dangerous. If a playground has a large slide or tall jungle gym that may be used safely only when a supervisor is present, there must be fencing around the area to restrain children from using it when it is unsupervised. The greater the danger, the more secure the fencing must be.

In cases related to facilities, the courts have shown that an important factor is whether the school officials, including coaches and teachers, knew a hazard existed over time and did nothing to correct it (actual notice). In these cases, the district consistently has been found to be negligent. Even if it cannot be shown that school officials knew of the hazard, the fact that the dangerous condition existed for an extended period will tend to cause the district to be considered negligent (constructive notice).

Facilities and Legal Problems. Tennis courts must be well designed and well maintained. In a case related to tennis court construction, a player ran into a side fence that was up against a stone wall so it would not "give" when hit. In another case, a professional player tore cartilage in her leg when her body went forward but her foot stuck in a "dead space." A youngster at a camp fell and injured her leg when she slipped into a depression. Although the poor condition of the courts was obvious, the suits were filed nevertheless.

Swimming pools provide immense opportunities for lawsuits. In one swimming pool, a lifeguard was electrocuted when he touched the metal ladder to climb out of the water because the underwater lights were turned on and an electrical short occurred. A student was crushed to death when she attempted to retrieve her clothes from the top of a heavy wooden dressing bench; it was not fixed to the wall and toppled over on her. A lifeguard was electrocuted when he stood in the pool office with wet feet and switched on the public address system to make an announcement.

Lifeguards can best avoid lawsuits in these ways:

1. Ensure that there are written emergency procedures, and rehearse them.

2. Be qualified, hold a current certificate, and understand responsibilities.

3. Ensure that adequate numbers of lifeguards are present.

4. Ensure that the facility is properly designed and maintained.

5. Keep accurate records.

6. Maintain a well-understood communication system.

7. Develop and post rules for use and safety.

The most common areas for lifeguard litigation are injuries from sharp objects, failure to perform prompt rescue, inadequate supervision, inadequate rescue equipment, inadequate qualifications or training of lifeguards, and poor maintenance of facility (Osinski, 1988).

It is possible to find a great variety of injuries and suits due to design or maintenance problems in gymnasiums. A large number of suits involve slippery floors, glass or other hazards near the edge of the court, or courts too close to each other. A basketball player was completing drills, which required running to the endline. He crashed through a glass door, was injured, and sued. It was determined that the school had waived its immunity when it purchased liability insurance. But the court found the school not negligent because of the contributory negligence of the student. Because he had played in the gymnasium for three years, the court ruled that he did not take reasonable care to avoid injury.

Basketball courts too close together can result in dangerous situations. In New York an injury occurred when 48 students were playing on eight basketball playing areas in a space 43 feet by 80 feet.

A variety of injuries occur at outdoor facilities. A player tripped over the curbing along the edge of a cement softball area in New York City and was injured. The court upheld the city, citing the assumption of risk by the player. At a similar cement field, a player tripped over broken glass and was injured. In another case, the coach made the mistake of placing pole vaulting standards on top of two boxes; the plaintiff vaulted and landed on one. There are frequent cases due to bleachers with broken boards, jagged ends, unsteady bases, and lack of proper side or rear safety railings.

Administrators need to regularly inspect outside playing areas. A high school football player was injured during a game played on synthetic turf in a stadium owned by the Chicago Board of Education. The athlete claimed he was required to play on a surface that was improperly constructed, installed, and maintained. The Illinois School Code protects coaches from liability; however, the plaintiff claimed that the coaches should not be included because athletics are not a regular educational program. To illustrate the lack of agreement of the courts on these matters, the lower courts agreed with the coaches, but a higher court reversed this stand and held for the plaintiff. The coaches appealed to an even higher court and won. That court ruled that under Illinois law, the coaches were immune from liability for negligence due to defective equipment.

Equipment and Legal Problems.   According to Wolohan (2002a) "one of the most fundamental obligations an athletic administrator owes his or her athletes is to provide them with the proper equipment for each activity" (p. 24) When equipment is improperly used or poorly maintained, injuries and lawsuits often result. Inherent in cases related to defective equipment is the theory of "failure to warn," which requires manufacturers to warn of possible defects in equipment or hazards in its use. The degree of duty to warn is determined by the age and experience of the user (Cotton and Wilde, 1997).

Whether a warning is necessary for a product does require some judgment. If the hazard is obvious, there is no duty to warn. Thus, if there is a four-foot-tall snow-making machine in plain view along the edge of a ski slope, there is no need for a warning. If, however, it was on the slope and in a dip and was not visible from a distance, a warning would be necessary. There must be warning when there is no reason to expect a dangerous condition.

In *Dunne v. Wal-Mart*, 1996, the Louisiana appellate court reversed the lower court regarding a warning. It held that Wal-Mart (or the manufacturer) failed to warn that an exercise bicycle sold was not designed for persons weighing over 250 pounds, and found Wal-Mart liable for injuries. A person weighing over 400 pounds was hurt when such a bicycle collapsed (Abbott and Wong, 1997).

Coaches are usually in a key position to ensure that proper and safe equipment is purchased, fit, and maintained. A hockey coach was found negligent for ordering dangerously defective helmets (*Everett v. Bucky Warren*, 1978).

> This does not mean that the coach must personally purchase the necessary equipment when the school or parent refuses to do so. But the coach's responsibility goes much further than merely requesting particular equipment. If the proper equipment is not provided, it may be necessary for the coach to forbid a particular student's participation, or perhaps cancel a game. (Schubert, Smith, and Trentadue, 1986, p. 223).

Liability may exist when defective equipment is provided or when suitable equipment is not even supplied. An Oregon high school football player was injured and claimed it was caused by defective equipment. The boy had selected his own equipment from stock available. His helmet subsequently developed a crack, so he selected another helmet despite the fact that it was a little loose. The court found the school not negligent because the player did not complain about the equipment, and by selecting a second helmet, he showed he knew he could have returned to select other equipment. What do you think would have been the court's verdict if the player had reported that the helmet was loose, or if he had been issued the helmet without an opportunity to change?

In another football helmet case, Richard Austria (*Austria v. Bike*, 810 P.2d. 1312) alleged that the helmet he was wearing at the time of his injury was defectively designed. The court ruled in Richard's favor, noting that the helmet in question was not safe for its intended purpose.

In *Neal v. Fayette County Board of Education*, 1996, a fifth-grader partially amputated a finger in attempting to dunk a basketball during a physical education class. Neal sued on the basis that two students had previously been injured on the basketball hoop, claiming it was defective and dangerous and that the class was not properly supervised. The court held for the school, reporting that the two previous injuries did not prove that the goal was defective, and that two teachers were present and warned students not to dunk. The court further reported that the schools are not the insurer of safety ("Student Injured," 1996).

In another case, a shop rented a pair of in-line skates to a novice and allowed him to go outside and put the skates on without instruction (Brink, 2002). Although the court found the user mostly responsible for his injuries by not waiting for an instructor, the rental shop was also held to be at fault.

Supervision

From a legal point of view, the quantity and quality of supervision of all aspects of the program will be of the highest priority. Even a poorly funded program, with proper supervision, can be made safe, although it may not be up to the desired academic level. On the other hand, well-funded programs might depend even more on proper supervision for safety. In well-financed programs, there is frequently more sophisticated equipment, such as weight-training machines and gymnastic equipment, and a more diversified curriculum, including adventurous activities, such as swimming, gymnastics, or outdoorsmanship.

When clear standards and guidelines have been adopted by national organizations, failure to meet them will put the agency or organization in a dangerous position. The first edition of ACSM's *Health/Fitness Facilities Standards and Guidelines* was published in 1997. Among other things, it states that exercise clubs must provide a tour of the club and instruction on how to use all equipment. Further, the standards require that fitness areas must have continual supervision and provide a "relatively safe and motivating environment." In *Reeder v. Bally's Total Fitness Corporation,* 1997, a woman was hurt when she used a stomach curl machine. When she joined

she attended two orientation sessions, but that machine apparently was not included. Fortunately for the club, the plaintiff produced no expert witnesses, nor any credible evidence of the lack of supervision, so the judge ruled in favor of Bally's (Herbert, 1997).

In *Vonungern v. Morris Central School,* 1997, a six-year-old student fell from a monkey bar and fractured her elbow during recess. She sued, claiming another student pried her fingers off the bar causing the fall, and that the surface under the bars was not safe. Although two teachers were assigned to recess duty, they spent most of the time planting a garden by the playground. They saw no horseplay. The court ruled that the school did not have the duty to ensure the safety of the students, but it did have the duty to adequately supervise the students. The school was held liable because the injury was foreseeable and the teachers did not adequately supervise the children. There were also questions as to the safety of the surface ("Student Falls from Monkey Bars on School Playground," 1997).

Guidelines for Supervision. The administrator must determine the quantity and the quality of supervision required for each activity and situation. It might be adequate for a paraprofessional to supervise 25 youngsters on a playground without any complex equipment, but not on a playground with moving and climbing equipment, or if their activity includes something like soccer.

As the risk of the activity increases, the level of supervision must also rise. Obviously, activities requiring higher levels of skill, or that include contact, require more and higher levels of supervision. In addition, if the activity is required, or if a grade is based on competitive performance, supervision must be increased. The amount of supervision is also predicated upon individual differences and characteristics of the youngsters in the group. It must be assured that proper skill instruction in progression is achieved. The supervision must include quality controls on the skills and techniques used by teachers and coaches. Are they using proper warm-up, conditioning, progression, and teaching or coaching methods?

Inadequate or Incompetent Supervision. A class or athletic team should have the supervision of a certified person at all times. Students should never be left unsupervised without a serious reason. One should become a defensive thinker when such an occasion arises: "Would a jury think it was a reasonably prudent act to leave the class?" In most cases brought to court involving a teacher or coach being absent from the activity, the students have been instructed to sit and do nothing or to continue doing something considered safe, such as shooting baskets. As professionals educated in child development and the psychology of education, however, teachers should know that groups of students will likely not continue to play in a safe manner, or sit and do nothing when the teacher or coach leaves. In fact, it would be surprising if they did.

Two situations, settled out of court, but in which one of the authors served as expert witness, illustrate the major issues. In one case, three wrestling coaches were supervising a junior high school wrestling practice. A total of 12 boys were wrestling; in one of the matches, an illegal hold was used, which ultimately resulted in a dislocated elbow on one of the boys. The question that arose at discovery was "Who was supervising *these* two boys?" While it could be argued that there were enough supervisors, no supervisor was assigned this area or match to watch. In another case, a high school volleyball coach asked her players to set up the nets for practice. While the players were moving the standards into position for attaching the nets, the base of the volleyball standard came loose and cut off two toes on one of the players setting up the equipment. The coach was not in the gym at the time and had not instructed the players to be cautious about the base of the standards.

Additional cases involving improper supervision include these: (1) A high school football player was seriously injured while participating in a summer weight program. The plaintiff successfully sued the school's athletic director and principal (*Vargo v. Svitchan*, 1980). (2) A junior high school student was successful in a suit against the school for failing to properly super-

vise a "powder puff" football game (*Lynch v. Board of Education of Collingswell Community School District*, 1979). (3) Teachers were held liable (but not the school board) in the death of a student with mental retardation en route to participate in a Special Olympics basketball practice. It was held that insufficient numbers of teachers were present to properly supervise the athletes with mental retardation (*Foster v. Houston General Insurance Co.*, 1981; Wong, 1994). (4) A plaintiff has sued owners of a fitness club for, among things, failure to adequately supervise the use of free weights. The plaintiff alleged that he suffered a partial amputation of a finger after being struck by a free weight (Herbert, 1993). Students are referred to Chapter 2 for additional material on supervision.

Assault and Battery

There has been a staggering rise in on and off the court injuries to athletes and fans from cases of assault and battery. From an NBA player strangling his coach at practice to an Olympic figure skater arranging for an attack on a competitor, the problem of assault and battery is ever-present. At every level of sport, reports of fans attacking officials, coaches, or other fans can be read in too many newspapers. In 2002 a parent was convicted and sentenced to 6–10 years in prison for killing his son's hockey coach in a fistfight after a practice (Wolohan, 2002a). Sport managers must act responsibly to prevent or reduce these occurrences.

Although *assault* and *battery* are often used as synonyms, they are not. *Assault* indicates the threat of harm, while *battery* includes direct cause of harm. According to Cotton and Wilde (1997, p. 151), three elements must be proven to establish assault: (1) the defendant intended to cause harm, (2) the plaintiff felt reasonable apprehension of immediate harm, and (3) there was lack of consent from the plaintiff.

As a sport manager you will probably not often be directly involved in assaults and battery; however, you must be prepared to deal with them and may be held liable if you have not adequately prepared. In the landmark case *Bearman v. Notre*

Dame (453 N.E.2d 1196), the facility managers were held liable when a spectator was injured in a parking lot fight between tailgaters. Cotton and Wilde noted "Facility managers need to know that they may be found negligent if such incidents do occur and if the incidents were foreseeable" (p. 153).

Corporal Punishment

Although all teachers must be quite knowledgeable about corporal punishment, it would appear that the dynamic, emotional, and physical aspects of physical education and sport require a special awareness of the legal parameters of corporal punishment.

There remains, however, an inconclusive final stand on what specifically constitutes deprivation of "due process." An increasing number of states have banned corporal punishment. The most damage to a teacher's legal position occurs if the student is permanently injured as a result of corporal punishment. If the student is disabled or disfigured, the punishment could *not* have been moderate or reasonable.

Physical education teachers and coaches must keep in mind that corporal punishment includes many physical acts—not just "paddling." *Never touch a student or player when you are angry.* If the touching results in an injury, the courts will consider whether there was anger present. Individualize punishment—don't treat all students the same. The courts will give special consideration to whether the student has any disability. It goes without saying that anytime there is abusive punishment resulting in battery, the teacher or coach has a serious problem.

■ SPORT AND THE LAW

The basis upon which disputes in amateur athletics are judged is derived from *public* or *private* law. In the past, most have been seen as private law disputes between, for example, an athlete and an association over some rule or regulation. The trend, however, has been for more cases to be decided according to public law, which is based on constitutional provisions that supersede private law. In private law, disputes are viewed as a disagreement over binding rules or regulations. Because the courts are not as likely to question the rule or regulations, the plaintiff usually does not fare well. The trend, therefore, is for more cases to be judged on a constitutional basis, and for the regulatory bodies (associations, conferences) to be subjected to more supervision by the courts and legislative bodies.

In the past, it was assumed that participating in extracurricular activities was a privilege, not a right. In recent years, this tradition has been tested in the courts with mixed results. The Tenth Circuit Court of Appeals stated that regular school attendance could not be denied without due process safeguards, but this did not apply to each component of education, such as the athletic program.

The landmark case of *Ross v. Creighton University* centers on whether Ross was provided the education that he alleges he was promised while he played basketball. The district court held for the university on the basis of the difficulty in determining causation and the duty owed, the nature of education being collaborative, and the possibility of a deluge of education malpractice suits. On appeal, in 1992, the court upheld the district in rejecting Ross's claim of educational malpractice and negligent admission, but reversed the district court in finding that he could return to the lower court to have the contract violation claim be heard. This ruling opened the door for athletes to challenge universities as to whether specific promises made in the recruitment process were honored (Yasser, McCurdy, an Goplerud, 2000).

How Is Amateur Athlete Defined?

Each amateur organization has developed its own definition of "amateur athlete." In the past, many organizations allowed the athletes to receive no money. Most now allow the athlete to earn living expenses, and many allow full participation of professional and amateur athletes in any competition.

The NCAA has not been as quick to change as many other sport bodies. While considerable debate continues over the rights of collegiate athletes to earn money, the NCAA and the courts are hesitant to change. One case involved a University of Colorado athlete, Jeremy Bloom, a member of the 2002 U.S. Olympic freestyle ski team and the CU football team. Although the U.S. Skiing Association would allow Bloom to earn money from equipment suppliers and other sponsors through endorsements, the NCAA (and the Colorado courts) would not allow Bloom to receive these payments without jeopardizing his NCAA eligibility (Sanchez, 2002).

Institutions of higher education received a jolt on the workers' compensation issue with scholarship athletes. A former athlete at Texas Christian University who was seriously injured 17 years earlier was allowed to file a workers' compensation claim in 1991 because the statute of limitations in Texas does not start until an employer initiates an injury report, and, of course, TCU had never done so. The Texas Workers' Compensation Commission ruled in behalf of Kent Waldrep, awarding him $500,000 for past and future medical bills and a weekly salary, retroactive to 1974 for $115 per week for the rest of his life, which was based on the value of his scholarship at that time. If this challenge stands, it could have widespread implications, not the least of which are income tax payments on grant and aids and whether scholarships meet minimum-wage requirements (Wolohan and Wong, 1993).

An interesting legal problem in eligibility of high school athletes is on what basis "home school" students are allowed to participate. In states such as Oregon, New Mexico, and Pennsylvania, home schoolers who meet various basic criteria must be allowed to compete. The old premise that one had to attend a school to represent it vanishes. Because the majority of home schools are based on religious fundamentals, some assume that parents of some gifted athletes will go through religious conversions to be able to circumvent various eligibility controls. It is assumed that there will be tests on this issue from parents as well as schools and activity associations (Cohen, 1993).

Legal Requirements to Properly Educate

Closely related to discipline and supervision is the duty to properly instruct. This relates to the skills and techniques, methodology (planning, lessons, rules and regulations, facilities and equipment), conditioning, and, if appropriate, the duty to warn. Adams (1993) reports that correct and proper instruction in techniques must be taught; incorrect techniques must be corrected; progressive skill development and conditioning must occur; proper techniques must be demonstrated; the risk of the activity should be matched by the level of skill and training of the instructor; detailed lesson plans should be written and filed; and all staff should be required to keep abreast of new developments. All of these elements apply to athletics, health–fitness programs, and physical education.

Rules and Regulations in Athletics

Several cases have supported the thesis that athletic participation is an integral part of students' education and is entitled to the same protection as other educational experiences. In addition, the fact that participation has economic implications for college scholarships and professional pursuits is also important. This right to participate brings up serious questions about due process and procedural problems for the coach and administrator to consider. It may become necessary to provide due process and procedures to be followed when an athlete is dropped from a squad. The coach in athletics is understood to have broad authority over players, including the power to establish conduct and training rules along with penalties for infractions. Coaches do not have the right, however, to regulate aspects that do not directly relate to athletic performance.

Rules relating to important skills and techniques, as well as the rules of the sport, must be *established, communicated,* and *understood* by participants. The coach must be able to prove that all three elements occurred. If rules are not both communicated and understood, it is as if they didn't exist. Having players (of reasonable age) sign rules under a statement that they have read and understood them is helpful. Being able to call on *any* team member to verify that the skills, techniques, and rules were clearly explained, not once, but many times, is essential. For example, a high school baseball player crashed into a catcher, causing serious injuries to the catcher. Depositions showed that the players of the team at bat had never been instructed that this was not allowed by rules. The week after the accident, they were so instructed for the first time. Needless to say, the insurance company for the defendants settled out of court. "Not only must rules be taught, they must be discussed and examined. Rules must be taught, retaught, and practiced" (Gaskin, 1993, p. 27).

Can a coach set dress or personal grooming standards? Unless the standard would directly affect performance on the playing field, such rules would probably not hold up in court. In *Long v. Zapp,* a coach set a rule about hair length in and out of season. A player who grew long hair after the season was denied a letter award, and he sued. The court upheld the player, stating that his First Amendment rights had been violated.

Case law appears to support the thesis that college athletes have some degree of "property right" to participate, and thus are probably entitled to greater "due process" than high school athletes. It has been held, however, that a college athlete does not have constitutional rights protection when demoted from the first team to the second team, or to participate in a postseason or televised game.

In *Bonner v. Lincoln Parish School Board,* 1996, two unopened bottles of beer were found under the jacket of a basketball team member on an extracurricular field trip. After various hearings, including one by the basketball coach, the student was suspended from school and the basketball team. The court found the student did not have a constitutional right to be on the basketball team ("Student Is Suspended and Thrown off the Basketball Team for Having Alcohol on a School Trip," 1997).

Contracts

Can a coach refuse a coaching assignment? Can a teacher refuse an extracurricular assignment? Several cases have supported the school district's authority to require a teacher to coach if it is a reasonable assignment. One case was contested on the basis that there was no extra pay for extra duty. The court ruled that this made no difference. In Utah, the supreme court upheld the school district when it dismissed a teacher and coach who had resigned from his athletic position but wanted to continue to teach. Generally, the courts have upheld school districts in cases in which teachers have contested extracurricular assignments, such as taking tickets at athletic contests, when the assignments were within statutory limits and were reasonable in amount and nature. In *McGrath v. Burhard* in California, a teacher filed suit for having to supervise six contests a year, which he claimed was nonprofessional. The court upheld the school district even though reference to such duties was not specifically included in the contract.

In the past, college coaches were frequently fired before the completion of existing contracts. This situation has changed following the expulsion of Pepper Rodgers from Georgia State, after which he sued for damages he lost due to salary and outside contracts with the media and other outside sources (*Rodgers v. Georgia State Athletic Association,* 1983). He gained a substantial settlement. The courts have held that before a teacher–coach can be discharged for questionable personal indiscretions, it must be clear that the conduct had a direct adverse effect on the performance of duties. Coaches have been removed from positions of both teaching and coaching when convicted of larceny.

The concept that makes nonteaching coaches and sport administrators vulnerable to termination is called *employment at will.* This concept allows either party to terminate the contract without showing cause—for any reason, or no reason at all. In *Tramontozzi v. St. Francis College,* 1996, the plaintiff sued for being terminated over a dispute with his supervisor, claiming that his contract was for an indefinite period. The lower court held for the defendant, which was upheld in the state court. The legal exception that might apply (each state is different) to protection from such termination is violation of public policy, an implied contract, and an implied covenant of good faith and fair dealing. To avoid such termination, employees should insist on a contract for a period of time, or stipulate a clause that requires the employer to show cause for termination (Wong and Duncan, 1997).

In another contract dispute, Katalin Deli, a gymnastics coach at the University of Minnesota, was dismissed when a sexually explicit video tape of her was distributed among the players. One clause in her contract stated duties under the contract included "positively representing" the university and the university's athletic programs in private and public forums. Based on the contractual language, the court upheld her dismissal (*Deli v. University of Minnesota*, 511 N.W.2d 46).

As schools have had difficulty filling all coaching positions, many have turned to either one contract for both or two interrelated contracts. In 1990 the South Dakota Supreme Court ruled that teachers must accept these dual-duty contracts ("School Board Requires Teachers to Accept Extracurricular Duties," 1992).

A high school soccer coach was quoted in the local newspapers as stating that the team had lost a game because the players "gave less than their best effort." He described the players as "cowards." He was suspended from coaching, but not from his teaching position. He sued, claiming that his constitutional right of free speech had been violated. The court held for the school, stating that the First Amendment protected public employees' right to speak only on matters of public concern. The degrading comments did not fall under public concern. Such issues under public concern would help citizens "to make informed decisions about their government, to disclose misconduct or generate public debate on some issue of significant public interest" ("School Gives Soccer Coach the Boot after Calls Team Cowards," 1997).

A high school football coach's contract was not renewed in *Marschall School District v. Hill* (1997), and the coach sued the district for not following the state's Teacher Fair Dismissal Act. He claimed the district failed to notify him of the problems that could have led to nonrenewal and provided no efforts to help him correct the deficiencies. The court held for the coach and awarded him retroactive earnings and earnings from the several years after the nonrenewal

("Fired Football Coach Says Court's Award Falls Short of the Goal Line," 1997).

Due Process

The Fifth and Fourteenth Amendments to the U.S. Constitution guarantee due process.

> Two minimum requirements of due process are the right to a hearing and notice of the hearing time, date, and content. Although an individual may enjoy the guarantee of due process, the actual process is rarely spelled out. The type of due process protections guaranteed in a given situation are determined by a consideration of the importance of the right involved, the degree of the infringement, and the potential harm of the violation. As a general rule, the more an individual has at stake, the more extensive and formal are the due process requirements. (Wong, 1994, p. 58)

Two cases illustrate the application of due process in sport. In *Conard and Fudzie v. University of Washington* (814 p. 2d, 1242) two football players argued that their scholarships had been revoked without due process. In another case, the court found that the New Jersey State Interscholastic Athletic Association had not provided due process in waiting two years to rule on an appeal of a high school quarterback's eligibility. As you can see, following the proper protocol in due process is critical for sport managers (Booth, 2002).

Athletic Associations

Do high school activity associations, conferences, or national organizations, such as the NCAA, fall within the classification of "state action"—thus covered by the Equal Protection Clause of the Fourteenth Amendment, which provides that "no state shall make or enforce any law which shall . . . deny to any person . . . the equal protection of the laws"? This issue is far from settled.

In 1988 the U.S. Supreme Court ruled in *NCAA v. Tarkanian* that the NCAA did not assume the role of the state when it directed a state institution to take action against one of its employees (488 U.S. 179). Also in 1988, the federal court found, in the case of *Anderson v. Indiana High School Activity Association*, that the IHAA was not engaged in state

Title IX requires that institutions provide equal athletic opportunities for both sexes.

action. But in the case of *IHAA v. Schaffer*, a junior withdrew from school at the end of the basketball season because of a sinus infection and was subsequently not allowed to play. The Indiana Court of Appeals ruled in 1992 that the IHAA *was* a state actor "because the association's existence depends on the support of the public school systems, and rules enforcement has a substantial impact on the rights of the students" (Wong and Craig, 1993). The court ruled that the rules of the IHAA were overly broad, arbitrary, and capricious, and that Schaffer had been denied an opportunity to participate through no fault of his own. The Indiana Supreme Court subsequently refused to hear the case, so the ruling stands.

The case law on the issue of "state action" is mixed. In 2001 the Supreme Court ruled in *Brentwood Academy v. Tennessee Secondary School Athletic Association* (530 U.S. 1, 295) that TSSAA was involved in state action primarily on the grounds that there was an intertwining of objectives and that TSSAA board members met during state working hours, thus expending state funds for their operation.

A special consideration in "association law"

is that frequently courts follow this body of law even when the case involves a dispute between an athlete and the association. The fact that the athlete is almost never a member of the association does not seem to be taken into account.

Can an association adopt "good conduct rules" for athletes? One athletic association adopted a rule that called for the loss of eligibility for any player who possessed, consumed, or transported alcoholic beverages or dangerous drugs. The rule included any athlete in a car stopped by authorities that contained these substances. During the "off season," an athlete was in a car that was stopped and that contained beer. Charges against the athlete were dismissed, but he was still declared ineligible, so he sued. The court upheld the athlete, stating that the rule was unreasonable and overinclusive. Similar rules for conduct related to assaultive conduct and improper grooming have also been successfully challenged.

Frequently an individual school or an athlete will challenge an association's right to restrict them from participating in some event. To withstand challenges, such sanctioning must be to support the overall good and development of athletes; to prevent exploitation; and to equalize competition. Generally the courts will interven only if the association violates the constitutional rights of an athlete, if the association violates its own rules, or to ensure fairness.

Another legal problem area in high school athletics is eligibility and residence. In the past, the majority of the contested cases of transfer of residence have resulted in the association's rules being upheld. However, with more open enrollment and home school scenarios, the court findings are mixed.

The control of eligibility based on test scores or grades has been another interesting area of sport law. If the rules are reasonable, they are usually upheld. When the rules apply academic achievement from a previous level (high school) to a new situation (college), however, the results from the courts have been inconsistent.

The courts have endorsed the use of academic standards to determine eligibility for athletics. In addition, the courts have supported rules that limit age and the length of time athletes can compete. In general, the courts have supported rules that limit eligibility for interscholastic competition to eight consecutive semesters, or four years, from the date of entrance into ninth grade.

Since the mid-1980s the NCAA has attempted to regulate the eligibility of entering freshmen through required high school coursework. While the overall impact of the legislation on minorities has been questioned, again, the court findings on this issue have been mixed. Early cases supported the requirements, yet more recent rulings have required the NCAA to refrain from enforcement.

Is it legal for an association to create rules that punish a home team if spectators are not controlled? To be within the association's authority, such rules would be required to be directly related to regulating disturbances or turmoil at athletic events. The rules should affect only those spectators whose conduct needs to be controlled. In the case of *Kelly v. Metropolitan County Board of Education* in Nashville, the court *did not* support the school board. At the end of a postseason basketball game, the losing team fans left the facility improperly and abused fans and officials physically and verbally. The board suspended the losing school from all interscholastic competition for one year. The court's decision was based on the fact that no rules specified the kind of spectator conduct that schools were required to enforce.

In light of the increasing sophistication of amateur athletic competition, along with the proliferation of cases contested in the courts, schools, conferences, and associations need to carefully analyze the legal grounds upon which they *enforce rules and regulations.* The primary element of due process is to allow the affected athlete a fair hearing. In a case in which the coach is suspending a player for one game for being late to practice, the due process might be to notify the player verbally that unless he or she has an excusable reason for being late, the suspension will follow. In a serious case, however, due process will require that written notice be given of a formal hearing so that the student has time to prepare a defense and to be represented by counsel.

Americans with Disabilities Act (ADA) and Sport

The Rehabilitation Act, enacted in 1973, is entitled Section 504. It protects the handicapped from being excluded, solely by reason of their handicap, from participation in any program or activity receiving federal financial assistance. The Americans with Disabilities Act (ADA) was subsequently enacted in 1990 to put teeth in Section 504; it extends the coverage to all but the "smallest employers, professional athletic teams, and probably college teams. . . . The Act prohibits employment discrimination against individuals with real or perceived disabilities; it also prohibits discrimination in employment against associates of the disabled" (Champion, 1993, p. 232). An example could be the refusal of a school to hire an otherwise fully qualified coach who was the spouse of an AIDS victim, or removing a physical education teacher because of his or her HIV status (Kelly, 1994).

Effective in 1992 for small businesses, and in 1993 for large businesses, Title III was added to the ADA. This "prohibits discrimination on the basis of disability by public accommodations and requires places of public accommodation and commercial facilities to be designed, constructed, and altered in compliance with the accessibility standards established by this part" ("Nondiscrimination on the Basis of Disability," 1994, p. 468). (Students are referred to Chapter 10 on facility planning for further details.) The ADA prohibits discrimination against the disabled in employment, public services such as public transportation and government facilities, public accommodations (buildings) and services provided by private entities, and telecommunications (Farmer, Mulrooney, and Ammon, 1996).

With the ADA now in effect for some years, there has been an increase in the number of cases involving students with disabilities who have been held back a grade or two during their school years and then face age limitations for participation in interscholastic athletics. In a review of such cases, Sikorski and Gibbons (1998) report that the jury is still out on this issue. In general, either the courts have found the cases moot—the students have already graduated or left school by the time the suit was heard—or the courts have found that age, not disability, was the key factor and held in favor of the association rules.

In *Beatty v. Pennsylvania Interscholastic Athletic Association*, 1996, a student, a member of the volleyball and basketball teams, turned 19 before his senior year, resulting in ineligibility. His participation was included on his Individualized Educational Plan. The court found in favor of the association, reporting that he was excluded because of age, not disability. In reporting this decision, the court noted that an "intolerable burden" would be placed on the school authorities if they were required to undergo the case-by-case analysis necessary to decide if a waiver for a particular athlete was in order ("Federal Court Upholds Age Eligibility Rule," 1997).

In *Rhodes v. Ohio High School Athletic Association*, 1996, the court rejected an ADA section 504 claim on the basis that the student was not excluded solely because of his disability. Further, it ruled that the association was not a public accommodation under Title III, and rejected the ADA claim as well, saying that there was no causal connection between the disability and the enforcement rule ("Sports Eligibility Rule Could Be Applied," 1996).

In *M.Ha. v Montana High School Association*, 1996, the court rejected the disabled student's suit to continue to participate based on the fact that such participation was not written into his IEP ("Student with Disability," 1997).

An interesting question is whether youth leagues fall under "place of public accommodation" in ADA Title III. If they do, then youths with disabilities can demand special adjustments to play in these leagues. In *Schultz v. Hemet Youth Pony League*, 1996, an 11-year-old with cerebral palsy asked to play baseball with a younger age group, which the league rejected. The court found that the youth did qualify under ADA Title III because "a place of public accommodation" was not restricted to physical structures, and that the league excluded the child without investigating whether plausible modifications could have been made to enable him to participate. The court motion was granted. In a similar case, a child who needed a walker was allowed to compete in a youth soccer program if his walker was padded.

In *Elitt v. USA Hockey*, 1996, the parents of a child who had been diagnosed with attention deficit disorder requested that the child be allowed to "play down" in a younger group. The court determined that it lacked jurisdiction because the club and organization were not places of public accommodation within the meaning of Title III. The child also would present a safety concern if he were allowed to play with younger children. His participation would fundamentally alter the program at issue and would result in an undue burden. The complaint was dismissed ("Court Split on Athletes with Disabilities and Age Rules," 1996).

Probably the most famous case in sport and ADA was *PGA Tour V. Martin* (532 U.S. 661). Casey Martin, a qualified golfer, had a disability that hamperd his ability to walk the golf course. The PGA claimed that its rules required all golfers to walk the course and that if Martin was allowed to use a golf cart, he would have an advantage over the other players. The Supreme Court ruled that the PGA had to allow Martin to use a cart as a "reasonable accomodation."

Public Law 94-142, enacted in 1975, is the Education for All Handicapped Children law. The law assures that all children with disabilities (from ages 3 to 21) receive free appropriate public education that emphasizes special education and related services designed to meet their unique needs (Kennedy, French, and Henderson, 1989).

As students with disabilities are more fully integrated into regular physical education classes, many will want to participate in intramural or interscholastic competition. This integration has occurred quietly in the past, and many students with disabilities have participated. But more and more cases will find their way to the courts. A New York Circuit Court upheld a school board's policy of excluding partially sighted students from contact sports. The appeals court reversed this ruling, however, stating that protective eyewear minimized the risk of injury.

Several challenges to NCAA requirements have been filed by student athletes with disabilities. The cases have ranged from athletes who did not meet the minimum entry standards because of a diagnosed learning disability to requests for reductions in the number of credits taken to ensure reasonable progress toward their degree. The findings of the courts have supported the ADA by requiring the NCAA to make reasonable accommodations for the athlete's disability.

Legal Aspects of Violence in Sport

Coaches are putting themselves in liable positions when they teach players to win at any cost. High school athletes, particularly, will take cues from coaches as to the right or wrong of playing violently. Coaches must take a firm and positive stand against violent behavior from their players.

There is ample evidence of coaches encouraging or at least allowing players to engage in excessive violence. Peer pressure adds to the use of intimidation and violent actions. Coaches at all levels must reduce these tactics or the courts will do it for them.

Based on reports of violence against sport officials, a new law took effect in 1997 in North Carolina that protects all officials, from Little League to professionals. Anyone convicted of assaulting a sport official could face up to two years in prison for the misdemeanor.

Both players and coaches may be liable when violence occurs in sport. When players have exhibited violence and uncontrolled anger and the coach takes no punitive action, that coach is not following reasonable, prudent, or professional action. If a coach directs a player to take violent action (for example, "slide into second with your spikes high and wipe out the second baseman"), the player could plead that he was simply acting as an agent of the coach and following directions.

Player-versus-Player Lawsuits

Two key cases that dealt with player-versus-player suits were *Nabozny v. Barnhill* (1975) and *Janovich v. California Sports* (1979). These cases exemplified the concept that players do not assume the risk of *reckless or wanton* attacks falling outside the rules of the game. In the former, Nabozny, a soccer goalie, was kicked in the head; in the second case, Janovich, a professional basketball player, was punched in the face, ending his career. The plaintiff was awarded over $3 million in the initial hearing (Van Der Smissen, 1990).

Two more recent cases also involved player-versus-player lawsuits. In a coed recreational soccer game, a female player sued a male participant for injuries resulting from a rules violation, in *Jaworski v. Kiernan*, 1997. Jaworski was shielding the ball waiting for the goalie to take it from her when she was fouled by being hit from behind by the male, Kiernan, resulting in a torn anterior cruciate ligament. Jaworkski claimed that the foul was reckless and wanton. The court held that the action of Kiernan was foreseeable, but it was not reckless or wanton. In addition, it stated that if every foul in sport were found to be negligence, sport participation would be severely compromised.

In *Dilger v. Mayles*, 1997, the plaintiff was struck in the mouth by a golf ball hit by the defendant. The fairways were divided by a row of trees that Mayles claimed blocked his view of the other fairway, while Dilger stated that Mayles did not warn of the errant shot by calling out "fore." The court held that errant hits are an inherent risk in golf, and that failing to call out "fore" did not raise the action to reckless or wanton status (Gibbons and Wong, 1997). This concept was reinforced in *Schick v. Ferolito* (327 N. J. Super. 530), where the court held that the standard of negligence in golf would be recklessness, not ordinary negligence. Thus a plaintiff would have to show that another golfer engaged in reckless or intentional conduct (Peach, 2001).

Match and Mismatch

Cotton and Wilde (1997) reviewed for negligence cases related to pairing of participants without regard for characteristics such as age, skill, size, or experience. Common sense dictates that if a mismatch resulted in injury the courts would hold for the plaintiff, but reports indicate otherwise. They identified 13 cases that involved mismatches, 9 of which resulted in the favor of the defendant. It appeared that most of these cases were poorly prepared, or the mismatch was very weak. For example, one case involved a 15-year-old being tackled by four boys from 10 to 12 years of age.

Lehr (1993) studied matching cases and stated, "When no negligence was found, the courts concluded that the teacher used an appropriate standard of care and adequate matching procedures. Students were paired by either mental comparison of weight or body structure and ability" (p. 25). In those cases in which the courts held for the plaintiffs, however, it was "concluded that the students were improperly paired and did not comprehend the nature of the risk" (Lehr, 1993, p. 25).

In *La Mountain v. South Colonie Central School District*, in 1991 on appeal, the court held for two school districts in a soccer case. A junior varsity player was injured during competition. She had undergone a physical examination, she had four years' prior experience, and her mother had signed a participation form. She was injured while planting her left leg to kick the ball with her right leg. She claimed she was run over by three opposing players; however, coaches from both teams contradicted her. In holding for the districts, the court stated that the schools were required to exercise reasonable care to protect students who voluntarily compete only from unassumed, concealed, or unreasonable risks.

Defamation

According to Cotton and Wilde (1997) *defamation* is that which tends to injure the reputation, esteem, or good name of another. There appears to be a trend toward more cases involving defamation; usually the coach is suing the administration or the media. The purpose for defamation law is to clear a good name and record, to obtain compensation, and to warn others. If a principal reports to a newspaper writer, "The coach has not properly prepared the players and he's too friendly with some," the principal is treading on dangerous ground. Defamation consists of two types. That which is written is called *libel*. That which is spoken is called *slander*. Defamation is an intentional tort, as opposed to negligence, which, of course, is unintentional. Statements that may be actionable are false, defamatory (public embarrassment or ridicule), and "published" (which legally simply means that it was spoken or written to a third party), and result in financial damage. However, if the statement related to moral turpitude, unchastity, loathsome disease, or professional misconduct, it is considered so damaging, per se, that financial damage proof is not necessary. Also note that public figures (well-known coaches and players) are harder to defame, because another required element states that the defamer must have demonstrated malice or at least reckless disregard for the truth (Cotton and Wilde, 1997).

Because of the frequency of nuisance suits, a recent trend has emerged called "let the plaintiff be aware." Some states, mostly in the West, have adopted this concept. When frivolous suits are filed, the plaintiff will be charged with the legal fees of the defendant.

Drug Testing

The legal challenges to drug testing of athletes have been consistent since its inception. Several challenges have been successful, but they have been specific to the particular case and circumstances, and thus cannot be extrapolated to have general implications. Sport administrators should have drug-testing programs reviewed by legal counsel before implementation to ensure that they do not violate the Fourth Amendment of unreasonable search and seizure, interfere with privacy, or violate the Fourteenth Amendment of due process.

Two cases with opposite conclusions are illustrative. The courts upheld the Oregon public school system in the *Acton v. Vernonia School District*. Substantial drug-related problems, along with many unsuccessful attempts at dealing with them, prompted the drug testing of all athletes at the start of the season. In addition, 10 percent of the team members were tested randomly each week in a system that respected privacy, but carefully controlled the sampling, maintenance, coding, and testing of urine. Second tests were given if results were positive. If the second test was positive, the school officials met with the parents and student privately to explain that the student could either enter a counseling program or be suspended for that season and the next. An important factor is that results are not reported to law enforcement officials (Sendor, 1993).

The system used at the University of Colorado failed a court challenge and an appeal (*Derdeyn v. University of Colorado*). The system, which was first instituted in 1984, was changed from time to time, but consent by athletes was always required. The action was brought on the basis of a violation of rights to be free of unreasonable searches and to privacy, due process of law, and equal protection of the law. The trial court ruled that the consents were invalid because they had been "coerced." The appellate court stated that the consents had been "compelled," since because of economic or other commitments to the university, the students had no choice but to sign. The appellate court indicated that the university could run a testing program based on "reasonable suspicion," rather than the higher standard of "probable cause" (Ross, 1993b).

The principles put forward in the *Vernonia* case were expanded in 2002 with the court's decision in *Board of Education v. Pottawatomie* (122 S. Ct. 2559). In this case, the drug testing was expanded from scholastic athletics to all extracurricular activities. The Supreme Court ruled that even "suspicionless" drug testing was within the school's purview and furthered educational objectives (Sharp, 2002).

Based on the prevailing litigation, three guidelines have emerged with which sport managers should review their drug testing procedures. The first guideline relates to the expectation of privacy. In the *Acton* case, the courts found that student athletes had a reduced expectation of privacy based, in part, on the nature of locker rooms and other athletic environments. The second guideline correlates to the nature of the intrusion. In the cited cases, the intrusion protocol differed. In *Hill v. NCAA*, although the California court upheld the NCAA's right to test, the court noted that having an observer witness the urination was very intrusive.

After the 2000 Olympic Games in Sydney, the USOC worked to establish an independent drug testing agency for Olympic athletes. The United States Anti-Doping Agency began operations in October 2000. As stated in its mission, the USADA "is dedicated to eliminating the practice of doping in sport, including U.S. Olympic and Pan American athletes" (www.usantidoping.org). In professional sport, drug testing protocols vary considerably. While some cases have been filed, the courts have generally upheld the league drug testing procedures because the athletes, through their player unions, have agreed to the testing parameters.

Spectators

The sport administrator must be concerned about the many ways spectators are injured. These cases involve persons being hit by balls and bats in softball or baseball, or falling from bleachers, or being injured during fights or by thrown objects. What is the responsibility of the coach or athletic director for injuries to spectators? Generally, if it can be shown that reasonable precautions have been taken to ensure the safety of spectators, the plaintiffs have not been upheld. An illustrative case involved a young girl who was seriously injured by a ball while she was watching a baseball game. She was sitting on a fence, 35 feet behind first base. The state supreme court finally heard the case and upheld the school. What do you think might have been the result if the girl had been sitting directly behind home plate with no backstop fencing? In California, a student was hit by a bottle thrown during an athletic event. The court ruled in favor of the school, stating that the school officials could not have foreseen this act and should not be held responsible for the misconduct of others. What would have been the outcome if the plaintiff could show that there was no effort to restrict fans from entering the stadium with bottles, even though there had been evidence at previous games of bottles being thrown or broken?

Many suits have involved injuries resulting from inadequate protective screening in ballparks. There is little agreement about the proper height or width for backstops or screening down the sidelines. Common sense is the best guide for administrators. For example, assume there will be overthrows at first and third bases; avoid placing seats in these trajectories unless there is protective fencing. The following cases illustrate these concerns. (1) A plaintiff attending a Chicago Cubs game was hit in the head by a wild pitch from the bullpen. Because it was impossible to watch the bullpen and the game at once, his case was supported against the Cubs, but not against the pitcher who threw the ball. (2) A woman who sat behind first base was struck by a foul ball and sued the Philadelphia Baseball Club. The court did not support her, stating that she had assumed the risk of sitting where she did.

Football sidelines and bleachers present special areas of potential lawsuits for the administrator. La Rue (2002) noted that almost 20,000 bleacher-related injuries occur each year. After two children were killed, the U.S. Consumer Product Safety Council introduced guidelines for bleacher safety (www.cpsc.gov).

Three cases illustrate the possible suits. (1) A student was injured in Alabama when the bleachers collapsed at a football game. She sued, and the state supreme court ruled that although the school board was immune from torts, it could be held liable for injury to ticket holders if conditions were not safe. (2) A grandmother of a high school player watched a game scrimmage from the sidelines and was severely injured when hit by players. Both the trial court and the court of appeals dismissed the case on the grounds of contributory negligence. (3) Another grandmother in Louisiana was watching a junior high school game from the sidelines and was seriously injured when she was hit by players. The trial court found on behalf of the school district, but the court of appeals reversed this decision because the woman was not asked to leave the sidelines. The state supreme court reviewed the case, however, and reverted back to the trial court decision, stating that it would be too expensive to install fences at junior high school fields to restrain crowds.

GENDER ISSUES IN SPORT

Gender Equity

In recent years documentation shows substantial increases in participation in sport by women, while there have been decreases in the number of female coaches, officials, and administrators.

Data indicate that the number of women participating in high school sports since the passage of Title IX has grown from 300,000 to 2.8 million (1 in 27 to 1 in 2.5). At the college level, participation has increased from 33,000 to 163,000 since 1972 (Berger, 2002; Gutner, 2002; Casey, Ballard, and Deitsch, 2002). However, relatively few major universities meet the equity requirements spelled out in the legislation. Each NCAA institution must file a report detailing the funding, opportunities, and benefits available to its student athletes in conformance with the Equity in Athletics Act. From these data, it was determined that in 2002, only 18 of more than 300 Division I NCAA institutions met the requirements (Solomon, 2002).

Title IX.   Much of the recent litigation by female teachers, coaches, and participants has been based on Title IX of the Education Amendments of 1972, which states that "No person . . . shall, *on the basis of sex,* be excluded from participation in, be denied the benefits of, or be subjected to discrimination under any education program or activity receiving federal financial assistance" (Yasser, McCurdy, and Goplerud, 2000, p. 154).

The case of *Grove City College v. Bell* restricted Title IX to be program specific. That is, the specific program (such as men's athletics) must have received federal funds to be held to Title IX standards. In 1988 Congress reversed that decision by passing the Civil Rights Restoration Act over President Reagan's veto.

In 1997 the U.S. Supreme Court let stand the lower court's ruling on the long-running *Cohen v. Brown University,* which began in 1992 when "Cohen and other members of the Brown University women's gymnastics and volleyball teams, which had just lost their funding, filed a class-action suit against the school alleging gender discrimination. Each level of the courts has ruled in favor of the athletes. The Supreme Court ruling ended any speculation about the intent of the law. It is now clear that the court's current interpretation of Title IX, with its three prongs of compliance with gender equity, is here to stay" ("Gender Equity Debate Heats Up," 1997).

Title IX applies to physical education by requiring coeducational classes—except that ability grouping without regard to sex may be used so long as it does not adversely affect one sex. Also, students may be separated by sex in contact sports or for religious beliefs of students.

In addition, this thoughtful question has been raised: "Have the equal participation and coeducational physical education classes been a benefit to girls?" The answer has been, in general, "yes" to athletic participation, but "perhaps" to coeducational physical education. Lirgg (1992, p. 9), for example, reported that her study revealed that "boys thrive in coed classes while girls perceive the same-sex environment more favorably."

In *Haffer v. Temple University,* originally filed in 1981 and reviewed after the Civil Rights Restoration Act and in 1988, the parties reached an agreement following the court's ruling in favor of a reconsideration of the plaintiff's claims. While the agreement affects no other school, note that Temple's athletic program agreed to include proportional scholarships, increased athletic opportunities, and increased budgets for females. The cost for men's football and basketball programs were included in the total athletic budget considerations (Wong, 1994).

Opening another front, the finding of the U.S. Supreme Court in 1992 in *Franklin v. Gwinnett Public Schools* declared that a former student could sue for *monetary* damages in a sexual harassment case. The important issue from this case is that monetary damages can be accommodated by Title IX (Cotton and Wilde, 1997).

To alleviate worries about litigation, develop a compliance report. The following tips should be kept in mind when putting together a report: As an administrator, do not wait for issues to surface, but be proactive. Compliance plans must be very specific and place the school in a position of being accountable. Sport-specific booster groups might unintentionally create compliance problems, but Title IX requires that athletic departments control booster contributions. This is so that all sport programs receive equal benefits. Survey the students and find out their athletic interests. Pep rallies and printed sport programs should be designed as promotional material for girls' and boys' programs. If school budgets are reduced and your athletic department finds itself in a position of retrenchment, be careful not to discriminate between the genders. Remember that Title IX looks at the total program and takes into consideration the unique nature of particular sports. It is possible to be in compliance even though some apparent discrepancies exist (Paling, 1996).

"The Department of Education's Office of Civil Rights, which is charged with enforcing Title IX, estimates that only 2 percent of complaints involve athletics" (Solomon, 2002, p. A1). The operational definition for determining gender equity used by the U.S. Office of Civil Rights includes the following:

1. Whether intercollegiate-level participation opportunities for male and female students are provided in numbers substantially proportionate to their respective enrollments.

2. Where the members of one sex have been and are underrepresented among intercollegiate athletes, whether the institution can show a history of this.

3. Where the members of one sex are underrepresented among intercollegiate athletes, and the institution cannot show a continuing practice of program expansion, whether it can be demonstrated that the interests and abilities of the members of that sex have been fully and effectively accommodated by the present program (Yasser, McCurdy, and Goplerud, 2000; Cotton and Wilde, 1997; Berger, 2002).

The three prongs covered above also pertain to benefits provided to men's and women's athletics in the following areas (Berger, 2002):

1. Equipment and supplies.
2. Scheduling of games and practice times.
3. Travel and per diem allowances.
4. Tutoring.
5. Coaching.
6. Locker room, practice, and game facilities.
7. Medical and training facilities and services.
8. Housing and dining facilities.

9. Publicity.
10. Support services.
11. Recruitment.

The three principal areas where equity is examined are participation opportunities, scholarships, and these other benefits noted above.

Will the increased funding for women's sports result in something like the men's current programs? This question has arisen as some issues like recruiting and bonuses to coaches have occurred. For example, several coaches of a successful women's basketball team have been granted a large bonus for winning and have salaries higher than the coaches of the men's teams.

Many arguments have surfaced over the last 30 years that Title IX has caused a reduction in men's sports. In the last 20 years, 170 college wrestling programs have been eliminated. It should be noted that "Title IX does not tell universities how to spend their sports budgets, it just says that both sexes must have equal access to the resources" (Casey, Ballard, and Deitsch, 2002, p. 21.) Gutner (2002, p. 144) notes that "while it is true that some less popular men's collegiate sport programs have been cut, such as Bowling Green State University's track team, it's certainly not the fault of Title IX. Each school chooses how to allocate its sport resources." Data indicate that despite claims of reductions in men's programs, the number of collegiate opportunities for men has increased over the past 20 years (Slezak, 2002).

The courts tend to support this thinking. In 2002 a suit by the National Wrestling Coaches Association (later joined by College Gymnastics Association and the U.S. Track Coaches Association) argued that Title IX discriminated against male student athletes. Their case, however, was dismissed by the Justice Department (Curtis, 2002). In related litigation, the 8th Circuit Court of Appeals upheld the University of North Dakota's actions dropping men's wrestling in order to meet Title IX requirements ("Proportionality Okayed for Title IX Compliance," 2002). A New York court dismissed a suit by males against their institution for dropping their sport as a part of compliance

with Title IX (Applin, 1997). Generally speaking, using Title IX in reverse discrimination cases has not had much success.

On the lower levels, gender equity issues center more on unfair practices at specific schools, such as the lack of qualified coaches, equal sports as men, or scheduling (Frankel, 1992). In a settlement of a complaint filed by a high school girls' field hockey coach, it was agreed to provide a band, cheerleaders, and concession stands at girls' activities and ensure that coaches of boys' and girls' teams received equal salaries ("Settlement Has Been Reached in a Title IX Complaint," 1996).

Sexual Harassment

Sexual harassment is defined as unwelcome sexual advances, request for sexual favors, and other verbal, nonverbal, or physical conduct of a sexual nature when (1) submission to such conduct is made either explicitly or implicitly a term or condition of an individual's employment or academic decisions; (2) submission to or rejection of such conduct may be reasonably construed by the recipient of such conduct as an implication that compliance or noncompliance will be used as a basis for an individual's employment or academic decisions; (3) such conduct has the purpose or effect of unreasonably interfering with an individual's work performance or creating an intimidating, hostile, or offensive working environment; or such conduct has the purpose or effect of emphasizing the sexuality or sexual identity of a student or an employee so as to impair the full enjoyment or educational or vocational benefits, climate, or opportunities (Colorado Civil Rights Commission, 2002).

Sexual harassment policy is difficult to write. Tension exists between free expression and those being harassed. For example, one faction of the ACLU is said to be supporting female employees objecting to suggestive pinups and offensive language, while another faction is supporting employees' freedom of speech and expression. The essential thing for management is to be committed to the strategy that harassment won't be tolerated or ignored (MacDonald, 1993).

Salt Lake Olympic Committee
Antidiscrimination and Harassment Policy (2002)

SLOC wants to provide its staff members with a workplace free of tensions involving matters that are not related to the services we offer. SLOC will not tolerate discrimination or harassment because of race, color, sex, pregnancy, childbirth or pregnancy-related conditions, age, religion, national origin, disability, or handicap in the workplace; such conduct may result in disciplinary action up to and including termination. Further, any such discrimination or harassment is a violation of state and/or federal law. If any staff member believes that he or she has been subject to any such discrimination or harassment, he or she must notify his or her supervisor, manager, the SLOC Human Resources Manager, or any other person with whom the staff member feels comfortable. Any officer, supervisor, or manager who has knowledge of any incident of discrimination or harassment prohibited by this policy is required to report such information to the SLOC Human Resources Manager. A staff member who makes a report of discrimination or harassment in good faith will not be adversely affected. The report will be properly investigated and any remedial action that is necessary and appropriate will be taken.

SLOC will not tolerate discrimination or harassment in the workplace because of race, color, sex, pregnancy, childbirth or pregnancy-related conditions, age, religion, national origin, disability, or handicap, and such conduct may result in disciplinary action up to and including termination. Further, such discrimination or harassment is a violation of state and/or federal law.

Definition of Harassment. Harassment in the workplace may include (but is not limited to) words, gestures or actions that annoy, alarm, or abuse another person or create an intimidating, hostile, or offensive working environment based on race, color, sex, pregnancy, childbirth or pregnancy-realted conditions, age, religion, national origin, disability, or handicap. Harassment includes derogatory or degrading remarks, inappropriate jokes, slurs, or comments. It includes harassment with a sexual connotation.

Definition of Sexual Harassment. Sexual harassment is a violation of federal law under Title VII of the Civil Rights Act of 1964, as amended, and of Utah law. Sexual harassment includes unwelcome sexual advances, requests for sexual favors, and any other verbal or physical conduct of a sexual nature, including, but not limited to

Engaging in offensive sexual flirtations
Leering or other offensive visual contact
Making sexual gestures
Offering graphic verbal commentaries about individuals or individuals' bodies
Using degrading words or names
Displaying sexually suggestive pictures or objects
Verbal abuse related to a person's gender
Distributing suggestive or obscene letters or notes
Making unwelcome physical contacts
Threatening or insinuating (explicitly or implicitly) that an employee's refusal to submit to sexual advances will adversely affect his/her work environment or any conditions of employment

Reporting Discriminatory or Harassing Conduct. Staff members are required to report discriminatory or harassing conduct immediately to their supervisor or manager, the SLOC Human Resources Manager, or any other managerial person with whom the staff member feels comfortable. Any officer, supervisor, or manager who has knowledge of any incident of discrimination or harassment prohibited by this policy is required to report such information to the SLOC Human Resources Manager.

Investigation of Reports of Discrimination and Harassment. The SLOC Human Resources function reviews and investigates reports of discrimination and harassment. An investigation may include interviews with the person who makes a report of discrimination or harassment, the person accused of discrimination or harassment, witnesses, and others as appropriate. Whenever practical, the identity of the staff member who has made the report is not disclosed, and investigation of the complaint is made under strict confidence. Information about the investigation is shared only with those who have a need to know. A staff member who makes a report of discrimination or harassment in good faith will not be adversely affected. Following an investigation of such a report, corrective action that is necessary and appropriate will be taken in a timely manner.

The sexual harassment policy must be clear and concise, the term defined, sanctions set forth, and the policy communicated and enforced. Evidence must be gathered, maintained, and documented; the time, place, and event must be cited; this must be corroborated; and it should reflect that the conduct was unwelcomed (O'Brien and Overby, 1993).

There are many situations when a sport administrator should be on the lookout for evidence of sexual harassment. Unwelcome situations with a sexual undertone can be construed as sexual harassment. These situations include sexual invitations, degrading language, innuendoes, insulting jokes or sounds, inappropriate touching, consensual relationships that lead to favoritism or affect others adversely, and placing sexual materials like pictures, videotapes, or literature in a place of work or a practice area (Miller, 1997).

In *Faragher v. City of Boca Raton* (118 S. Ct. 2275) Faragher and other female lifeguards claimed that their supervisors created a sexually hostile environment through uninvited touching and lewd comments. Eventually, after numerous complaints to the city, the supervisors were reprimanded, and under the law, the city was found to be liable for the offensive actions of its employees (Sawyer, 1999).

Well-meaning sport administrators find a very large gray area in what is and is not sexual harassment. School attorney Melinda Maloney suggests that the administrator consider many variables, such as the age of the person being harassed, the nature of the complaint, whether there are witnesses, whether the individual filing a complaint recorded the instances, and the credibility of the persons involved. To meet the standard of sexual harassment, the conduct must be severe, persistent, or pervasive, and it must have created a hostile work or educational environment. To judge this ask two questions (Maloney, 1997): (1) Did the harassment adversely affect the student's grade, work performance, or sport progress? (2) Did the harassment cause a person to drop out of a program, athletics, or extracurricular activity?

Sexual harassment has moved into a new domain in the elementary and secondary schools and recreation programs of child abuse and criminal felonious behavior, so a great deal is at stake. "Roles such as coach, physical education teacher . . . often require individual contact with students, often in private settings, and often in a capacity that builds trust and intimacy between adults and students" (Stein, 1993b, p. 7).

An important administrative concept is to break the casual approach to objectionable behavior (Stein, 1993a). One administrator recommends that students be assisted in writing a letter to the harasser that states three basic points. First, state what has happened, including what, when, and how often; second, relate how it made the victim feel; and third, request it cease immediately, and state that if it does not, it will be considered sexual harassment and will be subject to disciplinary action (Lydiard, 1993; Stein, 1993a; Penfield, 1993).

Some protective strategies for teachers include these: do not hold closed-door meetings with a student; do not hold after-school meetings with a student unless other adults are in the area; treat all students equally; do not touch students; do not invite students to your dwelling or take overnight trips unless other adults are present; and be professional in behavior and dress (Anderson, 1993).

A key element for successful sexual harassment containment is to train the appropriate number of people in the organization. It is not wise to have one investigating his or her own unit or school. Administrators need a cadre of such people that can be called on at any time. Experience shows that if such persons are available, administrators are more apt to start an investigation earlier. Some interesting strategies have been developed such as using a technique called an "environmental scan." This is obtained by talking to people around the person you suspect is being harassed to develop a profile. Another strategy is to not bring the alleged harasser and the victim together—this can be considered amplification of the original sexual harassment. "'If you haven't seen it yourself, it doesn't count,' is a mindset that school officials need to reject. That's not what the law says" (McGrath, 1997).

Sawyer (1999, p. 8) recommends the following guidelines for sport managers:

1. Managers need to have a formal mechanism in place to address complaints of sexual harassment.

2. Managers and their sport organization should establish a zero-tolerance policy toward sexual harassment and communicate it to their employees.

Critical Thinking

Testing athletes for drugs is a recent concern from a legal point of view. This is especially true at the junior high and senior high level. Based on results of legal cases, what is and is not acceptable is still being discovered. Yasser, McCurdy, and Goplerud (2000, p. 923) state, "To evaluate the legality of any drug testing scheme, it is important to consider who the tester is, why the test is to be conducted, who the test is to be conducted upon, how the test is to be administered, what drugs are to be tested for, and what procedures are to be triggered if someone 'fails' the test." Some of these questions were answered when the U.S. Supreme Court heard the case of a town in Oregon in *Vernonia School District v. Acton*, 1995.

This case grew out of ample evidence that more and more student athletes were using drugs. The drug use was causing increasing unruliness and absenteeism in the schools. Special classes were held, and speakers were invited to discuss the dangers of drug misuse. Various groups met to address the problem. Finally, a drug-testing program suggested that a random drug test like urinalysis be administered in junior and senior high schools. The program was presented at an open meeting, and it received unanimous approval from the parents in attendance.

The testing program consisted of each athlete receiving written permission from parents to be tested, and every athlete being tested at the beginning of the season. In addition, 10 percent of each team was randomly tested. Each athlete produced a sample monitored by an adult of the same sex. Each sample was labeled by code number, and the chain of custody was exact. It was sent to a certified laboratory, which sent the results back to the superintendent. Only the principal, assistant principal, and assistant director saw the results. If positive, the athlete was to be immediately tested again. If positive again, the student athlete and parents met and were given the options of (1) attending a six-week assistance program and weekly testing or (2) suspension from athletics for the season and the next season. The athlete was tested again when eligible, and a positive test resulted in automatic penalty.

Acton was in the seventh grade and signed up to play football. His parents refused to give written permission for drug testing, and he was denied participation. Acton filed a suit claiming a violation of his rights under the Fourth and Fourteenth Amendments to the U.S. Constitution. The Fourth Amendment prohibits unreasonable searches; the Fourteenth Amendment extends these searches to include those by state officers. The trial court denied the claims, but the appeals court reversed. The U.S. Supreme Court found that Vernonia's policy was reasonable and hence constitutional. How could the policy have been more favorable in light of the court? What are the weaknesses of the policy? If you went back to coach in the high school from which you graduated, would you favor such a policy? Would you have agreed with the policy when you were in high school?

---

3. Managers and their employees should receive training in issues related to sexual harassment on an annual basis, or as the situation requires.

4. The protocol for filing complaints involving sexual harassment should be clearly defined, and all complaints must be taken seriously by management without reprisal against the person filing the complaint.

Legal issues abound in the sport setting. With an understanding of the principles and guidelines set forth in this chapter, you will be able to provide a safe environment, conduct your programs in accordance with the law, and in the process, avoid litigation.

Exercises

1. If you have a rule that no one in a physical education class may touch a shot put during your track and field unit until you say so, from a negligence point of view, why is it important to determine whether you have enforced the rule once a student is injured by not following the rule?
2. Select a playground or sport facility with which you are familiar. List the specifically dangerous conditions that, in the event of an injury, would likely result in liability litigation.
3. Describe the most serious injury that ever occurred in one of your physical education classes. Assume that the injury would have resulted in a lifelong handicap. (For example, if the accident resulted in a broken or cut arm, assume that the use of that arm was impaired for life.) List the reasons the injured student might have given for suing the teacher or school district. List the reasons the coach could have given in his or her defense.
4. Repeat the previous exercise, selecting the most serious injury you witnessed in athletics.
5. If you as a teacher, coach, or administrator carry liability insurance, what difference does it make if you are sued?
6. Review the drug-testing program at your institution and evaluate its chances of standing up to a court challenge. If there is no drug-testing program, write one.

References

Abbott, S. W., and Wong, G. M. (1997). Storm warnings. *Athletic Business* 21, pp. 22–24.

Adams, S. (1993, February). Duty to protect. *Journal of Physical Education, Recreation and Dance*, pp. 22–23.

Anderson, P. L. (1993, June). Sexual harassment. *School Business Affairs*, pp. 14–17.

Applin, A. G. (1997, Summer). The Title IX battlefield. *USSA Sport Supplement* 5, p. 2.

Berger, J. (2002, June 15). Is Title IX equal to task? *Rocky Mountain News,* **www.rockymountainnews.com/ drmm/college.**

Berry, R. C., & Wong, G. M. (1986). *Law and business of the sports industries: Vol. 2. Common issues in amateur and professional sports.* Dover, MA: Auburn.

Booth, M. (2002, August 9). Sports officials ran stall play in disqualifying gridder. *New Jersey Law Journal*, pp. 23–28.

Brink, N. (2002, Sept. 27). Sport shop held negligent in renting in-line skates to novice. *The Lawyers Weekly,* v22, No. 20, pp. 1–2.

Bucher, C. A., and Krotee, M. L. (2002). *Management of physical education and sport* (12th ed.). St. Louis: McGraw-Hill.

Casey, S.; Ballard, C.; and Deitsch, R. (2002). Scorecard. *Sports Illustrated,* v96, i26, p. 21.

Champion, W. T., Jr. (1993). *Sports law.* St. Paul: West.

Clements, A. (1988). *Law in sport and physical activity.* Indianapolis: Benchmark Press.

Cohen, A. (1993, March). And the home schoolers take the field. *Athletic Business*, pp. 20–22.

Colorado Civil Rights Commission (2002). *Guidelines on Sexual Harassment.* Denver: Colorado Civil Rights Commission.

Cotton, D. J. (1992, September). Matching participants—Is it a real issue? *Sports, Parks, and Recreation Law Reporter*, p. 23.

Cotton, D. J., and Wilde, T. J. (1997). *Sport law for sport managers.* Dubuque, IA: Kendal Hunt Publishing.

Court split on athletes with disabilities and age rules. (1996, December). *Your School and the Law* 26, pp. 6–7.

Curtis (2002).

Farmer, P. J., Mulrooney, A. L., and Ammon, R. (1996). *Understanding sport organizations.* Morgantown, WV: Fitness Information Technologies.

Federal court upholds age eligibility rule governing sports. (1997, January). *Your School and the Law* 27, p. 11.

Fired football coach says court's award falls short of the goal line. *School Law Bulletin* (1997, September), pp. 3–4.

Frankel, E. (1992, November). Charging ahead—Putting gender equity into play. *Athletic Management* 4, pp. 15–19.

Gaskin, L. P. (1993, February). Establishing, communicating, and enforcing rules and regulations. *Journal of Physical Education, Recreation and Dance* 64, pp. 26–27.

Gender equity debate heats up (1997, August/September). *Athletic Management* 9, pp. 11–13.

Gibbons, M. G., and Wong, G. M. (1997, December). Player versus player. *Athletic Business* 21, pp. 22–24.

Gutner, T. (2002, Oct. 7). Women's sports could take a hit. *Business Week,* i3802, p. 144.

Herbert, D. L. (1993, March). Overcrowding and poor supervision litigated. *Fitness Management* 9, p. 24.

Herbert, D. L. (1997, November). Club case fails due to lack of evidence. *Fitness Management* 13, p. 44.

Hochberg, P. R. (1988a, January 25). The sports-bar scramble. *Sports Inc.* 1, pp. 42–43.

Hochberg, P. R. (1988b, February 22). Whose right is it anyway? *Sports Inc.* 1, pp. 44–45.

Kelly, P. (1994, May 16). EEOC sues Campbell for firing instructor with AIDS. *Charlotte Observer*, p. 2C.

Kennedy, S. O.; French, R.; and Henderson, H. L. (1989, October). The due-able process could happen to you! *Journal of Physical Education, Recreation and Dance* 60, pp. 86–93.

LaRue, R. (2002, Aug./Sept.). Safe in their seats. *Athletic Management*, pp. 61–63.

Lehr, C. (1993, February). Proper classification. *Journal of Physical Education, Recreation and Dance* 64, pp. 24–25.

Lirgg, C. D. (1992, August). Has coed physical education been a positive step forward for girls? *Journal of Physical Education, Recreation and Dance* 63, p. 9.

Lydiard, B. W. (1993, January). A decade of dealing with sexual harassment. *School Administrator*, pp. 20–21.

MacDonald, R. (1993, January). Sexual harassment is imprecise. *Ski Area Management* 61, p. 77.

Maloney, M. (1997, February). Sexual harassment. *Your School and the Law* 27, p. 3.

McGrath, M. J. (1997, February). Sexual harassment: Use training to limit your district's liability. *Your School and the Law* 27, p. 3.

Miller, L. (1997). *Sports business management.* Gaithersburg, MD: Aspen.

Nondiscrimination on the basis of disability by public accommodations and in commercial facilities. (1994, July). *Department of Justice,* 28 CFR, part 36.

O'Brien, D. B., and Overby, J. O. (1993, March). Legal aspects of sexual harassment in higher education with special reference to physical education and athletics. *Research Quarterly for Exercise Science* (Suppl.), A-110.

Osinski, A. (1988, May/June). Legal responsibilities of lifeguards. *Journal of Physical Education, Recreation and Dance* 59, pp. 73–75.

Paling, D. (1996, June/July). High school's Title IX story. *Athletic Management* 8, pp. 22–28.

Peach, R. J. (2001, March 19). Crawn's heightened-care standard is extended to non-contact sports. *New Jersey Law Journal,* v63, i12, pp. 7–9.

Penfield, C. (1993, March). Sexual harassment at school. *Executive Educator*, pp. 41–42.

Proportionality okayed for Title IX compliance. (2002). *Journal of Health, Physical Education and Dance*, v73, i7, p. 13.

Ross, T. C. (1993a). Unhappy basketball player takes university to court. *Sports and the Courts* 14, p. 10.

Ross, T. C. (1993b). University's drug-testing program fails constitutional challenge. *Sports and the Courts* 14, p. 7.

Salt Lake Olympic Committee (2002). Anti-Discrimination and Harassment Policy. *Team 2002 Training Manual.*

Sanchez, J. (2002, August 16). Judge rules against bloom. *www.denverpost.com/stories.html.*

Sawyer, T. (1999). Sexual harassment. *Journal of Health, Physical Education and Dance,* v70, i9, p. 7.

School board requires teachers to accept extracurricular duties. (1992, June). *Your School and the Law* p. 8.

School gives soccer coach the boot after calls team cowards. *School Law Bulletin.* (1997, June), pp. 2–3.

School liability. (1996, January). *Your School and the Law* 27, p. 6.

Schubert, G. W.; Smith, R. K.; and Trentadue, J. C. (1986). *Sports law.* St. Paul: West.

Sendor, B. (1993, March). Passing the test on drug testing. *American School Board Journal* 180, pp. 23–24.

Settlement has been reached in a Title IX complaint (1996, October). *Your School and the Law,* p. 16.

Sharp, L. A. (2002, October). Vial decision. *Athletic Business,* pp. 30–33.

Shepherd, R., Jr. (1993, February). Liability. *Parks/Grounds Management*, pp. 14–17.

Sikorski, E. J., and Gibbons, M. (1998, January). Old school. *Athletic Business* 22, pp. 20–22.

Slezak, C. (2002, Sept. 24). No easy answers. *Chicago Sun-Times*, p. 111.

Solomon, J. (2002, June 23). Title IX: 30 years later. *The Houston Chronicle*, p. A1.

Sports eligibility rule could be applied, according to court (1996, December). *Your School and the Law* 26, p. 7.

Stein, N. D. (1993a, January). Sexual harassment in schools. *School Administrator*, pp. 14–19.

Stein, N. D. (1993b, May). Breaking through casual attitudes on sexual harassment. *Education Digest*, pp. 7–10.

Student falls from monkey bars on school playground. *School Law Bulletin* (1997, September), pp. 7–8.

Student injured in gym class; school board not liable (1996, June). *Your School and the Law* 26, p. 10.

Student is suspended and thrown off the basketball team for having alcohol on a school trip. *School Law Bulletin* (1997, May), pp. 4–5.

Student with disability had no right to participate in sports (1997, February). *Your School and the Law* 27, pp. 8–9.

Van Der Smissen, B. (1990). *Legal liability and risk management for public and private entities.* Cincinnati: Anderson.

Wolohan, J. T., and Wong, G. M. (1993, June). Ruling may have a Texas-size impact. *Athletic Business* 17, pp. 22–23.

Wolohan, J. (2002, August). Happy landings. *Athletic Business*, pp. 24–28.

Wong, G. M. *Essentials of amateur sports law.* (2nd. ed.). 1994. Westport, Conn. Praiger Publishing.

Wong, G. M., and Craig, J. T. (1993, April). Start making sense. *Athletic Business* 17, p. 14.

Wong, G. M., and Duncan, K. L. (1997, November). All fired up. *Athletic Business* 21, pp. 20–24.

Yasser, R.; McCurdy, J. R.; and Goplerud, C. P. (2000). *Sports laws, cases and materials* (4th ed.). Cincinnati: Anderson.

9

Risk Management in Sport and Physical Education

Worse than being blind, is to be able to see and have no vision.

Helen Keller

Case Study: Torts in Sports

Marc Buoniconti was a sophomore starting linebacker at The Citadel. He injured his neck on October 5, 1985, in a game against VMI. Even though his neck was stiff, weak, and sore, he played the next week against Davidson. He took treatments for his stiff neck and played again against the University of Tennessee–Chattanooga, and hurt his neck again. The next week he wore a soft cervical collar and was excused from drills and contact at practice. X rays were taken, and the team physician found nothing that should restrict him from playing. The trainer concocted a piece of equipment that would restrict his head from bending backward, and the physician approved his playing the next game wearing the device.

During that game, against East Tennessee State University, he dove in to finish off a tackle that another player had already initiated—possibly "spearing" in the process. No penalty was called. Marc crushed his spinal cord. He has not been able to move any part of his body but his head since that moment.

The family sued The Citadel, the trainer, and the team physician. As the trial was in progress, the insurer of The Citadel and the trainer settled. The case went forward with the physician as the only defendant. After a long case, the court found for the defendant. South Carolina is one of the few states that has not instituted comparative negligence. This means that any contributory negligence on the part of a plaintiff operates as a complete bar to recovery. This apparently worked harshly against Marc Buoniconti.

The family requested a new trial, which was denied, and they filed for an appeal to state supreme court. In October 1988, almost three years after the accident, the family abandoned the appeal. Marc has taken graduate studies in psychology at Miami University, where the family has instituted the Miami Project to Cure Paralysis. The fund has raised over $20 million. In addition, the family has endorsed the "no practice, no play" rule to improve safety (Yasser, McCurdy, and Goplerud, 1997).

The reader should be able to

1. Describe risk management and crisis management as they apply to sport and physical education.
2. Explain the legal aspects of transportation in sport and physical education, and make recommendations for avoiding legal problems.
3. Describe the three legs of the insurance triangle and the recommendations for complying with responsibility for coverage.
4. Report on the administrator's responsibilities for emergency care in sport and physical education.
5. Identify the major components of safety programs for sport and physical education.
6. Explain how to apply exculpatory agreements and consent forms to sport administration.

■ RISK MANAGEMENT

A disaster not covered by insurance . . . being taken to court for negligence . . . adverse publicity due to a misjudgment by a staff member—all three of these prospects strike fear into the heart of any sports administrator. And for good reason, as most athletic departments don't have a plan for how to deal with potential catastrophes. (Buisman, 1992, p. 10)

The risk management process is ongoing and involves four stages: identify the risks, assess the risks, treat the risks (For example, changing a dangerous program, buying insurance, or requiring the signing of exculpatory/documents, which will be discussed later), and write standard operating procedures (Farmer, Mulrooney, and Ammon, 1996; Herbert, 1997a; Sawyer 2001c).

Risk management includes safety, accident prevention, and sound insurance policies, but also encompasses much more. Just as the modern definition of health is more than just the absence of illness, risk management is more than simply avoiding accidents. It is a total program that analyzes risks, identifies where and why injuries or accidents might occur, and specifies what to do about them. This includes identifying hazards that might be eliminated or controlled; pinpointing aspects requiring indemnification (insuring or otherwise protecting personnel or the organization from financial burden); or altering the program to eliminate activities judged to be professionally indefensible or too costly for indemnification. Managing risks includes inspecting facilities and equipment to predict and preclude accidents, but it also embraces an active program of accident investigation and follow-up. At the same time, it must be recognized that if physical education and sport are to remain exciting and challenging, a degree of controlled danger and risk must continue.

How Much Risk Is Too Much?

Due to a variety of factors, there are many injuries in physical education and sport. After any serious accident, there is frequently a cry to eliminate any activity that appears to be risky. Study shows, however, that many activities that have resulted in serious injury or death, such as gymnastics and swimming, can be safely conducted if handled properly. For example, bouncing on a trampoline may be perceived as dangerous, but when it is conducted properly with a safety belt, it is actually very safe.

How do we compensate with controls? Who decides which controls are acceptable? Here are some examples of controls: requiring racquetball players to wear protective eye guards; establishing antispear tackling in football; padding the underside of basketball backboards; and adopting rules such as shorter time periods for inexperienced or youth participants.

The implication for risk management is to increase care commensurate with increases in risk.

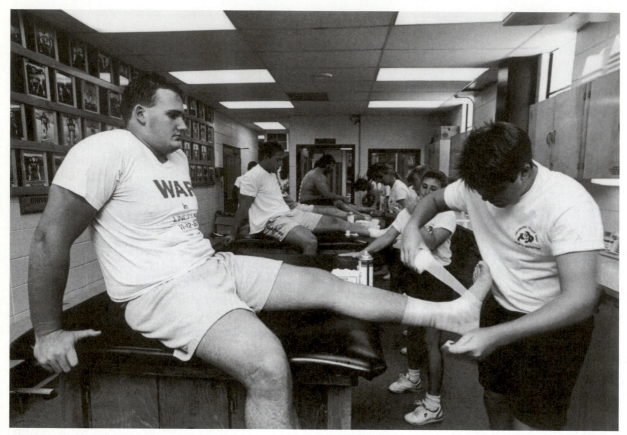

Certified athletic trainers play a vital role in sport risk management.
Courtesy of University of Colorado Athletic Department Public Relations.

If the activity is required, or the teacher or coach directs the activity to be completed, care must be proportionally increased. If the student has a history of injury, a propensity for accidents, or a disability, special care is necessary. The mental state, age, experience, and skill of participants dictates the amount and type of supervision and the standard of care.

The Risk Management Plan

Crisis management planning is a process that usually goes through a series of stages. First the sport organization must become aware of the risks. A chief administrator should form a risk management team. This team reviews risk management plans of similar organizations and writes a draft for their organization. The appropriate officials re-

view the plan and prepare it for a final draft. Most important, those elements on the plan that require personnel action must be practiced by the organization (Kramer, 1997/1998; Appenzeller, 1998, pp. 159–162).

Two important aspects of risk management for health–fitness operations are emergency response preparedness and preenrollment cardiovascular screening. A survey was sent to 102 Massachusetts clubs that were association members and 102 nonassociation members. Results found that 35 percent of all responding association clubs and 46 percent of all responding nonassociation clubs *did not* routinely screen or never screened new members. Emergency training was part of staff orientation at 81 percent of the clubs, but emergency response preparedness drills were *never* practiced at more than 40 percent of the clubs (Herbert, 1998).

Reports indicate that contact sports such as football show an injury rate as high as three-quarters of the participants sometime during each season. In noncontact sports the figure might be only about 10 percent. While amounts vary, generally the deaths and catastrophic injuries in football have steadily declined over the years. "According to data collected under the NCAA's Injury Surveillance System (ISS), there is a risk of injuries two to three times higher in spring football practice compared to fall football practice" ("New Proposal Aims to Reduce Spring Football Practice Injuries," 1997). Because of this, it has been recommended to reduce the number of spring practices in which tackling is permitted and full scrimmage is allowed.

Risk management guidelines are a must for football. Coaches must inform athletes that no one sets foot on the practice field without a physical examination. To prevent injuries, coaches have a legal duty to properly condition players. All players must prove that they have adequate insurance coverage in case of injury. Emergency plans should be practiced before the football season begins. Athletic trainers must be present at every practice and game. Make sure athletes have adequate supervision on the field and in the locker room and weight room. Additionally, coaches must check the equipment and facilities before the season begins to make sure everything is safe (Borkowski, 1996).

We should learn about risk management from other related industries that are more exposed to both the risk and an aggressive public. Recent changes in the ski industry, for example, might be precursors for changes in sport and recreation. The case of *Sunday v. Stratton* in the 1980s involving a ski area has resulted in changes in both risk management and legislation. Among other things, ski area managers have been urged to advertise skiing honestly as a hazardous activity for which participants need to be in condition, careful, and alert. Managers are attempting to advertise slope conditions truthfully. This truth-in-advertising is a dramatic change from the past,

when the advertising was all positive, but untrue, and the fallacy was revealed in court.

Does stretching truth ever occur in sport? For example, can you see yourself describing your coaching to a jury as child-centered and professionally prudent when you named your defensive unit the "death squad"?

The Right to Risk

Is the risk worth taking? This decision is frequently based on statistics reflecting the injury rate for a particular activity. As previously stated, the counterbalance to hazards in the risk management equation is the right to "reasonably" safe risks. If swimming pools are to be made "fail-safe" for injuries, there is only one alternative—to fill them in. (Appenzeller, 1998, pp. 51–52).

Very seldom do cases associated with high-risk activities materialize from well-organized and professional programs. Some reasons for this are that the activities are so obviously dangerous that only certified and well-trained people are involved; they insist on state-of-the-art equipment and facilities; and participants are constantly alert and attentive to instructions. But public governmental agencies such as schools and recreation departments have been hesitant to provide adventure-type activities. This is changing with increasingly strong safety records. An example is the At-Risk Youth Division in Phoenix (Colley, 1998).

If risk management is the art of balancing the control of hazards with the inclusion of controlled risks, we must understand the *actual danger* of adventure-type activities as opposed to the *apparent danger*. For example, a supervisor was astounded to see a concrete base under a very large jungle gym on an otherwise grassy playground. The principal said the area under the gym had been unsafe and had resulted in many accidents because it had been used so much that holes and uneven ground had developed under and around it. Why was rubberized asphalt not installed?

An infrequently studied area of the risk of sport injuries is the place of socialization in "playing hurt," thus resulting in more serious injuries and possible adverse litigation. Nixon (1993, p. 190) has reported, "When athletes are socialized, encouraged, pressured, or otherwise influenced to view pain and injury as a necessary or attractive part of the game, coaches may not have to try hard to convince them to play hurt. In fact athletes may be among the strongest opponents of efforts to introduce new rules or equipment to make sport safer."

Risk Management Decisions

In the end, the administrator must weigh the evidence and make a decision based on two questions: (1) How many hazards in the activity under consideration are controllable and how much control can the activity tolerate? (2) Given the preceding findings, will the benefits justify the calculated risks?

The strategy of getting a handle on risk management is similar to solving any other management problem. First, identify and evaluate the potential risks; second, select the best possible approaches to the risks. Next, initiate operational procedures to control the risks. And as always, evaluate the results. Identifying the risks can be grouped by *property* exposures; public liability in *program* services, with and without negligence; and risks in the *business* operations (Cotton, 1993).

To carefully prepare a risk management plan, modify or eliminate activities that involve too much risk. Transfer the risks through insurance or indemnity arrangements. Agencies or schools should consider self-insurance, but all should be covered for catastrophic accidents. National athletic associations, such as the NCAA and others, has reasonable rates (Appenzeller, 1998, pp. 39–47).

At the beginning of each year, select an emergency situation that could possibly occur, and test the crisis plan (Neal, 1996; Diles, 1996; Hessert, 1997). This might be a bleacher collapse with multiple serious injuries. Who will be in charge? How many victims can the local hospital emergency room handle at once? Where is the nearest air evacuation pad? Who will release information to the media?

Crisis Management

A *crisis* is "a significant disruption that stimulates extensive new media coverage and public scrutiny and disrupts the organization's normal business activities" (Irvine, 1997, p. 37). Crisis events are of two basic types: sudden and smoldering.

Crisis management programs and plans in sport organizations need to become far more sophisticated. "The question is not whether the costs can be afforded, but rather that the cost of not doing them could ruin the organization" (Frank, 1997, p. 34).

"Crisis management can take many forms—the death of an athlete or participant, a bus accident, a bomb threat, or a financial disaster. Crisis management is a new name for a good old idea—having a well-planned emergency strategy in place before catastrophe occurs" (Horine, 1987, p. 98). In the event of a crisis, release only *verified* facts to the media without any additional speculation or theories. Do not release the victims' names to anyone but the highest medical and law-enforcement authorities; respect the privacy of both victims and their families; and have one professionally trained spokesperson to which all are referred (Call, 1993).

In the past, media were slow to respond to a sport crisis, and when they did it was usually "friendly" coverage. No more! Such events are now "big news," and often the media are adversarial. "Decisions made in the first few hours of a crisis can make the difference between temporary setback and a long-term disaster" (Horine, 1986, p. 72). The guidelines for mitigating crises are to first establish a team. The team must include top management with authority to allocate resources as required. A highly individualistic, written crisis plan that reacts to the worst-case scenario must be set down.

Three characteristics occur in a crisis. It is sudden, it is urgent, and it is visible. Crisis experts suggest that the public must be informed in plain language as soon as possible; if not, rumors (usually worse than the actual fact) will fill the vacuum. Silence will imply guilt! Supply the public with details to justify the conclusion. Recognize that reporters face deadlines, and therefore give them accurate and timely information (Horine, 1986).

Standards and Risk Management

Standards refer to the levels of performance that are expected by those with similar amounts of education and training. It reflects accepted actions as defined by society and the consensus of experts in a similar field. In legal terms, it is called "the reasonably prudent person standard." The lawsuit attempts to prove that a person did not follow the standards expected in that field (Borkowski, 2000, p. 23).

Managers and administrators must follow the standards of care in the following categories:

- Properly plan the activity.
- Provide proper instruction.
- Provide a safe environment.
- Provide proper equipment.
- Properly match participants.
- Supervise the activity.
- Warn of inherent risks.
- Provide emergency and postcare help (Borkowski, 2000).

Sport administrators must be aware that standards of performance are not static—they change with time. A case in point is providing an automatic external defibrillator (AED) in almost all sport and recreational venues. Until recently, AEDs were very restricted in their use and would not have been a required standard. But now, if the need for the use of one occurs in any sport facility such as an arena, pool, fitness center, ski area, or golf course, and one is not available along with personnel trained in its use, the facility will be in a precarious legal situation. If the administrator cannot meet standards, it is best not to offer the activity at all. (Bynum, 2002).

■ TRANSPORTATION

In the case of *Jones v. Iowa Central Community College*, 1992, the plaintiff was a member of the basketball team riding in a college van driven by the coach. The plaintiff suffered injuries in an accident and brought a suit against the school and coach. The jury found the college negligent and awarded the plaintiff $270,000 (Appenzeller, 1998, p. 108).

From a management point of view, four options, listed from best to least desirable, are available when transporting teams. The best strategy is to use bonded, independent contract carriers. Almost as effective is to use regular school vehicles with regular drivers. The third option, carrying some additional risk, is to use inspected employee vehicles with licensed adult drivers. Not recommended is the last option—to use inspected nonemployee vehicles with adult licensed drivers (Borkowski, 2002). In *Foster v. Board of Trustees of Butler County Community College*, 1991, over $2 million was awarded to a basketball recruit who was injured when being driven in a personal car by a student employee who had no liability insurance (Pittman, 1993).

The following are some recommended bus rules:

- Review the record of the company, including accident reports, vehicle maintenance plans, and experience of drivers.
- Ensure that the company has adequate insurance.
- Ensure that the company is fully licensed.
- Have legal counsel review the contract.
- Ensure that the company has required drivers to be trained and that they have passed state examinations.
- Select a company that has experience in transporting athletic teams.
- The company should require that a coach or agency supervisor be on the bus (Borkowski, 2000).

Drivers

One of the problems in pupil transportation is the selection of drivers. The job usually pays a minimum wage; frequently the result is a shortage of highly qualified drivers. Even if a trip and contest has to be forfeited, never allow a driver who is not competent and properly licensed to take a team.

Coaches themselves must often drive vehicles to transport athletes. This may be the case with nonrevenue teams and teams with small numbers on the squad. The practice becomes outlandish when college coaches must drive vans hundreds of miles carrying up to 15 athletes and their gear back to campus during the winter or after night contests. How safe is this custom in climates where icy roads are common? Only the dedication, perseverance, and skill of countless coaches have limited the accidents in these situations.

Salt Lake Organizing Committee Driver Agreement Form

Full name (printed)   **Date of birth**

Social Security number

Driver license no.   **State of issue**

Expiration date

This information may be used to obtain your MVR (Motor Vehicle Report) to help determine your eligibility to operate a SLOC vehicle.

Driver Conduct Requirements

I understand the loan of any SLOC vehicle is subject to the following terms and verify that I am 18 years of age or older and am an employee, employee's spouse, agent, or representative of the USOC, SLOC, participating NGBs, or OPUS. I acknowledge that I must

1. Possess a valid operator's license, display such license to the vehicle key issuer at each vehicle exchange, and comply with all license restrictions.

2. Never drive while impaired by alcohol, drugs, medications, illness, fatigue, or injury.

3. Ensure proper use of safety belts and child safety restraints for all occupants.

4. Obey all applicable motor vehicle laws, codes, and regulations.

5. Drive in a defensive manner, anticipating situations where incidents are likely to occur.

6. Refrain, at all times, from using radar/laser detection devices.

7. Plan trips by selecting the safest route, depart early enough to observe posted speed and traffic regulations and be mindful of current and forecast weather conditions.

8. Report all incidents/crashes involving damage to the vehicle to SLOC Motor Pool – 212-2101. (A report form is provided in the glove compartment of the vehicle.)

9. Prohibit the use of the vehicle by other parties, including family members other than spouse.

10. Be personally responsible for the adjudication of all moving and parking citations.

Furthermore, by signing this acknowledgment, I verify that I have not been convicted within the past 36 months of any of the following motor vehicle violations:

a. Driving while operator's license is suspended, revoked, or denied.

b. Vehicular manslaughter, negligent homicide, felonious driving, or felony with a vehicle.

c. Operating a vehicle while impaired, under the influence of alcohol or illegal drugs, or refusing a sobriety or substance abuse test.

d. Failure to stop or identify after an accident (includes leaving the scene of an accident; hit and run; giving false information to an officer).

e. Eluding or attempting to elude a law enforcement officer.

f. Traffic violation resulting in death or serious injury.

g. Any other significant violation warranting suspension of license.

If you are NOT a SLOC employee/volunteer driving a SLOC vehicle and are injured in an automobile accident that you cause, SLOC's insurance will pay $3,000 for your medical expenses. If you an independent contractor or an individual from another country and wish more than $3,000 medical coverage for yourself, you should purchase additional insurance for your own protection.

Driver's Signature: **Date**

Courtesy of SLOC

Transportation Policies

The key to prudent administrative planning for travel entails carefully considered written policy. If calculated risks are necessary, for example, to travel to off-campus tennis courts for classes or practice, these trips must not occur on the spur of the moment.

To manage risks, consider the following precautions. If possible, travel in only bonded common carriers or school buses. The state laws regarding liability should be followed if students will travel in private cars. Student drivers should not be used unless they are authorized drivers of school buses. Avoid allowing students to drive private automobiles to transport teams or classes. Student conduct should be defined and controlled. Faculty supervision on school trips is mandatory. If, as a last resort, private automobiles must be used, insist on adult drivers, inspect vehicles to ensure safety, travel together with the leader absolutely following speed limits, and allow participants to choose cars and seats in which to ride. Coaches who receive expenses for transporting students should take out special insurance to cover this practice.

Transportation Recommendations for the Administrator

1. Learn the transportation law of your state regarding "guest" status and governmental immunity (which may be different from the remainder of the school areas) and whether it applies to athletics.

2. After consulting with appropriate people, write a risk analysis of the present operating procedures for transportation.

3. Present the risk analysis to the appropriate authorities for immediate action and for long-range plans. It may require several years of fundraising to make a substantial change, such as purchasing a new activity bus.

4. If risk analysis shows an unreasonable level of danger, but changes in number 3, preceding, are not administratively feasible and are rejected, forward this judgment to superiors and file a copy.

5. Form a study group to resolve the conflict, which may require both immediate changes in scheduling—such as eliminating an off-campus golf class or changing the time of an opponent's game a long distance away—and changes in programs, such as reducing numbers of students, eliminating certain sports, or strategies to obtain more favorable administrative support for improvement.

6. Maintain adequate personal liability insurance.

■ TRANSFERRING RISKS AND INSURANCE

Accidents are unavoidable in the fast-moving world of sport. Athletes and spectators are injured; equipment and facilities fail; and all kinds of unexpected actions, such as a criminal act, can result in litigation or necessary payments. One part of the whole risk management program is to carry appropriate insurance for the protection of the integrity of the sport organization and the peace of mind of leaders. For a variety of reasons, insurance coverage for sport, fitness, and recreational departments and businesses has become much more expensive. It has been suggested that for college programs, the three strategies for mitigating these increases are to aggressively reduce the risk exposure, apply higher deductibles, and communicate to athletes and parents that the institution's insurance is secondary. (Polanshek, 2002a and 2002b).

The cost of the insurance for any organization is important; however, it is not advisable to put insurance needs out for bids and to take the lowest bidder.

> Be suspicious of huge savings promised under a "group" plan and carefully question how the institution will fare in future years. Will schools with good loss control end up paying for those with poor experience? Will benefits be decreased to contain losses? Regardless of the size of the group, any reliable carrier must eventually consider premium taxes, claims paying fees, licensing fees, administrative fees, reinsurance, and carrier/company profit in their pricing. An initial discount could rapidly disappear (Polanshek, 2002c).

Each state has different laws regarding school insurance. In some states, the school districts are allowed to purchase liability insurance, but if it is not procured, governmental immunity is maintained. In others, the school district may purchase insurance related only to bus transportation and/or proprietary activities, which may include athletic programs. In most instances, the amount of claims is either limited to a fixed amount or may not exceed the coverage of the insurance. If the school district has insurance, it is more likely that claims will be filed against the district, and this tendency may lessen the chance of the school administrator or coach being sued. In addition, the statutes frequently limit or exclude some specific situations from coverage.

The Three Legs of the Insurance Triangle

A vital aspect of risk management, and the **first leg** of the insurance triangle, is *school or agency insurance.* This can be through a carefully selected firm, self-insurance (placing funds in escrow to cover costs if any should materialize), or a combination of the two by purchasing inexpensive, high-deductible insurance and putting small amounts aside to cover costs up to the deductible (Herbert, 1997a).

The Canutillo Independent School District near El Paso, Texas, purchased a "School Leaders Errors and Omissions" insurance policy covering such things as alleged violations of federal or state constitutional civil rights. The policy, however, excluded claims based on criminal acts, assault, or battery, or any claim arising out of bodily injury to any person. The parents of five second-grade girls claimed that Perales, a physical education teacher, had sexually abused their children. He was tried and convicted for sexual molestation. The parents then filed federal civil rights and state common law tort claims against the school district. The insurance company refused to handle the case, based on the exclusions in the contract. The school district unsuccessfully sued the insurance company and was left to fend for itself (Zirkel, 1997). In another example, the Westville riding club purchased spectator insurance that excluded rodeo participants. Aside from the regular rodeo events, there was a contest in which spectators were invited to remove a ribbon from the horns of a bull and earn $50. A spectator, Remaley, took them up on the challenge, but was butted and seriously injured. The club thought it was protected, but the insurance company successfully argued that Remaley changed from a spectator to a participant when he entered the contest. Rather than spending money on spectator insurance, the club might have been better off deciding that the "challenge" was too dangerous and not scheduling it, or might have had contestants sign a waiver, which will be addressed later in this chapter (Sawyer, 2001c).

The **second leg** of the triangle is the *insurance needs of teachers, coaches, and administrators.* In some states, the state pays part or all of the medical insurance for teachers. If not, coaches and physical education teachers need to join a group plan for medical coverage. Because of the emotional and physical demands and dimensions of these areas, it is also recommended that disability pay continuation be purchased so that in the event of a disabling injury or illness, a portion of the regular salary will continue. Since 1960 AAHPERD (American Alliance for Health, Physical Education, Recreation and Dance) has offered a disability income protection plan to its members. Finally, personal liability insurance should be obtained. In some cases this coverage might be included in homeowners' insurance. Also, the school district may take out insurance coverage on all administrators. If not, perhaps this issue can be pursued with the board. Many coaching or professional associations include liability coverage within the dues benefits, or make it available at a reasonable additional cost. For example, AAHPERD provides members with liability insurance for a small charge. As a last resort, commercial coverage can be purchased at an insignificant cost.

The **third leg** of the insurance triangle is *coverage of the students and athletes.* No athlete should be allowed on the practice field or court without medical insurance. Sometimes the school pays for all insurance costs or covers a portion of the costs, and sometimes the student is required to cover all costs. If the school cannot pay for the athlete's medical insurance, an aggressive attempt should be made to obtain a low-cost group plan to which student athletes can subscribe if they are not adequately covered by their parents' plans. Remember, plans must also be designed to confidentially finance the medical insurance for any athlete who is incapable of bearing the cost (Polanshek 2002a).

In the end, the best insurance for students, faculty, coaches, administrators, and the district is to insist on appropriate programs carried out in a safe environment with reasonable and professional instruction and supervision. Financial reimbursement will never pay for pain and suffering, the loss of the player to the team or the teacher to the system, or the personal anxiety and professional damage resulting from litigation.

Out-of-Court Settlements and the Effect on Insurance

Insurance executives defend the frequency of out-of-court settlements as a means of improving the goodwill of both parties and building the company's reputation as a liberal payer of claims, which will stimulate sales. Lawyers and insurance executives might be underestimating the negative and devastating effect of out-of-court settlements due to a lack of public trust in the coaches and administrators, company products, or the school. The school's image will affect booster club donations and athletic recruitment as well as purchasing equipment. Because businesses win the majority of the cases brought against them, many manufacturers ask for safeguards in their insurance policies so that more cases will be taken to court.

■ EXCULPATORY AGREEMENTS AND PARENTAL CONSENT FORMS

Exculpatory agreements are what some people erroneously call *disclaimers, waivers,* or *approval forms*. A *disclaimer* is used by a manufacturer to warn users that if the product is not used as specified, the company will not provide compensation for injuries. After an injury, if a party receives a settlement, it will be contingent upon signing a *waiver*. The *approval form* (consent) is to ensure that parents approve of the activities in which their children will engage, which does not restrict the right to sue should an injury occur (Borkowski, 2000).

An *exculpatory agreement or release,* on the other hand, is an agreement not to sue if an accident occurs in the future. Just because it is signed doesn't mean that it will hold up in court. Some refer to exculpatory releases as "express assumption of risk documents." Herbert (1997a, p. 46a) states, "Increasingly, the court system is giving le-

gal effect to such documents and allowing individuals to prospectively release facilities and their personnel from a variety of claims, including those which may be related to the active or passive negligence of those released by such documents. Claims related to willful/wanton/intentional conduct of those related to criminal acts will not be protected."

If an exculpatory agreement is signed by an adult to cover himself or herself, is clearly worded, is obvious in nature and not hidden in small print, and it excuses ordinary negligence and not gross, wanton, or intentional acts, it will hold up in court. Even if conditions are met, it will not hold up if a parent signs for a minor, or if the minor signs it. (Wolohan, 2002; Appenzeller 1998, pp. 63–65). See Table 9.1.

Do exculpatory contracts hold up in court? It depends on how well they are written and in what state they are processed. Each state law is different. To one degree or another, it is reported that waivers are effective in about 45 states (Cotton, 2000). Yasser and others summarize the tug-of-war of waivers as follows:

> Those cases that uphold enforceability of exculpatory agreements: *Kotary v. Spencer Speedway, Inc.,* 341 N.Y.S. 2d 45 (1973, spectator in the infield); *Lee v. Allied Sports Assocs., Inc.,* 209 N.E.2d 329 (Mass. 1965, spectator in pits); *Winterstein v. Wilson,* 293 A 2d 821 (1972, driver injured when racer struck object on the track). Those cases that do not uphold enforceability of exculpatory agreements: *Wade v. Watson,* 527 F. Supp. 1049 (N.D. Ga. 1981, release may not as a matter of law apply to gross negligence); *Santangelo v. City of New York,* 66 A.D. 2d 880, 411 N.Y.S.2d 666 (1978, minor not bound by release signed by father in connection with ice hockey clinic); *Scheff v. Homestretch, Inc.,* 60 Ill. App. 3d 424, 377 N.E.2d 305 (1978, release not effective to eliminate potential dram shop liability). It should also be noted that waivers and releases are often used to insulate the owner from liability to participants as well as to spectators. Here, too, the results are mixed. (Yasser, et al., 2000, p. 728).

Recently reported cases further illustrate the unpredictable outcome of defenses based on releases. In *Skotak v. Vic Tanny International,*

Table 9.1 Guidelines for Writing Exculpatory Agreements

- Involve an attorney. Don't use a universal "boilerplate" form.
- Individualize the form for each specific activity.
- Make the waiver itself and specific exculpatory language conspicuous in bold, uppercase, or underlined, print.
- The signature space should be on the same page as the exculpatory language. If the participant is a minor, make space for the signature of the guardian or parent. Provide spaces for witnesses and the date.
- Make the language clear, straightforward, easily understood, and suitable as a stand-alone document.
- Specify all parties who are intended to be protected by the waiver.
- Ensure that the title is descriptive as to a waiver, release from liability, or an indemnity agreement.
- Use language that will broaden the interpretation of what injuries are intended to be covered.
- Include language to make it clear that the waiver is intended to protect against negligence of the provider by referring specifically to "negligence."
- Include reference to loss or damage of property as well as to liability for personal injury.
- Outline to the signer the inherent risks of the activity, but distinguish clearly between the inherent risks of the activity and those risks presented by negligence; include an affirmation of voluntary participation.
- Insert a severability clause (a clause declaring that if any part of the waiver is deemed void, this will have no effect on the remainder of the waiver) with the waiver.
- Insert a statement by which the signer affirms having read the agreement.
- State the duration of the waiver.
- Include an indemnification clause (the signer agrees to indemnify, reimburse, hold harmless, or save harmless) (Sawyer, 2002; Cotton, 2000).

---

513 N.W. 2d 428, 1994, a club was protected by a signed release even though it did not include a provision releasing the facility for its own "negligence." The court of appeals reported that the release did include "all claims," and the word "all" leaves no room for exceptions (Herbert, 2000a). In the case of *Universal Gym Equipment v. Vic Tanny International*, 526 N.W. 2d 5, 207, 1994, the court determined that despite a release signed by the member, the club could be liable for gross negligence due to an action filed by the equipment manufacturer (Herbert, 2000b).

The case of *Feeney v. Manhattan Sports Club, Inc.*, 642 N.Y.S. 2d 674, Supreme Court of New York, Appellate Division, First Department, 1996, illustrates the importance of membership agreements. "When the plaintiff began using the facility, he was assigned a personal trainer. He asked his trainer whether his use of free weights would reinjure his shoulder, and was advised that 'he would have no problem.' However, he later suffered a shoulder injury while lifting weights." (Herbert, 2000d, p. 60). Because the membership agreement stated that employees were not quali-

fied to diagnose, examine, or treat any medical condition, and admonished members to see a physician before using the facility, upon appeal, the court found for the club. (Herbert, 2000d).

In the case of *Sanchez v. Bally's Total Fitness Corporation*, Court of Appeals of California, Second Appellate District Division Four, 79 Cal. Rptr. 2d 902, November, 1998, the court found that the release and assumption of risk provision document that the plaintiff signed was clear, explicit, and comprehensible, and therefore held in favor of the corporation. The plaintiff had slipped when walking across an aerobic slide mat and injured her wrist (Sawyer, 2001a).

Parental Consent Forms
A form that plainly describes the activity or field trip and solicits the needed information serves the purpose better than one drafted with complex legal terms. Probably at least two forms are needed to cover the usual interscholastic team membership, and another for special field trips. The form should communicate the care and safety of the activity, but also acknowledge the danger.

In *Risk Management in Sport,* edited by Herb Appenzeller, it is stated, "Risk warning is essential to reducing injury risk. Athletes are key participants in the prevention process but must possess the appropriate knowledge for doing so. Warning of the risk of injuries, particularly the most serious types, lays the foundation for teaching athletes how to prevent unnecessary harm" (1998, p. 50).

The following items of information should be obtained: (1) permission to participate, along with a simple honest statement of the danger or risk; (2) the medical insurance company and member number; (3) telephone numbers of parents or guardians at home and at work, along with an alternative number of someone who would be likely to know their whereabouts if they cannot be located at regular numbers; (4) the name of the family physician with work and home telephone numbers; (5) a list of special conditions or medications; and (6) permission for the student to be given emergency medical treatment in the event of an injury. Parents or guardians of team members should meet at the beginning of each season to complete the form and to hear the teacher or coach explain its purpose and answer questions. A notary public should be there to legally verify signatures. If a player requires emergency treatment while on a road trip, notarized signatures will clear the way for prompt and unquestioned treatment.

The question of whether a physician can treat an athlete is called *informed consent.* A physician who treats without the consent of parent or guardian might be charged with assault and battery. For example, a girl 17 years of age caught her finger in a door; without surgery, she was in danger of losing it. Her parents were not available to approve the surgery, but the girl consented. She sued, and the Kansas State Supreme Court rejected her case on the grounds that she was close to legal age and knowingly consented to the operation. In a similar situation, an underage athlete fractured an arm during volleyball practice. The girl's parents were away on a trip, and the local hospital refused to treat the fracture until her parents could be tracked down. The physician's statement was that a fracture was not an emergency of sufficient degree to justify nonconsent treatment.

For field trips, the permission form must specify the precise destination of trip, the route to be traveled, and the estimated time and exact location of return. Many field trips end late at night, so the drop-off location is very important. Many times people will be waiting alone for the students to return, and this can be dangerous. Never leave the return location until the last student leaves. Plan very accurately to return at the estimated time. Returning too early will lead to discipline problems while students lounge around waiting to be picked up, and a late return will cause great concern to parents. If, because of an emergency, the return will be delayed by more than a short time, stop enroute and telephone that information to someone who will notify the appropriate people.

■ SPORTS MEDICINE

The growing field of sports medicine has generated improvements in preventing injuries, treating ailments, and improving training and conditioning procedures. Physicians in greater numbers each year have developed special competencies in sports medicine, and through the certification standards of the National Athletic Trainers Association (NATA), the quality and quantity of athletic trainers is improving. Although more high schools have athletic trainers on their staffs, the numbers are still inadequate. Many authorities believe that secondary schools should be required to employ NATA-approved athletic trainers, even if only part-time. It has been reported that the injury rate for programs with athletic trainers is about half of those for which the coaches are responsible.

Athletic Trainers and Education of Teachers and Coaches

In its efforts to improve the emergency care athletes receive, the NCAA's 1997–1998 *Sports Medicine Handbook* stated,

> Each scheduled practice or contest of an institution-sponsored intercollegiate athletic event, as well as out-of-season practices and skills sessions, should include the following: (a) The presence of a

person qualified and delegated to render emergency care to a stricken participant; (b) The presence of or planned access to a physician for prompt medical evaluation of the situation, when warranted; . . . and (f) Certification in CPR, first aid, and prevention of disease" ("NCAA Ups Coverage Requirements of Sport Practices," 1997; Rochman, 1997).

It is absolutely vital that every physical education major program include courses in first aid, cardiopulmonary resuscitation, and the care and prevention of athletic injuries. In a further refinement of the sports medicine field, there are now programs for women's sport medicine at the Hospital for Special Surgery in New York and at Duke University. ("Duke Launches," 2002). Because many coaches in interscholastic athletics will not be trained professionally in physical education and thus are not likely to be competent in first aid, administrators must arrange in-service training for them. When it comes to hazardous activities, the administrator must stand by the axiom, "If we can't do it safely, we won't do it!"

Physical Examinations

Correct medical practices in physical education and sport start with adequate health data and appraisals. This information must be used—not filed away. Even with the large numbers of students assigned to a typical physical education teacher, it takes but a short while to review the current health record of every student, keeping an eye out for impairments that necessitate adapted programs, or conditions that might require emergency action. Before athletic practice begins for the season, team members should have an appropriate physical examination, with a careful review of these results by the coach and, if possible, the trainer.

Both the American College of Sports Medicine (ACSM) and the American Heart Association call for screening participants prior to their participation in fitness activities. In spite of this, a fitness club did not require screening prior to a racquetball tournament. In the case of *Rutnik v. Colonie Center Club,* 672 N. Y.2d 451, 1998, a participant in the tournament collapsed and in spite of CPR that

was performed, he died. Surprisingly, the club was fortunate and won the case (Herbert, 2000c).

The duties and responsibilities of the team physician should be negotiated by the AD with the coordination of the athletic trainer, business manager, and legal counsel. The contract should stipulate that the physician is an independent contractor. Consider giving the team physician responsibility for arranging emergency coverage of both games and practices, with a written plan for emergencies; this plan should be tested. Arrangements should include providing preparticipation physical examinations, evaluating and treating all injured athletes, prescribing and supervising athletes during recovery, coordinating with the trainer when athletes can resume competition, providing recommendations as to practice and games in adverse weather, and making athletes and coaches aware of sound nutritional approaches and conditioning methods.

"While preparticipation physical exams must test the immediate health status of a student athlete, they can also include a complete overall assessment, with both a musculoskeletal and fitness component" (Bonci, 1992, p. 22). In *Stineman v. Fontbonne College,* a deaf softball player was hit in the eye, and, even though the college health service was across the street, she was sent to her room to rest and apply cold. Several days later, her vision blurred; she sought medical evaluation and was diagnosed as having traumatic hyphemoa. While normally this is treated with success, because of the time lapse, she lost vision. The court awarded her $800,000 in damages (Gray, 1993).

Other good medical practices include

- Using sound equipment, conditioning, and scientifically based teaching and coaching techniques.
- Administering proper first aid, but not offering treatment.
- Insisting on medical clearances for injured students or athletes prior to their return to class or practice.
- When an athlete is removed from a contest because of an injury, having a physician clear the student to return to action.

- Having a physician and specially trained first-aiders such as a rescue squad with a vehicle on hand that can be used as an ambulance at every contact sport event, or when large numbers of participants will be gathered.
- Ensuring that a means of emergency communication is present at practice fields and game sites.
- If student trainers are utilized, ensuring that they are trained *and* certified but work only under the supervision of a certified instructor.

An emerging sport risk management concern in sports medicine relates to asthma. There has been a substantial increase in asthma, and because it is so easily controlled, many asthma patients exercise and compete in sports. A recent asthma-related death of a university football player has heightened the need for administrators of sport programs to have specific action plans to handle an asthma emergency (Metz, 2002).

The case of *Kleinknect v. Gettysburg College* is important in determining what is reasonably foreseeable in medical emergencies in college sports. A 20-year-old student athlete with no history of severe medical problems, who had been recruited to play lacrosse, died of cardiac arrest at a nontraditional fall practice. His parents sued for wrongful death, claiming that the college breached its duty by failing to provide proper medical services. No trainers were present, neither coach was certified in CPR, and there was no emergency communication system from the field. The district court granted summary judgment for the defendant, stating that the college could not foresee such an event. The court of appeals, however, reversed this because the student was recruited to play lacrosse and was stricken while engaged in that activity; thus a jury should determine the question (Wong and Barr, 1993).

Accident Reporting

Teachers and coaches should view the accident report form as a protective device, a simple and quick method of gathering facts and witnesses when things are fresh in mind. Remember, cases frequently come to court years after the accident.

The statistical management of injuries and accidents in sport and physical education in each school should be a part of a coordinated district plan. As a part of the total risk management concept, the district should have standard operating procedures related to accident reporting including the following: a definition of a reportable accident; a system of reporting; one person in the district responsible for collecting and analyzing data; a person or committee to review, and when necessary, investigate accidents; and a follow-up, along with necessary administrative action for discipline, change of regulations or policies, or corrective equipment or facility action.

Our profession could learn valuable lessons about accident reports from the National Ski Patrol System's accident reporting procedures. Every injury is considered to be a potential negligence suit, and the report reflects this. If the skis were rented from the ski area, a separate form is completed about the skis' condition, and they are tested in the rental shop. (Why aren't football helmets tested by experts after a head injury?) The report is signed by the injured person. If available, witnesses are recorded; and, if the injury appears serious, photographs are taken of the accident scene.

In addition to the obvious requirements such as the date, time, exact location of the accident, and the full name of the injured person, the following important items should be included in the accident form:

- The nature and extent of injuries.
- A description of the accident from the teacher or coach.
- A description of the accident in the victim's own words.
- The victim's signature, indicating that his or her description is accurate.
- A description of the accident environment (for example, the floor, the field, the equipment, or the lighting).
- Witnesses with addresses, and if the injury is serious, their descriptions of the accident.
- The full name and address of the teacher or coach.

The form should be in duplicate, and its arrangement should be conducive to computer processing. It is suggested that the definition of a *reportable injury* be one that results in treatment by a physician. Experience has shown that if all accidents are considered reportable, some teachers or coaches report accidents that are insignificant, and others report almost none.

AIDS and Risk Management

The team physician should play a major role in helping an HIV-positive player decide whether to participate in physical activities. This should be based on the individual's health status. A participant who is asymptomatic and is without evidence of immunologic deficiencies should not be automatically prohibited from play. A review of the literature reveals no known occasion wherein HIV transmission has occurred in an athletic setting.

> "There is no evidence that exercise and training of moderate intensity is harmful to the health of HIV-infected individuals. No research data are available for looking at the effects of intense training and competition for the elite athlete with HIV. The administrative issues are of great importance. The identification of individuals with a blood-borne pathogen must remain confidential. Only those persons in whom the infected student chooses to confide have a right or need to know" (Appenzeller, 1998, p. 156).

BloodBorne Pathogens

In the changing nature of society, protecting athletes, teachers/coaches, or athletic trainers from diseases transmitted by bloodborne pathogens (germs) is now a necessity. The primary diseases readily transmitted through blood and body fluids are human immunodeficiency virus (HIV) and hepatitis B, C, and D. Also of concern is the transmission of herpes simplex virus. The employees who may be exposed to the pathogens must be provided immunization injections for hepatitis B. The first line of defense is for all who may be exposed to these diseases to use body substance isolation (formally called universal protection), which most frequently takes the form of wearing protective gloves. Also important is the management of any blood on participants, clothing, or the ground. Biohazard bags should be readily available at all practices and contests (Appenzeller, 1998, pp. 153–158).

The case of *Silver v. Levittown Union Free School District* illustrates that while the transmission of these diseases through contact in sport is very rare, it is possible. Silver was allegedly directed to wrestle with a former wrestler (Clover), who was visiting practice and who allegedly had blisters and rashes on his head and face. Silver contracted herpes and sued. The case ended up in the New York Supreme Court, which upheld the appellate court in favor of Silver (Sawyer, 2001e).

In 1992 the standards in *Occupational Exposure to Bloodborne Pathogens* by the Occupational Safety and Health Administration (OSHA) became effective. This prescribes duties that affect risk management in first aid rooms, training rooms, and on-site first aid in such areas as ski slopes, swimming pools, and playfields and courts. How do you think this could affect the equipment room? OSHA has a variety of requirements regarding exposure to bloodborne pathogens (germs). One of the most important to sport administrators is the requirement to adopt and employ a hazard communication plan if any units would be expected to render emergency care.

▉ SAFETY

There's an old saying that "if accidents gave warnings, there wouldn't be any." A sound safety program is based on almost everything covered in this text, from the quality of instruction and programs to the facilities and equipment purchased. Although there are many reasons why lawsuits are detrimental, the most important reason is that they usually result only when a student is injured. The safety programs are vital cogs in the total risk management machine.

Sport and Safety

Throughout the history of sport there have been periods where violence or injury have caused athletics to be banned or severely limited. Because of the number of deaths, football was saved from ex-

Table 9.2 Standard Health Operating Procedures for Football	
1. Preseason conditioning must be emphasized, especially for participants who have been working or living in air-conditioned areas. 2. No students will be allowed to practice until the physical examination is completed. 3. No contact will be allowed until after five days of organized team practices. 4. The uniform for the first five days of practices will be shorts and T-shirts with helmet. 5. When there are two practices a day, the first practice must end by 10 A.M. and the second must not begin until after 4:30 P.M. During the first two weeks, night practices are encouraged. 6. Players experiencing muscle cramps, general weakness, or dizziness will be removed from practice or games and may not return until they are evaluated by a physician. 7. Coaches must know the symptoms of heat illness along with first-aid procedures. 8. No practice may continue for more than one hour without a water break.	9. No practice may last more than two hours. 10. Practice games may not be held until after the end of the second week of practice. 11. No player absent from school for health reasons on the day of a contest shall be allowed to suit up for the game. 12. No player removed from the contest because of injuries may return to the game without a physician's approval. 13. At game time, the home coach will ascertain that a physician is present, a stretcher is near each bench, and an ambulance is in place. The principal of the home school will decide whether to delay the game if the ambulance or physician is not present. 14. The physician will check with both coaches in the dressing rooms after the games. 15. Coaches will not leave the dressing room area until the last player leaves.

tinction at one time only by presidential intervention. If sport is to hold the high sociocultural place it now maintains, administrators must insist that injuries be controlled. (See Table 9.2).

Two cases illustrate the seriousness of failing to be cautious. After playing several football games with an injured neck, Marc Buoniconti fractured his neck and was paralyzed. In another case, after being on medication Hank Gathers died from heart failure during a basketball game, which resulted in several suits (Yasser, McCurdy, and Goplerud, 1997).

The facts show that sport is a high-risk program. Generally, about half of all athletes are injured sooner or later, about 10 percent seriously. In the past, the average has been 18 deaths each season. An eight-year study showed that there were 105 deaths in sport in children from 5 to 14 years of age. The results indicated that two-thirds of the deaths were from injury from impact with a secondary object such as a baseball or puck.

Sport injuries are costly, both directly and indirectly. Direct costs are those paid by the in-jured player, the athlete's family, or a third party (such as an insurance company) to cover such services as the hospital and doctor's or dentist's bills. Also included in direct costs are funds for research and training for sport injury detection, treatment, prevention, and related facilities and equipment. Indirect costs are those that occur because of the injury, but are not directly associated. In college programs, these injuries could adversely affect gate receipts, alumni donations, future recruiting, and even television contracts.

April has been designated National Youth Sports Injury Prevention month. According to the National Youth Sports Foundation for the Prevention of Athletic Injuries, sport injuries occur because of inadequate preparticipation exams, improper or poorly fitted equipment and inadequate facilities, grouping by age instead of size, inadequate training, lack of safety equipment, and fatigue. The following sport injury surveillance strategies have been recommended. First, develop a uniform system. Coordinate data from

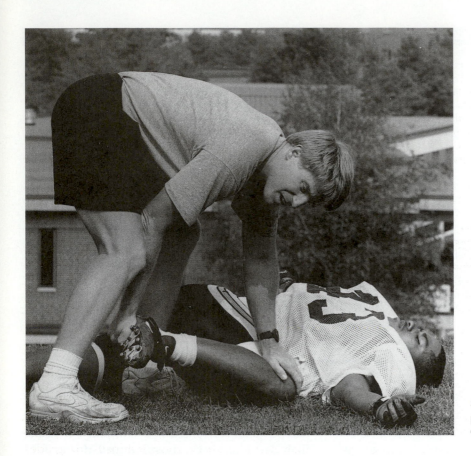

Stretching is a must for injury prevention.
Courtesy of Watauga Democrat

insurance firms, hospitals, athletic organizations, and records generated from litigation. Identify common injuries characteristic of individual sports. Analyze injury data as they relate to external factors such as equipment and rules, and develop effective interventions. For more information, contact the National Youth Sports Injury Prevention Month, NYSFPAI, 10 Meredith Circle, Needham, MA 02191; and NIAM Information Clearinghouse, Box AMS, 9000 Rockville Pike, Bethesda, MD 20892.

A strategic plan to control accidents should center on several areas. To control the *physical environment,* have safely designed and maintained facilities and equipment, including safe playing surfaces and lighting. Ensure that the *program* is appropriate for the age and skill level of the participants. Control the *leadership* involved to ensure

that proper coaching techniques and supervision are provided. (See-Table 9.3). Last, the *participants* must be controlled as to preactivity (approval forms, insurance, physical examinations, conditioning) and during the activity season by monitoring continuing conditioning, injury treatment, and training codes.

Sport and physical education administrators should think of when accidents are most likely to occur, and then draft plans to cover that period. For example, one situation that we all know is chaotic and dangerous is when inclement weather forces all classes or teams inside. Develop a plan that addresses this so that every instructor or coach knows ahead of time what space will be available, and for how long. Be sure to address all safety concerns in the plan (Borkowski, 1997).

Table 9.3 Standard Operating Procedures for Field Trips to Swimming Areas	
1. Permission for such trips must be secured from the principal. 2. Advance arrangements must be made to ensure that authorities in the area to be visited know the number and age range of the students involved. These authorities must have sufficient lifeguards for the group, or arrangements must be made to take the necessary number of qualified lifeguards along. 3. Parental approval forms must be completed. Only children who have passed at least the beginning swimming test may go on such trips. 4. Each such group must be under the leadership of a physical education teacher or sport supervisor,	who may be assisted, if necessary. Each person will have clearly assigned duties. 5. At a minimum, a modified "buddy system" will be followed. Children will be paired, and they will be clearly instructed that they must stay together in or out of the water. Each one will be responsible for the other. 6. Before leaving the bus, the person in charge will clearly describe the swimming area's hazards and emphasize the necessity for safety. At this time, students will be informed when the first "person count" will be taken and what kind of a signal will be given to initiate it.

As a result of research on football injuries, the following recommendations have been made:

1. Medical examinations and medical history should be taken before allowing an athlete to participate in football.

2. All participants should be properly conditioned, with special attention given to neck strengthening.

3. A physician should be present at all games and practices (if this is not possible for practices, arrange for emergency coverage).

4. All football personnel should understand the problems and emergency care for heat-associated illness.

5. Each school should have an athletic trainer.

6. Cooperation and communication between coaches, trainers, physicians, manufacturers, and administrators should be maintained.

7. Administrative regulations, game rules, and the conduct of the game officials should be strictly enforced.

8. Renewed emphasis should be given to employing athletic personnel who have good professional education, and to providing good equipment and facilities.

9. Football safety research should continue.

10. Proper fundamentals of blocking and tackling should be emphasized.

11. Rules of the game should be strictly enforced.

Physical Education and Safety

In some ways, the need for an aggressive safety program in physical education is greater than for athletics. A major reason for this difference is that students are, for the most part, required to participate. Second, they must compete for grades. Third, physical education students vary enormously in their abilities. Fourth, these students will have, on the average, much lower motor ability, endurance, and strength, all of which will increase the chances for injuries.

To provide the appropriate safety program for physical education, safety must be emphasized from the top. The superintendent and the principal (or the equivalent in higher education) must insist that safety be given a high priority. Most important, the chairperson of the department must believe that a strong safety program is vital. The safety emphasis must permeate the entire program, including curriculum planning, staff evaluations, the design and maintenance of facilities, and the purchase and maintenance of equipment. Inspections must be made every week; problems should be solved immediately. The same accident reporting system used in the remainder of the system should be followed.

Safely constructed and properly supervised play areas are essential.
Photo courtesy of Gary Hemsoth, Watauga Democrat.

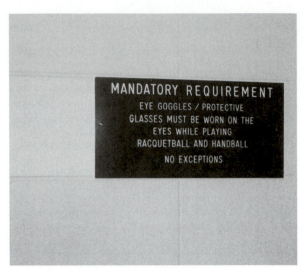

Signs must be precise.
Photo by L. E. Horine.

Gymnastics requires great control and evaluation. Class size, appropriate and progressive instruction, excellently maintained equipment, and a "ready" emergency care plan are all necessary. In recognition of these needs, the U.S. Gymnastics Safety Association has published the *Gymnastics Safety Manual*. One of the association's most important goals is to certify all gymnastics instructors, just as water safety instructors are certified. Younger children must be taught safety procedures before beginning gymnastics. The natural reaction of young children to gymnastics equipment is exuberance and experimentation, which must be safely controlled.

Great care must be taken with the trampoline. The standards produced by organizations such as the U.S. Gymnastics Safety Association or AAH-

PERD must be followed. In general, use of the trampoline requires the following precautions:

1. The activity should be elective.
2. An instructor who has professional preparation in teaching trampolining should supervise.
3. Spotters should be trained and in position.
4. The somersault should not be permitted in regular classes; in advanced classes it should be allowed only from feet-to-feet and with a safety belt.
5. The trampoline should be locked when not in use.
6. It should be regularly inspected and maintained.
7. Emergency care plans should be known and understood.
8. Statistics on its use and the number of accidents should be maintained.

Another facility area that requires constant risk management attention is the swimming pool. There have been numerous successful suits resulting from improper construction, number and placement of lifeguards, lack of depth and other warning signage, improper depth and slope configuration of the diving well, and the height of starting blocks related to the depth of the water. Recent changes have mandated a minimum of four feet of depth for the use of the standard 18-inch starting blocks (Popke, 2002). Two recent cases involve supervision and security. Two youth trespassers drowned in an Old Dominion University pool in a strange set of circumstances. Damaging to the university position was that there appeared to be evidence that officials were aware that unqualified youth had been breaking into the pool (Cohen, 2002). In the case of *Barnett v. The Zion Park District,* 665 N.E. 2d 808, 1996, a youngster slipped near a diving well, hit his head on a board, and fell into the water. Lifeguards were apparently alerted to this accident, but had not seen it and did not respond. A patron extricated the boy, who later died, from the water. The Illinois Supreme Court upheld the appellate court's ruling of governmental immunity for the district. Had this been a private swimming pool, the result would have likely been different (Sawyer, 2001d).

In Ohio, a city attempted to claim immunity, but the Supreme Court of Ohio reversed the lower courts and remanded the case back to the trial court. In the case, *Cater v. City of Cleveland,* 697 N.E. 2d 610, August 18, 1998, a boy 12 years of age died from complications of a near drowning at a municipal pool. Two of the four lifeguards were away at lunch, and employees couldn't dial 911 because they didn't know that they had to dial a 9 for an outside line (Sawyer, 2001b).

Safety Standards for Sport Equipment
The primary agency establishing equipment standards for sport is the American Society for Testing and Materials (ASTM), a nonprofit organization of manufacturers, consumers, and technical experts. Of the 130 technical committees of ASTM, F-8, the National Operating Committee on Standards for Athletic Equipment (NOCSAE), is of most concern to sport.

A major effort of the NOCSAE has been directed toward helmets and face guards for football, baseball, and hockey. Of these, the work associated with football helmets has been most noted. In 1977 helmet guidelines were revised to specify standards for reconditioning helmets, which in turn led to the formation of a 27-member National Athletic Equipment Reconditioners

Association. The advent of testing software has increased the accuracy and consistency of the testing process. "The reconditioning process entails complete examination of every helmet component, as well as the shell itself. Worn components are easily replaced, but shells with visible cracks (typically near a helmet's hardware, or at its base after being subject to the undue stress of a player sitting on it or excessive gouging (common on the helmets of lineman) must be retired" (Steinbach, 2002, p. 14). Since most manufacturers void warranties if the helmet is not reconditioned in two years, a good plan is for half of all old helmets to be reconditioned each year. While reconditioning firms have multimillion-dollar insurance policies, this does not free the schools from liability.

The risk management concerns with helmets go further than reconditioning. Recent deaths in skiing and pole vaulting have caused a serious debate on whether wearing helmets should be mandated in many other areas of sport. It is a complex question (Kahl, 2002).

In 1981 the standards expanded to recommend that the certification seal on the outside of the helmet and chin strap be modified to include the wording "See Warning Inside." The technical testing of helmets used since 1981 seems to justify little change in helmet construction. The major cause of injury is the compression or flexion loading of the top of the helmet, especially if in combination. The various helmet crown designs have had little effect on this problem. The committee has studied the possibility of transferring the compression loads from the helmet to the shoulder pads or the flexion loads from the face guard to the chest pads.

Safety Inspections
Regular inspections are necessary. To have all facilities inspected each week, however, the administrator must delegate much of this duty to others. Written records in simple checklist form are recommended. At one large junior high school, a very active student safety council made inspections under the principal's supervision. Standard inspection forms should be developed for each special area, such as the weight room and stadiums.

Critical Thinking

A Crisis in the Media

At a medium-size university most of the football players lived in one dormitory. From time to time they held rousing parties. A 19-year-old woman stated she attended such a party with her football player boyfriend and consumed six mixed drinks. The woman stated she could not remember parts of what happened that night, but the next day she reported to the campus police that six students at the party had taken turns raping her. She did not press criminal charges with the local police. The university held a hearing within its usual student judiciary process and found the six football players guilty of lewd, indecent, obscene conduct, but not guilty of rape. The university put all except the boyfriend on various terms of probation and suspension.

The football players employed an attorney and filed civil suits against the woman for slander that caused them ridicule, public hatred, contempt, embarrassment, and disgrace. The woman countersued. Through an independent mediator, these two suits were settled out of court. The university was sued by the football players for violating their civil rights by listing their names in media releases. The university stated that the players had included the records of the student judiciary hearing with the suit, which was illegal because they were confidential. The trial court agreed with the university. The players appealed.

Five of the six players and the woman left the university. Local and regional media covered the story in great detail. Various faculty and student groups publicly voiced their dissatisfaction with the way events were handled. The students' and administrator's lives were changed in negative ways ("Woman Settles out of Court," 1998).

1. In hindsight, what do you think the athletic department might have done differently?
2. Was controlling the behavior of the students the responsibility of the athletic department or of the officials of the dormitory organization?
3. If there had been a crisis management plan in place, would things have been handled differently?
4. A review committee recommended that the continuation of coaches' contracts be dependent on their athletes' not being involved in any criminal behavior. What is your opinion of this recommendation? What are the dangers?

The need for regular maintenance and firm rules was brought home in the case *Claveloux v. Downtown Racquet Club Association,* 1997. An experienced 57-year-old racquetball player was paralyzed from an accident of slipping on a court. The day before he and another player had slipped in another court. The trial court would not allow the evidence of the prior slips, but the appellate court did, even if the floors were not slippery for the same reasons (Herbert, 1997b).

Recommended guidelines are as follows:

- Put the safety and welfare of the participants first. In the excitement of competition, it is easy to get caught up in the desire to win. Emphasize long-term goals, values, and beliefs.

- Warn participants about the dangers and inherent risks of the activity. Depending on the age and experience of the athlete, for catastrophic or life-threatening situations, these warnings must be repetitive, not just before the first practice.

- Teach proper technique and correct skills. A coach in North Carolina was successfully sued when he encouraged his players to crash into catchers at home plate, and one was seriously hurt doing so.

- Explain and demonstrate safety rules. Emphasize the demonstration: youth learn by seeing and doing, not by listening to verbiage.
- Check facilities and equipment regularly. Don't expect athletes to report deficiencies or problems—they just want to play. This is the job for the leaders.
- Utilize appropriate warning and behavior signage. See further information in Chapter 10.
- Establish appropriate supervision. The younger the participants and the more complex or dangerous the activity, the greater the level the supervision must be. If the participant is disabled, the supervision must also be increased. In the case of *Miami v. Cisneros*, 1995, a 10-year-old mentally retarded athlete was killed in a traffic accident walking to a practice site with 10 others. The court found that one coach was not sufficient for supervising such a group and awarded the family $65,000 (Appenzeller, 1998, p. 133).
- Develop and practice an emergency plan. An interesting way to develop such a plan is to have the staff discuss "what if" situations. For example, what if a sudden lightning strike occurs during football practice and because of wet ground, five players are knocked unconscious? What do we do, and who does what?
- With children, be prepared for the unexpected. Anticipate possible problems and take action to mitigate them (Appenzeller, 1998, pp. 133–135).

Exercises

1. In risk management as it relates to activities, an important concept is the difference between perceived danger and real danger. Select a common physical activity that represents each of these two types of dangers.
2. Assume that you are a middle school soccer coach. Draft a risk management plan for your sport.
3. Assume that you are the athletic director of a large high school. A female athlete has a disfiguring scar on her face from a softball injury. You believe that the evidence will show clearly that the school and coaches were not negligent. However, the insurance company is leaning toward an out-of-court settlement. Although this settlement will not result in direct costs for the school, the coaches, or yourself, list the adverse effects or the indirect costs of an out-of-court settlement.
4. Some legal authorities state that liability releases may not hold up in court. If this assessment is accurate, are the releases still recommended?
5. Design an accident report form for use in junior high school physical education programs.
6. A school safety committee composed of mostly students may be extremely useful on the middle school level. List the duties that might be assigned such a group.
7. You are a football coach at a high school. One of your better players insists on spear tackling. What would be your strategy for correcting the situation? What specific arguments could you use, particularly when he states that no catastrophic injury will ever happen to him?

References

Appenzeller, H. ed. (1998). Risk management in sport, issues and strategies. Durham, NC: Carolina Academic Press.

Bonci, C. (1992, July). Anatomy of a physical. *Athletic Business* 16, pp. 22–30.

Borkowski, R. P. (1996, October/November). Focusing on football. *Athletic Management* 8, p. 18.

Borkowski, R. P. (1997, August/September). Insiders advice. *Athletic Management* 9, pp. 16–17.

Borkowski, R. P. (2000, June/July). Fair warning. *Athletic Management* XII, pp. 20–21.

Borkowski, R. P. (2002, Feb./Mar.). Who needs wiper blades? *Athletic Management* XIV, pp. 20–23.

Buisman, K. (1992, July). Risk management. *Athletic Management* 4, pp. 10–16.

Bynum, M. (2002, March). Shock wave. *Athletic Business* 26, pp. 55–59.

Call, M. D. (1993, March). How to keep cool in a news crisis. *Cleaning Management Institute* N-1.

Cohen, A. (2002, April). The deep end of the pool. *Athletic Business* 26, p. 9.

Colley, J. A. (1998, January). Risky business: Innovative at-risk youth programming. *Journal of Physical Education, Recreation and Dance* 69, pp. 39–43.

Cotton, D. J. (1993, February). Risk management: A tool for reducing exposure to legal liability. *Journal of Physical Education, Recreation and Dance* 64, pp. 58–61.

Cotton, D. J. (2000, March). Liability waivers. *Fitness Management* 16, pp. 50–54.

Diles, D. L. (1996, August/September). Expecting the unexpected. *Athletic Management* 8, pp. 36–38.

Duke launches. (2002, April, May). *Athletic Management* 14, p. 10.

Farmer, P. J.; Mulrooney, A. L.; and Ammon, R. (1996). *Sport facility planning and management.* Morgantown, WV: Fitness Information Technologies.

Frank, W. (1997, July). Key to crisis management. *Communication World* 14, pp. 34–35.

Gray, G. R. (1993, February). Providing adequate medical care to program participants. *Journal of Physical Education, Recreation and Dance* 64, pp. 56–57, 65.

Herbert, D. L. (1997a, September). Managing risk. *Fitness Management* 13, pp. 45–47.

Herbert, D. L. (1997b, December). Slippery floors leads to trials. *Fitness Management* 13, p. 42.

Herbert, D. L. (1998, January). Survey finds neglect of standards. *Fitness Management* 14, p. 44.

Herbert, D. L. (2000a, January). Clubs protected from wrongful death suit. *Fitness Management* 16, p. 28.

Herbert, D. L. (2000b, February). Clubs may be liable despite release. *Fitness Management* 16, p. 56.

Herbert, D. L. (2000c, April). Club wins case despite failure to screen tournament participant. *Fitness Management* 16, p. 63.

Herbert, D. L. (2000d, May). Personal trainer's advice leads to lawsuit. *Fitness Management* 16, p. 60.

Hessert, K. (1997, April/May). Vigilant thinking. *Athletic Management* 9, pp. 10–11.

Horine, L. (1986, August). Are you prepared for a real-life crisis? *Athletic Business* 10, pp. 72–74.

Horine, L. (1987). Crisis management. In Bronzon, R. T., and Stotlar, D. K. (eds.), *Public relations and promotions in sport.* Daphne, AL: U.S. Sports Academy.

Irvine, R. B. (1997, July). What is a crisis, anyway? *Communicating World* 14, pp. 36–42.

Kahl, R. (2002, May). The helmet issue. *Ski Patrol Magazine* 41, pp. 48–50.

Kramer, L. (1997/1998, December/January). Crisis planning's most important element: The drill. *Communicating World* 15, pp. 27–30.

Metz, G. (2002, June/July). Breathing easy. *Athletic Management* 14, pp. 43–46.

NCAA ups coverage requirements of sports practices (1997, October/November). *Athletic Management* 9, p. 9.

Neal, T. (1996, February/March). This is only a test! *Athletic Management* 8, pp. 50–53.

New proposal aims to reduce spring football practice injuries. (1997, October/November). *Athletic Management* 9, p. 10.

Nixon, H. L. (1993). Accepting the risks of pain and injury in sport: Mediated cultural influences on playing hurt. *Sociology of Sport Journal* 10, pp. 183–191.

Pittman, A. T. (1993, February). Safe transportation—a driving concern. *Journal of Physical Education, Recreation and Dance* 64, pp. 53–55.

Polanshek, K. (2002a, February). Insurance climate. *Athletics Administration* 37, p. 32.

Polanshek, K. (2002b, April). Insurance will survive. *Athletics Administration* 37, p. 48.

Polanshek, K. (2002c, June). Buyer beware. *Athletics Administration* 37, p. 59.

Popke, M. (2002, July). Deep trouble. *Athletic Business* 26, pp. 30–33.

Rochman, S. (1997, February/March). Coach on call. *Athletic Management* 9, pp. 49–53.

Sawyer, T. H. (2001a, January). Release of liability. *Journal of Physical Education, Recreation and Dance,* 72, pp. 11–13.

Sawyer, T. H. (2001b, March). Planning for emergencies in aquatics. *Journal of Physical Education, Recreation and Dance,* 72, pp. 12–13.

Sawyer, T. H. (2001c, April). Specator insurance and contest participants. *Journal of Physical Education, Recreation and Dance,* 72, pp. 9–10.

Sawyer, T. H. (2001d, September). Supervision: willful and wanton misconduct. *Journal of Physical Education, Recreation and Dance,* 72, pp. 9–11.

Sawyer, T. H. (2001e, Nov./Dec.). Negligent transmission of communicable disease. *Journal of Physical Education, Recreation and Dance,* 72, p. 8.

Sawyer, T. H. (2002, August). Release from liability. *Journal of Physical Education, Recreation and Dance,* 73, pp. 16, 17, 27.

Steinbach, P. (2002, January). Headgear overhaul. *Athletic Business* 26, p. 14.

U.S. Department of Labor. (1991). *All about OSHA (OSHA 2056).* Washington, D.C.: U.S. Government Printing Office.

Wolohan, J. T. (2002, May). The parent trap. *Athletic Business* 26, pp. 16–19.

Woman settles out of court. (1998, February 4). *Watauga Democrat,* 1–2.

Wong, G. M., and Barr, C. A. (1993, July). Practice and malpractice. *Athletic Business* 17, p. 16.

Yasser, R.; McCurdy, J. R.; and Goplerud, C. P. (1997). *Sports law.* Cincinnati: Anderson.

Yasser, R.; McCurdy, J. R.; Goplerud, C. P.; and Weston, M. A. (2000). *Sport Law, Cases and Materials* (4th ed.). Cincinnati, Ohio-Anderson.

Zirkel, P. A. (1997, April). Insurance liability: Don't make an error about omission. *Phi Delta Kappan* 78, pp. 658–659.

10

Facility and Equipment Planning, Designing, and Management in Physical Education and Sport

Management Thought

Never assume the obvious is true.

William Safire

Case Study: Sport Facility Design Bloopers

In a $19 million college facility, four locker rooms were designed so that they would all have both a dry hallway and swimming pool wet access. However, because of poor planning, the locker rooms did not have sufficient egress, and users were required to leave the pool area doors unlocked anytime the locker rooms were in use. Obviously, college locker rooms are open many hours of the day and night, whereas pools have very selective hours. How could people be restricted from entering the pool when it was closed?

In another college facility, the design called for a women's team locker room within the general women's locker room. The problem with this design was realized when the male coach for the women's basketball team had to walk through the women's locker room each time he met with his team in their team locker room. The women's volleyball and soccer teams also had male coaches. In addition, the men's team room was designed the same way, so that ultimately when a woman coaches a male team, she will have to pass through the men's locker room.

In a new college swimming pool design, the fixed starting blocks were installed at the shallow end, where the water was four feet deep, the exact NCAA minimum. If the contractor made a minute error on depth, or if the water level fell a fraction of an inch, the pool could not be used for competition. In the same pool, the lighting was designed to produce 60 foot-candles per square foot, which is the NCAA minimum. A meet could not be held if one light burned out. Also, the pool deck did not have any faucets, which are required for hosing down decks (LaRue, 1997).

Chapter Objectives

The reader should be able to

1. Show the steps necessary to identify a facility problem, assess the program and facility needs, and plan a solution.
2. Identify the major considerations involved in planning a facility, from establishing a committee to funding the project.
3. Identify the strengths and weaknesses of the three methods of sport facility project approaches.
4. Explain the special energy problems and opportunities associated with physical education and sport facilities.
5. Describe the site selection and primary planning needs associated with indoor, outdoor, and aquatic areas.
6. Become familiar with standards for sport facility surfaces, walls, ceilings, lighting, acoustics, seating, and climate control.
7. Enumerate the important factors in making a locker room functional, aesthetic, and efficiently maintained.
8. Compare natural grass to artificial turf.
9. Compare encapsulated structures to traditional facilities.

For a teacher, coach, or administrator, becoming involved in building a new facility is an awesome and immensely rewarding experience. The amount of money required to build is so enormous that most educators have difficulty comprehending the reality of the process. Yet one assumes the responsibility of judging what the public will want and need for many years. There is nothing quite as final as having a decision poured in steel and concrete. The rewards of the effort are to see dreams emerge in mortar and brick that are likely to outlive the builders. Nothing in the professional life of a sport manager can approach the need for planning, studying, thinking, and consulting that is necessary in the construction of a facility.

Although limited facilities for sport were built by many of the ancient civilizations, the Greeks were the first to build mammoth facilities dedicated to sport and entertainment. In 776 B.C. the first Olympic Games were held, with pageantry and spectacle that would rival today's major sporting events. The Greeks pioneered the U-shaped stadium. They built the Olympic Stadium in Athens in 331 B.C. and reconstructed it in A.D. 160 to hold 50,000 spectators. The Romans were the first to build stadiums using concrete and vault techniques. The largest was Circus Maximus, which was constructed in 46 B.C. and held 200,000 spectators (Farmer, Mulrooney, and Ammon, 1996).

■ NEEDS

A Problem

Most facility needs become known as a result of problems. Some of the problems that will alert the administrator include

- Not enough teaching stations to accommodate students.
- Insufficient practice space to handle existing teams.
- Injuries resulting from inadequate areas.
- Inability to host home meets, matches, or games.
- Inability to add new sports or activities because of the lack of appropriate space even though there is support and demand.
- Complaints from students, parents, members, or staff related to inadequate facilities.
- Escalating repair and maintenance bills.
- Consistent inability to accommodate all spectators.

Assessment

When it has been determined that the facility problems are real and that simply rescheduling or adjusting practice times will not solve the problem, the whole situation requires an in-depth needs assessment. The basic scientific problem-solving method can be applied.

Through a strategic assessment, the planning committee should follow a set of planning guidelines. The Council on Facilities and Equipment of the American Alliance for Health, Physical Education, Recreation, and Dance has recommended the following steps. Comply with the Americans with Disabilities Act (ADA). Develop an overall plan, which may be called a master plan, comprehensive plan, or case study. Use participatory planning with all groups associated with using the facility. Growing more important is the need to research all funding opportunities and possibilities. Develop a program statement for the architect, which may be called a building program or educational specifications. Use necessary planning professionals such as consultants (Sawyer, 1999, pp. 13–21).

The firm of Burt Hill Kosar Rittelmeann Associates uses a high-involvement, interactive system to achieve the comprehensive plan. This approach is called "discovery through viewpoint and diagram," or DVD. They solicit input from all interested groups and parties in a series of open hearings and discussions. They produce rough drawings first for further discussions, and then more complete schematic renditions that show traffic patterns relationships between spaces, efficiency of the project, and sketches of how the building may look; then they get more feedback. With further refinements from that information, they hold formal presentations to show all constituents what has developed along with schedules, building dimensions, and materials. The process is then put on hold until financing is settled (Kosar, 2002). This sort of process takes a great deal of time. One design firm reported that multisport complexes can take anywhere from 2 to 15 years to complete (Bynum, 2002b). "Each design firm will employ different strategies to collect input from the community. Open round-table discussions and interactive workshops are among the most common research tools" (Bynum, 2002b, p. 72).

Planning should be both macro and micro. *Macro planning* relates to the big picture, including demographic and marketing projections, the future of the educational program and how it impacts on sport, an audit of all sport facilities in the community, community attitudes toward education and sport, and the future socioeconomic variables of the community. *Micro planning* involves items with which the sport specialist will be more directly related, such as design, project construction method, budgets, environmental concerns, aesthetics, safety, utility, maintenance, security, equipment, contextualism (how the facility fits with other structures), and consultants (Horine, 1987).

Solution

From the needs assessment, information necessary to postulate various solutions will evolve. It may be that economics, growth patterns, or future changes in curriculum and sport show that construction is not justified. Let us assume that the data suggest that some kind of additional facilities may be necessary. The next step is to obtain authorization from higher authorities to formally investigate and plan for the additions. Nothing could scuttle an emerging facility faster than the president of the school or the superintendent of the district learning about such plans indirectly.

■ PLANNING FACILITIES

Planning Committee

When planning a sport facility, be creative and innovative—be the first of the new rather than the last of the old. New innovations in sport facilities will continue to evolve. These will range from miniaturization of electronic parts, to facilities needed for sports not now in existence, to the continual evolution of improved building materials. However, planners should be aware that utilizing the newest material could have a downside. If the material has not been used long enough to have a track record, it could be inferior. Also, if the

Not even synthetic playing fields last forever. Removal without damaging the pad is difficult.
Courtesy of Watauga Democrat.

material is new to an area, the contractors will never have applied it before, which might result in imperfect installation. In addition, in the highly competitive business of producing sport materials, such as synthetic flooring, firms may change a product for the sake of marketing rather than substantive improvement (Dilullo, 2002).

An extremely valuable aid in structuring early meetings is the use of checklists for various facilities. All persons involved in the project should be encouraged to add items to these checklists before they are utilized.

The structure of the planning committee—so vital to the success of the project—must be individualized to fit the specific situation. If the project approach will be design/build, or if the architect is very experienced in sport facilities, a smaller committee gives better results. This demands highly experienced persons representing the three elements of the project as follows: (1) the owner or user, (2) the designers and builders, and (3) the central business office or owners who are fiscally responsible for the project (Gimple, 1992).

For example, selecting a planning committee for a new high school gymnasium might include the following: the chair of the physical education department and/or the athletic director; the architect; someone from the office who is financially responsible for the project, such as the principal or business manager for the school system; someone representing maintenance, such as the school's chief custodian; a student athlete; and at least two teachers or coaches, both male and female, who are experts in the primary sports to be included in the facility. In addition, at several steps in the process, three specialists—in special education, safety, and education facility law—need to be brought in to review the plans (Horine, 1987, p. 25).

Planners and Consultants

Because no two projects are alike, no pat answer exists as to whether a planner or consultant should be employed. In part, this decision depends on the size and complexity of the project, the experience of the program specialist and institution business officials, and the type of contracting system followed. The design professionals might include an architect, a general or specific consultant, a design firm, or a construction manager. Experience emphatically points out that time spent in the selection process proves to be a good investment—consultants or architects who are following their own agenda rather than the needs of the committee, or who are either incompetent or inexperienced, will bear rotten fruit.

Two organizations offer helpful resources. The Facilities and Equipment Council of the American Alliance for Health, Physical Education, Recreation, and Dance at 1900 Association Drive, Reston, VA 22091, has printed a directory of architects, builders, and consultants for sport facilities. It can be obtained from AAHPERD Publication and Sales, P.O. Box 385, Oxon Hill, MD 20750-0385; 800-321-0789 (LaRue, 1997). You can also contact the Association for Sports and Leisure Facility Development and Management, Richmond Bridge House, 417-421, Richmond Road, Twickenham, Middlesex, TW1 2EX, England ("Getting Organized," 1993).

For every sport complex, a sport facility consultant should be employed. Frequently the cost will be minimal and involve the consultant meet-

One way to avoid surprises is not to build on a floodplain. This photo illustrates the effect of a flood on tennis courts built on low-lying ground.
Photo by L. E. Horine

ing with the planning committee during the preliminary stages and reviewing the blueprints, the schedule of construction, and the construction documents (LaRue, 1997).

> The number of specialists needed depends on the experience of the members of the committee, the size and complexity of the project, the project approach selected, and the philosophy of the leaders. Some people believe it impossible to complete a major facility without a construction manager or a consultant, while others think these two individuals are a waste of money. If the project approach is the design/build system, the architect and equivalent to a construction manager will be included in the basic contract (Horine, 1987, p. 25).

Selection of the design/build firm, or the architects and consultants, requires a series of steps similar to those followed in selecting a new chief executive officer:

1. Define needs—geographical location, type of building, budget, schedule, and unusual requirements.

2. Identify five or six available professionals.

3. Prepare and send each firm a request for proposal, asking for three references from similar projects.

4. Set up interviews for the best three firms and notify each they will be expected to address

similar project experience, capacity to handle project, cost and schedule, firm's track record, personnel, in-house resources, and fee structure.

5. Design a standard rating instrument, using a uniform system of evaluation.

6. Rate the firms on each category by each person on the team, and then compute the total scores.

The selection of the firm should not necessarily be based on volume or size of the firm. A very busy firm may present problems, and sometimes a small specialized firm can give more attention to your project. The primary consideration must be the firm's reputation.

> *Business's Athletic Business's* online buyers' guide currently lists 319 architecture firms and 129 sports facility consultants/specialists. Along with the jump in quantity has come a corresponding leap in quality—or, more accurately, in architects' understanding of the needs of sports facility owners and users. These buildings look better, but more important, they function better than the facilities of 25 years ago (Cohen, 2002b).

Avoid Surprises

Before purchasing land, ensure that there are no noise limitations or other building restrictions that might cause problems in the future. Be sure that utilities, sewer capacity, and other basic services are sufficient. Is there adequate space for parking development? Confidentially arrange for the land purchase after the carefully selected surveyor has completed that task.

Insist on appropriate soil sampling prior to developing construction details. As the bids are developed, also make sure that the general contractor and all subcontractors are sufficiently bonded. Build penalties into the contract for late completion of work, but recognize that this could cause higher bids as contractors protect themselves.

Plan to accomplish an environmental impact study whether it is required by law or not. Educational agencies should set an example. Will the facility change vehicular patterns and create traffic problems? Will it create any problems in watershed, noise, wind patterns, or field of vision interferences? Will it set an example for aesthetics and energy conservation?

Project Approaches

There are three main approaches to controlling the entire fiscal process of construction: lump sum bidding, the construction management system, and the design/build method. (See Figure 10.1.) Traditionally, governmental institutions have followed the *lump sum bidding* approach. In this method, after the institution has formal approval for a project, an architect or design firm creates schematic drawings of the facility for the owner or user to approve. Once approved, working drawings are produced and competitive bids are received. If the bids are within approved limits, the project is awarded to the lowest bidder. If the bids are too high, very complex maneuvers ensue. The choices for the owner are to delay the project while more funds are raised, which will raise costs because of inflation; negotiate with the low bidder by eliminating extras and hope for cost reductions; ask the architect to redesign, which again will raise costs; or abandon the project.

Construction management (CM) is achieved by paying the general contractor to be part of the planning team right from the start. This manager, now working for the builder, assumes the general leadership and supervision of the whole project.

The construction manager will put all areas out for bid and coordinate their work. By being a member of the building team, the goals and interests of the builders are represented at every stage. However, this service will cost an additional amount of about five percent of the cost of the project, and the construction manager doesn't really have full control over the subcontractors. Some districts report overall savings of three percent with this method (DuBray, 1993).

The third method of building the new facility is called *a design/build package.* In this system, one firm handles the entire process of design and construction. The dangers are real, but the potential benefits are enormous. Because one firm takes all responsibility for the project, few safeguards exist to protect the owner except the professional integrity of the firm. Obviously, it is absolutely essential that the firm be investigated and have strong recommendations from previous clients. In addition to being professionally competent, the firm must have the financial strength to survive unforeseen problems such as acts of God or labor strife. At its best, however, the design/build method is highly efficient because a line manager may attack building problems on all fronts. A variation of design/build is called *fast tracking.* It is used in large projects in which contracts are let incrementally or sequentially so that the construction time may be reduced.

Decision Making in the Planning Process

The decision-making process in facility construction can be summarized in five steps: (1) determine that an addition is needed, (2) understand program needs, (3) determine space needed, (4) find out what others are doing, and (5) develop a master plan.

At the beginning of the chapter, it was recommended that the need for the facility be established through a self-study needs assessment. Assuming the need existed, formal planning approval was obtained from higher authorities and the planning committee was established. This committee would then address the second step of the decision-making process—understanding program needs. A facility planning axiom is that *program dictates facilities.*

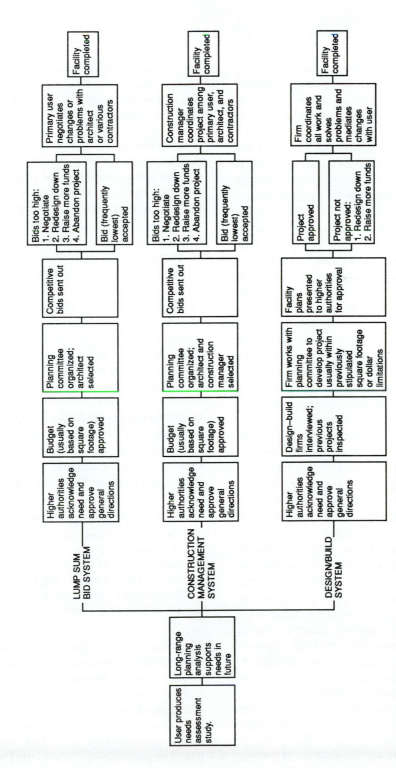

Figure 10.1 The process of developing a sport facility.

213

The third phase, determining the space needs, is vital and can include using facility references with tables showing recommended square footage for specific areas, determining standards required by federations asking expert consultants, and obtaining the advice of the specialists who will use the space.

After estimating the space requirements, the next step is to estimate the cost of the project. A study of 22 university recreation centers recently built revealed a cost from $68 to $158 per square foot. Based on these figures, Bernard (1997, p. 34) estimated the benchmark construction costs for university recreation centers to be $105 per square foot, and $110 a square foot for community recreation centers. Gymnasiums were estimated to cost $900 per seat; a basic arena with 6,000 or more seats, $2,250 per seat; and college/municipal arenas with suites, $3,400 per seat. A basic stadium with 3,000 to 6,000 seats, $950 per seat; and a college/municipal stadium with more than 6,000 seats, $1,800 per seat. The characteristics that will affect the benchmark cost are the components and amenities, the quality of the materials and finishes, and the degree of site work, which includes the parking lot, utility improvement, and retaining walls. The committee should use the benchmark cost, and then add or subtract based on cost-consuming characteristics (Bernard, 1997).

The fourth phase is to determine what others are doing. Usually the program specialist should assume the responsibility for arranging visits to other facilities. Make sure that the architect or designer accompanies the team and that notes and/or photographs are taken. If possible, obtain floor plans and photographs of the facilities before the visit. Seek out schools with comparable size, geographic factors, demographics, and economics. Also include, if possible, several futuristic and innovative facilities to stretch the imagination of the team. While on visits, chat with personnel responsible for cleaning the facility and distributing equipment. The building should be designed for efficient maintenance and cleaning.

Finally, make a master plan. This, of course, will bring everything together, taking into consideration previously discussed concerns and decisions, such as what method or approach to follow (lump sum bid, CM, or design/build), whether to have a planner or consultant, and whether to have a committee—and if so, a large or small one. Additional concerns that need to be included in the master plan follow.

The Architect

Although the cost for designing a facility is substantial (frequently approximately 6 percent), the selection of the architect should depend more on the past record of the firm than on the architect's fee. Unfortunately, an architect seldom is selected because he or she is renowned for the design of gymnasiums, stadiums, or swimming pools. Usually architects have experience with municipal buildings or general educational structures. If this is the case, both the program specialist and the architect need to spend more time looking at and talking about similar facilities. It will help a great deal if the program specialist is knowledgeable in building construction. The process for selecting an architect must be thorough and similar to a search for the replacement of a key administrator for the organization (Graves, 1993).

Selecting a competent and experienced architect is essential. In addition to designing a facility that meets all the demands of function, you want the project to be aesthetically pleasing. Architects use

(1) Form . . . the handling of the solid geometry of the building and the empty space surrounding and with it; (2) Scale; people are attracted to forms they can understand and are repulsed by forms that are forbidding; (3) Color . . . preferably a primary color and two neutral colors that are complementary; and (4) Light (Hughes, 1997, pp. 70–71).

If the architect is not experienced in sport facility design, the program specialist must build interest and excitement about the project. Architects are artists, and, as such, they want to create attractive and creative structures. They are concerned with style, scale, proportion, and rhythm while also creating a facility that meets functional requirements. To achieve the desired goal, the program specialist must find ways of getting the architect excited about the project and emo-

Table 10.1   The Job Progress Chart

The following section of a construction timetable is based on the chart used for a facility built at Southern Illinois–Carbondale. The exact jobs are specified in the far left column and their month-by-month status is charted by percentages in the boxes to the right. Before groundbreaking, the contractor figures out what percentage of each job should be completed by the end of every month. This percentage is put on the chart with small dashes (--) before it. At the end of every month, it is determined what percentage of each job is completed, and this percentage is written on the chart, with a long dash (—) in front of it. For example, by the end of December, 67 percent of the work was supposed to be completed. But when December 31 arrived, only 16 percent of the structural steel work actually was finished. By the end of February, all structural steel work was supposed to be completed, but it was not until April that this phase was actually finished.

This chart is only one section of a much larger chart. A complete job progress schedule includes every contract item and every month in which the project is under construction. In this example, we have taken just two of the contract items and 5 of the 14 months this project was being worked on.

	A	B	C	D	E	F
1	**Items**	December	Jananuary	February	March	April
2	*Metals*					
3	Structural steel	-- 67—16	-- 96—36	-- 100—74	—90	—100
4	Steel joists	-- 40—15	-- 80—15	-- 100—15	—100	
5	Metal deck	-- 35—25	-- 80—25	-- 100—25	—77	—100
6	Misc. steel	—10	-- 50—16	-- 75—43	-- 100—57	—100
7	*Heating*					
8	General items	-- 29—29	-- 42—42	-- 55—55	-- 70—70	-- 86—86
9	Temp. controls			-- 0—29	-- 0—29	-- 50—50
10	Insulation				-- 50—0	-- 100—50
11	Equipment		-- 25—0	-- 50—0	-- 75—0	-- 100—25
12	Chilled water	-- 25—0	-- 50—0	-- 75—10	-- 100—24	—50
13	Heating water	-- 25—0	-- 50—0	-- 75—10	-- 100—29	—55

-- = Percentage of scheduled progress
— = Percentage of actual progress

Source: Dunn, McMinn, and Meyer (1989, May).

tionally involved, especially emphasizing the need for function.

Companies specializing in large sport design projects believe that users select design firms based mostly on their track record and audio-visual presentations rather than on price (Raber, 1988). Is it important to select the best design firm? In taking over a large project from a design firm that was released from completing the job, the new company sued for $4 million based on "delays caused by incomplete specs and plans, frequent design revisions, and inadequate coordination among the project teams . . . found problems in the 48 concrete beams supporting the upper level . . . that reinforcement rods, embedded in each beam and attached to welding plates, were cut off and improperly installed" (Rosner, 1987).

Timing and Tracking the Project

Sport facility construction requires a thoughtfully and carefully constructed timetable. A timetable that is updated each month indicates when different phases of the job are supposed to be completed. (See Table 10.1, for example.) The schedule should be completed by the architect, general contractor, or construction manager at least 30 days before the start of the project. The phases of construction are frequently divided into site work; concrete work; masonry (walls); wood and plastics; thermal and moisture protection; doors, windows, glass, and hardware; specialties such as folding partitions and bath accessories; mechanical (plumbing, heating, air conditioning); and electric (Dunn, McMinn, and Meyer, 1989).

Frequently the athletic or physical education specialists will force an unrealistic timetable on the contractor and then be upset when it is not met. Build in "catch-up" periods. "Rework" frequently represents the majority of the project time and thus should be built into the work schedule if the project timetables are expected to be realistic (Cooper, 1993).

Weather problems, labor disruptions, or delays of deliveries of equipment (frequently by something happening in a distant location, even overseas) can delay the project. The "sport specialist" can assist in smooth tracking and effective advocacy for the users by diligently studying the book of specifications; limiting access to the work site; and clarifying with whom one should deal, and when the proper time is to talk and when to put problems or changes in writing. It is suggested that the chief specialist should negotiate a "punch list" with the general contractor to inspect with him or her all critical work at the completion of each phase. Once work has progressed past that point, it may be impossible to inspect or change an item without great cost or slowing down the whole project (Gordon, 1989).

Legal Considerations and Special Populations

Potential litigation can be reduced by considering legal aspects during the planning and design phase. The planning period is the time to envision the structures, space, and facilities needed to comply with building codes and Title IX requirements. Also, avoid physical barriers to persons with disabilities. Frequently gymnasiums have more barriers than anywhere else on a school campus. Be particularly mindful of the needs of persons with

disabilities in the dressing and shower rooms (Seidler, Turner, and Horine, 1993). Just as geologists have been included on planning teams for building on unstable sites, lawyers should be consulted on facilities being built for physical activity. A program specialist knowledgeable about legal problems can be of great service.

Both seniors and people with disabilities require special consideration when designing facilities. The Americans with Disabilities Act (ADA), Public Law 101-336, requires full accommodation for the disabled. This is comprehensive, strong, clear, and enforceable (Seidler, Turner, and Horine, 1993). An estimated 50 million individuals with disabilities are unemployed or underemployed because of the lack of accommodations. Failure to design a facility accommodating persons with disabilities is an act of discrimination subjecting owners and others associated to civil liability (Farmer, Mulrooney, and Ammon, 1996). All public accommodations "shall remove architectural barriers in existing facilities, including communication barriers that are structural in nature, where such removal is readily achievable, i.e., easily accomplishable and able to be carried out without much difficulty or expense" (*Nondiscrimination on the Basis of Disability*, 1994, p. 476). New facilities, must be designed to be "readily accessible to and usable by individuals with disabilities" (p. 480).

Restoring Existing Facilities

A typical American reaction is that "new" is always better than "old," but in recent years planners have tended to look to restoration. If it will cost 50 percent or more to rebuild than to build new, it is probably best to construct a new facility. This choice depends on many variables, such as historical significance, the type and quality of the original construction, and the specific use the new facility will have (Viklund, 1993). The analysis of the present facility should cover the structural condition of the facility; the moisture-protection capability and potential for new energy-saving adaptations; site constraints, including expansion or improvement of parking and vehicular and pedestrian traffic flow; and availability of adequate utility services (Gimple, 1992).

Colleges are also adapting existing structures more frequently. Appalachian State University rebuilt an archaic basement men's dressing room by bulldozing all the internal walls and even the concrete floor to rebuild from the ground up. This resulted in a modern locker room with an open atmosphere that was very well received (Horine and Turner, 1979). Harvard's Briggs Cage fieldhouse was renovated in a similar way.

Concrete floors in sport facilities wear out and become unsafe; this is particularly true in swimming pool decks, locker rooms, hallways, and weight rooms. This can be solved by replacing the entire floor or by utilizing a new technology of epoxy surfacing. First the floor has to be inspected to ensure that it is structurally sound. The next step is to remove existing coatings and repair cracked areas. After ensuring that there is no dust or dirt remaining, a leveling compound is applied. At this point, a primer is rolled on the scarified surface, followed by an epoxy surfacing, and a leveling compound is used for its compressional strength, abrasion qualities, and impact resistance. Two finishing coats are applied with a 100 percent solids, self-leveling epoxy. It is chemical resistant and hygienic, and does not need to be waxed. The whole process can be done in four weeks (Hart, 1997).

■ FINANCING FACILITY DEVELOPMENT

After initial planning, the new project cannot move forward without finding adequate financing. Frequently overlooked are five areas that also need to be considered when searching for total financing: (1) projecting inflation forward to when bills will be actually paid; (2) costs for operation including marketing; (3) a contingency percentage for cost overruns; (4) equipment and supplies; and (5) maintenance costs. All facility financing originates from private, public, or private/public sources (Sawyer, 1999, p. 43).

Public Facility Financing
There are generally two types of public financing for school or recreational sport facilities: taxes

and bonds. There are a variety of taxes, of which lodging and auto rental are the favorites because local taxpayers incur little of the expense. For facilities that will be used primarily by local citizens, property or sales tax increases are fairest. For professional sport facilities, granting tax abatement (exemption of property tax for a period) to the organization is an indirect way of taxing. Municipal bonds are the primary means of financing local school sport or recreational facilities. In the past, the most common bonds used for this purpose were general obligation full-faith and credit obligation. This means that the money advanced must be paid back with interest within a set period from property taxes. The disadvantage is that municipal bonds must be voted on for approval, which is no easy task in today's fiscal environment; bonds also increase the local debt. In recent years, nonguaranteed bonds have been most popular. In general, they do not require voter approval, and repayment is tied to resources other than property taxes. In addition, financing can be arranged through tax-free foundations or governmental agencies. Many states have governmental agencies that provide funding (most must be matched from local funds) for greenways and other recreational facilities (Sawyer, 1999, pp. 43–44. Bynum, 2002b and 2002d; Dudziak, 2002).

Private Facility Financing
This form of financing can be used for public or commercial facilities. There are a multitude of avenues from private sources. (See Chapter 5 for specific projects.) For school and college sport facilities, raising money through cash donations, in-kind contributions, and advertising rights is very common. Large institutions and expensive recreational facilities have frequently turned to sponsorship packages such as supplying the football team with shoes, food and beverage rights or exclusivity, preferred/premium seating or luxury suites, bequests and trusts, real estate gifts, life insurance packages, endowments, and securities donations. Along with using many of these strategies, professional organizations have utilized such additional avenues as restaurant

rights, lease agreements, parking fees, merchandise revenue, vendor/contractor equities, and asset-backed securities. Using naming rights to raise revenue has become controversial. Many feel it is demeaning to put a product or company name on a sport facility (particularly if it is a public facility); but because several of the largest firms who paid the most for naming rights have gone bankrupt, the amount of money that companies will pay will likely shrink (Sawyer, 1999, pp. 44–45).

Public/Private Financing

By combining the previous two types of financing, many projects can be achieved. For example, when a community was attempting to identify where sufficient funds would come from to build a new swimming pool, a person who had been on the local high school swimming team offered to donate $1 million if the county and city would contribute the remainder. In addition, professional franchises may contribute some portion of the funds to build a new stadium or arena if the city funds the remainder.

An example of multisource funding may be found in a California community, where new and renovated facilities were achieved by funding through a booster club, school funds, a YMCA, a soccer association, a construction company, and even a provider of cellular communications equipment, which provided new lighting poles that double as cell towers. (Popke, 2002a).

■ FACILITIES AND ENERGY

Did you know that the average community recreation center uses more energy per square foot than an average urban hospital? It's true (Flynn and Schneider, 1997, p. 51). Administrators must insist that energy conservation be a primary consideration in every facility decision. Improperly constructed sport facilities consume inordinate amounts of energy. During periods when energy costs happen to be low, society tends not to give this critical area its due share of attention. It doesn't take an engineer to see that running hot water into the sewer system or exhausting hot or chilled air into the outside environment doesn't make sense. *Capture energy anywhere and everywhere,*

such as from lighting systems; it saves money in addition to setting the proper environmental conservation example.

Loss of energy can be averted by correctly orienting the building to take advantage of sunshine, with high-performance glazing (windows) to capture passive heating. The exterior shell should be constructed with the maximum recommended levels of insulation (Flynn and Schneider, 1997). Consider utilizing heat wheels, energy recovery units, or heat-exchanging "run-around" coils. In new facilities, insist on energy-conserving light fixtures and dimming controls, and be aware of the increased energy requirements of indirect lighting (DiLullo, 2002; Cohen, 2002a).

One of the greatest problems in ice rink design is to counteract the huge costs for energy. The majority of the energy used in ice rinks is the refrigeration system. Radiation through the ceiling makes up over a quarter of the heat lost in rinks, while the next highest cost is to maintain the arena air temperature.

Maintaining the correct humidity is a delicate equation in ice rinks. One system is to dehumidify air with "desiccant" systems, which remove water from the air without cooling it by passing the air over a desiccant (a substance that absorbs humidity) before returning it to the arena (Vivian, 1997). (Also see the section on ice rinks.)

Solar

Solar energy technology should be utilized more in sport and recreation facilities. Examples are the use of solar panels on the roofs of gymnasiums, arenas, and swimming pools to heat buildings and hot water. In cold climates, solar panels can heat the swimming pool water, which can serve as a huge storage tank of energy.

The Geodesic Dome and Energy

The geodesic dome has been successfully used for energy-efficient sport structures. Because of its configuration of not having internal walls or columns, the number of square feet of play space can be generated at a much smaller energy expenditure than with a traditional structure. Maintaining a low profile by partially locating the dome underground and installing heat reclaiming units further enhances energy savings. In addition, experience has shown that spraying the underside of the roof with one inch of urethane foam under one-half inch of cellulose fiber adds to fire protection, sound absorption, and energy savings.

Lighting and Energy

Authorities estimate that about half of the energy used in schools is for lighting (Lewis, 1993). In addition, elite sport competition has increased the demands for illumination levels, and if there is to be television coverage, extremely high lighting intensities are required. Designers have found that if the underside of a ceiling has a degree of reflective capacity, energy savings (as well as aesthetic quali-

ties) can be realized by directing the lamps upward for indirect lighting and at the same time capturing heat from the system for use in climate control.

Energy savings can be generated in lighting systems by maintaining tightly sealed and gasketed floodlights and the most efficient location of the lights to the playing area. The greatest savings can be obtained by switching to high-pressure sodium, quartz, or metal halide systems. In one school, the mercury vapor lights were replaced with high-pressure sodium fixtures (HPS), reducing the needed wattage from almost 41,000 to 9,000. The exterior lighting was changed to tungsten halogen, resulting in more light for less cost and energy. (See Tables 10.2 and 10.3.)

Table 10.2 Types of Lighting—Advantages and Disadvantages			
Type	Description	Advantages	Disadvantages
Incandescent	Common light bulbs	Low initial cost, shows good color, no sound, not affected by how many times turned off and on, light is instantaneous	Short lamp life, inefficient, high spot brightness, gives off much heat, difficult to achieve high levels of illumination
	Quartz lamps	Slightly more efficient than incandescent	Bronze color
Fluorescent	Commonly found in workrooms, usually in the form of long tubes	Longer life than incandescent highly illuminating, little color distortion, gives about 2 1/2 times more light than incandescent lamps for the same amount of energy	Frequently have distracting hum; if not installed correctly, may flicker with strobe effect
High-intensity	Mercury vapor	Longest lamp life, less expensive to operate than incandescent	Slow starting, high initial cost, distorts colors, bluish tint, slow starting
	Metal halide	Better light output and operates more more efficiently	Don't last as long as mercury vapor
	High-pressure sodium	Long life expectancy, highly efficient	Yellow-bronze hue
	Metalarc (clear)	Most resembles daylight	

Source: Sawyer, T. H., ed. (1999). *Facilities planning for physical activity and sport: Guidelines for development* (9th ed.), pp. 110–112. Dubuque, Iowa: Kendall/Hunt Publishing Co.

Table 10.3 Energy Uses for Various Types of Lighting		
	Average Lumens per Lamp Watt	Energy Savings Comparison
Incandescent	23	0%*
Quartz	31	16
Mercury vapor	61	66
Fluorescent	70	71
Metal halide	110	80
High-pressure sodium	140	85

*Based on energy required to maintain identical lamp lumens

Source: Sawyer, T. H., ed. (1999). *Facility planning for physical activity and sport: Guidelines for development* (9th ed.), p. 113. Dubuque, Iowa: Kendall/Hunt Publishing Company.

Because of peak-load electricity pricing, institutions should study how to control usage according to time. It was reported that Louisiana State University saved $85,000 a year after installing a $200 light that glows to different colors or flashes red to signal when particular actions require avoiding peak usage costs.

Energy Systems

The following typify some of the interesting energy systems reported in sport facilities. A cost-saving feature of the new recreation center in Kingston, Pennsylvania, is a geothermal system that uses mine water for heating, domestic hot water, and air conditioning. The same principle is utilized for heating and air conditioning at the Activities/Resource Center at Pratt Institute in Brooklyn, New York. This geothermal system paid for itself in 3.5 years and might underwrite the whole facility in 20 years. A heat exchanger was installed in Ainsworth Gym at Smith College in Northampton, Massachusetts. Because enormous amounts of exhaust air are required in swimming pools, gymnasiums, and locker rooms, the Smith College officials determined to pick up this energy and reuse it. The $40,000 cost of the installation is expected to be offset by energy savings in six or seven years. Tapping the heat expelled from the heat rejection apparatus of the ice hockey rink at Amherst College in Massachusetts essentially heats the entire athletic complex. An addition to

the athletic center of Brown University in Providence, Rhode Island, added 100,000 square feet to a 50,000-square-foot facility. The whole new facility is heated for the same cost as heating the old small one by utilizing energy reclamation devices.

If a complex is not going to be tied into an existing central power plant for heating, several new or reoriginating plant systems are possible. Returning to burning coal is one alternative, and burning wood chips has potential. East Stroudsburg State University in Pennsylvania is constructing a pilot system utilizing an advanced fluidized bed coal boiler that will allow it to convert anthracite waste into efficient energy. With heat recovery wheels, waste heat can be scavenged from high-ventilation areas and recycled, conserving energy.

■ INDOOR FACILITIES

Site Selection

While detailed checklists should be used to avoid overlooking a planning feature, this section covers some general guidelines for locating indoor facilities. The level of the institution is the first factor. At institutions of higher education, planners should take into consideration where the students live and their vehicular and pedestrian traffic patterns. On the other hand, on the lower

The interior of WCU Ramsey Center.
Western Carolina University Media Relations Office.

grade levels, noise will be the highest consideration. In addition to the education level, site selection depends on whether the facility will be utilized for spectator sports. Obviously, parking and crowd flow patterns are vital if large crowds are expected. It would be wise planning to envision a new facility as multipurpose and versatile. If it is a school facility, plan for its use as afternoon and evening recreational activities. If it is a community or higher education facility, plan for a variety of entertainment and public programs such as ice shows, concerts, and trade shows (Bynum, 2002a, Popke, 2002c).

If the type of indoor structure has not been predetermined, the topography of the site might influence this decision. A swampy area may preclude an underground facility, and a hilly area might lend itself to an encapsulate. Frequently sites are selected that don't allow for appropriate future expansion. Plan for the future!

Teaching Stations and Activity Space

A *teaching station* is a space in which a physical education class can be safely conducted. *Activity space* could refer to varsity team practice space, an intramural competition area, or a room for individual recreational activity. Indoor and outdoor teaching stations are computed in the same manner.

There is a great deal of room for judgment in determining the teaching stations. In part the following factors will influence the decision:

- The weather—how many classes or activity units might require inside space at each hour of the day or night during inclement weather.
- Whether activity units will be provided with a space just to "get by" inside (softball team space to play catch) or space for an indoor practice (softball team space to take infield practice).
- The size of the classes or activity units (space provided may dictate this,which is incorrect).
- The type of classes and/or activities related to space.
- The type of class and/or activities related to equipment.

Floor Surfaces

Once again, the surface of the indoor facility must be predicated on the expected activities and ability levels of the participants. (see Table 10.4.) As previously reported, most basketball and volleyball coaches prefer hardwood playing surfaces.

In the past, installation of hardwood floors used either a floating floor or an anchored floor. Each of these systems was flawed. "Today, the benefits of both are found in a hybrid, called the restrained floating floor, which uses metal pins, channels, straps or other mechanical fasteners to loosely fasten the subfloor system to the concrete beneath it. Each of these systems provides the floor with enough stability to deter buckling during moisture-induced expansion and contraction of the system, while also controlling the amount

Table 10.4 Suggested Indoor Surface Materials

Rooms	Floors							Lower Walls								Upper Walls						Ceilings			
	Carpeting	Synthetics	Tile, asphalt, rubber, linoleum	Cement, abrasive and nonabrasive	Maple, hard	Terrazzo, abrasive	Tile, ceramic	Brick	Brick, glazed	Cinder block	Concrete	Plaster	Tile, ceramic	Wood panel	Moistureproof	Brick	Brick, glazed	Cinder block	Plaster	Acoustic	Moisture-resistant	Concrete or structure tile	Plaster	Tile, acoustic	Moisture-resistant
Apparatus storage room				1	2			1		2	1	C													
Classrooms			2		1					2		1		2				2	1			C	C	1	
Clubroom			2		1					2		1		2				2	1			C	C	1	
Corrective room		1		2				2	1					2		2	2	1	2					1	
Custodial supply room				1			2																		
Dance studio			2		1																	C	C	1	
Drying room (equip.)				1		2	2	1	2	1	1					1		1							
Gymnasium		1			1			2	1					2		2	2	1	2	"		C	C	1	
Health service unit			1		1					2		1		2				2	1					1	
Laundry room			2				1	2	1	2	2		1	C	"						"			"	"
Locker rooms		3	3			2	1	1	2	2	3	1			"	1		1	2				C	1	
Natatorium		2					1	2	1	3	2		1		"	2	2	1		"	"	C	C	1	"
Offices	1	3		2						2		1		1				2	1					1	
Recreation room		2			1			2		2		1		1		2		1	2		"		C	1	
Shower rooms			3			2	1	1	3	3	2	1	3		"	2	1	2	2		"	3	3	1	"
Special activity room			2		1				2				1	1		1		1	1				C	1	
Team room	1		3			2	1	2	1	2	2	3	1		"	1		1	2				C	1	
Toilet room			3			2	1	1	2	2	2	1			"	1		1	1					1	
Toweling-drying room			3			2	1	1				2	1		"	2	1	2	2		"			1	"

Note: The numbers in the table indicate first, second, and third choices. "C" indicates the material as being contrary to good practice. A " indicates desirable quality.

Source: Sawyer, T. H., ed. (1999). *Facilities planning for physical activity and sport: Guidelines for development.* (9th ed., p. 91). Dubuque, Iowa: Kendall/Hunt Publishing Company.

of vertical deflection the floor imparts upon the athletes" (Steinbach, 2002c, p. 82).

Synthetic floor surfaces have been evolving for several decades. One innovation is the use of prefabricated mats made of recycled tire rubber coated with a poured layer of urethane to create a durable, seamless playing surface. Poured urethane floors were not very resilient, so another recent change has been to mix finely ground rubber into the lower layers to add shock absorbency. Injection-molded polypropylene tiles, previously limited to outdoor application, have now been used indoors. These snap-together modular tiles result in multipurpose functionality and immunity to moisture damage. Another option is based on vinyl sheets, some of which include vulcanized rubber that can be formulated in colors or a wood-grained look. Advanced heat-welding techniques have mostly eliminated the evidence of the seams in the sheet applications (Steinbach, 2002a; "Surfaces and Covers," 2000).

Don't overlook the importance of color on surfaces. Color may influence attitudes and energy of patrons as well as assisting in traffic flow (McDonnell, 2000; Steinbach, 2002a).

An important factor is how much shock absorbency is optimal for the user. The American Society for Testing and Materials (ASTM) has developed procedures for testing the shock-absorbing properties of sport surfaces, but no standards have been produced. Europe, on the other hand, has led this research by producing criteria for hardwood and synthetic floors called the DIN (Deutsches Institute Für Normals) standards. This measures the "specific performance qualities for shock absorption, deformation, area of deflection, ball bounce, rolling shear, and friction" (Ellison, 1993, p. 55).

In this country, the buzz words for aerobic flooring surfaces have been *flotation, suspension,* and *spring system.* A less favorable choice is rubber. If it is smooth, it gets slippery easily; and if the rubber surface is granular, perspiration can be absorbed. On the positive side, the cost for rubber flooring has been greatly reduced in recent years, down to about $3 to $5 a square foot. The higher-priced rubber flooring could be appropriate for weight areas (Cioletti, 1998). Few clubs are still

carpeting over a concrete slab (Hauss, 1993). For "cardio" rooms, many administrators prefer a high-grade nylon carpet for its resiliency and sound-absorbing qualities. Because of its propensity to absorb perspiration, it should receive antimicrobial treatment (Cioletti, 1998).

At the other extreme, for foyers and hallways, a popular hard surface product is Torginol. It is a poured surface with either vinyl chips embedded in multiple coats of liquid resins topped with polyurethane glaze, or quartz granules embedded in clear epoxy (Williams, 1993). New products, such as floor hardeners or impregnators called thermal adhesion activators (Ames, 1993), and new high-speed spray buff machines that operate from 1,000 to 3,000 rpm for burnishing and glazing, have greatly improved the length of life, looks, and time between stripping of surfaces (Weeks, 1993).

For some multipurpose facilities, vinyl tiles can provide an inexpensive, long-lasting alternative. Vinyl tile flooring with permanently inlaid lines, as shown in Figure 10.2, has been installed in several elementary schools and has served very well over the years.

Walls, Doors, and Windows

Gymnasium walls should be easy to maintain, smooth enough to serve rebounding purposes (tennis, volleyball), and serve as sound absorbers. Frequently all these requirements can be met by constructing the lower and upper walls of different materials.

Consider utilizing color and graphics on the walls. Having inlaid or painted signage on the walls will prevent vandalism later. Utilize colors that won't show handprints and foot scuff marks. Recessed electrical outlets should be placed at regular intervals around any physical activity space. Recessed drinking fountains should be located in hallways adjacent to activity areas. Permanent and heavy-duty padding should be installed as appropriate and not an "add-on" after occupancy. All exit doors must open outward, conform to codes, have proper safety bars, and be constructed of safety or wired glass. In cold climate areas, install double-door entrances and design overhang roofs for all outside doors. Utilize as much

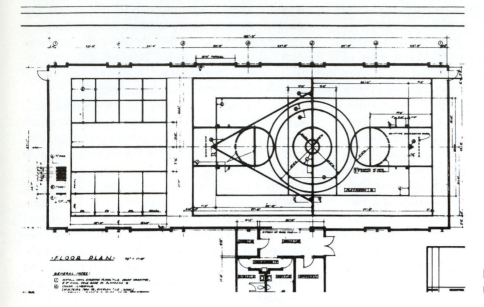

Figure 10.2 Sample elementary floor markings.

glass as possible in nonactivity areas, but be selective in glazing activity areas such as swimming pools. (How many students can recall gymnasiums that had glass windows painted black?) In areas where the outside environment is of high quality, consider installing awning type windows beneath fixed windows.

Ceilings

The primary purpose of the ceiling is to absorb sound and reflect light. After meeting these objectives, the most aesthetically pleasing and easy-to-maintain ceiling should be installed. Carefully consider what activities might damage the ceiling. For competitive volleyball and basketball, the low side of beams should be 24 feet high. Avoid pure white ceilings because of the difficulty of following white implements such as shuttlecocks. Ceilings should be treated to prevent condensation and for acoustics. Ensure that plans are made for catwalks or other means to service light fixtures in high ceilings (Sawyer, 1999, pp. 89–92).

Acoustics

The major problem with indoor acoustics is too much noise. To reduce noise, select rough or textured surfaces as often as possible. Acoustical en-

gineers should certainly be consulted. Metal ducts may transmit unwanted sound into teaching spaces. Some methods of reducing noise include using double-wall construction, filling wall spaces with sound-absorbing materials, covering pipes, installing baffles in ducts, laying blankets over partitions in suspended ceilings, and installing motors on rubber mountings. In the design of sport or recreational facilities, give careful consideration to the placement of "noisy" activities and those requiring quiet. For example, place the weight areas far from offices and classrooms. Sound travels spherically (Sawyer, 1999, p. 117).

Sound levels for teaching areas are recommended to be between 40 to 50 decibels (dB). But in athletic facilities, the sound levels average over 70 dB. Reverberation times (the number of seconds required for the energy of a reflected sound to decrease to 60 dB) in athletic facilities range from about two to over eight seconds. The range recommended for educational areas is 0.5 to 1.5 seconds. Many modern materials and methods are available for reducing noise in sport facilities, including installing acoustical clouds; utilizing heavy carpeting and sound-absorbing lockers; and installing perforated tiles, sound-absorbent vercoustic panels for walls, or sound-absorbing units in the ceilings.

An example of an open locker room, "tree" showers, and a handicap shower.
Photo by L. E. Horine

Most arenas are designed for basketball, and then users do the best they can for adapting to other special events such as concerts. This oblong layout presents major problems for high-quality sound and acoustics. One firm has designed an arena to seat 10,000 that is shaped in convocation configuration to function with higher qualities for sound and acoustics. Named the Alpha Center, it incorporates 28 patent-pending claims (Thompson and Riley, 2002).

Environmental Graphics (Signage)

Signs can have a powerful, positive impact on the appearance, functionality, entertainment value, and revenue for a facility. When a facility is being completed, various signs should be installed, such as directional signs both inside and outside the facility, a directory, accessible entrances for emergency purposes and persons with disabilities, bulletin boards with activity listings and facility hours, and signs identifying entrances, rooms, seats, and gates (Pearce, 1998).

Service Areas and Changing Rooms

Service areas may need to be improved or replaced faster than other areas. This may be the case because of the impact of equal opportunity laws, which have opened the gymnasium to previously excluded populations. Other factors include changing health and hygiene standards and the need for more efficient energy utilization. For example, in the past, training rooms were generally reserved

for elite male athletes, whereas now the law mandates equal access to women and to athletes of all levels, including athletes with disabilities.

The next step in planning is to carefully study the possibility of renovating or adding to the existing locker and shower rooms (Horine and Turner, 1979). Remember that the two areas most frequently given insufficient space are the offices and storage rooms. Adding a few extra feet to an office will make a significant impact on the ability of the teacher and coach to function professionally, and the cost will be insignificant. The locker room is one of the most important facilities. Because of the personal nature of changing and showering, and the fact that almost every student in the school is frequently in and out of locker rooms, it is an essential area. This area lends itself to both cleanliness and innovation (McDonnell, 2000).

The traditional locker room is no more. The trend is for changing rooms to also include lockers. The changing rooms are now more like living rooms for the athletes. They are more open and airy, and have satellite facilities for team meetings (with full media installations with large screens) and reading areas. In some there are computers, adjacent fitness rooms, training rooms, and equipment rooms. The lockers have become larger. Because sweat is absorbed into the pads and gear of some sports, designers are including a separate small locker for just street clothes, sometimes in a different area. Most lockers for athletes now include a separate lock box inside the locker for expensive shoes and valuables. A room dedicated to the media is a valuable asset. Lighting and ventilation systems are much improved. In some cases diffusers are installed to blow air through the lockers to dry out uniforms (Dillon, 1996; Viklund and Coons, 1997; Cohen, 1998).

Some specific guidelines relate to locker room planning:

1. Consider mounting lockers on six-inch metal bases so that lockers can be moved by removing a few bolts, or mounting lockers on a cement pedestal.

2. Consider having some bays of lockers on wheels to maintain flexibility.

3. Design lockers so that either they are low enough for equipment managers to see over, or the long axis of the rows is open to supervisory personnel.

4. Avoid shower curtains or partitions and instead slope the floor 1 percent for drainage.

5. Consider benches that are bolted down.

6. Plan for lockers 15 inches deep rather than 12 inches, as listed in many references.

7. Install expanded metal or screened lockers to increase ventilation; also have screening on top or slope the tops so dust does not collect.

8. Install heavy-duty steel (16 gauge or heavier) on end panels of lockers.

9. Utilize recessed handles on lockers to avoid their being kicked.

10. In high-humidity areas, investigate stainless steel unpainted lockers.

11. Consider indoor/outdoor carpeting in at least some of the areas.

12. Request nylon catches and stops to reduce noise.

13. Paint walls with polystyrene or acrylic paints, or tile them.

14. Avoid low-level suspended ceilings that are natural targets to "pop up" with a baseball bat or tennis racquet, and install moisture-resistant and acoustically treated ceiling tiles.

15. On all levels, install a few "modesty" showers.

16. Some modular showers should be considered so that they can be used for isolated teams, men, or women as needs change.

17. Wall-bar or pole-mounted showers are possible, but many planners are finding the latter, frequently called "tree" showers, are preferred.

18. Consider installing modular dressing rooms with connecting (lockable) doors so rooms can be used for either sex, or for special team or visitors' dressing rooms (Cohen, 1993a; Dillon, 1996).

Fitness centers or clubs have somewhat different locker room requirements. Suggestions include making sure that enough space and lockers are planned with an appropriate ratio of day-use lockers to long-term rentals. Ensure that maintenance and cleaning considerations are heavily weighed when the area is planned because club members demand "squeaky" clean facilities. Separating the wet and dry areas will assist in the cleaning routine. Properly conditioned air to accommodate peak crowds during hot and humid summer months must be designed, along with energy-saving devices and equipment. Decor, signage, and privacy appropriate to the membership are necessary to create a sanctuary for your members so they enjoy and look forward to showering and changing. This can be a positive social period if the facility is designed and maintained properly.

Lighting

Lighting has been previously discussed as it relates to energy. If in doubt, plan for more illumination and central switching so that there can be low levels of light for general teaching and recreational play; medium levels for specific teaching activities that require more light (for example, badminton) and varsity practice; and very high levels for special programs and contests (see Tables 10.2 and 10.3).

For elite sport competition, metal halide lighting sets the standard. It provides excellent intensity for television and is more economical, lasting 5 to 10 times as long as incandescent lamps (see Table 10.3). From Table 10.2 note that both the highly efficient high-pressure sodium and metal halide lamps require a few moments to start or restart after an electrical interruption or turning the system off. Thus backup incandescent emergency lights are necessary. If lights will be routinely turned off and on (for example, at halftime shows), consider installing an instant restrike metal halide system, although this is more expensive. If an arena will be used with less than capacity crowds, plan lighting that allows for darkening the higher unoccupied seats to give the illusion of full capacity. Install automatic dimming systems to save costs. Indirect lighting has become very popular because it is aesthetically pleasing, but recognize that this produces a great amount of heat that must be captured, and it may be more difficult to recognize details on three-dimensional objects (Cohen, 2002a; DiLullo, 2002). The Alpha Arena lighting "comes from dimmable high-intensity discharge lamps whose ballasts are electronically controlled to avoid noise associated with HID lighting"—(Thompson and Riley, 2002, p. 102).

Because school and municipal sport facilities are used for decades, many forms of lighting are out of date. "Because they cost far less than new fixtures, reflectors are an ideal way to refurbish existing fluorescent fixtures without major rewiring or tearing up the ceiling. They increase the usable light emitted by the existing lamps, giving you the option of reducing the number of lamps—and electrical costs" (Dorr, 1997, p. 82). In addition, fluorescent lamp replacements can be installed in incandescent light sockets without rewiring. These lamps can reduce electricity costs by 75 percent and can last 10 to 13 times longer (Dorr, 1997).

Mechanical (HVAC)

For obvious reasons; heating, ventilation, and air conditioning are vital in locker rooms, swimming pools, ice rinks, and all other interior spaces where activity takes place.

The strategy for developing optimal thermal environment is to achieve ": (1) radiant temperature where surface and air temperatures are balanced, (2) air temperature between 64° and 72° F, (3) humidity between 40 and 60 percent, and (4) a constant air movement of 20 to 40 linear feet/per/min. at a sitting height. "(Sawyer, 1999, p. 120).

To plan "intelligent" facilities, HVAC should be connected with fire protection, access systems, security, elevators, and communication systems to a central computer. Buildings are likely to last longer than the latest HVAC system because of rapidly changing technology in this area. An example of this is that heat pumps installed in colder climates in the past could not produce sufficient heat in the winter, but with great technical advances, these heat pumps are now vastly more efficient. The best way to overcome this inevitable HVAC obsolescence is to design with ample space (vertical and horizontal) to allow new systems to be easily installed (Sawyer, 1999, pp. 119–122).

Climate control includes designing to achieve a personal comfort environment for every occupant of every area within the complex. To achieve this, one must design a system that will provide air conditioning, heating, ventilation, and humidity control in an automatic manner, regardless of the number of people in each area. We have all been in public places where it is quite comfortable when few people are present only to become quite unpleasant when the place becomes crowded. In a well-designed system, this should not occur. The architect should follow the standards promulgated by the American Society of Heating and Ventilating Engineers.

As previously mentioned, and emphasized at this time, climate control is a major energy consumption factor. Remember that it takes energy to produce air conditioning, and heat is energy. Thus, anytime heat can be captured, energy is saved to heat, ventilate, or air condition. In the past, to control humidity and odors, it was necessary to vent air to the outside and bring in fresh air. If the air in the dressing room or gymnasium was warmer than comfortable, the new air had to be cooled; if too cold, it had to be heated. At the same time the energy of the outgoing air was literally going out the window. Today these constraints are gone. As previously discussed, the energy can be reclaimed from the outgoing air, or circulating air can be dehumidified as necessary.

Experience has shown that climate control systems frequently create noise. Be cognizant of this problem and locate the units far from offices and classrooms; and utilize baffles, sound blankets, and floating motor mounts. Install tamper,

The interior of the Dean Smith Center at the Univesity of North Carolina, Chapel Hill.
Photo by L. E. Horine

vandal-proof thermostats in appropriate areas. Either install sealed windows, or keep thermostats away from window areas. Avoid installing air-conditioning units on roofs. Be aware that humidity control is highly sensitive—dehumidifying the air in a locker room may feel great when entering after a workout, but feel freezing when coming out of the shower.

Seating

The type and quantity of spectator seating will depend on the program and activities. The large coliseums for high-level competition are installing individual theater-type seats that fold up, although some institutions have returned to bench-type seating in the lower rows next to the playing floor to pack in more students and to give themselves more home court advantage from the noise they can generate. The trend in arenas is to install more retractable and power-folding movable seating for flexibility for various types of events.

A major effort has been made to improve the safety of bleachers. The state of Minnesota has been a leader (with impetus from the death of a child falling through an open space in bleachers) by enacting the Minnesota Bleacher Safety Act in 1999. In 1998 the United States Consumer Product Safety Commission (CPSC) estimated that there were 19,200 bleacher-related injuries requiring emergency care. Administrators must be concerned about five areas:

1. Restrict gaps to four inches or less.
2. Guardrails should be in place where the top row is 30 or more inches off the ground; the top surface of the guardrails should be no less than 42 inches from the highest point of the bleachers; gaps in the guardrails should be no more than four inches; the design of the guardrails should discourage climbing.
3. The structural integrity of all bleachers must be sound. If movable the mechanisms for moving must work perfectly, and the bleachers must be properly anchored.
4. Patrons must have safe access into and egress out of bleachers with appropriate width of aisles, nonskid surfaces, signage, and enforced rules about blocking aisles.
5. Either block off the space under bleachers or have the area supervised (LaRue, 2002; Popke, 2002b).

The minimum width of seats is 18 inches, but 22 inches is recommended for adults. Standard bleachers include up to 23 rows; however, over 16 rows increases difficulties for safety and crowd control. On balconies, telescope the bleachers

An example of a well-conceived weight room.
Photo by L. E. Horine

from back to front so that they form a dividing wall to create a teaching station.

Strength and Cardiovascular Training Areas

These centers have become the heart of the fitness and recreation centers as well as school and campus recreation and athletic facilities. The planner must perform the same needs assessment study as listed earlier for other new facilities. The assessment, however, must be narrow and address the following: What are the training goals? What types of equipment and space will be required for each group? Determine the age, training experience, and hours or seasons that will result in peak demands. How should the equipment be placed for most efficiency, safety, and supervision? Note that in the following references there is an excellent summary of the advantages and disadvantages of various types of cardiovascular equipment (Sawyer, 1999, pp. 251–252; Bynum, 2002c).

Weight-training facilities should be included in all new secondary, community, or college athletic facilities. Ensure that weight training is available for both sexes. The choice of a free-weight facility or a system of machines depends on philosophy, space, sex of users, how much time users have for workouts, and the ultimate outcomes desired. Most prefer a rubber floor wherever weights might touch. Rubber is easy to maintain, provides pleasing aesthetics (it can be purchased in black or in colors), is forgiving for both the weights and the participants, and has a long life. It can be installed in continuous sheets or in interlocking squares. In areas not directly involved with the weights, an industrial-grade carpeting should be installed (Sherman, 1997a; Steinbach, 2002a and 2002c; Popke, 2002d).

Fitness weight rooms should have the following range of densities of equipment to allow for safe passage and uncongested use:

- Free weights: 55 to 65 square feet per unit.
- Machine weights: 70 to 80 square feet per unit.
- Cardiovascular equipment: 30 to 35 square feet per unit.

Install indirect lighting since much of the activity will be in a reclining position and glare will present problems (Lavoie, 1989; Sherman, 1997a).

Weight and fitness rooms should be light and airy and should have as many views as possible. Because the facility participants will be preoccupied with horizontal and vertical lines of sight when they exercise, pay close attention to attractive wall and ceiling details. To alleviate odor buildup in a weight room, make sure there is a high rate of air exchange (Sherman, 1997a).

Special Areas

Depending on the size and level of the school, recreation complex, or spa, careful planning needs to be provided for special areas. These might be dance studios, martial arts/wrestling rooms, climbing walls, gymnastics room, hydro pools/steam rooms/saunas, handball courts, squash courts, racquetball courts, concessions, offices, training rooms, storage/maintenance areas, or laboratories.

Health clubs and community recreation centers have included juice bars and pro shops for some time. Now patrons are ready to pay extra for new high-tech gadgets such as hypoxic chambers to emulate high-altitude training. Another is the "Bod Pod" to accurately measure body composition (Steinbach, 2002d).

Ice Rinks

Most ice rinks are privately owned, and schools and recreation departments have rented a considerable amount of time from these facilities. With expanding interest in ice skating and ice hockey, schools and colleges are adding ice hockey as varsity sports. This has resulted in more partnerships (Sherman, 1997b).

To get an accurate estimate of costs of building an ice rink, the following information should be gathered: In what geographic location do you plan to build? Is your rink for public skating or theatrical use? Is the rink to be a permanent structure? If it will be portable, what will be the range of temperatures? Will the rink be indoor, outdoors, or a combination of both? How will the building be insulated? What type of construction will be planned (masonry, metal, air structure)? What is the average temperature in winter and in summer? What is the elevation? What is your power source? If the rink is to be installed in an existing building, what type of floor exists in this building? What will be the maximum spectator seating requirement? (Ice Rink Engineering and Manufacturing Co., 1997; Steinbach, 2002c; Bynum, 2002e).

Examples of Constructed Indoor Facilities

Cited as another wonder of the world is the first arena built as a pyramid. The home of the Memphis State University basketball team is 32 stories (320 feet) high at the apex, almost three times higher than other arenas with similar seating. It seats 20,000 for basketball or hockey with 26 private suites. An original problem was acoustics, but this was solved by adding 30-by-4-foot soft acoustical blankets (Cohen, 1993b).

A student recreation center was completed at a cost of $17.25 million at the University of Toledo. A colorful open plan allows students to relax or study in the center and see activities throughout the 149,000-square-foot facility. It contains "five full-sized basketball courts, an enclosed multipurpose court with a synthetic floor, a natatorium, six racquetball courts, a large machine weights room, a free-weight area, locker rooms, an aerobics area, and an upper-level running track" (Schmid, 1993, p. 44). The facility also includes a table-games area, television lounge, multipurpose rooms, and deli.

The builders of the The Gym in Washington, D.C., decided that what would set it apart from the other centers was to make it all above ground, and light and bright. The 25,000-square-foot award-winning facility allows each area of the gym to receive natural lighting. It is unique in space-to-member ratio, providing 12.5 square feet per member, which is double what the competition was offering. Innovations like swinging and pivoting mirrors attract members (Renner, 1998).

Security

Predesign your facility for security! Protecting your facility investment from vandalism and misuse is not only good stewardship of funds, it may keep the institution out of court. Some common-sense strategies include these: Avoid windows within reach of the ground. Have no windows in storage areas. Install well-placed security lights, and cover outside lights with vandal-proof guards. Avoid recessed doorways. Be sure that landscaping does not create hiding places or a means of entry to the building.

During the design period, analyze the traffic patterns that will occur when the facility is in full use and try to locate specialty areas so they can easily be secured. Install locks, surveillance devices, and electronic entry systems. If possible, eliminate lockers and make roof areas as inaccessible from the grounds as possible (Pappalrdo, 2002). See Chapter 7 for details.

OUTDOOR FACILITIES

As in other facilities, the program needs dictate the quantity and quality of the outdoor facilities needed. Specialized facilities used infrequently can be accommodated by having permits to utilize another agency's facility or contracting to use another space. Cooperative planning between schools and community park and recreation agencies is strongly recommended (Zawadski, 1993).

Outdoor Site Selection and Development
The factors that should be considered in site selection include the number of participants and spectators, the interrelationships of spaces and traffic patterns, space and environmental rankings of various activities, special equipment needs, and the future needs and expansion potential of each area.

An almost universal problem with outdoor facilities is insufficient drainage. Frequently poor site selection initiates the problem. Two other factors that require serious early study (particularly for baseball fields) are wind patterns and the orientation of the field to the sun (Bynum, 2002).

Establishing grass baselines from home to first and third, rather than the traditional dirt, has been shown to reduce maintenance and daily chalking. On the other hand, creating a dirt path between the pitcher's mound and home plate has also reduced maintenance time. This is particularly true when it is required to move the pitching rubber up and back (Dirty, 2002).

Grading and drainage planning requires the utmost consideration. For hard-surface areas, a slope of one inch to eight feet is recommended. For field drainage, the type and quantity of use as well as the soil composition and type of grass will

A new track installation is put on hold. When designing sport facilities, build weather delays into schedules.
Courtesy of Watauga Democrat.

determine the system. Subsurface drainage systems are an exact science, and it is strongly recommended that an engineer be consulted.

Fencing must also be carefully planned. The characteristics required are stability, durability, economy, ease of maintenance, attractiveness, and effectiveness. The fencing used most often is woven wire, commonly called chain-link. Gauge 11 or more in weight is recommended, with H-shaped or round posts. Tops of fences should be smoothed unless it is necessary to install barbed wire. If there is any possibility that someone's foot could slide under the fence, the bottom must also be smooth. Note that fencing can be made with plastic coatings of a variety of colors, which makes it more attractive and smoother to touch.

Natural Grass
Although grass fields generally cannot withstand the same amount of constant use and abuse as synthetic surfaces, many players and coaches prefer grass. Research to improve grass fields, particularly for football, has been extensive. Dr. William Daniel, an agronomist from Purdue University, developed Prescription Athletic Turf (PAT), a sand-based system. The PAT system has been improved by adding a three-dimensional nylon webbing to reinforce the soil. This system has fostered deeper root growth and still allows excellent drainage. Another stimulant to deeper

root growth has been the Warren Turf Nursery system of washing the sod from grass before planting it in sand-based soils.

For baseball and other such fields, Bermuda (Hall, 1993a) and zoysiagrass grow best in warm areas with temperatures between 80°F and 95°F. For cooler areas, use bluegrasses or fescues, which grow best between 60°F and 75°F (Polk, undated). As many as one-fifth of all injuries that occur when playing outside result from poor playing surfaces, so a great deal of attention must be devoted to their installation and maintenance (Dorsch, 1993). Because most of the country has more clay in its natural state than is beneficial for drainage, growth, and noncompaction, usually more sand should be mixed in the subsurface (Berg, 1993). Of course, year-round top quality requires proper mowing, fertilization, moisture, and weed control and, depending on use and environmental factors, other treatments of de-thatching, aeration, disease and insect control, and supplementals such as iron and lime (Hall, 1993b; Ashman, 1993). In heavily used fields, a damage repair schedule must also be maintained (Horman, 1993; Outdoor Facilities, 2000).

The drainage of natural turf fields is one of the most important aspects. To avoid costly rebuilding, administrators must insist on proper initial installation. "A typical sand-based field includes 3 to 4 inches of pea gravel over the subgrade, topped with 12 to 14 inches of soil for the seedbed" (Watson, 1998, p. 60). Drainage can be improved by installing underground tubing, frequently placed in a herringbone pattern running from the center to the sidelines. Crowning also assists in drainage—18 inches for football, or, if the facility must be used for both football and soccer, 8 to 10 inches. Baseball fields drain from the mound to the bases with a four-inch drop (Watson, 1998).

Hybrid Turf

Hybrid turf might be too expensive for school installation, but it appears likely that it will be more extensively used in universities and professional facilities. An example is Memorial Stadium for the Baltimore Ravens. "The field is a combination

The last piece of the puzzle in the installation of a new artificial-turf soccer/field hockey/football field.
Courtesy of Watauga Democrat.

of natural and synthetic elements, sophisticated drainage, and a system that heats the field during cold weather" (Schmid, 1997a). The field is sand-based consisting of a shallow 6-inch root zone, rather than the usual 12-inch zone. The synthetic aspect consists of a layer of polypropylene fibers woven together to make an "open-weave" backing system. Three-inch polypropylene fibers were punched to create a backing with 1.5-inch-long artificial grass blades. The sand is filled in around these synthetic fibers to provide the medium for natural grass growth. The result was a turf that had a consistent surface with good traction and a field that did not freeze (Schmid, 1997a).

An example of an award-winning outdoor facility development is the Bullock Memorial Soccer Field Complex in Butte, Montana. As a result of the tragic death of a youngster, the community raised funds to construct a 20-acre complex next to the high school on donated land. The complex contains seven soccer fields, two of which can be converted to baseball fields, and a nature walk (Bradley, 1997).

Outdoor Synthetic Surfaces

Synthetic turf has been in use since 1964. Although it will continue to be used for baseball, football, field hockey, and soccer areas, it appears that future refinements will see synthetic turf being used in special areas, such as putting greens.

The number of contests that can be held on a natural grass field is severely limited by compaction and turf deterioration; the number that can be played on a synthetic field is limited only by scheduling. Estimates suggest that an artificial field can accommodate 15 times more wear than a natural grass field with about one-third the maintenance cost.

One persistently reported problem for artificial playing surfaces is their capacity to absorb heat. This factor is important in regard to possible heat illness. Research has shown that the temperatures of the turf surfaces were slightly higher (1° to 4°) than grass, but the humidity above the surfaces was slightly lower. It appears that no significant difference exists between natural grass and synthetic turf as to the propensity for heat illness.

The debate continues as to relative safety between natural and artificial turf. To date, no definitive study has been accepted, although several studies seem to show greater incidence of injuries from artificial turf on the higher levels of football, and players have consistently favored the natural grass. An important key is the quality of the shock pad under the artificial turf, which has been improved greatly in recent years. This probably invalidates all previous studies.

> Attractions for operators include that the surface is repairable, picturesque, portable, durable, stable, and paintable, and drains rapidly. However, the greatest detractor of synthetic surfaces for the operator is the life of the surface, approximately 15 years (Sawyer, 1999, p. 315).

Synthetic turf systems provide the most durability and allow for the greatest field-use flexibility, but critics have believed that injury rates are higher from the hardness. Firms have concentrated on producing a synthetic surface that feels and plays like natural turf without increasing injury rates. One company, FieldTurf, Inc., claims to have achieved this (Patterozzi, 1997).

Students seeking detailed information related to artificial playing surfaces should consult the Sports Turf Managers Association, Box 1926, Appleton, WI 54913.

To Light or Not to Light?

A planner's dilemma is whether to build two unlighted fields, or one lighted field; or two banks of tennis courts, or one bank of lighted courts. For teaching purposes, the more fields or courts the better. For intramural and community use, the lighted facilities are more advantageous for late afternoon and night use. At colleges in particular, lighted recreational facilities will be effectively used even late into the night. (See Tables 10.2 and 10.3.)

In most school and recreation settings, lighting will be for multipurpose applications, or multiple fields in the same location—for example, a cluster of softball/youth baseball diamonds, or a field for soccer/football/field hockey. Lighting levels and pole placement become extremely important planning factors. Limiting light pollution and controlling spill and glare are also vital. It has been reported that sharing light poles and fixtures among several sports can reduce initial costs by 40 percent. Some of the technical aspects to address include selecting the type and height of poles, quality and quantity of lights, number of luminaire assemblies, and the type and number of switching controls. The system must comply with the National Electric Code and local and state codes and have Underwriters Laboratory approval. For further information, contact The Illuminating Engineering Society of North America (IESNA) at www.iesna.org (Sawyer, 1999, p. 115). For material on lighting, write to the National Lighting Bureau, 2101 L Street, N.W., Suite 300, Washington, D.C. 20037 (Moon, 1987).

Pole locations and heights of the lamps are very important. Locate the poles so the glare of the light does not impair play. For baseball, light should be directed from between four and eight locations with the poles set back 30 feet or more. For football, locate four to six poles along each side, set back about 75 feet with each holding a dozen or more lights. Computers should be used to determine the best combination of beam spreads to obtain the most uniform lighting (Frier, 1988).

Tracks

There are two general types of tracks: natural and synthetic. Natural tracks can be composed of dirt, clay, cinders, or grass. Grass tracks are common in some other countries, and grass training tracks (sometimes only one lane around outside of the regular track) are recommended by some authorities.

Synthetic tracks are of two types: (1) asphaltic and rubber composition, which includes sand-asphaltic; and (2) elastomeric, which includes polyurethanes, polyvinyl chlorides, and rubber composition tracks. All tracks should slope 1 percent from outside to inside. Although the running surface is very important, careful planning of the field event areas is also necessary. Frequently, the vaulting and throwing areas are not within sight of the viewing stands and are too far from the other areas for the coach to supervise. Unless the complex is in a region without appreciable rainfall, ensure that substantial water traps are on the inside of the track. For throwing circles, install a drain adjacent to the circle, and have a small recessed drain in the middle. One nice advantage of synthetic applications is the great choice of colors (Steinbach, 2002a).

It might be helpful for a track and field planning committee to divide the project into four basic phases: needs and space assessment, organizational structure, track design, and construction. The largest commitment of time and money is likely to be in the selection of the track surface. It might be helpful to develop a "specific weighted percentage for different categories such as price, timeliness, material content, contract completion history, etc." (Tollison, 1996, p. 40). For specifications, refer to the Track Construction manual, U.S. Track and Tennis Court Builders Association, 720 Light St., Baltimore, MD 21230.

As new multipurpose arenas are constructed, many are incorporating indoor tracks. The greatest limitations on many are the extremely short and dangerous "run-outs" at the end of the sprint sections, and the lack of spectator seating unless the track is on floor level inside the arena. An example of an excellent design is that at Penn State, with a 200-meter hydraulically banked track, six 42-inch outside lanes, and eight 48-inch sprint lanes down the middle (Wilson, 2000).

Outdoor Seating

The location of outdoor seating depends on the sport, the geographic placement of the facility,

and the time of day the contests will be viewed. For example, for tennis viewing, the preferred seats are at the end lines. For football, it is important whether the games are played at night or day. In a cold climate with afternoon games, fans prefer to be in the sun, whereas in warm climates, fans prefer the shade. The same applies to baseball; however, because it is usually warmer in baseball season, the prime consideration is how to avoid having fans look directly into the sun during late afternoon games.

Careful safety inspections must be performed on all seating facilities. Fans will be distracted while moving in and out; the crowd noise masks normal walking sound cues; and trash builds up quickly and causes obstacles. Special attention to color cues for steps and other locations should be utilized. Substantial railings at the ends and rear should be installed. If bleachers must be used, it is recommended that they be raised so that people in the first row can see clearly over people walking in front of them. Careful measurement of the sight lines for all seats must be calculated so that sufficient vertical rise between rows is planned (Sawyer, 1999 p. 251; Popke 2002c).

Tennis Courts

The planning and construction of tennis courts offer a unique challenge. Planners need to consider who will use the courts and within what kind of program, and what kind of surface the geographical and climate conditions necessitate. The user specialist must question surface details, including glare, ball skid, spin, discoloration, and foot slide.

The majority of Americans play on outdoor hard courts, which make up about 80 percent of all tennis courts. These courts are usually made of a rough asphalt base coated with a smooth, sand-textured acrylic. As the concentration of sand increases, the slower the courts play, which promotes learning an all-around game and is better for beginners and seniors. Most courts today are two-tone green (Steinbach, 2002a).

It is recommended that core samples be taken before multiple courts are constructed. For school installations, banks of eight courts are recommended to provide enough space for effective teaching and to host matches efficiently. In laying out the courts, pay particular attention to the wind and sun. Heavy-duty fencing, 10 feet high, is required, with the bottom wires bent over. Use "H" type or round poles with fencing placed on the inside. Nonporous courts should drain from side to side with a slope of from .5 percent to a maximum of 1.5 percent depending on the type of surface. The minimum size of double courts, including the perimeter space, would be 122 feet by 66 feet. The minimum distance between side-by-side courts is 12 feet (Sawyer, 1999, p. 274). Details may be obtained from the U.S. Tennis Association, 729 Alexander Rd., Princeton, NJ 08540; and the U.S. Tennis Court and Track Builders Association, 720 Light St., Baltimore, MO 21230.

Stadiums

The trend in recent decades in stadium design has shifted from new concepts to adopting new technologies and refinements in construction and materials and combining existing designs. Stadiums are being designed to be more fan-friendly and more of a total entertainment center. To accomplish this, concourses have been widened and established on each level. Rest rooms have been increased, and some have been designed for either sex so that depending on the expected sex mix of a crowd, the rooms can be adjusted by just changing the entrance signs. Increasing attention has been paid to meeting the demands of the Americans with Disabilities Act, as well as providing more club seating and luxury suites (Sawyer, 1999, pp. 395–396).

In renovating existing stadiums, or building new, locating the field at below grade has been successfully utilized, Colorado University, Washington State, and New Mexico State at LasCruces have followed this path, Ohio State recently renovated their stadium by lowering the field by over 13 feet (Wilson, 2000).

Much publicity has been devoted to various multimillion-dollar superdomes. Several colleges, however, have spent a modest amount to build domes in which football and most other activities take place. Although originally plagued by a very difficult roofing problem, the minidome

at East Tennessee State University has proved an excellent addition. Kibbie Dome at the University of Idaho seats 21,000 for football and 10,000 for basketball in temporary seats. When the 400-foot roof was installed, the asphalt floor base was covered with a synthetic surface, suitable for track, tennis, volleyball, and physical education classes. This surface is permanently marked for eight tennis courts, 11 volleyball courts, 16 badminton courts, and a 300-meter, five-lane running track.

Air Structures

Air structure facilities are commonly called "bubbles"; actually, they are pneumatic structures based on pressurized construction. The air structure operates on the principle of a balloon. The fabric is anchored to the ground, and air is then pumped in to inflate it. The door is constructed as an air lock to retain the pressure. This pressure is not noticed by participants.

The following are the advantages of air structures: low initial cost; speed of erection; ease of deflation, inflation, and repair; portability; adaptability for temporary functions; long-span and high-ceiling features; integrated heating, ventilation, and air pressure systems; maximum utilization of daylight illumination; possibly lower energy costs; less maintenance; and full utilization of space. The following are the disadvantages of air structures: limited portability in some applications; short life span; poor thermal insulation; acoustical problems; pressure problems; uncertain performance over a long period; restrictions due to wind; and high cost for liability insurance because of widely publicized deflations of large arenas (Sawyer, 1999, pp. 399–400).

Because heat gain is more a problem than heat loss, air structures have more potential in colder climates. When the span to be covered is greater than 300 feet, this type of structure becomes more economical than regular roofs. In addition to the air structures described previously, note that there is a variation called air-supported structures. These are designed so that air-filled fabric columns support the membrane.

Open up aquatic ccenters and let the sun in. Madison Recreation Facility. Madison, AL.
OpenAire, Inc.

Tensile Structures

Although air structures are frequently shaped with cables, tensile structures are not pneumatic and thus are not inflated. Instead, cables are strung from supports, and a fabric or membrane is laid over the cables. Frequently the cables are anchored to steel or concrete towers, or earthen berms are built up around the facility from which the cables are fixed. The primary advantages of the tensile design are open access from the sides; the potential to leave the facility unattended; and the great spans can be enclosed without center supports (Sawyer, 1999, p. 400).

> *Cable domes*
> Through a complex system of cables and girders, very large spans can be inexpensively covered by a fabric roof without the need for columns or fans to maintain integrity. Engineers predict that the cable dome concept is feasible for spans of at least 1,000 feet (Sawyer, 1999, p. 405).

■ AQUATIC CENTERS

At best, aquatic facilities are inflexible and so require diligent planning. Unfortunately, many swimming pool complexes are planned primarily for elite competition, even though such competition is only a small part of the pool's intended use.

The following are some of the other activities that require consideration in early planning stages: teaching; recreation; fitness; therapy; water volleyball and basketball; water polo; diving; synchronized swimming; scuba diving; kayaking and canoeing; sailing; windsurfing; lifesaving; swimnastics; flycasting; and underwater photography. In addition, forward-looking designers should allow for weight-training areas, hydropools, and underwater viewing windows.

Aquatic centers use tremendous amounts of energy. The Colorado Office of Energy Conservation adapted the following ideas (Steinbach, 2002b):

- Turn off special water features when they are not needed and when energy demand rates are high.
- Try reducing the water temperature in the lap pool.
- Wait 30 minutes to backwash the filter after turning off the circulation system.
- Backwash filters only when needed—that is, when the manufacturer's recommended pressure is reached.
- Cover the pool to block evaporation, keep in the heat, and reduce room ventilation needs.

- Buy a vacuum that returns water to the pool instead of sending it down the drain (Flynn and Schneider, 1997).

"Each year nearly 700 spinal cord injuries occur in the United States as a result of recreational diving" (DeMers, 1994, p. 17). Angela Dudziak states, "An average of 4,000 people drown each year. Recent technological advances have upgraded the safety of the 'open' pool by the invention of monitors. These high-tech detection systems have literally opened the eyes of many facility directors to new and revolutionary means of preventing pool fatalities" (Dudziak 2002 p. 18).

"Aquatic facility design has undergone a complete makeover during the past 10 to 20 years, responding to the changing demographics and interests of the swimming public. Once defined by rectangular competition pools with separate diving tanks and kiddie pools, the industry has welcomed a new generation of family-friendly aquatic facilities characterized by larger shallower free-form bodies of water with zero-depth entry, water slides, current rivers, and interactive play features" (Hunsaker, 2002, pp. 68–69). Details regarding swimming pool design are beyond the scope of this text. The rapidly changing design features of such items as movable bulkheads, vortex or wave pools, hydraulic lifts, movable bottoms, and automatic water- and air-conditioning systems are but a few of the technical advances. Those interested in design details should refer to the National Swimming Pool Institute and current periodical references (Hughes, 1993).

Water Treatment

When it comes to chemical treatment of the water in swimming pools, the single most important variable is the number of swimmers using the facility. The operator of a residential pool, an agency/school pool, or a commercial pool can have very different requirements. Many myths about maintaining the chemical balance in water in swimming pools exist. For example, sand filters do not need to be run 24 hours a day. Swimming pools with sand filters do not have to "back wash" every day. Indoor pools will benefit from utilizing pool coverings. It is not necessary to use large amounts of acid to sanitize pools and maintain an acceptable pH level (Schmid, 1997b; Ward and Hunsaker, 1997).

Water in swimming pools is kept clean by sanitation and filtration. The former is achieved by using agents such as bromine, ozone, or chlorine to kill microscopic bacterial debris. There are three filtration media: sand, diatomaceous earth, and cartridge filters. Sand is the most commonly used in commercial operations. Gravity, rapid-rate, and high-rate are three types of sand filters used (Ward and Hunsaker, 1997).

■ FACILITY MANAGEMENT

During the approval stage for the construction of the facility, ensure that appropriate budgeting is provided for the staffing of the arena or stadium. It is folly to build a new or expanded facility and expect the existing staff to operate it. Whether that staff is made up of a creation director and specialists, or athletic director and usual staff and coaches, these people are already fully occupied with their present positions. Depending on the complexity and size of the facility, staffing for administration, ticket sales, maintenance, security, and most important, marketing and public relations needs to be planned. Facility management is entertainment business. Trained professionals are required to effectively administer booking and event operation for circuses, speakers, concerts, exhibitions, trade shows, job fairs, and tournaments as well as in-house contests and special events (Popke, 2002c).

There are numerous job opportunities in facility management. Many of these positions will grow out of internships, which are highly recommended and should be an integral part of sport management programs. One student secured a nonpaying one-semester internship with a professional football franchise. After graduation, she was employed as a full-time tour director for the stadium. The next year, she was promoted to the administrative position of director of tours and hospitality. See Chapters 2 and 4 for further material on personnel, training, and staffing.

Table 10.5 Organizations Advancing Standards	
American National Standards Institute (ANSI)	National Fire Protection Association (NFPA)
American Society of Testing and Materials (ASTM)	**www.nfpa.org/Home/index.asp**
www.astm.org	European Committee for Standardization (CEN)
International Environmental Health and Safety	**www.cenorm.be/**
www.lbl.gov/ehs/	International Standards Organization (ISO)
American College of Sports Medicine (ACSM)	**www.iso.ch/**
International Recognized Association of Quality Clubs	National Spa and Pool Institute (NSPI)
(IRSA)	**www.nspi.org**
United States Tennis Association (USTA)	World Waterpark Association (WWA)
www.usta.com	**www.waterparks.com**

Source: Sawyer, T. H., ed. (1999). *Facility planning for physical activity and sport: Guidelines for development* (9th ed., pp. 48–63). Dubuque, Iowa: Kendall/Hunt Publishing Company.

■ PLAYGROUNDS

Because of safety and Americans with Disabilities (ADA) concerns, there is increased interest and pressure for safe, well-conceived playground design and construction. The Access Board for ADA had developed a set of guidelines for play areas. They are published in Section 15.6 of the ADA Accessibility Guidelines (Malkusak, Schappet, and Bruya, 2002). "Designing playgrounds to encourage dynamic play is about creating a sense of place or belonging. It should invite exploration through sight, sound, touch, and smell. A playground is the very essence of the 'Art of Play,' as opposed to the 'Function of Play' " (Hendy, 2002, p. 65). There are some who feel the solution is to eliminate playgrounds. Children, however, " . . . need the physical, social, and multisensory experiences that take place during play. What they don't need are playgrounds with hidden hazards" (Peterson, 2002).

A driving force to produce better playgrounds comes from the injury statistics. The U.S. Consumer Product Safety Commission (CPSC) reports that each year almost 204,000 preschool and elementary children receive emergency care for injuries that occur on playground equipment. About three-quarters of these injuries occur on public equipment. There is now national demand for states to adopt laws based on the safety guidelines outlined by CPSC in *A Handbook for Public Playground Safety* ("Legislation Proposed," 2002).

Two important factors in the design of playgrounds are the ground surface and equipment height. Rubber surfaces result in injury rates about half those of bark and one-fifth of concrete. A general recommendation is that with resilient surfaces, the height of climbing equipment and slides should not exceed six feet for school-age children and a maximum of four feet for preschool children (Frost et al., 2002). The safety of the playground also depends on how well it is maintained. Uncompacted surface material will compact in time and will need tilling or replacement. Even the best playground should be regularly maintained and reviewed (Christiansen, 2002).

Standards established by professional organizations apply to all facilities & equipment. Architects and planning committee members should contact appropriate associations listed in Table 10.5.

Critical Thinking

In this and previous chapters, you have learned about the Americans with Disabilities Act, and some of its ramifications for sport administration. The case of *Paralyzed Veterans of America, et al. v. Ellerbe Becket Architects, P.C., et al.,* 1996, involves the specific area of providing accommodations for wheelchair patrons in the new MCI arena in Washington, D.C.

The ADA requires new public facilities to provide wheelchair areas that "provide people with physical disabilities a choice of admission prices and lines of sight comparable to those for members of the general public." In a 1994 supplement to its Title III, it amplifies this: "in assembly areas where spectators can be expected to stand during the event or show being viewed, wheelchair locations must provide lines of sight over spectators who stand." The new guidelines require that new facilities must adhere to the "1 percent plus 1" formula. Thus MCI should provide 181 accessible spaces for basketball, 173 for hockey, and 186 for staged events. The district court ruled that a substantial number of these must have "enhanced sight lines."

The plaintiffs contended that the MCI Center fell short on both the number of spaces with clear lines of sight when patrons stood, and the proper dispersion in all prices of seating. It was undisputed that the lower bowl would have 64 enhanced spaces, while the club level would have 6 or 7. The defendants claimed that there were enough wheelchair spaces with enhanced sight lines, but the plaintiffs rebutted that 110 of these clear-sight-line spaces were in luxury boxes not available for the public. The court ruled that luxury suites do not constitute general seating areas. The defendants suggested that they would either cover and not sell some of the seats in front of the wheelchair spaces, or post and enforce "no standing" rules for people sitting in these seats. The court rejected these proposals. The court further ordered that the 72 upper bowl seats be redesigned to comply with enhanced sight line requirements. The court did not define a "substantial" number of enhanced sight spaces, but it was agreed that 78 to 88 percent of the spaces would meet the standard.

Both parties appealed the court's rulings, with the plaintiffs wanting all spaces to have enhanced sight lines, and the defendants stating that the court erred in interpreting the required sight lines. The appellate court rejected both parties and affirmed the trial court's findings. For information on ADA, visit the U.S. Department of Justice ADA home page at www.usdoj.gov/crt/ada/adahoml.htm or call 800-514-0301 (Wong and Goering, 1997).

1. Do you agree with the trial court's findings?
2. Why did the trial court refuse to accept the proposal to cover and not sell some seats, or enforce "no standing" rules, for those who sat in those seats to achieve the enhanced lines of sight?
3. The plaintiffs objected to the fact that the majority of the upper bowl spaces were in the end zone. According to ADA requirements, on what basis was the contention made?
4. If you were the defendants, what action would you suggest to meet the court's demands?

Exercises

1. Tour your facilities; list problems or inadequacies.
2. You are the AD and chairperson of the physical education department of a 2,000-student high school.

An old gymnasium has been destroyed by fire. The principal has arranged for you to make a presentation to the school board on how to plan for the replacement of the facility. Either write the report you would make or present the report to the class.

3. Contrast the three approaches for controlling the fiscal process of a project—lump sum bidding, the construction management system, and the design/build method.
4. Outline how the complex you are now in could be made more energy efficient.
5. Assume it has been determined that a gymnasium at the institution you are attending needs to be replaced or renovated. Using the appropriate factors, analyze whether you would build new or renovate.
6. Prepare a report as to how you would recommend selecting the architect for the project in Exercise 5.
7. Describe a situation in which a new sport facility could be built in such a way that the institution would likely lose a lawsuit even though the structure itself was safe.
8. List how the beauty or functional use of one of the gymnasiums in your present institution could have been improved by utilizing a different approach for walls, ceilings, windows, doors, or surfaces.
9. List the ways acoustics could be improved in the room you are in.
10. Select any sport facility with which you are familiar. Identify the ways it could have been built more efficiently for security and maintenance.
11. Redesign all of the lighting (inside and out) currently in use at your college or university sport facilities.
12. Using a scale of one inch equals 25 feet, cut out of construction paper various colors to scale to represent the following areas for a 1,500-student middle school, grades 4 through 9: (a) multipurpose gymnasium with one regulation basketball court and two smaller cross courts, (b) a multipurpose gymnastics/dance/wrestling room, (c) a small playfield for softball, and (d) a playfield large enough for soccer.

References

Ames, A. (1993, April). Cleaning problem. *Cleaning and Maintenance Management* 9, p. 10.

Ashman, D. (1993, May). Greener pastures. *Athletic Management* 5, pp. 23–29.

Berg, R. (1993, May). High tech turf. *Athletic Business* 17, pp. 47–50.

Bernard, A. W. (1997, August). What recreation facilities cost. *Athletic Business* 21, pp. 32–41.

Bradley, M. (1997, February/March). A safe place, Butte High School. *Athletic Management* 9, pp. 22, 38.

Bynum, M. (2002a, Jan.). After school special. *Athletic Business* 26, pp. 30–33.

Bynum, M. (2002b, Jan.). Space odyssey. *Athletic Business* 26, pp. 67–73.

Bynum, M (2002c, April). Custom fit. *Athletic Business* 26, pp. 60–71.

Bynum, M. (2002d, April). Wishes granted. *Athletic Business* 26, pp. 34–38.

Bynum, M. (2002e, May). Warming up to ice. *Athletic Business* 26, pp. 36–46.

Christiansen, M. (2002, April). Playground needs assessment: initial steps. *Parks and Recreation* 37, pp. 84–91.

Cioletti, J. (1998, January). From the ground up. *Club Industry* 14, pp. 23–30.

Cohen, A. (1993a, March). Locker rooms: What works, what doesn't. *Athletic Business* 17, pp. 61–66.

Cohen, A. (1993b, April). Another wonder of the world. *Athletic Business* 17, pp. 49–51.

Cohen, A. (1998, January). Team needs. *Athletic Business* 22, pp. 47–52.

Cohen, A. (2002a, May). Reflections. *Athletic Business* 26, pp. 48–55.

Cohen, A. (2002b, July). A crowded field. *Athletic Business* 26, pp. 48–56.

Cooper, K. G. (1993, March). The rework cycle: Benchmarks for the project manager. *Facilities and Strategic Planning* pp. 17–21.

DeMers, G. (1994, April). To dive or not to dive: What depth is safe? *Journal of Physical Education, Recreation and Dance* 65, pp. 17–22.

Dillon, J. (1996, August/September). Changes in the changing room. *Athletic Management* 8, pp. 45–49.

DiLullo, D. (2002, Feb.). The new sports architecture design and technology. *Coach and Athletic Director* 71, pp. 100–105.

Dirty. (2002, March). *Athletic Business* 26, pp. 72–73.

Dorr, M. (1997, October). Show your facility in a better light. *Cleaning and Maintenance Management* 34, pp. 82–83.

Dorsch, G. (1993, January). Safe sports turf is well-maintained. *Parks/Grounds Management* 8, p. 20.

DuBray, B. (1993, April). Master builder. *American School Board Journal* 180, pp. 37–38.

Dudziak, A. (2002a, Feb.). The building blocks of athletic facilities: Fund raising. *Athletic Business* 26, pp. 26–29.

Dudziak, A. (2002b, April). Pool safety and technologies. *Athletic Business* 26, p. 18.

Dunn, M.; McMinn, W.; and Meyer, W. (1989, May). It's all in the timing. *College Athletic Management* 1, pp. 59–60.

Ellison, T. (1993, April). Sport floors. *Athletic Business* 17, pp. 54–60.

Farmer, P. J.; Mulrooney, A. L.; and Ammon, R. (1996). *Sport facility planning and management.* Morgantown, WV: Fitness Information Technologies.

Flynn, B., & Schneider, R. (1997, August). Energy audit. *Athletic Business 21*, 51–58.

Frier, J. P. (1988, March). Keeping users out of the dark. *Athletic Business 12*, pp. 38–43.

Frost, J.; Sutterby, J.; Therrell, J.; Brown, P.; and Thornton, C. (2002, April). Does height matter?, *Parks and Recreation 37*, pp. 73–83.

Getting organized. (1993, September). *Athletic Business 16*, p. 12.

Gimple, J. (1992, September). Laying the foundation. *Athletic Management 4*, pp. 32–38.

Gordon, C. (1989, March). Constructive help. *College Athletic Management 1*, pp. 35–38.

Graves, B. E. (1993, April). Choosing the right architect. *American School Board Journal 180*, p. 22.

Hall, J., III. (1993a, February). Bermudagrass athletic fields. *Parks/Grounds Management 46*, pp. 8, 23.

Hall, J., III. (1993b, July). Expanding the "window of opportunity" for turf applications will help. *Parks/Grounds Management 46*, pp. 8, 11–19.

Hart, T. (1997, September). Level the playing field, save money. *Cleaning and Maintenance Management 34*, p. 65.

Hauss, D. S. (1993, February). Flooring. *Club Industry 9*, pp. 39–45.

Hendy, T. (2002, June). Playgrounds for the mind, body, and spirit. *Parks and Recreation 37*, pp. 64–71.

Horine, L. E. (1987, January). Planning sport facilities. *Journal of Physical Education, Recreation and Dance 58*, pp. 22–26.

Horine, L. E., and Turner, E. T. (1979, December). Appalachian State's locker room renovation provides open atmosphere. *Athletic Purchasing and Facilities 3*, pp. 20–23.

Horman, W. (1993, January). A turf timetable. *Athletic Business 17*, pp. 51–54.

Hughes, W. L. (1993, February). Maintaining your balance on the facility design tightrope. *Parks and Recreation*, pp. 44–47.

Hughes, W. L. (1997, August). The aesthetic effect. *Athletic Business 21*, pp. 69–72.

Hunsaker, D. S. (2002, Mar.). Accidents will happen. *Athletic Business 26*, pp. 61–71.

Kosar, J. E. (2002, June). Cultivating dialogue before building. *The School Administrator 59*, pp. 28–30.

Ice Rink Engineering and Manufacturing Co. (1997). [Personal correspondence with the author.] 1727 E. Salufa Lake Rd., Greenville, SC 29611.

LaRue, R. J. (1997, October). That's a job for a consultant— a facility specialist! *Focus on Facilities 3*, pp. 1–4.

LaRue, R. (2002, Aug.). Safe in their seats? *Athletic Management XIV*, pp. 61–63.

Lavoie, H. R. (1989, January). Weight rooms that work. *Athletic Business 13*, pp. 28–32.

Legislation proposed to make playgrounds safe. (2002, summer). *Focus on Facilities V*, p. 1.

Lewis, E. J. (1993, May). Energy efficiency yields savings. *School Administrator*, p. 43.

Malkusak, T.; Schappet, J.; and Bruya, L. (2002, April). Turning accessible playgrounds into fully integrated playgrounds: Just add a little essence. *Parks and Recreation 37*, pp. 66–69.

McDonnell, A. (2000, Aug.) Flooring color and design. *Fitness Management 16*, pp. 54–56.

Moon, D. V. (1987, May). 1 lighted field = 2 unlighted fields v. cost savings. *Athletic Business 11*, pp. 40–46.

Nondiscrimination on the basis of disability by public accommodations and in commercial facilities (1994, July 1). Department of Justice, 28 CFR Part 36.

Outdoor facilities. (2000, April/May). *Athletic Management XII*, pp. 52–57.

Pappalardo, W. (2002, June). Proofing schools against vandalism. *The School Administrator 37*, p. 32.

Patterozzi, V. (1997, September). Turf tech. *Athletic Business 21*, pp. 41–48.

Pearce, B. (1998, January). Sign sense. *Athletic Business 22*, pp. 39–44.

Peterson, J. A. (2002, April). Eliminate playgrounds? *Parks and Recreation 37*, pp. 92–95.

Polk, R. (undated). *Baseball playbook*. P. O. Drawer 5327, Mississippi State University, Miss. 39762.

Popke, M. (2002a, Jan.). California dreaming. *Athletic Business 26*, pp. 26–29.

Popke, M. (2002b, May). After the fall. *Athletic Business 26*, pp. 56–62.

Popke, M. (2002c, May) Versatile venues. *Athletic Business 26*, pp. 72–80.

Popke, M. (2002d, July) Evolution. *Athletic Business 16*, pp. 69–76.

Raber, T. R. (1988, March 14). America's architects. *Sports Inc. 1*, pp. 18–19.

Renner, M. (1998, January). Results: The gym. *Fitness Management 14*, p. 30.

Rosner, D. (1987, November 16). Trouble in the building. *Sports Inc.*, pp. 71–72.

Sawyer, T. H., ed. (1999). *Facilities planning for physical activity and sport* (9th ed.) Dubuque, Iowa: Kendall/Hunt Publishing Company.

Schmid, S. (1993, April). Student attraction. *Athletic Business 17*, pp. 44–48.

Schmid, S. (1997a, September). Year-around turf. *Athletic Business 21*, p. 42.

Schmid, S. (1997b, October). Pool maintenance. *Athletic Business* 21, pp. 47–56.

Seidler, T. L.; Turner, E. T.; and Horine, L. E. (1993, January). Promoting active lifestyles through facilities and equipment. *Journal of Physical Education, Recreation and Dance* 64, pp. 39–42.

Sherman, R. M. (1997a, October). Strengthening weight rooms. *Athletic Business* 21, pp. 73–80.

Sherman, R. M. (1997b, November). Ice age. *Athletic Business* 21, pp. 32–34.

Steinbach, P. (2002a, Jan.) Beauty and brawn. *Athletic Business* 26, pp. 58–65.

Steinbach, P. (2002b, May). Water utility. *Athletic Business* 26, pp. 63–68.

Steinbach, P. (2002c, July). Great planes. *Athletic Business* 26, pp. 79–86.

Steinbach, P. (2002d, July). Money machines. *Athletic Business* 26, pp. 40–44.

Surfaces and Covers, (2000, Aug./Sept.). *Athletic Management* XII, pp. 58–65.

Sutterby, J.; Therrell, J.; Brown, P.; and Thornton, C. (2002, April). Does height matter? *Parks and Recreation* 37, pp. 73–83.

Thompson, G. and Riley, K. (2002, April). *Athletic Business* 26, pp. 97–106.

Tollison, S. (1996, April/May). Tracking an installation. *Athletic Management* 8, pp. 36–41.

Viklund, R. (1993, July). This old gym. *Athletic Business* 17, pp. 29–34.

Viklund, R., and Coons, J. (1997, September). Locker rooms. *Athletic Business* 21, pp. 63–71.

Vivian, J. (1997, December). Reining in rink costs. *Athletic Business* 21, pp. 79–88.

Ward, K., and Hunsaker, S. (1997, December). Filtration fundamentals. *Athletic Business* 21, pp. 91–98.

Watson, J. R. (1998, January). Waterworks. *Athletic Business* 22, pp. 59–64.

Weeks, A. B. (1993, April). Smart stripping. *Cleaning and Maintenance Management* 30, pp. 34–36.

Williams, T. (1993, April). How to care for Torginol floors. *Cleaning and Maintenance Management* 30, pp. 49–50.

Wilson, S. (2000, Oct./Nov.). Crowd pleasers. *Athletic Management* XII, pp. 47–54.

Wong, G. M., and Goering, J. R. (1997, September). Sitting targets. *Athletic Business* 21, pp. 20–23.

Zawadski, M. (1993, January). Saving through sharing. *School Business Affairs* 59, pp. 8–11.

11

Evaluation in Physical Education and Sport Administration

——————————— **Management Thought** ———————————

Good leaders are like baseball umpires:
they go practically unnoticed when doing their jobs right.

——————— **Case Study: It Is Necessary to Evaluate Equipment** ———————

In sport, a great amount of resources are devoted to equipment. Sufficient equipment of the proper quality influences the success of the program, whether it is physical education, athletics, recreation, or a fitness center. An administrator must ensure that purchased equipment is evaluated.

A school system has four high schools, six middle schools, and 10 elementary schools. Physical education is required for all students daily through the ninth grade, and offered as an elective for grades 10 through 12. Between these 20 schools, a tremendous amount of equipment is purchased each year. Each school has been ordering its own equipment each year. The assistant superintendent for business and the coordinator of physical education and athletics for the district completed a review of the purchases and concluded that buying equipment in bulk

would save money. The chairpersons of all the schools gave recommendations to identify their schools' needs. The committee then identified two models of basketballs that were to be used for each level. Bulk orders were placed after receiving competitive bids from national vendors, and each school received equal numbers of both models.

The committee asked each chairperson to solicit opinions from all physical education teachers, students, and equipment managers at the end of the school year. The high schools greatly favored one model over the other, the middle schools equally liked both models, and the elementary schools showed no interest in either model. This was an ongoing process, taking on a different area of equipment each year, but continuing to evaluate previous selections.

——————————— **Chapter Objectives** ———————————

The reader should be able to
1. Discuss how programs in physical education and sport might be evaluated.

2. Describe the major areas of evaluation of student performance in physical education and sport from the administrative perspective.

3. Describe the systems of evaluating faculty and coaches.
4. Describe how facilities and equipment used in physical education or sport can be evaluated.
5. Discuss performance evaluation of the professional staff.
6. Describe a system of evaluating administrators in education and sport.

▪ EVALUATION

From an administrative perspective, evaluation has many facets. The following areas need to be targeted:

- Personnel—physical educators, staff (clerks, maintenance workers, and so on), coaches, recreation supervisors, and fitness leaders.
- Programs—physical education curriculum, interscholastic sports program, intramural program, fitness workouts, and recreation program.
- Equipment and facilities.
- Students, athletes, recreators, and fitness participants.
- Administrators and managers.

Planning for the future requires gathering information to know what has happened in the past and where the organization is presently. In addition, evaluating people in meaningful ways will result in higher levels of performance.

> Measurement takes place when a test is administered and a score is obtained. If the test is quantitative, the score is a number. If the test is qualitative, the score may be a phrase or word such as "excellent"; or it may be a number representing a phrase or word. The process of evaluation involves the interpretation of a score . . . measurement is an objective, nonjudgmental process, whereas evaluation requires that judgments be made (Safrit and Wood, 1995, p. 5).

A manager of a fitness center might utilize the data from a survey of opinions of members to plan purchases of new equipment. An athletic director could utilize the results of a coach's evaluation to justify a merit pay increase.

Accountability through Evaluation

Several years ago, administrators, elected officials, and the public demanded accountability. "Justify how our dollars are being spent," they said. "Justify why the football team should have new uniforms." This has led to a renewed interest in measurement and evaluation. The following are macro-strategic approaches: Gather information in a systematic order on how well teachers, students, coaches, administrators, facilities, programs, and equipment have performed; learn how they are viewed by parents, participants, and members; do cost–benefit analyses of money spent related to spent program components; and regularly obtain evaluations from middle management to ascertain how well objectives are on target or are being met.

> Without convincing evidence of a program's contribution to goals held by national; state, or local authorities, it should not be surprising that . . . programs struggle to justify a claim to necessary resources (Doolittle and Fay, 2002, p. 24).

Lund and Kirk (2002) have suggested that such evaluation can be approached on a micro basis through criterion-referenced tests and surveys; performance and self-evaluation tests and surveys; objective written tests; anecdotal records; portfolios (especially for faculty/coaches/supervisors); interest inventories; and files of completed work, awards, honors, and accomplishments.

Develop an Evaluation Plan

Sport managers must be careful to plan evaluations *with* the staff and not attempt to autocratically thrust evaluations on them. The staff must be told precisely how the results will be used. If the results will be used for adverse personnel actions, as well as for promotions, this information should be communicated. Guidelines for an evaluation plan should include

1. Identification of the areas to be evaluated (coaches, teachers, curriculum, managers).
2. Identification of the evaluators.
3. Identification of those who will compute data.
4. Determination of who will see the results.
5. Establishment of a system of distribution, collection, and dates for accomplishing the process.
6. Selection and reproduction of the evaluation instrument.
7. Computation and organization of results in the most usable form.
8. A review of the results with appropriate people.
9. Utilization of the results to improve personnel and programs. Follow up on any action such as merit raises if this was outlined in the first step of the process.

Evaluating Equipment, Facilities, and Security

Evaluating the quality of equipment received against required standards or written specifications must take place. Inspection of existing or new facilities to evaluate needed corrections or to see if they meet specifications or security needs was covered in Chapter 10.

Student Evaluation

The product of the physical education and athletic program is the student. It is expected that every coach and teacher will complete an entire course in tests and measurement. From an administrative point of view, students should be aware that in recent years there has been considerable debate over how to evaluate students. Formative assessment, authentic assessment, performance assessment, portfolio assessment, and outcome-based assessment have all been touted (Zhu, 1997; Hensley, 1997; Lund, 1997; Lund and Kirk, 2002; Doolittle and Fay, 2002;

Kirk, 1997; Melograno, 1997; Joyner and McManis, 1997; Gréhaigne and Godbout, 1998). Thus, while this is an area of great importance to administrators, the details pertaining to student evaluations will be omitted.

The real problems that hinder effective assessments of elementary, middle, and secondary physical education and athletic programs include large classes, poor facilities for testing, unsupportive colleagues and higher authorities, too many classes, too few support staff, and lack of teacher preparation in meaningful measurements. All but the last of these are problems that require administrative action on the appropriate level to solve or at least reduce their severity.

Fitness testing falls within the area of student evaluation, but whether or not to schedule, and the choice of tests, *is* an administrative decision. For several decades, large numbers of students were tested with performance-based tests that emphasized motor fitness. In the 1990s health-related tests were favored. The validity of such tests, however, is debatable. More recent trends in assessment have developed around student achievement and criterion-referenced measures as opposed to content-based curricula. In this environment, the focus is on student performance against an established level, not against fellow students. The end result of this process is to have a "reverse curriculum mapping planning process" achieved through a five-step course of action. Lund and Kirk (2002, p. 142) identified those steps as

1. Establishment of major unit themes.
2. Culminating product and rubric.
3. Essential knowledge, skills, and abilities.
4. Learning activities and performance-based assessments.
5. Critical resources.

In summary, "when schools can demonstrate that through their program students have achieved standards endorsed by state and school officials, they are more likely to gain both the social and administrative support for better quality programs" (Doolittle and Fay, 2002, p. 24).

Another interesting management concern in student evaluation is whether higher education seniors should be required to pass an exit test of physical skills and techniques and/or a comprehensive written examination before being approved for graduation. If not, why not? Should candidates for master's or doctoral degrees be required to pass comprehensive examinations? A study on the master's level showed that 25 percent of degree programs required an oral examination only, 45 percent required a written examination only, and 30 percent required both. The average length of the oral examination was 1.6 hours, and 4.6 hours for the written. The average number of examiners for the oral was 3.2, and 3.9 for the written examination (Horine, 1992). Many states have also developed content-based exams for physical education graduates who desire certification to teach.

From an administrative position, it is not enough to work with the faculty or staff to devise a well-conceived student evaluation plan, but all client groups must understand and support the initiative. In a school situation, this includes the parents, students, all teachers, and the higher administration. Many people have a general disdain and fear of testing, and when it has a strange-sounding new name like "performance assessment," it can automatically arouse a negative attitude. "Success or failure often depends on how well you have informed parents and the general community of impending changes" (Alvestad, 1997, p. 16).

Evaluation of Programs

The primary purposes of evaluating the physical education and/or athletic program are to improve them and to provide accountability. Whatever method or instrument is used, the basis for evaluation should be to measure the degree to which the program's stated goals are attained. The first step in program evaluation is to review existing goals or objectives of the unit and, if there is no such statement, to write one.

Methods of Evaluating Programs

One method of program evaluation is *system analysis*. In this method the various subunits or sections are examined to determine how well each is meeting its goals. For example, in a college physical education major program, comparisons might be made among health, physical education, recreation, and dance on how many credit hours are generated in relation to the number of faculty.

Cost–benefit analysis, previously mentioned, is discussed further in financial management (Chapter 6).

Program evaluations are most effective when they are either ongoing or planned for periodic intervals. This type of evaluating is referred to as *formative*. The feedback of the evaluation during the program allows administrative adjustments to improve results. Evaluation at the end of a program is called *summative*. In well-managed sport organizations both formative and summative evaluations exist.

Ultimately, program evaluation must be based on the strategic planning activities of the organization. Just as in student assessment, program assessment must begin with the end product in mind. Thus program assessment is tied to organizational planning. Bridges and Roquemore (2000, p. 146) define strategic planning as "the process of determining an organization's long-term goals and objectives in compliance with its mission and formulating the proper plan of action (strategy), policies, and programs with which to ensure that sound decisions will be made about internal resources and environmental factors that affect all effort to achieve the desired end results in the long run."

Following this pattern, managers must utilize the prescribed plan and a guide to assess the current situation. Management by Objectives (MBO) evolved in the late 1950s and has been a force in business management for the ensuing decades. According to Bridges and Roquemore (2000), the use of MBO allows managers to move directly from organizational planning to assessment. This assessment can be applied to the organization as a whole, units of the organization, and even individuals within the organization. Specifically, they cite the essential requirements for an MBO program as

1. The primary objectives (why the organization exists).

2. The operating objectives (annual or 12-month objectives).

3. Unit objectives (annual objectives for divisions, branches, departments, and so on).

4. Individual managerial objectives.

5. Individual nonmanagement employees' objectives (p. 125).

The essence of MBO is to set measurable standards and criteria for organizational success. Program appraisal naturally follows through the measurement of those standards and criteria. It's relatively straightforward: "measure performance; then compare performance to the standards" (Bridges and Roquemore, 2000, p. 334).

An excellent example can be seen in the planning and assessment of the U.S. Figure Skating Association's (USFSA) Strategic Plan for 2002–2006 (2002a). After a very successful 2002 Winter Olympic Games, the goals were set for the coming quadrennium. First they assessed skaters from 2002 that were committed to returning to Olympic competition for Turin in 2006. The 2002 medalists and the top 15 finishers were all queried regarding their plans. Next USFSA managers profiled the best prospects from the junior ranks that had legitimate chances for success at the Olympic level through an athlete talent identification and development pipeline program. Systems for scientific research and development, biomechanics, injury tracking, elite coach education, and organizational political influence were crafted with specific strategies and tasks. Finally, exact medal targets for Turin 2006 were set, with a goal of one gold and three other medals (U.S. Figure Skating Association, 2002b).

■ PERFORMANCE EVALUATION

Although performance evaluation of teachers, coaches, and fitness personnel is generally supported by boards and management, it is still controversial. Too many ill-conceived and even capricious evaluation schemes have been established, based on poor systems and instruments.

> To ensure they are of benefit to both the employee and the sport organization, appraisals should first and foremost be relevant. That is, there should be a link between what is expected in the job and the criteria used to evaluate the individual doing the job. Performance appraisals should also, like selection devices, be reliable. Reliability here essentially means that whatever method is used, different raters evaluating the same person should arrive at a somewhat similar conclusion. Finally, the effectiveness of a performance appraisal system is enhanced if it has the support of all members of the organization (Slack, 1997, p. 243).

In referring to the mandatory summative evaluations of all teachers every year, Duke (1993, p. 703) stated,

> If there is a less meaningful ritual for the vast majority of experienced teachers, it would be hard to find. The idea of evaluating all competent teachers every year according to a common set of performance standards that, at best, represent minimum or basic expectations is little short of institutional insult. Teachers and administrators both know that these evaluations are a terrible waste of time and energy.

For many years, performance evaluation was based on traits and attributes. Thus traits such as good grooming and looks, good speech, or a pleasant personality were believed to be related to high capability for teaching, coaching, and supervisory superior performance. These lists were further expanded to include such traits as enthusiasm, flexibility, humor, judgment, originality, initiative, persistence, self-control, integrity, cooperation, morality, and the like. Research has not supported the validity of such systems. Before 1980, performance evaluation research was primarily directed toward developing valid and reliable rating scales, training raters to reduce rating errors, and improving observational skills. Since that time, research has focused on understanding the rating process itself more clearly.

If teaching, coaching, and fitness instructors have achieved the requisite level to be called professionals, a mandatory requirement is evaluation by each area. It is not an option to take a position that performance evaluation is too difficult or too costly—we must do the best we can—it is a required administrative duty. Only through evaluation can weaknesses be identified and corrected, and achievements and positive results be validated, recognized, and awarded.

Performance appraisals determine the extent to which the individual employee and/or his work group are contributing to the overall purpose of the sport organization. More specifically, appraisals contribute to enhancing the effectiveness and efficiency of sport organizations by guiding management in making decisions about promotion, compensation, and the allocation of other forms of reward. They are also a means of identifying employees who are not performing up to the required standard and either removing them from the organization, disciplining them, or providing training to rectify their deficiencies. Performance appraisals are, in short, the key input into an organization's reward-and-punishment system (Slack, 1997, pp. 242–243).

In recent years *product evaluation,* or student achievement, has been a popular basis for teacher evaluation. Student achievement is so dependent on extraneous, uncontrolled factors that this method of teacher evaluation doesn't appear to be effective. In some districts and in most institutions of higher education, teacher evaluations also take into consideration contributions to the community and professional organizations, research, leadership, and service.

Evaluation of Faculty and Professional Staff

Jackson and Schuller (1999) defined performance appraisal as "a formal, structured system for measuring, evaluating, and influencing an employee's job-related attributes, behaviors and outcomes. Its focus is on discovering how productive the employee is and whether he or she can perform as or more effectively in the future, so that the employee and the organization both benefit" (p. 453). With this in mind, conducting appropriate personnel evaluations is a critical skill for sport managers. In our society, salaries, promotions, and career advancement often depend on a person's evaluation. As such, evaluation is key to both the organization's and the employee's future.

Unfortunately, many sport managers are not well trained in employee evaluation. To date, no universally accepted protocol has emerged. The challenge for sport managers is to develop and conduct employee appraisals that are objective and valid. Historically, many forms of evaluation have been used. Some have used ranking, where

employees are placed in order from best to worst. Unfortunately, this system places no value judgment on how good the best employee is or how poorly the worst employee performs. Rating scales have also been a popular evaluation method. In this system, the evaluator assigns a numerical rating to different aspects of employee performance measures. Terms such as *excellent, good,* or *below average* are typical with this method. The problem with this method is that there are different opinions of what *good* means and how it may differ from *excellent.* It also provides little information to the employee about how to advance from *good* to *excellent.*

Maiorca (1997) recommends that managers develop a set of performance dimensions and a subsequent set of descriptors for each dimension that represent a wide range of actual job behaviors from poor performance to outstanding performance. The following steps will assist the development of these *behaviorally anchored rating scales (BARS):*

1. Managers and employees familiar with the job should create a list detailing the activities that are essential to effective job performance. These become the performance dimensions.

2. The same people must also develop statements that accurately describe the range of performance from poor to excellent on each dimension.

3. A reference group of employees (also familiar with the job) should be used to clarify the wording and judge the appropriateness of the items.

4. Managers next review the information obtained from step 3 and revise the instrument accordingly.

5. The dimension performance descriptors are subsequently paired with a numerical rating such that each description also has a number assigned. In this case a person who is assigned a "2" on a factor can associate that number with a performance statement.

6. The resulting document is a behaviorally anchored rating scale with ordered and scaled descriptors related to the performance standards of the position. (See Figure 11.1 for sample statements.)

For an employee of a fitness center:		
Performance Dimension	Poor Performance	Outstanding Performance
Product knowledge	Insufficient knowledge about programs and services available to members	Extremely knowledgeable of all aspects of club programs and services
Dependability	Too unreliable to be retained without improvement	Always regular and prompt; volunteers for overtime when needed

For a coach in an athletic department:		
Performance Dimension	Poor Performance	Outstanding Performance
Skill instruction	Coach shows little or no evidence of appropriate teaching techniques	Coach demonstrates a variety of unique and effective teaching techniques
Staff relations	Does not communicate well with administration or other staff members	Consistently exhibits regular and effective communication with administration and staff

For a sport event manager:		
Performance Dimension	Poor Performance	Outstanding Performance
Planning	Consistently lax in developing plans for the conduct of events	Develops, implements, and adapts plans for the effective conduct of events
Public relations	Seldom paticipates in PR activities and performs inefficiently in public forums	Exhibits mastery level public speaking skills and consistently manages sensitive situations well in public forums

Figure 11.1   Sample Statement for a Behaviorally Anchored Rating Scale.

Another benefit of BARS is that it serves as an excellent document if personnel evaluation decisions result in litigation. As noted earlier in Chapter 8, we are a litigious society. People, if fired, will often file suit against supervisors and the sport organization. The use of BARS has been very effective in showing that termination decisions have been based on objective evaluations of job-specific components ("Minimize Performance Evaluation Legal Risks," 1998).

MBO is comprised of four steps: (1) performance standards are established for each person; (2) the standards are monitored; (3) a remediation process is established for those failing to achieve standards; (4) validation of achievement is established (qualitative and quantitative) concentrating on results rather than personality characteristics or individual skills.

Peer Evaluation.   Peer evaluation has several positive elements. Some authorities believe colleague evaluation is required to achieve true professional status. Peers are in the best position to evaluate the quality of performance, and administrators generally endorse peer evaluation to broaden the base of ratings and reduce the impact of the administrator's evaluation. When peer evaluations have been endorsed by associations and used to help staff improve, but not for adverse action, the system has had good results.

However, peer evaluations also have negative elements. It is difficult to arrange for in-class visitations. Personality problems may enter into the evaluation, and there is no agreement as to what constitutes quality teaching. Teachers generally dislike evaluating colleagues. Peer evaluation frequently requires considerable time and paperwork; and if evaluation is done honestly, friendships are jeopardized.

Student Evaluation of Faculty.   Possible purposes and uses for student evaluations include providing data for accountability to boards or councils; assisting in improving the competencies of the instructors; providing data to students so they can make more informed selection of instructors; and making decisions on merit pay increases, employment retention, removal, promotion, or granting tenure.

The use of student evaluations of professors in higher education is quite common. One study of 200 institutions showed that 86 percent utilized student evaluations; most schools informed ad-

ministrators of the results. Another study of 100 teacher education programs showed that 84 percent used student evaluations. Neither research nor expert opinion, however, agrees on the usefulness of student evaluations.

Reasons for not supporting student evaluations include the lack of experience and maturity of the students as well as many variables such as class size; amount and difficulty of the subject matter; sex of the teacher or student; rank of the teacher; level of the class; whether the course is required or elective; grades awarded in the past; time of the day and days of the week; and instructor's personality. Also, student evaluations take valuable class, clerical, and computer time, and they require the cost of the materials. Finally, little evidence supports the idea that instruction improves because of student evaluations; however, they may inhibit academic freedom and encourage "enjoyable" rather than rigorous course content.

What's right with student evaluations? There is no evidence that extraneous variables such as class size, teacher's sex, or grade point average of the rater bias evaluations. Because the student *is* the consumer, she or he is in the best position to judge the quality of the experience. To provide accountability, student evaluations must be included—it is better to have imperfect data for administrative action than no data. And there is no evidence that student evaluations have decreased teaching performance, and they might motivate some instructors to try harder to improve.

The following are recommended steps for initiating student evaluations:

1. Unless the instrument and procedures are handed down from top officials, involve the staff in designing them.

2. If possible, emphasize that the major purpose of the evaluations is to improve instruction.

3. If the purpose is for administrative personnel action (such as merit pay, promotion, tenure), design the instrument so that one or two general statements relate to the professor, such as "The overall rating of the instructor is . . ." and use only these generalized statement results for personnel action.

Student Evaluation Form

Scale:	Awful			Poor			Average			Good			Excellent		

Scale: Awful   Poor   Average   Good   Excellent

      0   1   2   3   4   5   6   7   8   9

Darken only ONE circle for each statement.

1. The instructor's ability to stimulate increased student interest in the subject matter is
2. The instructor's preparation for this class is
3. The instructor's use of outside resources is
4. The instructor's daily utilization of highlighting, reviewing and summarizing is
5. The instructor's ability to encourage students to think is
6. The instructor's accessibility to students is
7. The instructor's effective utilization of class time is
8. The instructor's enthusiasm for the subject matter is
9. The instructor's ability to evaluate students on the material covered in the course is
10. The instructor's ability to involve students in class participation discussion is
11. The instructor's presentation of different points of view is
12. The instructor's ability to provide thorough evaluation feedback is
13. The instructor's discussion and presentation of current developments relating to subject matter is
14. The instructor's ability to use a variety of teaching styles is
15. The instructor's use of new and creative ideas in the class is
16. The instructor's ability to show a genuine interest in students is
17. The instructor's ability to provide an intellectual learning environment is
18. The instructor's ability to communicate the subject material on the students' level is
19. The instructor's ability to present course material in an organized manner is
20. The instructor's knowledge in the subject matter is
21. The instructor's ability to return evaluated materials promptly is
22. The instructor's fairness in evaluation is
23. The instructor's ability to accept students' ideas is
24. The instructor's comprehensive coverage of the subject matter is
25. My overall evaluation of this instructor is

Copyright 1989 Appalachian State University Department of Health, Leisure, and Exercise Science.

Figure 11.2 A sample student evaluation form used in higher education.

4. Carefully plan details with the staff as to the day evaluations should be given, how many classes should be included, the word-for-word instructions to students, and whether instructors should leave the room.

It is not a good policy to adopt in total an evaluation form used elsewhere, but starting with a tried and proved one is advised. Many published instruments can be used as guides; see Figure 11.2 for an example. The evaluation should take place about one-third into the course, and again at the end so that corrections and improvements can take place and be measured.

Administrative Evaluation. Faculty must be evaluated regularly. "Public education is an enterprise in which competence and incompetence are largely ignored. . . . the most egregious example is paying the best employees the same as the worst" (Murphy and Pimentel, 1996, p. 74). Some methods that can be utilized to evaluate teachers or professional staff are portfolio records, outcomes performance assessments, professional peer evaluation, administrator evaluations, and student evaluations. Within each of these types, there are myriad forms, instruments, and systems. Recently there has been a great deal of interest in using "authentic assessment" (Safrit and Wood, 1995; Darling-Hammond, 1998). The level of the organization (elementary, secondary, undergraduate higher education, or graduate higher education) dictates, to a great degree, which methods will be most effective. In the end, the administrator must make judgments based on assessments.

MBO, previously discussed, is ideal for designing an individualized administrative performance evaluation instrument for professional staff. The key to creating this program is for the faculty and administrator to jointly list all of the employee's professional efforts. For a physical education teacher, this will include measurable teaching achievements, but also many other factors. For a coach, it will include objectives such as student graduation rates, staff relations, and compliance with governing rules, in addition to the record of wins. Similarly, in fitness settings measurable components of the person's job description would be used as the basis for evaluation. Next, these activities must be weighted as to relative worth for achieving organizational goals. The result is that the person who engages in the areas felt to be most important will have higher scores. By motivating employees through the use of the instrument, the organization will move toward achieving its objectives while identifying employees who are not producing. Naturally, this process takes several years to become effective.

One such instrument is illustrated in Figure 11.3. Note that this form is designed for use in a college department, but the concept could be easily adopted for use in athletics or for other levels. The totals are not important in themselves—only in relation to the department range. One might want to try to envision the most outstanding performance a person might achieve and arrange the weights so that a perfect score would be 100. (Of course a superachiever would try to surpass this.) As an example of computation (Figure 11.3), if one has two courses at an "awkward time," the "2–3 courses"

under column 2 would be circled; this 2 would be multiplied times the weight of 10 for a total of 20 points for the first item. An arbitrary maximum of 75 points for any one line item was established to avoid encouraging faculty overspecializing. For example, refer to item number 5 in figure 11.3, publications. If an instructor published two articles in a national professional journal, the computation would be a performance rating of 3 times the weight of 10, or 30, computed twice—once for each article, for a total of 60 points. If three were published the total would be 90 points, but only 75 would be credited. Such a form requires only about 15 minutes for most instructors to complete.

The athletic coach contributes significantly to the development of a large segment of every school population in many vital ways, and yet the only common evaluation of the coach's performance is the win–loss record. Winning is important, but not the most important factor in coaching. Although it must be recognized that emulation of the professionals has resulted in more pressure for the high school coach to produce a winner, frequently most of that pressure comes from within the coach. Even if it is pressure from outside the organization sport managers (ADs, GMs, and the like) must ensure that evaluation is based on sound program goals and objectives and not on winning alone.

On what basis do coaches receive the "Big T" (termination)? In all the areas of evaluation in administration, this area represents both the greatest need and the best opportunities. A small-college AD recommends setting consistent expectations, setting goals, analyzing tasks, and performing year-end evaluations (Bey, 1993). Steir (1993)

| Area of Evaluation | Weight | Performance Rating | | | Supportive Data | Earned Points (Weight × Performance) |
		3	2	1		
		(CIRCLE APPROPRIATE CATEGORY AND COMPUTE POINTS)				
1. MA Thesis	10	Chairman Committee		Member		
2. Classes at "awkward" time (8:00 A.M., Saturdays, any after 3:00 P.M.)	10	4 courses or more	2–3 courses	1 course	No supportive data	

Figure 11.3 Faculty performance evaluation instrument.

Area of Evaluation	Weight	Performance Rating 3	Performance Rating 2	Performance Rating 1	Supportive Data	Earned Points (Weight × Performance)
3. Master's Comprehensive Examination	10	5 or More	3–4	1–2	Names not necessary	
4. Research	10	Research proposal approved	Submitted proposal but not approved or completed self-supported research	Draft of research written for "supported" or "self-supported"		
5. Publications	10	Each article published in national professional journal	Each article published state/regional journal	Each published series in lay publications or a newsletter		
6. International/National (Computed as many times as appropriate)	6	Presented paper or speech	Discussant, panelist, or program involvement at meeting	Attended meeting		
7. District/State	5	Presented paper or speech	Discussant, panelist, or program involvement at meeting	Attended meeting		
8. Committees or Officer in National/International Associations or Publication Editor	6	Major office holder or chairman of **major committee**	Major committee member or chairman of minor committee	Minor committee or minor office holder		
9. Committee or Officer in State/District Associations or Publication Editor	5	Major office holder or chairman of **major committee**	Major committee member or chairman of minor committee	Minor committee or minor office holder		
10. Department Colloquy, Clinics or similar meeting	5	Presented one paper and attended another, or served as director	Attended two or presented at one	Attended one	No supportive data needed	
11. University- or College-Level Committees/Councils	10	Faculty Senate **committee chair**person	Faculty senator	Member of university task force, council, or committee		
12. Departmental Committees	5	Chairman of committee(s)		Member of committee(s)		
13. Department Personnel Committee	5	Elected **member**			No supportive data needed	
14. Coordinator of Area	5	Swim Pool		Other areas		

Figure 11.3 *(Continued)*

Area of Evaluation	Weight	Performance Rating 3	Performance Rating 2	Performance Rating 1	Supportive Data	Earned Points (Weight × Performance)
15. Student Activities	5	Official advisor to a major student club with active involvement	Advisor to other student organizations or clubs such as Letterman Club, Ski Club, Hiking Club, etc., or slight involvement in a major club	Participated in student activities		
16. International/ National/District/ State Professional Organization	10	Paid member of 4 *or more*	Paid member of 3	Paid member of 1 or 2		
17. Professional Service to Civic Public (Nondenominational unless involvement is based on profession and not membership)	5	One speech to state or regional group, or two or more to local groups, or president of such an organization	One speech to local group, or chairman of a committee of such an organization. Directed short-term clinic	Active membership in such a group or organization. Assist with clinics, etc.		
18. Advising Students	2	Points per official advisee listed on records				

SUBJECTIVE (CHAIRPERSON WILL EVALUATE ITEMS IN THIS AREA. FACULTY SHOULD LIST PERTINENT INFORMATION BUT LEAVE EVALUATION BLANK.)

Area of Evaluation	Weight	Performance Rating 3	Performance Rating 2	Performance Rating 1	Supportive Data	Earned Points (Weight × Performance)
19. Instructional Innovation	10	Major involvement		Minor involvement		
20. Department Administrative Support (reports, deadlines, etc.)	10	Always prompt	Normal	Reasonable, but has missed a few	No supportive data needed	
21. Meeting Attendance (Graduate Department, General Department, General College, General University Committee) (conflicting duties considered)	10	Superb attendance	Normal attendance	Reasonable, but has missed a few	No supportive data needed	
22. Other contributions not covered in any of the preceding such as . . . work with community group for extended time, publishing a book, President of Faculty Senate, or Chairperson of University Task Force, producing an instructional movie, etc.						

TOTAL POINTS _____

Signature of Faculty Member

Figure 11.3 *(Continued)*

recommends that the process should first settle the issues of why the coaches should be evaluated; on what they will be judged; for what criteria the coaches should be held accountable; who should be involved in the process; where and how they should be evaluated; and how the results will be utilized (see Figure 11.4).

Because findings indicate that only about one-third of professional football players had college degrees while almost all were recruited from college programs, there has been considerable pressure for increasing the number of graduates among athletes. One study assessed to what extent head football coaches, ADs, and college presidents of NCAA Division 1-A supported the use of student athlete graduation rates as a criterion in head coaches' evaluations. Each group favored this, but all believed that the graduation rate criterion should represent less than 40 percent of the head football coach evaluation (Waggoner, Ammon, and Veltri, 1993).

The following steps in the evaluation process will provide the communication necessary to assess coaches:

- During the preseason, develop a written job description.
- Prior to the season, develop the criteria for performance evaluation in consensus with the coach.
- Prior to the season, set goals.
- Directly observe the team during the season.
- After the season, provide quantified written evaluation with a narrative.
- Give the coach a copy in advance of an open discussion and allow for a subsequent written reply by the coach if desired (Leland, 1988).

Self-Evaluation. Perhaps self-evaluation is the most efficient and powerful way to improve effectiveness. The initial step in the process is for the coach to complete one form while the supervisor does the same; then they are compared in a conference. Coaches should write a personal evaluation at the conclusion of each season, assessing problems and reflecting on the means to improve

for the next season. An anonymous semistructured opinionnaire for players (especially graduating seniors) to complete after the season is highly recommended. Frequently teachers will design their own course evaluations. One of the simplest and most effective is to include a question on the final exam to be graded just the same as other questions: "List the ways this course could be made more effective in the future."

Unfortunately, the best teachers, coaches, and employees are often too hard on themselves while those performing poorly many times have a false sense of their performance. When used with employees that can honestly reflect on their performance, self-evaluation can be beneficial.

Evaluating Administrators. Just as a coach and teacher want to learn how they can improve, so does the administrator. However, significant differences exist. One is that frequently it will be left up to the administrator whether he or she wishes to be evaluated. Also, an administrator will have taken adverse action with some employees, teachers, or coaches, and it can be expected that these persons' evaluations of the administrator will be extremely negative. Most administrators believe it most fair to be evaluated by those to whom they report, partly because personnel below them do not know the facts and situations behind many administrative decisions. But many leaders welcome evaluations by the personnel they supervise if no one sees the results but themselves. If improvement is the objective, this is probably the best course.

One study used the Center for Creative Leadership's instrument called Benchmark to assess the performance of 2,000 managers. "A manager who engages in the Benchmark's assessment receives information on how multiple others perceive his or her performance and, most importantly, on how his or her own assessment differs or agrees with these others. This process is known as 360-degree feedback" (Brutus, McCaulley, and Fleenor, 1996).

High School
Coach's Evaluation Form

Rating scale:

1=unacceptable   2=poor   3=average   4=good   5=excellent

Name: Sport:

I. Human relations
   A. Personal
      1. Enthusiasm
      2. Role model
      3. Language
      4. Sportsmanship
      5. Interaction with parents
   B. Personal conduct
      1. Ethical behavior
      2. Emotional control
      3. Places welfare of athlete above winning

IV. Coaching
   A. Methods
      1. Applies skills, techniques, and rules
      2. Teaches fundamentals
      3. Builds team spirit & morale
      4. Builds discipline
      5. Makes students aware of behavior expectations
   B. Strategy
      1. Assesses player objectively
      2. Consequences for behavior are explained and uniformly enforced
   C. Rules and regulations
      1. Abides by above
      2. Demonstrates knowledge of rules and officiating

Comments: Comments:

II. Administrative
   A. Practice organization
      1. Well-planned sessions
      2. Timely information to players and administration
   B. Financial
      1. Budget policies & procedures
      2. Remains within budget

V. Personnel management
      1. Monitors student's academic achievement
      2. Develops and maintains a positive attitude among athletes

Comments: Comments:

III. Medical/legal aspects
      1. Conduct in preventing and handling injuries
      2. Follows advice of physician regarding participation of injured athletes
      3. Teaches and enforces school athletic code
      4. Reinforces school drug policy

VI. Public relations
      1. Communication with assistant coaches
      2. Cooperation with AD
      3. Cooperation with media
      4. Appreciates concerns of parents of athletes and general public
      5. Communication with parents
      6. Communication with AD
      7. Communication with director of transportation

Comments: Comments:

Figure 11.4 The ins and outs of evaluating coaches.
Adapted from: Steir, W. F. Jr., (1993, May). Athletic Management, 35.

Critical Thinking

Research and experience clearly show that professional staff perform at higher levels when fair, timely, and meaningful assessments are made of their work. A chairperson of a department of health, physical education, recreation, and dance decided to embark on a long-term process of faculty evaluation. (In actuality, this process has been evolving for over 25 years in the same department.)

Stage I was to receive approval of the initiative from higher authorities, and then to establish a faculty committee to investigate research and practice to share with the total faculty. The first step recommended and supported by the faculty was to utilize a short student evaluation program. The trend was to add more questions each year. As this was done, the results improved, but the problems of time and expense grew. To solve this, it was decided to shrink the assessment and ask only one question concerning the overall teaching effectiveness for administrative ranking.

Stage II was to add alumni evaluation. It was thought by some that vigorous classes and grading standards might adversely affect some faculty, and that graduates "out in the real world" would look back more favorably and realistically. Evaluation forms were sent to all graduates of the previous three years for them to assess the faculty who had taught their classes. These data were added to the administrative judgment.

Stage III was to add the element of peer evaluation because many faculty believed that the system was too weighted on student opinion. This was a large department where many faculty were specialists; some faculty did not know others' disciplines, and some who did were not privy to their accomplishments. To overcome this, and to restrict the system from being too overbearing, it was decided that each faculty member would select four others who knew his or her discipline and work. Of the four, the chairperson would secretly assign two to accomplish the evaluation. Thus faculty did not know who did their evaluations.

Stage IV was to add a strictly administrative evaluation based almost entirely on objective data. Such areas as attendance at faculty and university meetings; number of department and university committees; publications; attendance to state, regional, and national professional conferences; election to professional posts; and the number of classes taught were included.

1. After two years, two of the first three stage initiatives were found to be in such close correlation that one was dropped. Which two do you think were essentially the same?
2. What do you think were the greatest problems with each system?
3. Which system do you believe was least supported by the faculty and dropped as soon as the chairperson was changed?
4. If you were a faculty member, rank the four systems with your most preferred first.

Any system of evaluating administrators should be based on these assumptions: the results of the evaluations should be used to improve performance, assess, and modify roles; those participating in the evaluation must have a thorough knowledge of the responsibilities of the position and factual data about accomplishments; the rating instrument should be as simple but as valid as possible.

Exercises

1. Assume that you are the AD of a 2,000-student high school. You intend to establish an MBO program with all coaches. Select any sport with which you

are familiar. Prepare a list of measurable objectives for the coach of that particular sport to consider establishing as goals.

2. Student evaluation of teachers is a controversial issue. Let us assume you are a physical education teacher in a middle school of grades seven to nine and you do not have tenure. The principal has suggested that student evaluations may be used as part of the data to be considered for granting tenure. The principal has directed all nontenured teachers to prepare a position paper on the subject. Do so.

3. Assuming that no supervisor or administrative officer in your high school has time to sit in on your classes frequently, and the school policy is against student evaluations, discuss how the principal might arrive at a fair administrative evaluation of your work for the year.

4. Evaluations of coaches have not been very effective. Design a system for evaluating coaches in a large high school.

5. You are a new physical education teacher at a junior high school. Several parents have complained to the chairperson that the curriculum in physical education is weak. The chairperson assigns you the task of recommending how to evaluate the program. How would you go about doing this?

6. You have inherited a medium-size fitness center. Records show that it hasn't made a profit in the last four years. How would you go about determining the reasons for its profitlessness?

References

Alvestad, K. (1997, December). Communicating new initiatives. *School Administrator* 54, pp. 16–18.

Bey, L. W. (1993, March). The fairness doctrine. *Athletic Business* 17, pp. 55–59.

Bridges, F. J., and Roquemore, L. L. (2000) *Management of athletic/sport administration: Theory and practice* (3d ed.). Decatur, GA: ESM Books.

Brutus, S.; McCaulley, C. D.; and Fleenor, J. W. (1996). Age and managerial effectiveness. *Issues and Observations, Center for Creative Leadership* 16, p. 5.

Darling-Hammond, L. (1998, February). Standards for assessing teaching effectiveness are key. *Phi Delta Kappan* 79, pp. 471–472.

Doolittle, S., and Fay, T. (2002). *Authentic assessment of physical education activity.* Reston, VA: National Association for Sport and Physical Education.

Duke, D. L. (1993, May). Removing barriers to professional growth. *Phi Delta Kappan* 74, pp. 702–711.

Gréhaigne, J. F., and Godbout, P. (1998, January). Formative assessment in team sports in a tactical approach context. *Journal of Physical Education, Recreation and Dance* 69, pp. 46–51.

Hensley, L. D. (1997, September). Alternative assessment for physical education *Journal of Physical Education, Recreation and Dance* 68, pp. 19–24.

Horine, L. (1992). *Survey of master's degree comprehensive examinations in physical education and human movement studies in North America.* Unpublished manuscript. Department of Health, Leisure, and Exercise Science, Appalachian State University, Boone, NC 28608.

Joyner, A. B., and McManis, B. G. (1997, September). Quality control in alternative assessment. *Journal of Physical Education, Recreation and Dance* 68, pp. 38–40.

Kirk, M. F. (1997, September). Using portfolios to enhance student learning and assessment. *Journal of Physical Education, Recreation and Dance* 68, pp. 29–33.

Leland, T. (1988, November/December). Evaluating coaches—formalizing the process. *Journal of Physical Education, Recreation and Dance* 59, pp. 21–22.

Lund, J. (1997, September). Authentic assessment: Its development and applications. *Journal of Physical Education, Recreation and Dance* 68, pp. 25–28.

Lund, J. L., and Kirk, M. F. (2002). *Performance-based assessment for middle and high school physical education.* Champaign, IL: Human Kinetics Publishers.

Maiorca, J. (1997, August). How to construct behaviorally anchored rating scales (BARS) for employee evaluations. *Supervision* 58, pp. 15–18.

Melograno, V. J. (1997, September). Integrating assessment into physical education teaching. *Journal of Physical Education, Recreation and Dance* 68, pp. 34–37.

Minimize performance evaluation legal risks (1998, February). *Journal of Accountancy* 185, pp. 85–96.

Murphy, J. A., and Pimentel, S. (1996, September). Grading principals. *Phi Delta Kappan* 78, pp. 74–81.

Safrit, M. J., and Wood, T. M. (1995). *Introduction to measurement in physical education and exercise science* (3rd ed.). St. Louis: Mosby.

Slack, T. (1997). *Understanding sport organizations.* Champaign, IL: Human Kinetics.

Steir, W. F. (1993, May). The ins and outs of evaluating coaches. *Athletic Management* 5, pp. 34–38.

U.S. Figure Skating Association Strategic Plan (2002a). Colorado Springs, CO: U.S. Figure Skating Association.

U.S. Figure Skating Association Winter Games Assessment (2002b). Colorado Springs, CO: U.S. Figure Skating Association.

Waggoner, R. G.; Ammon, R., Jr.; and Veltri, F. R. (1993, March). Perceptions of student-athlete graduation rates as an evaluation criterion for head football coaches. *Sport Marketing Quarterly* 2, pp. 27–34.

Zhu, W. (1997, September). Alternative assessment for physical education. *Journal of Physical Education, Recreation and Dance* 68, pp. 17–18.

12

Data Processing and Office Management in Sport and Physical Education Administration

Management Thought

It is never too late to give up our prejudices. No way of thinking or doing, however ancient, can be trusted without proof. . . . What old people say you cannot do, you try and find that you can. Old deeds for old people, and new deeds for new.

Henry David Thoreau (Everhart, 1997, p. 36)

Case Study: Overrun with Students

Jose Fuentes was a first-year physical education teacher at a junior high school. His teaching schedule consisted of five classes every day with about 40 students per class. He had one 50-minute period each day for planning and paperwork. There were constant demands on his time for forms to complete, items to order, questions to answer from students and parents, and committee assignments. At first he used his planning period to accomplish these tasks and would do his paperwork and planning after school. As the year progressed, he found that he had to take these tasks home each night. During the second semester the district required giving all students physical education activity tests and then health–fitness tests. He was overwhelmed. Doing the testing was no problem since he had excellent coursework in evaluation and measurement in his physical education teacher preparation program. His problem was the enormous amount of statistical recording and computation.

His seventh-grade classes met three times a week, and his eighth-grade classes met twice a week, so he actually had 240 total students. Each of the tests

he had to give consisted of six different items. He organized each class with recorders, and arranged for some of these to volunteer to stay after school to help him compute and record the results. Even though they were good students and meant well, they were just young teenagers and made mistakes and, after the first few sessions, had a hard time staying on task. It became a mess. Every night he had to take the work home to straighten things out, which put him behind in all the rest of his work. At the end of the year he was exhausted and was thinking about quitting.

He met with the chairperson of the department and vented his frustration and asked for help. The chairperson acknowledged that even the experienced teachers had been overwhelmed and everyone was asking for help, and she had an idea that might help. They made an appointment to see the principal the next day and floated an idea to structure a system of using data processing for the two tests. The principal was supportive and arranged a meeting for them with the data processing officer in the district central office. In a matter of a few hours they had worked out a plan to use an existing reporting form for which his computer was set up for optical scanning. The specialist also agreed to work out the program during the summer that would handle the computing of the data for each class, with printouts for each instructor. Jose met several times during the summer to finalize plans and write the instructions for each teacher to follow. The next year was a breeze, and for his work in the project, Jose received a substantial salary raise as part of the district merit pay plan.

Chapter Objectives

The reader should be able to

1. Define common terms associated with computers and office management.
2. Describe the characteristics of computers, the computer central processing unit, and the input, output, and media devices used in computers.
3. Differentiate mini, micro, and large computers.

4. Name a variety of practical uses for computers for teaching physical education, sport research, athletic coaching, and sport and physical education administration.
5. Discuss the concepts of office management.
6. Identify the practical uses of word processing, electronic messaging, and other modern office technologies in physical education, recreation, and sport management.

◾ COMMON OFFICE MANAGEMENT, COMPUTER, AND DATA PROCESSING TERMS

Definitions

Algorithm. A step-by-step procedure that guarantees a correct outcome.

Artificial intelligence. An academic discipline. A broad research program aimed at improving what computers can do. It is not a product.

Audiotex. A system or service that presents information via telephone in a natural voice from the caller.

Bubble memory. A memory device that utilizes magnetically charged crystal chips to store information.

CAD. Computer-assisted design.

Central mainframe computers. The large CPUs that control institutions' major data processing needs.

Collate. To arrange separate sheets of paper into a specific order.

Computer graphics. Graphic representations produced on the computer.

CPU. The central processing unit—the information storage area shared by multiple data- or word-processing terminals.

Electronic filing. The storage of information on magnetic media rather than hard copy.

Electronic mail or messages (e-mail). A system of communicating electronically to a recipient who receives either a hard copy or a visually displayed message on a screen.

Facsimile (fax). A process that involves the transmission of an exact copy over communication lines.

Fiber optics. The use of ultrathin glass fibers to guide and project light beams used as a communication medium.

Floppy disk. A storage medium in which information is recorded magnetically on the surface of a flexible disk.

Hardware. A basic piece of equipment, such as the mechanical, magnetic, electrical, or electronic devices.

Laser printing. The same as image printing, except it operates only on laser control rather than on direct image.

Microfiche. A sheet of film containing many microimages arranged in a grid pattern.

Online processing. Is associated with access to computers for both input and output from the point of data origination via remote terminals.

Programmer. One who writes the specific instructions for the computer.

Programs. Instructions for the computer itemizing exactly what kinds of data will arrive, what calculations to make and in what order to perform them, and what form the output will take.

Robotics. Enable computers to "see" and manipulate objects in their surrounding environment.

Software. A program that instructs a computer to perform operations it ordinarily cannot perform based just on its operating system program.

Spreadsheets. A grid containing information arranged in horizontal rows and vertical columns. The electronic equivalent of an accounting worksheet.

Systems analyst. One who studies the data processing needs of an organization to design the most efficient means of meeting its requirements.

Word processing. The transferring of an idea or thought into a final, error-free document by means of an automated system of word productivity.

■ COMPUTERS

The following distinctive characteristics allow the versatile and efficient computer to be used in many ways:

1. Flexibility. The computer can be used to solve a great variety of problems and provide many direct services.

2. Speed. Problems or services impossible to perform before computers can be accomplished in a very short time.

3. Accuracy. Not only will the computer not make a computational error, but modern programs have built-in instructions to correct errors or identify them.

4. Reliability. In properly organized systems, the data processing will continue even if some components fail.

5. Capacity. This is measured both in speed and amount of data that can be stored.

6. Expandability. Various units are modularized so that additional units can be easily added.

7. Cost efficiency. Whereas the cost of manually processing data increases with volume, the cost of computerized data processing is reduced by greater volume.

Basic Components of Computers

Input Devices. Input devices include the keyboard (and usually a mouse), disk drives, and a modem. Disk drives are both input and output devices. Computer programs that are magnetically stored on disks can be transmitted to the computer memory via the disk drive. Several types of disk drives can be built into the computer, such as floppy disk or ZIP drives. Most computers also have a hard drive, which contains more information and can be accessed faster than floppy disks. The modem is both an input and an output device that allows computers to communicate across telephone or cable lines. It is also common for computers to have an optical disk drive to read from and write to CDs or DVDs.

Memory. "Computer memory can be classified as *primary memory* and *secondary memory.* Primary memory is memory that is contained on the computer's circuit board in the form of integrated circuits or chips. Primary memory can be further classified as random access memory (RAM) and read-only memory (ROM)" (Safrit and Wood, 1995, p. 108). ROM is static, unchanging, and preprogrammed by the manufacturer. On the other hand, RAM chips provide memory space for storage of data and programs transmitted by the user.

Central Processing Unit (CPU). The core of the computer system is the central processing unit (CPU), which consists of three primary segments:

1. Control unit. This interprets instructions directed from the program and issues the appropriate signals to the other units.

2. Storage unit. This is the common link between the various parts of the system that maintains data and instructions for use in any unit.

3. Arithmetic-logic unit. Obviously, this unit provides the computational operations required to achieve meaningful output.

Output Devices. These devices include the monitor (display screen), printer, and drives. Originally monitors were black and white; now color monitors are universal. The resolution and size of monitors have continually grown and improved. Such items as antiglare screens have been added. The resolution depends on the number of the *pixels* (dots). The greater the quantity of pixels, the better the resolution.

Printers are primarily of three types: laser, dot-matrix, and inkjet printers. Laser printers are similar to photocopy machines, produce high-quality results, and cost more. Dot-matrix printers work by firing pins against a ribbon, while inkjet printers work by injecting the ink through nozzles onto the paper. Of the latter two, most users prefer inkjet printers (Safrit and Wood, 1995).

Microcomputers and Minicomputers

A few decades ago there were distinct differences among large mainframe computers, minicomputers, and microcomputers. With incessant technological advances the differences have blurred. The smallest microcomputers now have the power and speed that used to be limited to mainframes. In physical education and sport administration, use is almost completely limited to microcomputers, usually referred to as *desktop* or *laptop* computers (Picciano, 1994).

Security

Security in computer use has become more important. One of the first lines of defense is the selection of an appropriate password. Most people tend to select familiar names, words, or important dates, all of which are easy to guess. Experts say that a password should be a combination of letters and numbers. Or pick two or more unrelated words with punctuation marks in between, and misspell them. Also, utilizing both upper- and lowercase words and reverse spelling of words will help foil those attempting to break into your computer (Kenworthy, 1997).

What Should the Administrator Do before Buying a Computer or Software?

Many administrators in physical education or sport will be involved in decisions about what type of computer or microcomputer to purchase. Just as in any other area of specialization, the first order of business is to learn as much as possible about the products and how they could meet the needs of the organizations. After determining the purpose, get the assistance of an expert consultant.

Before purchasing a microcomputer, make sure that the model allows for adding additional input or output components. Because this field represents such a dynamic and changing technology, flexibility and adaptability are the most important considerations. Be sure to consider the following variables: memory capacity (RAM), disk capacity, speed, quantity and quality of available software, reliability and maintenance, adaptability for adding new features, ability to accept specific needed software, and cost. Each year magazines rate computers and components. Administrators should refer to the latest ratings before purchasing ("Desktops," 2002; "Monitors," 2002; "Printers," 2002; "Laptops," 2002).

Software has become more of the percentage of costs involved in data processing than hardware, and selection of software should be made carefully. Some questions to answer are these:

- Cost?
- Will it run on existing hardware?
- How fast does it process data?
- How easy is it to install?
- What is the quality of the technical operation information?
- Is it user-friendly?
- Can a backup copy be made?
- Can it be upgraded at a low cost?
- Will it accomplish what you need?
- Can it be previewed?
- Can you get adequate technical support in a reasonable time?

- How much training does it require?
- Can it be stored on a hard disk? (Safrit and Wood, 1995)

Many administrators face the problem of what equipment to purchase when establishing computer workrooms for faculty or students. Two lines of consideration should be processed. One is *educational*, consisting of student and faculty preferences, homework compatibility, ability to operate, educational software availability, and future computing requirements. The other line is *functional*, consisting of purchase and repair costs, space limits, staff skill, availability of peripherals, compatibility with networks and software, ease of upgrading, and vendor relationship and market standing (Djang, 1993). Bay (1993) suggests four Cs: establish a *commitment* from all using units and the administration; establish *communication* links between users, using units, and the administration; establish *control* to ensure that individuals and groups maintain the focus on the goals and objectives of the data processing system; and establish reasonable *costs*.

■ ADMINISTRATIVE COMPUTER APPLICATIONS IN PHYSICAL EDUCATION AND RECREATION

Computer Uses in Physical Education Management

Most authorities agree that one of the highest priorities for the computer is to identify the many possible ways it can directly assist the instructor or teacher. Computerized information retrieval systems are valuable for teachers and researchers. General databases such as ERIC are available, as well as specialized ones such as MEDLINE, SIRLS, SPORT DISCUS, and SPORTDOKUMENTATION.

One of the most important direct services to the academic staff is test construction and computer grading. Computerized systems can be developed to print out achievement test questions from a permanent memory bank. Most computer centers have a standard program available to grade objective examinations written on special

"op-scan" sheets. Any type of question that results in up to five responses can be automatically processed. This includes true and false questions, multiple choice, diagram identification, and matching. Depending on the computer schedule, tests can be graded in a short time with a printout frequently reporting the raw score, the percentage, the Z score, the T score, and a standard deviation for the group. In addition, most programs call for a listing of the percentage each question is answered correctly, and a point biserial coefficient is recorded for each question. The point biserial coefficient is an excellent means of determining the validity of questions. The percentage each question is answered correctly is also known as the *difficulty index*. Some programs also report discriminant score (D score), which provides how each item discriminates the scores from the students who did well in the test (top 75th percentile) from the ones who did not (bottom 25th percentile).

There are many software suppliers to write various types of tests. One can easily produce a generic test construction bank by simply using a word processor. The automatic numbering system provided on most computers will make this an easy task. Also, with the graphics available, one can enliven tests with diagrams and drawings. An alternative to test banking is to use database software where questions developed on a word processor can be imported to a database, coded for content, and sorted and retrieved at a future date.

Because fitness testing encompasses enormous numbers of students and data, several organizations have prepared software for tabulating results and providing individual profiles. FITNESSGRAM (Institute for Aerobics Research); Physical Best (AAHPERD); and the Chrysler Fund–AAU Physical Fitness Program are among those providing such programs.

Grading in physical education is a major administrative problem because of the many students in each class and the fact that classes meet only two or three times a week. Simple but effective report cards can be produced on a word processor. Student scores can be stored in a database and then merged, producing an individualized report card. Many vendors produce software to accomplish this.

In physical education, computers have numerous applications in the activity areas, laboratory, and theory classes. Computer-assisted instruction (CAI) will be accelerated through greater use of microcomputers. Specific uses are to teach personalized lifestyle fitness courses, health, nutrition, sports officiating, and professional foundations of physical education. Self-paced courses in physical education and strategies for activities such as racquetball have been programmed through the PLATO system. The same system has been used to present a special biomechanics unit on projectiles in a kinesiology class. Further examples of incorporating the computer in the instructional process have been to enhance teaching movement notation, four-dimensional profiles of dance teachers, and a simulation program to be used in a class on curriculum planning.

For bowling classes, the computer can relieve the instructor of the tedious task of recording scores and provide feedback to the student that would otherwise be impractical. Video games can be used for motor learning research. It appears, however, that the most logical of all classes to utilize the computer would be in the tests and measurement classes. By using programs already written, students would need to learn only a few basic commands on how to "log in" in order to use the computer. Future coaches and physical education teachers need this hands-on experience.

In any situations where great amounts of data are handled for large numbers of students, such as physical education class attendance, height, weight, body fat composition, heart rates, and flexibility, measurements could all easily be computer-processed and analyzed. In college courses in administration, measurement, adaptives, and curriculum, the computer could be involved.

> Exercise physiologists are becoming dependent on computers to monitor and record stress tests, compute body composition parameters from hydrostatic weighing and bioelectric impedance techniques, and to determine bone mineral density. Biomechanists rely on computers to estimate the kinetic and kinematic parameters of body movement, while sport psychologists are beginning to explore the use of sophisticated statistical techniques to model the factors that contribute to exercise adherence and motivation to participate in physical activity. Athletic trainers and exercise specialists share the need for efficient record keeping and the means of providing information to clients on their health and physical status—tasks well suited for computers. (Safrit and Wood, 1995, p. 104)

In biomechanics study, data processing is regularly utilized to obtain velocities from stroboscopic photography of a golf swing. Computers are used to control cardiovascular fitness testing. For example, the speed and grade of a treadmill could be controlled according to any protocol.

From the early 1970s, computer programs have been available to analyze energy expenditure from the raw data collected in oxygen consumption testing. The computer increases the accuracy, and of course, is much faster. It is now common and less expensive to process data on oxygen consumption analysis through the use of a portable programmable calculator and small printer. Once the program is stored in the calculator's memory, it can be transferred to magnet cards; programming is then accomplished by inserting the cards into the computer.

Calculating percentage of body fat from skinfold measurements can be done much more quickly and accurately using microcomputers than by hand calculations. It is relatively simple to develop a computer-controlled cardiovascular fitness testing center.

Student performances in an activity could be evaluated by computer. Students could write programs or otherwise be involved in planning strategies of play in various simulated situations with feedback from the computer as to the choices made. When computers are utilized, the dropout rate will likely be lower because students can be given periodic feedback on their progress.

With the use of a microcomputer, hundreds of student reports could be generated in a short time. Student performance management systems can address evaluation of whether objectives of the course were met, and whether the instruction led to gains in student performance. A program that accommodates this is dBase III Plus.

Administrative Applications for the Computer

Annesi (2002, p. 43) states, "A large number of administrative functions are facilitated by the software that keep reliance on memory, note taking, journal entries, and stacks of paper to a minimum. For example, tasks to be completed with each fitness professional/exerciser session are derived by the computer from a number of personal, psychological, and behavioral factors. The software not only establishes them instantaneously, but presents them as a convenient 'checklist' for use by the fitness professional."

Curriculum planning is an area of management in which the computer can be effectively utilized. For example, if the physical education requirement is changed from required to elective, or new activities are offered, the administrator must know the impact ahead of time on equipment, staff, and facilities to decide whether such a change is even possible. Problems such as this could be simulated with the computer showing what results would be likely to occur. To calculate the long-term effects on curriculum planning for physical education, researchers designed a computer program to simulate a long-term scenario to analyze the effects of varying economic, governmental, educational philosophy, and community actions. Uses for computer technology in managing sport facilities include locker records, equipment inventories, student aid and payroll records, recruiting files, and utility consumption. The innovative lighting system in the Michigan State arena is controlled by a computerized control system that is preprogrammed for different lighting levels (Rabin, 1993).

Computer programs can be effective for scheduling students, teams, or facilities. The time that can be saved in scheduling in large departments is enormous. In school systems where flexible scheduling is used, it is imperative to utilize the computer. The computer could be valuable in a variety of other administrative tasks. With a computerized advanced registration, each department can be given not only the numbers of students enrolled in each section of each class, but a "demand analysis" that tells the administrator how many students had requested each class. This data is invaluable in adding sections and planning for the future. Computerization of the graduates of a department could provide important data. While almost all colleges register for physical education classes by computer, secondary schools have been slower to utilize this method.

Maintaining equipment records through data processing is extremely efficient. This is particularly necessary if purchasing is done for a number of schools. At a moment's notice, an inventory and budget analysis can be obtained for any school. Keeping track of equipment assigned to students or checked out for short-term use could be greatly simplified through use of microcomputers. In addition, all of the retrievable data related to the use of facilities and equipment could then be used to build and justify budgets.

Microcomputers can be programmed to turn other controls on and off, such as security lights and hot water, and also to act as sensors to alert the administrator when the gymnastics, swimming pool, or equipment doors are not locked. Textbook inventories and library acquisitions can be routinely maintained via computerization. Recreation and physical education departments should all have computer laboratories. In addition to utilizing them for a variety of courses and out-of-class assignments, computer laboratories can be used for hosting computer camps and teaching unique courses, such as entrepreneurship.

Student evaluation of faculty, or evaluation of leaders in any sport situation, requires the use of data processing. There has been an enormous quantity of research published in this area with many companies producing evaluation systems for profit. One system that has been successfully used is the Individual Development and Educational Assessment Center's (IDEA) student rating of instruction program. This firm offers a short form that is primarily useful for administrative evaluation purposes, and a long form that contains extensive diagnostic information that could be effectively used for instructional development. For further information, call (800) 255-2757 or www.idea.ksu.edu.

Electronic Mail

Utilizing electronic mail (e-mail) as a quick form of communication lessens the distance between various locations. The University of Virginia established such a program with a large grant to arrange for students, cooperating teachers, and the university supervisors to operate through the mainframe for e-mail. Many usually time-consuming activities such as schedules for visits, lesson plans, and meetings were all handled through the system. In addition, all three of the entities could communicate with all others on mutual problems. East Carolina University and Appalachian State University have instituted a similar program in which the cooperating teachers, student teachers, and university supervisors all receive training and access to the system (Everhart, 1997; Wittenberg and McBride, 1998).

A study of 26 teacher education programs that included physical education majors revealed that only 8 (30.8 percent) used e-mail in their student teaching program. The majority of respondents were interested in adding e-mail to their programs in the future. For those already utilizing e-mail, Everhart (1997, p. 37) reports that "student teachers correspond weekly with university supervisors, sending them weekly logs and journals as well. Also the student teachers can communicate with each other and with their cooperating teachers. This communication is helpful so that lesson plans can be critiqued by cooperating teachers and supervisors when necessary."

Computer Uses in CAD and Facilities Management

Computer-assisted design (CAD) was previously mentioned in connection with planning facilities. CAD software creates three-dimensional views of floor plans, furniture layouts, and walls or shapes of rooms. This can all be done in a moment, and the software has become very inexpensive. At the time of this writing, a handy CAD compact disk

with an instructional booklet cost less than $20. Of course, hard copies can easily be made (Parkhouse, 2001, p. 81).

Key features of such programs are built-in dimensioning tools, easy positioning utilities, libraries with hundreds of symbols, a variety of printing sizes, metric and imperial measurements, multiple tolerance levels, and adjustable fills, colors, and patterns. They can be used for mechanical/architecture design, electrical and plumbing schematics, flowcharts/diagrams/ network schematics, civil engineering, and circuit boards (*Key CAD Complete*, 1997).

Developing a database for maintenance and cleaning will allow the manager to retrieve all kinds of necessary information at a moment's notice and to have a feeling of being in control of what is being managed. For example, the facility manager must control great numbers of keys to very sensitive areas, document records as to how hazardous wastes have been processed, and control grounds or building maintenance or cleaning schedules. Of the many programs commercially available, one recommended which is user-friendly on IBM compatibles is the Alph4 database. An example of use of this program is the tracking of the electrical consumption and costs of various areas and the development of long-term cost–benefit analysis studies and projected trends (Jonigan, 1993).

Software in Recreation and Fitness Center Management

Computers are used for controlling music, maintenance schedules, inventory, billing, research studies, and collections.

> With the advent of computerized exercise data collectors, fitness equipment can now, for example, recall exercise prescriptions, encourage exercisers to stay within a given heart rate range, and report estimated caloric expenditures—generally summarize what has been accomplished by an exerciser. To take the exercise support process forward, computer technology plays a central role. The process of developing and refining a computer application that is specifically designed to support new and returning exercisers extends the present

limits of what technology can bring to the health and fitness industry. . . . A computerized exercise support program (ESP) that focuses on goals that emphasize sticking with the exercise program rather than goals that emphasize results, strengthens the connection between members and staff and better serves the individuals' needs (Annesi, 2002, 38).

Assessing the risk of a member dropping out is an important management task. Utilizing ESP generates information obtained from the 15-item self-report inventory. From a touch screen, data can estimate how much a member is at risk of dropping out, what factors make the member vulnerable, and what action should be taken to prevent the drop out (Annesi, 2002). Gathering data from patron check-in will also provide information for using highly active clients for referrals for new members, and necessary contacts for those who have not been using the facilities to reactivate them (Cherry, 2002).

Some principles for effective exercise support software include

- It should appear straightforward, concise, and nonthreatening.
- It should have a high degree of flexibility.
- It should be based on research-driven best practices.
- It should improve the delivery and effectiveness of services.
- It should enhance the quality of interpersonal contacts.
- It should clearly document results (Annesi, 2002).

Many vendors now supply excellent software to accommodate these needs. Ross and Wolter (1997, p. 63) recommend that the following factors be considered in addition to price:

1. Identify what you want the software and registration system to accomplish and prioritize those items.

2. Establish a timetable for implementation of the computerized recreation registration system.

3. Be knowledgeable of specific hardware and software requirements for the recreation registration software.

4. Determine the level of technical support, documentation, and maintenance support required.

The following vendors have provided registration software packages (Ross and Wolter, 1997):

- A.E.K. Computers, (800) 666-4AEK.
- Aspen Information Systems, (281) 320-0343.
- THE-Programmed for Success Inc., (800) 488-7374.
- Overtime Software Inc., (800) 467-0493.
- Sierra Digital Inc., (888) REC-WARE.
- Vermont Systems Inc., (800) 377-7427.

Software continues to evolve, but there are a number of packages available to assist in managing workouts. Typically they provide an initial health–fitness evaluation and subsequent periodic assessments. These systems can measure and track cardiovascular endurance, muscular strength, flexibility, and body composition. ("Business and Fitness," 1997):

A service to consider is that of providing a computer center within the larger fitness and recreation centers. Colleges and universities have long provided computer "labs" distributed about campuses and in dormitories and sometimes adjacent to fitness centers. In particular, fitness chains could capitalize on this concept because many patrons maintain their memberships through travel and need to utilize them while on the road. Having computing capabilities during these trips would greatly enhance membership (Handley, 1993).

Once a website is in operation, how does one know if it's worth the cost? One way is to install a "counter" that will measure the number of contacts (hits) each day. This is an interesting statistic, but unless these people contact the organization in some way, it doesn't measure the worth. In addition to constant updating and the use of catchy graphics, another way to get those follow-up contacts is to use "push" technology. "Push software allows updated information on websites to be automatically sent to the site's subscribers. . . . this technology is a powerful and, as of recently, free tool" (Tucker, 1998, p. 44; Sherman, 1997).

Deciding what software one needs to monitor patron check-in is a daunting task because of the variables and number of packages available. It has been suggested that the staff brainstorm to identify everything you want the program to do. Gondolfo (1997, p. 33) recommends considering "areas like usage tracking, member identification, guest tracking, customer service function, service support, billing and collections, and reporting capabilities." Include details such as a photograph identification feature that would allow member telephone messages to be viewed on the screen at the time of check-in. Check with others to learn from their mistakes, and search the industry journals. When a vendor has been identified, request names of organizations in your area that are using the programs and check with them. Raise questions such as these: What kind of staff training do they offer? Is their technical support available 24 hours a day? Will they allow you to test the program in your own organization? Ensure that your existing hardware will accommodate the software (Gondolfo, 1997).

Club management software has been designed to keep total control of an operation. In addition to tracking membership and check-in, programs are available that can provide inventory control, general ledger functions, and custom reports. Software can also provide billing and point-of-sale data ("Business and Fitness," 1997).

Collecting funds has undergone a revolution in the last decade. Several options are available for collections, but the first decision to make is whether to handle these accounts internally or by outsourcing. If it is to be a new operation, checking with several similar organizations that handle it each way is suggested. The trend is to turn to *electronic funds transfer (EFT)*. This refers to debiting a bank account with the funds being transferred from the member's account to the organization. No billing or mailing is involved by either party. While there is a transfer fee, it is small, and the collection rates are substantially higher. Another option is for a debit to be applied to a credit card. A third method is to presell coupons that are sent in each month, which usually require a slightly extra fee. It is only a matter of time until payments will be accommodated through the Internet by electronic mail. Many new fitness centers will accept members only with electronic transfer arrangements (Cioletti, 1998).

■ ADMINISTRATIVE COMPUTER APPLICATIONS IN SPORT AND ATHLETICS

It appears that data processing is used more in sport than in the academic setting. If this is an accurate observation, it may be because of the nature of athletics—it is competitive and it has more financial resources. The computer has been used in athletics to prepare

- Calendars, memos, schedules, letters, and electronic mail.
- Financial reports and travel arrangements.
- News releases, desktop publishing, programs, and media guides.
- Fund solicitations and acknowledgment of gifts.
- Injury reports, and forms generation.
- Equipment inventories, equipment purchasing records, and maintenance management schedules.
- Letters of intent, graphics, and playbooks.
- Printing of tickets and direct mail solicitations for ticket sales.
- Letter and mass mailings for marketing or sponsor development.
- Squad lists and athletic compliance progress reports, eligibility lists, and grade reports.
- Sport information statistical reporting and press releases.
- Scoring computation for events with large numbers of participants, such as cross-country meets.

See Table 12.1.

As in the academic setting, if the administrator desires to implement data processing in athletics, it would be wise to first plan on how the program would help the individual coach. The computer could help high school coaches store large quantities of information, perform many

Table 12.1   Types of Activities Handled by the Computer

Departmental Area	Functional Operations		
	Communications	Database	Math
Athletic director's office	Calendar, memos, schedules, letters, electronic mail	Donor database, departmental directory	Budgeting, special financial reports
Athletic business office	Financial reports, travel arrangements	Vendor's database, purchase order database	Spreadsheets, accounting, reconciliations, budgeting, revenue trend analysis
Sports information office	News releases, desktop publishing (programs, media guides, etc.)	Media database	Game statistics
Development office	Funds solicitations, acknowledgment of gifts	Donor database	Fund-raising trend analysis, pledge accounts receivable
Training room	Injury reports, forms generation	Insurance records, student athlete physical status records, supply records	Budget control, budget preparation, insurance claims administration
Equipment room	Calendar, memos	Inventory control	Budget preparation, budget control
Coach's office	Letters of intent, memos, graphics, playbooks	Recruitment database, team member database	Game analysis, sport's budget control
Athletic ticket office	Printing tickets, mass mailings of ticket applications	Season ticket holders database, ticket inventory	Sales reports, game settlement reports
Marketing and promotions office	Letters, mass mailings, printouts of sponsors	Corporate sponsors database	Event attendance statistics
Compliance office	Squad lists, academic progress reports, other compliance reports and forms	Student athlete database, prospective student athlete contracts	Financial aid calculations, housing and meal allowance accounting

Source: Sharon Andrus, The Andrus Group.

operations in little time, and provide consistent accuracy while maintaining versatility. Programs have been developed with sufficient versatility to be used by all coaches, but specific enough to meet needs. Five areas of application have emerged: simulation, scheduling, scoring, statistics, and scouting.

Instant computations for indexed scored sports, such as gymnastics, diving, or the decathlon, are all candidates for microcomputer application. With their myriad statistics, baseball and softball are made for computerization.

An example of computerized scouting on the high school level revealed that the coaches utilized the personal microcomputers owned by the school for math classes. The system included a keyboard, a cassette recorder for program storage and input, a monitor, and a printer. Information was collected on each offensive play as to hash mark, yardline, down, distance, formation, play, player, result, hole, and type of play. Each play was diagrammed as to blocking schemes, specific backfield actions, and pass routes. In less than one hour the data were entered into the computer, and all the offensive material necessary to prepare a game plan was ready in a few minutes. One coach could do this in one hour, whereas it would take several coaches several hours to complete the results by traditional methods.

Another use of data processing has been the National Collegiate Athletic Association's committee for selecting teams for the national basketball tournament. The computer is used to rank each of the Division I basketball teams based on winning record, opponents' winning record, strength of opponents' schedules, and success on the road. Under new rules, fewer teams receive automatic berths—so the data from the computer are even more important.

Consider a variety of additional avenues for computer use in athletic administration. Microcomputers have been used to control lighting in large centers for athletics. The same applies to sound effects. For example, it is possible to program a system so that sounds come out of speakers at different times and in varied orders. An operator would only have to touch the terminal keyboard to play the national anthem or school fight song.

Computers should be routinely used in ticket management to minimize personnel costs and eliminate unwieldy operational procedures. Farmer, Mulrooney, and Ammon (1996, p. 188) report that the following information can be provided:

- Point-of-sales patron information by zip code.
- Computerized mailing lists.
- Update of daily financial information.
- Solicitation of patron response for specific events.

- Monitoring of ticket sales versus marketing efforts.
- Comparison of demand fluctuations to the type of advertising or marketing program employed.

The computer has been used in intramurals in several ways. Students have utilized the computer for recreational games and to maintain statistics for their teams. Teachers have surveyed interest levels for various extracurricular activities. The greatest potential for computers in intramurals is probably for scheduling and computing standings in large programs. In colleges and universities, it is common to have over a hundred teams in several sports being scheduled during the same period. Programs have been written so that the director has only to type in the team names on the terminal, and with a few simple commands, the entire tournament schedule is printed out ready to post. Such testy problems as seeding and byes are easily handled, as well as the court or field location and time for each contest.

The ski industry has utilized computers extensively. As in many growing businesses, the computer has been employed in administrative and financial operations. But it has also been used in other areas that could serve as a model to school and college athletics. For example, computerizing ticket sales has reduced human error and given management feedback on sales progress. In manual accounting methods, the manager of a ski area had about a 45-day lag time in accounting. That is, the manager knew where he stood 45 days ago, but not last week. Through computerization, the manager can analyze operations from moment to moment.

Registration for sport camps, intramurals, and recreation programs often inundates a small staff with thousands of responses all at once. The answer is to automate registration. But like all data processing systems, it must be done correctly and for the right reasons. Courtney (1993) recommends the following test questions: What is the current volume? How much does it cost to do it manually? Are funds available to automate? Does cost–benefit analysis show that it's justified? What resources will be required to handle the operation? Does automation fit within the organization's long-range strategic plans?

World Wide Web and the Internet

> The Internet and the World Wide Web provide intra-enterprise and inter-enterprise connectivity and application access on a scale unimaginable just a few years ago. By exploiting the broadly available and deployed standards of the Internet and the Web, companies are able to build client/server applications for internal use (Intranets) or for external use (public Internets) to reach and interact with customers, business partners, and suppliers in numerous ways (Kalakota and Whinston, 1997, p. 93).

The Web is so popular because it consists of such a wide range of concepts and technologies. The concepts include global hypertext publishing, universal readership of content, and the client–server interaction. This interaction allows the Web to grow without any centralized control.

With economic difficulties, many companies that had been operating website hosting services for colleges and high schools have retracted. Others firms have weathered the storm. Official College Sports Network (formally Fansonly), iHigh, eteamz, and HighWired are looking to expand coverage. The firm iHigh services about 5,500 active high school sites. It hopes to expand into higher education business. eteamz.com offers a free website service that includes many recreation departments and youth leagues, but also 120,000 high school teams. HiredWire.com offers broader services directed at the entire school. They include scheduling and communication programs ("What's New," 2002).

Most institutions of higher education have established websites, including pages for the athletic department. As a normal progression, athletic departments have established their own sites, and some have developed sites for just women's sports or for just one sport. In the beginning most included just text, but subsequently sound and graphics have been incorporated. The sites have been successful in extending marketing, promotion, advertising, recruiting athletes,

and communicating with alumni living too far to receive normal media transmissions. In addition, recreation departments, conferences, associations (such as the NCAA), and high school activity associations have established websites (Catalano, 1996; Sherman, 1997; What's New, 2002).

Deciding whether to establish a website depends on philosophy as well as cost, in both equipment and personnel. Some organizations have decided that websites are going to grow and the cost of not jumping on the bandwagon may be more in the long run than doing so. The primary purposes of the Web are information exchange, sales, and advertising. For example, some health clubs have established home pages, recognizing that they are unlikely to sell many new memberships but that they will likely be of great importance to membership communication; thus they can help retain members and motivate members to be more active. If the establishment of a home page is being considered, the first step should be to talk to other similar organizations that have taken the step (Tucker, 1997; Sherman, 1997).

A relatively new administrative concern is employees utilizing computers for recreational pleasure. "Managers and employees should strive together to harness online recreation toward positive ends, rather than condemning or seeking to stifle it completely. Online recreation has already served many supportive purposes in organizations; games can be used to help decrease computer anxiety and encourage experimentation. . . . Constructive recreation is also in keeping with legal and technical constraints . . . allowing online recreation but placing specific limits concerning content and timing" (Oravec, 2002, p. 61).

■ OFFICE ORGANIZATION AND MANAGEMENT

Since desktop computers have become so much faster and more cost effective, the face of office management has changed drastically. Along with the basic computer, the office support technologies of faster and more efficient word processors and desktop publishing, laser printers, intelligent copiers, facsimile machines, and the Internet with e-mail have transformed office management.

Networking by creating direct electronic links between offices, or sections within an operation, is greatly expanding. For example, administrators or approved staff can easily pull up the academic records for students. Hard copy forms for documents such as purchase orders should be eliminated by using electronic means of communication. The submission of manuscripts or grant applications should be accomplished electronically.

The days of an organization being structured with the boss having the largest office with the private bathroom, and the remainder of employees following the same hierarchy of large to small self-contained cubicles, are changing to organizing the workplace according to what is most productive and efficient.

The positive physical, psychological, and emotional status of employees depends on ergonomics of the workplace. Many studies have shown that improving the ergonomics for employees pays dividends for greater work output, less time off, and more satisfied employees. As employees spend more time at computers, more effort must be made to ensure that chair height, back support, and lighting are correct. The total overhead cost of maintaining office support has increased through the years, requiring more attention to this area.

Organizing the Workplace

> Organization ecology is about how an organization's leaders choose to convene their employees in space and time in pursuit of a long-term competitive edge. (Becker and Steele, 1995, pp. 11–12)

The key elements of organizational ecology are as follows:

- Decisions about the physical settings in which work is carried out.
- Decisions about the processes used for planning and designing the workplace system.
- Decisions about how space, equipment, and furnishings are allocated over time.

These decisions are based on the following factors (Becker and Steele, 1995):

- The nature of the work and business processes themselves.
- The particular organizational culture and values in which the work is carried out.
- External factors, such as air quality and transportation demand, that affect how employees come to work and where they work.
- Real estate supply and demand.
- Safety, security, and other quality-of-life issues.
- Workforce demographics such as age, gender, and lifestyles.

Research and experience have shown that automating or adding electronic gadgets to an office will not ensure greater efficiency or productivity. How many of us have purchased scanners or digital cameras only to have them never used? To design the modern office one must perform a needs assessment, select the technological products that will achieve the desired results, and provide the proper training to ensure use:

- Determine the interconnections and relationships within the whole organization.
- Emphasize that technology is to provide more efficient means for the workers to accomplish their goals.
- Office technology cannot be seen as the sum of isolated applications or as affecting only some workplaces.

Examples of applying these suggestions are academic departments in physical education, leisure, exercise science, and health promotion in which students register for classes via modems in their rooms or at computer laboratories, while secretaries and administrators can pull up counts of numbers of students enrolled in each section, and access student records to assess their progress in meeting requirements. Instructors can communicate with students in their classes by establishing a website for each class listing the syllabus, assignments, test schedules, and other information. Student teacher supervisors can communicate with their charges along with the cooperating teachers everywhere—even overseas. An interesting addition is that instructors can print out electronic photographs of students in their classes.

In athletics, authorities can check on the academic progress of the athletes for eligibility matters at the flick of a switch. Athletic training administrators can follow the injury and treatment progress of the athletes. Equipment managers can track who has what equipment checked out, as well as all kinds of background information about the equipment, such as how old it is and what size each item is.

Office Structure and Personnel

The modern office is an informational processing system. It is a network of component parts developed to provide a flow of information to decision makers. The functions of an office are carried out through the following five activities:

- Receiving data and information.
- Recording data and information.
- Preparing data and information.
- Communicating data and information.
- Safeguarding information.

Sport managers must be cognizant that incorporating technology into an office has a profound effect on employees using the equipment. Automated workstations frequently put employees in more isolation. This is not better or worse than the traditional office desk arrangement. But it is vastly different. There will likely be more pressure for independent thinking and decisions. Also, technical equipment has a way of forever changing and improving, requiring a never-ending cycle of retraining. To be productive and happy in this new work environment, employees must have the attitude that they will continue to learn and adjust every work day until retirement.

■ WORD PROCESSING

Word processing is the most frequently used application of the microcomputer (Picciano, 1994). As stated at the start of this chapter, word processing is the transferring of an idea or thought into a final, error-free document by means of an automated system of word productivity. It is a system because it uses automated fast equipment, skilled operators, and revised procedures. Word processing software production continues to be a highly competitive business with new systems coming on board to dominate the market.

Word processing is simply a better way to type. It is better because of two major characteristics. First, you can see what you have typed before it is transferred to paper. You can see the material on a screen and then very easily correct errors, add or delete material, relocate information, change margins, center material, and perform other formerly time-consuming tasks. Second, word processors have "memory"—they remember everything you type. Documents can be stored as files and used over and over. In most word processing systems, the actual printing on paper is done on a separate printer.

A major capability needed for athletic offices is the feature of assembly/merge. This allows for the production of originally typed, multiple copies with appropriate changes in names, addresses, or special paragraphs or sentences. This is sometimes referred to as "boilerplate" document production.

The common uses of word processors in a school or athletic program are as follows:

1. Producing typed (printed) material faster and more professionally. Estimates show that the system is three to four times as fast as traditional typing because of ease of correction; automatic features such as carriage return, hyphenation, margins alignment, and centering; and ease of material reorganization.

2. Test editing and document assembly. The word processor eliminates retyping. Chores such as alphabetizing a list of names can be done automatically. Or, if the list is alphabetized by name, but you need the list numerically by Social Security number, it can perform that task. A large bank of test questions could be maintained in the memory; an instructor could call for any specific questions desired, and a test could be printed in a matter of minutes.

3. Records management. The word processor works efficiently in maintaining grade lists, team rosters, eligibility lists, schedules, physical fitness scores, equipment inventories, and textbook inventories.

4. Statistical/science applications. Word processors can be purchased that have extensive mathematical capabilities and are also programmable. Obviously, word processors have a place in the laboratories of researchers in biomechanics and the physiology of exercise. The statistical use of word processors has revolutionized sports information data on all levels. Think of the applications of word processors to the college intramural and campus recreation programs, where it's necessary to maintain records and point totals for hundreds of teams.

■ OTHER COMMON OFFICE TECHNOLOGY

It seems as if some new device in office technology comes out every day. There are, however, three items that should be considered in planning the modern sport management office. The microfiche reader is a very handy device that is going to become common in sport management in the future. With the explosion of printed material inundating us, it is believed that more and more sport management data will be stored and transmitted on microfiche. Microfiche readers are inexpensive, have no operating expenses, and are almost maintenance-free. Special copy machines, which are rather expensive, may be purchased in association with microfiche readers.

Almost every office has a copy machine, which correctly should be termed a xerograph. Plain-paper electrostatic processing now dominates the market. The most important information needed before shopping for a copy machine is how many copies per month will be made. Other needs that will determine the type of machine to purchase are reduction or enlargement; sorting, collating, or binding; automatic duplexing (printing on both sides); large paper capacities; control panel operation; document feeder that accepts paper of various sizes; computer forms feeder; color capability; and built-in service diagnostics.

The facsimile machine (fax) is vital in sport management. This machine transmits printed material (including graphics) via regular telephone lines to a receiving machine. The receiving machine prints a duplicate copy. Fax machines are almost maintenance-free. The cost of fax machines dropped dramatically when the volume of sales increased substantially. Almost everything in sport, except legal documents, will be transferred by fax, such as purchase orders, schedules, and eligibility lists. Fax machines are organized by class. Class I, the oldest and slowest, are extinct. Class II are the oldest mass-produced machines, which probably represent about 2 percent of those in operation. Class III are those now in operation. Class IV are the new generation, which are very fast and expensive. The most inexpensive models are portable and lightweight and are suitable for small offices that expect to send about 10 or fewer messages a week. The more substantial models are considered commercial and have a variety of added options, each of which increases the price. Delayed dialing will allow messages to be sent after-hours, saving on long-distance costs. Autodialing allows speed dialing of frequently used numbers. Especially important for offices that will be calling overseas numbers, or others frequently difficult to get through, is automatic repeat dialing.

Those who have used e-mail for some years tend to take it for granted, which can minimize its effectiveness. One problem is people who create new addresses without deleting the old one. A solution is to sign up for a service, such as "Bigfoot," which will copy and forward your e-mail. Another reported problem is setting the limits on the length of input too low, causing a normal transmission to be rejected. Finally, if you will be away for a week or more, arrange for someone to check your e-mail, or have the server automatically respond to input with an "answering machine" type of note that tells people when you will again be available (Grinzo, 1997).

A necessary tool for the sport information office is a scanner. This will allow utilizing photographs and printed materials or pictures from newspapers, magazines, or books to be scanned

Critical Thinking

Jane Fong was delighted to find that she had been approved to do her student teaching the following fall in a high school. She had a double teaching major in physical education and computer science. Jane met with the university student teaching supervisor to whom she had been assigned and learned that a minimum of six visits were required. Because her assigned high school was so far away, the supervisor said she would come three times to observe her twice on each trip, once in the morning and once in the afternoon on each visit.

Jane learned that a major part of the protocol was a requirement to deliver or mail weekly logs to the supervisor summarizing activities, problems, and successes. Also, Jane was required to deliver or mail a lesson plan of the activity she would be teaching for each of the observation periods. In addition, the supervisor would be sending detailed written results of each of the observation periods to Jane and her cooperating teacher. Jane was informed that she would be expected to visit with the supervising teacher each week in person or by telephone to chat. Jane started to lose her enthusiasm as she contemplated the cost and time required for preparing and delivering or sending all this material.

She described her anxiety to Dr. Johnson, one of her computer science professors, who said, "Why don't you meet with the director of student teaching and offer your expertise to set up a program wherein all the communication between the student teaching office, the student teaching supervisor, the cooperating teacher, and you be accomplished through e-mail and the Internet?" The director of student teaching thought it was a great idea, but asked Jane to meet with her computer science professors and come back with answers to the questions here. Your professors came up with plans to overcome all of them. How?

1. Your university supervisor and the cooperating teacher do not have computers, so how would they be able to get online?
2. Since you don't have a computer of your own, how would you communicate?
3. How could sending lesson plans and weekly logs be simplified through e-mail?
4. How could the weekly "chat" session be accommodated through e-mail?
5. Since neither your university supervisor nor your cooperating teacher has learned to use e-mail, how could this be accommodated?
6. What would it take to initiate this for all student teachers?

right into documents. Like all hardware, the price of scanners is falling each year while the quality and speed of operation increase ("Scanner Gives SOHO a Personal Touch," 1997).

Exercises

1. List some examples of existing uses of the computer in sports. Now list other ways it might be used.
2. Since there appears to be little material presented in the professional literature on computerized scouting for basketball, pretend you are a coach talking to a programmer who will prepare a program for you to use in basketball scouting. List the five most important factors or tendencies about your opponents that you want the computer to analyze.
3. Describe some way data processing could be used in this course.
4. Assume you are the athletic director of a large high school program. The principal requests a list of ways you and the coaches could utilize a central computer if a terminal and screen were installed at the athletic office. Prepare a list.
5. Describe how a university sports information office could utilize a word processing system.

6. You are chairperson of a physical education department at a junior high school with about 2,000 students. There are a total of four physical education teachers. The responsibilities of the department include modest intramural and interscholastic programs. List the ways you or your staff would utilize a personal computer.

7. Draw a diagram of the physical education and/or athletic offices of the school you are attending. Draw a second design with your own ideas about how it could have been designed to improve operations.

8. Describe how networking could be incorporated into a large high school athletic department to improve operations.

References

Annesi, J. (2002, January). Using computers to solve the exerciser dropout problem. *Fitness Management* 18, pp. 38–43.

Bay, R. (1993, May). The four Cs for computer success. *School Business Affairs* 59, pp. 10–13.

Becker, F., & Steele, F. (1995). *Workplace by design.* San Francisco: Jossey-Bass.

Business and fitness. (1997, August). *Club Industry* 13, pp. 32–33.

Catalano, J. (1996, June/July). The Web. *Athletic Management* 8, pp. 42–47.

Cherry, D. (2002, January). Handling your atrocious attrition. *Fitness Management* 18, pp. 44–48.

Cioletti, J. (1998, January). Top billing. *Club Industry* 14, pp. 17–22.

Courtney, R. (1993, June). Automating your recreation department. *Parks and Recreation* 33, pp. 66–70.

Desktops. (2002, September). *Consumer Reports* 68, pp. 20–22.

Djang, P. A. (1993, Spring). Selecting personal computers. *Journal of Research on Computing Education* 32, pp. 327–338.

Everhart, B. (1997, August). Using e-mail in student teaching. *Journal of Physical Education, Recreation and Dance* 68, pp. 36–38.

Farmer, P. J.; Mulrooney, A. L.; and Ammon, R. (1996). *Sport facility planning and management.* Morgantown, WV: Fitness Information Technologies.

Gondolfo, C. (1997, November). Check out the check-in. *Fitness Management* 13, pp. 33–34.

Grinzo, L. (1997, October). E-mail heaven. *Windows* 8, p. 45.

Handley, A. (1993, February). Management notebook. *Club Industry* 9, pp. 51–54.

Jonigan, M. L. (1993, April). Get instant answers with a database. *Cleaning and Maintenance Management* 30, pp. 29–33.

Kalakota, R., and Whinston, A. B. (1997). *Electronic commerce.* Reading, MA: Addison-Wesley.

Kenworthy, K. (1997, October). Keep out! Private. *Windows* 8, pp. 218–226.

Key CAD complete. (1997). TLC Properties, Inc., a subsidiary of The Learning Company, Inc.

Laptops. (2002, March). *Consumer Reports* 68, pp. 28–31.

Monitors. (2002, September). *Consumer Reports* 68, pp. 23–25.

Oravec, J. A. (2002, January). Constructive approaches to Internet recreation in the workplace. *Communications of the ADCM* 45, pp. 60–63.

Parkhouse, B. L., ed. (2001). *The management of sport.* Dubuque, Iowa: The McGraw-Hill Company.

Picciano, A. G. (1994). *Computers in schools: A guide to planning and administration.* New York: Macmillan.

Printers. (2002, September). *Consumer Reports* 68, pp. 26–28.

Rabin, J. (1993, July). Light years ahead. *Athletic Management* 5, p. 6.

Ross, C., and Wolter, S. (1997, October). Registration information. *Athletic Business* 21, pp. 59–65.

Safrit, M. J., and Wood, T. M. (1995). *Introduction to measurement in physical education and exercise science.* St. Louis: Mosby/Yearbook.

Scanner gives SOHO a personal touch. (1997, March). *Windows* 8, p. 176.

Sherman, R. M. (1997, November). World wide worth. *Athletic Business* 21, pp. 45–53.

Tucker, R. (1997, November). Clubs on the Web. *Fitness Management* 13, pp. 29–32.

Tucker, R. (1998, February). Pushing your message. *Fitness Management* 14, p. 44.

What's new in Web services? (2002, June/July). *Athletic Management* XIV, pp. 6–8.

Wittenberg, D. K., and McBride, R. E. (1998, March). Enhancing the student-teaching experience through the Internet. *Journal of Physical Education, Recreation and Dance* 69, pp. 17–20.

13

Administrative Issues Specific to Physical Education and Campus Recreation

───────── **Management Thought** ─────────

*Law of Energy: Children have more energy after a
hard day of play than they do after a good night's sleep.*

Steve Jarrell

───── **Case Study: Teacher Determined That Physical** ─────
Education Will Not Be a Spectator Sport

Bill Smith, who won the teacher of the year award for his school, was in his fifth year of teaching physical education in a middle school. He was doing well, but still wanted to improve. He recalled that his teaching had not been videotaped since he was student teaching. He thought it would be interesting to see what his teaching looked like now, so he set up a camera in the corner of the gym and let it roll. As he studied it later, he noticed that he remained in one area of the gym most of the period, and he also noticed that a few students were dominating his time—some because they were the best, and some apparently because of behavior problems.

For the fun of it, he made a grid of the gym and plotted how much time he spent in each section. He then listed the students, and after their names marked an "S" each time he had an interaction with a student for a skill or technique and a "B" each time he interacted with a student because of behavior. When he compared the two forms, he noticed that the good students who dominated much of his time gravitated to the sections in which he spent most of his time, while the students with behavior problems

stayed as far away as possible. He also noticed that several shy students, who were not as active, managed to stay far away. He also saw that several students were always eager to respond to questions and dominated the verbal interaction of the class. Thus he decided to develop some strategies to rectify the situation.

First, Bill decided that a partial solution was to make a conscious effort to move about the teaching area in a random order throughout each period. Second, he evaluated his disciplinary strategies for those repeaters and decided to tighten up discipline for the first offense by instituting an immediate five-minute "time-out" instead of verbal warnings. Third, he gave the talkative students each two tokens. Each time they responded or asked questions, they handed in a token—when their "two cents" were spent, that was it for the period. He did the same thing for the shy ones, but they had to "spend" their tokens by the end of the period. He noticed that he had been asking many questions that required only yes and no answers, so he decided to rephrase questions to require thinking and in-depth answers or discussion. He also found that if he always waited several seconds after asking a question to slow responders, he was able to draw out more responses from the shy students. Another strategy he tried from time to time was to ask a question and have the class pair off to discuss the answer, and then call on several pairs to jointly share their thoughts with the class.

All in all, his classes improved even more, and he had a great deal of fun knowing that he was keeping his students from making physical education classes into a spectator sport (Colvin, 1998).

Chapter Objectives

The reader should be able to

1. Outline the constructs for planning a physical education curriculum.
2. Identify primary administrative strategies for dealing with areas of special concern in physical education.
3. Identify the major requirements of the Individuals with Disabilities Act (IDEA) of 1996 for physical education and intramurals, write an IEP for a student with disabilities that includes both of these programs, and report the competencies required for an adapted specialist.
4. Identify the primary aspects of an intramural program for a middle school, a secondary school, and an institution of higher education.
5. Identify the objectives and structures of intramural programs.
6. Demonstrate the appropriate tournament organization for a variety of sport competition in team and individual situations.
7. Compare and contrast the intramurals, extramurals, and club sport programs.

▇ REFORM AND CHANGE IN PHYSICAL EDUCATION

There is nothing more difficult to plan, more doubtful of success, nor more dangerous to manage than the creation of a new system. For the initiator has the enmity of all who would profit by the preservation of the old institution and merely lukewarm defenders in those who would gain by the new one. (Machiavelli)

When we hear about a good idea, but know that it will be difficult to overcome inertia to achieve change, we may think, "If we keep on doing what we have always done, we will keep on getting what we have always gotten—poorly conceived programs of learning in physical education and the associated poor learning results" (Lambert, 1998, p. 13).

In perusing the current literature, one is overwhelmed with the proliferation of material on standard-based curriculum reform. Most authorities seem to agree that if standards are used to direct teaching toward worthy goals, to promote teaching that is responsive to the ways students learn, to evaluate school practices, and to apprise students and parents of progress and special help if needed, that standard-based reforms can be supported. But if standard-based reform just results in tougher hurdles, it should not be supported. Nor should we support such practices such as lockstep curricula; increased testing, especially in the primary grades; tracking by "ability"; and retention and promotion decisions made on the basis of single test results, all of which are detrimental to learning (Falk, 2002). In 1940, one of the great leaders of physical education, Charles McCloy, "criticized school programs and teachers for too much duplication of material from year to year, low levels of engaged time in physical activity, poor student motivation for active participation, and subjective grading systems that were not correlated with individual differences" (Lee, 2002, p. 118).

In reviewing what research has told us about teaching, learning, and leading physical education, Amelia Lee has reported these findings:

- High levels of engagement lead to higher levels of achievement, and the quality of practice rather than the quantity is most important.
- The role students play in their learning is powerful as they make decisions about the extent to which they pay attention, the effort they will put forth, and whether the activity is enjoyable.
- Students who have adequate skill and positive feelings about their competence are more likely to learn the activities.
- Competency beliefs vary as to age, gender, and the type of activity; but younger children have higher, but not necessarily realistic, beliefs about how good they are.
- Teacher practices are linked to students' beliefs about values of physical activities, and which are more appropriate for boys and girls.
- Boys are more active than girls, activity levels decrease as children move through the grades, and confidence in one's ability leads to increased activity.
- There is an abundance of research that should help prepare physical education teachers, but it should be acknowledged that this is a complex endeavor that requires a long-term developmental process.
- Students entering the physical education teacher training process have strong experiential beliefs, good and bad, about what goes on in physical education, which may differ from content being presented in training programs. These students must be introduced to strategies that go beyond equitable treatment of boys and girls to overcome the sex bias in beliefs and behaviors (Lee, 2002).

The conundrum is that the president of the United States, the National Centers for Disease Control, and most of the health and medical societies and associations have endorsed strong statements for more exercise and activity, and polls have shown that parents want more; in contrast, however, less time has been dedicated to physical education, less money has been invested in facilities and equipment; generally classes in physical education are far too large; and school boards and school administration have provided meager support. Why the paradox? Can it be fixed?

Siedentop (1992) suggests that rather than poor marketing, as some have suggested, the cause is that physical education programs have not performed in ways that are valued by the consumers—the students. He agrees with breaking the mold. Rather than small incremental improvements of programs, assessment, and instruction, he recommends changing the system to jump into the future. For example, he recommends experimenting with more flexible scheduling of periods, time and length of day, and length of the year.

It should be noted, however, that many entire schools had modular scheduling in the 1960s, and it didn't "stick." Since the 1970s, many higher education physical education activity programs have been scheduled on flexible meeting times. This has been beneficial for some classes and for some students, but will not in itself "reform" physical education. Experimentation could also be given to changing from presenting a wide variety of activities to doing a few better and with more depth; having students more responsible for their own programs and outcomes; and building on the awareness that sport and fitness are sought and valued because of social outcomes.

The National Association of Sport and Physical Education (NASPE) developed *National Standards for Beginning Physical Education Teachers* in 1995. This prescribes the knowledge and performances a beginning physical education teacher should possess (see Table 13.1). The process shifted from a focus on what teachers should know (content) to what they should be able to do (performance based). In association with this effort, NASPE developed standards for what students should know and be able to do. These standards were reported in *Moving into the Future: National Standards for Physical Education* in 1995,

Table 13.1 How Sport Education Meets the NASPE Standards	
NASPE Standards	**Sport Education**
1. Demonstrates competency in many movement forms and proficiency in a few movement forms.	Builds competence through • Longer seasons. • Small-sided competition. • Practice sessions during preseason. • Formative assessment—focuses student practice. • More practice trials results in more learning. • Teamwork and cooperative learning. • Learning tactics and skills that promote proficiency.
2. Applies movement concepts and principles to the learning and development of motor skills.	Helps apply concepts and principles by • An assessment focus on critical elements of skills. • Helping students understand how practice improves skill. • Providing preseason opportunities for skill preparation. • Providing opportunities for more skilled students to help less skilled students. • Exposure to application of biomechanical principles (force). • Tactics and skills instruction. • Allowing students to occupy roles of statistician and referee.
3. Exhibits a physically active lifestyle.	Helps students exhibit an active lifestyle by • Encouraging everyone to be a player. • Helping students achieve a feeling of competence so that they are more likely to be active. • Encouraging students to become and feel "capable."
4. Achieves and maintains a health-enhancing level of physical fitness.	Promotes achievement of fitness through • Opportunities for fitness testing/assessment. • Individual feedback of fitness results through use of heart rate monitors. • Record keeping and goal setting. • Encouragement of team warm-ups and preparation for play. • Increased opportunities to participate in small-sided competitions.
5. Demonstrates responsible personal and social behavior in physical activity settings.	Encourages responsible personal and social behavior by • Tallying team fair play points. • Focusing on team play rather than individual play. • Offering opportunities for officiating. • Allowing opportunities for multiple roles/responsibilities. • Emphasizing the value of becoming a member on whom others depend.
6. Demonstrates understanding and respect for differences among people in physical activity settings.	Promotes understanding and respect for differences through • Development of character and a sense of social responsibility. • Multiple student roles and responsibilities. • Diverse teams and balanced selection process.
7. Understands that physical activity provides opportunities for enjoyment, challenge, self-expression, and social interaction.	Builds understanding through • Integration of arts and other academic areas in the culminating experience. • Availability of multiple student roles that support game play. • Affiliation with a team. • Opportunities, particularly for less skilled students, to be a full participant.

Source: Veale, M. L.; Johnson, D. J. ; Campbell, M.; and McKethan, R. (2002, April). The North Carolina PEPSE Project. *JOPERD* 73, p. 21.

which provides target points, or benchmarks, that should be achieved throughout the K–12 programs (Senne and Housner, 2002). The new NASPE/NCATE standards for physical education are required in February 2003 (NASPE News, 2002). In addition, NASPE has released the first-ever physical activity guidelines for infants and toddlers:

- Infants should interact with parents and/or caregivers in daily physical activities that are dedicated to promoting the exploration of their environment.
- Infants should be placed in safe settings that facilitate physical activity and do not restrict movement for prolonged periods.
- Infants' physical activity should promote the development of movement skills.
- Infants should have an environment that meets or exceeds recommended safety standards for performing large muscle activities.
- Individuals responsible for the well-being of infants should be aware of the importance of physical activity and facilitate the child's movement skills.
- Toddlers should accumulate at least 30 minutes daily of structured physical activity, preschoolers at least 60 minutes.
- Toddlers and preschoolers should engage in at least 60 minutes and up to several hours per day of daily unstructured physical activity and should not be sedentary for more than 60 minutes at a time except when sleeping.
- Toddlers should develop movement skills that are building blocks for more complex movement tasks; preschoolers should develop competence in movement skills that are building blocks for more complex movement tasks.
- Toddlers and preschoolers should have indoor and outdoor areas that meet or exceed recommended safety standards for performing large muscle activities.
- Individuals responsible for the well-being of toddlers and preschoolers should be aware of the importance of physical activity and facilitate the child's movement skills (NASPE News, 2002).

The traditional secondary physical education unit of instruction has been the multiactivity program. The primary limitation of this curriculum approach is the assumption that secondary students need very little skill work prior to engaging in games. Typically, students receive limited instruction on skills and proceed to game play. The consequence of this approach is that many students become competent bystanders. They are left out of game play because either they lack the skills or more skilled players engage with other skilled participants and leave out the marginally skilled participants (McKethan, 2002). Some have described this as "managed recreation." If the goal is to prepare students for lifelong participation, these programs are invalid and possibly negligent (Veal et al., 2002).

The sport education model of delivering secondary school physical education (Siedentop, 1994) has been selected to reform a failing program in North Carolina. It was selected because it presents a good fit for the NASPE standards and meets the general objectives required for secondary physical education programs in the state (see Table 13.1). Workshops were held to provide information on both the sport education concept and the NASPE standards. Ten schools representing all regions of the state were selected as pilot programs for the 2000–2001 school year. Each school was required to compare the effectiveness of new programs versus the old. Expansion of the program will depend on these results, but very positive reports have been received from each of the sites (Veal et al., 2002).

Authorities generally agree that there is a range of physical education programs from excellent to abysmal. Far too many are at the wrong end. Because this text is primarily concerned with administration, it is beyond our scope to delve into curriculum theory and construction. Instead, a few generalities of special concern to administrators will be covered.

Many other nations have a national curriculum for all subjects, and some authorities are calling for a national curriculum with standardized tests for use in this country. "The National Board for Professional Teaching Standards has convened the standards committee to delineate what accomplished teachers of physical education should know and be able to do. This is the beginning of a 2–3 year process which will culminate in a certification for recognition of physical educators" ("National Teaching Board Calls for Physical Education Standards," 1998).

Several national initiatives have been mounted to assist in the promotion of the need for daily physical activity and physical education. One of these was the National Coalition for Promoting Physical Activity (NCPPA), which was established in 1995 by six organizations to encourage Americans to lead more active lifestyles (Hudgins and O'Connor, 1997). In 1996 the U.S. surgeon general issued a report, *Physical Activity and Health,* that attempts to stimulate Americans into greater physical activity (U.S. Department of Health and Human Services, 1996). The Centers for Disease Control and Prevention released a report in 1997 calling for the same (*Promoting Lifelong Physical Activity,* 1997). NASPE recently stated that few states are meeting the recommendations of these reports for daily physical education. Illinois is the only state to do so; Colorado, Mississippi, and South Dakota are the only states that have no requirement ("Shape of the Nation Report," 1998).

■ PROGRAM PLANNING

Basis

The physical education program does not exist in a vacuum; therefore, it must reflect the philosophies of the community and the school district. To plan long-range programs, the initial task must be to have groups study these prevailing attitudes and prepare a statement that lays the basis for future programs.

Next, the planners need to establish how the community's future physical education programs will interface with the general educational objectives of the district. After this, it is possible to identify the general physical education objectives. At this point, there must be serious discussion about what objectives should be emphasized, and to what degree, for physical education to contribute to the general education objectives of the district and to reflect the community's philosophy. See Figure 13.1, which illustrates the program planning pyramid.

Curriculum Planning

For many years, curriculum planning was based on broad goals such as developing strength, endurance, motor ability, rhythmic skills, sportsmanship, health, and sport skills. Educators believed that certain activities made it possible to achieve these goals; these became specific objectives. These were listed and scheduled to be accomplished in each grade with a progression from basic to more complex. Students that remained in the system throughout their schooling, it was hoped, would achieve the end goals.

However, many of these goals and objectives were stated in a way that was not measurable; individual interpretations of them varied greatly. Thus the movement to state them in behavioral objective terms based on competency emerged. Stating the objectives in these terms required specific words that were measurable and universally interpreted. They dealt in the affective, cognitive, and motor domains. This shift brought an emphasis on movement education in the lower grades. There still doesn't appear to be an agreement on whether the emphasis should be on movement education throughout the lower and secondary grades, or if the curriculum should be sport-skill oriented or fitness centered. Because of large classes, students not ready or interested to learn, poor facilities and equipment, and teachers not well-prepared or motivated, the results have generally not been very successful. As previously stated, some authorities believe we can fix the problems by incrementally improving specific areas, while others believe the present system is fatally flawed and needs to be abandoned.

Kirk (1993) suggests that curriculum work is a *craft,* not a collection of specific behavioral objectives. He contends that developing curriculum based on behavioral objectives trivializes the educational process and emphasizes divergent

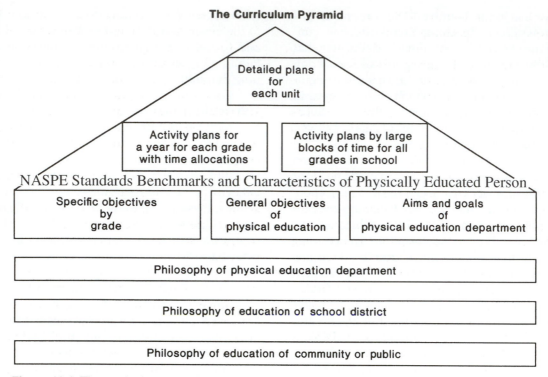

The Curriculum Pyramid

	Detailed plans for each unit	
Activity plans for a year for each grade with time allocations		Activity plans by large blocks of time for all grades in school

NASPE Standards Benchmarks and Characteristics of Physically Educated Person

Specific objectives by grade	General objectives of physical education	Aims and goals of physical education department

Philosophy of physical education department

Philosophy of education of school district

Philosophy of education of community or public

Figure 13.1 The curriculum pyramid.

learning outcomes. He recommends, instead, that the curriculum be crafted to involve "systematic and reflective processes promoting individuality and personal involvement in teaching and learning. This process also creates the possibility of divergent learning outcomes" (Kirk, 1993, p. 244).

Another approach is developing the physical education curriculum based on *learning goals.* A learning goal is simply a statement of expectations for student learning or a benchmark. Guidelines to follow when preparing learning goals include identifying realistic goals, writing the goals based on what three-quarters of the students will achieve, preparing goals for each unit and each grade, and concentrating the goals on overlearning in depth.

Authentic assessment has stimulated interest in building a more *integrated curriculum,* both within physical education (internal integration) and between physical education and other subjects (external integration). Within physical education, it has long been held that such skills as

problem solving and critical thinking have been taught. The problem has been that it has been largely left to incidental learning (assuming that the learning was occurring because the students were engaged in the activity). An integrated program has to be actively planned, taught, and assessed (Placek and O'Sullivan, 1997).

Because of the recognition of the need for diversity and that there is no one best teaching style, the "Spectrum" teaching styles system originated by Myuska Mosston (1992) has been implemented in some schools. The spectrum is an integrated model of teaching styles in which each style is located on a decision-making continuum. This allows students and teachers decision-making responsibilities in one or more of the three phases of teaching: planning, activation, and evaluation. The spectrum is also grounded in some very traditional concepts—such as that the teacher must know the subject matter thoroughly, as well as the learners' developmental stages, ranges of abilities, learning styles, needs, and interests (Mueller and Mueller, 1992).

Health–Fitness in Program Planning

Should a major emphasis of the physical education program be based on physical fitness, health–fitness, or both? It is a question that has been wrestled with for decades. As new research and public opinion polls are released, opinions can flip-flop.

For example, the past recommendation was for students to engage in cardiovascular activity at or above the target zone for *20 minutes, three times a week.* In 1990 the ASCM reported that lower levels of activity might have beneficial results for health, but not for fitness. "The ASCM now promotes the health benefits of longer periods of exercise at lower intensities, emphasizing a more moderately *sustained activity on a daily basis, totaling at least 30 minutes* combined activity durations" (Ward et al., 1998, p. 33). In March 1997 the Centers for Disease Control and Prevention (CDC) published guidelines for school and community programs for promoting lifelong physical activity. The guidelines cite a litany of benefits of regular activity, and list the consequences of inactivity. Three statistics, as follows, are alarming to those in physical education:

1. Seventy-two percent of 9th graders participate in vigorous physical activity on a regular basis, compared with only 55% of 12th graders.
2. Daily participation in physical education classes by high school students dropped from 42% in 1991 to 25% in 1995.
3. The time students spend being active in physical education classes is decreasing; among high school students enrolled in a physical education class, the percentage who were active for at least 20 minutes during an average class dropped from 81% in 1991 to 70% in 1995 (*Promoting Lifelong Physical Activity*, 1997, pp. 1–2).

Ward and others (1998) have stated that it is questionable whether the necessary target heart rates can be achieved in regular physical education classes, given the number of constraints (length of class, numbers of students, limited facilities) and the fact that many secondary programs are sport activity oriented. They state, however, that with slight modification and creative programming, the fitness objectives can be met along with the other objectives.

The media have reported that parents and children desire fitness programs, which schools are not delivering, so that commercial health–fitness centers that market fitness programs for youth are emerging. In addition to the difficult question of whether physical fitness is possible to effect, substantial disagreement exists on how to measure it. In recent years, the testing has switched from physical fitness to health fitness. In addition to the actual testing difficulties, there must be more evidence that those who test high on health fitness tests do in fact maintain better health later in life.

Sport/Games in Program Planning

It has been suggested that physical education classes in higher education institutions have been problematic. Many of these "activity" or "service" classes have been taught to a substantial extent by graduate teaching assistants, many of whom were not physical education majors or had no teaching experience. Many such classes have the reputation of "show up, try hard, and get an easy Satisfactory or 'A'." A perennial problem has been that the classes frequently attract two types: students who have engaged in the activity for years and perform at a high level (former or present varsity athletes), and those who have never engaged in it and want to learn how to do it. The resulting heterogeneity is enormous. One suggested solution is to base these courses on a "sport education model," which will provide a more "authentic" approach and be more motivational. (See Chapter 11 for a discussion of "authentic" assessment.) Basically, these classes act as a team preparing for, and subsequently engaging in, formal competition interspersed with regular practice. Rules, scorekeeping, coaching, strategy, and skills and technique are all included (Bennett and Hastie, 1997; Mohr, Townsend, and Bulger, 2001 and 2002). Siedentop's sport education model, previously discussed, has also found favor in many secondary physical education programs (Veal et al., 2002).

It's never too early to start.
Courtesy of Watauga Democrat.

Fitness testing at Flamingo Elementary School, Hialeah, Florida.
Courtesy of Bill Reeves.

To others, the question is not whether the curriculum should be based on fitness attainment or sport skills, but whether the sport/games programs are based on competition or cooperation. Emphasizing cooperation rather than winning is difficult for most Americans. For example, instead of playing "four square" to win, it might be played to see how many consecutive times the ball could be hit. It would appear that research results favor cooperative games, especially for young children, over competitive games in physical education (Henkel, 1997). Student needs must drive curriculum decisions.

Curriculum Delivery Schemes

Flexible scheduling in physical education allows the class period to vary three ways: in length, in the number of classes per week, and in the total number of class periods for each semester or session. The extreme of flexible scheduling is modular scheduling, in which the school day is divided into small segments called modules, frequently 15 minutes long. To be completely flexible, the students' schedule of modules would be arranged differently every day. At the other end of the flexible scheduling range is when large blocks of time are set aside for sustained activity. Examples of this are outdoor courses in skiing or camping that might meet over a weekend or vacation period. In higher education, some classes are scheduled for eight weeks of double periods, others are scheduled for double periods on Friday afternoons all semester, and some are scheduled on weekends only. Rather than scheduling physical education in the traditional seven-period days in secondary schools, some have changed to block scheduling to bring more sustained time to each activity.

Proficiency testing and credit by examination are other curricular innovations. The primary objective is to allow students to "pass" out of activities in which they are already proficient. The problems in proficiency testing are primarily from the reliability and validity of the tests, the time it takes to test, and the philosophical conundrum of exempting students from physical education.

Continuing physical education has become more important each decade as the mean population age advances and the scientific evidence grows in support of aerobic exercise throughout life. Descriptions of continuing education range from adult lifelong learning, to extended education, to recurring education, to elder hostel. The tremendous interest in aerobic dance, martial arts, and yoga, as well as the growth in the commercial health spas, display ample evidence of the market and the need. Special adult populations also require trained leadership, such as for cardiac rehabilitation programs.

Competency or performance-based courses grew out of the movement in several states to base teaching certification on the achievement of competencies rather than the successful completion of courses. Many school districts are still experimenting with competency or performance-based courses. The objectives to be met in the competency-based courses are stated in behavioral terms as previously discussed. An example of a performance-based physical education course would be to grade the high jump in a track-and-field unit according to the height jumped.

Contract courses and other forms of independent study have been organized. In higher education, contract courses are usually limited to nonactivity courses, although individual programs of activity for adaptive physical education are frequently on a contract basis. Students are motivated by the personal attention in smaller teaching situations and the opportunity for independent practice.

Fads or capturing current interest is always an interesting question. If a new activity comes along that is in vogue, is fun and exciting, *and achieves the goals and objectives* of the curriculum without extra expense, it seems incredible not to include it. Such activities as Ultimate Frisbee and aerobic dance are examples.

Character Development in Physical Education

Most agree that we no longer have the luxury of deciding whether character education should be a part of physical education. As we can see from the terrible tragedies in some schools to terrorist actions to mandates from the NASPE standards, character education must be included. In the NASPE standards this emanates from standard 6, to develop respect for individual similarities and differences through positive interaction (Doolittle and Demas, 2001; Issues, 2001).

What is character development? Some view it as "moral reasoning." They are emphasizing moral education (thinking and then making a moral decision) as opposed to moral training, which involves merely conforming to rules without understanding the principles involved (Stoll and Beller, 1998). One definition is that character consists of three dimensions: (1) moral knowing, or knowing what is good; (2) moral feeling, or desiring the good; (3) moral behavior, or doing the good. Some believe that the first two aspects can be reinforced and practiced in physical education within the existing curriculum.

In practical terms, the teacher would offer many opportunities to discuss and practice "doing good" things—for example, following rules and being courteous. If teachers would reinforce good behavior in physical education, then good behavior would become second nature and automatic. This might be virtue education or moral training, but not moral education. Is either type a part of the mission and objectives of physical education? Should it be? (Gough, 1998; Fisher, 1998; Docheff, 1998; Stoll and Beller, 1998).

To accomplish teaching for character education and respect, it has been suggested that for middle school physical education the following concepts be discussed with specific behaviors offered by both students and teachers:

- Altruism.
- Compassion and sympathy.
- Respect, regard, esteem, or valuing something.
- Tolerance.

Teachers should create lessons that focus directly within the affective domain. The following steps have been suggested:

- Define the concepts and related student behaviors.
- Act and observe—design activities in which affective learning can be observed in both positive and negative behaviors.
- Debrief—discuss the activities and observations.
- Assess—provide opportunities for assessment of student behavior.
- Apply—provide additional activities in which students apply new understanding and insights (Doolittle and Demas, 2001).

If character development is accepted as an objective, it has to be measured to see if it is attained. Many doubt that it can be measured. Others believe that universal moral values do exist, that moral reasoning based on universal values can be learned, and that if it can be learned it can be measured. They also "believe that the learning process is affected by three factors: environment, modeling, and specific, formal educational process" (Stoll and Beller, 1998, p. 22).

■ UNIQUE AREAS OF CONCERN FOR PHYSICAL EDUCATION ADMINISTRATORS

Discipline

What are the special problems of discipline in physical education? Because the subject matter is physical, there is a danger that both students and teachers may transfer the physical aspect into uncontrolled action. There are no easy answers. What should a teacher do when two ninth-grade boys are fighting and class members will not intercede? What should a teacher do when a student is engaging in behavior that will surely lead to injury, but will not stop when ordered to? Few textbooks recommend the correct response for a teacher who has been hit by a softball bat thrown by an angry student.

Although it is beyond the scope of this text to suggest disciplinary actions, the following administrative guidelines offer some preliminary considerations:

1. Establish sound programs.
2. Strive to maintain a reasonable teacher/student ratio.
3. Provide adequate facilities and equipment.
4. Create clear written policies for discipline and see that both teachers and students understand them.
5. Insist that all teachers enforce the rules consistently and fairly.
6. Back teachers *publicly* when policies are followed, no matter what pressure is brought to bear.
7. Firmly and consistently discipline teachers *privately* who fail to enforce policies; establish a "paper trail" verifying the disciplinary action.
8. In the discipline policy, include only those actions that are enforceable and that are likely to be followed.
9. Involve all teachers and student leaders in the establishment of discipline policies.
10. Make sure that higher authorities understand and will back the discipline code.
11. Through staff development programs, show the inadequacy of negative forms of punishment in physical education (requiring lap running or calisthenics as discipline, removing students from the activity, or verbally assaulting students) and instead develop practical methods and techniques of positive reinforcement.
12. Suggest that teachers use short time-outs.

Dressing for Physical Education and Showering

Whether all students are required to wear a prescribed uniform, or whether they are allowed to wear whatever they want, there are always some students who do not dress for physical education class. Why? What should be done about them?

There could be a variety of reasons, but a common cause is because they don't enjoy or value the program. Others may be self-conscious of their undeveloped bodies, or even deformities. A very few avoid dressing because of religious beliefs, but perhaps many more to defy authority.

1. All students are expected to dress out and participate every day of physical education class. Students who do not bring workout clothes may rent shirts, shoes, and shorts for a nominal fee ($.50) from their teacher. Students who choose not to dress for class will be removed from class immediately and cited for direct disobedience to a teacher.

2. Each student will be graded as follows: cognitive 30%, skills 30%, fitness 30%, and affective 10%. Each time a student does not dress or participate completely with the class, he/she will lose 7% from his/her nine-week average.

3. Each student is to be dressed out and seated on his or her assigned area by the time the gym clock counts down to zero. Failure to do so will count as tardy. Each tardy will result in a loss of 2% from the nine-week average.

4. Students are reminded *not to bring any valuables* to the gym. If you do so, you do it at your own risk.

5. Students with a doctors' excuse *must dress out* unless physically disabled. In order to receive credit, students with short-term disabilities will be given a different assignment.

6. Dressing consists of: PE shirt, red shorts, shoes (tennis, basketball, running, or aerobic shoes). When the weather is cold, students may wear red, black, or gray sweats.

7. Students should respect other students, teachers, and staff at all times.

8. Students will take the Fitnessgram, a fitness test given three times per year (August, October, and December). Students must meet minimum age and gender requirements.

9. Students are responsible for these rules, school rules, and general commands.

First Offense................................Warning
Second Offense............................Lunch Detention
Third Offense...............................Phone call to parents
Fourth or more offenses..............Referral to the office

Direct disobedience will result in immediate removal from class and referral to the office for in-school suspension. A parent-teacher conference will be required for students to be allowed to return to class.

Parent Signature   _____   Date _____

Student Signature _____   Date _____

Example Dress Code Agreement
Source: Mitchell, M. & Hewit, P. (2002, August). Not Dressing Is Disobedience, Not Just a Nuisance. JOPERD, 73, 28–31.

What are the solutions? Develop a sound and exciting program and ensure that the teacher is a role model for dress. Develop flexible dress requirements that reflect hygiene, movement, and safety as their basis. If a strict dress code is to be established (perhaps involving school colors) do so only with the authority of the school administration, and with a great deal of planning as to cost and discipline procedures if not followed. Raise the question: Why are we doing this? Ensure that there are adequate reasons. It is somewhat questionable that grades should be affected by not dressing in a prescribed uniform if the student could effectively and safely take part in other attire. Unless the uniforms are provided free of charge, ensure that some method is arranged to provide uniforms for poor students. For students who do not dress out, try to determine why before issuing punishment or discipline. Arrange for referrals to the guidance counselors to assist those students who have a serious problem with dressing out. If the problem is embarrassment because of poor skills, arrange for special help sessions (Mitchell and Hewitt, 2002).

Showering after class is another consistent problem. With proper facilities, time, and numbers, showering should be a pleasant experience. But most students will find one or two of these factors missing, and showering will be a constant problem. A fundamental point that should be discussed (particularly if classes are large or facilities less than needed) is whether showering should be required or included in the grading. Certainly, taking a shower is not physical education. In addition, the type of activity completed should be considered. Every effort should be made to satisfy the necessary requirements for showering—showering should be dissociated from grading, and an ongoing positive effort should be made to encourage it.

Lesson Plans

Lesson plans are for the teacher what strategic management plans are for the businessperson—a guide or map on how to get the job done. There are many different forms to follow, but experience has shown that if the form is too complex, it won't be used.

One form is a traditional "six-point plan": (1) focus and review; (2) statement of objectives; (3) teacher input; (4) guided practice; (5) independent practice; and (6) conclusion. A form recommended by Harrison and others (1996) for secondary physical education includes these headings: (1) time; (2) teaching and learning experiences; (3) teacher and student class organization; (4) skill analysis—description of skills and activities; (5) teaching cues; and (6) safety, motivation, and individual differences. Pangrazi (1998) reports a lesson plan for elementary phys-

Self-defense classes are becoming more popular but require small classes for safety.
Photo by L. E. Horine.

ical education with the following headings: (1) movement experience and content; (2) organization and teaching hints; and (3) expected student objectives and outcomes.

Class Size

Proper class size depends less on any magical number than on the homogeneity of the students, the activity, and on the facility and equipment. Some authorities have begged the question by stating that physical education classes should be no larger than classes in other subjects. The degree of homogeneous grouping (class made up of students with similar abilities) is vital in determining appropriate class size. This factor has become more important for safety and instructional success with mainstreaming and the higher-risk activities. One might justify scheduling 50 students for a jogging and conditioning class while maintaining that 15 to 20 might be the maximum for weight training or self-defense.

Grading

Grading is a powerful tool and complex, from an administrative perspective (Kleinman, 1997). (See Chapter 11.) Safrit and Wood (1995, p. 214) state, "With all the advances in education, no one has developed a foolproof system of grading. Each system has its advantages and disadvantages." Regardless of the system or form grading takes, the end result should be based on the objectives of the program. An administrator must ensure that all understand and agree on what the grade means. It is important to consider whether the grade reflects improvement, attitude, achievement, attendance, cognitive skills, effort, affective skills, or sportsmanship (Safrit and Wood, 1995). Whatever the system, ensure that it meets the approval of your supervisor and that the students are informed about the system and understand it. Also be aware of systems of grading other than letter grades. Pass–fail or satisfactory–unsatisfactory are frequently used in higher education. In elementary grades, frequently a checklist of objectives is used, with the notation that the student has met each at a level of "outstanding," "satisfactory," or "needs improvement."

Class Organization and Attendance

Class organization also relates to how the teacher groups students for record keeping, attendance, and team activities. Other than the first day or two, there is no reason for calling out roll. Some of the methods used are (1) assigning students numbers and having them count off; (2) standing on assigned numbers that have been painted on the edges of courts and outside play surfaces; (3) dividing students into squads and have one person in each squad maintain attendance for that squad; (4) having the person in the equipment area take roll by noting the baskets used; (5) assigning students seat numbers (when seat numbers are already painted on

bleachers); and (6) having tags on a board lettered or numbered for students to turn over as they come into class.

Dividing classes into squads greatly expedites organizing activity. One very practical method is to carefully structure squads of six students. Each week, change the student leaders of all groups. Frequently, activity units change every six weeks (except for lower grades), so every student will experience the leadership position for a week of every activity. Many drills and sports fit nicely into multiples of six. If the activity is softball, for instance, squads can be paired together. Instructors are urged to be flexible with sport rules to create better learning situations. It makes very little difference for instruction whether a softball team has 8, 10, or 12 players, but it makes a tremendous difference to two students to sit out an activity to meet game rules.

Classes can be quickly grouped through a variety of other methods, such as month of birth or favorite color. An innovative method is to use a deck of playing cards for organization. By carefully assigning students their cards, this would allow for equal groups. A variety of groups is immediately available such as odds and evens, colors, or suits.

■ ADMINISTRATIVE CONCERNS

What are the major administrative problems in physical education in higher education? Members of the College and University Administrative Council (CUAC) of the AAHPERD surveyed its membership who were chairs of departments. The results showed the most serious perceived problem was the lack of awareness of the HPERD mission within the campus and community, especially as to confusion with athletics. The next two most serious problems were the specialization and special interests of faculty replacing a sense of community and collegiality, and balancing the individual interests of HPERD in a combined administrative unit.

An administrative concern is that when physical education is offered as an elective in high schools, not many students take these courses. In a survey of high school seniors in Nebraska, Idaho, and Utah, it was found that 73 percent had opted to avoid physical education. Thirty-one percent thought that there was too much emphasis on winning in physical education; 35 percent reported that they did the same things over and over in physical education; 42 percent said that athletes got preferential treatment; 31 percent reported that males tried to dominate; 32 percent that showering was a hassle; and 30 percent said that they didn't like to dress out in activity attire (Scantling et al., 1995).

What's in a Title?

Except for marketing, department titles were not considered greatly important. Now, however, when departments that include physical education don't contain the old titles of human performance, sports science, or human movement, the field loses identity. Kleinman (1992) believes that the name problem is a "pseudo issue" and that the emergence of the subdisciplines such as sport sociology, sport history, or sport psychology have been a disaster for physical education. Even if the field accepts some new name such as kinesiology, he does not think it will bring unity.

Reports indicate that more than a hundred names were used in various combinations in the 1980s. Justification included changes in academic focus, greater institutional acceptance, better marketing to students, grant acquisition, and, for a couple of states, a result of legislative action. Corbin (1993) argues that physical education should be a "field" representing a combination of disciplines and professions. These would have disciplinarians and professionals, each serving different roles but working toward common goals.

Student Leaders

On all levels, developing a student leader system is highly recommended. The experience will greatly benefit the teacher, the student leader, and the general students. The student leader will gain leadership training that will be beneficial for any vocation in the future, and if a career in physical education is selected, the training will have a positive and long-lasting impact. By encouraging and training high school seniors to be cadets, teachers report that it regenerates them and instills a process of self-development toward professionalism (Havens, 1993).

Students in a leadership program might be called student assistants, student aides, peer teachers, or cadet corps, but whatever the name, faculty must offer strong supervision. It is important that the school administration approve of the system and that the duties and guidelines be clearly outlined in writing. For professional reasons, the extent of the duties must be carefully planned. Certainly, there should be no suggestions that physical education can be taught by any layperson, student or adult. The duties need to be carefully delineated for legal reasons.

It is suggested that the program be quite selective and based on both objective and subjective criteria with no favoritism shown to athletes or to men rather than women. Experience has proved that if such a group maintains very high entrance requirements, more, not fewer, students wish to join.

The following features might be considered:

1. Create several levels or ranks within the system (with expanded duties for higher ranks).

2. Establish special attire.

3. Correlate the system with other school organizations so that the students receive recognition in yearbooks and other publications.

4. Hold special training sessions so the group develops high motor-skill competence for demonstrations.

5. Establish clear evaluative criteria to quickly cull incapable students.

6. Maintain high visibility for the group by posting action photographs on school and gymnasium bulletin boards, as well as by releasing the photos to school and commercial newspapers.

7. Set high standards and assign extra work loads; consistently explain their value.

8. Find outreach projects several times a year, such as acting as officials for Special Olympics, elementary track meets, or a Little League clinic.

Regular duties that might be considered include demonstrating skills; record keeping; monitoring the dressing room; issuing student gear; preparing class equipment; maintaining and repairing equipment; maintaining bulletin boards; assisting individual students; escorting students with minor injuries or illness to the first-aid room; sitting in on curriculum planning meetings; and officiating in class or possibly in intramurals.

Social Concerns for the Physical Education Administrator

It has long been recognized that the leadership acumen of the physical education administrator has significant bearing on social factors, such as leadership development and inhibiting sex-role stereotyping. Childhood obesity is another vital concern. Administrators must also bring their attention more to using physical education to combat child abuse and neglect. Dropouts from elective physical education require study, and administrators also need to study how physical education might mitigate the student from dropping out of school altogether.

Increased attention to diversity is a definite trend in physical education. This relates to students, teachers, and administrators. As previously stated, empowerment also appears to be a major need and trend. These two factors are interrelated. Education for empowerment requires serious consideration of the strengths, experiences, and goals of oppressed minorities. "Multiculturism may be viewed as a means of empowerment, promoting self-help and social responsibility" (McDonald and Fairfax, 1993, p. 78; Scott, 1993).

■ PHYSICAL EDUCATION FOR SPECIAL POPULATIONS

Preschool Children

Physical education programs for preschool youngsters have been generally neglected—a serious mistake. As the number of single-parent families and families with both parents working increases, the number of day care nursery schools will also increase. As this occurs, more

and more children will spend several years in such schools.

There is evidence that later mental and physical competence are determined to a significant degree by the motor learning that occurs in the preschool years. Infants' capacity to learn rather complex motor skills has been demonstrated. Their abilities to hang and climb are easily seen. Considerable research in areas such as perceptual motor training and neurological organization for infants has been conducted, but much more effort is recommended for practical programs of movement education for preschool centers, such as the Main Street Early Education program (McCall, 1994).

As previously outlined, NASPE has published activity guidelines for infants and for toddlers. Many physical education teacher training institutions have initiated projects that serve as demonstration centers for serving these youngsters while providing practical hands-on experience for their trainees, providing a public service, and allowing basic research. An example of this is Kindergym, operated by The University of Northern Iowa, an early childhood motor laboratory model (Marston, 2002, pp. 35–39).

Older Adults and Lifelong Activity

The average age of the population in the United States is advancing; at the same time, more adults have greater resources and time to devote to physical activities. To devise and monitor such programs requires a professional physical educator with specialized training. These specialists will be part of a significant growth industry as the "baby boomers" join others in retirement. In part, this can be seen by the active marketing by universities and colleges sponsoring elder hostel programs, states allowing seniors tuition-free courses, and colleges for seniors at the University of North Carolina at Asheville and Appalachian State University (Macneil, 1998).

The U.S. Department of Health and Human Services recently "indicated that 25 percent of adults do not participate in any physical activity, and 60 percent of adults do not participate regularly in physical activity" (Parr and Oslin, 1998, p. 72). It is generally believed that if students are exposed to a variety of activities and sports, they will find things they will enjoy lifelong. However, little research supports this contention. In many countries, youth are encouraged to participate in fewer sports, but are reinforced to maintain these activities for life.

Despite the fact that it is now common to see athletes in their sixties and seventies competing in long-distance runs and swims, we still concentrate the bulk of research for adult activity on groups in their forties and fifties. Research must focus on what kinds of activities are recommended for various types of older sport participants, in addition to establishing recommendations for frequency, duration, and intensity. Physical education administrators should be aware of and support senior and master competition.

At-Risk Students

Perhaps at-risk students could be helped through physical education more than any other area in the school. They are turned off to school, hostile, troubled with low self-esteem, and likely to have low motor skills. Recall the previous discussion of the Pygmalion effect—students will be what you expect of them; this has great importance with the at-risk student. As many successful experiences as possible must be provided. Activities that build self-esteem, such as martial arts and weight training, would be important (Sparks, 1993).

Adapted Physical Education for the Disabled

> If you treat an individual as he is, he will stay as he is, but if you treat him as if he were what he ought to be and could be, he will become what he ought to be and could be. (Goethe [1749–1832])

The goal is to provide the opportunity for all individuals with disabilities to reach their full potential through individualized education programs. The mandates for inclusion derive from several federal acts. The Rehabilitation Act

of 1973 is general civil rights legislation that applies to social services and schools. It refers to all disabilities collectively, while each state may have differing definitions. "Section 504 of the Rehabilitation Act (PL 93-112) defines a school-age person with a disability as anyone who has a physical or mental impairment that substantially limits one or more life activities, such as caring for one's self; performing manual tasks; walking; seeing; hearing; speaking; breathing; learning; or working" (Auxter, Pyfer, and Huettig, 1997, p. 7).

The Individuals with Disabilities Education Act (IDEA), 1996, expands the Education of the Handicapped Act of 1975 (PL 94-142), which focuses on educational settings and is designed to provide equal educational opportunities for individuals with disabilities. The 1983 amendment (PL 98-199), the 1986 amendment (PL 99-457), and the 1990 version of IDEA (PL 101-476) were all added to expand and refine the original act. For many years, the impetus for adapted physical education programs was PL 94–142, and these definitions were adapted into IDEA. Also fitting into the legislative puzzle is the Americans with Disabilities Act (ADA) of 1990, which has been covered previously in our discussion of prohibiting discrimination in places of public accommodation (Schilling and Coles, 1997).

IDEA replaced the term *handicapped* with *disability*. It also expanded the services required to include transition services to promote movement from school to postschool activities; assistive technology of evaluating and supplying equipment; recreation therapy; and social work. IDEA also expands services to children with autism and traumatic brain injury.

The role of the adapted physical educator (APE) "is to develop physical and motor fitness, fundamental motor skills and patterns, team sport skills, and knowledge of rules and strategies that go with participation in physical activity" (Auxter, Pyfer, and Huettig, 1997).

The laws require schools to provide the least restrictive environment for physical education. This phrase describes the inclusionary process of integrating disabled students wherever possible into regular classes and is referred to as *mainstreaming*. Progressive schools were mainstreaming special education students since the 1960s.

While it has been reported that APE specialists who helped draft IDEA never intended for all disabled children to receive their physical education with the general program, pressure from parents and administrative units for "inclusion" have resulted in most disabled children being mainstreamed. "Adapted physical education consultants—like general physical educators—are torn to meet the excessive demands made daily on their talent and time" (Huettig and Roth, 2002). From an administrative perspective, however, problems must be recognized and ameliorated. The administrator must recognize that one or more students with disabilities cannot simply be placed into an already overburdened physical education class. Either numbers must be reduced or assistants must be added. Modifications in the changing and showering areas might be required, and means of getting from the changing area to the class site might need to be provided. Information and education must be supplied to the existing class prior to the arrival of the student with a disability, to minimize rejection. Physical education teachers must be creative and proactive in making adjustments to ensure that students with disabilities are included successfully. Administrators must recognize the difficulties of the situation and be supportive and encouraging throughout the process.

As a result of the "inclusion movement" there has been a shift in the role of the APE specialists from providing direct service to students with disabilities to serving as a consultant to the general physical educator (Block, Brodeur, and Brady, 2001). This has resulted in excessive caseloads of over 300 students for the consultant (Huettig and Roth, 2002). The APE consultant assists the generalist in providing information about the following:

- Specific disabilities.
- Medical and safety issues.
- Modifications to the specific activities.
- Behavioral and instructional strategies.
- The Individualized Education Plan (IEP) process.
- How to assess students with disabilities.
- How to be an advocate for these students (Block, Brodeur, and Brady, 2001).

There should be a concerted effort in physical education to instill in teachers and students that disabilities are not handicaps. Administrators must sensitize physical educators to the tendency for both teachers and students to develop "handicapism"—the stereotyping, prejudice, and discrimination practiced against people with disabilities. While labeling of some children is necessary and required by law, it should be as subtle as possible and not emphasized. Administrators in physical education must be aware that "the major barriers faced by disabled children are not their physical and mental disabilities but the attitudes of others" (Shapiro and Barton, 1993, p. 54).

Since most disabled students receive some type of accommodation within the general physical education class, grading may present some difficulty. Because these students must receive progress reports to provide feedback relative to their progress toward meeting IEP goals or benchmarks, "contract grading" has been gaining in popularity. The physical education teacher, student, and the APE consultant write a contract outlining the goals and objectives (which will correlate with the IEP) that the student will achieve. The student is subsequently evaluated relative to the extent to which these goals and objectives were met (Henderson, French, and Kinnison, 2001). See Table 13.2. With more inclusion, disabled students are being mainstreamed into special areas such as gymnastics and aquatics with perhaps more severe challenges for risk management for catastrophic events. But with proper training of the personnel, collaboration

	Table 13.2 Sample IEP Grading Contract		
Annual Goals	**Specific Educational Services Needed**	**Present Level of Performance**	**Person Delivering Service**
Goal 1. Trevor will improve abdominal strength.	Special physical education consultant services	Performs eight bent-leg sit-ups with assistance	Morgan Stewart, special physical educator
Goal 2. Trevor will improve throwing skills.	Special physical education consultant services	With a tennis ball, Trevor hits a 2' × 2' target five feet away on 2 of 10 trials	Morgan Stewart, special physical educator

Short-Term Objectives	**Date Completed**	**Special Instructional Methods and/or Materials**	**Grade**
Goal 1. Objectives			
1. In the gym, with assistance, Trevor will perform 10 bent-leg sit-ups.	10-12-01	Mat; social praise; a performance graph	C
2. In the gym, without assistance, Trevor will perform eight bent-leg sit-ups.	11-7-01	Same	B
3. In the gym, without assistance, Trevor will perform 25 bent-leg sit-ups.	Progressing; can do 21	Same	A
Goal 2. Objectives			
1. With a tennis ball, Trevor will hit a 2'×2' target five feet away on 6 of 10 trials.	11-14-01	Tennis ball and target	C
2. With a tennis ball, Trevor will hit a 2'×2' target 10 feet away on 6 of 10 trials.	11-21-01	Same	B
3. With a tennis ball, Trevor will hit a 2'×2' target 20 feet away on 8 of 10 trials.	12-10-01	Same	A

Signatures and titles of appropriate team members (signatures indicate approval of this IEP):

_____   _____   _____
(Parent)   (Teacher)   (Administrator/Supervisor)

Source: Henderson, H. L.; French, Ron; and Kinnison, L. (2001, August). Reporting grades for students with disabilities in general physical education. *JOPERD* 72, pp. 50–55.

with the APE consultants, and adaptations of the curriculum and environment, significant success can be achieved (Block and Conatser, 2002). A wealth of information is available through the National Center on Physical Activity and Disability (NCPAD); telephone (800) 900-8086; website at http://www.ncpad.org/mediassets/; or e-mail at ncpad/news@listserv.edu.

The cornerstone of the education program for a student with a disability is the Individualized Education Plan (IEP), which is required by the Education for the Handicapped Act. This document requires that teachers and administrators be accountable for the education of a child with a disability. (See table 13.3 for an example of an IEP.)

Table 13.3   Individualized Education Plan (IEP)

Prime Exceptionality   Fourth Grade Student with an Orthopedic Impairment   **Active**

Student's Name	Grade 04	School		Birthdate	IEP Begin Dt.	IEP End Dt.	Active ☒

Exceptionality/Rel. Service	Teacher/Provider	# Sessions per	Minutes per Session	Hours per Week
OI	Williams	1 per Week	60	1.00

Present Level of Performance (include specific descriptions of strengths and needs that apply to academic performance, behaviors, social/emotional development, learning styles, physical limitations, and other relevant information).

Student participates in regular physical education 3 days per week and adapted physical education 1 time per week. He interacts well with peers and the adults at the school. He requires a wheelchair or walker for ambulating due to an orthopedic impairment. Gross motor skills in throwing and striking are functional. He needs to improve object handling skills and to maintain his current level of fitness in order to participate fully in physical education and community recreation.

Identified Area: Motor   Skill Area: Object handling skills/catching

Annual Goal #: _1_ Student will improve object handling skills in catching. All objectives will be performed from the wheelchair.

Short-Term Instructional Objectives	Criteria for Mastery	Evaluations Objectives (How) Procedure	Evaluation Schedule	Date Reviewed (See Progress Reports)
With eyes open, student will self-toss and catch a wiffle ball, 10/10x.	With 100% accuracy	Teacher checklist	10/97 1/98 3/98 5/98	
With eyes open and in the ready position, student will receive a basket and ball bounce pass from a partner. He will anticipate the pass and catch it 8/10xs.	In 8 out of 10 trials	Teacher checklist	10/98 1/98 3/98 5/98	
With his eyes open, student will catch a 6 inch ball thrown to him from 10 feet.	In 10 out of 10 trials	Teacher checklist	10/97 1/98 3/98 5/98	
In a four square game, student will receive and pass the ball to other players, imparting the needed force for it to travel to the opponent's square, 3 consecutive times during the game.	In 8 out of 10 trials	Teacher checklist	3/98 5/98 10/98 11/98	

Identified Area: Motor   Skill Area: Physical Fitness

Annual Goal #: _2_ Student will improve his current level of physical fitness, to include strength, agility, muscular endurance, and cardiovascular endurance.

Short-Term Instructional Objectives	Criteria for Mastery	Evaluations Objectives (How) Procedure	Evaluation Schedule	Date Reviewed (See Progress Reports)
With his legs supported on a gymnastik ball, and his trunk extended, student will complete 10–13 assisted push ups.	With 100% accuracy	Criterion-referenced test	5/98 10/98 1/99 5/99	
Using his walker, student will complete one pass of the shuttle run, placing the eraser in a pocket or pouch, in under 18 seconds.	With 100% accuracy	Criterion-referenced test	5/98 10/98 1/99 5/99	
Assisted as needed to the upright position, student will complete 28 to 35 bent-knee sit-ups in 1:30 seconds.	With 100% accuracy	Criterion-referenced test	5/98 10/98 1/99 5/99	
Riding a 3-wheel bike, student will complete one mile around the track in under 10 minutes.	With 100% accuracy	Criterion-referenced test	5/98 10/98 1/99 5/99	

A progress report that relates directly to the goals and objectives is sent to parents four times a year.

Courtesy of Mary Powell Williams, Appalachian State University.

■ INTRAMURALS AND RECREATION SPORTS

Development

Intramurals and recreational sports at both higher education and lower levels have grown out of the natural desires of students to play and compete. Originally, units of competition were clubs or classes and the contests were loosely organized and primarily based on challenges from one team to another. Institutions gave little support or direction to the programs. In some cases, the intramurals (within the walls) gave way to extramurals (outside the walls or between schools) and gradually grew into varsity athletics. In 1913 the first intramural programs under administrative control were established at the universities of Michigan and Ohio State. By 1916, 140 institutions had followed suit. In 1917 the Intramural Sports Section was formed within what is now the AAHPERD; in 1923 intramurals for women originated in higher education; by 1925, intramurals were established in secondary schools. In 1950 the National Intramural Recreational Sports Association (NIRSA) (originally the National Intramural Association) was founded by William Wesson at Dillard University in New Orleans. This organization publishes the *NIRSA Journal* three times a year (Bucher and Krotee, 2002).

Terminology Related to School and Campus Recreation Programs

Intramurals include a variety of activities and tournaments, ranging from chess to team sport seasons. Participation is limited to students (and frequently staff and faculty) from *within* the school.

Extramurals involve competition between teams or people from different schools. Frequently these teams have a higher level of skill than the typical intramural team. Teams or individuals are frequently either winners from intramurals, an all-star team, or a "club team" chosen after tryouts open to the whole institution.

Play day is when participants from several schools meet to engage in one or more sports but schools do not retain their identity.

Sports day is the same as a play day except that schools do retain their identity.

Club sport participation involves groups that organize because of a common interest in an activity or sport. "Self-administration and self-regulation are characteristics common to all clubs . . . those who desire club sport membership seek regular participation under a more coherent design than informal, intramural, or extramural programs offer" (Mull and others, 1997, p. 148). There are usually no paid coaches or scholarships, and the club members frequently have to help pay for uniforms, travel, and officials.

Objectives, Organization, and Structure of Intramural Programs

The general objectives of the intramural program should be to offer a variety of activities. The emphasis should be on enjoyment, camaraderie, challenge, and physical activity.

Intramural programs in the lower schools usually fall under the direction of the physical education department. In higher education the trend moves away from this arrangement; instead the control is shifting to student services or student affairs, and, to a lesser extent, to athletic departments.

This shift appears to be based on finances. Support for these programs is usually based on student fees paid to the general fund. At the elementary and secondary level, the funding comes from the district or student government.

Student involvement plays a major role in the internal organization of intramurals on all levels. A professionally trained administrator of the program (the director) must be appointed to give the program continuity and proper leadership. On all levels, paid coordinators or program supervisors (faculty or graduate assistants) supervise the actual activities. In addition, councils comprised mostly of students should be established to set policy and hear appeals and protests. On the elementary and secondary levels, it is suggested that either several faculty sit on the council or an advisory council of faculty members be formed to review the work and policies recommended by the student intramural council.

Units of Competition and Eligibility

The type of units used depends greatly on the local situation and tradition, along with staff and facilities. The units selected should be based on a "common bond" and "equalized competition." The former refers to something in common that holds a group together—a gang spirit or loyalty. On the lower levels, this bond may be class, homeroom, clubs, or living in the same area. In colleges, the bonding may be dormitory floor, sorority or fraternity, club, major, or class. Equalizing competition is more difficult to achieve. In some activities such as golf and bowling, handicapping may be used. On the lower levels, the units of competition might be based on skill testing.

On the middle school level, classifying participants into leagues (A,B,C) based on height, weight, and age has been successful.

Finances, Equipment, and Facilities

It's nice to have strong financial support for intramurals, and one should continue to strive for it; but many fine programs have existed with almost no support. It may be possible to solicit funds from the business community, by having a local business sponsor part of the program, for example; offering noncredit classes or lessons in unusual activities for fees; or best of all, showing the administration facts and figures to generate more funding.

Equipment and facilities always seem to present problems for intramurals. Cooperation and coordination are the keys. The intramural director must work closely with athletics and physical education to share equipment and facilities.

Most policies on the use of facilities call for class use first, athletics next, and intramural and free play last. Where strong leadership has been present, secondary schools have established policies that put intramurals first in priority for facility use after school. In many institutions of higher education, facilities have been constructed primarily for campus recreation, and, of course, intramurals have first priority, or exclusive use of these facilities. Intramural directors must be creative when facilities are limited. Some programs use hallways and lobbies for such activities as bowling, shuffleboard, bocce, or marbles. Large closets or storerooms can be effectively used for darts or quiet games such as checkers. At other times parking lots or cafeterias can be utilized for roller skating, dancing, and the like. In colleges, students often prefer to use facilities after all other activities are finished. At many institutions, the time slots between 9:00 P.M. and midnight are the best attended.

Program of Activities and Scheduling

Activities taught in the physical education program could form the basis for the intramural program, but many more creative sports and activities can be included. The important concept is to provide a variety of activities to attract widespread participation. A balance of traditional sports with higher levels of competition, such as a track-and-field meet or basketball, should be tempered with activities such as checkers, tug-of-war, or an inner-tube race down a river. Adapting traditional sports to a new environment or different equipment is an excellent way to create interest and excitement. For example, play ice hockey on ice but with brooms for hockey sticks, football in a swimming pool in inner tubes, or basketball with one hand tied in back.

When possible, schedule intramurals after school. In some districts, a late bus to generalized dropoff locations has been arranged for days when intramurals are held. On the high school and college level, however, many strong programs utilize facilities late in the evening. At many elementary and junior high schools, programs before school, during lunch hours, or on Saturdays have been successful.

Club Sports and Adventure Recreation

Club sports and adventure recreation activities have been growing rapidly in recent years. Club sports have been expanding for a variety of reasons. In some cases, colleges have dropped varsity sports such as baseball, wrestling, swimming, and gymnastics due to financial exigencies, and these sports have been reconstituted as club sports. Little direct financial support is provided to club sports, so it is a cost-effective means of providing a competitive experience. In many cases, colleges will allow club sports to request modest funding for officials and travel. In other cases, the club sport teams will raise funds through typical low-level efforts such as car washes or equipment sales. One ski and snowboard racing club makes several thousand dollars each year selling used equipment in which the club retains a percentage of the sales. In many cases, leagues are formed that would never function in a traditional college conference—which might involve competing against company teams, town teams, and a mix of two-year colleges, small four-year colleges, and large universities. Many students are under the impression that some of these leagues are sponsored by national associations such as the NCAA and take the competition very seriously. Other examples of club sports that have become popular in recent years are rugby, tackle football, and ice hockey for women; and lacrosse and field hockey for men. For both men and women, equestrian, fencing, Ultimate Frisbee, body building, weight lifting, long-distance running, and triathlon teams have become common.

In addition to regular club teams, recreational adventure activities have become popular. In many schools and colleges, competitive and recreational climbing have a growing following as more colleges and high schools are installing climbing walls. Groups also regularly meet or have outings in such activities as caving, kayaking, hiking, canoeing, water rafting, orienteering, sailing, and cross-country skiing.

Officials, Protests, and Forfeits

Securing competent officials is a major problem for the intramural director on all levels. On the college level, officiating costs cripple many budgets. The obvious solutions are to pay sufficient fees, advertise widely, and support the authority of officials through consistent administration. Frequently, however, sufficient funds are not available, in which case the following may be tried:

1. Give ample credit to college students for taking courses in officiating for which laboratory work is calling intramural games.

Officials must be prepared to call contests involving persons of the opposite sex.
Courtesy of the Appalachian State University Intramural Department.

2. Solicit help from varsity sport players, especially to officiate at the lower levels.

3. Require each team to provide an official.

4. Play without officials.

A great deal of time and effort is frequently expended dealing with protests and forfeits in intramurals. An effective means of dealing with forfeits in higher education is to require that a "forfeit" deposit be paid at the start of a season. If a team forfeits, it looses a portion of the deposit. Teams that do not forfeit any games receive the deposit back at the conclusion of the season. Strong policies regarding protests should be established to reduce the number. An extreme version is to allow protests based only on ineligible players. Whatever the policy, it should require that protests be submitted in writing and in a timely manner. Protests normally are not allowed if based on the judgment call of an official. A proven method of restricting protests is to require a fee to post a protest that is returned only if the protest is upheld (Mull and others, 1997).

Statistics and Awards

An incredible amount of statistical computation is required in well-managed intramural programs. To encourage year-round participation, rather complex point systems involving numbers of par-

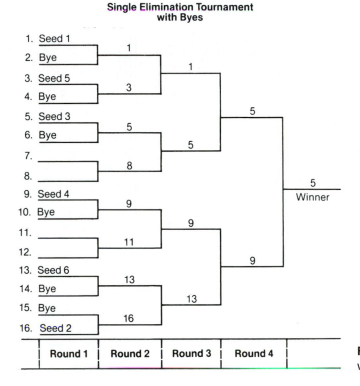

Single Elimination Tournament with Byes

1. Seed 1
2. Bye
3. Seed 5
4. Bye
5. Seed 3
6. Bye
7.
8.
9. Seed 4
10. Bye
11.
12.
13. Seed 6
14. Bye
15. Bye
16. Seed 2

| Round 1 | Round 2 | Round 3 | Round 4 |

Figure 13.2 Single elimination tournament with byes.

ticipants, numbers of contests, and win–loss records of all activities need to be maintained.

Rewards based on self-motivation are much preferred to materialistic awards. But to motivate students to become involved, it is realistic to utilize awards of some kind. The greatest reward students can receive is publicity and recognition. Having a team picture in the paper is probably valued much more than a trophy. Frequently, innovative and inexpensive awards can be handmade. Many businesses will be willing to donate T-shirts as awards with the business name on one side and the name of the school and perhaps the sport on the other side.

Organization of Competition— Tournaments and League Play

League play and tournaments are frequently organized into five types: single elimination, double elimination, consolation elimination, round-robin or league play, and challenge.

Single Elimination Tournament. This type of tournament is the most common in intramurals because the winner is determined in the shortest time. Participants compete until they lose or one is declared the winner. Half of the entrants are eliminated after each round. The single elimination tournament is drawn into brackets as shown in Figure 13.2.

This structure is based on the power of two such as 4, 8, 16, 32, and so on. When the number of entrants does not fall into the power of two, "byes" (free wins to move to second round) are given. The number of byes is computed by subtracting the number of entrants from the next power of two. For example, as shown in Figure 13.3, there were 10 entrants, so a bracket for 16 was drawn and thus six byes were given. If the strength of the entrants is known, the strongest should be given the byes and these "seeded" entrants should be placed so as to meet each other as late in the tournament as possible. Thus no byes are used after the first round.

Double Elimination Tournament

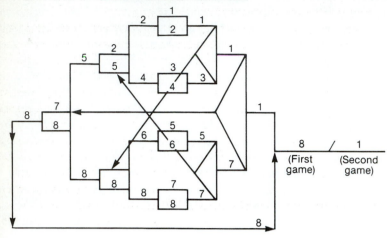

Figure 13.3 Double elimination tournament.

Consolation Tournament

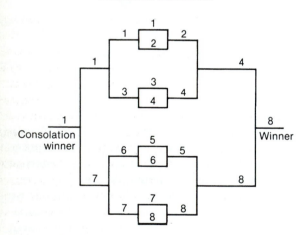

Figure 13.4 Consolation tournament.

Obviously, in Figure 13.2, entrant "5" wins, and "9" is second. How the third and fourth winners should be determined must be decided before the tournament starts. Frequently it will be stated that the entrant losing to the ultimate winner in round three ("1") will be third and the other loser in round three ("13") will be fourth. Sometimes the losers in round three will play each other to decide third and fourth. The total number of matches required to determine the winner will be one less than the total number of entrants. (In Figure 13.2, six contests will be required.)

Double Elimination Tournament. This is one of the fairest types of tournaments because all entrants must lose twice before being eliminated. The structure, however, is awkward to draw. When teams must travel far enough to stay overnight, they prefer this type of tournament because every team is guaranteed at least two games. The drawbacks are the length of time to complete the tournament, the number of courts or fields required, and some difficulty in precisely stating when entrants will play. First-time losers drop into the losers' bracket as shown in Figure 13.3. Seeding, byes, and the determination of the size of tournament brackets is the same as for the single elimination type. The total number of contests is computed by doubling the number of entrants and subtracting one or two. (One if the winner's bracket entrants beats the loser's bracket; two if not.) Thus, in Figure 13.3, with eight entrants, there would be either 14 or 15 contests.

Consolation Elimination Tournament. This kind is similar to the preceding, except that the losers stay in a separate tournament playing only other losers. For this reason, it is not usually popular. If decided in advance, the winner of the consolation tournament (loser's bracket) may play the winner of the winner's bracket. Figure 13.4 illustrates this tournament.

Table 13.4	Round-Robin Rotation System for Even Number of Contestants			
Round 1	Round 2	Round 3	Round 4	Round 5
A vs. F	A vs. E	A vs. D	A vs. C	A vs. B
B vs. E	F vs. D	E vs. C	D vs. B	C vs. F
C vs. D	B vs. C	F vs. B	E vs. F	D vs. E

Note: Team A remains fixed while all other teams are rotated counterclockwise.

Table 13.5	Round-Robin Rotation System for Odd Number of Contestants			
Round 1	Round 2	Round 3	Round 4	Round 5
X vs. E	X vs. D	X vs. C	X vs. B	X vs. A
A vs. D	E vs. C	D vs. B	C vs. A	B vs. E
B vs. C	A vs. B	E vs. A	D vs. E	C vs. D

Note: Team X represents a bye since there are an odd number of teams and the X remains fixed while all teams are rotated counterclockwise.

Round-Robin or League Play. This is the most common and the fairest of all kinds of competition because all entrants meet all other contestants. The formula used to determine the total number of contests required is N (N − 1) divided by 2. Thus, with six entrants, 6 × 5 divided by 2 equals 15 matches. If there are eight or more teams, it is suggested that the teams be grouped into leagues of four to six teams in each, with league winners playing off for the championship. The method of organizing an even or odd number of teams is illustrated in Tables 13.4 and 13.5. Note that the rotation system is based on revolving the entrants counterclockwise; the first team in the fixed position is a bye.

Challenge Tournaments. This type of competition continues for a prescribed period. The contestants attempt to advance up the hierarchy by challenging opponents in a higher position. This form is effective for individual activities such as racquetball and tennis. Frequently the contestants arrange the time and place to play. Some of the most common types are the ladder (see Fig-

ure 13.5), the pyramid (see Figure 13.6), and the funnel (see Figure 13.7). The ladder tournament is also excellent for determining positions of players on teams such as tennis. Usually, rules in ladder tournaments stipulate that contestants may challenge "up" one or two positions, and must play one person below before challenging again above. The pyramid is similar but accommodates more contestants. In the pyramid, contestants usually must defeat one person on their level before challenging above. The funnel-type tournament combines the above two types.

Competition for the Disabled
It would appear that intramurals, extramurals, and club sports would be rich venues for providing opportunities for persons with disabilities to compete. By proactive and affirmative actions, there might even be sufficient numbers of students, staff, and faculty with disabilities to create leagues. In some sports, administrators need to initiate creative innovations and adaptions to enable students with disabilities to compete against regular participants.

Ladder Tournament

1 _____
2 _____
3 _____
4 _____
5 _____
6 _____
7 _____
8 _____

Figure 13.5 Ladder tournament. Seed entrants if possible Contestants usually may challenge up one position and must play one below before challenging up a second time. A deadline should be set for end of tournament.

Pyramid Tournament

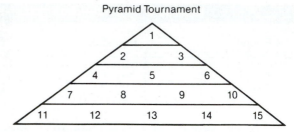

Figure 13.6 Pyramid tournament. Seed entrants if possible. Contestants must challenge and defeat someone on their own level before playing someone on the next higher level.

Funnel Tournament

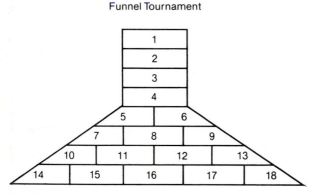

Figure 13.7 Funnel tournament. Seed entrants if possible. Contestants must challenge and defeat someone of the same level (if in funnel) before challenging next higher level. Once in a ladder at the top, contestants must play and defeat a participant from below before challenging "up" a second time.

Exercises

1. Outline the steps you would follow in revising the curriculum if you were the chairperson of a high school physical education department.
2. Write a lesson plan for one period of physical education for an activity with which you are most familiar.
3. Assume that students are required to take at least some physical education each year in grades seven through nine. Outline a three-year plan for soccer instruction in these grades.

4. Describe how flexible physical education program scheduling might be utilized in a high school program.
5. Explain how you would advise the teacher who was the target of an angry student's softball bat.
6. Write a standing operating procedure for junior high school physical education teachers to follow in regard to students showering after class.
7. Identify the procedure you would recommend for taking attendance in a middle school in physical education.
8. Describe what *mainstreaming* means in physical education and relate how it has come about.
9. Write an IEP for a ninth-grade student who is greatly overweight and has a learning disability.
10. Should physical fitness be the dominant component of the public school physical education curriculum? Refer to "Issues," 1992c.
11. Should there be one standard fitness assessment nationwide? Refer to "Issues," 1992d.
12. Should all physical educators be expected to have a common set of performance skills and competencies for teaching? Refer to "Issues," 1992b.
13. What is the place for competition in the elementary and high school physical education programs? Refer to "Issues," 1992e and 1992a.
14. Is it possible to serve normal, at-risk, and disabled boys and girls in the same class effectively? Refer to "Issues," 1993.
15. Present a list of standard operating procedures you would recommend to an intramural director to formulate a student intramural advisory council for a high school program, and one for a university intramural program.
16. Set up a round-robin tournament bracket for volleyball teams A through J illustrating how the

Critical Thinking

During her college days, Mary Sheryl was an active participant in campus intramurals and officiated several sports. Upon graduation she landed a job as a physical educator and assistant coach in two sports at a large high school. She developed an excellent reputation in both teaching and coaching, finally moving up to be the girls' head basketball coach. Her teams had winning records and went to the state finals one year. During these years, she had tried to get various intramural sports started, but each time they fell by the wayside.

At this point she was offered the position of chairperson of the physical education department. She resigned from the coaching position and accepted the chair position with the agreement that she would also be in charge of intramurals and receive an appropriate stipend for the extra work. Soon after, she worked out a compromise that intramurals and varsity sports would have equal access to facilities after school and at night, and gained a modest budget for intramurals from the student association.

During the next few years the program grew, with some standard team sports and some highly innovative special events and individual sports. To help drive the program she got some businesses to sponsor various sports. As the complexity and size of the program increased, four problems started to dominate her time and resources: officials, protests, forfeits, and injuries.

Mary Sheryl was not able to get enough officials, and some of those she did recruit were eager to do a good job but lacked officiating skills and experience. The student association even put a special item into her budget so she could pay a small stipend for officiating. The primary problem with protests was that there were too many, and many resulted from questionable judgment calls by the officials. Her aim was that the intramural competition should be enjoyable with a high level of sportsmanship, and she was afraid that the number of protests was evidence that this objective was not being met. The major problem with forfeits was when they occurred on a weekend or at night when students and officials had made considerable sacrifices to come back to school for the contests only to find that the other team hadn't shown up. The primary concern with injuries was that one life-threatening injury not treated properly could wipe out the whole program. Team members and officials seemed to be able to handle all the minor injuries.

1. How could the problems with officiating be ameliorated?
2. Outline some policies that would reduce the problem of protests.
3. Identify some strategies to lessen the problem with forfeits.
4. How could the possibility of life-threatening injuries being improperly treated be mitigated?

teams could move through to an ultimate winner of team A. Identify how many total contests would be held. Establish a schedule for the contests assuming it is a high school program and the tournament must be completed within six weeks.

17. Set up a double elimination tennis tournament for individuals 1 through 15 with number 1 winning and number 2 second.

18. List three club sport teams or activities of a recreational and instructional nature that would be suitable for a 1,000-student junior high school, a 1,500-student high school, and a 10,000-student college.

References

Auxter, D.; Pyfer, J.; and Huettig, C. (1997). *Principles and methods of adapted physical education and recreation* (8th ed.). St. Louis: Mosby.

Bennett, G., and Hastie, P. (1997, January). A sport education curriculum model for a collegiate physical activity course. *Journal of Physical Education, Recreation and Dance* 68, pp. 39–43.

Block, M. E., and Conatser, P. (2002, May/June). Adapted aquatics and inclusion. *Journal of Physical Education, Recreation and Dance* 73, pp. 31–34.

Block, M. E.; Brodeur, S.; and Brady, W. (2001, October). Planning and documenting consultation in adapted physical education. *Journal of Physical Education, Recreation and Dance* 72, pp. 49–52.

Bucher, C. A., and Krotee, M. (2002). *Management of physical education and sport.* Dubuque, Iowa: The McGraw-Hill Company.

Colvin, A. V. (1998, February). Learning is not a spectator sport: Strategies for teacher–student interaction. *Journal of Physical Education, Recreation and Dance* 69, pp. 61–63.

Corbin, C. (1993, January). The field of physical education—common goals, not common roles. *Journal of Physical Education, Recreation and Dance* 64, pp. 79–87.

Docheff, D. (1998, February). Character in sport and physical education—summation. *Journal of Physical Education, Recreation and Dance* 69, p. 24.

Doolittle, S., and Demas, K. (2001, November/December). Fostering respect through physical activity. *Journal of Physical Education, Recreation and Dance* 72, pp. 28–33.

Falk, B. (2002, April). Standards-based reforms: problems and possibilities. *Phi Delta Kappan* 83, pp. 612–620.

Fisher, S. (1998, February). Developing and implementing a K–12 character education program. *Journal of Physical Education, Recreation and Dance* 69, pp. 21–23.

Gough, R. W. (1998, February). A practical strategy for emphasizing character development in sport and physical education. *Journal of Physical Education, Recreation and Dance* 69, pp. 18–20.

Harrison, J. M.; Blakemore, C. L.; Buck, M. M.; and Pellett, R. L. (1996). *Instructional strategies for secondary school physical education* (4th ed.). Madison, WI: Brown & Benchmark.

Havens, B. (1993, March). Teaching "cadet teachers." *Education Leadership*, pp. 50–52.

Henderson, H. L.; French, R.; and Kinnison, L. (2001, August). Reporting grades for students with disabilities in general physical education. *Journal of Physical Education, Recreation and Dance* 72, pp. 50–55.

Henkel, S. A. (1997, February). Monitoring competition for success. *Journal of Physical Education, Recreation and Dance* 68, pp. 21–28.

Hudgins, J. L., and O'Connor, M. J. (1997). Let the surgeon general help promote physical education. *Journal of Physical Education, Recreation and Dance* 68, pp. 61–64.

Huettig, C., and Roth, K. (2002, January). Maximizing the use of APE consultants. *Journal of Physical Education, Recreation and Dance* 73, pp. 32–35, 53.

Issues: Competition in physical education: An educational contradiction? (1992a, March). *Journal of Physical Education, Recreation and Dance* 63, pp. 10–11.

Issues: Should all physical educators be expected to have a common set of performance skills and competencies for teaching? (1992b, April). *Journal of Physical Education, Recreation and Dance* 63, pp. 9–10.

Issues: Should physical fitness be the dominant component of the public school physical education curriculum? (1992c, May–June). *Journal of Physical Education, Recreation and Dance* 63, p. 15.

Issues: Should there be one standard fitness assessment nationwide? (1992d, September). *Journal of Physical Education, Recreation and Dance* 63, pp. 8–9.

Issues: Does competition improve performance skills of high school students? (1992e, October). *Journal of Physical Education, Recreation and Dance* 63, p. 12.

Issues: Is it possible for a physical education teacher to serve all students well? (1993, February). *Journal of Physical Education, Recreation and Dance* 64, p. 11.

Issues, (2001, May/June). Can physical educators do more to teach ethical behavior in sports? *Journal of Physical Education, Recreation and Dance* 72, p. 12.

Kirk, D. (1993). Curriculum work in physical education: Beyond the objectives approach? *Journal of Teaching Physical Education* 12, pp. 244–265.

Kleinman, I. (1997, May–June). Grading: A powerful teaching tool. *Journal of Physical Education, Recreation and Dance* 68, pp. 29–32.

Kleinman, S. (1992, May–June). Name that discipline. *Journal of Physical Education, Recreation and Dance* 63, p. 11.

Lambert, L. T. (1998, January). This too shall pass—or will it? *Journal of Physical Education, Recreation and Dance* 69, pp. 13–14.

Lee, A. M. (2002, June). Promoting quality school physical education: Exploring the root of the problem. *Research Quarterly for Exercise and Sport* 73, pp. 118–124.

Macneil, R. D. (1998, February). Leisure, lifelong learning, and older adults: A conceptual overview. *Journal of Physical Education, Recreation and Dance* 69, pp. 26–28.

Marston, R., (2002, May/June). Addressing the university's tripartite mission through an early childhood movement program. *Journal of Physical Education, Recreation and Dance* 73, pp. 35–41.

McCall, R. (1994, January). An inclusive preschool physical education program. *Journal of Physical Education, Recreation and Dance* 65, pp. 45–47.

McDonald, J. M., and Fairfax, J. L. (1993, March). Meeting the needs of a multicultural society: Implications for professional preparation programs. *Journal of Physical Education, Recreation and Dance* 64, pp. 77–79.

McKethan, R. (2002, October). Personal correspondence: reform and change in physical education.

Mitchell, M. and Hewitt, P. (2002, August). Not dressing is disobedience, not just a nuisance. *Journal of Physical Education, Recreation and Dance* 73, pp. 28–31.

Mohr, D. J., Townsend, J. S., and Bulger, S. M. (2001, November/December). A pedagogical approach to sport education season planning. *Journal of Physical Education, Recreation and Dance* 72, pp. 37–46.

Mohr, D. J., Townsend, J. S., and Bulger S. M. (2001, January). Maintaining the PASE: a day in the life of sport education. *Journal of Physical Education, Recreation and Dance* 73, pp. 36–44.

Mosston, M. (1992, January). Tug-o-war, no more: Meeting teaching–learning objectives using the spectrum of teaching styles. *Journal of Physical Education, Recreation and Dance* 63, pp. 27–28, 56.

Mueller, R., and Mueller, S. (1992, January). The spectrum of teaching styles and its role in conscious deliberate teaching. *Journal of Physical Education, Recreation and Dance* 32, pp. 48–53.

Mull, R. F.; Bayless, K. G.; Ross, C. M.; and Jamieson, L. M. (1997). *Recreational sport management* (3rd ed.). Champaign, IL: Human Kinetics.

National teaching board calls for physical education standards. (1998, Winter). *NASPE News* (National Association for Sport and Physical Education) 50, p. 1.

Pangrazi, R. P. (1998). *Dynamic physical education for elementary children* (12th ed.). Boston: Allyn & Bacon.

Parr, M. G., and Oslin, J. (1998, February). Promoting lifelong involvement through physical activity. *Journal of Physical Education, Recreation and Dance* 69, pp. 72–76.

Placek, J. P., and O'Sullivan, M. (1997, January). The many faces of integrated physical education. *Journal of Physical Education, Recreation and Dance* 68, pp. 20–24.

Promoting lifelong physical activity. (1997, March). Atlanta: USDHHS, Centers for Disease Control and Prevention.

Safrit, M. J., and Wood, T. M. (1995). *Introduction to measurement in physical education and exercise science.* St. Louis: Mosby.

Scantling, E.; Strand, B.; Lackey, D.; and McAleese, W. (1995). An analysis of physical education avoidance. *Physical Educator* 52, pp. 197–202.

Schilling, M. L., and Coles, R. (1997, October). From exclusion to inclusion: A historical glimpse at the past and reflection of the future. *Journal of Physical Education, Recreation and Dance* 68, pp. 42–44.

Scott, M. W. (1993, March). Faculty diversity: A crucial link to the successful recruitment and retention of minority students. *Journal of Physical Education, Recreation and Dance* 64, pp. 74–80.

Senne, T. A., and Housner, L. (2002, March). NASPE standards in action, introduction. *Journal of Physical Education, Recreation and Dance* 73, pp. 19–20.

Siedentop, D. (1992, September). Thinking differently about secondary physical education. *Journal of Physical Education, Recreation and Dance* 63, pp. 69–73.

Siedentop, D. (1994). *Sport education.* Champaign, IL: Human Kinetics.

Shape of the nation report. (1998, Winter). *NASPE News* (National Association for Sport and Physical Education) 50, p. 1.

Shapiro, A., and Barton, E. (1993, March). Disabilities are not handicaps. *Principal* 73, pp. 54–55.

Sparks, W. G., III. (1993, February). Promoting self-responsibility and decision-making with at-risk students. *Journal of Physical Education, Recreation and Dance* 64, pp. 74–78.

Stoll, S. K., and Beller, J. M. (1998, January). Character development: Can character be measured? *Journal of Physical Education, Recreation and Dance* 69, pp. 19–23.

Timeline announced for phase-out of current NASPE/NCATE standards (2002, Spring). *NASPE News*, p. 11.

U.S. Department of Health and Human Services. (1996). *Physical activity and health: A report of the surgeon general.* Atlanta: U.S. Department of Health and Human Services.

Veale, M. L.; Johnson, D. J.; Campbell, M.; and McKethan, R. (2002, April). The North Carolina PEPSE project. *Journal of Physical Education, Recreation and Dance* 73, pp. 19–23.

Ward, B.; Everhart, B.; Dunaway, D.; Fisher, S.; and Coates, T. (1998). Emphasizing fitness objectives in secondary physical education. *Journal of Physical Education, Recreation and Dance* 69, pp. 33–35.

14

Administrative Issues Specific to Athletics and Health–Fitness Centers

Management Thought

Of all our social institutions, sport uniquely brings together people across age, class, regional, and ethnic boundaries and gives them a shared focus for discussion and, perhaps especially, an opportunity to express identification, commitments, and emotions . . .

Lever and Wheeler

Case Study: Where Were the Administrators?

Athletic administrators who manage programs must walk through all facilities (or delegate others to do so) every day to ensure their safety and that they are being used safely. That didn't happen in one school.

A high school softball player was unable to recover damages for injuries she sustained when a ball hit in a practice drill took an erratic hop and hit her in the face. The student knew of the danger of the rough playing field and was aware that other players had been hit by balls taking similar hops on the field, according to a North Carolina appellate court.

The student, a member of her high school varsity softball team, was participating in a practice drill on a field owned by the board of education and leased and maintained by the city. Because the field was being constructed, the playing field was rough, with intermittent spots of grass and numerous rocks in the outfield. During the drill, the coach hit a ground ball toward the student. The ball took an erratic hop and hit the student in the face, knocking out one of her teeth and loosening another. The student sued the board of education, as well as the city and her coach. The trial court granted the defendants' motions for summary judgment, and the student appealed.

The appellate court affirmed the lower court's decision, finding that the student's own negligence barred her from recovery. Because the student knew of the danger on the rough playing field, the board of education did not have a duty to warn the student of the condition of the field, the court noted. Further, the board's insurance policy clearly excluded liability for injuries to sport participants.

As for the team's coach, the court held that, although she was negligent in conducting practice on a dangerous field and telling her players that it would improve their game, the student was also negligent in participating in a practice held on a field where she knew such participation could result in injury. Likewise, even if the city had been negligent in maintaining the field and allowing the rough condition to remain, the danger posed by the field was obvious to the student and no duty to warn arose (*Daniel v. City of Morgantown*, NC Ct. of App., 1997) ("Student Could Not Recover Damages for Softball Injuries", 1997, pp. 8–9).

The reader should be able to

1. Identify the problems and possible solutions of interscholastic and intercollegiate athletics.
2. Describe the organization and control of athletics on various levels.
3. Discuss coaching preparation, certification, compensation, and staffing.
4. Discuss special management concerns related to sport, such as athletes' conduct, eligibility and scholarship, awards, scheduling, officials, concessions, contest control, and women in sport.
5. Describe concerns and solutions for youth sport programs.
6. Describe the typical health–fitness club.
7. Predict the future direction of the health–fitness industry.

■ ATHLETICS

Problems

While there appears to be a consistent barrage of reports of "big-time" college athletic teams and a few high schools violating rules, in general the status of youth, and high school, athletics is similar today to what it has been for almost a century. That is not to state there are not problems. No, there have been, are now, and will be problems.

An examination and analysis of the characteristics of sport will reveal why problems are inherent.

1. Sport has intangibilities—that is, it cannot be touched, smelled, seen, or heard before the activity occurs.
2. Sport develops emotional attachments in participants, leaders, and fans.
3. Sport is perishable in that it is produced and consumed at the same time.
4. Sport is unpredictable with the outcome of each event unknown (Stotlar, 2001).

Many Americans think that sports are out of control, from players attacking coaches, fans attacking officials, and parents pushing their kids too hard in youth sport 1991). On the other hand, it should be recognized that the great majority of athletes and coaches are hardworking and honest participants and professionals. The good lessons for life, pursuit of excellence, fitness, fun, and entertainment far exceed the ills.

The 29th annual Phi Delta Kappa/Gallup poll of the public's attitudes toward public schools included for the first time three questions about athletics. The first was about the amount of emphasis placed on such sports as basketball and football. A small majority (53 percent) believed that the emphasis is about right. An interesting side statistic is that 58 percent of public school parents thought the emphasis was about right. Almost all (96 percent) agreed that there should be minimum grades required for athletic participation, with the same percentage agreeing that the grade-point average should be C or higher (Rose, Gallup, and Elam, 1997).

Although nationally publicized problems relate to collegiate athletics, the same ills plague junior and senior high schools. One problem is that some junior high students request to repeat the eighth grade to gain a year of maturity before starting their high school athletic careers. Allegedly, both parents and coaches have encouraged this procedure. Unless there is legitimate educational justification, this practice is extremely unfair to the student. It encourages the athletes to bank their futures entirely on athletics at the expense of their educational and social growth as well as their self-esteem. About 1 million youngsters play high school football, about 30,000 are awarded some scholarship assistance to higher education, about 300 are drafted to try out for the professionals, and a fraction of these are retained; the average career is but a few years.

On the secondary level it is often reported that athletics assist greatly in building school spirit. The sports programs are something tangible students can identify with whether they are on the teams or attend the games. Where schools have broad-based programs, frequently over half of the student body will directly participate, and all but a handful will become involved by attending games and pep rallies. On the other hand, some of the problems cited with secondary athletic programs are as follows:

1. Citizens questioning whether educational funds should be allocated for athletics.

2. Injuries—particularly in contact sports.

3. The continuing inequities of funding sports that favor males.

4. The inordinate proportion of money spent on football as opposed to lifetime sports.

5. Negative coaching techniques, such as not playing all team members and abusive verbal attacks on immature students.

6. The interference with academics caused by athletics.

7. Problems created by employing teachers who are more qualified to coach than to teach.

8. The high cost—particularly to buy "extras" for football and basketball.

As was briefly mentioned in Chapter 8 on law and sport, students being educated at home are requesting eligibility to participate in interscholastic and intercollegiate athletics. It is now legal to educate at home in all 50 states, and more than a million students are now in this process. Without meeting criteria for attendance, conduct, and grade achievement, should they be allowed to participate? Naturally, most associations don't believe so. The courts and parents have other ideas. A major problem cited by school administrators is the difficulty of documenting appropriate grade averages for conferences and associations. A danger is that some schools could bring in "ringers" through this avenue, so most associations have required home-schooled students to participate within the district they reside. In the late 1990s about 20 states allowed home-schooled students to participate in interscholastic athletics, and it appears that this trend will continue (Ashley, Landrum, and Dollar, 1996).

The home-schooled student issue has also arrived at the college level. To be eligible for the NCAA Division I or II, they must have their academic portfolios evaluated through a special individual waiver process and must meet the same initial eligibility standards as other students. They must show evidence that they have completed the required core courses and meet the established minimum scores on the SAT (*School Law Newsletter*, 1997).

Reform

Most authorities believe that athletic reform on all levels must start with administrators (athletic directors, principals, superintendents, and presidents) becoming directly involved and holding a firm and consistent educational position. A good place to start in the reform of specific sport programs is with an honest, measurable strategic mission statement with input from all levels. Use this as a cornerstone to frame a five-year strategic plan. List the key objectives that would be needed to achieve the plan. Outline the necessary actions for the department to achieve those objectives (Hamhill, 1997).

Coaches are on the front line. Sport managers need to instill a higher ethical standard so they reject the pressures to shortcut. "Any coach who knowingly cheats or otherwise advocates unethical standards is a blight upon the reputation of many thousands of honest, upright coaches in the profession. When even one coach cheats, he makes all of us look bad" (Warren, 1988, p. 52). "When the tide comes in, all boats rise!" That is, when one coach or school engages in unethical behavior, all athletics suffer.

What long-range strategies will change the tide? Required in-service courses in ethics and values must be developed by national organizations such as the NCAA or NAIA. Because many high school coaches are still educated as physical educators, a similar course on the undergraduate

Soccer has been increasing in participants for both girls and boys.
Courtesy of NCHSAA, photo by John Bell.

level should be offered as an elective for those who intend to coach. In addition, note that the standards for degrees in sport management already call for such a required course. Continued emphasis should be given to evaluating coaches on more than winning, but especially on their graduation rates and the behavior of their athletes off the fields and courts. Coaches should be required to reimburse schools if they break multi-year contracts, and cheating should result in automatic dismissal. In addition, colleges should receive more severe penalties if they seriously violate rules so that they put more pressure on coaches to operate within rules to balance the pressure to win.

Evidence indicates that reform measures with the NCAA are moving in the right direction, but some believe that collegiate athletics are caught between irreconcilable aims, and that the only solution is to scuttle the program or abandon the education-academic pretense (Lawry, 1991). A study revealed that the higher the classification (e.g., Division I), the less satisfied the faculty were with athletic departments (Cockley and Roswal, 1993).

From a management perspective, perhaps the problems of college athletics could be remedied if the focus was expanded beyond sales and marketing, if revenue generation was eliminated as the mission, if long-range strategic planning was required, and if the role of the AD was redefined (Maloy, 1993).

Youth Health and Behavior Concerns in Sport

Imitation, it has been said, is the sincerest form of flattery. When this applies to youth imitating major league sport heroes, it may also be the most dangerous. While health is frequently listed as one of the goals or results of youth sport activity, it is difficult to document that such is the case. Some areas of concern for administrators require greater proactive education and attention.

According to the Centers for Disease Control (2002), "The popularity of youth sports in the United States continues to explode. That is why sports activities are great ways to reach our nation's young people with information about how to make important health decisions related to tobacco use, physical activity, and good nutrition."

The CDC has joined forces with many high-profile athletes and coaches in forming a tobacco-free sports movement. "CDC is proud to have on its winning team such stars as Jackie Chan and international skateboarder Tony Hawk, as well as Olympic gold medalists and world record holders Stacy Dragila (pole vault) and Picabo Street (alpine skiing)." Through these endeavors the tobacco-free sports movement has positively affected thousands of young people. The global SmokeFree Soccer program jointly sponsored by the CDC and the World Health Organization (WHO) worked with the Federation Internationale de Football Association (FIFA) to promote worldwide tobacco-free messages in soccer. The program included the production of posters featuring women and men soccer stars from the United States, Australia, Brazil, China, and Canada. FIFA also organized World No-Tobacco Day on May 31, 2002, with the theme "Tobacco-Free Sports" during the 2002 World Cup in Korea and Japan. Furthermore, all venues and participants in the Salt Lake Olympic Games (2002) and the 2000 Sydney Olympic Games were smoke-free, and messages about tobacco-free and healthy lifestyles were promoted throughout the event.

The CDC has also published a downloadable book, *The Tobacco-Free Sports Playbook*, "designed to help coaches, school administrators, and state and local health departments reach out to young people with messages about the importance of choosing a healthy, active, and tobacco-free lifestyle" (www.cdc.gov/tobacco/sport_ initiatives/overview.htm, 2002). While the NAIA and the NCAA have banned the use of smokeless tobacco outright, even for coaches on the sidelines, it remains a problem for youth, especially when they emulate professional stars.

The dramatic increase in skin cancer also causes concern. A study has revealed that more than 80 percent of teenagers spend most weekends in the sun, and, of course, athletes in outdoor sports spend almost every afternoon in the sun. Only 9 percent, however, always use sunscreen, and 33 percent never do. Sport managers must insist that coaches of outdoor sports include this problem in their educational components. Visit the American Academy of Pediatrics website at www.aap.org for more information about health issues and youth sport.

Aggressive and criminal actions of athletes have been in the news for some time, and, in some cases, have cost the coach a job according to Kadlecek (2001), athletic directors reported that the most common crisis they encounter was the off-field misbehavior of athletes. Thousands of high school and college athletes have been tested for moral development, and the results have shown that the athletes were reasoning on a level about five years under the general student population. "While the general students were taking other people's views and feelings into account when making behavioral decisions, the student-athletes were not. The student-athletes were acting according to what was best for them. They were so engulfed in what they were doing, they didn't think about anybody else" (Bradley, 1992, p. 17).

In another study, the importance of physical achievement, social–rational, and experiential concerns were measured in 9- through 14-year-old competitive gymnasts. The lowest factors were socially based enjoyment, positive social relationships, and social–competitive achievement. "The interaction of children's goal orientations and perceptions of relevant competence or goal attainment has been theoretically and empirically linked to adaptive and maladaptive

patterns of responding in academic–intellectual, athletic, and social contexts" (Lewthwaite and Piparo, 1993, p. 115).

The National Institute of Mental Health found that athletes participated in about one-third of the sexual attacks on campus; another study revealed that the majority of gang rapes on a campus over a 10-year period involved varsity athletes or fraternity members; and another study found that athletes were 5.5 times more likely to be involved in date rape than nonathletes (Melnick, 1992). So what should be done? Melnick (1992) suggests that colleges should abolish special residences for athletes. One of the authors served as a resident director for one year and as an academic adviser for another year for two nationally ranked football teams and cannot emphasize strongly enough his agreement with this suggestion. Also, sport managers should work to eliminate all sexist talk from the sport environment; impose tough, swift punishment for athletes who are found guilty; educate for greater sensitivity to the problem; and reformulate the male sport experience. Wiederg (1998) found that from August 1, 1997, to August 1, 1998, 175 NCAA Division I athletes were arrested. This effectively means that college athletic directors must deal with this type of situation once in every two days (Kadlecek, 2001).

Several institutions have initiated programs that examine the social/behavioral forces impacting the lives of student athletes. While some have questioned the wisdom of such programs for just athletes, especially with no evidence of problems at a particular campus, others believe that the malbehavior is there but not reported or is just under the surface waiting to happen. Marchell and others (1992) report three reasons why athletes are involved in a disproportionate number of sexual assaults. One factor is the group dynamics, in which the assault is actually carried out for the approval of others in the group; the victim is incidental. The possible carryover of aggression associated with team sports may also play a part. The last factor is the understanding of freedom from punishment built up in athletes by the social status afforded them and previous experiences of having been protected when engaging in minor social misbehavior. Based on these data, it is imperative that sport managers prepare to handle such crises. Unfortunately, many sport administrators are unprepared. Kadlecek (2001) found that while many college athletic directors encountered problems with athlete behavior, only one AD in his study actually had developed a crisis management plan.

The concern of contracting HIV, the AIDS virus, through sport participation will continue to be an administrative concern. Two factors need to be considered. Almost half of the college athletes surveyed in one study were worried about HIV-infected opponents in contact sports who had not been tested, while three-quarters felt that all contact sport participants should be tested before competing. On the other hand, there has never been a documented case of anyone contracting HIV through athletic participation ("HIV Fears vs. Reality," 1994).

Most mission statements for athletic organizations and textbooks in athletic administration cite "character building" as a major result or objective (Stoll and Beller, 1998). In looking both at the material presented in the previous section on "reform" and at these problems, it would appear that there is an incongruity in operation. Sage (1998, pp. 16–17) states,

> There have been few well-conceived and implemented empirical research studies of the effects of organized sport involvement on the social development of young athletes. . . . Perhaps the sport setting is merely a particularly good setting for enabling persons to exhibit preexisting character traits; that some athletes or former athletes display culturally valued personal and social characteristics cannot be wholly attributed to their sport experiences without an enormous leap of faith. Recent research actually suggests that contrary to building character, organized sport for youth may actually be detrimental to moral development, a key component of character.

Stoll and Beller (1998, p. 21) state that "an overwhelming research database of qualitative

and quantitative research supports the theory that something is occurring in the competitive arena that negatively affects an individual's ability to consistently reason or judge morally." "Morality is learned and we, as teachers and coaches, can positively affect the learning process of others who participate in sport" (Stoll and Beller, 1998, p. 23).

Organization and Control of Athletics

The most common administrative structure on all levels for athletics is for an AD to report to the head administrator of that institution. On the lower levels, the top administrator is usually the principal; in higher education, it's the president or chancellor. In many secondary schools and in most colleges, an advisory group of some sort recommends athletic policy to the head administrator. Frequently, on the secondary level the council includes coaches, students, and faculty. In higher education, faculty frequently make up the largest representation along with students and alumni.

The control of athletics on all levels is through associations. On the lower levels, the state associations govern sport. There are three types: voluntary; associations affiliated with state departments of education; and those administered through a university. The National Federation of State High School Associations was formed in 1920 and adopted its present name in 1922. The national federation never attempted to take over the state associations, only to promote adherence to eligibility rules for interstate competition, to standardize playing rules, and to be a national advocate for high school athletics. One of its main contributions has been the publication of rule books for 16 sports for boys and girls along with the supporting case books and other publications.

In higher education, institutions voluntarily join one of several associations. Which association joined is determined by the institution's level, type, and size and the organization to which similar colleges nearby belong. The associations serving intercollegiate athletics are as follows:

1. National Junior College Athletic Association (NJCAA). This organization was founded in 1937 and serves two-year colleges. The official website is www.njcaa.org. The organization is based on regional entities, each with an elected director. Each region operates under the constitution and bylaws of the parent organization, which is operated by an elected executive committee. It sponsors national tournaments in many sports and invitational tournaments in others.

2. National Association of Intercollegiate Athletics (NAIA). This association was established in 1940 as a basketball association and expanded to all sports in 1952. It serves over 300 smaller institutions of higher education and holds national tournament championships in many sports (www.NAIA.org).

3. National Collegiate Athletic Association (NCAA). This organization grew out of a meeting in 1905 of administrators concerned with the number of serious football injuries. A constitution and bylaws were adopted the next year with the original organization called the Intercollegiate Athletic Association; the current name (NCAA) was adopted in 1910. It now consists of over 1,000 institutions with about 100 conferences. Violations can result in probations, exclusion from television or postseason games, and expulsion (www.ncaa.org).

4. National Association for Girls and Women in Sport (NAGWS). A major aspect of the mission of this organization (one of six associations within the structure of the AAHPERD) is to encourage the development of full access to sport participation and leadership opportunities. Some have argued that with laws such as Title IX on the books, this organization may be redundant. Supporters state that the need for NAGWS is evident in the following statistics:

- Only one-third of our nation's school-based athletes are females.
- Girls are provided with inadequate equipment, insufficient coaching, less practice and scheduled competition, and less administrative commitment.
- Fewer than half of the head coaches of women's teams are female.

- Fewer than 2 percent of head coaches of men's teams are female.
- Fewer than 20 percent of the head administrators over women's programs are female. (Carpenter and Acosta, 1997).

At the time of printing, a new "blue ribbon" report was due, addressing many of these issues 30 years after the passage of Title IX.

In addition to the national and state associations, much of the direct and specific control derives from conferences. High school conference rules pertain mostly to scheduling and officials, whereas in higher education, conferences frequently become more involved. For example, both the Big 10 and the Ivy Conferences have established standards over and above those of the associations to which they belong (www.AApherd.org/NAGWS).

■ COACHING AS A PROFESSIONAL CAREER

Preparation

Coaching can be practiced in association with teaching or can be independent of it. Many people who combine coaching and teaching experience role conflicts. In fact, research suggests that combining coaching with teaching physical education results in greater role conflicts than if the coaching is associated with teaching other subjects. Administrators need to take this potential problem into account when they assign duties to coaches.

A greater emphasis should be placed on the human relations aspect of the coaches' preparation. They need to be prepared to handle the inevitable complaints and critics as well as to appreciate the trust and special relationships they have with athletes and their parents. Rarely do coaches have difficulty with their own staffs or the technical aspects of the sport; rather, handling the individual personalities of players, parents, fans, and administrators presents difficulties.

The results of suits against coaches are evidence of the importance of good teaching on all levels. But this is especially important on the middle and high school levels. One area that seems to be lacking in this regard is the ability to observe and correct motor skills in athletes. This is particularly vital in highly skilled acts, where poor motor skills frequently lead to injuries. To more effectively evaluate and correct poor motor skills, coaches should use video recordings in slow and stop action. Understanding and being able to apply basic principles of physics are important for good motor skill observation and correction. Coaches need to develop better skills of providing useful feedback rather than yelling. Start with something positive; use analogies of known actions; make use of aids such as taping a balloon under an arm as a reminder of correct arm position away from the body; go from simple to complex; and use overcompensation for directional or depth problems (Turner, 1998).

Sage (1989) has reported that high school coaches essentially learn the job through socialization while they are in their first years of coaching. He found that "reality shock" was the enormous work load that accompanies the high school coach—often 30–40 hours a week during season—all this on top of a full-time teaching job that alone exhausts most people.

It becomes obvious that the major problem of secondary school coaches is that they have two full-time jobs. Kneer (1987, pp. 28–29) suggests four possible strategies to handle this dilemma:

1. Continue to combine teaching and coaching jobs but include coaching as part of the teaching load.
2. Continue to combine teaching and coaching but reduce practice time and schedule length.
3. Separate the teaching and coaching occupations within the school and employ full-time coaches.
4. Separate teaching and coaching as occupations and remove athletics from the school.

In most of the rest of the world, elite athletics (what we would call varsity or intercollegiate athletics) are not associated with secondary or higher education.

Certification of Coaches

Institutions of higher learning do not offer majors in athletic coaching, and only a few have offered minors in coaching. Although there have been considerable interest and discussion about coaching certification through the years, only a few states actually require such. In the past, administrators could rely on physical education teachers to perform much of the coaching. But there has been a trend of greater athletic participation; more sports are being added; and women's programs have greatly expanded. The result is that physical education teachers make up only a small percentage of the coaches needed. In addition, as the physical education teachers grow older, they frequently don't want to coach at all. This leads administrators to assign coaching duties to people not properly prepared.

Why not require certification? Guidance counselors, driver education instructors, and other "special" educators are certified. Little professional control is being exerted on personnel assignments to coaching. Why not require all coaches to meet a certification standard? Many national organizations have been actively working on the establishment of national standards for athletic coaches. While there will likely be refinement and adjustments, five levels of proficiency from entry level to master are now planned. The competencies include 37 standards in the following domains:

- Injuries—prevention, care, and management
- Risk management
- Growth, development, and learning
- Training, conditioning, and nutrition
- Social/psychological aspects of coaching
- Skills, tactics, and strategies
- Teaching and administration
- Professional preparation and development (www.aapherd.org/NASPE 2002; Carney, 1997; "Coaching Education Update," 1998).

The problem is that if staffing coaching is difficult, how could it possibly be done if standards are increased? It is recommended that states phase in certification standards on three levels. The highest requirements would be for head coaches of contact sports. The next highest would be for head coaches of other sports. Minimal requirements would be established for assistant coaches.

For certification to be practical, statewide salary standards for coaches would need to be increased considerably.

Several other independent organizations have developed coaching certification programs. The Program for Athletic Coaching Education (PACE) was developed through the Institute for the Study of Youth Sports at Michigan State University. This program was designed to provide schools and administrators with the programs and materials needed to maintain effective coaching programs. It is utilized in many states and has produced thousands of qualified coaches (http://edweb3.educ.msu.edu/kin/certificates/cert_pace.htm). The National Alliance for Youth Sports (www.nays.org) has also created coaches' associations and certification programs. Established primarily to assist with the training and education of volunteer youth sport coaches, NAYS developed training materials used by many Boys and Girls Clubs as well as park and recreation districts. At the elite level, most of the national governing bodies in the Olympic movement conduct their own coach training and have extensive testing and certification programs advancing from entry levels to Olympic and national certification.

Staffing Coaching Positions

As previously discussed, an increasingly difficult job for the administrator on all levels is to hire and retain highly qualified coaches for all sports. In higher education, fewer coaches are teaching, and therefore the full salary must be borne by the athletic budget. More and more frequently, non-revenue teams are being coached by part-time staff not otherwise associated with the institution. The inherent problems are obvious. On the secondary level, the problem centers on not enough teachers qualified or interested in assuming the coaching assignments.

High school staffing of coaches frequently turns to alternatives such as employing "paraprofessionals" or "lay coaches," neither of which have full-time teaching positions in the school system. Usually they are assistant coaches. Recently it was reported that 49 states allow nonfaculty coaches.

In some states, as many as 30 percent of the positions available in high school athletics are filled by paraprofessionals. The highest percentages are found in the metropolitan areas and in women's sports (Gillentine and Bryant, 1997).

Coaching Compensation

The pragmatic position for administrators to take at the secondary level is to campaign for the greatest amount of extra pay for coaching duties. But from a philosophical point of view, this is a prostitution of the teaching profession because the basic teaching assignment (whether physical education or any other subject) is a full-time professional occupation. Paying such a person extra is acknowledging either that teaching does not require a full professional effort, or that the coach is going to cheat on the time and effort devoted to teaching or coaching. Of course, one could take the position that the time and effort the coach expends comes from time otherwise used for family and recreation. Unfortunately for the health of coaches, this is frequently the case.

The following are other means of compensating coaches:

- Release time from teaching.
- Reduced student load per class.
- Clerical assistance.
- Special office or dressing room provisions.
- Professional recognition from school administration or board (special titles, awards).
- Personal–social recognition or incentives (honorary membership in a country club, passes to college or professional athletic contests or movie theater).
- Special out-of-season extra pay opportunities, such as summer school teaching.
- Special attire, such as coaching shirts, pants, and shoes.
- Media appearances.
- Free use of automobiles.
- Attendance at conferences and workshops.
- More assistants.
- Improved team traveling arrangements (providing a professional driver).

- Controlling the length of the season and the distance of trips.
- Special teaching and coaching equipment and facilities (such as videotape or a pleasant environment in the gymnasium).
- Consistent positive feedback from the administration.

From a professional point of view, reducing the teaching load to compensate for coaching is the most attractive alternative. From a fiscal perspective, however, this method actually is much more expensive for the school district. If released time is used, the first periods in the morning should be those released. Coaching stipends are the most commonly utilized method in high schools. In addition to being cheaper for the district than released time, it attracts more qualified coaches. Although it may increase the cost to the athletic department slightly, it is better to pay using a graduated scale. That is, compute the pay on a percentage of the regular teaching salary, or on a step scale based on the number of years the person has coached the sport. Either of these methods will reward the more experienced coaches and maintain greater continuity in the staff and program.

It is imperative that supplemental coaching pay scales be carefully planned. To initiate a new system, or to revise an existing plan, a committee should be established with representatives from revenue and nonrevenue sports, the AD, the school administration, and the school district's central office. Suggested criteria to consider include

- Hours involved in activity.
- Hours involved in preparation.
- Number of participants.
- Experience required.
- Special training or knowledge required.
- Spectator numbers.
- Injury potential for participants.
- Injury potential for the coach.
- Physical energy demanded of the coach.
- Pressure.
- Equipment and facility responsibilities.
- Environmental conditions in which the activity will be conducted.
- Responsibilities for travel and supervision.

High school volleyball is being played at a higher level and with more participants.
Courtesy of Watauga Democrat.

- Administrative responsibilities.
- Number of people to supervise.
- Level of assignment (freshman, JV, varsity).
- Initiative required.
- Degree of judgment required.
- Extent of creative ability required.
- Mental and visual concentration required.

■ SPECIAL ATHLETIC MANAGEMENT CONCERNS

Many management concerns about athletics have been discussed in the previous chapters. The following major facets are unique to athletic administration.

Conduct of Athletes and Teams

The administrator is concerned about conduct from four perspectives: fairness to the participants;

Table 14.1   Code of Conduct for Coaches

- The coach has tremendous influence on student athletes and shall never place winning above the value of instilling the highest desirable ideals of character.
- The coach shall strive to set an example of the highest ethical and moral conduct with the student athlete, officials, athletic directors, school administrators, the state high school athletic association, the media, and the public.
- The coach shall discipline athletes who display unacceptable behavior.
- The coach shall know the game rules and be responsible for their interpretation to team members. Additionally, the coach shall not try to seek an advantage by circumvention of the spirit or letter of the rules.
- The coach shall promote and work in harmony with the entire interscholastic program of the school.

- The coach shall respect and support contest officials by avoiding conduct that will incite players or spectators against the officials.
- The coach shall actively promote good sportsmanship of spectators by working closely with administrators, cheerleaders, pep club sponsors, and booster clubs.
- The coach shall meet and exchange greetings with the opposing coach before and after each contest to set and maintain a positive tone for the event.
- The coach shall take an active role in preventing the use of alcohol, tobacco, and other drugs, while stressing the importance of a healthy lifestyle.

Adapted from Handbook of the North Carolina High School Athletic Association, p. 35 (1997–98). 222 Finley Golf Course Rd., Box 3216, Chapel Hill, NC 27515; (919) 962–2345; http://www.nchsaa. unc.edu.

effect on the esprit de corps of the team and student body; relationship to maximum team effort; and reflection on the competence of the coach, administrator, and school. Two generalizations affect codes of conduct. First, participation on teams is extracurricular and voluntary; therefore it's a privilege and not a right. Second, as long as rules are reasonable and relate directly to the sport, they will be generally upheld in courts. This is particularly true if the rule is a conference or association rule. If the punishment is severe, such as loss of eligibility, it is important that due process was provided. It is recommended that broad rules of conduct be established for all school athletes through the school athletic council, for example, if the council has student representatives. The administrator must be careful to evaluate these suggested rules to ensure that they are reasonable and enforceable.

Consideration should be given to unique cases, such as the poor, minorities, and those with impairments or special religious affiliations. These broad rules can then be augmented by specific rules as necessary. It is suggested that

coaches work out rules with squad members, and then allow the participants to vote for their adoption. Such rules should reflect what happens when they are violated and what options of appeal are available to students. Once established, the rules must be applied consistently and uniformly. The code should be signed by the athlete and, on the high school level, by the parents as well. The problem with code of conduct violations is not unique to interscholastic and intercollegiate sports. Significant problems arose in the 1994 Winter Olympic trials when figure skater Tonya Harding arranged an attack on fellow competitor Nancy Kerrigan, violating U.S. figure skating's good conduct rules along with the law.

Unfortunately, no matter how reasonable conduct rules are, ultimately they will be broken. The sport manager must ensure that coaches discipline athletes prudently and consistently. If the discipline is serious enough to generate public interest, the sport manager should be involved in the process.

An example of a general code of conduct for high school coaches is shown in Table 14.1.

Eligibility and Scholarship

Eligibility rules that are thoughtfully conceived and reasonable have been consistently upheld in the courts. They are established to provide fair and equal competition and to ensure that athletics are part of the general educational program. Maintaining exact control of eligibility procedures is a paramount duty of every athletic director.

Studies of high school athletes appear to support the conclusion that athletes earn higher grades than nonathletes. If this is so, does athletic participation enhance academic achievement or does the athletic program attract above-average students? In a study of scholarship, absences, and tardiness among male high school athletes, results showed no significant difference between athletes and nonathletes regarding absences and tardiness, and athletes earned significantly higher grades than nonathletes (Horine, 1968). The trend has been to increase the number of "basic" courses that athletes are required to pass to be eligible to participate in interscholastic athletics.

Athletic Awards

Athletic awards have long been used to encourage students to participate, as well as to recognize those who excel; but many authorities are concerned about this form of *extrinsic motivation.* They believe more effort should be directed toward increasing *intrinsic* or *self-directed motivation,* without trophies and plaques. This is especially important in pre-senior high school competition. It is essential that all awards be financed and controlled through the school. Frequently the most treasured awards will be those with little expense, such as a certificate or plaque presented in a public ceremony, a photograph in a newspaper, or even a homemade personal award.

High school associations often do not allow participants to receive monetary awards or valuable goods, such as rackets, balls, or shoes. Typical association rules allow gifts if they are available to every member of the team, are entirely consumable and nontransferable (meals, trips) or are permanently labeled, and are approved by the principal and superintendent.

Parental Involvement in Athletics

For many years coaches and athletic administrators have tried to keep parents involved in secondary school sport. Apparently in recent years this has become easier to the point of creating a problem in some areas as parents want to become too involved. To encourage parents but to draw the line where involvement becomes interference, it is recommended that a meeting at the beginning of each sport season be held with athletic administration, coaches, and parents.

One format that has proved successful is for parents from all sports to meet together with the sport and school administration to go over administrative rules and standard operating procedures. Information that applies to all sports should be covered, such as physical examinations, insurance, and fees or costs such as banquets, transportation policies, nutrition advice, academic requirements for athletics, and general information about how parents are needed for volunteer work and positive reinforcement for their children. It should be clearly enunciated that the policy for dealing with any problems related to a specific sport is that parents speak to the coach first to resolve conflicts. If this can't be accomplished, the AD, parents, and coach will meet to discuss the issue.

At the conclusion of the general information period, the coaches of each sport in season should meet with the players to go over any material specific to that sport. For sports like football, showing the details of the equipment is always well received by parents. Covering the time and length of practices, a summary of the strategic system used by the coach, and any special training requirements or suggestions are other topics proved successful (Catalano, 1997).

Scheduling

In general, scheduling evolves from two bases. The first is the philosophy of the district, school, and athletic department. These views affect the size of schools outside the conference to be scheduled, the allowable distance to travel, time of day or night, days or nights of the week, and the number of contests. The other factor is the conference requirements. Frequently conference contests are scheduled first and many times automatically.

Scheduling should take into account the following considerations:

1. Schedule home and away in same or alternate seasons when possible.
2. Are potential opponents competitive?
3. How are their facilities?
4. How far away are they?
5. What reputation do they have for sportsmanship?
6. Do they draw sufficient spectators at home?
7. Would fans follow them when the contest is at your school?

Related to scheduling, state athletic associations may limit contests to two-year periods; the lengths of seasons are usually specified. Sometimes no contests may be held on Sundays; and out-of-state contests require advance approval.

A definite and well-conceived policy must be written regarding the postponement or cancellation of contests. For example, it is suggested that if a change in a night football game is being considered, by 10 A.M. the AD should notify his counterpart of the possibility and promise a decision by 1 P.M. By then, after consulting with the principal and head coach, the AD should make the decision. The visitors' AD and local media should be called immediately.

Officials

No job of the athletic administrator is more important than to find and retain good sport officials.

In some states, booking agents from the state athletic association assign sport officials. Primarily, these agents control sports such as football, basketball, soccer, and wrestling. General regulations pertaining to officials are as follows:

1. Coaches should not talk to officials about complaints before contests, during the half-time, or after the game.
2. Coaches should never enter the officials' dressing room.
3. Coaches or school officials should never criticize officials in the media.
4. Officials should be met as they arrive with a reserved parking place and be escorted to a private dressing room.

5. Officials should be paid before the game.
6. Officials should be provided with an escort off court or field and from the dressing room to the car.
7. Maintain written contracts with officials; if a booking agent is not responsible for assignments, remind the official of the contest a couple of days in advance.
8. Follow standardized fees and never engage an official for less.
9. Never hire a relative of the coach or AD.
10. Avoid using the same officials for several contests in a row.
11. Make sure that officials are registered and certified by appropriate body.
12. If no booking agents are used, have opponent approve officials.

Coaches should rate every official, and, in turn, the officials should evaluate coaches. Although this takes time and effort, only through honest and frank evaluation can improvements occur. Many conferences now require this procedure. It is recommended that coaches become involved in some officiating early in careers to gain a balanced perspective on the demands placed on officials.

Contest Management

It is not possible to discuss in detail the great variety of factors that should be carefully considered if large crowds are expected for an event. Many of the areas of concern listed here might require several meetings of a task force or committee to structure a well-conceived, workable written policy:

- The schedule itself.
- Game officials.
- The game site.
- Parking.
- The public address system.
- Communication (media, opponents).
- Transportation.
- Limitation of crowd.
- Conduct of cheerleaders.
- Personnel on field or court.
- Security forces and enforcement of rules and law.
- Postgame activities.
- Emergency crisis plans and medical services.

Crowd Management

At its worst, poor crowd management leads to injury, death, and lawsuits; at its best, the spectator has a poor experience and doesn't return. Factors that escalate rowdyism are seating large groups together rather than dispersing them; selling alcoholic beverages (or not stringently prohibiting their intrusion); allowing crowded seating; lack of proper aisles or divided section; lack of barriers to keep fans away from the playing area or from falling off the sides or rear of stands; lack of sufficient ushers or security forces; poor officiating; allowing coaches to behave in such a way as to incite the crowd; and scheduling boring contests (Farmer, Mulrooney, and Ammon, 1996).

From a risk management perspective, the key word is *foreseeability*. The sport administrator must ask whether a particular scenario or episode is plausible or predictable under the particular circumstances. The classic case of *Bearman v. Notre Dame*, 1983, illustrates the test of foreseeability. The institution encouraged tailgating before football games, but didn't detail sufficient security in the parking lots. A spectator was injured as a fight broke out between two intoxicated spectators, and Notre Dame was held liable (Miller, 1997).

The following are some specific strategies that have been successfully employed to mitigate crowd control problems:

1. Pass laws against bringing alcohol into events or body passing.

2. Train security forces and ushers in proper ways to meet the public and how to diffuse anxious situations.

3. Plainly communicate rules of behavior through signs and the media.

4. Utilize group dynamics techniques, such as the type and loudness of music, brightness of lights, and colors.

5. Rectify physical or structural problems of the facility.

6. Amply light and patrol parking lots.

7. Prepare and practice a disaster plan including how to evacuate stadiums and arenas (Miller, 1997).

8. Consider using metal detectors.

9. Have all school officials wear something distinctive such as armbands or vests with appropriate lettering.

10. Prepare a behavior intervention plan and have all supervisory staff, ushers, and police briefed on the procedures—use police only as the last resort.

11. Segregate visitors and home students.

12. Segregate home and visitor adults and families from each other and students (Rochman, 1997).

13. Ensure that barriers between visitors and home spectators are substantial, and not a simple railing that can be stepped over.

Women's Sports

As noted earlier, the number of female participants in high school athletics increased significantly over the last decade. Corresponding increases also have been reported for higher education. At the same time, the number of female coaches has declined. For a variety of reasons women leave positions, and also for a variety of reasons, many positions have been filled with men. While it is dangerous to oversimplify, it is believed that this situation has resulted from supply and demand; a perceived notion (primarily by men) that Title IX has caused women's sports to be at a higher level and men can stand the pressure better; lack of training and experience opportunities for young women; and a lack of societal reinforcement of the rewards for a woman to coach.

One study revealed that the importance of same-gender coaches as role models in a coaching situation was inconclusive, but more female-coached athletes aspired to be head coaches in high school than did male-coached athletes (Lirgg, DiBrezzo, & Smith, 1993).

Food and Beverage Concessions

Food and beverage sales are a major generator of income at all levels of sport, from Little League all the way to the major leagues. There are three types of operations (see Table 14.2):

- *Completely in-house.* This type is frequently used in smaller operations where service

	Table 14.2 Favorable and Unfavorable Factors Affecting Concession Performance	
Factor in Concession Performance	Favorable	Unfavorable
In-house concession management	Flexibility	Outside agencies handle greater volume
Utilize volunteers as staff	Labor costs greatly reduced	High turnover, not operated cost-efficiently
Use waitstaff	Premium price charged for this service	Depends on extravagant patron attendance
Use cash boxes only	Low initial cost	Less accurate
	Ease of operation	No financial statements
Wish for more operating space	More serving and supply storage space	Raises overhead costs
Utilize portable units	Concessions placed at best sales locations	Added overhead and maintenance costs
Use moving vendors	Convenience generates more sales	Sales not covering operational costs
Utilize franchised restaurant vendors	Brand-name recognition generates sales	Shared profits
Sell alcohol	High markup, high revenue potential	Potential patron behavioral problems on site

Adapted from Motsinger, Turner, and Evans, 1997, p. 46.

clubs, volunteers, or various team members do the selling.

- *Full contract.* This type of arrangement is usually used in large operations where the various concessionaires take the risks, do the work, and provide the owner with 30 to 50 percent of the profits (Motsinger, Turner, and Evans, 1997). In the last few years, several companies have begun to dominate the concession businesses at the professional level. ARAMARK and Volume Services America are the established leaders in the industry.

- *Management contract.* This is a combination of the previous two types and is frequently used by mid-size operations where the organization may maintain sales over some sites or some high-profit items such as popcorn, but contract other sites out to concessionaires (Farmer, Mulrooney, and Ammon, 1996).

■ YOUTH SPORT MANAGEMENT

Although it is not possible to devote a great amount of space to exploring sports for youth, it is certainly of vital concern. The upper elementary and middle schools are becoming more directly involved in competitive sports, but the majority of such programs are administered by recreation departments or volunteer service organizations.

Estimates suggest that more than 35 million youth participate in organized sport, yet only a few of the coaches have formal training. Professional educators need to become more directly involved in policy-making for youth sport, if not in the direct management.

A summary of the research related to physiological functions and youth sport has showed that growth and development, in general, has not been adversely affected by sport participation; cardiovascular demands of youth in sport are accommodated without difficulty; and that while youth are sturdy, youth sport managers

Soccer—an ever-increasing youth sport activity.
Courtesy of Watauga Democrat.

must emphasize that they are children—not miniature adults—and training should respect the differences.

Administrators of youth sport programs are also concerned with psychosocial influences. Some suggest that in youth sport, most learning takes place through modeling and reinforcement. The values and philosophy of the program are transmitted through the coaches. The improvement, certification, and licensing of coaches have been aggressively attacked through various sport organizations noted earlier.

Youth Development

"Youth development is a pro-social philosophical concept directed toward influencing positively the well-being of youth" (Edginton, 1997, p. 15). There appears to be an initiative to bring together programs that have been operated before, but in a new direction. That is, in the past youth sport, leisure, intramural, dance, and health programs have operated as separate entities. "Youth development" programs attempt to merge these into planned initiatives to positively influence competencies in the health/physical, personal/social, cognitive/creative, vocational, and citizenship areas. Developing such programs after school is

worthy of more attention, particularly for "at-risk" youth (Edginton, 1997; Hudson, 1997; Witt and Baker, 1997). Research in leisure studies supports the thesis that "leisure is an important context for young people in terms of identity formation. Identity formation refers to the development of both personal identity (individual, core characteristics) and social identity (self in relation to others, group membership, and social identification with a group" (Kivel, 1998, p. 36).

■ THE FITNESS INDUSTRY

Since Kenneth Cooper released his first book *Aerobics* in 1967, the fitness industry has experienced consistent growth. Some believe it has reached its maturity, while others believe it to be in adolescence. Several trends appear to be consistent, one of which is a continued increase of stricter regulations, controls, and standards. (See the previous discussion of standards in Chapter 9, Risk Management.) Another trend is greater association with the health care industries. Additional clients will likely consist of youth and seniors. Participants are also much more educated about health and exercise, which puts more pressure on the preparation and training of the staff (Gantham, Patton, York, and Winick, 1998).

The International Health Racquet and Sportsclub Association (IHRSA) has been the leading professional body in the management of fitness facilities for many years. Their reports on the industry have been utilized across the nation as a guide for determining performance and efficiency. In 2001 they reported that the number of fitness centers and sports clubs in the United States grew by 10.5 percent. Other data indicated that the number of people belonging to health, fitness, and sport facilities had grown to 32.8 million. IHRSA also produces valuable information for managers and investors. Their reports detail overall revenue, revenue after taxes, revenue by facility type, and average revenue per square foot. These benchmarks can be used to measure an operation against industry averages. Additional data show average salaries for fitness management positions and hourly wages typically paid to fitness center staff. Of further interest to sport managers is their report on the popularity and profitability of club programs (IHRSA, 2001).

The most commonly offered programs were personal training, aerobic dance and exercise, fitness testing, yoga, cardio-kickboxing, child care, Spinning massage, and nutritional counseling. It should be interesting to note that many of these programs are "extra" services, not included in basic monthly membership dues. In fact, the average annual revenue per member was found to be over $1,000, far in excess of the standard $50 per month that many members pay in dues (IHRSA, 2001).

As in all types of sport management, the health–fitness business also requires astute long-range strategic planning. Clubs have five strategic elements: a defined purpose and direction; an organizational structure; information and control systems; a resource allocation system (budgeting); and a reward and recognition system. "Clubs have historically been strong in the operation phase of management, but weak in the planning stage. Knowing yourself and the conditions of business helps build your vision into a system for success" (Faust and Carim, 1993, pp. 33–34).

Wellness Programs

> As the lines continue to blur between health care and fitness, clubs are playing a more visible role in the wellness arena. In some facilities that has meant a greater emphasis on wellness programs and nutritional counseling. Other facilities have introduced physical therapy or targeted population with special health needs, such as people with arthritis. (Handley, 1998, p. 36)

Wellness programs have been initiated at many businesses, agencies, and institutions and provide new opportunities in sport management. The well-rounded program should offer employees or students a variety of activities: behaviorally oriented programs such as smoking cessation, stress management and relaxation classes, nutrition counseling, back care clinics, blood pressure and cholesterol screenings, and cooking classes; along with activities such as walking, jogging, aerobics, weight training, yoga, tai chi, self-defense, and sports (Cioletti, 1997).

Gradually the public has become educated to understand that health care and fitness programs are interrelated. It has become accepted in the scientific community as well as by the public that exercise is a way of preventing many health problems and treating others. Many health–fitness centers are now establishing a medical advisory board. Frequently potential members are already members and familiar with the club and can make immediate recommendations. Rather than pay them for the service, it is better to absorb some or all of their membership dues. Keep the board small (three to five members), meet two to four times a year along with top management and supervisors, and listen to and follow their advice (Handley, 1998).

What's in a name? Some award-winning centers reflect merging of health and fitness activities with their very names. The Good Samaritan Health and Wellness Center of West Palm Beach, Florida, was awarded the "best innovation" in wellness and health promotion. After operating an unsuccessful, complex, and expensive weight management program, managers talked to the consumers to learn what went wrong and designed a less expensive program with less individual attention and more group activity that has been highly successful (Renner, 1998a). The Winter Park Health Foundation Center for Health and Wellness was selected as best in promotion, sales, and marketing. Their slogan was "More Than a Health Club." In addition to the usual marketing methods, this club went out to service clubs to give talks on the new center; had a private open house for the media, physicians, and board members; and had an open house for the public (Renner, 1998b).

Exercises

1. Assume that you are the AD for a large high school. The football coach has included a $10,000 budget item for a new, sophisticated videocamera on the basis that the higher-quality pictures would better the chances of players receiving scholarships. A group of parents has publicly questioned the proposed purchase. How would you handle the situation?

Critical Thinking

In most states it is legal for students to be educated at home; however, it is not clear whether these students are eligible to participate in interscholastic athletics. Some cases have found in favor of allowing home-schooled students to participate, but the following case illustrates that this isn't always so.

A home-schooled student was not eligible to participate in interscholastic sports in the school district in which she resided. The student's parents provided home schooling to their daughter pursuant to state regulations. The parents brought action against the commissioner of education, seeking a declaration that home-schooled students are eligible to participate in interscholastic sports in the school districts in which they reside. The Supreme Court, Albany County, dismissed the complaint, and the parents appealed.

The appellate court affirmed the decision, noting that the regulation regarding eligibility for interscholastic sports unambiguously requires that the student be enrolled in the school

district in order to participate in a school's sports program. Here the home-schooled student clearly was not "regularly enrolled" in a public school, as required by the regulations. Moreover, the commissioner's refusal to allow the student to participate in interscholastic sports is merely an expectation and no fundamental right is involved (*Bradstreet v. Sobol*, N.Y. App. Div, 1996) ("Home-Schooled Student Not Eligible to Participate in Sports," 1997).

1. Do you think that future cases will reflect the same opinions?
2. Can you think of any other ways that the parents might have approached the case to make it stronger?
3. Why do you think that the commissioner of education did not grant the position that the parents sought?
4. What problems do you see as possible if future cases are reversed and home-schooled students are declared eligible?

---

2. You are the basketball coach for the boys or girls at a large junior high school with a rather high-powered interscholastic program. The PTA has requested your presence at its next meeting to justify spending so much time and money on 12 players. Present a defense.

3. List the pros and cons for the coach and the school district of the following methods of compensating a coach: (a) granting two extra free periods, (b) paying a fixed $1,000 coaching supplement, and (c) paying 5 percent of regular teaching salary as a supplement.

4. Assume that you are the AD of a high school that does not have a general conduct code for all sports. The principal asks you to draw up a general code to present to the athletic council. Prepare the code you would suggest.

5. You are the AD in a high school classified as "3A" in a state in which the largest schools are "4A." The coach in one sport insists on scheduling all "2A"

opponents for all non conference games. What would be your position? Why?

6. Assume that you are the AD of a high school with a home basketball game scheduled in three weeks with an arch-rival school. The last football game caused bad feelings between the schools. You have every reason to expect that, unless steps are taken, the crowd could get out of hand. List all the strategies you could take to avert this potential problem.

7. In previous chapters, information about the Americans with Disabilities Act (ADA) has been presented. Should students with disabilities be allowed to try out for and compete on school athletic teams? Should schools be responsible for providing extracurricular athletic options for students with disabilities?

8. Structure a "start-up" operations budget for the first year for an average health–fitness center assuming a $2,000 per month payment for leasing the facility.

9. Draw the floor plans of a typical health–fitness facility with machine and free weights, resistance machines, aerobic space, and two racquetball courts.

10. What would be the program and marketing differences between a "fitness center," a "health–fitness center," and a "wellness center"?

References

Ashley, F. B., III; Landrum, K; and Dollar, J. (1996, October/November). A threat from home? *Athletic Management* 8, pp. 45–50.

Bradley, M. (1992, September). Great expectations. *Athletic Management* 4, pp. 14–21.

Carney, S. R. (1997, Winter). Coaching information on the Web. *U.S. Sports Academy Sports Supplement* 5, p. 6.

Carpenter, L. J., and Acosta, R. V. (1997, February). Statistics on females in athletics. *Journal of Physical Education, Recreation and Dance* 68, p. 10.

Catalano, J. (1997, October/November). Parents on the field. *Athletic Management* 9, pp. 47–52.

Cioletti, J. (1997, December). All's well. *Club Industry* 13, pp. 19–24.

Coaching education update. (1998, Winter). *NASPE News* 50, p. 10.

Cockley, W. T., and Roswal, G. M. (1993, March). A comparison study of faculty members' perceived knowledge and satisfaction regarding NCAA athletic programs. *Research Quarterly for Exercise Science* (Suppl.), p. A109.

Edginton, C. R. (1997, November/December). Youth development: Enabling the future. *Journal of Physical Education, Recreation and Dance* 68, pp. 15, 20.

Farmer, P. J., Mulrooney, A. L., and Ammon, R. (1996). *Sport facility planning and management.* Morgantown, WV: Fitness Information Technologies.

Faust, G., and Carim, R. (1993, March). Managing clubs in the mid-1990s. *Fitness Management* 9, pp. 33–38.

Gillentine, A., and Bryant, L. G. (1997, May/June). Paraprofessionals: The answer to staffing problems. *Coach and AD* 67, pp. 4–6.

Grantham, W. C.; Patton, R. W.; York, T. D.; and Winick, M. L. (1998). *Health Fitness Management,* Champaign, IL: Human Kinetics Publishers.

Hamhill, G. (1997, October/November). Speaking on style. *Athletic Management* 9, pp. 55–57.

Handley, A. (1998, February). Wellness integration: Establishing a medical advisory board for your club. *Club Industry* 14, pp. 36–38.

HIV fears vs. reality. (1994, December/January). *Athletic Management* 6, pp. 4–8.

Home-schooled student not eligible to participate in sports. (1997, January). *Your School and the Law* 27, p. 8.

Horine, L. (1968, April). Attendance and scholarship of high school athletes. *Athletic Journal* 48 pp. 52–53.

Hudson, S. D. (1997, November/December). Helping youth grow. *Journal of Physical Education, Recreation and Dance* 68, pp. 16–17.

Kadlecek, J. C. (2001) Crisis management response to NCAA Division I student athlete arrests. Greeley, CO: University of Northern Colorado. Unpublished doctoral dissertation.

Kivel, B. D. (1998, January). Adolescent identity formation and leisure contexts: A selective review of literature. *Journal of Physical Education, Recreation and Dance* 69, pp. 36–38.

Kneer, M. E. (1987, February). Solutions to teacher/coach problems in secondary schools. *Journal of Physical Education, Recreation and Dance* 58, pp. 28–29.

Lawry, E. G. (1991, May 1). Conflicting interests make reform of college sports impossible. *Chronicle of Higher Education,* p. A44.

Lewthwaite, R., and Piparo, A. J. (1993). Goal orientations in young competitive athletes: Physical achievement, social–relational and experiential concerns. *Journal of Research in Personality* 61, pp. 103–117.

Lirgg, C. D.; DiBrezzo, R.; and Smith, A. N. (1993, March). Who should coach? *Research Quarterly for Exercise Science* (Suppl.), p. A103.

Maloy, B. P. (1993, January). Beyond the balance sheet. *Athletic Business* 17, pp. 29–31.

Marchell, T.; Hofher, J.; Parrot, A.; and Cummings, N. (1992, November). Prevention by education. *Athletic Management* 4, pp. 44–48.

Melnick, M. (1992, May/June). Male athletes and sexual assault. *Journal of Physical Education, Recreation and Dance* 63, pp. 32–35.

Miller, L. K. (1997). *Sport business management.* Gaithersburg, MD: Aspen.

Motsinger, S. E.; Turner, E. T.; and Evans, J. D. (1997). A comparison of food and beverage concession operations in three different types of North Carolina Sport venues. *Sport Marketing Quarterly* 6(4), pp. 43–52.

Renner, M. (1998a, January). Good Samaritan Health and Wellness Center. *Fitness Management* 14, pp. 32–33.

Renner, M. (1998b, January). Winter Park Health Foundation Center for Health and Wellness. *Fitness Management* 14, pp. 36–41.

Rochman, S. (1997, April/May). Prepare for the worst. *Athletic Management* 9, pp. 14–21.

Rose, L. R.; Gallup, A. M.; and Elam, S. M. (1997, September). The twenty-ninth annual Phi Delta Kappa/Gallup poll of the public's attitudes toward the public schools. *Phi Delta Kappan* 79, pp. 41–56.

Sage, G. H. (1989, March). Becoming a high school coach: From playing sports to coaching. *Research Quarterly for Exercise and Sport* 60, pp. 81–90.

Sage, G. H. (1998, January). Does sport affect character development in athletes? *Journal of Physical Education, Recreation and Dance* 69, pp. 15–18.

School Law Newsletter. (1997, Winter). 18, p. 830.

Stoll, S. K., and Beller, J. M. (1998, January). Can character be measured? *Journal of Physical Education, Recreation and Dance* 69, pp. 19–24.

Stotlar, D. K. (2001). *Developing Successful Sport Marketing Plans.* Morgantown, WV: Fitness Information Technology.

Student could not recover damages for softball injuries. (1997, February 28). *Your School and the Law* 27, pp. 8–9.

The International Health Racquet & Sportsclub Association (2001). *Profiles of Success.* Boston, MA: IHRSA.

Turner, E. T. (1998, March). A concise guide for the teacher–coach to successfully observe and correct motor skills. *Journal of Physical Education, Recreation and Dance* 69, pp. 7–9.

Warren, W. E. (1988). *Coaching and winning.* West Hyack, NY: Parker Publishing.

Wiederg, S. (1998, September 18). Special report: colleges confront athletes' crime. *USA Today*, pp. 17C–20C.

Witt, P., and Baker, D. (1997, November/December). Developing after-school programs for youth in high-risk environments. *Journal of Physical Education, Recreation and Dance* 68, pp. 18–20.

www.aapherd.org/NAGWS (2002, October 30). Department of Education's Blue Ribbon Panel—Commission On Opportunity In Athletics.

www.aapherd.org/NASPE (2002, October 30). National standards for athletic coaches.

www.cdc.gov/tobacco/sport_initiatives/overview. htm (October 30, 2002). Sports Initiative Overview.

15

The Future in Physical Education Administration and Sport Management

---
Management Thought

He turns not back who is bound to a star.

Leonardo da Vinci

Case Study: A True Case, and It Could Be You

Armed with a new bachelor's degree in health and physical education and lettered in several college sports, Bill applied for positions. He was offered two: (1) assistant football coach and teacher of subjects other than his major or minor at a large metropolitan football high school, and (2) the head football coaching position (with one assistant) at a rural school with 55 boys, teaching in both his major and minor, with a salary less than the former. He took the latter. His teams won most of their games and the principal and superintendent asked him to stay on. Instead he returned to school for a master's degree, and became a graduate assistant in football.

Upon completion of graduate work, Bill was recruited to be the assistant football coach, head baseball coach, and teacher of physical education and health education at an excellent large high school. His baseball team won and his teaching received high evaluations. The head football coach liked the drive and willingness Bill had in putting conditioning and discipline above his popularity. The principal, a former coach, also highly valued these attributes. After the first year, the head football coach was promoted to AD, and Bill was promoted to head football mentor along with baseball. For three years Bill, the AD, and the principal became a mutual admiration society as the teams won and as the school spirit and discipline were at their best.

The principal was promoted to assistant superintendent starting the next year, in charge of curriculum for a school system with five high schools, five junior high schools, and 23 elementary schools. He had a staff of directors under him in charge of various major areas, one of which was health, physical education, safety, and athletics. Bill's former principal asked him to apply, and he was the youngest of the many applicants. To his surprise he was selected, primarily through the endorsement of his former principal. In his first private meeting with the new assistant superintendent, he was told three things: (1) His effectiveness will be judged by how little he is in his office and how much he is out in the schools. (2) Just as he delegated a great deal of authority to his assistants and players in football, he will do the same in this position to principals and athletic directors. And (3) after about five years of experience in this position, he must earn a doctorate and then go on to a university and become the chairperson of a physical education department or athletic director, and then write a textbook on how to do it all. He did, and you can too.

The reader should be able to

1. Identify the major changes in society and in data processing likely to occur in the future.

2. Demonstrate an understanding of the future changes in sport, leisure, and physical education that will affect administration.

3. Predict the future expansion of administrative or sport management positions.

■ PREDICTING THE FUTURE

It is said that the record of experts predicting the future hasn't been very accurate. One journal, *The Futurist*, is dedicated to this subject. The editors looked at what their experts predicted in their first issue 30 years before:

1. In predictions about space, they were about half right.

2. In medicine they were all correct, primarily predicting the regular use of transplants.

3. In leisure there were only two predictions, and both were correct—working hours per week would be decreased and expenditures on sport and leisure would double.

4. In communication, three out of five predictions were true.

5. In all categories, the predictions were correct in 23 out of 34 cases. (Cornish, 1997)

What are the experts saying about the future now? The editors of *The Futurist* have selected the following as the top 10 forecasts in Outlook 2002:

• Future farmers could make more money from the air than the land by installing wind turbines and selling power.

• Automated translation systems may allow people to communicate freely with others speaking different languages.

• Natural disasters could become more disastrous as the world's wetlands dry up.

• Schools may solve behavior problems with better nutrition.

• There will be 1 billion elderly people (age 60 and older) by 2020, and three-fourths of them will be in developing countries.

• Vaccinations will be gained through eating genetically modified foods.

• Water shortages will become more frequent and more severe over the next two decades.

• Time-pressed workers will increasingly seek leisure pursuits packed with intensive experiences that don't take up much time.

• Printed and bound textbooks will disappear as more interactive coursework is developed.

• Fish farming will overtake cattle ranching as a food source by 2010 ("Top 10 Forecasts from the Outlook 2002," 2001).

The university of the future will have an increasingly important role. The president emeritus of Cornell University, Frank Rhodes, sees the following changes for universities:

• The library will become a web of information networks and data banks.

• A worldwide pool of lifelong learners may outnumber traditional students as they take advantage of distance learning.

• Universities will be more privately supported, but publicly accountable.

• Colleges will be more internationally oriented.

• Information technology will not only benefit and impact the teaching and research on campus, but also bring electronic learning tools to the surrounding community.

• Universities will be forced into reality checks on financing programs with administrative efficiency and cost–benefit analysis being more rigorously applied ("The University of the Future," 2002).

What will jobs look like in the future? It is reported that 90 percent of white-collar jobs will be destroyed or greatly altered in the next 10 to 15 years. Some job titles that will emerge will have titles like bioinformationalists, geomicrobiologists, cybrarians, and e-mail counselors. The U. S. Department of Labor Statistics reports that jobs "related to personal appearance, and physical health, communications, and travel will be particularly fertile. . . . Work related to physical conditioning is becoming more prominent . . . more jobs will be available in exercise instruction, for example. . . . 25% of the industries with new and emerging occupations are involved in health, social, and educational services" ("Economics, Tomorrow's Job Titles," 2002). Another trend worldwide that will directly impact physical education, sport, and fitness programs is global obesity. While obesity has been a steadily increasing problem in the United States, statistics now show that large-population countries such as Russia and China have joined the problem as fast food increases and technology lessens physical activity. It is believed that this trend will spread to all of the developing countries, causing a worldwide greatly expanded need for expertise in health and physical education ("Demography, Trends in Global Obesity," 2002).

Students who seek more information on the future are directed to the website www.wfs.org. This site provides exclusive interviews with authorities and Web Forums in the following areas:

- Cyber society.
- Methodology.
- Opportunities.
- Social innovation.
- Study of the future.
- Wisdom of the world ("Special features on the Web," 2001).

Cyberspace
Anyone looking back to the early 1980s would find it daunting to project from then to what is commonplace in the 2000s. Could anyone predict that the Internet would reach more than 500 million users, 150 million serving computers, and 300-plus million laptops? The network was then still sponsored wholly by the U.S. government, and it was not even clear that public or commercial access would be granted (Cerf, 2002).

A problem that will become more serious in the future is the disposal of old computers. Processor speed is doubling every 18 months (this is described as Moore's Law). There will be 150 million dead but not decaying (because of the lead, mercury, and chromium inside them) computers buried in landfills by 2005 (Pescovitz, 2002).

Virtual Reality and Robotics
"More and more, physical reality looks like it jumped off the computer screen, imitating computer-generated models and simulators. Even our bodies are beginning to reflect the genetic engineering and virtual anatomy simulations first realized on a screen. The real and the virtual are even beginning to blend together augmented reality interfaces" (Rosenbloom, 2002, p. 29). "The Tiles system seamlessly blends virtual and physical objects to create a work space that combines the power and flexibility of computing environments with the comfort and familiarity of the traditional workplace" (Poupyrev et al., 2002, p. 44).

It appears that robotics will continue to be used extensively. Miniaturization and increased technical sophistication will allow robotics to be incorporated into uses that now cannot be visualized. "Expect robots to function on their own with other people and each other under whichever environmental conditions they happen to find themselves" (Sukhatme, and Mataric, 2002, p. 30; Cook, 2002; Pauli, 2002).

Every higher education department of leisure studies, sport science, human performance, and health promotion should possess a virtual reality laboratory. This will be used for everything from teaching anatomy by traveling inside a living body and through the various organs to playing all sports and teaching movements by feel. Varsity athletes will practice their foul shooting, batting, or golf strokes in the virtual reality laboratory.

Practical Applications of Computers Now
A perusal of current literature reveals some current uses of the computer that will be greatly expanded. There is no question that every student expecting a career in sport administration or sport management needs to become immersed in computer use and data processing capabilities.

One previously reported use will be expanding student teaching supervision by e-mail on a routine basis through teacher education websites to be used through the first few years of novice teaching (Everhart, 1997).

Electronic fund transfers (EFT) for all kinds of transactions should be used. For example, special extra fees for laboratory or a course such as scuba would be handled in this manner, along with bills for lost or damaged equipment. Monthly bills for commercial fitness centers are already processed in this way in many clubs ("Keep an Eye on the Operation," 1997).

It is likely that networking through the Internet has many immediate applications. For example, the ski industry has learned that when several areas open in close proximity, the synergy results in more, not less, business for each. Where there are four or five operations in one area, forming a network for mutual cooperation and coordination might make sense even if each is owned by separate entities. With fitness centers owned by the same company but located far away from each other, networking is mandatory (Tucker, 1997). Local area networks (LANs) for recreation departments that can perform management, marketing, and financial operations should already be in use universally (Ross & Wolter, 1997).

Computers will become commonplace in team changing suites. Athletes will have computers built into their lockers where they can check their daily weight, practice schedules, class assignments, research paper searches, equipment needs, or friendly advice from their academic advisers. The equipment manager will use electronic bar codes on everything and will be able to retrieve a complete history of each piece of equipment at the press of a computer key (Dillon, 1996).

Fitness Trends

These fitness programs have showed the greatest recent increase in participation:

- Core conditioning classes.
- Flexibility/stretching classes.
- Group strength training.
- Yoga.

- Pilates.
- Combination/hybrid classes that combine several of the above into one class.

The following specific activities have increased in popularity recently:

- Other mind-body modalities.
- Group personal training.
- Sport-specific training.
- Stability ball training.
- Indoor cycling.
- Walking.
- Water training.
- Wellness/lifestyle classes.
- Outdoor activities.

The following activities have seen decreased interest recently:

- Boxing-based classes.
- Kickboxing.
- Martial arts–based classes.
- Indoor rowing.
- Mixed impact classes ("IDEA Survey Discloses Leading Fitness Trends in 2001," 2002).

■ OTHER SPORT ADMINISTRATION INITIATIVES

With the ever-increasing numbers of retired citizens in vibrant health and willing to become involved, the use of volunteers in sport has not even begun to be tapped. Organizations like hospice and hospital administration use volunteers extensively. If it were not for volunteers, such operations would be far more expensive. It has been shown that professionals in midcareer who are dues-paying members in fitness centers will volunteer if asked in the right way (Sattler and Doniek, 1998a, 1998b). Parents are easy volunteer recruits for middle and senior high schools. In higher education, faculty outside the physical education/sport areas are willing volunteers for recreation and sport programs.

The saying "Children are our future" may have a great deal of meaning for fitness clubs. Dual working parents looking for a chance to blend a workout into their cramped schedules and also provide the benefits of movement and exercise for their children will be willing to pay to enroll their children into well-conceived programs at the same time. Baby-sitting is not what they will want. Parent/toddler programs in the middle of the morning will be popular (Price, 1998).

Because of the increased participation by such groups (youth, women, adults), there will be increased opportunities and positions in sport management. In addition, it is expected that the trend of enormous expenditures in leisure and sporting equipment will provide many opportunities in retail and wholesale.

New sports or activities (perhaps some that are not now known) will provide new management opportunities. Recent examples are climbing and snowboarding. Within a few years most institutions of higher education and even small communities will have commercial or municipal climbing walls. The dramatic increase in numbers of snowboarders has created an entire industry along with the retail outlets, technical representatives, wholesalers, instructors, and professional riders.

Some futurists have been increasing their attention to building down rather than up. This is interesting because there have been interest and experience in underground sport and school facilities for decades. Underground sport facilities provide many natural advantages such as very low energy costs, no sun glare problems, and great possibilities of reducing the environment degradation that huge above-ground stadiums and arenas cause. "In an 'underground utopia,' buildings could still come in any shape and size, from wildflower-adorned noise barriers to underground stadiums and airports. Nature would nurture us" ("An Underground Utopia," 2002).

■ THE FUTURE OF SPORT MANAGEMENT/SPORT ADMINISTRATION

Physical education and athletic participation numbers will likely grow modestly. Even if these numbers remained constant, these programs represent a tremendous number of positions in administration.

Professional sport organizations offer many sport administration positions. These jobs allow for a great deal of vertical promotion and lucrative salaries within each organization. While some believe these major sport operations will price themselves out of existence, looking at the long-term growth of the past does not seem to support this view.

Commercial sport areas such as golf courses, ski areas, water parks and beach and lake operations, leisure parks, and recreation camps are likely to mirror population growth. Each of these industries offers many opportunities for management positions.

The opportunities for commercial and nonprofit programs in exercise, leisure activities, and sport for the older adult are enormous. All statistics point to more of the adult population having more disposable income, interest, and time to devote to these pursuits. Jobs in management operating these programs will be plentiful for those properly trained.

The impetus for expanding opportunities in sport management and athletic administration comes from several fronts. Powerful stimuli have come from the previously outlined reports from the U.S. surgeon general and the Centers for Disease Control and Prevention. These reports will carry more weight than any that have come from professional organizations within sport or exercise science. In addition, one cannot peruse a medical journal in any discipline without seeing positive recommendations for regular physical activity to mitigate problems with a wide variety of serious medical problems, such as diabetes, cancer, heart disease, osteoporosis, depression, immune deficiency, high blood pressure, and weight control ("Preventing Hypertension," 1998). These reports will change the motivation for many from exercising to look or feel better, to exercising for health, which will likely cause a higher sustainability rate.

■ GENDER AND SPORT

Gender equity and Title IX have been discussed in various sections of this text. Title IX was 30 years old in June 2002. It would take an entire book to fully describe and analyze this controversial topic. But since gender equity and Title IX permeate all phases of youth, school, and college sport and physical education administration, this justifies summarizing the present status and guessing at the future. From the lack of critical essays in the professional literature, it would appear that gender equity in physical education in schools and colleges has achieved a good deal of balance. Certainly equitable salaries of instructors, equipment, and facilities seem to be no problem primarily because of coed classes. In the past there has been some concern that less skilled females were not apt to have a positive experience in coed classes, but instructors should try to work around this potential problem in the future.

In sport, on the school level, strides have been achieved in adding sport opportunities for females. Even though the lack of scholarships on the school level lessens the overabundance of spending for football, compared to the college level, football still gobbles up much of the equipment budgets in high schools as well as coaching stipends. With no comparable sport to football for females, it is assumed that this imbalance will continue. Perhaps sports to which females are more attracted, such as competitive dance, gymnastics, water ballet, and ice figure skating, could be the answer. It has been, and will continue to be, a concern that there are very few females coaching men's sports while there are too many men coaching female sport teams on the school level. And females are much underrepresented in the athletic administrative positions in school sport.

In sport college administration, the number of athletic directors who are female has declined. In the 2002 study of NCAA administrators, it was reported that there were "27 female athletic directors in NCAA Division I, the same as in 2000 and down from 30 in 1998. In Division II, there were 41, down from 45 and 48 in previous surveys. In Division III, 108 women held the title, up from 99 in 2000 but down from 110 in 1998. . . . there were 3,210 administrative jobs in NCAA programs that offer women's athletics,

an increase of 282 jobs since 2000. The average number of administrators per school was 5.08 in Division I, 2.52 in Division II, and 2.36 in Division III. The average number of females in athletic administration in 2002 was 1.59 in Division I, .87 in Division II, and .95 in Division III. Furthermore, 18.8 percent of NCAA athletic administrations have no women at any level, which is down from 23 percent in 2000" ("Acosta-Carpenter Study Shows Decline in Female ADs, Coaches," 2002, p. 10). In the NCAA administrative positions for head athletic trainers have been about one-quarter female on all levels, and about 12 percent for sport information directors. In 1977, 90 percent of the head coaches for women's teams were female, while the 2002 study revealed that only 44 percent were female. This represents a dismal record, and better progress in the future must be made. For further information, contact www.AthleticSearch.com ("Acosta-Carpenter Study Shows Decline in Female ADs, Coaches," 2002).

The number of participants by sex in sport on both the school and college levels greatly impacts administration socially, emotionally, and financially. The arguments for and against fully implementing Title IX are both numerous and complicated. There is no question that progress has occurred. But has it been fast enough and far enough? Will this progress plateau in the future without agreement on how to handle the football conundrum? Eliminating nonrevenue or Olympic sports for men to reach achievement is a sad solution, and blaming Title IX and sport for women for following this avenue does not stand in the face of logic (Boyce, 2002; White and Sheets, 2001).

Exercises

1. Consider fitness centers and health–fitness–wellness centers. Which will likely grow most in the next decade? Why?
2. What is the growth potential for school and higher education physical education administrative positions in the next decade?
3. What is the growth potential for school and higher education athletics administrative positions in the next decade?

Critical Thinking

Refer to the case study at the start of this chapter. Several concepts were critical to this success story, without which the coach would have remained "stuck" at any spot. Answer these questions, and you will learn the vital concepts for success.

1. What paved Bill's way to being offered two jobs right out of college? What could have been substituted?
2. Why did he accept the lower-paying position for his first job at a smaller school? What difference did it make in his being selected for the next job?
3. Was it wise to return to graduate school after only one year of teaching/coaching? What difference did it make in landing the second job?
4. What were the important factors in being promoted in the second job to head football coach?
5. What were the important factors in being promoted to the administrative position? How does the saying "riding on the coattails" fit in?
6. What is the importance of each of the three "charges" the assistant superintendent gave?

4. Which of the following operations do you think will offer the best future in management positions: aquatic parks, swimming pools, ski areas, golf courses, tennis complexes, or recreation camps?
5. If you had a choice, which of the following majors do you think would have the greatest potential for entry positions and for highest terminal salary: sport management; athletic administration; fitness management; facility operations management; or leisure management?

References

Acosta–Carpenter study shows decline in female ADs, coaches (2002, June/July). *Athletic Management* XIV, pp. 10–11.

An underground utopia (2002, March–April). *The Futurist* 36, pp. 33–36.

Boyce, A. (2002, September). Title IX: what now. *Journal of Physical Education, Recreation and Dance* 73, pp. 6–7.

Cerf, V. (2002, September). Looking ahead. *Computing Reviews* 43, cover.

Cook, D, (2002, September). Artificial intelligence through use of robotics. *Computing Reviews* 43, p. 305.

Cornish, E. (1997, January/February). Futurist forecasts 30 years later. *Futurist* 31, pp. 45–50.

Demography, trends in global obesity (2002, May–June). *The Futurist* 36, p. 10.

Dillon, J. (1996, August/September). Changes in the changing room. *Athletic Management* 8, pp. 45–49.

Economics, tomorrow's job titles (2002, May–June). *The Futurist* 36, p. 9.

Everhart, B. (1997, August). Using e-mail in student teaching. *Journal of Physical Education, Recreation and Dance* 68, pp. 36–38.

IDEA survey discloses leading fitness trends in 2001 (2002, Winter). *The AAALF Active Voice* 7, p. 11.

Keep an eye on the operation. (1997, August). *Club Industry* 13, p. 20.

Pauli, J. (2002, June). Learning-based robot vision. *Computing Reviews* 43, p. 189.

Pescovitz, D. (2002, January). Please dispose of properly. *Computing Reviews* 43, cover.

Poupyrev, I.; Tan, D.; Billinghurst, M.; Kato, H.; Regenbrecht, H.; and Tetsutani, N.; (2002, March). Developing a generic augmented-reality interface. Computer, 35, 44–50.

Preventing hypertension: A new urgency. (1998, February 28). *Patient Care* 32, pp. 64–80.

Price, L. (1998, February). Energize kids (and families) with exercise. *Fitness Management* 14, pp. 37–40.

Rosenbloom, A. (2002, July). How the virtual inspires the real. *Communications of the ACM* 45, pp. 29–70.

Ross, C., and Wolter, S. (1997, October). Registration information. *Athletic Business* 21, pp. 59–65.

Sattler, T. P., and Doniek, C. A. (1998a, February). How to recruit volunteers. *Fitness Management* 14, p. 20.

Sattler, T. P., and Doniek, C. A. (1998b, February). Revise your vision with volunteers. *Fitness Management* 14, pp. 18 19.

Special features on the Web (2001, Winter). *Future Times*, p. 5.

Sukhatme, G. S. and Mataric, M. D. (2002, March) Robots: intelligence, versatility, adaptivity. Robotics, 45, pp. 30–63.

Top 10 forecasts from the Outlook 2002 (2001, Winter). *Future Times*, p. 11.

Tucker, R. (1997, November). "Net"working your club's data. *Fitness Management* 13, p. 42.

The university of the future (2002, May–June). *The Futurist* 36, p. 7–8.

White, E. A. and Sheets, C. (2001, April). If you let them play, they will . . . . *Journal of Physical Education, Recreation and Dance* 72, pp. 27–28, 33.

Appendix A
Selected Sport Products and Services Suppliers

Air Structures American Technologies; airbldg@aol.com; www.airbldg.com; (914) 937–4500

Amerec Sauna & Steam; AMEREC@amerec.com; www.amerec.com; (800) 331–0349

American Athletic, Inc.; info@americanathletic.com; www.americanathletic.com; (800) 247–3978

American Body Building Products; michaelFU@weider.com; www.americanbodybuilding.com; (800) 453–9542

American Leisure Corp.; amerleisco@aol.com; www.americanleisure.com; (800) FIT-MGMT)

American Locker Security Systems, Inc; 103303.1432@compuserve.com; www.americanlocker.com; (800) 828–9118

Aqua Products, Inc.; aquainfo@aol.com; www.aquaproducts.com; (800) 221–1750

Aqua Vac Systems, Inc. info@aquavacsystems.com; www.aquavacsystems.com; (800) 327–0141

ASF International; info@asfinternational.com; www.asfinternational.com; (800) 227–3859

ASICS Tiger Corp.; www.asicstiger.com; (800) 333–8404

Association Insurance Group; www.clubinsurance.com; (800) 985–2021

AVOCET/PHASE Heart Rate Monitors; sales@avocet.com; www.avocet.com; (800) 227–8346

Bailey Mfg. Co.; baileymfg@baileymfg.com; www.baileymfg.com; (800) 321–8372

Balanced Body Pilates Equipment; info@pilates.com; www.pilates.com; (800) 745–2837

Barker Rinker Seacat Architecture; rozschneider@brsarch.com; www.brsarch.com; (303) 455–1366

Befour, Inc.; befour@execpc.com; www.befour.com; (262) 284–5150

Beta Technologies, Inc.; sales@langecaliper.com; www.langecaliper.com; (800) 858–2382

Brownell Sports Products; brownell@cyberzone.net; www.brownellco.com; (860) 873–8625

BSA Architects; bsa@bsaarchitects.com; www.bsaarchitects.com; (415) 781–1526

Burlington Socks; www.burlingtonsocks.com; (800) 575–3497

Cap Barbell, Inc.; www.capbarbell.com; (800) 225–0505

Century, Inc.; info@centuryfitness.com; www.centuryfitness.com; (800) 626–2787

Clamshell Buildings, Inc.; sales@clamshell.com; www.clamshell.com; (805) 650–1700

Clubrunner, Inc.; sales@clubrunner.net; www.clubrunner.net; (800) 554-CLUB

CMS International (Club Marketing and Management Services); clubdoc@cms-clubweb.com; www.cms-clubweb.com; (406) 449–5559

Comtec Indust.; info@comtechindustries.com; www.comtechindustries.com; (800) 455–5148

Concept 2; rowing@concept2.com; www.concept2.com; (800) 245–5676

The Court Company; build@racquetballcourts.com; www.racquetballcourts.com; (901) 682–2600

Covermaster, Inc.; info@covermaster.com; www.covermaster.com; (800) 387–5808

Cox Target Media, Inc.; contact_sales@coxtarget.com; www.coxtarget.com; (800) 782–5725

CSSI Resilient Surfacing Products; jfy@carlsurf.com; www.carlsurf.com; (800) 851–4746

Cybex International, Inc.; www.ecybex.com; (888) GO-CYBEX

Cytech (USA), Inc.; usa@tomahawk.de; www.indoorcycling.com; (941) 596–8861

Dinoflex Rubber Flooring; dinoflex@dinoflex.com; www.dinoflex.com; (877) 713–1899

Dur-Flex, Inc.; info@dur-a—flex.com; (800) 528–9838

Durkan Patterned Carpet; durkan_sales@mohawkind.com; www.durkan.com; (800) 241–4580

Eltron Card Printer Products; cards@eltron.com; www.eltroncards.com; (800) 452–4056

Entre Prises Climbing Walls; paulp@epusa.com; (800) 580–5463

Environmental Coating Systems, Inc.;
info@alldeck.com: www.alldeck.com; (800)
ALL DECK

Exerflex Aerobic Floor Systems; exerflex@exerflex.
com; www.exerflex.com; (800) 428–5306

Fawn Vendor, Inc.; gbahr@fawnvendors.com;
www.fawnvendors.com; (800) 548–1982

Ferno Ille; twells@ferno.com; www.ferno.com; (800)
733–3766

Fiberesin Indus., Inc.; info@fiberesin.com;
www.fiberesin.com; (262) 567–4427

Fibre Tech, Inc.; resurface@fibretechinc.comgn.
com; www.fibretechinc.com; (800) 393–7283

Fleet Insurance Services. LLC; erik_henricksen@
fleet.com; (800) 526–4458

Flexo; info@flexcofloors.com; www.flexcofloors.
com; (800) 663–3151

Fortress Lockers Systems; sales@
fortresslockers.com; www.fortresslockers.com;
(800) 683–2624

Game Time; info@gametime.com;
www.gametime.com; (800) 235–2440

Gold's Gym International, Inc.; www.goldsgym.com;
(800) 457–5375

Grizzly Fitness Accessories; mail@grizzlyfitness.
com; www.grizzlyfitness.com; (800) 265–4504

Hayes Large Architects; altoona@hayeslarge.com;
www.hayeslarge.com; (814) 946–0451

Health Fitness Corp.; info@hfit.com; www.healthfit-
nesscorp.com; (800) 639–7913

Healthtrax; trax@healthtrax.net; www.
healthtrax.net; (860) 633–5572

Heat Pumps Unlimited; shari@poolheating.com;
www.poolheating.com; (800) 533–5087

Helo Sauna & Steam; helo@saunatec.com;
www.helosaunas.com; (800) 882–4352

Hillier; ggeier@hillier.com; www.hillier.com; (212)
629–4100

Hoist Fitness Systems; dsbragia@hoistfitness.com;
www.hoistfitness.com; (800) 548–5438

HRH Insurance of Mass.; bryan.dank@hrh.com;
www.insurefit.com; (800) 445–4664

Humane Mfg., LLC; humane@midplains.net;
www.humanemfg.com; (800) 369–6263

Indoor Courts of America; info@indoorcourts.com;
www.indoorcourts.com; (800) 373–4262

Integrated Architecture; tspaulding@intarch.com;
www.intarch.com; (616) 574–0220

Jewell Insurance; staff@fitnessinsurance.com;
www.fitnessinsurance.com; (800) 881–7130

Junckers Hardwood, Inc.; js@junckershardwood.
com; www.junckershardwood.com; (800) 878–9663

K & K Insurance; shelly_myer@kandkinsurance.
com; www.kandkinsurance.com; (800) 440–5580

Keiser Kiser Corp.; sales@kiser.com; www.kiser.
com; (800) 888–7009

Kiefer (Adolph) & Assoc.; catalog@kiefer.com;
www.kiefer.com; (800) 323–4071

Kiefer Specialty Flooring; kfloor@mindspring.
com; www.kieferfloors.com; (800) 322–5448

L. Robert Kimball & Assoc., Inc.; aande@lrkimball.
com; www.lrkimball.com; (814) 472–7700

Koala Corp.; koalaco@koalabear.com; www.koal-
abear.com; (888) 733–3456

Kraiberg Flooring; kraiburg@aol.com;
www.kraiburgflooring.com; (888) 382–6767

KZF Design, Architects, Engrs.; kzfinfo@kzf.com;
www.kzf.com; (513) 621–6211

Lady of America; charles@ladyofamerica.com;
www.ladyofamerica.com; (800) 833–5339

Landice Treadmills; sales@landice.com;
www.landice.com; (800) LANDICE

L & T Health and Fitness; ltwell@ltwell.com;
www.ltwell.com; (703)204–1355

Langdon Wilson Achitecture; langdonwilson@
lw-oc.com; www.langdonwilson.com; (949)
833–9193

Lee Tennis Products; hartru@leetennis.com;
www.leetennis.com; (800) 327–8379

Leo A.Daly, Planning, Architecture; mjriordan@leoad-
aly.com; www.leoadaly.com; (402) 391–8111

Life Fitness; webmaster@lifefitness.com; www.lifefit-
ness.com; (800) 634–8637

McArthur Towels, Inc.; sales@mcarthur-towels.
com; www.mcarthur-towels.com; (800) 356–9168

MediFit Corporate Services; rbaldwin@medifit.
com; www.medifit.com; (973) 540–1800

M-F Athletic Company; performbetter@
mfathletic.com; www.mfathletic.com; (800) 556–7464

Mikasa Sports; info@mikasasports.com;
www.mikasasports.com; (800) 854–6927

Mondo USA; mondo@mondousa.com; www.mon-
dousa.com; (800) 441–6645

Murria & Frick Insurance Agency; jfrick@
murriafrick.com; www.fitnessandwellness.
com; (800) 395–8075

Muscle Dynamics Corp.; trogan@
muscledynamics.com; www.muscledynamics.
com; (800) 544–2944

Musson Rubber Co.; info@mussonrubber.com;
www.mussonrubber.com; (800) 321–2381

Nautilus Human Performance Systems; sales@nau-
tilus.com; www.nautilus.com;
(800) 628–8458

New Balance Athletic Shoe; www.newbalance.com;
(800) 343–4648

Osborn Architects & Engineers; bax@osborn-eng.
com; www.osborn-eng.com; (216) 861–2020

Paragon Aquatics; info@paragonaquatics.com;
www.paragonaquatics.com; (888) KDI–SWIM

Pawling Corp.; sales@pawling.com;
www.pawling.com; (800) 431–3456

Pellerin Milnor Corp.; mktg@milnor.com; www.mil-
nor.com; (800) 469–8780

Peter Burwash International Tennis; pbihq@pbiten-
nis.com, www.pbitennis.com; (800) 255–4707

Plexipave Sport Surfaces; info@plexipave.com;
www.plexipave.com; (800) 225–1141

Polar Electro, Inc.; www.polarusa.com; (800) 290–6330

Precor, Inc.; commsls@precor.com; www.precor.com;
(800) 786–8404

Prochaska & Assoc.-Planning Architecture;
prochaska@earthlink.net; www.cmdg.com/
profile; (402) 334–0755

ProMaxima Mfg., Inc.; dpayne@promaximamfg.
com; www.promaximamfg.com; (800) 231–6652

R-B Rubber Products, Inc.; fitness@rbrubber.com;
www.rbrubber.com; (800) 525–5530

Reebok International Ltd.; info@clubreebok.com;
www.clubreebok.com; (800) REBOK1

S & S Architects & Planners; jmoyer@sasarch.com;
www.sasarch.com; (847) 564–8333

Santana Products Co.; roger.smith@
hinyhinder.com; www.santanaproducts.com; (800)
368–5002

Schwinn Cycling & Fitness, Inc.; www.schwinn.com;
(800) SCHWINN

Sentinel Security Lockers; sentinel@tiffinmetal.com;
www.tiffinmetal.com; (800) 537–0983

StairMaster Health & Fitness Products, Inc.; commere-
cialsales@stairmaster.com; www.stairmaster.com;
(800) 635–2936

Structures Unlimited, Inc.; info@
structuresunlimitedinc.com; www.
structuresunlimitedinc.com; (800) 225–3895

Sun Ports International, Inc.; isaacson@sunports.
com; www.sunports.com; (800) 966–5005

Sussman Lifestyle Group; slg@sussmancorp.com;
www.sussmanlifestylegroup.com; (800) 767–8326

SwimEx LLC; simex@tpicomp.com;
www.swimex.com; (800) 877–7946

Texacraft Indoor & Outdoor Furnishing Mfg.;
jsrega@aol.com; www.texacraft.com; (800)
231–9790

TKDA Engineers Architects Planners; janncs@
tkda.com; www.tkda.com; (800) 247–1714

TMP Architecture; info@tmp-architecture.com;
www.tmp-architecture.com; (248) 338–4561

Total Gym/EFI; sales@totalgym.com;
www.totalgym.com; (800) 541–4900

Troy Barbell & Fitness; bob@troybarbell.com;
www.troybarbell.com; (800) 872–7767

True Fitness; info@truefitness.com;
www.truefitness.com; (800) 426–6570

Tuflex Rubber Flooring; info@tuflex.com; www.tu-
flex.com; (800) 543–0390

Ultimate Power Fitness Equip.;
mrudolph@rudco.com; (800) 828–2234

Universal Gym Equipment; www.universalgym.
com; (800) 843–3906

USFilter Stranco Products; stranco@usfilter.com;
www.stranco.com; (866) 766–5987

Vita Tech International, Inc.; gregw@vitatech.com;
www.vitatech.com (714) 832–9700

W. A. Schmidt; sales@waschmidt.com;
www.waschmidt.com; (800) 523–6719

W2A Design Group/Wallace & Watson Assoc.;
info@w2a.com; www.w2a.com; (610) 437–4450

Yeadon Fabric Structures, Ltd.; yeadon@
yeadon.on.ca; www.yeadondomes.com;
(888) 493–2366

York Barbell Company; echaillet@yorkbarbell.
com; www.yorkbarbell.com; (800) 358–9675

Source: 2002 products and services directory, *Fitness Management* 18, pp. 1–81; 2002 buyer's guide for high school and college athletics (2002, Dec./Jan), *Athletic Management* XIV, pp. 28–145; Recreational sports and fitness resource buyers' guide (2002, May),
Recreational Sports and Fitness 4, pp. 14–54.

Appendix B
Sample Student Athlete
Physical Form

_____   __ __

(Last name),   (First)   (Middle)   (Soc. Sec. no.)

_____   _____

(Sport)   (Date of preparticipation physical)

Pertinent history: _____

_____

_____

I. INITIAL PREPARTICIPATION PHYSICAL:

[Indicate Normal: (U);   Abnormal: (*)   and comment below]

Height:	Weight:	Pulse:	B/P:	Urine:

GENERAL:		ORTHOPEDIC:	
ENT		Upper extremity	
Dental			
Heart		Lower extremity	
Hernia/Rectal			
Abdomen		X ray	
Skin			

Comments: _____

_____ Physician signature: _____

II.   ANNUAL SCREENING RECHECKS:

Date:		Height:	Weight:	Pulse:
B/P:	Urine:	Comments: _____		
ATC signature:		MD approval:		

Date:		Height:	Weight:	Pulse:
B/P:	Urine:	Comments: _____		
ATC signature:		MD approval:		

Date:		Height:	Weight:	Pulse:
B/P:	Urine:	Comments: _____		
ATC signature:		MD approval:		

Index